6,

HEALTH CARE
FINANCE

HEALTH CARE FINANCE

Economic Incentives and Productivity Enhancement

STEVEN R. EASTAUGH

AUBURN HOUSE
New York • Westport, Connecticut • London

Library of Congress Cataloging-in-Publication Data

Eastaugh, Steven R.
  Health care finance : economic incentives and productivity
enhancement / Steven R. Eastaugh.
      p. cm.
    Includes bibliographical references and index.
    ISBN 0–86569–044–8 (hc : alk. paper). — ISBN 0–86569–049–9 (pbk.
: alk. paper)
    1. Medical economics.   2. Managed Care Programs—economics.
I. Title.
    [DNLM: 1. Financial Management, Hospital.   2. Health Services—
economics.   3. Long Term Care—economics.   4. Marketing of Health
Services—organization & administration.   WX 157 E127h]
RA410.E27   1992
338.4′33621—dc20
DNLM/DLC
for Library of Congress   91–26255

British Library Cataloguing in Publication Data is available.

Library of Congress Catalog Card Number: 91–26255
ISBN: 0–86569–044–8
      0–86569–049–9 (pbk.)

First published in 1992

Auburn House, 88 Post Road West, Westport, CT 06881
An imprint of Greenwood Publishing Group, Inc.

Printed in the United States of America

The paper used in this book complies with the
Permanent Paper Standard issued by the National
Information Standards Organization (Z39.48–1984).

10 9 8 7 6 5 4 3 2 1

This book is dedicated to my wife,
Janet A. Eastaugh, M.D.

Contents

Figures and Tables

TABLES

Preface

Americans want incompatible results: unlimited access to the best care at affordable prices. Health care has priced itself into the public eye and has assumed an increasing proportion of the American economy. The antecedents of this book, my two texts *Medical Economics and Health Finance* and *Financing Health Care*, parallel the evolution of this field. In 1980 economic issues and talk of national health insurance or deregulation dominated the discussion. In 1987 financial issues and the corporate growth of for-profit multihospital systems seemed of paramount importance. In 1992 productivity and quality are paramount issues for managers and policy makers. In each of my previous books one major prediction failed to happen. If I had to second-guess one major prediction in this current volume, I would guess that by the late 1990s the Deming method for quality improvement (chapter 11) will be relegated to the dust bin of failed ideas; joining two other things that did not happen: the popularity of Japanese quality circles and Paul Elwood's concept of supermed corporations providing the majority of the nation's health care.

A single individual working within our health care system may feel that his or her contribution is infinitesimal, but it is infinitely important that each person make a real contribution. I hope that the reader will develop admiration (1) for what a manager can do to enhance productivity, market strategy, quality, and profitability, (2) for what a financial manager can do to manage capital structure, investment decisions, and financing decisions, (3) for what a policy maker can do to enhance access, promote managed care, and learn from technology-assessment studies, and (4) for what a payer can do to act as a prudent buyer, yet preserve the biomedical capacity of the nation and meet the rising demand for long-term care. We must respond to the challenges ahead to make sure that our health care systems, ranging from long-term care to acute hospital care, serve in the most effective and efficient way possible.

In preparing this book, I have intentionally cast a wide net to include managers, policy makers, health care providers, and graduate students. I anticipate that this wide audience is more interested in a synthesis of currently available study results and potential policy ramifications than in new research methods. However, portions of five chapters (2, 4, 5, 8, and 13) are intended for functional specialists and scholars with interests in technical issues. My hope is that the reader will come away with a better understanding of the medical economics and financial management literature and a renewed appreciation of the fact that the behavior of consumers and medical providers is only partially understood at this time.

The various cost-containment proposals that have been advanced in the 1990s are examined against the backdrop of the empirical research available to date. In part 1 we define the elements that make up the medical cost-inflation problem and survey a number of models of providers concerning their accounting habits, purchasing behavior, and product-line specialization. In part 2 we discuss health maintenance organizations (HMOs) and other managed-care systems, the wide variety of long-term-care systems, long-term-care insurance, and financial management issues (chapters 3 and 4). Part 3 considers market analysis, diversification trends, strategy selection, and pricing for hospital care and ambulatory care (chapters 5 and 6).

In part 4 the focus shifts to physician reimbursement, managing physicians, expenses related to operating teaching hospitals, and the management of medical schools (chapters 7 and 8). One-quarter of my former students work in this market niche (and almost 20 percent of our recent graduates work in the fast-growth long-term-care market). While some information concerning ways to enhance productivity are contained in chapters 1–4, part 5 (chapters 9–11) considers the link between productivity enhancement, cost control, and quality control. Chapter 11 discusses the Deming method of continuous quality improvement and the controversial topic of public disclosure of quality ratings. The topics in parts 3, 4, and 5 (chapter 5–11) are obviously interrelated: enhanced productivity will cut costs and improve financial position, and enhanced quality will improve market share and hopefully increase institutional profitability.

Part 6 (chapters 12–14) focuses on the institutional manager and the impact that cost containment has had on all hospitals. Most of the emphasis is on hospital finance. Hospitals have an excessive reliance on debt relative to other sectors of the economy—for example, 80 percent of total new capitalization is debt financed. Public utilities borrow on the average about 60 percent of new capitalization, and manufacturing firms borrow only 40–50 percent. A number of financing alternatives are evaluated, including two types of leasing options. Chapter 13 considers investment decisions, financing decisions, and the impact of the new Medicare capital payment system for hospitals. Chapter 14 considers capital structure decisions. Part 7 asks whether the nation is ready for a systematic reform of the health care system that offers universal coverage, universal access, cost control, and sufficient flexibility to allow steady quality-of-care improvements (chapter 15).

This book contains 1,200 published references. However, since not everything worth knowing is published in the journals, a second source of information is utilized. For two decades I have sought to accumulate, through management consulting work, firsthand accounts of ways to improve economic efficiency, productivity, quality, and access. As an economist I grew tired of sterile econometric measurement of a cost function and wanted to jump into the tougher task of cutting costs while enhancing service quality. Such real-world experience helps improve the text by reporting success and failure (authors seldom advertise failures in the journals). Under the coming era of barebones reimbursement, learning from our failures and the failures of the competition will become increasingly important for managers.

ACKNOWLEDGMENTS

I acknowledge, first of all, my wife Janet, who provided me with a provider perspective and the life-sustaining critical review of this book during the long preparation period. I have depended on the ideas and assistance of others in writing this book, including Professors Philip Reeves, Warren Greenberg, Richard Riegelman, Ruth Hanft, Duncan Neuhauser, Jim Begun, and former student David Dranove. A number of research assistants over the years deserve special thanks for their help: Ascanio Terracciano, Susan Labovich, Bonnie Horvath, Susan Clark, Kevin Smolich, Juan Acevedo, Carolyn Lankford, Jay Higham, Tina Kao, Tom Caldwell, Michael Jernigan, Steven Klapmeier, Gary Selmeczi, Susan Cosgrove, and Nancy Bohn. I acknowledge the invaluable help of the two editors Charles Eberline and Lynn Flint. For any errors that remain in the book I am responsible.

Part One

MANAGERIAL CONCERNS FOR PAYERS AND PROVIDERS

Chapter 1

Payment Incentives, Provider Behavior, and the Need for Better Cost Management

Cost management means the delivery of all the care that is medically needed, for as long as it is needed, but not for a day or a dollar more.

—Robert Shelton

Change is already here, like it or not. More change is in view. Change breeds doubt. Doubt kindles choice. Choice is opportunity, opportunity to do better or worse.

—Steven Muller

Saving money will require a reduction in the number of beds and in the number of employees in the hospital; not their redeployment to provide yet another untested treatment. We need a leaner, trimmer health care economy.

—John E. Wennberg, M.D.

The need for better information, active cost management, and better financial management is widely accepted. Only with better financial management can we preserve the duality of our health care institutions as both a charity and an efficient service provider for the community. The focus will be both micro (institutional) and macro (better payment options for the future). The initial focus of the first two chapters will center on the hospital economy. We start with the hospital economy because it is the largest segment of the health care sector, representing 4.7 percent of the gross national product (GNP). Prior to beginning a discussion of hospital cost inflation, it is essential first to explain how it is known that costs are in fact increasing each year. In other words, it is necessary to identify the indexes of cost inflation being used and to understand their implications. One broad indicator of the *relative* quantity of resources devoted to health care is the percentage of the GNP devoted to health expenditures. National health expenditures rose from 4.5 percent of the GNP in 1950 to 7.2 percent in 1970, 10.7 percent in 1983, and 11.8 percent in 1990 (see table 1.1).

An estimated 12.66 percent of GNP ($735 billion) will go to health care expenditures in 1992. Hospital services represent 39.5 percent of the total, and physician services represent 20.3 percent ($149 billion). Nursing home expenditures are estimated at 8.45 percent of the health budget ($62 billion) in 1992 (financed 47 percent by Medicaid, 1.8 percent by Medicare, 1.4 percent by private insurance, and 49.8 percent by out-of-pocket spending). In 1992 home health care should exceed $7.1 billion (financed 45 percent from Medicare and 35 percent from Medicaid). Prescription drug spending will reach $36 billion, and nonprescription drugs and other medical nondurables should cost $19.5 billion. Commercial research expenditures should exceed $10 billion, while government-sponsored research and other noncommercial research should exceed $17 billion. Dental services will represent $39.5 billion, vision care products $10.1 billion, and other durable medical products $4.4 billion in 1992.

DISTRIBUTIONS OF HEALTH CARE EXPENDITURES

Hospital expenditures, excluding physician billings for services performed in the hospital, represented 39.5 percent of health care spending in 1991. In 1992 hospitals will receive an estimated $290 billion in revenue. Public funds finance 55.2 percent of all hospital care: Medicare represents 29.8 percent, Medicaid 10.8 percent, state and local tax subsidies represent 6.8 percent, and the Department of Defense and the Veterans Administration provide 7.3 percent. Private funds finance 44.8 percent of hospital services: Employer-based health insurance represents 32.3 percent, consumer cost-sharing and individual-insurance plans represent 7.9 percent, and 4.7 percent of revenues comes from nonpatient sources (philanthropy, gift shops, office space rental, educational programs, and so on).

Although the explosion in health insurance during the past 40 years is the single most important factor in the increased demand for medical care, other factors have had an influence as well. Growth in population and increases in the average life span have contributed to the demand for medical care. The fastest-growing age group is the 65-and-older category, whose per capita expenditures on health care are four times those of adults 19 to 64. In addition, many innovations in medical technology are extremely expensive and increase the demand for medical care in a multiplicative fashion. Although the development of antibiotics and other drugs has been cost-effective in saving lives, new developments in medical technology, such as chemotherapy and organ transplantation, require expensive equipment and skilled personnel; by prolonging life instead of curing illness, such technology can be radically cost-increasing (Eastaugh 1990a). The cost-increasing nature of medical technology will be discussed in chapter 8.

Despite the tighter reimbursement climate in the 1980s, more and more community hospitals purchased expensive medical technologies. The percentage of community hospitals having magnetic resonance imaging (MRI) increased from 3.1 percent in 1984 to 17.7 percent in 1991. The percentage of community

Table 1.1
National Health Expenditures (Aggregate and per Capita)

Year	GNP (in billions)	Health Expenditures (in millions)	Health Expenses per Capita	Health as a Percentage of GNP	Hospital Care as a Percentage of GNP[a]
1929	$ 101.3	$ 3,589	$ 29	3.5	0.7
1935	68.9	2,846	22	4.1	0.9
1940	95.4	3,883	29	4.1	0.9
1950	264.8	12,027	78	4.5	1.0
1955	381.0	17,330	104	4.5	1.1
1960	498.3	25,856	142	5.2	1.5
1965	688.0	38,892	198	5.9	1.9
1966	722.4	42,109	212	5.8	1.9
1967	773.5	47,897	238	6.2	2.2
1968	830.2	53,765	264	6.5	2.3
1969	904.2	60,617	295	6.7	2.4
1970	960.2	69,201	333	7.2	2.7
1971	1,019.8	77,162	368	7.6	2.9
1972	1,111.8	86,687	410	7.8	3.0
1973	1,238.6	95,383	447	7.7	3.0
1974	1,361.2	106,321	495	7.8	3.1
1975	1,487.1	127,719	588	8.6	3.4
1976	1,667.4	145,102	663	8.7	3.5
1977	1,838.0	162,627	737	8.8	3.5
1978	2,107.6	192,400	863	9.1	3.6
1979	2,346.5	216,500	964	9.3	3.7
1980	2,631.7	247,500	1,049	9.4	3.7
1981	2,957.8	285,200	1,197	9.6	3.9
1982	3,069.2	321,200	1,334	10.5	4.2
1983	3,304.8	355,100	1,461	10.7	4.3
1984	3,662.8	387,400	1,580	10.6	4.1
1985	4,015.1	420,100	1,701	10.6	4.1
1986	4,232.0	450,500	1,806	10.7	4.1
1987	4,524.0	488,800	1,941	10.8	4.2
1988	4,881.1	544,000	2,124	11.1	4.3
1989	5,209.0	604,400	2,398	11.6	4.5
1990	5,455.3	633,000	2,488	11.8	4.5
1992 est.	5,764.0	735,000	2,820	12.7	4.9
1995 est.	6,753.0	934,000	3,285	13.9	5.4
2000 est.	8,779.0	1,334,000	4,212	15.2	6.0

Sources: Health Care Financing Review 12:4 (Fall) 1991; author estimates for 1992, 1995, and 2000.

[a]This is an underestimate of the hospital sector's share of GNP because the figure does not include services provided by nonsalaried physicians within hospitals. Because physicians have increasingly pursued subspecialty careers that demand increased reliance on the hospital, the magnitude of the hospital-sector underestimation bias has undoubtedly increased since the 1950s.

hospitals having organ transplantation nearly tripled, from 4.4 percent in 1984 to 11.2 percent in 1991. The percentage of community hospitals having Computerized Tomography (CT) scanners increased from 47.9 percent in 1984 to 68.9 percent in 1991. The percentage of community hospitals having Extracorpeal Shock-Wave Lithotripsy (ESWL) went from zero in 1984 to 7.6 percent in 1991. The percentage of community hospitals having open-heart surgery increased from 11.8 percent in 1984 to 15.9 percent in 1991.

COST-EFFECTIVENESS ANALYSIS: CAN IT DAMPEN THE TECHNOLOGY-BASED COST INFLATION?

The need for more cost-effective clinical decision making is clear when one considers the burden of a demand inflation in tests and procedures. In 1991 dollars the nation annually spends $5.4 billion on 280 million blood cholesterol tests, $4.5 billion on 230 million urinalysis tests, $7.4 billion on 126 million sequential multiple analyzer (SMA) tests, $3.2 billion on 115 million blood counts, $4.2 billion on 49 million chest X rays, $2.6 billion on 35 million ultrasound exams (for pregnancy and for heart and gallbladder problems), $2.7 billion for 32 million annual electrocardiograms, $1.8 billion on 26 million endoscopy exams, and $1.8 billion for 6.6 million stress/treadmill tests. Utilization review and prior-certification programs have done little to slow the inflation rate in demand and dollars for these tests and procedures. Media coverage has helped foster the explosion in patient demand for repeat cholesterol tests. One could speculate that adoptions of Medicare physician fee schedules in 1992 for certain procedures like endoscopy may dampen the volume for those procedures. Even little-ticket expenditures like Pap tests are a $1.0-billion item if we perform 46 million annually. Ultimately education based on the evolution of cost-effective preferred practice patterns is the number one tool we have to control physician ordering habits (Eastaugh 1990a).

Medical technology has moved into the public eye as a culprit in rising health care costs. However, there is a wide range of opinions as to whether technology is, on balance, a major or minor source of rising costs. Technology can sometimes be cost-decreasing, although this is less frequently the case in the medical sector of the economy. One wonders whether technology explains 5 or 40 percent of the cost-inflation problem. For Wilensky (1990) and other data analysts, technology has been implicated as a substantial cause of increased cost (30 to 40 percent) through increasing intensity of services and utilization. Other economists suggest that technology plays a more minor role in rising health care expenditures. What could society remove or ration to make a substantial reduction in the $700-billion annual health care bill?

If the cost problem were technology driven, would not the sectors of the medical economy that are high-tech grow the most? The data do not support this hypothesis. Even with 865 magnetic resonance imaging (MRI) facilities set up in the last seven years, one cannot argue that imaging technologies have driven up the cost of health care. Indeed, diagnostic imaging has increased from 3.1 to 3.5 percent of health care expenditures. Substitution for old techniques and prudent utilization controls to hold down variable costs have made MRI a costly burden. Many technologies would perform more cost-effectively with the aid of more stringent utilization review, for example, fiber optics. Inappropriate utilization makes a technology less cost-effective.

Some medical technologies appear cost-decreasing, such as visualizing gallstones with ultrasound and crushing the stones with lithotripsy. This is also clearly quality-enhancing in comparison to traditional exploratory surgery. Unfortunately, the public is not well versed in life-cycle costing or the risks of old-style invasive medicine (with iatrogenic infections and prolonged lengths of stay). The media tend to focus excessive attention on initial capital outlays rather than on long-run cost-benefit and cost-effectiveness. The public reads that MRI technology costs $1 to $2 million more than traditional X-ray equipment, or that IBM is trying to bring a $20-million compact synchrotron to market in the 1990s, and concludes that health care costs must be 90 percent technology driven. This is simply not true. Much of the administrative technology that hospitals have added since 1984 is cost-decreasing in pharmacy or nursing (e.g., automated nurse-scheduling systems to create workload-driven staffing patterns; see chapter 9).

Clinicians also have an incomplete understanding of life-cycle costing, product maturity, and development. Some physicians find technology a convenient bogeyman to blame for increasing health care costs. If technology and demanding patients are tagged as 90 percent of the cost-control problem, then organized medicine proceeds to lobby for higher fee schedules, claiming that its members, as professionals, are not getting enough money for their value. Advocates for either price competition or tight fee schedules reverse the perspective and ask if consumers are getting enough value for their money. Many agree with Wilensky (1990) that consumers and third-party payers need better-funded high-quality assessments of the costs, risks, and benefits of medical technology. The argument that technology cannot be evaluated because it presents a "moving target," constantly improving and efficiently circumscribing the indicators for clinical usage, is not to be believed. As Wilensky (1990) suggested, careful analysis is especially needed in those grey areas where technology attempts to improve quality-adjusted life years (QALYs) without extending life expectancy.

Nonclinicians are not familiar with the cascades of hypotheses to be tested in the severely ill teaching hospital patient (Eddy 1990). Physicians do not live in a world of perfect knowledge concerning certain probabilities (Haug 1989). Bayes theorem is the operating axiom implicit in most clinical decision making: Statistical inference concerning probabilities is associated with individual events (tests, clinical results) or qualitative statements (judgments, guesses) and not merely with sequences of events (as in frequency theories developed by statisticians studying only plants). An economist may have an easier time describing his or her body with exact numerical probability, but the tendency for most members of the human race is to describe things in qualitative categories (likely, unlikely, and in between). Conventional use of simple categories of probability is acceptable for a Bayesian diagnostic system in the academic medical center because the target conditions have a relatively high prior probability. For example, Chard (1991) studied pelvic infection to compare the effects of quantitative and qualitative probability estimates on the diagnostic accuracy of Bayes's theorem. For the commoner conditions (prior probability greater than 20 percent), the use of a two- or three-category system was virtually equivalent to the use of exact probability. However, uncommon conditions (with prior probability under 3.0 percent) were completely ignored by the qualitative system.

HOW MANY AMERICANS ARE UNINSURED?

Most health care professionals are familiar with statistics that demonstrate the paradox of deprivation amid excess (e.g., excess acute-care beds and almost $2 billion per day spent on health services). Roughly 31.5 million Americans lack health insurance, even when the unemployment rate dips to 5.3 percent, and this figure includes over 8.3 million children (U.S. Congress 1991). The uninsured as a percentage of the nonaged population changed from 13.8 percent in 1977 to 14.6 percent in 1980, 16.1 percent in 1983, and 18.4 percent in 1986 (Brown 1990), declined to 15.5 percent in 1990, and increased to an estimated 17 percent during the economic downturn in 1991. In 1986, 36.5 percent of the uninsured worked in jobs earning more than $10,000 per year, and 15 percent worked in jobs earning over $25,000 per year (Brown 1990). Monheit and Short (1989) reported that 75 percent of the uninsured had jobs or were dependents of those who worked. One-third of the uninsured were children (under 18), and another one-third were between the ages of 18 and 24. Brown (1990) indicated that 92 percent of the firms without employee health plans had fewer than 25 employees.

Uncompensated care is one of the forgotten stepchilds of our increasingly competitive medical marketplace. Hospitals compete for market share of the paying-patient business, but no one competes for nonpaying patients (Eastaugh 1987). The debate over indigent care will lead nowhere until we reach some consensus on whether our top priority is institutional financial support or providing access to a minimum standard of care for underinsured citizens. Institutional managers argue in terms of minimizing uncompensated care and mainstreaming the poor to all hospitals, no matter how costly and inefficient. The tenet of faith among managers and some researchers (Hadley, Steinberg, and Feder 1991) that equity, efficiency, and access are a zero-sum equation is certainly open to question. Moreover, one could question whether we can promote affordable managed-care systems for the uninsured and still maintain the dream of mainstreaming all people into "best-quality" service-delivery systems. We hear reports on how the poor are dumped from hospitals. Policy makers insist that indigent care is a vexing problem and demand that providers do "it" better—with hardly any consideration of the "it" we want improved. Good care for our population is the answer. But what is the question?

Indigent care is service provided to those who are incapable of paying for all or part of their medical bill and do not qualify for medical assistance programs. Care for the medically indigent includes charity care and some fraction of the bad debts. Sloan, Blumstein, and Perrin's (1988) analysis of American Hospital Association (AHA) data found that billed charges to "self-pay" patients were likely to be uncompensated care. In their Tennessee sample the self-pay patients were most likely to be maternity or accident cases. At their local Vanderbilt teaching hospital most uncompensated-care patients had incurred small bills. However, patients with hospital bills over $25,000 accounted for 35 percent of total hospital expenses (and only 2 percent of the patients).

A number of analysts (Cohodes 1986; Eastaugh 1987) have pointed out that the terms "uncompensated" or "indigent" care lump both charity care and bad debt into a single category. It is hard to get any accurate national estimate as to what fraction of bad debt involves poor people financially incapable of paying their bills, in contrast to nonpoor people unwilling (because they are dissatisfied) to pay some fraction of their bill. In affluent suburban markets bad debt might involve less than 10 percent charity care, whereas in the ghetto bad debt is 95 percent charity care. In 1991 an estimated $4.4 billion of charity care was provided by hospitals, and there was $8.6 billion of bad debt (1.6 and 3.15 percent of hospital gross revenues, respectively). While $13 billion of free care to the poor may seem an insignificant amount in macroeconomic terms within a nation that spends over $14 billion per week on health care, it represents an ethical and financial problem for one-third of the hospitals (Eastaugh and Eastaugh 1990).

Point-in-time data on the uninsured population are skewed toward the demographic traits of those individuals who have periods of being temporarily uninsured. Swartz and McBride (1990) reported that over half of the uninsured periods last less than five months. If only uninsured spells at a point-in-time survey are reported, 59 percent last longer than two years, and only 13 percent end within four months. From the more realistic longitudinal viewpoint, observing people over time, only 15 percent of uninsured periods last longer than two years. Employed people and higher-income people are more likely to experience uninsured spells than point-in-time data on the uninsured indicate. One in every five uninsured individuals has family income exceeding $3,100 per month. Two-thirds of the people who lose employer coverage, but do not lose employment, have uninsured spells that end within four months. The majority of this employed/uninsured group lack insurance while serving as probationary employees on new jobs. The hard-core uninsured/unemployed population, lacking insurance for over two years and not eligible for Medicaid, may represent less than 5.4 million Americans. An expanded Medicaid program could help these 5.4 million citizens. Can we afford to allow one in seven nonelderly Americans to want for lack of health insurance? Are we our brothers' keeper with respect to health care? Having raised the basic question concerning equity in the health field, we must define the three basic efficiency questions vital to the cost-management process.

INSURANCE AND THE DEMAND FOR CARE

How does the tremendous increase in expenditures on hospital care relate to the out-of-pocket costs borne by the consumer of hospital care at the time of illness? In other words, how is it that consumers are willing to bear the costs of such an increase in the intensity of hospital care without an equivalent return in the form of better health? Part of the answer lies in the fact that although there has been a great increase in the amount of national resources devoted to hospital care, there has been very little change in the cost of hospital care to the consumer at the time of illness.

In 1950 approximately 50 percent of the cost of hospital care (short-term, nonfederal) was paid directly by the consumer and 50 percent was paid by third parties, including government and private insurance. By 1983 the proportion of costs paid directly by the consumer had dropped to 13.9 percent, and by 1987 to a record low of 12.9 percent. However, since 1988 this figure has increased, reaching an estimated 16.3 percent in 1991 because of the hikes in cost-sharing provisions (e.g., Medicare, table 1.2). (Out-of-pocket consumer payments as a percentage of hospital revenues are two-thirds lower because of the fraction of consumer copayments, deductibles, and coinsurance channeled through third parties.) The result of the deep insurance coverage of hospital services is summarized as follows: The average cost of a patient day to the consumer has doubled in constant dollars since 1950, whereas the 1991 Average Cost Per Patient Day (ACPPD) was 579 percent what it was in constant dollar terms in 1950. Ideally one should not use hospital list price per diem, even if it is a component of the Consumer Price Index (CPI), as an index of inflation. List price inflation has greatly exceeded actual inflation (Dranove et al. 1991) as more patients receive discount prices, and the negotiated discounts are larger in recent years. However measured, the inflation in health care costs is more substantial than any other sector of the American economy. In this context it is not surprising that our health care sector could grow to $1.5 trillion (15.2 percent of GNP) by the year 2000 (Ginzberg 1990). There is substantial evidence to indicate that when a large proportion of medical costs are offset by insurance, doctors will recommend more services, and consumers in turn will demand more and better services. Thus as insurance increases, a higher quantity and quality of care are demanded.

DEFINING TYPES OF EFFICIENCY

Any attempt to lower costs while not reducing the quality or intensity of care is an attempt to improve efficiency. Efficiency can be identified in three forms: technical, economic, and allocative. *Technical efficiency* refers to the relationship

Table 1.2
Cost Sharing under Medicare, 1991

	Beneficiary Liability
Medicare Part A	
Hospital deductible	$628 per spell of illness
Hospital coinsurance	
Days 61-90	$157 per day
Days 91 on (for 60 lifetime reserve days)	$314 per day
Skilled nursing facility coinsurance	
Days 21-100	$78.50 per day
Medicare Part B	
Premium	$29.90 per month
Deductible	$100.00 per year
Coinsurance	20% of allowed charge
Balance bills	All excess up to 125% of the allowed charge, with the exception of evaluation and management services, which are limited to the lower of 140% of the allowed charge or the physician's 1990 maximum allowable actual charge (MAAC) percentage.

between input and output, irrespective of cost. If one cannot reduce the amount of input and still produce the same amount of output, then maximum technical efficiency has been achieved. In a hospital context, for example, inputs might be full-time-equivalent employees, and outputs would be days of care. *Economic efficiency* refers to the relationship between inputs and cost. When a day of care is provided at the minimum possible cost, there is economic efficiency. *Allocative efficiency* in health care involves determining from among which inputs the allocation of resources would be least costly for achieving an improved level of output (health status). A health production function is necessary to describe the relationship between combinations of inputs and the resulting output. Fuchs (1986) reviewed the findings and limitations of a number of studies whereby improved levels of health output were produced using different combinations of inputs. The reader should be careful to differentiate production functions from a closely similarly labeled concept—the production possibility curve—which describes the trade-off between different outputs from a given set of resources.

We shall consider in the coming sections the impact of pricing policies and capacity (size, equipment) decisions on efficiency.

The advent of federal and private prospective pricing has placed hospitals at risk for their cost behavior and has created a revolution in two senses. First, and for the first time, hospitals that are the most successful in holding down costs receive the advantages of higher operating margins and retained earnings for future capital replacement and growth. Second, the term "price" no longer refers to the old friendly concept of "charges" set by the hospital or in negotiation. Price has been exogenously thrust upon the sellers—in this case hospitals—by third-party payers interested in price competition. However, the seller could rightfully complain that the Health Care Financing Administration (HCFA) has offered something other than a free-market-determined price. HCFA has utilized its monopsony power to administer a form of price controls and to act as a "prudent buyer" on the taxpayers' behalf.

Many clinicians and hospital managers have found that the transition from reimbursement to payment and from cost-based to price-based financing has been far from smooth. The past two decades of blank-check, pay-hospitals-what-they-spend financing arrangements have done little to control costs. In fact, under cost payment, voluntary efforts to cut costs became a voluntary suicide program to shrink the assets and prestige of the hospital.

Health-services delivery is emerging as a market-driven industry. The current administration at the U.S. Department of Health and Human Services (DHHS) seems to be moving in the direction of more competition through competitive bidding and capitation contracts. Health care payers should work to devise a bidding scheme that manages cost reductions without harming quality. Before suggesting a quality-enhancing bidding system, it is necessary to survey why federal officials think that the hospital industry is currently too profitable because it earns a 12 percent profit margin per prospective payment system (PPS) case, according to the DHHS inspector general, Richard Kusserow (1989).

SUFFICIENT PAYMENT RATES: OUR MONEY OR THEIR LIVES?

This section discusses some of the basic issues that limit the smooth transition to prospective hospital payment. This highly regulated industry suffers from uncertainty as to how payment rates will change. In addition, hospitals are experiencing problems in product-line planning, unbundling of services, cost accounting, and explaining these new developments to their medical staffs. Regulators and payers are enjoying the benefits of declining admission rates and duration of stay, but the equity of the payment scheme is questionable. Improvements in PPSs are suggested as a way to reap scale economies of quality and efficiency, preserve access, and encourage hospitals to develop a balanced portfolio of service lines that foster regionalization. In terms of improving efficiency and effectiveness, the hospital sector has one leg over the fence of change and the other dangling. With so much cost-containment activity, it is reasonable to ask, "Are hospital costs under control?" The answer is a complex mix of good and bad news.

The 1976–90 trends from the AHA panel survey of 1,260 hospitals in all 50 states provide a useful sample, including all patients (not just Medicare) and more than 17 states (the sample universe for the DHHS inspector general's audited Medicare hospital cost reports; Kusserow 1989). One "good-news item" in table 1.3 is that inpatient days declined 8.9 percent (line 8) in 1984 because of a 0.3-day decline in average length of stay and 1.45 million fewer admissions. Inpatient days declined an additional 6.2 percent in 1985 as a by-product of a 0.1-day decline in length of stay and 1.46 million fewer admissions. In addition, total hospital inpatient costs increased only 3.2 percent in 1984 (line 9), the lowest rate since 1963. Hospital admissions per 1,000 citizens declined 19.7 percent from 1983 to 1991 (table 1.4, column 4). Hospital occupancy rates nationwide declined by 8 percent in 1984 to 66.8 percent and to a record low of 63.4 percent (350,000 empty beds) in 1986. Inpatient costs increased 4.4 percent during 1985. While economists could savor these declines in hospital cost inflation and utilization, there were reasons for doubting that the improvements would be either real or long lasting.

The skepticism of the mid-1980s was warranted (Eastaugh 1987), as total inpatient costs (table 1.3, line 9) inflated at 8.5 percent in 1988, 9.9 percent in 1989, and 11.8 percent in 1990. This return of hospital cost inflation happened despite the restructuring of the insurance marketplace and the frequent pleas from the hospital industry to increase prices to prevent hospital closures. HMO fee schedules and other managed-care systems also put pressure on the hospital industry (Fox and Heinen 1989). The number of empty beds should decline to 300,000 by 1992.

The public may be misled into undersupplying debt or equity funds to hospitals if it continues to read doom-and-gloom rhetoric about the hospital industry. The popular press often produces doom-and-gloom statistics as if the end of the world is at hand for American hospitals. For example, the *Washington Post* listed 698 fewer hospitals in the 1980–90 period as if "698 hospitals closed" (Eastaugh 1990b), but in fact only 107 hospitals closed, 84 restructured into long-term-care facilities, 118 mergers swallowed 123 hospitals, 262 hospitals consolidated with other hospitals, and 127 restructured into specialty hospitals (e.g., psychiatric facilities). Young health care managers need not fear an insufficient future job market, and the public need not avoid purchasing hospital bonds, because hospitals do not always go bankrupt. A consolidation occurs when two or more hospitals join to form an entirely new hospital (with a new name). Mergers involve separate firms that combine, with one hospital absorbing the other facility.

Akin to the airline and banking industries, hospitals are overstaffed and overbuilt. Closures are a healthy sign because they get some of the pathology out of the system, eliminate fixed costs, and stimulate control over the total health care bill. As Egdahl (1984) observed, in the labor-intensive hospital business,

Table 1.3
Trends in Hospital Capacity, Utilization, and Cost, 1976–1990

				Mean Annual Change (except lines 14-17)					
	1976-1982	1983	1984	1985	1986	1987	1988	1989	1990
Capacity									
1. Staffed beds	0.8	0.6	-1.1	-1.8	-1.2	-0.9	-1.3	-1.3	-1.0
2. Total personnel FTEs	5.0	1.4	-2.3	-2.3	-1.1	0.4	0.9	1.9	2.5
3. FTEs per 100 patient days	3.2	3.8	7.3	4.1	0.4	0.3	1.4	2.3	3.2
Elderly utilization									
4. Admissions (65 and over)	5.1	5.5	-2.9	-5.0	-2.1	-1.1	0.4	1.2	2.0
5. Length of stay (65 and over)	-1.5	-4.3	-7.6	-2.0	0.4	1.0	-0.7	-0.1	-1.6
Utilization and costs, all patients									
6. Admissions	1.9	-0.5	-4.0	-4.6	-2.9	-0.6	-0.4	-0.9	0.2
7. Length of stay	-0.4	-2.0	-5.1	-1.6	0.2	0.8	0	-0.1	-1.5
8. Inpatient days	1.5	-2.5	-8.9	-6.2	-1.4	0.2	-0.5	-1.0	-0.9
9. Total inpatient expense	15.8	10.2	3.2	4.4	7.5	8.6	8.5	9.9	11.8
10. Expense per day	14.1	12.9	13.3	11.0	9.1	8.4	8.9	9.3	12.8
11. Expense per admission	13.7	10.2	7.5	9.4	10.3	9.2	9.0	9.3	10.2
Market-basket price trends									
12. HCFA input price index	10.0	6.3	5.6	4.8	4.0	5.2	5.8	6.1	5.6
13. Consumer price index (CPI), all items	8.4	3.8	4.0	3.8	1.9	3.7	4.1	4.8	5.4
Trends in hospital cost-per-unit-of-output in real terms relative to CPI									
14. $ per day % Δ/CPI	1.5 fold	3.4 fold	3.3 fold	2.9 fold	4.8 fold	2.3 fold	2.2 fold	1.9 fold	2.4 fold
15. $ per admission % Δ/CPI	1.2 fold	2.7 fold	1.9 fold	2.5 fold	5.4 fold	2.5 fold	2.2 fold	1.9 fold	1.9 fold
Profitability (absolute values for the year, not % changes)									
16. Total operating margin (% of total revenue)	4.1	5.1	6.2	5.9	5.2	5.0	4.8	5.0	4.8
17. Patient operating margin (% of patient revenue)	-0.5	1.0	2.0	1.5	1.2	0.9	0.4	0.5	-0.1
Outpatient activity									
18. Outpatient visits and outpatient surgery	1.1	3.3	1.1	4.8	6.0	5.9	6.3	5.9	6.8
19. Outpatient revenue	19.3	16.0	13.0	16.0	16.8	16.6	17.2	15.8	17.9

Source: "American Hospital Association Panel Survey" (over 1,270 hospitals), *AHA Economic Trends*, 1991.

Table 1.4

Growth Rates in the Demand and Supply of Nonfederal Short-Term Hospitals, Selected Years, 1950–1991

Year	FTE Personnel per Adjusted Patient Day[a]	Patient Days (millions)	Admissions per 1,000 Citizens	Number of Hospitals	Number of Beds	Bed Occupancy (percent)	Outpatient Visits (millions)
1950	1.62	136	111.4	5,031	505,000	73.7	
1955	1.85	149	117.3	5,237	568,000	71.5	
1960	2.06	174	129.2	5,407	639,000	74.7	
1965	2.24	205	138.8	5,736	741,000	76.0	93
1966	2.37	215	138.9	5,812	768,000	76.5	96
1967	2.41	223	139.0	5,850	788,000	77.6	103
1970	2.65	242	145.6	5,859	848,000	78.0	134
1974	2.89	256	157.8	5,977	931,000	75.3	195
1978	3.23	263	161.1	5,935	980,000	73.5	204
1979	3.28	267	162.4	5,923	988,000	73.8	204
1980	3.34	279	165.8	5,905	992,000	75.4	207
1981	3.47	281	161.9	5,879	986,000	75.9	207
1982	3.52	284	156.7	5,863	982,000	75.2	214
1983	3.59	277	154.4	5,843	988,000	73.4	231
1984	3.67	254	147.1	5,814	961,000	66.8	232
1985	3.85	236	139.0	5,774	940,000	64.0	234
1986	3.92	229	133.7	5,720	920,000	63.4	245
1987	4.00	226	131.7	5,650	909,000	64.2	268
1988	4.04	225	130.0	5,570	897,000	64.7	287
1989	4.11	223	127.7	5,487	884,000	65.5	301
1990	4.18	221	126.4	5,408[b]	873,000	65.7	319
1991	4.33	213	124.0	5,358	863,000	63.9	333

Source: American Hospital Association panel survey, includes over 1,270 hospitals each year.
[a]Full-time-equivalent (FTE) personnel adjusted for outpatient visits rendered.
[b]If figures include specialty hospitals and federal and state hospitals, 698 closed in the period 1980-90.

bringing about significant cost savings without reducing staff and closing facilities is no easy task. Layoffs, or "managed attrition" that avoids firing people, are necessary to draw staffing into line with declining workloads. Hospitals, like airlines and banks, will continue to adapt to deregulation, trim their staffs, and close unnecessary service sites. At the same time, they will be diversifying into newly identified service product lines (see chapter 5). A net-present-value (NPV) analysis of the costs and benefits of each product line is required in most situations.

NET-PRESENT-VALUE ANALYSIS: DISCOUNTING

The uneven distribution of costs and benefits over time poses little conceptual difficulty for the analyst. One simply reduces the stream of future costs and benefits to net present value by discounting. The most common rationale for discounting social programs to present value reflects the uncertainty of the future: A benefit in hand is worth two in the future (Robinson 1990; Lipscomb 1989). In contrast, health economists have downplayed the business-sector rationale for discounting, which is the time value of money. In the business sector uncertainty is always incorporated through the use of decision trees. A form of discounting, net-present-cost analysis, will be used in chapter 13 to evaluate buy/lease decisions for new equipment.

Most studies offer a sensitivity analysis of the impact of discounting on cost per year of life saved: $31,300 for heart transplants discounted at 10 percent (but $27,200 if they are discounted at 5.0 percent), or $50,600 for liver transplants discounted at 10 percent (but $44,000 if they are discounted at 5.0 percent (Evans 1986). A discount rate of 10 percent produces a discount factor of 0.3855 after 10 years and 0.0085 after 50 years. In other words, benefits accruing a decade from now are worth just under two-fifths as much as comparable benefits accruing today; benefits accruing 50 years from now are worth one-eighty-fifth as much as comparable benefits accruing today.

The discount rate is designed to reflect the opportunity cost of postponing benefits or expenditures for an uncertain future. Economists posit that the yield on private investment can be properly regarded as the appropriate opportunity yield for public investment only if the subjective cost of risk bearing is the same for the average taxpayer as it is for the private investor. Musgrave (1969) indicated that the benchmarks should be a function of the source of financing; private consumption has a higher discount rate than public investment. Ten percent is the most frequently used discount rate. Opportunity-cost principles argue for a high discount rate. The true cost of a health care investment is the return that could have been achieved if the resources had gone elsewhere in the private sector. For Mishan (1976), the relevant comparison is not the expected rate of return but the expected rate of return net of the subjective costs of risk bearing. The corporate discount rate is obviously overinflated since it includes both a risk premium and a markup for corporate taxes. In order to achieve equivalent after-tax investor earnings, a corporation must offer stockholders a 10 percent return (that is, a 15 percent before-tax gross return) to compete with a riskless municipal bond returning 7.25 percent. Operationally, the second choice, government borrowing rates, serves as the upper bound in most analyses. Given the implicit assumption that the discount rate is not changing over time, the most prudent course of action is to perform a sensitivity analysis of the net present value under a range of discount rates. If a sensitivity analysis can demonstrate that selection of a discount rate does not affect the recommendations, then the tenuousness of the assumption will not be a source for concern.

The last discounting issue that must be considered is the selection of an appropriate downward adjustment to reflect the degree to which the medical price index exceeds the consumer price index (CPI). Klarman, Francis, and Rosenthal (1968) were the first to incorporate a net discount rate adjusted downward by 1 to 2 percent to reflect the extent that growth in medical prices exceeded the growth in the CPI. Jackson et al. (1978) utilized a downward adjustment of 5 percent to reflect the excess of medical inflation relative to inflation in the general economy. This net-discount-rate factor reflects the value of direct health-service forgone costs (benefits) that would also have increased by the excess of the medical price index over the CPI. If cost-containment programs were to bring the medical inflation rate to parity with the CPI, then this adjustment would be unnecessary.

UNNECESSARY UTILIZATION INTENSITY?

Insurance companies go beyond experience rating and demand side strategies (like higher coinsurance) to constrain health care costs. Insurance companies use utilization review and preadmission certification to trim annual premium increases by one-eighth (Gabel et al. 1990), but premiums still grow by more than double the rate of inflation in the general economy. According to the Lewin/ICF study (1987) about 40 percent of admissions to hospitals were avoidable. While non-hospital care was probably necessary, the hospital admissions would have been avoidable if the system had offered (1) gatekeepers to prevent unnecessary care, (2) consumer education, and (3) preventive care and access so conditions could be treated soon (prior to the need for hospitalization). Two important points seem clear: (1) Declines in admission rates predated PPS, and (2) we appear to have returned to 1960 admission rates (with more ambulatory care, compensating for the increased demands of a more aged population). If admission rates continue to decline, there are no easy, reliable answers to the questions "Are we saving much money?" and "Is any harm being done to patient health status?" We shall consider these issues in subsequent chapters.

Ginsburg and Hackbarth (1986) concluded that professional review organizations (PROs) may also contribute to continued declines in admission rates, but they will not be as cost-effective as those HMOs and preferred provider organizations (PPOs) facing the immediate threat of financial failure. PROs face the less immediate threat that they will lose their federal contracts. However, well-managed HMOs, PPOs, and the full spectrum of managed-care alternatives could produce further declines in admission rates (discussed in chapter 3).

Inpatient costs are down, but much of the forgone costs may have simply been shifted to outpatient settings. Many of these alternative care sites are owned by diversified and restructured hospitals and may be providing a healthy contribution to total operating profit margin of the parent companies. Also, the credit for much of this decline in inpatient expenses may rest with the fall in the basic national inflation rate—that is, the consumer price index (CPI). Many state rate-setting programs were set up to reduce unnecessary utilization and bring the annual rate of hospital cost inflation to less than double that of the CPI.

LOCAL STATE HOSPITAL RATE-SETTING PROGRAMS

A practical rate-setting system should try to limit regulatory costs (1) by limiting the cost of compliance for small, less sophisticated hospitals and (2) by limiting costly detailed review only to the hospitals asking for big rate increases. Some rate regulators assume a presumption of economic efficiency within peer groups of providers and only red-flag the inefficient 25 percent of each peer group. Those facilities with greater than average efficiency may be allowed to keep 50 to 100 percent of the gains from their internal cost-reduction efforts (incentive carrots); but the 25 percent of highest-cost, least efficient facilities in a peer group are offered "sticks" (low rate increases) to penalize inefficiency. Rate-setting methods range from annual review of budgets to formula or formula with appeals.

To be fair, a rate-setting system should pay for outlier cases and also adjust for appropriate changes in patient volume. Some states pay for volume changes at marginal costs (60 percent of average costs in the cost studies summarized in this chapter), while other states are less generous (paying for marginal additional patient volume at 40 percent of average costs); and some states mimic Medicare high-cost outlier payment rules and reimburse for additional patient volume above the baseline period at 80 percent of average cost.

Some state rate-setting programs are an arm of state government, while others function as independent commissions. Many state rate-setting programs have very limited budgets and low salaries (and thus inexperienced staff). The style of the rate-setting program varies from cooperative (e.g., Maryland) to adversarial (e.g., New York and Massachusetts). Cleverley (1990) outlined the need for hospitals to preserve their capital position. As a rule of thumb, the price-level-adjusted return on investment (ROI) should at minimum be 10 percent for an urban teaching hospital and 6.5 to 7.0 percent for a small rural hospital.

Maryland

The rate-setting program with the highest level of stability and effectiveness is the Maryland Health Services Cost Review Commission. The Maryland system promotes performance (cost control) without capital erosion because it offers a sufficient ROI to assure financial viability. Effectiveness is measured in two dimensions in this context: (1) long-run cost control (percentage increase in cost per adjusted admission, 1977–91), and (2) payer equity (percentage markup of charges over costs). Over the years 1985–91 Maryland had the lowest percentage markup of charges over costs (8.4 percent) in the nation, followed by New Jersey (11.3 percent), New York (14.9 percent), Washington (15.8 percent), and Massachusetts and Maine (19 percent). Maryland also had the best rate of long-run cost control, that is, the lowest percentage increase in cost per adjusted admission during the period 1977–91 (176 percent), followed by New York and New Jersey (198 percent), Massachusetts (200 percent), and Maine and California (255 percent).

The Maryland system was initiated in 1975 from a proposal written by the Maryland Hospital Association. Consequently, the program was cooperative in nature from its inception. In being cooperative, the Maryland system is also highly flexible. With regard to the unit of output, which is subject to rate control, Maryland has a mixed system, recognizing the differences between hospitals, both in terms of their ability to deal with a complicated rate-setting system and the nature of the market in which they are operating. Some rural hospitals are regulated by means of a total-patient revenue system. The constraint on most hospitals is an approved charge per case, but some small and all specialty hospitals have rates set per unit of service. The system is partly customized to the needs of the particular hospital (Atkinson and Eastaugh 1991).

Total-patient revenue system (TPR): A few rural hospitals with relatively self-contained service areas are given a total revenue budget based on the approved revenue of the hospital for some base year. This is increased each year for inflation plus 1 percent for new technology and new services (recently increased to 2 percent) and 1 percent for population growth and aging (unless the hospital can justify a greater factor for population growth and aging). Certain appeal adjustments are also made—for example, for malpractice insurance costs. There is no adjustment for change in the volume of patients treated. This system provides a predictable revenue to the hospital. The hospitals charge patients on the basis of the actual services provided within the total approved revenue; for example, a patient who stays for only two days will be charged less than a patient who stays for five days and has more services. If the hospital generates more than the approved revenue in one year, then the excess is deducted from its approved revenue for the subsequent year. Conversely, if the hospital generates less than its approved revenue in one year, then the shortfall is added to its approved revenue in the subsequent year.

Guaranteed inpatient revenue system (GIR): The system that applies to the majority of hospitals sets a guaranteed revenue per case for inpatient services. The hospitals continue to charge patients on the basis of the itemized charges for the services provided, but are constrained to be within the approved revenue per case after adjustment for the volume and case mix experienced. The rates are normally increased each year using a formula that provides for inflation plus 1 percent for new services (recently increased to 2 percent). Volume adjustments are made, with hospitals getting 85 percent of the average cost per case for each case above the budgeted level and losing 85 percent of the average cost per case for each case below the budgeted level. The guaranteed revenue per case, which is both a floor and a ceiling on the revenue per case, is automatically adjusted for change in the case mix experienced by the hospital, as well as for change in the mix of payers experienced by the hospital.

Rate per unit of service system: Some small rural hospitals and all the specialty hospitals have rates per unit of service. Units of service have been defined for each revenue center, and the hospitals are required to report to the commission the number of units of service and the revenue for each revenue center. Examples of units of service are days of care in routine daily patient-care centers like obstetrics, psychiatry, pediatrics, or medical surgical rooms, minutes of operating-room time, and workload units of the College of American Pathologists for laboratories. Again a volume adjustment is made using an 85 percent variable-cost factor.

The hospitals in Maryland bill patients on the basis of the itemized charges for the services provided for that case, no matter which mechanism is used to control the total revenues. The Maryland Hospital Association (1991) has prepared a book that describes in more detail the workings of the rate-setting system in Maryland. This is recommended for readers who wish to better understand the reasons for the success of the Maryland rate-setting program.

New Jersey and New York

New Jersey was the first state to use diagnostic related groups (DRGs) to set hospital prices. The state sets a rate for each DRG in each hospital. This rate is a blend of a hospital-specific cost and a statewide average cost for the case, with the percentage of the statewide average component dependent on how homogeneous the costs are within the given DRG. The more consistent the costs are within the DRG, the more the standard cost component is built into the rate. Until 1989 all payers (including Medicare and Medicaid) were charged using these DRG prices, with some payers receiving discounts (Rosko 1989). An appeal mechanism was set up for self-pay patients who considered that they had been overcharged, but this appeal method has been abandoned in favor of a new formulaic system where patients with a short length of stay are charged a high per diem, patients with a long length of stay are charged a lower per diem, and patients between the two thresholds are charged the DRG price. Medicare is no longer paying the rates established by the New Jersey commission.

The rates are adjusted each year for inflation, change in payer mix, change in volume, and other appeals. This system is more formulaic than the Maryland system, but less than the Medicare system. One recent evaluation of the New Jersey program (Broyles 1990) suggested that per case payment reduced length of stay and daily use of radiological procedures. Unfortunately, the New Jersey system was accompanied by an increase in daily use of lab procedures and the volume of lab tests per case.

The New York State rate-setting system has changed a couple of times in the past decade. During the late 1970s and early 1980s it was a per diem system, with the approved per diem rate based on the actually incurred costs of the individual hospital from three years prior to the year for which the rates were being set, with various penalties and adjustments. Blue Cross and Medicaid paid the same per diem rate, Medicare paid according to its own system, and most other payers were charged on the basis of the itemized charges for the actual services provided, with a control on the relationship between the average charge per day and the Blue Cross per diem rate. In 1983 the way in which the per diem rate for Blue Cross and Medicaid was calculated was changed. The base from which the per diem was developed was kept constant at the approved 1981 base costs, and inflation and other adjustments were applied each year to increase the per diem rates.

New York State started a DRG-based system effective January 1, 1988. This system is a blend of DRG pricing and DRG revenue limits. For each hospital a rate is set for each DRG. The rate for 1988 was 90 percent hospital specific and 10 percent of a group standard. In 1990 the rates were 55 percent standard and 45 percent hospital specific. The base year for the rates is 1981, with rates increased by an inflation factor each year, and capital, malpractice, and some other costs still paid at actually incurred levels. New York State has pools to pay for charity care and bad debts, and also a pool for distressed hospitals. The major payers for hospital services all pay a DRG price. Medicare and Medicaid pay the same rate, and insurance companies pay a rate that is 113 percent of the Blue Cross rate. Self-pay patients are billed the detailed charges for the services they receive, with a cap on their billing at 120 percent of the rate that an insurance company would pay for the DRG. Thus if Blue Cross would pay $2,000 for a case, then an insurance company would pay $2,260 for the same case, and a self-pay patient would pay the detailed charges, but not more than $2,712.

The rates do not include any recognition of differences between hospitals in the Medicare payment rates or Medicare percentages of revenue. It is of interest to note that New York State appropriately decided that the Medicare DRGs were inadequate for its purposes and greatly expanded the number of DRGs for new-born babies and acquired immune deficiency syndrome (AIDS) cases. It also developed DRG weights that were specific for the non-Medicare population of New York State.

Maine and Washington State

The system in Maine is unusual in that it was established in the 1980s, well after most of the other programs. In Maine there was a particular concern about ensuring access to hospital care. The system set the allowable gross revenue of each hospital, and the hospitals charged patients on the basis of the itemized charges for services rendered. The revenue was established based on the costs incurred by each hospital in a base year, with the usual adjustments for change in volume of service, inflation, and new projects. In 1989 some changes were adopted by the legislature that bifurcated the system. The system to be used for the regulation of the revenues of most hospitals will be more responsive to change in volume of service than the previous system, but certain hospitals in isolated areas that are needed for access to care will be provided some protection from revenue reductions due to volume declines.

Washington State is an interesting contrast to the rate-setting that took place in the northeastern states. The enabling legislation that established the Washington Hospital Commission was almost identical to that in Maryland (basically only the names were changed), but the outcome has been dramatically different. The Washington Hospital Commission took a very different approach to rate setting from that of the Maryland Health Services Cost Review Commission. Where Maryland relied upon incentives in the payment system to control the hospitals, Washington relied more upon a detailed annual review of the costs and charges of each hospital to control expenditures. Although the allowances provided by the Washington Hospital Commission were quite generous, and the rate of inflation in hospital costs in Washington State exceeded the national average over the period of the regulation, the hospital industry was quite antagonistic toward the regulatory system and in 1989 managed to bring it to an end (the same problems plague the West Virginia system, a copy of the Maryland system, which may ''sunset'' in 1992). This antagonism is an almost-inevitable outcome of a system that involves annual budget reviews. Such detailed reviews substitute the judgment of the regulators for the judgment of the hospital administration and arouse the ire of hospital administrators, who feel that they are being second-guessed.

Rate setting, when done effectively, can reduce the rate of inflation in hospital costs below the rate that would have been experienced otherwise and can also improve the fairness of the payment system. However, it should not be expected to reduce that rate of inflation below the rate of inflation in the general economy, and it should not be expected to control growth in medical technology.

The Maryland rate-setting process may not remain an all-payer system. Maryland has only maintained its Medicare waiver to operate the only single-payer (all-payer) rate-setting system by counting pre-1985 savings for the Medicare program to offset slightly higher than average absolute dollar costs per admission in 1991. New York, New Jersey, and Massachusetts all lost their Medicare waiver and capacity to operate a single-payer statewide system in the 1980s. The demise of the single-payer system in Maryland in 1992–93 would be sad in two basic ways. First, the state commission could no longer redistribute $270 million of funds (1991) from the wealthy areas to the 23 hospitals with the highest charity-care patient volume. Second, the demise of the last experimental all-payer state program would be a setback for policy advocates offering reform proposals that focus on a unified payment system (see chapter 15). However, Maryland will probably not retain its Medicare waiver, given that the state's average length of stay is 0.8 days higher than the national average. If Maryland Medicare patients are thrust onto the national DRG system, the incentive to trim length of stay will become much stronger (see chapter 8).

HEALTH PLANNING BY EXTERNAL AGENCIES: DID IT SAVE MONEY?

All the multiple regression studies of certificate-of-need (CON) programs suggest that health planning did not reduce the supply of hospital beds, plant assets, or total assets per bed (Eastaugh 1987, 1982; Sloan and Steinwald 1980; Salkever and Bice 1976). For this reason, corporate planning has replaced community-based health planning as a topic in the literature; and 23 states have dropped the CON process for hospitals since 1984.

Planners might have had some limited effect of increasing the cost of a capital project by delaying the date of project initiation with paper roadblocks. However, the investor community largely determines the size of a firm's debt capacity (and net available capital stock), and the firms simply bombard the planners with spending proposals until the funds are exhausted. Health planning may still prove cost-effective in a cost-reimbursed market (e.g., nursing homes), but in a price-payment hospital market the business risk associated with a proposal will determine whether the capital venture is good or bad for the institution. Corporate planning imperatives have essentially replaced community-based planning. Moreover, as many hospital chain managers can attest, only an idiot builds financially unnecessary bed capacity and equipment.

Eastaugh (1987) reported some adaptive responses that hospitals might pursue in highly regulated situations. Hospital administrators have three methods of co-opting the regulatory process. First, they can purchase equipment that is below the CON program review ceiling (figure 1.1, section D). Depending on the state, these are items costing less than $100,000 to $200,000. Second, if the administrators cannot spend money on new bed construction or modernization, they can bombard the CON agency with a number of capital equipment requests (figure 1.1, section F). Failing at either of these strategies, the administrator can hire an excessive number of licensed practical nurses (LPNs) or grant above-average wage increases (figure 1.1, section G).

This third phenomenon is consistent with all nonprofit models of hospital behavior and has been observed in a sample of 1,228 hospitals by Sloan and Steinwald (1980). In summary, the compensatory response to regulation can occur on both the capital and wage sides of the patient-care production process.

RATIONAL EXPECTATIONS AND EFFICIENCY

The theory of rational expectations has been widely heralded in the popular press as one of the most exciting advances in economic theory. However, older

Figure 1.1
Conceptual Framework for the Hospital Investment Decision-making Process

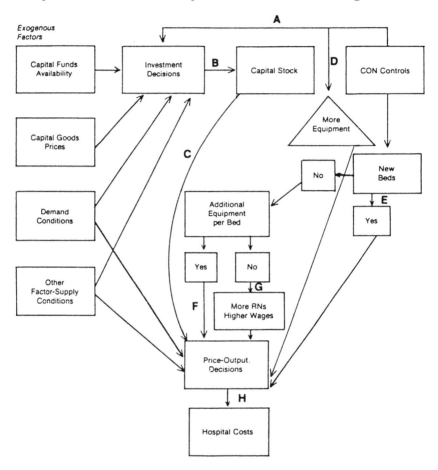

economists have always considered anticipatory behavior and announcement effects as being key hypotheses within the classical theory of the firm. Social scientists will find this "new" theory of the firm entitled "rational expectations" to be similar to the more familiar concept of the self-fulfilling prophecy (Eastaugh 1979). Simply stated, the theory of rational expectations postulates that people and institutions will take action based on how they expect outsiders, including government, to behave. In the process of attempting to predict or foresee the timing and details of new regulations, hospital administrators, commensurate with the theory, are believed to behave with anticipatory actions. Administrators who rush into new purchases of hospital equipment are eschewed as "irrational" by regulators, but if their behavior stems from anticipatory actions designed to increase the reimbursement base, such behavior may be considered a rational measure of self-protection. The smart administrator learns to anticipate future edicts from the rule makers and merely devises a new set of games for co-optation of future rules.

It was a rational expectation to predict that hospitals would change medical record-keeping habits to enhance reimbursement following the introduction of Medicare DRGs in 1983. Steinwald and Dummit (1989) outlined the importance of DRG creep or case-mix creep. The creep has been faster in the teaching hospitals, but the level of creep seems to be approaching diminishing returns; that is, the rise has been less substantial since 1986 (Carter, Newhouse, and Relles 1990). Teaching hospitals' Medicare index crept up 4.3 percent in 1985, 3.1 percent in 1986, and 2.3 percent in 1987. The rate of creep was lower for nonteaching hospitals: 2.8 percent in 1985, 1.7 percent in 1986, and 1.7 percent in 1987. Because the DRG prices are adjusted to the creep in a revenue-neutral way, the hospital sector does not benefit from DRG creep. However, individual hospitals with a higher than average rate of DRG creep do profit from reporting a higher, more resource-intensive Medicare case mix. Many hospitals have down-sized (reduced bed capacity), because financial managers have been incapable of reaping scale economies (size advantages), and demand is slack (low occupancy rates). Hospital managers have been doing less inpatient care as a proportion of revenues, and more outpatient care since 1983 (see Table 1.5).

ECONOMIES OF SCALE

In considering what happens to the level of output as the level of input increases, we are addressing the issue of economies of scale. If output grows at the same rate as inputs are increased, then there are constant returns to scale (per unit costs are the same at any given level of output). If output increases at a rate greater than inputs are increased, then there are increasing returns to scale (per unit costs decrease at high levels of output). If output grows at a rate less than the corresponding increase in inputs, then there are decreasing returns to scale (per unit costs increase as output rises).

Hospitalwide economies of scale are typically small. Within individual hospital departments and product lines there are substantial economies of scale to be observed. The most common problem faced by the analysts is that of comingling case-mix effects with unit cost; there tends to be a correlation between more difficult case mix and size (Keating 1984). Schaafsma (1986) studied 40 hospitals and concluded that in medium-size hospitals (60 to 293 beds) the economies-of-scale effect (12 percent) was more than offset by a case-mix effect, and hence costs increased slightly with volume. However, in hospitals with over 300 beds the economies-of-scale effect was sufficiently powerful to swamp any case-mix effect.

Economies of scale are generally illustrated by the long-run average cost curve (LRACC) in figure 1.2. Hospital size is measured either by number of beds or by average daily patient census. Output is typically measured by patient days

Table 1.5

Change in Hospital Revenue and Proportion of Revenue, by Source 1980–1991 (In Percent)

Year	Change in Revenue			Proportion of Revenue		
	Inpatient Revenue per Admission	Outpatient Revenue per Visit	Other Revenue per Adjusted Admission	Inpatient	Outpatient	Other
1980	14.5%	15.8%	9.7%	83.2%	12.5%	4.3%
1981	17.3	19.2	23.6	82.7	12.7	4.5
1982	16.2	16.8	12.9	82.7	12.9	4.4
1983	10.4	11.5	5.5	82.4	13.4	4.2
1984	8.6	12.4	10.9	81.3	14.4	4.3
1985	8.9	13.2	15.6	79.3	16.1	4.6
1986	8.5	8.3	6.9	78.0	17.5	4.5
1987	8.9	10.7	11.2	76.8	18.6	4.6
1988	8.5	11.4	14.5	75.2	20.0	4.8
1989	9.4	11.5	12.0	74.0	21.1	4.9
1990	9.2	11.7	10.1	72.5	22.5	5.0
1991	8.9	11.2	9.9	71.1	23.8	5.1
Averages:						
1980-1983	14.6	15.8	12.7			
1984-1991	8.9	11.3	11.6			

Source: American Hospital Association Panel Survey.

Figure 1.2
Relationships between Hospital Size and Cost

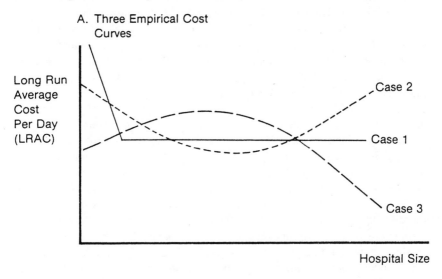

A. Three Empirical Cost
   Curves

Long Run
Average
Cost
Per Day
(LRAC)

Case 2

Case 1

Case 3

Hospital Size

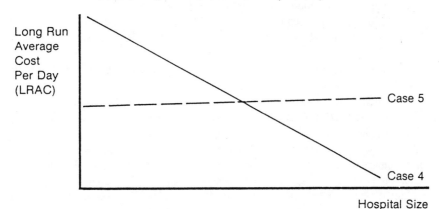

B. Classical Economy of Scale Curve (Case 4) and
   Constant Returns to Scale Curve (Case 5)

Long Run
Average
Cost
Per Day
(LRAC)

Case 5

Case 4

Hospital Size

Note: Case numbers are those of table 1.6.

and in some cases by patient discharges or admissions. The classic configuration of the LRACC is the U-shape illustrated in figure 1.2A, case 2. Generally, average costs are expected to decrease as output increases up to a point of minimum average costs, after which diseconomies of scale may take over. This point of minimum average costs is the optimal size for a firm or hospital (or the optimal level of output). Diseconomies beyond a certain point may be the result of inefficient management in large-scale facilities, or they may reflect the costs of increased travel time for physicians and patients (Fuchs 1986; Eastaugh 1987).

The central problem with applying the concept of economies of scale to hospital size is that hospitals do not produce a uniform product. Generally, the larger hospitals tend to treat more complex cases and to provide a much broader spectrum of care; thus a patient day in a small hospital is not equivalent to a patient day in a large hospital. Accordingly, any study of economies of scale must take case mix into account.

Research studies on economies of scale in the hospital sector have found five different shapes of the LRACC (see table 1.6). Failure to account for case mix results in a U-shaped LRACC. When adjustment for case mix is made, the LRACC is found to be slightly downward-sloping or flat for larger hospitals, indicating that economies of scale may exist, although the economies may not be great enough to justify much larger hospitals. An additional criticism of studies of the LRACC is that highly aggregated cost data make it impossible to separate the diseconomies due to size from those due to inefficiency, thus potentially leading to wrong conclusions regarding the optimal hospital size (Finkler 1979).

Much more significant economies of scale have been found on a departmental basis, under conditions where the product is homogeneous, by Hospital Administrative Services (HAS) researchers. Consequently, one would presuppose that if we could perform a perfect study adjusting for heterogeneous product mix of patient cases, then economies of scale would be more significant than the 16 percent difference between the smallest and largest hospitals in figure 1.2B, case 4. In summary, the data on economies of scale are not persuasive enough to suggest that we close all hospitals below a certain size. The increased travel time to consumers and staff associated with closing all below-average-size hospitals would probably outweigh the benefits accrued in increasing returns to scale.

In a study for the Federal Trade Commission Bureau of Economics, Sherman (1988) reproduced the Grannemann et al. (1986) study for a sample of hospitals. Updating the Sherman study, including some regulatory variables (Eastaugh 1982), table 1.7 reports the scale economies and marginal costs for two equations on a random sample of 232 hospitals with more than 75 beds. The long-run cost equation is the better specification; that is, it is more reasonable because the weighted cost estimates obtained from a full cost specification are much closer to the actual revenue figures for the 232 hospitals. Short-run equations are always lower estimates and represent only a fraction of total revenue and the expense of operating a facility. Marginal cost is the increase in total costs of producing an extra unit of output (the five hospital outputs listed in table 1.7), holding other outputs constant. As a rule of thumb, marginal costs equal 0.6 to 0.66 of average total cost in the studies in table 1.6. However, average total cost differs from the average incremental costs listed in table 1.7. The incremental cost of producing output 5 is the difference between the costs of producing all outputs and the costs of producing all the other outputs listed (table 1.7, 1 through 4). Dividing the average incremental costs by the marginal costs yields the product-

Table 1.6
Survey of Studies Concerning Economies of Scale in the Hospital Sector

Case 1.   L-Shaped Average Cost Curve Found:

Feldstein, M. S., and J. Schuttinga. "Hospital Costs in Massachusetts: A Methodological Study." *Inquiry* 14:1 (March 1977), 22–31.

Francisco, E. W. "Analysis of Cost Variations Among Short-Term General Hospitals." In H. E. Klarman (ed.), *Empirical Studies in Health Economics*. Baltimore, Maryland: Johns Hopkins University Press, 1970, pp. 321–332.

Lave, J. R., and L. B. Lave. "Hospital Cost Functions." *American Economic Review* 60 (June 1970), 379–395.

Case 2.   U-Shaped Average Cost Curve Found:

Schaafsma, J. "Average Hospital Size and the Total Operating Expenditures for Beds Distributed over H Hospitals." *Applied Economics* 18:1 (April 1986), 279–290.

Carr, W. J., and P. J. Feldstein. "The Relationship of Cost to Hospital Size." *Inquiry* 4:2 (June 1967), 45–65.

Cohen, H. A. "Variations in Cost Among Hospitals of Different Sizes." *Southern Economic Journal* 33 (January 1967), 355–366.

Feldstein, M. S. *Economic Analysis for Health Service Efficiency*. Amsterdam: North-Holland Publishing Co., 1968.

Case 3.   Inverted U-Shaped Average Cost Curve Found:

Ingbar, M. L., and L. D. Taylor. *Hospital Costs in Massachusetts*. Cambridge, Mass.: Harvard University Press, 1968.

Case 4.   Downward Sloping Average Cost Curve Throughout:

Baron, D. P. "A Study of Hospital Cost Inflation." *Journal of Human Resources* 9 (Winter 1974), 33–49.

Berry, R. E., Jr. "Returns to Scale in the Production of Hospital Services." *Health Service Research* 2 (Summer 1967), 123–139.

Feldstein, P. J. *An Empirical Investigation of the Marginal Cost of Hospital Services*. Chicago, Illinois: University of Chicago, Center for Health Administration Studies, 1961.

Case 5.   Constant Returns to Scale:

Bays, C. "Specification Error in the Estimation of Hospital Cost Functions." *Review of Economics and Statistics* 42:2 (February 1980), 302–305.

Evans, R. G. "Behavioral Cost Functions for Hospitals." *Canadian Journal of Economics* 4 (May 1971), 198–215.

Lipscomb, J., I. E. Raskin, and J. Eichenholz. "The Use of Marginal Cost Estimates in Hospital Cost Containment Policy." In M. Zubkoff, I. E. Raskin, and R. S. Hanft (eds.), *Hospital Cost Containment: Selected Notes for Future Policy*. New York: Prodist Press, 1978, pp. 514–537.

Table 1.7
Estimated Long-Run and Short-Run Cost Equations and Economies of Scale for a Sample of 232 Hospitals

Output	Long-Run Cost Equations, 1970-90			Short-Run (1 year) Equations		
	Marginal Costs	Average Incremental Costs	Scale Economies[a]	Marginal Costs	Average Incremental Costs	Scale Economies
Emergency department visits	390.29	476.18	1.22	116.02	142.73	1.23
Other outpatient visits	81.64	88.96	1.09	50.19	54.72	1.09
Subacute inpatient days	528.53	539.10	1.02[b]	126.02	124.80	.99[b]
Acute inpatient days	819.93	844.56	1.03	108.98	121.01	1.11
Intensive care days	1,175.26	1,267.48	1.07	297.60	328.25	1.10

[a]If this number exceeds 1.0, economies of scale exist.

[b]Not significant at the 0.05 level; other variables significant at the 0.01 level.

specific economies-of-scale factor listed in table 1.7, columns 3 and 6. In agreement with previous studies, shallow economies of scale exist (under 12 percent), except for one output—emergency-department visits.

DEMAND-PULL IN EMERGENCY-DEPARTMENT VISITS

The fact that substantial scale economies exist for emergency departments may be a by-product of the stressed urban hospital. In many urban areas the emergency department functions as the only available clinician for the poor. From 1983 to 1990 the number of emergency departments in the nation declined by 6.1 percent (from 5,406 to 5,077), and yet the number of annual visits increased by 19.6 percent (from 77.5 million to 92.7 million).

A number of complex factors have contributed to emergency-department (ED) overcrowding. With 15,000 beds closing each year, fewer beds translate into a lowered capability to shift sick ED patients into inpatient beds. A more complex patient mix, including an increased number of AIDS patients utilizing the ED department for primary care, is a major problem in urban hospitals. In 1985 people with AIDS accounted for 2.0 percent of patient ED workload in New York City hospitals. By 1991 this figure surged to 60 percent in New York City and 20 percent in Washington, D.C. Why do patients without AIDS use the ED for primary care? The answer is that the number of persons eligible for Medicaid shrank to 31 percent of poor citizens in the 1980s (Eastaugh and Eastaugh 1990). Inappropriate low staffing levels, due to a shortage of ED-qualified health care professionals, adds to the problem of overcrowding. Low Medicaid reimbursement policies contribute to all four of these problems.

On average, Medicaid spending is financed 57 percent by the federal government and 43 percent by state governments. Medicaid spending is the most rapidly inflating budget item for federal and state governments. From 1987 to 1990 annual Medicaid spending inflated at 17 percent per year, reaching $72 billion in 1990. From 1990 to 1992 Medicaid spending is expected to inflate at 23 percent per year (reaching $105.3 billion in 1992). There is considerable inefficiency in the Medicaid system, yet the prices paid to providers are substantially lower than average prices in most states. Half of the cost inflation is good news: it is the result of more uninsured individuals becoming eligible for Medicaid and willing to utilize Medicaid. Medicaid participation has jumped from 23.5 million citizens in 1989 to an estimated 28.8 million in 1992, but one in every seven citizens is still uninsured.

THE AGENDA

In the following chapters we shall consider in some detail various aspects of social and institutional cost-containment issues. In chapter 2 we shall outline changes in hospital accounting, purchasing, and specialization behavior. The problems of rising demand, consumer expectations, and the issue of unnecessary care are the subject of chapter 3. Viewed in this light, no sensible analyst could conclude that medical technology *per se* is the cause of rising costs. However, curtailment of overcapitalization and inefficient physician ordering habits form an increasingly important set of issues (chapters 7–11). Certain chapters will focus on a given market segment: HMOs and PPOs (chapter 3), long-term care (chapter 4), diversification and marketing (chapters 5 and 6) physician reimbursement (chapter 7), and multihospital systems (chapter 12). The critical issue of service quality will be discussed in chapters 11 and 15. Financing and debt issues will be discussed in chapters 13 and 14. The concluding chapter 15 will enable us to critically review and interrelate the disparate economic and financial management issues raised in the text. One final word of caution is in order for those who believe that the unplanned medical economy is a "nonsystem" of scattered parts: Observe how systematically providers resist government attempts to institute change.

REFERENCES

Arnett, R., McKusick, D., Sonnefeld, S., and Cowell, C. (1986). "Projections of Health Care Spending to 1990." *Health Care Financing Review* 7:3 (Spring), 1–36.

Atkinson, G., and Eastaugh, S. (1991). "State Rate Setting Programs." Working Paper, Department of Health Services Management and Policy, George Washington University, Washington, D.C.

Bays, C. (1980). "Specification Error in the Estimation of Hospital Cost Functions." *Review of Economics and Statistics* 62:2 (February), 302–305.

Berki, S. (1990). "Approaches to Financing Care for the Uninsured." *Henry Ford Hospital Medical Journal* 38:3 (Fall), 119–122.

Boxerman, S., and Gribbins, R. (1991). "Technology Management in the 1990s." *Healthcare Executive* 6:1 (January–February), 21–23.

Bronow, R., Beltran, R., and Cohen, S. (1991). "The Physicians Who Care Plan: Preserving Quality and Equitability." *Journal of the American Medical Association* 265:19 (May 15), 2511–2516.

Brook, R. (1991). "Health, Health Insurance, and the Uninsured." *Journal of the American Medical Association* 265:22 (June 12), 2998–3002.

Brown, L. (1990). "The Medically Uninsured: Problems, Policies, and Politics." *Journal of Health Politics, Policy, and Law* 15:2 (Summer), 413–426.

Broyles, R. (1990). "Efficiency, Costs, and Quality: The New Jersey Experience Revisited." *Inquiry* 27:1 (Spring), 86–96.

Carter, G., and Ginsburg, P. (1986). *The Medicare Case Mix Index Increase: Medical Practice Changes, Aging, and DRG Creep.* Rand Corporation Report R-3292 (June). Santa Monica, Calif.: Rand Corporation.

Carter, G., Newhouse, J., and Relles, D. (1990). "How Much Change in The Casemix Index Is DRG Creep?" *Journal of Health Economics* 9:4 (December), 411–428.

Chard, T. (1991). "Qualitative Probability versus Quantitative Probability in Clinical Diagnosis: Study Using a Computer Simulation." *Medical Decision Making* 11:1 (January–March), 38–41.

Cleverley, W. (1990). "Improving Financial Performance: A Study of 50 Hospitals" *Hospital and Health Service Administration* 35:2 (Summer), 173–187.

Coddington, D., Keen, D., and Moore, K. (1991) *The Crisis in Health Care*. San Francisco: Jossey-Bass.

Cohodes, D. (1986). "America: The Home of the Free, the Land of the Uninsured." *Inquiry* 23:3 (Fall), 227–235.

Congressional Budget Office. (1991). *Rising Health Care Costs: Causes, Implications, and Strategies*. Washington, D.C.: CBO, U.S. Congress.

Cornelius, L. (1991). "Access to Medical Care for Black Americans with an Episode of Illness." *Journal of the National Medical Association* 83:7 (July), 617–626.

Dunham, N., Kindig, D., and Ramsey, P. (1991). "Uncompensated and Discounted Care Provided by Physician Group Practices." *Journal of the American Medical Association* 265:22 (June 12), 2982–2986.

Eastaugh, S. (1992). *Health Economics: Efficiency, Quality and Equity*. Westport, Conn.: Auburn House.

———. (1990a). "Financing the Correct Rate of Growth of Medical Technology." *Quarterly Review of Economics and Business* 30:4 (Winter), 54–60.

———. (1990b). "Defining Rates of Hospital Closure." *Washington Post*, September 18, H2.

———. (1987). *Financing Health Care*. Dover, Mass.: Auburn House, 657–683.

———. (1984). "Hospital Diversification and Financial Management." *Medical Care* 22:8 (August), 704–723.

———. (1982). "Effectiveness of Community-based Hospital Planning: Some Recent Evidence." *Applied Economics* 14:5 (October), 475–490.

———. (1979). "President's Hospital Cost Containment Proposal." Subcommittee on Health Hearings, Committee on Ways and Means, 96th U.S. Congress, First Session, April 2, 1979, Part 2, Serial 96–19, 396–418. Washington, D.C.

Eastaugh, S., and Eastaugh, J. (1990). "Putting the Squeeze on Emergency Medicine: Pressures on The Emergency Department." *Hospital Topics* 68:4. (Fall), 21–25.

———. (1986). "Prospective Payment Systems: Further Steps to Enhance Quality, Efficiency, and Regionalization." *Health Care Management Review* 11:4 (Fall), 37–52.

Eddy, D. (1990). "Clinical Decision Making: From Theory to Practice." *Journal of the American Medical Association* 263:2 (January 19), 441–443.

Egdahl, R. (1984). "Should We Shrink the Health Care System?" *Harvard Business Review* 62:1 (January–February), 125–132.

Evans, R. (1986). "Cost Effectiveness Analysis of Transplantation." *Surgical Clinics of North America* 66:8, 603–616.

Fetter, R. (1991). *DRGs: Their Design and Development*. Ann Arbor, Mich.: Health Administration Press.

Finkler, S. (1979). "On the Shape of the Long Run Average Cost Curve." *Health Services Research* 14:4 (Winter), 281–289.

Fox, P., and Heinen, L. (1989). *Determinants of HMO Success*. Ann Arbor, Mich.: Health Administration Press.

Freeland, M., and Schendler, C. (1984). "Health Spending in the 1980s: Integration of Clinical Practice Patterns with Management." *Health Care Financing Review* 5:3 (Spring), 1–68.

Fuchs, V. (1986). *The Health Economy*. Cambridge, Mass.: Harvard University Press.

Gabel, J., DiCarlo, S., Sullivan, C., and Rice, T. (1990). "Employer Sponsored Health Insurance." *Health Affairs* 9:3 (Fall), 161–175.

Garrison, L., and Wilensky, G. (1986). "Cost Containment and Technology." *Health Affairs* 5:2 (Summer), 46–59.

Ginsburg, P., and Hackbarth, G. (1986). "Alternative Delivery Systems and Medicare." *Health Affairs* 5:1 (Spring), 6–22.

Ginzberg, E. (1990). *The Medical Triangle: Physicians, Politicians, and the Public.* Cambridge, Mass.: Harvard University Press.

Grannemann, T., Brown T., Pauly, M. (1986). "Estimating Hospital Costs: A Multiple-Output Analysis." *Journal of Health Economics* 5:2 (June), 107–127.

Gustafson, D., Catsbaril, W., and Alemi, F. (1992). *Systems to Support Health Policy Analysis: Theory, Models, and Uses.* Ann Arbor, Mich.: Health Administration Press.

Gutterman, S., Altman, S., and Young, D. (1990). "Hospital Financial Performance in the First Five Years of PPS." *Health Affairs* 9:1 (Spring), 125–133.

Hadley, J., Steinberg, E., and Feder, J. (1991). "Comparison of Uninsured and Privately Insured Hospital Patients: Condition on Admission, Resource Use, and Outcome." *Journal of the American Medical Association* 265:3 (January 16), 374–379.

Haug, P. (1989). "Revision of Diagnostic Logic Using a Clinical Data Base." *Medical Decision Making* 9:2 (April–June), 84–90.

Health Insurance Association of America (HIAA). (1991). *Source Book of Health Insurance Data, 1991.* Washington, D.C.: Health Insurance Association of America.

Hiatt, H. (1990). *Medical Lifeboat: Will There Be Room for You in the Health Care System?* New York: Harper and Row.

Institute of Medicine. (1989). *Effectiveness Initiative: Setting Priorities for Clinical Conditions.* Washington, D.C.: NAS Press.

Jackson, M., LoGerfo, J., Diehr, P., Watts, C., and Richardson, W. (1978). "Elective Hysterectomy: A Cost-Benefit Analysis." *Inquiry* 15:3 (September), 275–280.

Keating, B. (1984). "Cost Shifting: An Empirical Examination of Hospital Bureaucracy." *Applied Economics* 16:3 (July), 279–289.

Kellermann, A., and Ackerman, T. (1988). "Interhospital Patient Transfer: The Case for Informed Consent." *New England Journal of Medicine* 319: 8 (August 29), 643–647.

Klarman, H., Francis, J., and Rosenthal, G. (1968). "Cost Effectiveness Analysis Applied to the Treatment of Chronic Renal Disease." *Medical Care* 6:1 (January–February), 48–54.

Kusserow, R. (1989). "Report of the HHS Inspector General: Performance under the Prospective Payment System, Results from Hospitals." Inspector General, U.S. Government.

Latta, V., and Helbing, C. (1991). "Medicare Short-stay Hospital Services by DRGs." *Health Care Financing Review* 12:4 (Summer), 105–139.

Levit, K., and Cowan, C. (1991). "Burden of Health Care Costs: Business, Households, and Government." *Health Care Financing Review* 12:2 (February), 112–122.

Lewin/ICF. (1987). "Medically Preventable Hospital Admissions." Report to the DHHS. Washington, D.C.: Lewin/ICF Inc.

Linton, A., and Naylor, C. (1990). "Organized Medicine and the Assessment of Technology." *New England Journal of Medicine* 323:21 (November 22), 1463–1467.

Lipscomb, J. (1989). "Time Preference for Health in Cost-Effectiveness." *Medical Care* 27:3 (March), S233–S253.

Maryland Hospital Association. (1991). *A Guide to Rate Review in Maryland Hospitals.* Lutherville, Md.: Maryland Hospital Institute.

Mishan, E. (1976). *Cost-Benefit Analysis.* New York: Praeger.

Monheit, A., and Short, P. (1989). "Mandating Health Coverage for Working Americans." *Health Affairs* 8:4 (Winter), 22–37.

Musgrave, R. (1969). "Cost-Benefit Analysis and the Theory of Public Finance." *Journal of Economic Literature* 7:3 (September), 797–806.

Office of National Cost Estimates (ONCE). (1991). "National Health Expenditures." *Health Care Financing Review* 13:4 (Fall), 1–35.

Pauly, M., and Held, P. (1990). "Benign Moral Hazard and the Cost-Effectiveness Analysis of Insurance Coverage." *Journal of Health Economics* 9:3 (December), 447–461.

Perry, S., and Pillar, B. (1990). "National Policy for Health Care Technology." *Medical Care Review* 47:4 (Winter), 401–418.

Prospective Payment Assessment Commission (ProPAC). (1991). *Medicare Prospective Payment and the American Health Care System: Report to Congress.* Washington, D.C.: ProPAC.

Robinson, J. (1990). "Philosophical Origins of the Social Rate of Discount in Cost-Benefit Analysis." *Milbank Quarterly* 68:2 (Summer), 245–265.

Rosko, M. (1989). "Impact of the New Jersey All-Payer Rate-setting System: An Analysis of Financial Ratios." *Hospital and Health Services Administration* 34:1 (Spring), 53–69.

Salkever, D. (1975). "Hospital Wage Inflation: Supply-Push or Demand-Pull?" *Quarterly Review of Economics and Business* 15:33 (Autumn), 33–48.

Salkever, D., and Bice, T. (1976). "The Impact of Certificate-of-Need Controls on Hospital Investment." *Milbank Memorial Fund Quarterly* 54:2 (Spring), 195–214.

Schaafsma, J. (1986). "Average Hospital Size and the Total Operating Expenditures for Beds Distributed over H Hospitals." *Applied Economics* 18:1 (April), 279–290.

Schwartz, W., and Mendelson, D. (1991). "Hospital Cost Containment in the 1980s." *New England Journal of Medicine* 324:15 (April 11), 1037–1042.

Sherman, D. (1988). *The Effect of State Certificate of Need Laws on Hospital Costs.* Washington, D.C.: Federal Trade Commission.

Siegel, J. P. (1989). "Interhospital Patient Transfer." *New England Journal of Medicine* 320:3 (January 19), 258–259.

Sloan, F., Blumstein, J., and Perrin, J. (1988). *Cost, Quality, and Access in Health Care: New Roles for Health Planning in a Competitive Environment.* San Francisco: Jossey-Bass.

Sloan, F., and Steinwald, B. (1980). "Effects of Regulation on Hospital Costs and Input Use." *Journal of Law and Economics* 23:1 (April), 81–109.

Soderstrom, N. (1990). "Are Reporting Errors under PPS Random or Systematic?" *Inquiry* 27:3 (Fall), 234–241.

Steinwald, B., and Dummit, L. (1989) "Hospital Case-Mix Change: Sicker Patients or DRG Creep" *Health Affairs* 8:2 (Summer), 35–47.

Stern, R., Weissman, J., and Epstein, A. (1991). "Emergency Department as a Pathway to Admission for Poor and High-cost Patients.'' *Journal of the American Medical Association* 266:16 (October 30), 2238–2243.

Stevens, R. (1989). *In Sickness and in Wealth: American Hospitals in the Twentieth Century*. New York: Basic Books.

Stockwell, S. (1991). ''One Step Forward, Two Steps Back: Labor Issues.'' *Emergency Medicine News* 13:6, 8–11.

Swartz, K., and McBride, T. (1990). ''Spells without Health Insurance: Distributions of Durations and Their Link to Point-in-Time Estimates of the Uninsured.'' *Inquiry* 27:3 (Fall), 281–288.

Thompson, R. (1991). ''Total Quality Management.'' *Healthcare Executive* 6:2 (March–April), 26–27.

Thorpe, K. (1988). ''Why Are Urban Hospital Costs So High? The Relative Importance of Patient Source of Admission, Teaching, Competition, and Case Mix.'' *Health Services Research* 22:6 (February), 821–836.

Truman, D. R. (1951). *The Governmental Process: Political Interests and Public Opinion*. New York: Alfred Knopf.

U.S. Congress. (1991). *Medicaid Source Book: Background Data and Analysis*. House Committee on Energy and Commerce, Subcommittee on Health. Washington, D.C.: U.S. Government Printing Office.

Wennberg, J., Freeman, J., and Culp, W. (1987). ''Are Hospital Services Rationed in New Haven or Over-utilized in Boston?'' *Lancet* 1:8543, 1185–1187.

Wilensky, G. (1990). ''Technology as Culprit and Benefactor.'' *Quarterly Review of Economics and Business* 30:4 (Winter), 45–49.

Chapter 2

Hospital Accounting, Purchasing, and Product Specialization

In some cases hospital administration tended to go off on its own, saying "worry not, cost reimbursement will pay for everything." The attitude prior to 1984 was you trustees and physicians tell us what you want to do, we will spend the money, and somebody will pay us for our costs. With DRGs the new ball game had to include good cost analysis.

—Alex McMahon

Specialization helps trim unit cost, and improve service quality.

—Malcolm Baldridge

Beware of little expenses; a small leak will sink a great ship.

—Benjamin Franklin

Hospital accounting and financial reporting conventions have undergone two basic revolutions. The first revolution, during the years 1966 to 1968, following the passage of Medicare and Medicaid, required that tax-exempt hospitals keep more information than a simple one-page balance sheet. The state of tax-exempt financial reporting at this time was decades behind that of the business world. Investor-owned hospitals also lagged behind, but not as far behind as the tax-exempt hospitals. Former Speaker of the House of Representatives Carl Albert once related a marvelous story of how far hospital accounting has developed in the past decade. After the passage of Medicare and Medicaid, 30 hospital "superintendents" (no one was called an executive in those days) descended on his office to "protest this socialist concern for accounting ledgers and keeping records." The prevailing wisdom was that nonprofit organizations were too "charitable in character" to waste time keeping accounting records. Hospital superintendents began to be called administrators, and hospitals slowly discovered generally accepted accounting principles (GAAP).

The second revolution, in 1986–87, followed the Healthcare Financial Management Association's (HFMA) recommendation that hospitals record their income like any other business concern. In the spirit of true cost and revenue accounting, the hospital industry began to report revenue at expected payment levels. In the past, hospitals had recorded revenue as gross revenue, as if every patient paid list price (charges), with deductions for bad debt, charity care, and contractual or courtesy allowances (e.g., clergy). The pressure for this change in reporting conventions emanated from the need for the hospital's books to make sense for trustees with knowledge of the business world and from external relationships with five other key actors: lawmakers, state regulators, discount payers (e.g., Medicaid, PPOs, and so on), bankers, and bond-rating agencies (Schlag 1986).

Prior to 1987 the bond-rating agencies (Moody's, Standard and Poor's, and so on) and commercial bankers had to make numerous piecemeal extrapolations to assess a hospital's creditworthiness or financial health. Since modern hospital executives are clearly troubled about possible insufficient access to capital, communication with these external users of hospital financial reports is a critical area of concern. One could speculate that if the hospital industry had been more proactive, it would have changed its reporting conventions much sooner. For example, if hospitals had been reporting charity and bad debt as expenses prior to 1987, rather than as a "hidden" deduction from gross revenue, two things might have resulted: state lawmakers might have included indigent care in more of their payment schemes (Eastaugh 1990a), and federal lawmakers might have included expenses for indigent care in Medicare DRG rates. If legislators have no accurate estimate on the size of a problem (such as indigent care) because reporting conventions are deceptive, the problem often goes unresolved.

Since 1990 an increasing number of hospitals have been reporting gross patient revenue as the actual amount that the payers provide, that is, true revenue. The industry should have enacted this policy independent of any external reporting concerns. Such information is important for meeting the internal fiduciary responsibility to stay viable and up-to-date as an institution (Cleverley 1989). For example, internal decision making requires one to know how much PPO payer A is paying in relation to Blue Cross plan B. A hospital may not have any leverage negotiating better prices with Medicare, but the leverage to trade-off discounts for improved patient volume does exist on a local level. Having a more accurate estimate of the benefits and costs of alternative arrangements is better than forcing the finance department to mimic the extrapolations that bond raters are put through.

Hospitals have recently come to adopt the business-sector convention of product-line and net revenue reporting. If the hospital sector has experienced quantum leaps in financial reporting policies, the progress in managerial cost accounting has been more gradual and steady in the last few years (Eastaugh 1991).

Some ambulatory-care products are easily process costed, like diabetes control. However, other items have a wide range of customizing, including the addition of various "options" along the treatment process. As a rejoinder to interested medical staff, one might add that in order to avoid a reductionist "cookbook" standardization of medicine, it is necessary to quantify the cost-behavior ramification of the options (professional review organizations [PROs] tend to ignore the subtleties of marginal costing and to jump to the larger question of whether much of this care is "necessary"). For some DRGs, variability of costs within a DRG depends largely on the level of patient severity, which in turn determines the degree of customization (options selected). For example, within major reconstructive vascular surgery, including DRG 111, and to a greater degree for the more prevalent DRG 110, a wide coefficient of variation exists in cost per case, even when the surgeries are done by the same provider team (Rhodes, Krasniak, and Jones 1986). The range of customized options varies from proximal bypass to distal bypass for limb salvage to multiple ipsilateral surgery. The word "customized" is not intended to be pejorative, nor are the "options" frivolous.

The term "customized" denotes a situation that offers a wide range of options within the given DRG and thus a wide range of final product costs (e.g., DRGs 25, 82, 108, 169, 231, 243, 254, 296, 324, 421). Horn's (1986) computerized severity-of-illness index provides a four-level measure to improve on the definition of final products. Moreover, the Horn measure, or some other measure, could also be considered a custom option. For example, the daily room charge could be disaggregated into two basic components: (1) fixed per day hotel costs plus nursing costs at level-one severity and (2) variable costs for days in which the patient achieves severity level two, three, or four. In effect, hotel cost plus level-one severity costs could be process costed, and other severity levels (two, three, and four) could be job-order costed. Consider an extreme example: DRG 108 cardiothoracic procedures (except valve and bypass) might have a process-order cost of $7,000 per case, but a severity-level-two job order costs 3 times as much, a severity-level-three job order costs 7 times as much, and a severity-level-four job order costs 10 to 14 times as much, depending on the senior attending physicians. Regulators, including the PROs, may wish to claim that much of this extra care is questionable or could be provided more efficiently. In some cases, however, including DRGs 108, 110, and 111, there appear to be relatively narrow differences in the selection process of customization options among equally board-qualified surgeons where case mix (DRG) is adjusted for severity level.

From the more limited perspective of cost accounting, as long as the institution can isolate the custom options in serving a patient and standardize unit cost, cost accounting is a simple matter of arithmetic. The two difficult steps in cost accounting are (1) developing standard costs for each service-item option initially and (2) keeping these standards updated. We shall next consider standard costing methods. Standard costs are the direct patient-related costs in hospital operations. Today, methods for handling indirect costs are well established (Suver and Neumann 1985). Indirect costs are simply allocated from overhead departments to patient care (revenue) departments. The four basic cost-allocation techniques for handling indirect costs, ranging from the direct method to multiple apportionment, have been well established for two decades (Berman, Weeks, and Kukla 1990). Some hospitals still have problems appropriately assigning the fixed assets and labor costs of dietary or housekeeping to their respective work center of origin (Hogan and Marshall 1990). However, this measurement error in the cost-assignment process of indirect overhead departments is dwarfed by the potential specification and measurement problems in calculating variable standard costs (Botz 1989).

IMPROVEMENTS IN HOSPITAL COST ACCOUNTING

The introduction of PPSs and aggressive managed-care systems has had a large effect on the hospital industry. One area influenced by the change in payment methods has been cost accounting and its level of sophistication. The results of a survey of 232 hospitals suggest that larger hospitals and teaching hospitals have been more innovative in upgrading their cost-accounting systems. However, all hospitals in the sample either maintained the same method of cost accounting or upgraded their system. None of the 232 hospitals downgraded their cost-accounting approach in the period 1985–1990.

This section considers a repeat of the November 1987 *Healthcare Financial Management* survey of cost-accounting methods in six states (Eastaugh 1987). This mail survey expanded the scope of the 1987 study to a national sample. The surveyed hospitals represent a 20 percent sample of short-term nongovernmental hospitals with more than 75 beds. Only 58 percent of the hospitals responded to the survey concerning their cost-accounting approach in 1985 and 1990. The response rate was considered good, and no statistically significant bias was present in the sample respondents, compared to the hospitals that did not respond, based on seven variables (size, teaching status, urbanicity, ownership control, disproportionate share of patient volume, Medicare case-mix index, and length-of-stay index) (Eastaugh 1991).

The focus of this survey was how hospital cost accounting has changed over the period 1985–90. Cost accounting analyzes what it costs to bring together inputs into intermediate and final products. A taxonomy for cost-accounting methods will be outlined, followed by consideration of three basic questions: Has hospital cost accounting improved since 1985? Do certain types of hospitals take a more sophisticated approach to cost accounting? How valid is the taxonomy for cost-accounting methods?

A Typology for Cost Accounting

Six types of cost accounting will be outlined, in increasing order of sophistication, starting with the most basic approach.

1. Ratio of costs to charges (RCC) is the most basic top-down approach to costing. It handicaps hospitals because financial decisions get made on adjusted

charge data rather than on actual costs incurred. The RCC method estimates procedure-level costs by computing an overall ratio of departmental aggregate costs to charges and applies this ratio to the charges for individual procedures. As Neumann and Suver (1990) have demonstrated, RCC suffers because charges are poorly correlated with costs, and this aggregation of information does not correlate with the expense of a given procedure within a specific department. RCC was sufficient in the old days of cost reimbursement, when a dollar spent was a dollar paid.

2. RCC with some job-order costing in a few departments is the second approach to hospital accounting. Under this advanced RCC approach most of the hospital still uses aggregate cost data and RCC multiplication, but a few departments try procedure-level costing of actual expense per unit of service (e.g., the manual lab test done with a specific number of resources consumed). Most of the hospital is still doing top-down RCC cost guesstimates, but a few departments are actually trying to track specific costs at the event level, as in industry (bottom-up costing) (Horngren and Sundem 1991).

3. Job-order observation of actual costs tracks specific costs at the event level, including labor inputs, capital equipment, and indirect fixed costs (see Goldschmidt and Gafni 1990) to arrive at a real cost concurrent with the service production. In some sense this method of actual costing is the purest form of bottom-up costing, but it is costly and is most appropriate for departments with a wide variety of resource intensity per procedure (otherwise, the same information can be collected at lower administrative expense using method 4).

4. Process costing of relative value units (RVUs) initially allocates costs to the components (materials, labor, and indirect fixed costs) associated with performing a service in a department, then incorporates the relative share of the cost components required to perform the procedure (Eastaugh 1991). The advantage of this second form of bottom-up costing is that decision makers can look across services and procedures in a specific department to assess process efficiency (the resource costs and related expenses across intermediate products and subproducts) (Baptist 1987).

5. A hybrid costing approach uses RVUs in most departments but standard costing (approach 6) in some departments.

6. Standard costing is the recognized most sophisticated approach to cost accounting. Standard costing mirrors the RVU approach in allocating costs to the components (materials, labor, and indirect fixed costs) associated with performing a service in a department, then incorporates the relative share of the cost components required to perform a procedure (Meeting, Saunders, and Curcio 1988). But standard costing goes beyond the RVU approach by utilizing variance analysis to measure performance against normative standards. The costing standards are developed by industrial engineering studies to peg the production efficiency yardstick for comparison. Such standards are often microcosted at far greater than ''micro'' expense, but more accuracy often costs more.

Table 2.1
Shifts in the Six Basic Cost-Accounting Approaches, 1985 and 1990

		1985		1990	
		Number of Hospitals	*Percentage of Sample*	*Number of Hospitals*	*Percentage of Sample*
1.	Ratio of costs to charges (RCC)	137	59.1	86	37.1
2.	RCC with some job order costing in a few departments (advanced RCC)	40	17.2	44	19.0
3.	Job-order observation of actual costs in over five departments (Actual job-order)	22	9.5	41	17.7
4.	Process costing of relative value units (RVU/process)	17	7.3	26	11.2
5.	Hybrid approach of RVU process costing[a] (Hybrid standard RVU)	14	6.0	24	10.3
6.	Standard costing with variance analysis to measure performance (standard)	2	0.9	11	4.7
	Total	232	100	232	100

[a]Standardized costing in a few departments, but little use of industrial-engineered standards or variance analysis.

Rising Interest in Standard Costing

The survey results in table 2.1 suggest that more hospitals have upgraded their cost-accounting approach since 1985. The most primitive approach (RCC) was done by 59.1 percent of sample hospitals in 1985 but declined to 37 percent in 1990. The fraction of hospitals doing the more sophisticated bottom-up approaches to cost accounting (approaches 3 to 6) increased from less than one in four hospitals (23.7 percent) in 1985 to nearly half in 1990. One could speculate that it is more important to measure costs in the more competitive marketplace in the 1990s. Anecdotal reports have suggested that larger teaching hospitals have the resources to invest in better cost-accounting systems, and in turn sell their systems (e.g., New England Medical Center).

What Do Larger Teaching Hospitals Do?

To test whether large teaching hospitals do better cost accounting, the results for the teaching hospitals are displayed in table 2.2. Teaching hospitals were more advanced in accounting methods in 1985, and the gap widened in 1990. Both assertions are confirmed at the 0.05 level by a statistical test (chi-squared). In 1985, when 31.9 percent of the 300-plus-bed teaching hospitals used primitive RCC costing, 71.3 percent of the other hospitals (114 out of 160) used RCC. In 1990, when 12.5 percent of the 300-plus-bed teaching hospitals used primitive RCC costing, 48.1 percent of the other hospitals (77 out of 160) still used RCC. Nine of the 11 hospitals using standard costing with variance analysis were large teaching hospitals. Six of these 9 hospitals were large academic medical centers.

One could speculate that financially stressed teaching hospitals with a high indigent patient mix have had to invest more in controlling their cost behavior by acquiring more sophisticated cost-accounting methods. Upgrading the cost-accounting system may be an example of the adage "Necessity is the mother of invention." The sample appears to be representative and includes 12 percent of nonteaching hospitals, 12.3 percent of academic medical centers, and 11.9 percent of the nonteaching hospitals with more than 75 beds. One would predict that cost-accounting methods will continue to improve for all types of hospitals during the 1990s as necessity requires them to cope with the challenges brought on by prospective payment and managed care.

One may ask how good the typology is at scaling sophistication (whether method 6 is better than method 1). If in fact one method were better than a lower-numbered approach, one would predict that no hospital would downgrade its system during competitive times (Sokal 1974). This is confirmed in table 2.3, where none of the 232 hospitals downgraded their approach in the period 1985–90. Across line 1 of Table 2.3, 62.8 percent of RCC hospitals in 1985 stuck with RCC, 26.3 percent upgraded to approach 2 prior to 1990, 10.2 percent upgraded to approach 3, and one hospital upgraded to RVUs by 1990. Across line 3 of table 2.3, 18.2 percent of actual costs (job-order) hospitals in 1985 stuck with that approach, 36.4 percent upgraded to approach 4 prior to 1990, and 45.4 percent upgraded to approach 5 by 1990. At the bottom right corner of table 2.3, the two hospitals with standard costing in 1985 continued with that approach in 1990. Of the 14 hospitals doing hybrid method 5 in 1985, 35.7 percent stuck with that approach, but 64.3 percent (nine hospitals) upgraded to standard costing (approach 6) by 1990.

Standard Costing

Standard costs represent established yardsticks that should be achieved by an efficient institution and thus can be used normatively to assess economic effi-

Table 2.2
Teaching Hospitals with More Than 300 Beds: Shifts in the Basic Cost-Accounting Approaches, 1985 and 1990

		1985		1990	
		Number of Hospitals	*Percentage of Sample*	*Number of Hospitals*	*Percentage of Sample*
1.	Ratio of costs	23	31.9	8	11.1
	to charges (RCC)	(1)			
2.	RCC with some job-order costing in a				
	few departments	12	16.7	8	11.1
	(advanced RCC)	(1)			
3.	Job-order observation of actual costs in				
	over five departments	12	16.7	16	22.2
	(actual job-order)	(1)		(1)	
4.	Process costing of				
	relative value units	9	12.5	16	22.2
	(RVU/process)	(4)		(2)	
5.	Hybrid approach of RVU process costing				
	and standard costing[a]	14	19.4	15	20.8
	(Hybrid standard RVU)	(6)		(6)	
6.	Standard costing with variance analysis to				
	measure performance	2	2.8	9	12.5
	(standard)	(2)		(6)	
	Total	72	100	72	100

Note: Numbers in parentheses are for the 15 academic medical centers. The national random sample included 12 percent of teaching hospitals and 12.3 percent of academic medical centers.

[a]Standard costing in a few departments, but little use of industrial-engineered standards of variance analysis.

Table 2.3

Transition Probability of Changing from One Cost-Accounting Approach in 1985 to a Different Approach in 1990

1985 Approach	1990 Approach					
	1. RCC (86)	2. RCC advanced (44)	3. Actual costs (41)	4. RVU process (26)	5. Hybrid 4&6 (24)	6. Standard Costing (11)
1. Ratio of cost to charges (RCC) (137)	0.628 (86)	0.263 (36)	0.102 (14)	0.007 (1)	0	0
2. RCC with some job-order costing in a few departments (advanced RCC) (40)	0	0.200 (8)	0.575 (23)	0.225 (9)	0	0
3. Job-order observation of actual costs in over five departments (actual job-order) (22)	0	0	0.182 (4)	0.364 (8)	0.454 (10)	0
4. Process costing of relative value units (RVU/process) (17)	0	0	0	0.471 (8)	0.529 (9)	0
5. Hybrid approach of RVU process costing and standard costing[a] (hybrid/standard-RVU) (14)	0	0	0	0	0.357 (5)	0.643 (9)
6. Standard costing with variance analysis to measure performance (standard) (2)	0	0	0	0	0	1.0 (2)

Note: Numbers of hospitals are in parentheses. The probabilities sum to 1.0 across each row.

[a] Standard costing in a few departments, but little use of industrial engineered standards or variance analysis.

ciency and productivity. One cannot perform effective cost accounting without standards (Horngren 1982). The three techniques for identification of standards are nonscientific/inexpensive, traditional time motion, and the technically sophisticated input-output approach. The most long-standing management-sciences approach to standards involves time-motion activity-analysis (microcosting) standards. The second meaningful standards-setting approach involves input-output unweighted regression analysis, or, alternatively, exponential smoothing regressions that downweight the value of more historic (outdated) observations (McClain and Eastaugh 1983). Some hospitals attempt an even more sophisticated alternative for input-output analysis, utilizing Box-Jenkins time-series analysis (Coddington and Steiker 1986), but the results are no better than the exponential smoothing technique. A third variety of "standards" is an ad hoc negotiated opinion or standard, which for purposes of the survey instrument was defined as "cost accounting without standards." The following is a summary of the three basic categories:

1. Input-output regression measures of standard costs.
2. Time-motion work-sampling management-engineering approach to measuring microcosted standards.
3. Without empirical standards—ad hoc estimates of unit cost per service item based on informal work sampling (the nonscientific approach)

All three techniques in practice may involve some degree of negotiation between middle managers and senior managers, but the third technique is by definition a totally negotiated process. For purposes of our survey, we combined techniques 1 and 2 and labeled the result "cost accounting with standards." These two techniques are typically utilized simultaneously or alternating every few years. The standard-setting technique utilized varies by cost center, by service item within each cost center, and by year. Consider two examples. One might utilize management-engineered microcosting standards, done in an annual two- to four-week work sampling, for 85 percent of the routine service items (tests) within the laboratory department. For the nonroutine 15 percent of lab tests, one might perform input-output regression analysis. As a second example, one might microcost half of the service items in diagnostic radiology every three to five years to keep the standards current but perform input-output regression on the standards in other years. Actually, one-third (39 out of 124) service items in diagnostic radiology captured 95 percent of the expenses in that area at one teaching hospital.

As a last resort, the standards themselves could be externally adopted from other hospitals and adjusted with regression analysis to better fit the institutional application. One might borrow standards from the Maryland Health Services Cost Review Commission, the New York State resource monitoring standards (RMS), or some other source. Some hospitals have discovered that the search for analytical precision and theoretical perfection in microcosting is too expensive to do on a regular basis, but differentiating levels of refinement in cost accounting is key to determining the manner in which variable-cost items are identified and allocated. In other words, a one-time initial investment in microcosting five to nine large departments may pay off in increased accuracy but cost a significant amount of money and slow down implementation.

The basic question is this: Would one like a good product soon or a much better product for management in 12 to 24 months? As an academic, the author prefers the second road, as was done at Tufts New England Medical Center and at six departments at Georgetown Hospital. To avoid embedding levels of some other hospital's baseline inefficiency into the standards, these two hospitals "build up" standard costs with local firm-specific data. This route involves management-engineered yardsticks for how many full-time equivalents (FTEs) should really be in a department and offers targets (e.g., can we decrease direct productive worked hours to 85 percent?). The easy method, used in the majority of cases, is to "back in" costs based on the budget and external standards and thus absorb baseline inefficiency into cost standards.

Pilot cost accounting with microcomputers to allow management time to gain familiarity with costing methods before placing the best (reasonable) system up on the mainframe (Christensen and Stearns 1991) may offer the best option for avoiding strategic mediocrity. The concept of diminishing returns at increasing expense (administrative cost) is often summarized in the 90/10 Pareto principle: the first 90 percent of cost-accounting accuracy can be obtained with 90 percent of available resources, and the last 10 percent hypothetically requires an additional 90 percent effort (is too expensive to collect). Are the marginal benefits in microcosting accuracy worth the increased marginal costs ($100 to $180 per patient served), or could the system be validated and updated by sampling on a periodic basis? Is it necessary to microcost at the procedural level, or could one do it every three to five years on a 20 percent sampling basis, along with performing procedure costing for each and every newly initiated procedure? For example, at one teaching hospital 7 of 33 service items in hematology capture 90 percent of expenses. Therefore, effort should be concentrated on these seven items. A typical 200- to 400-bed Council of Teaching Hospitals (COTH) facility ($N = 116$ nationally) may treat 1,000 separate diseases and perform 9,000 separate procedures (50 new procedures were introduced in 1987–88 alone). Procedure costing would prove an onerous task. The problem is compounded in the case of academic medical center hospitals with 700 or more beds ($N = 45$) that offer 12,800 procedures, with 100 to 150 new procedures (service items) initiated each year.

Automation and expertise in management information systems are critical determinants of standard costing capacity. For example, the 840-bed Dallas Parkland Memorial Hospital invested $150,000 in the MEDSCAN bar-coding system that allows complete flow tracking (medical records, tests, and materials) throughout the entire facility. MEDSCAN can interface with any mainframe, meaning that bar coding can be applied to radiology, satellite clinics, and whatever else moves throughout the total hospital complex. A large hospital may require bar-code readers at 24 to 36 major distribution points, but smaller hospitals may need only 10.

Selective sampling and microcosting at the procedural/DRG level has allowed two innovative chief financial officers (CFOs) in our sample to develop software to reaggregate the cost information by 20 to 40 strategic product-line groupings (SPGs). These SPGs are utilized like strategic business units (SBUs) in the administrative-sciences literature (Eastaugh and Eastaugh 1986). Productivity and variance analysis are obviously more valid and reliable if costs can be combined at the procedural level. In this context the purist may state that inferior costing of profit and loss (P & L) by product line can do more harm than good if one opens or expands the ''wrong'' service misidentified as profitable. This statistical type-one error, rejecting the null hypothesis (unprofitable) when it is true (i.e., the product line is a poor bet, but the cost-accounting system cannot recognize this), is sometimes labeled ''failure to maximize specificity.'' Moreover, an inaccurate cost-accounting system can do harm if it closes or reduces the size of a product line misidentified as unprofitable. This is a statistical type-two error, accepting the null hypothesis (unprofitable) when it is not true. If, in fact, the product line is a good investment, this is a failure to maximize sensitivity. The only costing system that can achieve both a specificity and a sensitivity of 90 percent or higher in doing strategic financial planning is a procedural/DRG-based system. There is no such thing as a perfect system. However, misspecified costs yield poor short-run variance analysis, weak medium-run control, and inaccurate long-range financial planning.

Hospitals have never been able to charge uniformly for services in proportion to their costs. Without a measure of actual cost, it would be impossible to uniformly price markup relative to actual cost. Without standard cost accounting, charges have little association with costs. Consider the problems with such inaccurate RCC costing in the context of an American auto company. The company produces two models, ADRG and BDRG. The company produces car ADRG at $12,000 and sells it for $24,000. The company produces car BDRG at $8,000 and sells it for $12,000. The company sells three times as many model BDRG cars as model ADRG cars.

In our example, the ratio of costs to charges across the company is 0.6, or $[(3 \times 8) + 12]/[(3 \times 12) + 24]$. If the company had been so unsophisticated as to allocate costs by RCC, it would have claimed that car ADRG costs $14,400 (.6 × $24,000), and car BDRG costs $7,200 (0.6 × $12,000). Such a primitive RCC methodology overstates the profitability of a BDRG by $800 and understates the profitability of an ADRG by $2,400. The principles are the same when we attempt to cost-account patient care, with two exceptions: (1) Maintenance of technically up-to-date costing standards is more of a problem for medicine and surgery, and (2) health providers typically make a better net profit on the less expensive DRGs such as 86, 96, and angina pectoris (140), which exhibited a 57 percent increase in admissions in 1985. Obviously, with economies of scale any DRG can prove profitable with sufficient volume and reasonable levels of provider efficiency. However, certain high-cost DRGs are seldom reported as profitable: craniotomy (DRG 2), hepatobiliary shunt (191), kidney transplants (302), and extensive burns (457).

One should consider two final caveats in the cost-accounting process. First, charge items need to be refined into a multitude of service items. For example, one might develop a medical records service item, a discharge and/or admissions service item, and a routine (lowest level of severity or acuity) nursing service item per day. If medical records as a service item have 70 percent fixed and 30 percent variable costs, a seemingly homogeneous service item may subdivide into two separate cost accounts (fixed and variable). However, it may be more expensive to discharge a patient to a nursing home rather than to self-care, but the expense of microcosting this service item into multiple accounts may not justify the administrative expense.

The second caveat concerns reconciliation of standard costs as collected in an extended-charge master file containing data on all service items. Statistical discrepancies in the aggregate across the institution should be very small, amounting to under 1 percent of expenses at most. However, one cannot be unrealistic and expect to reconcile to the last dollar. In reconciling standard costs compared to actual cost information in the general ledger accounts, the difference can either be unfavorable or favorable. This variance can be attributable to management competence, system error, or exogenous events beyond management control. In any case, the variance information can be utilized to restructure future budgets.

Variance Analysis and Flexible Budgets

As Horngren and Sundem (1991) have pointed out, the essential strength of managerial cost accounting is that it links "promises" made during the budget process back to the responsibility center. For example, if a department chairperson claims that the purchase of certain equipment will result in labor savings, but no labor savings are experienced, then this shortfall in performance needs to be either (1) explained away by exogenous circumstances beyond the manager's control or (2) utilized annually to discount the judgment and/or budget of the manager in question. Budget variance is defined as the difference between the budgeted and actual amounts and can be favorable (under budget) or unfavorable (over budget). The traditional business technique as presented by Horngren (1982) is to separate total variance into three component parts: (1) price variance (input expense—what it costs to pay labor or purchase supplies), (2) mix variance, and (3) volume variance. In the hospital context Finkler (1982) neatly summarized this traditional analysis into an easy-to-calculate "pyramid model."

Consider a sample case where the actual radiology expenses for the month were $91,448, and the budgeted salaries were $90,576 (figure 2.1). The chief operating officer, unfamiliar with the new flexible budgeting software, claims

Figure 2.1
Variances in a Hospital with Flexible Budgets and Standard Cost Accounting

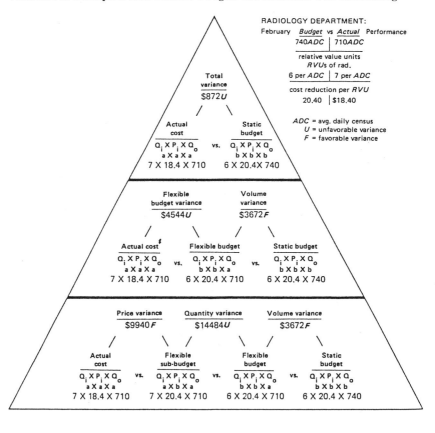

that the radiology manager does not deserve to go to a national conference because of this $872 unfavorable variance. To defend himself or herself, the radiology manager has to ask how this variance arose. Finkler's pyramid model (figure 2.1) provides a good analytical framework. The expectations when the most recent rolling budget was made were that, on average, 6 relative value units (RVUs) of radiology would be required per diem (Q_i) at an expense of $20.40 per RVU (P) with a patient census of 740 (Q_o). In actuality, there was an average of 7 RVUs per day, as the patients were more intensely treated in a shorter duration of stay, and more severely ill patients came from the recently closed public hospital's catchment area. Expense paid per RVU declined to only $18.40 per RVU thanks to the hard work of the radiology department manager to improve productivity and reduce costs. The number of patients declined to 710 (Q_o) following an 8 percent decline in predicted average length of stay and a 4.3 percent increase in admissions.

At the top of the pyramid in figure 2.1, the total variance is described as the difference between the static budget (6 × 20.40 × 740) and actual expense, for a net unfavorable $872. For simplicity, the lowercase letter a denotes actual costs and the letter b denotes budgeted costs. For the pyramid, any time an actual cost or budget figure on the left is smaller than the number on the right, it implies a favorable variance (e.g., radiology price variance); the opposite implies an unfavorable variance (e.g., quantity per patient day variance). One might suggest from the flexible-budget variance analysis that the utilization review committee consider the appropriateness of such a substantial increase in radiology services per diem. This medical-staff issue is certainly beyond the control of the radiology department manager. The volume variance in the lower right corner of the pyramid is the same as that in the middle level of the pyramid ($3,672 favorable). The flexible budget variance of $4,544 unfavorable has been subdivided in the bottom of the pyramid into changes in input efficiency (lower cost per RVU) and changes in radiology service mix utilized per case (more RVUs per patient, perhaps without any improvements in efficacy). The department manager is partially responsible for efficiency, in that she could purchase more cost-effectively or schedule better (and so reduce overtime hours). The senior management also has an impact on efficiency. The medical staff is largely responsible for efficacy and totally responsible for patient orders.

Both the subbudget and the flexible budget utilize the $20.40 expense per RVU and the 710 actual patient census. Thus, given the actual workload, the radiologists and other clinicians have produced an unfavorable $14,484 quantity variance. Some fraction of this might result from a more severe case mix. The remaining variance is the price variance, based on the actual cost and the sub-budget. Any difference between the actual cost and the subbudget is a result of paying a different amount per RVUs produced for the total radiology RVUs needed (one could be even more refined and subdivide the pyramid on a fourth level: increased [or decreasing] RVUs caused by deteriorating [or better] quality control per procedure versus increased RVUs caused by shifts in physician ordering habits). Since quality control was unchanged in our example, the radiology manager is largely responsible for a $9,940 favorable price variance. The radiology manager cannot be assigned any responsibility for the $3,672 favorable volume variance—that is, she did not decrease the average duration of patient stay.

Because flexible budgeting is not easily understood by many managers, the best software is so "user friendly" as to present the analysis in simplified language. One of the pioneers in this area was the Tufts New England Medical Center system. The strength of flexible budgets is that they focus on what expenses would have been had the workload output been forecast perfectly. The problem with a static budget is that it simplistically ignores variations that naturally occur as a result of circumstances outside of line-management control or in the control of others (e.g., medical staff, rate regulators, and other hospital management staff).

HOW EFFICIENTLY DO HOSPITALS PURCHASE ITEMS?

Hospital managers have become more sensitive to cost concerns in what they purchase. Inventory-related costs represent one-third of the costs of providing inpatient care (Eastaugh 1990b; National Purchasing Outlook [NPO] 1991). Nearly half of this cost is related to supply and movable-equipment expenses; to "buy smart" is to make the facility more price competitive in a competitive market (Watson 1991). Prior to the tightening of Medicare DRG prices and managed-care discount schemes over the years 1986 to 1991, the purchasing behavior and efficiency of hospitals were less than outstanding. For example, the General Accounting Office (GAO 1985) provided dramatic evidence of hospitals paying 200 to 300 percent more than the market price (e.g., what state institutions pay after seeking competitive bids) for a wide range of hospital supply items. Under cost reimbursement a facility would be reimbursed dollar for dollar for this excess expense. Thus there was no incentive to contain purchasing costs. Under prospective payment the hospital does not get paid more if it spends more. Pressures from payers to reduce costs led facilities to cut back on hospital supply expenses. Suppliers have felt the impact of these hospital cost-containment efforts (Eastaugh 1990b). In terms of stock-market price performance, hospital supply companies declined from the 92d percentile in 1985 to the 17th percentile in 1989. Drug companies also declined, from the 80th percentile in 1985 to the 47th percentile of American industry in 1989.

Marketing literature involving health-sector buyer behavior typically involves consumers or physicians (Folland, Ziegenfuss, and Chao 1988). However, the hospital supply sector desires to measure shifts in preferences among its buyers, hospital managers. This section employs the economists' concept of a utility function and the marketing-science concept of conjoint measurement techniques to measure dominant attitudes, opinions, and preference weights. Data were collected on a pretest/posttest basis at 50 hospitals from five different managers:

chief executive officer (CEO), chief operating officer (COO), electronic data processing (EDP) or management information systems (MIS) manager, director of nursing, and director of materials management. Three basic models describe the way managers spend facility funds: the economic buyer, the economic/ convenience buyer, and the quality/cost buyer. A preference function was developed utilizing conjoint measurement techniques (also see chapter 6 on marketing). A link between attitude and resulting financial performance is suggested. However, such a correlation does not prove a causal link (e.g., being economy-minded yields enhanced profit margins). The industrial marketing implication for this section is that hospital supply companies would better target their substantial price discounts to a certain group of managers, rather than operate an open-door policy. The open-door policy of small but universal discounts for all hospitals worked better in the pre-1984 era of cost reimbursement characterized by little price sensitivity in expenses (such as purchasing supplies) or in revenues (getting paid for insured patient costs). The academic marketing question for this section involves possible identification of segments of purchasers (hospital managers) whose decision rules may impact upon the profitability of the firm. The more narrow industrial marketing question for hospital supply firms is how they can segment and appeal to hospital managers' changing preference patterns (e.g., buyer behavior for purchase of inputs to the medical care process may be impacted by changes in how the business, hospital care, is reimbursed).

Hospital Population Sampled

A random stratified sample of tax-exempt voluntary hospitals was selected in 1985 based upon the 1984 American Hospital Association annual survey data. The sample was restricted to hospitals with over 100 beds, and teaching hospitals were oversampled in proportion to the degree to which they buy more hospital supplies. Hospitals were stratified based on two variables: size (100–299 beds, 300–599 beds, or 600 or more beds) and teaching status (medical center, other teaching hospital, or nonteaching hospital). The financial condition of the sample hospitals is summarized in table 2.4. In 1990 these same 50 facilities were resurveyed and subdivided into two types: low-profit hospitals with total net profit margins under 1.0 percent as of July 1990 (these 34 hospitals had an average margin of from 1.1 to 6.3 percent in 1985) and moderate-profit hospitals that had margins in excess of 1 percent in 1990 and 1985 (these 16 hospitals had an average margin of 5.4 percent in 1985 and 2.7 percent in 1990). This second category is labeled moderate-profit rather than high-profit because such margins are modest by historical standards (relative to those of other industries).

The results summarized in table 2.5 suggest that the dominant self-reported concern of COOs and EDP/MIS managers in moderate-profit hospitals was cost. 60 percent of those listing quality as their dominant purchasing concern in 1985 switched to cost in 1990. As observed in table 2.6, this figure was only 9.5 percent in low-profit hospitals. The results for directors of nursing and materials

Table 2.4
Summary of Financial Performance for the 50 Sample Hospitals in 1990 and the Original Stratification Variables (Bed Size and Teaching Status)

	Low Profit in 1990	Moderate Profit in 1990
Number of hospitals	34	16
Average profit margin in 1990	0.2%	2.7%
Average profit margin in 1985	5.0%	5.4%
Strata and sample size:		
Medical center, 600+ beds	2 hospitals	2
Medical center, 300-599 beds	3	2
Other teaching, 300-599 beds	4	2
Other teaching, 100-299 beds	4	1
Nonteaching, 300-599 beds	7	3
Nonteaching, 100-299 beds	14	6

managers indicate that 73 percent reporting quality as their prime concern in 1985 listed cost as their prime concern in 1990 in moderate-profit hospitals. The figure in low-profit hospitals was much less dramatic, 22 percent (table 2.6). Perhaps lack of concern for purchasing efficiency breeds low profit; however, correlation is not always causality. Conversion to cost consciousness as the dominant concern in buyer/agent behavior tends to be permanent (Parzen 1971) (tables 2.5 and 2.6, column 1, row 1). A test of the hypothesis "attitudes stayed the same over time" was rejected at the 0.01 level for each matrix in tables 2.5 and 2.6, using the McNemar three-way discordance test. In other words, one finds substantial change in managers' attitudes from 1985 to 1990.

One should not generalize too much from a sample of 250 managers in 50 hospitals. The intent of this research is to bridge the gap between academic and managerial perspectives. Over the 1980s health economists did not objectively measure hospital managers' preferences for cost control. Managers were told to cut hospital expenditures in response to the payment incentive without regard to values or objectives (Newhouse 1989). This study suggests that hospital managers' attitudes are in flux.

The individual approach of the five professional groups surveyed will involve, to varying degrees, three basic attributes or dimensions: cost, quality, and convenience. Buyer priorities in 1990 were compared using a multivariate analysis of manager conjoint weighted preferences. Conjoint measurement technique is a statistical approach to preference analysis borrowed from the marketing-science literature (Jain, Pinson, and Ratchford 1982). This type of information is of interest to external users (hospital supply firms), as well as being used internally

Table 2.5
Dominant Concerns among COOs and EDP Managers, and Directors of Nursing and Materials Managers, Attitude Matrix Transition, 1985–1990 (16 Hospitals, Moderate Net Operating Profit Margin in 1990)

		Dominant Attitude, Summer 1990[a]		
		(Number of Respondents in Parentheses)		
		Cost	Quality	Convenience
COOs and EDP managers		(24)	(7)	(1)
Spring	Cost (13)	1.00	.0	.0
1985				
dominant	Quality (15)	.60	.40	.0
attitude				
	Convenience (4)	.50	.25	.25
Directors of nursing and				
materials managers		(24)	(6)	(2)
Spring	Cost (11)	1.00	.0	.0
1985				
dominant	Quality (15)	.73	.27	.0
attitude				
	Convenience (6)	.33	.33	.33

aThe figures represent the probability of an individual in 1985 shifting to that matrix attitude by 1990. By definition, probability values sum to 1.00 across each line.

by managers interested in optimization and not merely satisficing (Weber, Eisenfuhr, and von Winterfeldt 1988).

The market research was originally funded by a hospital supply firm interested in ascertaining how prospective payment systems were affecting its business. Since the sponsor reported that teaching hospitals with a higher "dosage" of graduate medical education purchased more items from supply firms, the stratified sample oversampled teaching hospitals by twofold. The conjoint preference survey reported in table 2.7 is a much more sophisticated marketing technique than simply asking individuals to self-report their dominant attitudes and opinions (tables 2.5 and 2.6).

The characteristics of the purchase alternatives from which hospital managers must select are multidimensional. It is probable that no alternative is superior on every dimension of interest. Conjoint measurement is the technique of choice used by market researchers, although originally developed in the fields of psychometrics and mathematical psychology, to sort out the relative importance of

Table 2.6
Dominant Concerns among COOs and EDP Managers, and Directors of Nursing and Materials Managers, Attitude Matrix Transition, 1985–1990 (34 Hospitals, Net Operating Profit Margin under 1.0 Percent in 1990)

| | | Dominant Attitude, Summer, 1990[a] | | |
| | | (Number of Respondents in Parentheses)[b] | | |
		Cost	Quality	Convenience
COOs and EDP managers		(25)	(38)	(5)
Spring 1985	Cost (20)	1.00	.0	.0
dominant attitude	Quality (42)	.095	.81	.095
	Convenience (6)	.17	.66	.17
Directors of nursing and materials managers		(29)	(33)	(6)
Spring 1985	Cost (22)	.955	.045	.0
dominant attitude	Quality (37)	.22	.78	.0
	Convenience (9)	.0	.33	.67

[a]The figures represent the probability of an individual in 1985 shifting to that matrix attitude by 1990. By definition, probability values sum to 1.00 across each line.

[b]136 respondents in this table 2.6, 64 respondents in table 2.5, and the final analysis in table 2.7 will include 50 CEO respondents from the 50 sample hospitals. The total sample of respondents equals 250 hospital managers.

multidimensional attributes (Knight 1982). The technique breaks down the managers' ordinal observations into separate and compatible utility scales by which the original sequences can be surmised. The capacity to separate overall judgments into components provides valuable information for managers, suppliers, and policy analysts. One is provided information about the value of various levels of a single attribute or the relative importance between attributes. A number of conjoint studies have been published, including Noordeweir, Rogers, and Balakrishnan (1989) and Akaah and Becherer (1983).

Quantitative Marketing Techniques to Uncover Preferences

Managers were asked to select their single dominant concern in making purchasing decisions in 1985 and 1990. The three basic concerns were cost, quality, and convenience. The two most popular attributes listed under each of these three areas, along with their 1985 target levels of performance for 1990, were utilized to structure the 27 profiles for the conjoint measurement survey in 1990. The most popular attributes to capture cost concerns included product cost (mentioned by 100 percent of respondents), purchase-order processing costs (68 percent), and inventory costs (20 percent) in the 1985 survey. The attributes most often cited to describe quality concerns included product reputation (84 percent), supplier delivery quality without backordering (47 percent), and general manufacturer reputation (23 percent). The attributes most often cited to describe convenience concerns included convenience in ordering (68 percent), inventory accuracy (contrast of actual item count versus record count; 61 percent), stock availability (30 percent), and location accuracy (stored items in their assigned location as a measure of accuracy; 29 percent).

On the basis of pretest surveys in 1985 each of the six attributes was identified at three levels (table 2.7, levels a, b, and c). The written descriptions utilized to describe the levels may appear odd to the business marketing professional, but no hospital manager in the sample could conceive of buying a below-average product. Consequently, the levels in that example were identified as average, very good, or outstanding. The six attributes and the three levels were subsequently utilized in 1990 to survey the 50 hospitals (each with over 100 beds).

Information was collected utilizing a full-profile approach (Montgomery and Wittink 1980), rather than the more simplistic (unrealistic) bivariate approach. A factorial design was constructed to offer descriptive profiles of the product acquisition, delivery, and storage process. With three variables and three levels for each variable, the fractional factorial consists of 27 profiles. This allows estimation of the main effects (but omits interactions; see the Appendix to this chapter). The 27 profiles, constructed according to an orthogonal array, represented only 1 in 27 of the 729 possible combinations. The hospital managers' overall preference rating to a set of stimulus profiles (27) was used to derive part worths for each attribute level. The main-effects multiattribute preference model is expressed in the formula:

$$V_h = \sum_{j=1}^{3} \sum_{i=1}^{3} v_{ij} x_{ij}^{(h)}$$

where V_h is the manager's overall rating of stimulus profile h ($h = 1, 2, 3, \ldots$ 27), v_{ij} is the part worth associated with level i ($i = 1, 2, 3$) of attribute j ($j = 1, 2, 3$), and $X_{ij}^{(h)}$ is a dummy variable of value zero or one representing the base level i of the attribute that corresponds to stimulus profile h.

The 27 profiles were presented on separate index cards for the managers' evaluations. Each of the five respondents at a given hospital was shown the 27 cards, in a randomized order, and asked to rank the profiles from most liked to least liked. The dependent variable consisted of a respondent's preference rankings for the 27 profiles. These data from the 27 profiles were fitted to a main-effects-only utility model (Moore and Semenik 1988).

Computation of the utility scales of each attribute, which determine how influential each attribute is in the managers' evaluations of what to buy for the hospital, was carried out though a search procedure. The scale values for each level of each factor were chosen so that when they were added together, the total utility of each combination would respond to the original ranks.

Part worths (or utility values) for each level of each attribute were estimated by an ordinary least squares (OLS) procedure (using Conjoint Analyzer 1988). This procedure captures the relative importance of a respondent's overall evaluation ranking by selecting the best linear relationship between a dependent variable (rankings) and multiple independent explanatory variables.

Steps to Detect Preferences

The first step in our conjoint methodology involves regression analysis (ordinary least squares) to estimate the part-worth contributions of the measured attributes that underlie a hospital manager's multiattribute attitude. The six major attributes analyzed, listed in table 2.7, were the only features listed by more than one-third of the 1985 sample respondents. Because of the large amount of variability between managers in preferences, conjoint analysis is performed at the individual level of analysis (not the hospital level).

The second stage in conjoint analysis involves clustering attitudes. The issue is whether an underlying manager preference or utility function exists for trading off cost control, convenience, and quality. The hospital manager/buyer is interested in many things, including quality products, quality delivery, convenience in ordering, and convenience in inventory retrieval. Hospital managers increasingly interested in cost control compare last year's purchasing costs and ordering costs for supplies, drugs, and equipment. Conjoint analysis attempts to measure the depth and direction of the attitudes of buyers toward products and to cluster (bundle) the important attributes or features into homogeneous like-thinking market segments. Three clusters are reported in table 2.7 as the best representation of the three basic attitudes.

In the final stage of the conjoint analysis, the pooled evaluations for each of these three clusters were utilized for a segment-level analysis (similar to the individual OLS regressions) to determine part-worth utilities for each of the three clusters. The part-worth regression coefficients for each manager cluster segment, obtained from the dummy-variable regressions, are given in the initial three columns of table 2.7.

To assure comparability of the data across the sample, the standardization option of the Barr/Johnson clustering procedure was employed (Becker and Chambers 1989). This weighted hierarchical clustering program identified three stable, discrete, readily interpretable clusters. Figures on attribute importance, indicating the relative contribution of each feature to the judged overall profile score, are presented in columns 4 to 6 of table 2.7. Relative attribute importance was thus defined in terms of the range of the attribute's part worths relative to the total ranges of all other attributes combined. In estimating the structure of hospital managers' preferences, the traditional additive composition rule was used (McQuiston and Walters 1989).

The attribute-level weights resulting from transformation of the original unpooled regression coefficients through a conditional logit model are given in columns 7 to 9 of table 2.7. One attractive feature of this transformation is that the computed attribute-level weights are invariant over an additive constant applied to each of the part-worth coefficients within any specific attribute (McFadden 1976; see the Appendix for details on the transformation).

With respect to attribute preference, members of cluster 1 (the economic buyer group) considered purchase cost to be the single most important determinant (weight = .50 in table 2.7) of their behavior, with quality (.19) and processing cost (.13) ranking a distant second and third place, respectively. In the case of cluster 2, economic/convenience buyers, cost (.39) ranked first and inventory convenience (.19) ranked second in importance. For members of cluster 3, quality/cost buyers, quality of the product was still the principal concern (.39), followed distantly in order of importance by the cost of the product (.25).

Caveats

One possible threat to the validity of this conjoint analysis is the pooling of the five major management categories. One could hypothesize that attitudes differ as a function of job responsibility and the nature of the products one has to buy. For example, economic criteria would become a more critical attribute as the products become more standardized. However, the attributes did not vary significantly across manager types from the EDP directors to the directors of nursing. This finding is surprising, given the wide array of products a director of nursing has to purchase, from surgical-asepsis products to wound-closure products, critical-care products, and surgical instruments. One would not wish to generalize too extensively from this finding, given the limited sample sizes.

In order to measure the comparative validity of the results, a set of nine holdout cards not used in the original card sort was evaluated by the respondents. The utility scores from the two card sorts were used to predict the rankings of the holdout cards. The majority (82 percent) of the predicted ranks were within one rank of the actual rank. It was interesting that this check on comparable validity was slightly higher (89 percent) for those managers with graduate professional school training (MBA, MHA) than for those without graduate training (77 percent).

In large part, cluster membership did not depend on job status, but a three-group discriminant analysis indicated that COOs were 13 percent more likely to reside in cluster 1 (the economic buyer group). One hospital characteristic seemed to have an impact on cluster membership. Large medical centers (capacity over 600 beds) were 17 percent more likely to reside in cluster 2 (the economic/convenience buyer group).

Table 2.7

Comparison of Part Worths and Attribute Importances for the Two Respondent Groups in 1990 (Moderate Profit = above 1.0 Percent)

Attribute Levels	Part-Worth Regression Clusters			Attribute Importance Clusters			Attribute-Level Weight Clusters		
	1	2	3	1	2	3	1	2	3
Number of Observations[a] from									
•Low-profit hospitals	16	79	211	16	79	211	16	79	211
•Moderate profit	119	15	14	119	15	14	119	15	14
1-A. Cost of the product									
a. Discount 3-6%	0	0	0	–	–	–	.06	.17	.70
b. Discount 8-12%	2.79	1.36	.53	.50	.39	.25	.68	.58	.26
c. Discount 15-20%	1.01	1.00	.16	–	–	–	.26	.25	.04
1-B. Cost of processing a purchase order									
a. Typical, $55-$65	0	0	0	–	–	–	.15	.21	.32
b. Good, $35-$45	1.09	.91	.28	.13	.10	.06	.39	.38	.49
c. Outstanding, <$30	1.32	1.17	.20	–	–	–	.46	.41	.19
2-A. Quality of the product (reputation and/or prior experience)									
a. Average	0	0	0	–	–	–	.24	.27	.08
b. Very good	1.12	.92	1.84	.19	.13	.39	.41	.39	.29
c. Outstanding	1.25	.94	2.73	–	–	–	.35	.34	.63
2-B. Quality of delivery (percentage of an order shipped without backordering)									
a. Below average, 85%	0	0	0	–	–	–	.24	.26	.22
b. Average, 90-94%	0	0	0	–	–	–	.30	.31	.50
c. Outstanding, 97%+	.48	.26	.19	.06	.05	.11	.46	.43	.28

60

3-A. Convenience in ordering									
a. Below average	0	0	0	—	—	—	.18	.01	.24
b. Average (consolidate orders and shipments)	.38	.80	.49	.07	.15	.10	.34	.38	.47
c. Outstanding (computer-to-computer order and hard-copy confirmation)	.49	.75	.43	—	—	—	.48	.61	.29
3-B. Convenience in inventory									
a. Inventory accuracy average, 85-90%	0	0	0	—	—	—	.20	.14	.30
b. Inventory accuracy good, 92-95%	.19	.93	.35	.05	.19	.10	.34	.40	.39
c. Inventory accuracy outstanding, 98%+	.36	.59	.26	—	—	—	.46	.46	.31

[a]The total numbers of observations are 306 and 148 for low-profit and moderate-profit hospitals, respectively. The numbers of observations are based on a weighted cluster analysis. Consequently, the total number of observations is higher than the number of respondents (170 and 80, respectively).

Suggestions for Future Research

That management attitudes favor economic purchasing correlating positively with better financial outcomes is a suggestive, but not definitive, finding. More precise data, linking changing attitudes to changed behavior and improved financial status, would prove useful to policy makers. A second posttest in 1995 could be analyzed by subsamples: proactive managers (reacting prior to 1989), reactive managers, and nonreactive nonprogressive managers. One critical research question is whether to continue to sample on the basis of hospitals with minimal job turnover (18 percent in the 3.3-year period). One might attempt to track people through American College of Healthcare Executives membership rather than track just hospitals. One would expect that (1) proactive managers have a lower job-turnover rate than reactive managers (Eastaugh 1988), and (2) all types of managers will have a higher turnover rate in the 1990s compared to that in the relatively easy reimbursement climate before 1985. The payment climate under Pub. L. 99–372, the Gramm-Rudman-Hollings deficit-reduction bill, may lead to higher manager stress and turnover (Eastaugh 1990a). While the evidence is consistent with the general view that financial concerns have become more important in the last three years, the action linkage and behavioral implications of future changes in the prospective payment environment should be more fully examined by organizational theorists.

Given that the future pressures for cost control are not going to ease up, even if we move to capitated limited-access systems, the "economic buyer" manager (cluster 1 in table 2.7) will become increasingly prevalent. It would be helpful if information on quality were valid and reliable. Hospital buyers should never confuse supplier claims with facts. The developers and promoters of a given technology or product will always claim that their quality is the best and that the item does what it is purported to do. In this context it seems strange that the federal government in fiscal year (FY) 1991 will spend $7 billion on biomedical research, but only a mere $38 million on technology assessment.

The interaction between attributes has been assumed to be negligible in most health care marketing articles (e.g., Noordeweir, Rogers, and Balakrishnan 1989). The importance of any interaction effects should be examined in future research. The marketing-science techniques employed in this section have not defined the "correct" prototype of hospital manager. The wisest, most durable managers will spend the hospitals' money as if it were their own: with great care, as value-oriented shoppers looking for both price and quality. The next section will assess whether hospitals' product-line selection has shifted toward specialization.

SPECIALIZATION

With increased competition and discounting, hospitals may react like department stores in earlier times. In the 1950s every department store tried to operate with 450 product lines, from food to men's formal wear. The surviving department stores now specialize in 50 to 90 percent fewer product lines (Eastaugh 1988). Consider a second analogy. The national association of gas station owners in 1972 suggested that every gas station must be full service and have a mechanic on duty. Contrary to this viewpoint, the successful gas stations now sell self-service gas and food. Specialization and modest diversification may be an optimal strategy for American hospitals that are not sole community providers. A hospital with poor cardiac surgery or oncology might drop these services and acquire narrow specialized services like in vitro fertilization. A small sole community provider with 25 to 75 beds has a monopoly hold on the market and lacks the opportunity to specialize and reap economies of scale in high-volume specialty departments.

Specialization is never achieved by dumping market segments of people (e.g., the uninsured), but rather by dropping product lines better served by the competition and by recommitting resources to what a provider does best. Hospitals are not alone in the 1980s tendency to specialize. General Motors might be a better company if it became Specific Motors. Specialization has been the key to survival for American auto dealers, whose number has declined by 25 percent since 1985. In a decade where automakers and hospitals are experiencing fiscal troubles, no point of differentiation is likely to prove more powerful than quality.

Specialize or Offer a Wide Scope of Product Lines?

Finkler (1983) offered the traditional argument for avoiding specialization: Hospitals with a broad product scope attract more physicians. Many hospitals offer a broad range of prestige-maximizing high-technology services, often at low volume, and consequently do not financially benefit from the wide scope of product lines offered. Trustees and other interested individuals might accrue intangible benefits (e.g., pride) from being associated with a hospital that offers so many product lines. However, in the current climate of prospective payment many hospitals miss the era of cost reimbursement, where low-volume departments could be maintained. Low-volume departments with high unit costs do not get their inefficiency reimbursed under prospective payment. Hospitals operating HMOs have a limited ability to dump low-volume departments. The few dozen hospital-operated HMOs will have difficulty specializing because eliminating a product line may adversely affect their ability to serve enrollees or market their facility.

To maintain an equally high patient census, a hospital that specializes must open up the geographic range of its marketing effort. For example, when the 990-bed Memorial Medical Center of Long Beach decided to market its specialized advanced cancer-treatment program, it began to admit patients from a wider array of zip codes. The impact of consumer behavior is more obvious for smaller hospitals. As more hospitals specialize in fewer than 200 DRGs, patients will have to drive by a number of hospitals to get to "the hospitals right for them.'' The patient is increasingly going to the specialized hospital that creates a point of differentiation in his or her mind, rather than stopping at a full-service hospital offering every DRG.

The demise of cost reimbursement means that underspecialized hospitals are no longer protected from close scrutiny. Low-volume departments are under scrutiny for economic reasons (poor profit margins, poor productivity) and for quality reasons. It is difficult to establish cause and effect on the quality issue, given two alternative explanations. One is that volume is too low to maintain sufficient quality. Competition is a factor; that is, if some hospitals closed the service, market share and volume of those keeping this product line would rise. The other is that low-quality providers discourage doctors from sending patient referrals and so keep the volume low (Eastaugh and Eastaugh 1986). Irrespective of the cause-and-effect dynamics, specialization is associated with maintaining or enhancing the quality of patient care. Hughes, Hunt, and Luft (1987) indicated that specialization allows nurses and physicians to develop more expertise with respect to a specific category of patients.

Rational Behavior in the Hospital Marketplace

Robinson and Luft (1987) speculated that hospitals refuse to specialize because they would rather engage in a cost-raising ''medical arms race.'' This speculation appeared more relevant in the bygone era of cost reimbursement. Farley and Hogan (1990) reported that hospitals specialized 9.8 percent in DRG-weighted terms during the initial two years of the Medicare prospective payment system. They found a higher level of specialization (13.9 percent) during the same two years if the specialization was measured in terms of major diagnostic categories (MDCs, fewer in number than DRGs). Herrmann (1990) reported that 35 percent of CEOs in a survey of hospitals were considering product-line reductions in their facilities.

Quality and marketing are becoming increasingly important topics for hospital managers. Developing areas of specialization can bring prestige to a hospital and serve as a magnet for bringing in more patients. Special centers also assist hospitals in gaining access to capital (donors like giving to centers for treatment of a particular disease or ailment).

In addition to potential quality improvements, the benefits of hospital specialization for society include eliminating expensive duplication of services and underused technology. Internal corporate planning to cut duplication of departments and equipment in a marketplace can trim costs better than community-based health-planning regulations (Eastaugh 1982). External government planning does not prove effective in the American context because regulation operates at the periphery of the resource decision-making process. Internal cost control within the hospital is more effective than government planning guideposts, especially when the rise in discount payers and quality competition creates the need to trim product lines. Some demographic variables will be included in the analysis to assess the nature of the marketplace (competition and physician supply).

Sample and Study Methodology

The sample hospitals represent a 20 percent sample of short-term nongovernmental hospitals with more than 75 beds. Only 58 percent of the hospitals were willing and able to provide data for the two study years. The sample is explained in more detail elsewhere (Eastaugh 1991), but there was no statistically significant bias present in the sample based on seven variables (urbanicity, teaching status, size, ownership control, disproportionate share of patient volume, Medicare case-mix index, and length-of-stay index).

An unbiased information-theory measure of specialization has to be a scalar measure of output that is independent of scale (Barer 1982), so that the analyst can measure any nonlinear impact of economies of scale by including beds and beds squared in the equation. Utilizing the Farley and Hogan (1990) measure of specialization, let B_c be defined as the baseline proportion of cases in the category c, and let F_{cn} be the fraction of cases in the nth hospital observed in category c. The categories for inpatient specialization will be DRGs and MDCs, creating two alternative measures for specialization (DRG-based and MDC-based). The information-theory index I of specialization for hospital n collapses information about differences between B_c and F_{cn} as follows:

$$I_n = \sum_{c=1} F_{cn} \times \ln (F_{cn}/B_c),$$

where ln is the natural logarithm. This index equals zero when $F_c = B_c$ for all patient categories, and the index increases as case-mix fractions move away from one another. National case-mix fractions serve as the baseline. In each year (1983 and 1990) the specialization index was over 10 percent higher in western states and over 13 percent lower in two northeastern states. The results in table 2.8 suggest that specialization has been highest in competitive West Coast markets and lowest in the rate-regulated states (New York and Massachusetts). Hospitals have less incentive to contain costs by decreasing the array of services offered in stringent rate-setting states, like New York and Massachusetts, than in flexible rate-setting states (e.g., Maryland) that let the management reap the gains from any resulting cost savings. Because the MDCs are more heterogeneous categories and fewer in number than the DRGs, their information-theory index values are lower than the DRG index in table 2.8. For example, MDC 5, the circulatory system, is a grab bag of cardiac surgery (DRG numbers 103–9), pediatrics (137), vascular surgery (110–12, 119, 128, 130, 131), general surgery (113, 114, 120), and cardiology (115–18, 121–27, 129, 132–36, 138–45). The DRG-based measure of specialization increased 26.9 percent in the period 1983–

Table 2.8
Information-Theory Index of Case-Mix Specialization (I) by Geographic Location, 1983 and 1990

	Sample	1983	1990	Percentage Increase, 1983-1990
Index I DRG-based				
1. New York, Massachusetts	N = 26	.299	.371	24.1
2. Western United States	N = 50	.414	.508	22.7
3. Other 39 states	N = 156	.359	.458	27.6
4. United States	N = 232	.362	.459	26.8
Index I MDC-based				
1. New York, Massachusetts	N = 26	.102	.143	40.2
2. Western United States	N = 50	.158	.197	24.7
3. Other 39 states	N = 156	.107	.153	43.0
4. United States	N = 232	.117	.161	37.6

90. The MDC-based measure of specialization increased 37.6 percent in the period 1983–90.

What Drives Specialization?

A number of factors are hypothesized to impact specialization, including bed size, rate regulation, and ownership. For-profit hospitals have been found to specialize somewhat more (Eastaugh 1987; Farley and Hogan 1990), as have large teaching hospitals (those in the Council of Teaching Hospitals [COTH]; Eastaugh 1984; Farley and Hogan 1990). Melnick and Zwanziger (1988) reported that in the state of California inpatient costs, adjusted for inflation, decreased 11 percent in hospitals located in highly competitive markets. They used the Herfindahl index (Eastaugh 1984) by summing the squares of market shares for all the competitors in an area. If specialization is a reaction to competitive pressures, the index I should be lower in markets with a high Herfindahl index (in a monopoly single-hospital area the Herfindahl index is at the maximum value of 1.0). All else equal, specialization has been found to be higher in markets with a higher density of HMOs, hospital beds, physicians, and long-term-care units (Farley and Hogan 1990).

The DRG-based specialization index was regressed on the 13 variables outlined in table 2.9 to account for cross-sectional variations in case-mix proportions. The results in table 2.9 agree with the hypothesized signs from previous studies

Table 2.9
Variables Impacting Inpatient Case-Mix Specialization, 1983 and 1990

Variable[a]	Hypothesized Sign	Coefficient Estimate	Standard Error
A. Capacity (number of beds in 100s)			
1. Acute-care beds[b]	-	-.0984**	.0199
2. Acute-care beds squared	+	.0082*	.0040
B. Management focus (ownership, teaching status)			
3. For-profit hospital	+	.0703*	.0295
4. Member, COTH	+	.0961**	.0302
5. Affiliated with a medical school	?	-.0074	.0118
C. Competitive location and alternatives			
6. Herfindahl index bed concentration	-	-.1261**	.0292
7. In a metropolitan SMSA	+	.0329	.0204
8. Number of HMOs in the county	+	.0128*	.0047
9. Hospital beds/100 pop. in county	+	.0852	.0049
10. Physicians/100 pop. in county	+	.2596*	.1003
11. Fraction of beds in long-term care units	+	.0464*	.0214
D. State regulatory pressures			
12. Located in New York or Massachusetts	-	-.0409*	.0076
13. Located in western state	+	.0230*	.0080
E. Control for bias in index of specialization			
14. Inverse of the number of patient records	+	192.4**	49.8

[a]Ordinary least squares regression estimate with DRG-based information-theory index of specialization as the dependent variable.

[b]National sample of 232 hospitals with more than 75 beds.

*p < 0.05, two-tailed test

**p < 0.01, two-tailed test

R^2-adjusted = .628; F-ratio (14 d.f./216 d.f.) = 19.83

and support the DRG *I*-index as a measure of specialization. Specialization was high in moderately sized hospitals (100 to 300 beds) and declined up to 760 beds. Beyond 760 beds it appears that the scale of financial reserves or institutional slack enabled big hospitals to increase specialization for a wider scope of services (consistent with Dranove 1987 and Farley and Hogan 1990).

Does Specialization Reduce Cost per Admission?

To find out whether specialization can trim unit cost, one has to adjust for case mix in greater detail. One does not have sufficient sample size to introduce one variable for each product in the multiproduct firm, so the analyst does the second-best thing, which is to build a hedonic cost function (Eastaugh 1987; Barer 1982). The hedonic proxy measures for case mix include our DRG-based specialization index, a length-of-stay-weighted case-mix index, and three measures of emergency-department and outpatient-surgery volume. In building the cost function in table 2.10, one must include three measures of factor prices (if labor and debt are more expensive, then cost per admission will be more expensive) and admissions (as a measure for economies of scale in line 12, rather than bed capacity). The results in table 2.10 indicate that a 26.9 percent rise in specialization yielded a 6.9 percent reduction in cost per admission in the period 1983–90. Reducing costs 1 percent per year over seven years is a small, but not inconsequential, improvement in efficiency. The capacity for generating cost savings is one rationale for the rise in specialization. A second rationale for specialization involves shifts in technology and physician preference for certain procedures and product lines (Farley and Friedman 1991). From these regression equations one cannot ascertain how much of the specialization is provider/physician driven, management driven (by selection of product lines), or payment driven (either the reimbursement rates are too low or the inefficient departments have unusually high average cost).

The coefficients of the within-hospital regression equation explaining shifts in specialization over the period 1983–90 are given in table 2.11. The signs are consistent with the cross-sectional results in table 2.9, except that the fifth variable (affiliation with a medical school) and the ninth variable (bed density) have different signs. One cannot conclude much from the observation that the HMO density variable is more significant (0.01 level) but the Herfindahl index is slightly less significant (0.05 level) in table 2.11 than in table 2.9. Not surprisingly, the western states appear to be associated with more specialization, and the environment in New York and Massachusetts tends to retard specialization. The most substantial finding in table 2.11 is the large highly significant coefficient for cost per admission in line 7, suggesting that hospitals facing higher costs per DRG specialize more. One caveat should be introduced: It is difficult to assess reliability in going from such cross-sectional data to a comparison over time.

Table 2.10
Impact of Case-Mix Specialization on Inpatient Hospital Costs per Admission Based on a Within-Hospital Regression Equation

Variable[a]	Hypothesized Sign	Coefficient Estimate	Standard Error
A. Hedonic descriptors for case mix[b]			
1. ln (DRG-based I index)	-	-.1309**	.0285
2. ln (LOS-weighted case-mix index)	+	.7043**	.0920
3. Emergency-dept. visits/total visits	+	.0009	.0086
4. Outpatient-surgery visits/total visits	+	.0273**	.0072
5. Fraction of surgery done outpatient	+	.0601*	.0242
B. Competitive location and alternatives			
6. Herfindahl index bed concentration	-	-.1107	.0429
7. Fraction of revenue not from operations	+	.1968*	.0857
8. Number of HMOs in the county	-	-.0192**	.0037
9. Hospital beds/100 pop. in county	-	-.0684*	.0300
10. Physicians/100 pop. in county	?	-.0315*	.1798
11. Nonpatient-care revenue/total revenue	+	.1689	.0995
C. Economies of scale (impact of volume)			
12. ln (acute-care admissions)	-	-.2034**	.0462
D. Management focus (ownership, teaching status)			
13. For-profit hospital	-	.0612	.0352
14. Member, COTH	+	.0810*	.0345
15. Affiliated with a medical school	?	-.0036	.0129
E. Input factor prices (labor, debt)			
16. Ratio of long-term debt/total assets	+	.2070**	.0387
17. ln (total interest expense (long-term debt)	+	.0192**	.0051
18. ln (average payroll expense per FTE)	+	.1849**	.0220

[a]Least squares estimate with ln (average cost per admission) as dependent variable and instruments used for ln (I) and ln (admissions).

[b]LOS = length of stay; I = Information-theory case-mix index.

*p < 0.05, two-tailed test

**p < 0.01, two tailed test

R^2-adjusted = .397; F-ratio (18 d.f./444 d.f.) = 26.69

Table 2.11
Variables Impacting Within-Hospital Variance in Hospital Case-Mix Specialization, 1983–1990

Variable[a]	Hypothesized Sign	Coefficient Estimate	Standard Error
A. Capacity (number of beds in 100s)			
1. Acute-care beds[b]	-	-.0815**	.0217
2. Acute-care beds squared	+	.0059*	.0025
B. Management focus (ownership, teaching status)			
3. For-profit hospital	+	.0509	.0314
4. Member, COTH	+	.0702*	.0333
5. Affiliated with a medical school	?	.0058	.0118
C. Competitive location and alternatives			
6. Herfindahl index bed concentration	-	-.0652*	.0278
7. 1n (average cost per inpatient admit)	+	.1873**	.0319
8. Number of HMOs in the county	+	.0065**	.0016
9. Hospital beds/100 pop. in county	+	-.0369	.0208
10. Physicians/100 pop. in county	+	.2701*	.1144
11. Fraction of beds in long-term-care units	+	.0824*	.0292
D. State regulatory pressures			
12. Located in New York or Massachusetts	-	-.0641**	.0053
13. Located in western state	+	.0358**	.0051
E. Control for bias in index of specialization			
14. Inverse of the number of patient records	+	221.6**	35.7

[a]Ordinary least squares estimate with DRG-based index as dependent variable using an instrument for 1n (average cost per admission)

[b]National sample of 232 hospitals with more than 75 beds.

*$p < 0.05$, two-tailed test

**$p < 0.01$, two-tailed test

R^2-adjusted = .285; F-ratio (15 d.f./444 d.f.) = 21.06

CONCLUSIONS

Not so long ago there lived a happy paradigm that said that hospitals that specialized were too internally focused because they turned away patients and doctors in areas outside their limited product lines. Today the reduction of product lines in a more specialized hospital can reduce the inefficiency (unjustified costs) in individual hospitals (Berwick, Godfrey, and Roessner 1990; Eastaugh 1991). The new paradigm for the 1990s is that specialization breeds quality, and this section has offered evidence that efficiency is improved. The hospital offering every DRG is too internally focused and provides care at a higher unit cost (with less service quality). The obvious exception to this broad generalization is the few huge academic medical centers (AMCs) with departments already large enough to reap any possible economies of scale. About half of the 122 academic medical centers fall into this category (15 of the 232 hospitals in this study are AMCs). In the future the other 1,100 teaching hospitals may have to specialize or pool resources and become less full service (offering over 400 DRGs) but better positioned to survive in an era of cost competition and quality competition.

Studies of specialization should consider the direction in which the specialization is planned or driven. No current evidence exists to suggest that specialization has harmed access (Eastaugh 1991), but in the future specialization might produce less product differentiation, with every hospital moving in the same direction. Under such conditions all hospitals in a market area might vacate a necessary product line and perhaps harm the health of the population.

Future trends are hard to project from retrospective analysis. The observed 26.9 percent rise in specialization was associated with a 6.9 percent decline in unit cost (per admission) from 1983 to 1990. However, this does not mean that an additional 26.9 percent rise in specialization will yield a further 6.9 percent decline in cost per admission. One must not forget the role of the consumer. Travel time and search time to find that "right hospital" for a given condition will rise if the average hospital offers only 150 DRGs. Future research should consider whether the cost to consumers and physicians in the search process is worth the benefits in terms of (1) rising levels of quality and (2) declining unit cost per admission. With a good public information network and rising interest in value shopping (Eastaugh 1986), specialization may continue to be a bargain for providers and consumers. However, physicians may not like the fact that they have practice privileges to admit patients at a smaller number of specialized hospitals. On the upside for hospitals, they may have the economic power to charge high fees (like a condo fee or rent) to doctors in search of admitting privileges).

Future research should consider whether any future 7 to 10 percent improvement in cost efficiency per admission outweighs the cost to patients. If patients have to spend more time (travel time and lost wages) driving to fewer specialized providers, the monetary savings for payers may not be worth the resulting costs to the households. Judging by the quality-of-care studies surveyed in chapters

6 and 11, the gains in improved quality and efficiency more than outweigh the costs to consumers, but this generality may not be true in some unstudied rural areas where the opportunity costs for longer distances are more substantial.

APPENDIX

Two constraints in the conjoint analysis (Table 2.7) are readily apparent. First, the orthogonal array and the main-effects model omit interactions. This simplification is typical of many applied marketing studies (Green and Tull 1984). Second, the orthogonal experimental design involves only 27 of 729 possible combinations. As has been documented in the marketing literature (Johnson 1987), despite these limitations, the conjoint measurement program is capable of finding a reliable numerical measure of the utilities, thus providing an indication of each attribute's relative importance.

Given that the respondents' overall evaluation scores are known, the part-worth utility associated with each of the three attributes and the three levels can be solved (Green and Tull 1984) using a regression equation (ordinary least squares, OLS). In the cluster analysis three small clusters and three large clusters were collapsed down to three groups. From cursory inspection of each dendrogram in the cluster analysis, each of the three minor trees ($N = 8$, 6, or 3 observations) was "cut" to fit into the three large clusters. The original three clusters contained 93 percent of the sample before these final four minor groupings were "collapsed" back into the analysis. Given the goodness of fit (ranging from 0.54 to 0.46 v-restricted) and the correlations between attributes, the basic three clusters are the best representation of the sample.

To ascertain the validity of the three clusters in table 2.7, a discriminant analysis was performed and a discriminant function was estimated using 125 observations. This discriminant function was then used to classify the remaining observations into clusters. Only 2 observations were classified into a cluster different from the one assigned. This test confirms the stability and separation of the three clusters or market segments in table 2.7.

Attribute-level weights in table 2.7 were obtained by transforming OLS coefficients via a conditional logit model (McFadden 1976; Akaah and Becherer 1983). The attribute-level weights were obtained based on the transformation

$$P_j(i) = \frac{e^{u_j^{(i)}}}{\sum_{j=1}^{3} e^{u_j^{(i)}}}$$

where $P_j^{(i)}$ denotes the estimated weight for level j ($j = 1, 2, 3$) of attribute i ($i = 1, 2, 3$), $e = 2.718\ldots$, and $u_j^{(i)}$ is the regression coefficient (part worth) associated with level j of attribute i. The benefit of this transformation is that the computed attribute-level weights are invariant over an additive constant applied to each of the $u_j^{(i)}$'s within any specific attribute (Green and Tull 1984; Basu and Hastak 1990).

Because part worths in table 2.7 are expressed in terms of a common unit intervally scaled, an estimate of the total utility of any profile can be computed. (A zero part worth does not indicate the absence of utility.) Pooling respondents' part worths and working with a single overall utility function (often done by economists) unfortunately ignores any heterogeneity in preference among hospital managers (and reduces the predictive power of the model).

REFERENCES

Acito, F., and Jain, A. (1980). "Evaluation of Conjoint Analysis Results: A Comparison of Methods." *Journal of Marketing Research* 17:2 (February), 106–112.

Akaah, I., and Becherer, R. (1983). "Integrating a Consumer Orientation into Planning of HMO Programs: An Application of Conjoint Segmentation." *Journal of Health Care Marketing* 3:2 (Spring), 9–18.

American Hospital Association (AHA). (1991). Panel Survey Data, 1983–1991. Sample of over 1,270 AHA member hospitals. Chicago: AHA.

Baptist, A. (1987). "A General Approach to Costing Procedures in Ancillary Departments." *Topics in Health Care Financing* 13:4 (Fall) 32–47.

Barer, M. (1982). "Case Mix Adjustment in Hospital Cost Analysis: Information Theory Revisited." *Journal of Health Economics* 1:1 (Spring) 53–80.

Basu, A., and Hastak, M. (1990). "Multiattribute Judgements under uncertainty: a conjoint measurement approach" *Advances in Consumer Research* 17:1 (Spring), 454–60.

Becker, R., and Chambers, J. (1989). *Language and System for Data Analysis*. Murray Hill, N.J.: Bell Laboratories.

Berman, H., Weeks, L., and Kukla, S. (1990). *The Financial Management of Hospitals*. Ann Arbor, Mich.: Health Administration Press.

Berry, R., Varholy, S., Russell, M., Kelly, N., and Eastaugh, S. (1986). "A Study of the Financing of Graduate Medical Education." Arthur Young and Company Final Report (September), Contract DHHS:ASPE, DHHS-100–80–0155, chapters 4–5.

Berwick, D., Godfrey, A., and Roessner, J. (1990). *Curing Health Care: New Strategies for Quality Improvement*. San Francisco: Jossey-Bass.

Botz, C. (1989). "Weighting Case Mix Groups: The Fatal Flaw." *Healthcare Management Forum* 11:1 (Spring), 8–11.

Burik, D., and Duvall, T. (1985). "Hospital Cost Accounting." *Healthcare Financial Management* 39:3 (March), 58–64.

Carroll, N., and Gagon, J. (1983). "Identifying Consumer Segments in Health Services Markets: An Application of Conjoint and Cluster Analyses." *Journal of Health Care Marketing* 3:3 (Summer), 22–34.

Christensen, W., and Stearns, E. (1991). *Microcomputers in Health Care Management*. Rockville, Md.: Aspen.

Cleverley, W. (1990). *Handbook of Health Care Accounting and Finance*. Rockville, Md.: Aspen.

———. (1989). "Break-even Analysis in the New Payor Environment." *Hospital Topics* 67:2 (Spring), 36–37.

———. (1987). "Product Costing for Health Care Firms." *Health Care Management Review* 12:4 (Fall), 39–48.

Coddington, D., and Steiker, A. (1986). "New Tools for Healthcare Decision-making." *Healthcare Forum* 29:5 (September–October), 25–27.

Conjoint Analyzer. (1988). Version 2.0. New York: Bretton-Clark.

Cook, T., and Campbell, D. (1979). *Quasi-Experimentation: Design and Analysis Issues*. Boston: Houghton Mifflin.

Dranove, D. (1987). "Rate-setting by DRGs and Hospital Specialization." *Rand Journal of Economics* 18:3 (Autumn), 417–427.

Eastaugh, S. (1992). "Hospital Specialization and Cost Efficiency: Benefits of Trimming Product-lines." *Hospital and Health Services Administration* 37:2, 188–199.

———. (1991). "Improvements in Hospital Cost Accounting." *Healthcare Financial Management* 46:2, forthcoming.

———. (1990a). "Health Insurance Reform in the 1990s." *Journal of the American Academy of Physician Assistants* 3:5 (July/August), 384–395.

———. (1990b). "Financing the Correct Rate of Growth of Medical Technology." *Quarterly Review of Economics and Business* 30:4 (Winter), 54–60.

———. (1988). "Hospital Diversification Revisited." *Medical Care* 26:12 (December), 1115–1117.

———. (1987). "Has PPS Affected the Sophistication of Cost Accounting?" *Healthcare Financial Management* 41:11 (November), 50–52.

———. (1986). "Hospital Quality Scorecards: The Role of the Informed Consumer." *Hospital and Health Services Administration* 31:6 (November/December), 85–102.

———. (1984). "Hospital Diversification and Financial Management." *Medical Care* 22:8 (August), 704–723.

———. (1982). "Effectiveness of Community-based Hospital Planning: Some Recent Evidence." *Applied Economics* 14:5 (October), 475–490.

———. (1979). "Cost of Elective Surgery and Utilization of Ancillary Services in Teaching Hospitals." *Health Services Research* 14:4 (Winter), 290–308.

Eastaugh, S., and Eastaugh, J. (1990). "Putting the Squeeze on Emergency Medicine: Pressures on The Emergency Department." *Hospital Topics* 68:4 (Fall), 21–25.

———. (1986). "Prospective Payment Systems: Further Steps to Enhance Quality, Efficiency, and Regionalization." *Health Care Management Review* 11:4 (Fall), 37–52.

Farley, D., and Friedman, B. (1991). "Hospital Operating Margins: Noisy Equilibrium and Risk." Agency for Health Care Policy and Research, U.S. Department of Health and Human Services, Rockville, Maryland.

Farley, D., and Hogan, C. (1990). "Case-mix Specialization in the Market for Hospital Services." *Health Services Research* 25:5 (December), 757–783.

Finkler, S. (1983). "The Hospital as a Sales-maximizing Entity." *Health Services Research* 18:2 (Summer), 117–133.

———. (1982). "Increasing the Usefulness of Flexible Budgeting: The Pyramid Approach." *Hospital Financial Management* 36:2 (February), 30–39.

Folland, S., Ziegenfuss, J., and Chao, P. (1988). "Implications of Prospective Payment under DRGs for Hospital Marketing." *Journal of Health Care Marketing* 8:4 (December), 29–36.

General Accounting Office (GAO). (1985). *Hospitals in the Same Area Pay Widely Different Prices for Comparable Supply Items*. GAO Report 85–35 (January 21). Washington, D.C.: U.S. Government Printing Office.

Goldschmidt, Y., and Gafni, A. (1990). "A Managerial Approach to Allocating Indirect Fixed Costs." *Health Care Management Review* 15:2 (Spring), 43–51.

Green, P., and DeSarbo, W. (1978). "Additive Decomposition of Perceptions Data via Conjoint Analyzer." *Journal of Consumer Research* 5 (June), 58–65.

Green, P., Helsen, K., and Shandler, B. (1988). "Conjoint Internal Validity under Alternatives." *Journal of Consumer Research* 15 (December), 46–80.

Green, P., and Tull, D. (1988). *Research for Marketing Decisions*. 5th ed. Englewood Cliffs, N.J.: Prentice-Hall.

Herrmann, J. (1990). "New Strategies—Managing Hospitals in the 1990s." *Federation of American Health Systems Review* 23:4 (July/August), 14–23.

Hogan, A., and Marshall, R. (1990). "How to Improve Allocation of Support Service Costs." *Healthcare Financial Management* 44:2 (February), 42–52.

Horn, S. (1986). "Measuring Severity: How Sick Is Sick? How Well Is Well?" *Healthcare Financial Management* 40:10 (October), 21–32.

Horngren, C. (1982). *Cost Accounting: A Managerial Emphasis*, 5th ed. Englewood Cliffs, N.J.: Prentice-Hall.

Horngren, C., and Sundem, G. (1991). *Introduction to Management Accounting*. Englewood Cliffs, N.J.: Prentice-Hall.

Hughes, R., Hunt, S., and Luft, H. (1987). "Effects of Surgeon Volume and Hospital Volume on Quality of Care in Hospitals." *Medical Care* 25:6 (June), 489–503.

Interstudy. (1991). *The Interstudy Edge*. Excelsior, Minn.: Interstudy, 2nd volume.

Jain, A., Pinson, C., and Ratchford, B. (1982). *Marketing Research: Applications and Problems*. New York: John Wiley.

Johnson, R. (1987). "Adaptive Conjoint Analysis." Paper presented at the Sawtooth Software Conference on Perceptual Mapping, Conjoint Analysis, and Computer Interviewing (March).

Johnson, S. (1967). "Hierarchical Clustering Schemes." *Psychometrika* 32:1 (January), 241–254.

Knight, W. (1982). "Working Capital Management: Satisficing versus Optimization." *Financial Management* 11:2 (Spring), 33–40.

McClain, J., and Eastaugh, S. (1983). "How to Forecast to Contain Your Variable Costs: Exponential Smoothing Techniques." *Hospital Topics* 61:6 (November–December), 4–9.

McFadden, D. (1976). "Quantal Choice Analysis: A Survey." *Annals of Economic and Social Measurement* 5:1 (January), 363–390.

McQuiston, D., and Walters, R. (1989). "Preference Surveys." *Journal of Business and Industrial Marketing* 4:2 (Summer), 65–75.

Meeting, D., Saunders, G., and Curcio, R. (1988). "Using DRGs and Standard Costs to Control Nursing Labor Costs," *Healthcare Financial Management* 42:9 (September), 62–74.

Melnick, G., and Zwanziger, J. (1988). "Hospital Behavior under Competition and Cost-Containment Policies: The California Experience." *Journal of the American Medical Association* 260:18 (November 11), 2669–2675.

Montgomery, D., and Wittink, D. (1980). *Market Measurement and Analysis*. Cambridge; Mass.: Marketing Science Institute, 298–399.

Moore, W., and Semenik, R. (1988). "Measuring Preferences with Conjoint Analysis: Impact of a Different Number of Attributes in the Design." *Journal of Business Research* 16:2 (May), 261–274.

National Purchasing Outlook (NPO). (1991). *Healthcare Material Management*. Libertyville, Ill.: Mayworm Associates.

Neumann, B., Suver, J., and Zelman, W. (1992). *Financial Management: Concepts and Applications for Health Care Providers*. Baltimore: National Health Publishing.

Neumann, B., and Suver, J. (1990). *Management Accounting for Health Care Organizations* Chicago: HFMA.

Newhouse, J. (1989). "Measuring Medical Prices and Understanding Their Effects." *Journal of Health Administration Education* 7 (Winter), 19–25.

Noordeweir, T., Rogers, D., and Balakrishnan, S. (1989). "Evaluating Consumer Preference for Private Long-Term Care Insurance." *Journal of Health Care Marketing* 9:4 (December), 34–40.

Parzen, E. (1971). *Stochastic Processes*. San Francisco: Holden-Day.

Reisman, A. (1984). "Material Management Systems: A Means toward Significant Hospital Cost Containment." *Hospital Material Management Quarterly* 5:2 (February), 74–81.

Rhodes, R., Krasniak, C., and Jones, P. (1986). "Factors Affecting Length of Stay for Femoropopliteal Bypass: Implications of DRGs." *New England Journal of Medicine* 314:3 (January 16), 153–157.

Rizzo, J. (1992). "Supply and Demand Factors in the Determination of Expenditures," *Health Services Research* 26:6, 708–722.

Robinson, J., and Luft, H. (1987). "Competition and the Cost of Hospital Care, 1972 to 1982." *Journal of the American Medical Association* 257:23 (June 19) 3241–3245.

Schlag, D. (1986). "Providing Better Understanding of the True Revenues of the Organization—Impact of the Principles and Practices Statement No. 7." *Healthcare Financial Management* 40:4 (April), 72–81.

Snook, I. (1992). *Hospitals: what they are and how they work*, Gaithersburg, Maryland: Aspen.

Sokal, R. (1974). "Classification: Purposes, Principles, Progress, Prospects." *Science* 185 (September 27), 1115–1123.

Suver, J., and Neumann, B. (1985). *Management Accounting for Healthcare Organizations*. Oak Brook, Ill.: Healthcare Financial Management Association.

Watson, L. (1991). "Material Management in a Changing Environment: Reactive or Proactive?" *Hospital Material Management Quarterly* 12:2 (February), 33–40.

Weber, M., Eisenfuhr, F., and von Winterfeldt, D. (1988). "Effects of Splitting Attributes on Weights in Multiattribute Utility Measurement." *Management Science* 34 (April), 431–445.

Williams, S., Finkler, S., Murphy, C., and Eisenberg, J. (1982). "Improved Cost Allocation in Case-Mix Accounting." *Medical Care* 20:5 (May), 450–459.

Part Two

ACCESS TO LONG-TERM CARE AND PREPAID MANAGED CARE

Chapter 3

HMOs, PPOs, and Competition Health Plans

Medline Research Service does not list the word ''health'' in its index. In a teaching hospital there is no such thing as a healthy patient. A healthy patient is one who has not been sufficiently worked up at high cost. Come to a teaching hospital as a Medicare patient with the complaint of ''stiff hands in the morning'' and we will send you to rheumatology for a workup to discover Lupus in one case per 1,000 screened.

—John G. Freymann, M.D.

Consumers want value for their money, and that means shopping on the basis of quality and effective price. Much of the credit for lower rates of cost containment rests with private initiatives, not just the federal prospective payment system.

—Willis Goldbeck

PPOs are making inroads into the utilization advantage of HMOs. Where in the past HMOs had a hospital experience 50 percent less than that experienced by their fee-for-service competitors, that margin has now shrunk. As these managed care products continue to push down the utilization curve the price attractiveness of HMOs may decline.

—Donald Cohodes

The preference in Canada and Western Europe is for some degree of private management of the national health service or national health insurance plan. In the United States, Japan, and Korea, physicians and administrators who distrust regulatory approaches have advocated the injection of more competitive relationships between health care providers. However, not all physicians have a truly procompetitive bias. Many hospital managers and doctors who have had experience with competition and are now facing declining patient census and visits dream of returning to a less competitive era.

Nobody likes competition in what he or she produces, but we all like competition in what we buy. Physicians seeking fiscal security are increasingly cooperating with their local managed-care plans (American Hospital Association [AHA] 1990).

The basic rationale behind the competitive model is to keep the insurance companies, and hopefully providers, under constant pressure to find the means to provide care at lower costs (Atkinson and Eastaugh 1984). Third-party payers and HMOs will on occasion make management mistakes, create long patient queues, or provide unacceptable patient-care conditions, but the strength of competitive markets is that the good-quality, lower-cost operators will grow. Advocates of competition recognize consumer ignorance, insured consumers' indifference to costs, and strong physician influence on demands as three strong arguments for regulatory activity (Enthoven 1980; Hreachmack and Stannard 1990; Kirkman-Liff and Van de Ven 1989).

The public policy question is not simply one of whether to allow competition or regulation, but rather, what the proper balance of regulation and competition is and how much price and nonprice competition should be encouraged. As we have observed in chapters 1–2, the strongest argument for regulatory limits on competition—significant economies of scale leading to excessive monopoly power—does not exist in the medical sector.

A number of barriers impede competition in the health field. While there is sufficient time to shop for maternity care, there is seldom enough time to shop in most hospital "purchase" situations. Conventional analysis says that there is seldom a real "purchase" choice to be made, since the consumer, acting with minimal knowledge of medicine, goes to the doctor and says "save me." The doctor acts as the patient's agent. One might counterargue that an economist who purchases a jacuzzi has less knowledge of the equipment than the typical high-school graduate has concerning medicine. Yet the economist, with the aid of *Consumer Reports,* can make an intelligent purchase decision. The ignorance problem does not preclude competitive markets in the case of high-technology consumer goods. However, this problem is compounded in the medical sector when "rival" providers and hospitals act in a collusive fashion—for example, when they restrict advertising or quality-disclosure activities.

TYPES OF HMOs

There are four basic types of HMOs: staff HMOs, medical-group HMOs, independent practice associations (IPAs), and networks. Staff-model HMOs hire physicians as salaried employees—for example, Group Health Cooperative of Puget Sound in Seattle and Group Health in Washington, D.C.. Group-model HMOs function as a medical-group practice, with a number of physicians operating as a partnership or corporation that contracts with HMO management and the insurance plan to provide services, pool income, and redistribute income according to a predetermined formula. There are two basic variations of the group-model HMO. In the dual group model, the group contracts with a nonrelated HMO corporation for physician services (e.g., Kaiser Health Plan with Permanente Clinic physicians). In the single-entity group model, the physician group constructs its own HMO, health plan, and insurance entity as separate product lines, with a budget incorporated as part of the medical group. Because they are seldom sufficiently capitalized, the group HMOs in this second sub-category are few in number (e.g., Western Clinic in Tacoma and the former Palo Alto Medical Clinic corporation).

The third variety of HMO, the independent practice association (IPA), is a separate legal entity from the HMO that contracts with individual physicians practicing in a traditional office setting. There are two basic subcategories of IPAs. The oldest variation of IPA contracts with a separate entity (other HMOs) to provide physician services on a fee-for-service basis with a hold-back–risk-pool provision (10 to 25 percent of charges are held in the pool to be redistributed at the end of the year if the utilization experience has been sufficiently con-strained). The second variation of an IPA actually develops and controls its own separate HMO plan. This second type of IPA has been increasingly popular since the federal office of HMOs recognized this model as a legitimate federally qualified HMO in 1981 (e.g., CoMed in Cedar Knolls and Crossroads IPA in East Orange, New Jersey). Prior to 1981 the federally qualified HMO would have to operate two separate corporations, even if it had the same board and administrative staff. Both types of IPAs utilize the risk-pool–hold-back mech-anism in case utilization levels break the budget.

IPAs and staff-model HMOs are not frequently used with or by group-practice HMOs. IPAs were often marketed to physicians as a defensive reaction by organized medicine to the spread of group- or staff-model HMOs in the area. IPAs are formed from state or county medical societies or hospital medical staffs to create an economic bargaining unit to negotiate with all the managed-care brokers (nonprofit and proprietary HMOs).

To add further complexity to the issues, there is a fourth type of HMO called the network plan. Blue Cross/Blue Shield, five for-profit hospital chains, and two nonprofit co-ops or alliances have developed network HMO models to compete with smaller local HMOs for prepaid business. According to Shouldice (1987) and Boland (1990), the network HMO option is franchised to local providers, IPAs, and staff HMOs as potential partners with the regional network to provide prepaid care. For this reason, network HMOs are best labeled "mul-timodel franchises" that cover a city, state, or multistate region. Networks are especially attractive to multistate employers.

IPAs tend to be smaller HMOs (Interstudy 1991). IPAs represent 63 percent of the HMO plans, but only 41.9 percent of the national HMO enrollment. There are a few large IPAs, including Physicians Health Plan of Minnesota, Blue Choice of New York, HMO of Pennsylvania, Bay State Health Care, and Humana Health Plan in Kentucky. Group-model HMOs tend to be larger, including the three largest HMOs, Kaiser Northern California, Kaiser Southern California, and HIP (Health Insurance Plan of Greater New York). Group-model HMOs are

11 percent of the plans and have 28 percent of the national HMO enrollment (Interstudy 1991). Network HMOs are 15 percent of the HMO plans and have 17 percent of the enrollment. Large network-model HMOs include PacifiCare of California, Health Net in California, HMO Illinois, and the troubled Humana Medical Plan of Florida. Staff-model HMOs represent 11 percent of the plans and 13.3 percent of the enrollment.

Each of the four HMO types has for-profit and tax-exempt forms. IPAs and network HMOs tend to be for-profit, but nearly half the staff- and group-model HMOs are also for-profit. Nonprofit HMOs tend to be larger than average. Over 51 percent of HMO enrollees are members of the one-third of HMOs that are tax-exempt (nonprofit). The stock values of most for-profit HMO chains took a major nosedive in 1988 when Congress rewrote the 1973 HMO Act to allow a form of experience rating, thus permitting employers to pay less for HMO coverage than they do for indemnity insurance. For-profit HMOs had been earning record-high price-to-earnings ratios because of the high premiums HMO enrollees were paying relative to their expenses.

HMO GROWTH

President Nixon's vision of 40 million American HMO enrollees by 1980 has not been realized. Only 34.7 million Americans, 13.4 percent of the population, were in HMOs in 1990 (table 3.1). If Abramowitz's (1988) estimates are accurate, HMOs could cover 25 percent of the population by 1988. Certain geographic areas of the country tend to have higher HMO market penetration. Washington, D.C., has 78 percent of the population in HMOs, California 31 percent, both Massachusetts and Minnesota 25 percent, Oregon 24 percent and Rhode Island and Hawaii 23 percent (Interstudy 1991).

HMO enrollees are of two basic types: (1) locked-in members who only receive services from required participating HMO providers and (2) open-ended enrollees who can receive non-HMO care without prior referral authorization and pay a substantial cost-sharing requirement (e.g., 25 percent of the bill). Traditional "pure" HMO enrollees paid no cost-sharing requirement prior to 1980 and perhaps a $10 to $20 copayment per physician visit in the 1980s. Since 1986 open-ended enrollees have represented the HMO sector's reaction to PPOs: coverage to non-HMO doctors is financed similarly to that of a PPO, where the consumer pays higher deductibles and high coinsurance (e.g., 20 percent). Open-ended HMO membership grew from 100,000 in 1986 to 701,000 in July 1989 and an estimated 1.2 million in 1991. Pure HMO membership grew from 31.9 million in January 1989 to an estimated 36.5 million in 1991. Therefore, a combined total of 37.7 million Americans were in HMOs in 1991 (Interstudy 1991). By 1993 one in every six American employees will belong to an HMO.

While the enrollment of the HMO sector has outpaced general population growth by 4.2 percent per annum since 1986, the number of HMOs has declined (from 626 in 1986 to 653 at the beginning of 1988, 607 by January 1989, and

Table 3.1
Number of HMOs and Enrollment, Select Years, 1970–1991

Year	Number of Prepaid Plans (HMOs)	Enrollment (in millions)	Percentage of U.S. Population
1970	26	2.9	1.4
1973[a]	140	5.2	2.5
1975	178	5.7	2.6
1977	165	6.3	2.9
1979	215	8.2	3.6
1981	243	10.2	4.4
1982	265	10.8	4.7
1983	280	12.5	5.3
1984	306	15.1	6.4
1985	392	18.9	7.9
1986	585	23.3	9.4
1987	636	26.2[b]	10.4
1988	653	30.6	12.0
1989	607	32.6	12.7
1990	575	34.7	13.4
1991	555	37.7	14.4

Sources: Interstudy (1991) and the National HMO Census, Office of HMOs, U.S. Public Health Service.
[a]The HMO Act, Pub. L. 93-222, was passed in 1973.
[b]A small number of open-ended HMO enrollees have been included in the totals since 1987 (e.g., 858,000 in 1990).

565 in 1991). The reduction in the number of HMOs by 42 from 1989 to 1991 involved 11 consolidations, 12 mergers, and 19 closures (terminations). A consolidation occurs when two or more HMOs join to form an entirely new plan (with a new name); for example, Constitution Health Network consolidated with HealthCare Inc. in 1990 in Connecticut. Mergers involve separate firms that combine, with one HMO absorbing the other firm; for example, Bestcare merged into Health Maintenance Oregon in 1990.

Total enrollment in HMOs continued to grow even as the weak unstable plans were weeded out and closed or absorbed by stronger mature HMOs. After the shakeout in the HMO industry, profitability has returned to the HMO business. According to American International Healthcare, an HMO management conglomerate in Rockville, Maryland, the nation's 450 largest HMOs had net income of $243 million in 1989 and $268 million in 1990, compared to losses of $764 million in 1988. In a bad year (1988) 34 of the 37 California HMOs reported financial losses. The nation's 100 largest HMOs had operating profit margins of 2.2 percent in 1986, 0.5 percent in 1988, and 3.1 percent in 1990. Better utilization review procedures, improved productivity, and higher-than-average price increases (in premiums and copayments paid by patients) improved the profitability of the HMO industry. Between 1988 and 1990 the average copayments on office visits, emergency-department visits, and urgent-care visits more than doubled (Interstudy 1991). For most HMOs in the 1970s, free care with no copayment charges was typical.

HMO growth has received competition from a managed-care alternative, the preferred provider organization (PPO). PPOs offer a financial incentive for enrollees to go to the listed (contracted) providers, like an IPA, but unlike an IPA the patient can go to an unlisted fee-for-service provider and still have 75 to 80 percent of the bill paid by the HMO. Consequently, patients have more freedom to shop in PPOs compared to HMOs.

The number of PPOs peaked in December 1988, but the number of enrollees continues to grow. According to Marion (1991) the number of PPOs increased from 30 in 1983 to 73 in 1984, 369 in 1986, 674 in May 1987, and 678 in December 1988, then declined to 512 in 1991. Estimates of PPO enrollment vary from 28 to 32 million Americans, or 45 to 50 percent of the eligible employees working for employers that use PPOs. Blue Cross/Blue Shield had 12.4 million of its 72 million subscribers in PPOs in 1991. The multistate corporate PPOs have an additional 16.0 to 17.3 million enrollees. In summary, 36 percent of insured Americans under age 65 are in PPOs, and 41 percent are in HMOs. Pure fee-for-service health insurance declined from 95 percent of market share in 1983 to less than 10 percent in 1991. Even fee-for-service plans do so much utilization review that they have come to resemble PPOs.

HMO UTILIZATION RATES

For nonelderly populations, HMOs use 341 hospital-bed days per 1,000 enrollees, compared to 425 for PPOs and 542 for pure fee-for-service indemnity insurance. HMOs and the better PPOs utilize four basic approaches to controlling hospital utilization: (1) constraints on physician behavior, (2) physician incentives, (3) patient incentives, and (4) selection of physicians and a "style-of-practice" prototype profile for participation in the HMO. Different types of HMOs place varying degrees of emphasis on these four approaches. Homer (1986) in a survey of 93 HMOs reported these findings:

1. Seventy-three percent required prior approval of elective admissions.
2. Newer HMOs were more likely to utilize annual bonus schemes for physicians.
3. Smaller HMOs were more likely to use one type of bonus—ambulatory-care incentive payments for physicians.
4. Independent practice associations (IPAs) were less able to select physicians who

ordered fewer inpatient services and admissions (conservative practice style) for the plan because participation was nonexclusive (open to any medical society member in most cases).

5. IPAs were less able to confine treatment to ambulatory-care facilities because they did not directly operate such facilities.

Average hospitalization rates in 1991 reported for HMOs—375 bed days per 1,000 enrollees or 341 bed days for enrollees under age 65—as with any insurer, represent the days paid for by the HMOs. Mott (1986) listed 15 ways in which enrollees are hospitalized while their HMOs are unaware of or not reporting these days. The quantity of out-of-plan utilization is hard to estimate and may inflate actual hospital usage statistics from 5 to 20 percent. Luft (1981) was the first to point out that data concerning out-of-plan hospital usage, while seemingly objective, are really a hodgepodge of confusing, ill-defined figures. However, the days of hospitalization per 1,000 enrollees declined 3 to 4 percent each year from 1983 to 1991. A large part of this decline may have come about because of heightened competition between prepaid plans, but how much of this decline may have resulted from increased out-of-plan hospitalizations is impossible to estimate.

HMOs have obvious incentives to curtail hospital utilization and specialist referrals (Clancy and Hillner 1989). The model of the incentive-based physician as a "gatekeeper" places the clinician under some financial risk. For example, secondary resource pools (funds) are set up, and if the primary physician needs to refer, the cost comes out of his or her pocket up to a certain point ($1,500, $2,000). After that point, reinsurance kicks in, but the gatekeeper is still liable for enough financial risk to discourage inappropriate referrals. Some specialists argue that this creates restricted access to some appropriate referrals. Advocates of gatekeeper HMOs argue that underutilization is not a major problem and that specialists desire a continued supply of inappropriate referrals to guarantee their target incomes. Short-run profit taking may not lead to long-run inefficient referral patterns, assuming ethical clinician behavior. At the end of the year, if there is any money left in the primary pool, the primary-care physician gets a share. However, physicians realize that failure to make appropriate referrals often results in failure to obtain early diagnoses, resulting in more costly (and more frequent) inpatient expenses (and withdrawals from their risk-pool fund).

In staff-model HMOs the primary-care physicians are salaried. Capitated or salaried "gatekeepers" lack the direct financial incentive to improve earnings by restraining costs. They may still prove effective as gatekeepers for reasons of professional pride, preventive medicine, and long-run concern for balancing service and solvency in their HMO. However, in an understaffed staff HMO, the gatekeepers may refer too many inappropriate cases to the specialists, especially if they are very busy (or uncompensated for working any harder). Under no circumstances do HMOs offer an incentive to overhospitalize (Seaman 1990).

CONSUMER TASTE FOR MANAGED CARE

Concerns over the quality of HMO service have been brought up by government (General Accounting Office [GAO] 1989) and the general public. But HMOs appear to be performing quality control adequately, according to Berwick, Godfrey, and Roessner (1990) and Eisenberg and Kabcenell (1988). Consumers are also concerned with the time cost and restrictions of choice associated with HMO care.

From the patient perspective, the access to specialty referrals may pose a problem. Referrals are less of a problem for consumers in large staff- or group-model HMOs, where they can simply walk down the hall to the specialist's office. However, in an IPA-model HMO, the consumer often has to travel to a different office building. A second potential problem involves consumer expectations. Some consumers unrealistically expect a plastic surgeon for every small cut and a specialist for every minor complaint. This segment of the market would be wise to avoid enrolling in HMOs. Moreover, any HMO that caters to such whims must either go out of business or find subspecialists willing to work for $10 per hour.

Rural communities are less likely to be served by HMOs, presumably because of the lack of a critical mass (volume) of potential enrollees. This generality is not valid in all rural communities; for example, some rural areas have active business coalitions that have fueled the development of HMOs with sufficient initial start-up resources and promotional campaigns. A HMO offers certain rural areas the opportunity to retain resources and patients within the community. The percentage of rural communities served by HMOs has been on the increase: an estimated 15 percent of counties with fewer than 10,000 residents had HMOs in 1990 (up from only 4 percent in 1980); 25 percent of rural counties with 10,000–49,999 residents had HMOs in 1990 (up from 11 percent in 1980). Virtually 100 percent of urban communities had one or more HMOs available by 1985.

Do sick patients have a bias against HMO enrollment and instead prefer fee-for-service care? Feldman, Finch, and Dowd (1989) studied 6 HMOs and 17 employer groups and concluded that employees with poor health habits do not prefer fee-for-service plans to HMOs. They also speculated that HMOs have not gained long-term cost advantages by enrolling employees with favorable habits (nonsmokers, people who exercise, no heavy drinkers).

One major study has been done to assess the income elasticity of HMO enrollees. Welch and Frank (1986), using a national data set, reported a −.64 income elasticity of HMO enrollment and suggested that families of modest means are a natural clientele of HMOs. They found that families with lower reported health status are less likely to enroll in HMOs. One may never ascertain from retrospective analysis whether this is the result of favorable selection (by the HMO of the healthy), weak marketing of the HMO in areas with a sicker clientele, or simply a variant of natural selection (sicker people desire to remain with their current provider and not join an HMO plan). The limits of retrospective research designs are the major reason why the Rand health insurance study (Ware et al. 1986) of HMOs is so interesting to policy makers. On the positive side, the Rand study was a randomized controlled trial; however, the HMO portion of the study involved fewer than 1,000 individuals in one HMO in one city (Seattle).

For-profit HMO firms may increasingly have to worry about more aggressive competition from tax-exempt HMOs with stringent utilization review programs. Schlesinger, Blumenthal, and Schlesinger (1986) suggested that for-profit HMOs have average costs that are 10 percent higher than those of their tax-exempt counterparts, primarily due to higher expenses for ambulatory care. In addition to better utilization review, one strategy to control ambulatory-care costs is to initiate copayments. Welch (1986) reported that the demand for HMO enrollment was a negative function of the copayment charged by the HMO for an office visit. Therefore, the copayments must be balanced and modest in amount to make enrollment in the HMO desirable for the individual or the family.

Although most HMOs charge copayments per visit in the range of $10 to $25 on the East Coast, more modest copayments can have a significant impact on utilization. Cherkin, Grothaus, and Wagner (1989) indicated that introduction of a $5 copayment per HMO office visit resulted in an 11 percent decrease in primary-care visits and a 3.3 percent decline in specialty-care visits. These copayments had much greater impact on enrollees who were high users (more than 10 visits per year) during the year before the introduction of cost-sharing expenses. Since no decline in health status has been detected, Davis et al. (1986) referred to such forgone patient visits as an example of the "worried well" avoiding unnecessary additional visits to save the copayment expense.

A BETTER TAXONOMY FOR TYPES OF HMOs

Welch, Hillman, and Pauly (1990) outlined a better taxonomy for classifying HMOs by payment incentives and organizational structure. The five payment-incentive types in the 1991 context are the following: (1) Prepaid group-practice HMOs (42 percent of HMOs) have salaried physicians seeing only HMO patients (95 percent of staff HMOs and 80 percent of group HMOs do this). (2) Salary IPAs (4.9 percent of HMOs) have clinicians on salary and sharing a HMO-wide risk pool (holdout pool in case expenses exceed revenues, with the residual going to the providers at year's end) (15 percent of group-model HMOs). (3) Capitation IPAs (19 percent of HMOs) pay a fixed fee per enrollee per clinician each quarter or year. The doctors also see non-HMO private patients (35 percent of IPAs and 50 percent of network HMOs). (4) Fee-for-service IPAs with subgroup risk pools (18 percent of HMOs) have the clinician (self) or peers as a risk-pool subgroup (holdout pool to be distributed at year's end). The doctors are paid fee-for-service and see non-HMO patients privately (30 percent of IPAs and 35 percent of network HMOs). (5) Foundation-type IPAs (16 percent of HMOs) pay all the physicians fee-for-service, and they all share one risk pool as a group (33 percent of IPAs and 2.2 percent of group-model HMOs).

The five organizational-structure categories in the 1991 context are the following: (1) Prepaid group-practice physicians (42 percent of HMOs) see only HMO patients (95 percent of staff HMOs and 80 percent of group HMOs do this). (2) Two-tiered IPAs with a single risk pool (13 percent of HMOs) have physicians contract directly with the IPA and place doctors in a single risk pool, but the doctors can privately see fee-for-service patients (one-third of IPAs). (3) Two-tiered IPAs with subgroup risk pools (20 percent of HMOs) have physicians contract with the IPA and subdivide the physicians into risk pools by location and type of doctor (specialty, referral, or primary-care). The doctors also see their own fee-for-service patients (40 percent of IPAs). (4) Three-tiered IPAs with subgroup risk pools (19 percent of HMOs) pay medical groups that in turn pay their physician membership—the groups have specialty, referral, and primary-care risk pools, and the doctors also see their own fee-for-service patients (15 percent of IPAs and 4.5 percent of staff HMOs). (5) Three-tiered IPAs with a single risk pool (8 percent of HMOs) pay medical groups that in turn pay their physician membership, and doctors also see fee-for-service patients (4.5 percent of IPAs and 13 percent of group-model HMOs).

HMO physicians are concerned with the mechanism by which holdout risk pools are distributed. The physicians have full knowledge of the fee schedule or age-adjusted capitation rate of reimbursement from the HMO plan, but the risk pool can be handled a number of ways. Each clinician may have a referral fund to ensure that he or she does his or her work and does not shunt it off to other physicians (does not overrefer). Deficits in the referral fund might be covered with a 20 percent across-the-board holdout risk pool (a withhold), which means that the referral funds with a surplus are making up the loss. Each physician has a hospital fund, and the HMO absorbs 100 percent of all losses (because the HMO doctor cannot be held to blame for this "unexpected" event), but the HMO would pay 40 to 60 percent of any hospital-fund surplus to the physicians. Even HMOs without explicit risk pools or withholds offer some incentive to hold costs down. For example, a prepaid group-practice HMO like Harvard Community Health Plan may budget physician bonus pay at 5.5 percent of salaries, but depending on cost-control effectiveness, the bonus may vary from 0 to 10.5 percent of salaries. The decision to issue bonus pay is decentralized for a large three-tiered HMO like Health Insurance Plan (HIP) of Greater New York, which contracts with 8 physician groups and 49 hospitals.

CONTROLLING PROVIDER HABITS

The ordering habits of physicians appear to differ in HMO and fee-for-service settings. Epstein, Begg and McNeil (1986) studied ambulatory ordering behavior on comparable samples of patients among internists in large fee-for-service groups versus internists in a large HMO. After adjusting for age, sex, blood pressure, severity, and duration of illness, the authors reported that 40 percent more chest radiographs and 50 percent more electrocardiograms were obtained among fee-for-service patients. The size of the group was not a confounding variable in explaining these wide differentials. The comparison was not one of "raisins versus watermelons," in that the groups were large in both the prepaid and fee-for-service sector. Epstein, Begg, and McNeil (1983) showed that the use of ambulatory tests may be twice as high in large group practices as in smaller groups. Their 1986 study suggested that the use of high-cost, high-profit ambulatory tests is 40 to 50 percent higher in large fee-for-service groups than in large HMOs. Given that much of this extra service is medically unnecessary, revising the fee schedules to downweight the profitability of such tests seems appropriate for charge-paying patients.

The style of medicine may differ in the newer, less financially solvent HMOs compared to the older, large, established HMOs. In large HMOs, where the risks are widely shared and capital investment has been largely amortized, there may be no more denial of beneficial care than under a fee-for-service payment system (Yelin et al. 1985). There is an obvious incentive for all HMOs to curtail nonbeneficial care, but there is a presumption that weak HMOs may succumb to financial incentives and shave the costs of some beneficial care. We do not have any hard evidence in this area, but Medicare is attempting to improve rates to avoid "moral hazard" (Luft 1991; Langwell and Hadley 1990; Welch 1989).

The style of medicine practiced in HMOs may reduce expenditures by 15 to 25 percent, principally through a 25 to 40 percent reduction in hospital admissions (Luft 1981), but is this style of medicine quality neutral? In other words, for certain patient groups, does the quality of care seem to be worse (or better) in HMO settings than in fee-for-service care? One study by Ware et al. (1986) suggested that for one HMO the economical style of care might erode patient health status for the sick poor over a period of years. The Puget Sound HMO, a well-established plan, was studied as part of the Rand health insurance experiment from 1975 to 1982. The initially sick (at enrollment) low-income (bottom 20 percent of the population) participants appeared to fare better in the group randomized into fee-for-service settings than in the group in HMO care. However, the sick and nonsick high-income participants (top 40 percent of the income distribution) experienced a higher health-rating index in the group randomized into HMO care than in the group in traditional care. For the high-income enrollees, there are thus two reasons for joining an HMO: cost savings and gains in health status. The observed increases over time in bed days and serious symptoms were confined to the initially sick low-income HMO enrollees. The sick poor appeared worse off at the end of the study period than both the free-care and cost-sharing-care patients who were treated by traditional fee-for-service providers.

One lesson that could be drawn from the Rand study is that HMO care places more responsibility on the patient for compliance than the more aggressive and paternalistic fee-for-service system. Fee-for-service providers may cost more, but they have strong financial interests to coerce additional follow-up care by telephone and mail. A follow-up study by Davis et al. (1986) suggested that poor people in the Puget Sound HMO were less likely to maintain continuity with the same physician than Medicaid patients in the fee-for-service sector. In addition to problems in communication or continuity of care, the poor may also have greater difficulty in arranging transport to the HMO's centralized locations. What is disturbing about these two studies is that the Puget Sound HMO has two decades of experience in treating the poor and providing outreach programs. In HMOs without such an established track record and social orientation, the initially sick poor may not fare as well as the Puget Sound enrollees.

There are a number of study limitations in the Rand data base. Ware et al. (1986) pointed out that one should not conclude that Medicaid patients are better off in fee-for-service settings than in HMO care. The Rand experiment had a supply-side effect on Seattle physicians in that the researchers paid fee-for-service providers charges that were 20 to 60 percent more generous than those of the Washington State Medicaid program. Consequently, physicians would be potentially more aggressive in following up a more profitable Rand Medicaid patient than an ordinary Medicaid patient. That initially sick poor enrollees in the Rand study would have fared better under the standard Medicaid program seems unlikely. Underlying many media reports lurks the presumption that the quality of patient outcomes is directly related to the quantity of care provided. No such link that "more is better" has ever been established.

HMO RATE SETTING

Wrightson (1990) provided an excellent survey of HMO rate-setting methods and the technical issues behind the ongoing rancorous debate between employers, providers, and HMOs over the ways to determine premiums and prices paid to providers. Fiscal risk to the HMO is higher for community rating than for Kaiser's adjusted community rating. Risk is minimized through experience rating or group-specific rating. Community rating by patient class allows individual groups to have different rates depending on the composition by age, sex, marital status, and industry. Experience rating sets premiums that reflect the cost experience of the particular group enrolled. Most HMOs reduce risk by purchasing reinsurance: insurance bought from a large third party for catastrophic expenses, for example, insuring payment of 75 percent of hospital expenses in excess of $25,000 for one patient in a year. Sometimes reinsurance is purchased on an aggregate rather than catastrophic basis, insuring total HMO costs in excess of 115 percent of annual revenue. Because HMO revenues are fixed and prospective, managing costs and managing risk exposure are high priorities for the HMO corporation (Sutton and Sorbo 1991). Physicians in the medical group also seek to limit their risk by contractual arrangements with the HMO corporation (AHA 1990). Certain HMOs do not always behave in line with Enthoven's (1980) competition theory. Feldman et al. (1990) found two IPAs using more hospital days and not concentrating patients at hospitals that offered the lowest prices.

DO HMOs SAVE MONEY?

There is disagreement whether HMOs are more cost-effective than other insurance options. The GAO (1989) and Wrightson (1990) stated that HMOs today are more cost-effective than pure 1982 indemnity plans. The problem in this comparison of apples and oranges is that pure indemnity plans no longer exist. By 1990 every private insurance plan engaged in personal benefits management: an organized effort to identify high-cost patients as early as possible, access lower-cost quality treatment options, and manage the average-cost patients more cost-effectively. Over 130 million Americans are covered by managed-care plans that perform utilization review with varying degrees of effectiveness (half of these employees are in PPOs). In the period 1988–91 managed-care indemnity plans experienced annual cost inflation of 17.9 percent, in contrast to 10.1 percent for staff-model HMOs and 14.4 percent for other HMOs. Therefore, the 4.9 million Americans in the 50 largest staff-model HMOs (like Harvard Community Health, Group Health of Puget Sound, Group Health of Minnesota, CIGNA, and FHP Inc.) are receiving a real social dividend: a less inflationary style of quality medical care. But for the 32.8 million Americans in other types of HMOs there is less circumstantial evidence to suggest that HMOs save money in comparison to the competition (other managed-care alternatives).

There is no evidence that quality of care is any different in HMOs from that of traditional fee-for-service medicine. In the Rand health insurance experiment enrollee health status was tracked for eight years for a randomized cohort of enrollees in Group Health of Puget Sound and a control group. The researchers (Sloss, Keeler, and Brook 1987) reported that the cost savings achieved by this staff-model HMO through 30 percent lower hospitalization rates were not reflected in lower levels of health status after 1976. Another staff-model HMO, Harvard Community Health, has reported high levels of quality care resulting from the Deming method of quality control (Berwick, Godfrey, and Roessner 1990).

Business leaders are beginning to report a cost savings from certain HMOs. One unpublished study by A. Foster Higgins and Company in 1991 suggested that select HMOs save employers and employees $4.1 billion annually. Business leaders should also be equally concerned with the risk that HMOs might underprovide service. HMOs have a powerful incentive to avoid overusing services, but do some underutilize services? The federal professional review organizations (PROs) monitor HMO care to ensure that Medicare beneficiaries are protected, but most of the private-sector quality-of-care studies for all age cohorts of enrollees have been performed in staff-model HMOs. More quality-of-care research must be performed on the other types of HMOs to assure the public that certain plans are not "prepaid ghettos" (a few such unethical HMOs have been sanctioned in Florida). Ethical exclusive provider organizations (EPOs) that lock in a limited set of providers are an increasingly popular hybrid product. The EPO has stricter utilization controls than a PPO but does not do as much review as a HMO (and therefore has a lower administrative expense; Madlin 1991).

PREPAID MEDICARE

Medicare HMO volume in the form of Medicare risk contracts has grown since 1979. In 1985, 119 HMO plans had enrolled 560,000 elderly beneficiaries. Langwell and Hadley (1990) reported that risk contracting resulted in higher levels of satisfaction among Medicare beneficiaries. By 1991, 95 HMOs had enrolled 1.2 million Medicare beneficiaries. Congress and the health care industry are interested in two basic risk-contracting issues: price and equity. The risk-contracting program offered a slim 1.4 percent price rise in 1991, yet 11 new HMOs joined the risk-contracting program, and 13 dropped out (thus the number of HMOs in the program declined from 97 to 95 from 1990 to 1991). The second issue is more basic: How fair is the adjusted average per capita cost (AAPCC) methodology if it explains only 1.0 percent of the variation in cost per capita? Consequently, Congress specified in the November 5, 1990, budget bill that the HCFA come up with an improved AAPCC alternative by FY 1993 that explains at least 15 percent of the variation in cost and utilization among enrollees. Ash et al. (1989) reported that incorporating prior utilization by the individual into the model, defining nine distinct diagnostic cost groups (DCGs), helped to explain 4 to 9 percent of the variance in cost and utilization per capita. These results from a prior-use model were confirmed by Porell and Turner (1990), but the policy maker should still be left with a nagging question. Granted, using prior-year utilization data improves the statistical model, but how much of this prior utilization was unnecessary care, discretionary care, or required care? An alternative payment formula yet to be developed has the potential to reduce favorable selection bias in Medicare HMOs, ensure payer equity, and reduce fiscal risk for both parties (Riley, Rebey, and Kasper 1989).

A more comprehensive alternative to DCGs is the payment amount for capitated systems (PACS) developed at Johns Hopkins University. PACS establishes a payment rate for the HMO based on two factors: the health status of the individual who actually enrolls in the HMO and the input costs faced by the HMO. Anderson et al. (1990a) tested their model on random samples of Medicare beneficiaries from Florida and Pennsylvania and concluded that while DCGs may be four times as good as AAPCC, the PACS model beats DCGs in most closely approximating costs per capita. PACS performs well because it explicitly differentiates between acute and chronic conditions and offers higher payment rates for beneficiaries who experienced multiple hospitalizations during the prior year. PACS employs a continuous model, rather than clustering individuals into nine discrete groups like DCGs. The fourth advantage of the PACS model is that its incorporation of the Medicare Part B deductible variable helps differentiate those healthy people who have little or no contact with the health care system. Neither PACS nor DCGs can accurately predict which individuals will have multiple hospitalizations in the future. Therefore, Anderson et al. (1990b) suggested a separate payment mechanism to pay for high-cost outliers.

According to the theory of consumer choice, under the assumption of perfect information, the elderly would pick the HMO that best meets their needs. Unfortunately, the elderly are a high-cost cohort of individuals operating with less than perfect information (on their providers and concerning their future health needs). However, the HMO option may be a great deal for patients with serious chronic illnesses. Medicare supplemental insurance plans are poorly coordinated, overpriced, and poorly designed (Berenson 1986). Therefore, it would be difficult for the sick elderly not to find a better deal in joining prepaid plans. However, the elderly with many preexisting conditions seem most concerned with staying with their existing sources of care and not shopping for a HMO unless their current physician is a member of a plan. Participating in Competitive Medical Plans (CMPs) or HMOs offers an ethical dilemma for the clinicians, because to do what is best for the elderly may minimize their long-run income.

If low disenrollment rates are any indication of the enrollees' acceptance of HMOs and CMPs, it is apparent that the elderly are satisfied with the services they receive. Advocates of prepaid Medicare are fond of pointing out this fact, in addition to citing an actuarial phenomenon known as ''regression to the mean'' (Shafer and Gocke 1988). If the plan experiences adverse selection (expensive cases), its cost experience tends to regress down to the mean (get lower over time). Lubitz, Beebe, and Riley (1985) reported that high-risk elderly experienced Medicare costs 4.7 times higher than the mean, but by the next year their experience had fallen to 1.8 times the mean of all beneficiaries. On the other hand, favorable selection of the low-risk elderly also results in a regression up to the mean (in the first year the low-risk group may spend 1.8 percent of the national average Medicare expenses, but within a year this figure will have risen to 55 percent). Moreover, if the HMO or CMP can only selectively market to a small fraction of its enrollees, and if their behavior tends to regress to the mean, the question of selection bias may be labeled ''much ado about nothing'' by the health plans (Wilensky and Rossiter 1986). However, if the prepaid business evolves into a highly competitive market, a difference of a few percentage points in cost behavior could mean the difference between plan growth, stagnation, or closure. Four rural plans have already announced that they will stop their Medicare contracts because the rural AAPCC rate was $110 lower than the local urban rate, and their enrollees were heavy users of the expensive urban hospitals.

The General Accounting Office (GAO 1989) is obviously concerned with offering too much of a profit in the market with a generous AAPCC formula. However, the GAO will have a difficult task determining whether the plans underpromote to the sick elderly, overpromote to the low-risk elderly, or work with their physicians to improve utilization review activities. Is any reduction in utilization the result of patient selection or provider education?

APPROPRIATE ROLE OF INCENTIVE SCHEMES

In 1990 Congress prohibited HMOs with Medicare patients from using incentive payments to encourage physicians to meet utilization targets. According to one federal study, Congress may wish to ban arrangements that closely link financial rewards with individual treatment decisions and to limit profits earned by selective referral patterns for diagnosis or treatment (GAO 1989). Salary withholds and a bonus at year's end are still popular with 80 percent of the HMO primary-care physicians paid fee-for-service, 60 percent of the doctors paid through capitation, and 20 percent of the doctors paid through a salary arrangement (Interstudy 1991). A quota system of targets may be counterproductive, but incentive compensation for better productivity is good economics and good medicine (see chapter 10).

Physicians working part-time or full-time for a HMO claim that fiscal incentives do not affect their behavior, but most HMOs use incentives. One study suggested a cause-and-effect link between various incentives and the practice of medicine. Hillman, Pauly, and Kerstein (1989) surveyed 595 HMOs and reported that group-model or for-profit HMOs and salary and capitation payment mechanisms to physicians are all significantly associated with lower rates of hospitalization. The use of salary-based physician payment was associated with 13.1 percent fewer hospital days in comparison to fee-for-service payment plans (use of capitation had half this effect). Group-model and for-profit HMOs were associated with 9.6 and 8.2 percent fewer hospital days, respectively, than staff-model HMOs. The authors recognized the basic limitation of their study: Since no adjustment was made for patient case mix, one cannot be sure that the incentives induced the various rates of hospitalization. Future research should consider HMOs that change their physician payment scheme without significant shift in the HMO membership mix and study how rates of hospitalization, surgery, outpatient procedures, and tests adjust to the new incentives. Fee-for-service payment may entice physicians to overprovide care, but does financial self-interest cause some HMO physicians to underprovide care?

TRENDS: MARKET SHAKEOUT AND MORE FOR-PROFITS

Prior to 1981 the HMO industry was wedded to nonprofit ownership status. Since the elimination of federal grants in 1982, almost half of the HMOs have converted to for-profit status. If the two large HMO chains listed in table 3.2 are well-managed HMO chains, Maxicare is an example of overreaching, out-of-control costs, and poor planning. In 1986–87 Maxicare had administrative overhead and inpatient hospital payments that were 25 to 35 percent higher than

Table 3.2
Comparison of Operating Expenses as a Percentage of Premium Revenues in Two Large National HMOs, 1991

		U.S. Health Care	United Health Care
1.	Inpatient hospital	26%	29%
2.	Physician services	38%	37%
3.	Ambulatory care	5%	6%
4.	Other medical	8%	6%
5.	SGA overhead	10%	8%
6.	Total operating expenses	87.1%	86.3%
7.	Number of plans	6	16
8.	Number of states	6	10[a]
9.	Year the company became a national firm	1983	1979
10.	Inpatient days per 1,000 enrollees	331	342
11.	Physician visits per 1,000 enrollees	3.6	3.5

[a]Has IPA management contracts for physician groups in 18 other states.

the figures in table 3.2. Maxicare proved that a HMO could grow bigger and drive a business into the ground. In 1985 Maxicare had 686,000 enrollees in 9 states and made $20 million in profit, and the central office amassed $330 million in cash for further expansion. In 1986 Maxicare had 1.96 million enrollees in 19 states, but profits fell to under $4.8 million. In 1987 Maxicare had 2.3 million enrollees in 25 states and lost $71 million. Maxicare senior management still tried to retain the dream of approaching national employers with a national HMO network in 25 of the 30 largest cities in the nation. It is not a smart strategy to take on service-delivery burdens faster than the firm has learned how to contain the cost behavior of the providers. At the end of 1987 Maxicare's net worth was negative $29.3 million, Standard and Poor's credit rating declined to B − , and the firm was placed on the Credit Watch list. In 1988 the two senior managers in Maxicare resigned, 20 months after being profiled by *Fortune* magazine as "among the 50 most fascinating business people of the year." In March 1989 Maxicare filed for protection from creditors under chapter 11 of the Federal Bankruptcy Code. The good news is that the phoenix emerged from the ashes: Maxicare concentrated on operating in 7 states, emphasized cost control for its 405,000 enrollees, and reported its first quarterly profit in five years in the fall of 1990.

There has been a paucity of research concerning what an optimal scale is for

HMOs. Gurnick (1991) did a survival analysis of HMOs in the 1980s and concluded that (1) an optimal size for communication and fiscal survival is 40,000 to 60,000 enrollees; (2) to survive, a HMO should achieve a critical mass of 25,000 enrollees in four to five years; and (3) if the HMO is too large, it should subdivide into smaller segments (Kaiser Oakland subdivides into decentralized segments of 50,000 enrollees and thus produces better communication with the medical staff). Future research should consider long-run average cost curves and a more traditional economic analysis. Survivor analysis and market-share statistics (Gurnick 1991) only provide indirect evidence. But the HMO industry will not have the necessary uniform audited financial data until the mid-1990s.

CREATIVE PARTNERSHIPS

After going through a honeymoon period of rapid growth and remarkably receptive investors, the HMO companies are mimicking the insurance companies in pursuit of the "triple-option" strategy. A provider of triple-option insurance sells a full range of HMO, PPO, and traditional insurance. The key issues are what firms will be in control and who will be the senior and junior partners. Two national HMO firms have purchased insurance concerns to broaden their product offerings to all three of the options. Smaller, weaker HMOs, PPOs, and insurance companies will be bought out by stronger players in the other sectors over the coming years. However, it may not always be easy for a firm to control an unrelated venture, such as a small insurance company. Many firms might prefer joint venturing with a number of firms rather than owning an equity share in these companies (Larkin 1990).

In addition to the business risk of involving other companies, the triple-option strategy may not always be viewed as attractive by the employer community. Currently, employers prefer the simplicity in marketing for one firm that offers all three alternatives, but in the future the quality of some of these plans may erode their popularity in the eyes of the employees and the employers. From an economic perspective, the HMOs should come to realize that these products are substitutes. Meshing the three activities not only poses an obvious business risk but also a revenue risk. For example, offering a cheaper product like PPO care may cannibalize more profitable HMO enrollment bases (Eastaugh 1986). The market may quickly winnow out the losers, and many losers in playing the triple-option strategy may be acquired or recommit back to the base business in the 1990s.

PPOs AS A JOINT VENTURE

PPO growth has been rapid in recent years (Johns 1989). A number of hospitals have had success in joint ventures on PPOs with insurance companies and medical staff (Eastaugh 1986; Sabatino 1990). In this section we shall suggest how hospitals can form joint-venture partnerships to initiate a successful PPO, attain a critical mass of patients, and sell the plan to a HMO network at some future date in the 1990s. PPOs are less capital-intensive than staff- or group-model HMOs, are more akin to traditional group-insurance products, and are highly attractive to insurance companies and hospital chains initiating comprehensive networks of insurance and delivery (Graham 1986). A comprehensive network must offer employees the triple option of HMO care, PPO care, and traditional group insurance (Kuntz 1985; Berenson 1991).

PPOs have an intuitive appeal as a mechanism for attracting fixed blocks of business. For example, starting in 1991, AT&T selected Prudential Insurance, Travelers Corp., and Empire Blue Cross/Blue Shield to manage a preferred provider network across 23 metropolitan areas for its 100,000 nonmanagement employees. Those using the network will pay a deductible of $150 and a 10 percent coinsurance rate for nonhospital medical procedures; inpatient care will be 100 percent covered. Out-of-network coverage will have a $200 deductible and a 20 percent coinsurance rate for both inpatient and outpatient care. Taking on PPO patients is analogous to taking credit card business in that you absorb the 3, 6, or 9 percent discounts in hopes of increasing the volume of new users to the hospital. Any hospital initiating or joining a PPO should carefully weigh the strategic options, risks, and benefits, or it could find itself in severe financial difficulty. Generating new sources of revenues and new users of the hospital, not merely increasing the volume of patient days labeled as PPO users, is the desideratum.

The impact of a PPO on hospital financial position is twofold: (1) The PPO generates new revenue in excess of variable costs to create a net profit from pulling in new users (PPO-generated users) of the hospital, and (2) it forgoes revenue previously paid at charges by offering discounts in the context of the PPO to faithful "old users" of the hospital (a discount giveaway to those that would have used the hospital with or without a PPO). The critical question for a given hospital is whether the net profit (new user revenue above variable cost) exceeds the giveaways in discounts to old users (including any and all expected users of the facility, even if it is the first time the individual has ever been sick). This question will be addressed in the context of three fictitious hospitals initiating a PPO as a joint venture during 1991.

To make the venture work, all three partners must benefit from the PPO. The motivation for these three hospitals starting a PPO was threefold: (1) to be proactive in attracting more patients to offset the current declines in average daily census (ADC) and thus be better able to cover fixed costs (which was especially a problem at one hospital with a high debt-service burden, Charity Hospital), (2) to be reactive in blunting the impact of an investor-owned hospital that had the "advantage in being first" by starting a PPO, and (3) to take advantage of the fact that utilization per 1,000 citizens in this poor neighborhood was 82 percent higher than the national average (987 bed days per 1,000 citizens versus the average of 542). The more partners involved in the venture of initiating a PPO, the better their chance of success in achieving a critical mass of enrollees, and the better they are able to recoup the $400,000 initial start-up costs.

The market strategy for these three hospitals can be stated in either a positive or a negative way: to maintain or slow the decline in ADC, or to prevent continued erosion of their respective market shares by the competition. Our financial analysis will involve what accountants refer to as differential cost analysis and what economists refer to as marginal cost analysis. No statement can be made concerning the financial position of the entire hospital across all payers. Our only concern will be how viable the PPO strategy is at improving the profitability contribution by charge payers and reversing the downward trend in ADC.

As a hypothetical example, one could achieve an aggregate weighted discount across all PPO hospitals (DISTOTAL = 7 percent) in one of three ways: (1) an equal discount rate for all three hospitals; (2) an egalitarian discount rate under which one allocates higher discounts (e.g., 11 percent) to those better able to absorb them and lets the partner with the worst financial health offer a lower discount (e.g., 3 percent); (3) a meritarian discount rate based on an external standard from historical experience relative to one large payer that has required a discount (e.g., utilize Blue Cross as the yardstick). We shall consider all three methods for distributing DISTOTAL across the three hospitals. In the first few months of the market survey some employers indicated that they would consider a PPO only if DISTOTAL was equivalent to Blue Cross, and a few indicated that they would be unresponsive to entry of another PPO into the market unless the discount $D(x)$ at each hospital was at a parity with Blue Cross or better (higher discount).

In this market Blue Cross currently pays at cost plus 5 percent plus community service. De facto, these cost-based Blue Cross rates are equivalent to paying 0.84 of Oceanfront Hospital's charges, 0.97 of Charity Hospital's charges, and 0.98 of Suburban Hospital's charges, on average, during 1989–90. In 1991 Blue Cross started a prospective system that is de facto equivalent to paying 0.84 of Oceanfront's charges, 0.91 of Charity's charges, and 0.93 of Suburban's charges, on average. To achieve parity with Blue Cross, the potential PPO would have to offer discounts of 16, 9, and 7 percent, respectively, across the three hospitals, or a total weighted DISTOTAL of 10.5 percent. Two of the hospitals suggested a ''second-best'' pricing strategy by offering lower discounts in 1991, the initial year of the PPO (table 3.3, scenarios 2, 3, and 4), and achieving parity with Blue Cross in the future. Immediate parity with Blue Cross is defined as scenario 5 in table 3.3.

MARKETING TO EMPLOYERS AND CONSUMER CHOICE

Having a good estimate of the necessary ''critical mass'' of PPO enrollees to make the venture viable is a critical issue for all parties concerned. Just because employers in an area exhibit a great deal of general interest in the PPO concept

Table 3.3

Sensitivity Analysis of High-Low Estimates of the Impact of Discounts on PPO Daily Census by "Old Users" and PPO-Generated "New Users," 1991

Hospital, Discount Rate (DISC)	Low Estimate		High Estimate	
	ADO, Avg. daily Old User Census	ADN, Avg. daily New User Census	ADO, Avg. daily Old User Census	ADN, Avg. Daily New User Census
I. 1) Oceanfront Hospital				
Scenario 2, 9% discount	1.2	1.0	1.4	1.3
Scenario 3, 7% discount	1.3	1.2	1.5	1.5
Scenario 4, 12.5% discount	1.4	1.7	1.6	2.2
Scenario 5, 16% discount[a]	1.6	2.9	1.8	3.6
2) Charity Hospital				
Scenario 2, 4.5% discount	1.2	1.2	1.4	1.4
Scenario 3, 7% discount	1.3	1.4	1.5	1.7
Scenario 4, 7% discount	1.4	2.1	1.6	2.5
Scenario 5, 9% discount[a]	1.5	4.0	1.7	4.8
3) Suburban Hospital				
Scenario 2, 4.5% discount	1.2	0.8	1.4	1.0
Scenario 3, 7% discount[a]	1.3	0.7	1.5	0.9
Scenario 4, 4.5% discount[a]	1.3	1.0	1.6	1.2
Scenario 5, 7% discount[a]	1.5	2.0	1.8	2.4

II. Number of Enrollees in the PPO

Given assumptions on days per 1,000:[c]

	LL	HH	LL	HH
Scenario 2, 6.6% avg. discount	9,150	7,025	10,975	8,400
Scenario 3, 7% avg. discount[b]	10,000	7,650	11,950	9,150
Scenario 4, 9% avg. discount	12,350	9,475	14,850	11,375
Scenario 5, 10.5% avg. discount	18,750	14,350	22,350	17,125

[a] Equivalent to Blue Cross effective rate of discount under the new payment plan, July 1990.

[b] All three hospitals offer the same rate of discount, 7 percent.

[c] Under assumption LL the number of inpatient days per 1,000 PPO enrollees at PPO-member hospitals is 720. Under assumption HH it is 940 (or only 5 percent below current levels). In other words, the low estimate of scenario 2 could be produced by either 9,150 enrollees being hospitalized at the rate of 720 days/1,000 per year or by 7,025 enrollees being hospitalized at the rate of 940 days/1,000 per year.

does not mean that they have the capacity to easily add the PPO option to their benefit packages. In our situation the study area lacked a great number of self-funded employers with large numbers of employees. Fortunately, a number of companies are about to become self-funded or will soon become self-funded unless their commercial insurance carriers allow special arrangements for PPO participation. A second basic issue concerns what fraction of potential hospital users from a company offering the PPO option will actually walk into PPO facilities. The answer clearly is not 100 percent even with the "carrot" of waived cost-sharing requirements if one uses the three PPO hospitals. If the condition is very urgent, one might rather pay the extra dollar costs of going to a non-PPO hospital than pay the time and travel costs of driving to the closest PPO facility (McGuirk and Porell 1984). In our analysis we assume that PPO enrollees will utilize the three hospitals either 720 days per 1,000 per year (low estimate) or 940 days per 1,000 per year (high estimate). Obviously, one could perform a sensitivity analysis to a point where PPO usage by eligible employees is so low or the reduction in total days per 1,000 is so great due to aggressive utilization review that even this low estimate is unreasonably high (Schmitz 1990).

Given the prevailing lack of aggressive utilization review in medical practice in our marketplace, the range of estimates at the bottom of table 3.3 appears reasonable. The relative attractiveness of the PPO benefit option improves as the number of hospitals in the venture increases. If we only had a one-hospital PPO at Oceanfront, time and travel costs might so outweigh expected dollar cost savings in the consumer's mind that the PPO could only attract a 12 percent share. The distribution of hospitals and self-funded employers and employees is crucial information to gain in the market survey. The range of high-low estimates in table 3.3 would have to be adjusted if, for example, by 1993 utilization review brought charge-patient usage per 1,000 poor/lower-middle-class enrollees down from 1,100 to 770 days, with a net share of 70 percent going to the PPO hospitals, resulting in a net yield to the three partners of only 539 days per 1,000 eligible employees. The low estimate of 720 days per 1,000 working poor residents for 1991, compared to the 1989–90 experience of 1,100, could be achieved either by (1) a 10 percent reduction in days through utilization review (UR) and achievement of a 73 percent share of that market (720/990) or by (2) a 20 percent reduction through UR and achievement of an 82 percent share of the market (720/880), or by (3) any other linear combination that adds up to a 34.5 percent decline in bed usage at the three hospitals. One could run a PPO without discounts as long as one could convince employers ex ante that utilization review would be sufficient as a means of cost control (Grossman 1990).

DIFFERENTIAL COST ANALYSIS

Discounts are a two-edged sword in the sense that if the rates are too low, the PPO will fail to attract enough employers to test whether the venture can achieve true savings by means of utilization review and price discounts in combination. Second, if the discounts are too high, the hospitals will lose money. The differential costs and revenues of the PPO venture can be analyzed in the following framework. The formula for costs and forgone charges given away to sure users (old faithful patrons) of the hospital who now sign up for the PPO is

$$FR(X) = P(X) \times ADO(X) \times D(X), \tag{3.1}$$

where X = the hospital, $FR(X)$ = forgone revenue from discounts for patients that would have come to X irrespective of the PPO, $P(X)$ = average charges per diem at hospital X, $D(X)$ = fraction of charges (P) discounted at X, and $ADO(X)$ = average daily old-user census at X (listed in table 3.3).

Shifts in variable cost behavior will not be a factor in our analysis because we shall assume that physicians and hospitals do not treat old customers differently in intensity of service per day merely because they have joined a PPO. With experience in the area of utilization review one could modify the assumption. Such analysis depends on the size and cost structure of the facility under study. One analysis (Bridges and Jacobs 1986) suggested that marginal cost may be as low as 0.3 to 0.39 for 14 DRGs under study. However, employers traditionally have more confidence in a provider's ability to discount charges rather than to say with certainty that utilization review will save Y amount of money. The net profit from PPO-generated new users to the hospital is given by the following formula:

$$NR(X) = [P(X) \times ADN(X) \times (1.0 - D(X))] - [ADN(X)VC(X)], \tag{3.2}$$

where $NR(X)$ = net profit from new users, $ADN(X)$ = average daily new user census at X (listed in table 3.3), and $VC(X)$ = variable cost per diem at X.

Three basic estimates will have to be made in our analysis. First, we assume that PPO users have the same intensity of case mix and severity as previous charge-paying patients. Second, a range of variable-cost estimates is provided at all three hospitals. In our sensitivity analysis variable costs per diem as a percentage of total costs range from 50 to 60 percent (37 to 41 percent variable labor costs, 7 to 10 percent variable supply costs, and 6 to 9 percent variable overhead costs). Fixed costs account for 40 to 50 percent of average costs (5 to 10 percent depreciation, 16 to 22 percent fixed overhead, and 18 to 20 percent fixed labor costs), as is consistent with previous hospital cost function studies (Eastaugh 1986; Eastaugh 1982; Atkinson and Eastaugh 1984). Reporting one-third of labor costs as fixed might appear high. Economists tend to report a higher fraction of costs as variable and think in multiyear time horizons, whereas managers tend to think short-run and have a bias toward declaring more costs as fixed. Staff reductions are getting more prevalent in this industry. However, labor costs are variable only if they are managed in that manner (Eastaugh 1985). If it is hospital policy to accept 18 to 20 percent of average costs as fixed for a specified time period (e.g., 1991) regardless of variation in patient demand, then these costs are not variable. The estimated variable costs per diem range from $287.50 to $345 at Oceanfront Hospital, $290 to 348 at Charity Hospital, and $275 to 331 at Suburban Hospital.

The third area of concern involves refining estimates of *ADO/ADN*. Our market survey indicates that this ratio is a function of PPO growth, size, and population density. In a new, smaller PPO the old users are naturally the first to sign up, but if the PPO should expand, the new users of the hospital will eventually exceed the familiar old users. Moreover, the pool of potential new users is more unlimited in the dense urban environment, whereas the less populated rural areas would tend to have a higher *ADO/ADN* ratio, ceteris paribus. In our market the estimated old/new ratio equals 145/100 for Suburban Hospital and 100/100 for the urban Charity Hospital in the case of a fledgling PPO (8,000 enrollees). However, *ADO/ADN* equals 75/100 for Suburban Hospital and a projected 35/100 for Charity Hospital in the case of a mature PPO with over 20,000 enrollees. In each market situation a finely honed conjoint measurement survey of consumer preference would be in order (Rosko et al. 1983). Moreover, as Tresnowski (1985) pointed out, the consumers are interested in value for their money; that is, their choice is not always the least expensive alternative. Although this three-hospital PPO is for comprehensive health services, PPOs can be contracted for select limited services (like mental health—Wells, Marquis, and Hosek 1991).

OPERATIONAL PROJECTIONS

Differential costing—whether revenues from the venture would be in excess of variable costs, ignoring the $400,000 of start-up costs—is presented in tables 3.4, 3.5, and 3.6. The basic question asked by the three hospital chief financial officers (CFOs) is "Can our discounts be as generous as those of Blue Cross?" The answer seems affirmative over a wide range of assumptions. In other words, one need not hedge the bet and attempt discount scenarios 2, 3, or 4. Scenario 5, offering discounts at parity with Blue Cross, will attract between 14,000 and 22,000 PPO enrollees. The good news is that to move quickly and get into the PPO business in late 1990 may preempt the competition from starting PPOs and allow the venture to gain a sufficient scale of operations. The bad news is that average daily census may increase by only 13 to 16 days, helping to halt the projected rate of decline in ADC, but not growing enough to restore the occupancy rate to previous levels or raise it much beyond 72 percent. The $133,333 investment per hospital is of little concern since the expected payback period on the investment is under five years for the worst-case scenario at the weakest hospital.

Further analysis indicates a single-hospital PPO by any of the partners would only attract 2,500 to 6,000 enrollees. Initiating the PPO as a joint venture seems in order, but the discount policy should be reviewed after the first year of operation. If one or two other PPOs in the market go bust, the discounts may be revised downward. If competition from PPOs and HMOs heats up in the area,

Table 3.4
Net Impact on Profitability per Diem in 1991 under the Four PPO Scenarios at Oceanfront Hospital

Case Situation	Case A	Case B	Case C	Case D	PPO Daily Census Given the Demand Estimate	
					Low[a]	High[a]
Variable cost estimate per PPO patient day	Low ($287.5)	Low	High ($345)	High		
Demand estimate assumptions[a]	High	Low	High	Low		
Level of discount to PPO patients (DISC[b])						
Scenario number						
2	.09	$234.03	$173.65	$159.28	$116.15	2.2	2.7
3	.07	310.50	244.38	224.25	175.38	2.5	3.0
4	.125	359.38	265.94	232.88	168.19	3.1	3.8
5	.16	538.20	419.75	331.20	253.00	4.5	5.4

[a] The high estimate of demand assumes that PPO enrollees utilize 940 patient days per 1,000 members at the PPO-member hospitals. The low estimate of demand assumes a more effective utilization review effort, where PPO enrollees utilize only 780 patient days per 1,000 members per year.

[b] Revenue per patient day received by the hospital equals, on average, (1 - DISC) x $575.

Table 3.5

Net Impact on Profitability per Diem in 1991 under the Four PPO Scenarios at Charity Hospital

Case Situation	Case A	Case B	Case C	Case D	PPO Daily Census Given the Demand Estimate	
					Low[a]	High[b]
Variable cost estimate per PPO patient day	Low ($290)	Low	High ($348)	High		
Demand estimate assumptions[a]	High	Low	High	Low		
Level of discount to PPO patients (DISC[b])						
Scenario number						
2	.045	$332.92	$285.36	$251.72	$215.76	2.4	2.8
3	.07	363.08	296.38	264.48	215.18	2.7	3.2
4	.07	558.54	466.90	413.54	345.10	3.5	4.1
5	.09	1,052.70	872.90	774.30	640.90	5.5	6.5

[a]The high estimate of demand assumes that PPO enrollees utilize 940 patient days per 1,000 members at the PPO-member hospitals. The low estimate of demand assumes a more effective utilization review effort, where PPO enrollees utilize only 780 patient days per 1,000 members per year.

[b]Revenue per patient day received by the hospital equals, on average, (1 - DISC) x $580.

Table 3.6
Net Impact on Profitability per Diem in 1991 under the Four PPO Scenarios at Suburban Hospital

Case Situation	Case A	Case B	Case C	Case D	PPO Daily Census Given the Demand Estimate	
					Low[a]	High[a]
Variable cost estimate per PPO patient day	Low ($275.5)	Low	High ($330.6)	High		
Demand estimate assumptions[a]	High	Low	High	Low		
Level of discount to PPO patients (DISC[b])						
Scenario number						
2	$215.99	$170.81	$160.89	$126.73	2.0	2.4
3	155.38	115.71	105.79	77.14	2.0	2.4
4	261.17	218.97	163.37	195.05	2.3	2.8
5	499.21	416.01	305.81	366.97	3.5	4.2

(Level of discount values: Scenario 2 = .045, Scenario 3 = .07, Scenario 4 = .045, Scenario 5 = .07)

[a]The high estimate of demand assumes that PPO enrollees utilize 940 patient days per 1,000 members at the PPO-member hospitals. The low estimate of demand assumes a more effective utilization review effort, where PPO enrollees utilize only 780 patient days per 1,000 members per year.
[b]Revenue per patient day received by the hospital equals, on average, (1 - DISC) x $551.

one may have to raise the discount rates in 1991. An iterative approach to discount selection allows the multifacility-sponsored PPO to understand its market better over time and not give away too much in *ADO* charges relative to gains through *ADN* new users. Local business groups might even help underwrite the $400,000 start-up costs. As one business coalition executive put it: ''We are a marketplace looking for a product called PPOs, not a product looking for a marketplace.''

The enthusiasm of senior managers may have caused many PPOs to form, but the enthusiasm of utilization reviewers and operating managers will make PPOs a winning or losing proposition (Egdahl and Walsh 1989; Fielding 1985). The built-in cost-management incentives, not mere discounts, are the keys to PPO success (Boland 1990). Multiple-sponsor vertically related PPOs can be successful, but only if each partner makes a considerable effort to understand the activities of the other partners. In the example presented in this chapter, the partners are horizontally linked (three short-term general hospitals) and therefore understand the business activities of their neighbors. However, they lack business expertise in the insurance and employer-relations area. In all likelihood, as Graham (1986) suggested, the hospital-based PPO will wisely sell out to a vertically related senior partner at some future date. Sales prices in this area have ranged from $250 to 400 per enrollee, and some HMOs in their golden era (1988) received twice that price. Putting a price on a PPO is like putting a price on a rural radio station: Very little is tied up in assets. What is being bought and sold is good faith and continued operating relationships. In the interest of fiduciary responsibility, we shall select the low estimate ($250) and consider whether the hospital partners should sell their successful PPO at some future date.

PPOs are relatively easy to build in the physical sense that like radio stations or insurance companies, there are few fixed assets (e.g., computer software), and there is only cash flow to broker or manage. The buyer is purchasing your good will, existing relations with the provider community, and the public. Many insurance companies, HMO chains, and hospital chains are highly interested in purchasing successful PPOs. Hospital chains have become health care companies, viewing the insurance companies as their ultimate competition (chapter 12). Chains can make money from the insurance end of the business and channel patients to their half-empty hospitals. HMOs and insurance companies are quick to respond to the challenge and have gotten into the PPO business because employers strongly favor carriers that can offer the triple option: HMO plans, PPO plans, and traditional indemnity insurance. In considering make-versus-buy decisions, and after experiencing a number of disappointing acquisitions, all three sectors (hospital chains, HMOs, and insurance companies) are anxious to buy proven PPOs.

The first two questions PPO managers should answer are the following: (1) At what point do we begin to experience a positive cumulative cash flow? (2) At what point is the net present value of the investment in a PPO positive, with capital gains factored in? These questions are answered for two rates of discount and under two basic scenarios in tables 3.7 and 3.8. In scenario 1 (table 3.7) each of the three hospitals borrows $300,000 at an 8.5 percent interest rate because no employer group is forthcoming with the funds and physicians are unwilling to invest due to disillusionment over what federal tax reform has done to their tax shelters. The PPO enrollment is expected to peak at 18,000 enrollees in the seventh year of operation (1999). The enrollment in year one is expected to be 5,000, doubling in size by 1993. Expenses grow proportionately, yielding a net profit of −$925 after year one. The cumulative cash flow will not be positive until 1996, and the net present value (after paying 22 percent capital gains tax) will not be positive until 1998. The return on investment if the PPO is sold in 2000 (after two years of peak enrollment at 18,000) will be 315 percent (discounted at 8 percent, 2,832/900). The return on investment will still be a very healthy 235 percent if discounted at 12 percent (2,118/900) in table 3.7. The return on investment declines with declines in leverage. If the PPO is 100 percent equity financed, the return on investment discounted at 8 percent is 275 percent (table 3.8, 2,471/900); and discounted at 12 percent, the return on investment is 205 percent (1,843/900). We shall utilize these same discount rates (8 and 12 percent) in analyzing buy/lease decisions in chapter 13.

PPOs represent a mixed cost-control strategy—using provider discounts and consumer cost sharing as a disincentive against usage of nonpreferred providers. We have uncovered a second hospital-side motivation for initiating a PPO, other than the obvious motivation of providing annual patient revenues for the mothership. If the PPO is successful in attracting patients, it can be sold to a larger organization at a profit. Two caveats are in order. The return on investment in developing the PPO is sufficient by health industry standards if one presumes that a buyer willing to pay $250 per enrollee can be found. Second, many fledgling PPOs may be acquired from within by the medical staff or other buyers and converted into IPA-model HMOs.

CONCLUSIONS

None of the competition health plans promises substantial immediate relief from the medical cost-inflation problem. However, with medical costs inflating at approximately 2 to 3 points above the consumer price index, advocates of competition argue that society should not rush to a judgment on behalf of a more traditional regulatory approach. Many analysts see better potential long-run effectiveness in procompetition incentive schemes than in quick-fix, short-term regulatory intervention. Many liberals still argue that regulation in the form of global (health-sector) regional budgets is the better alternative.

One of the reasons why "competition" rhetoric is currently popular is that the idea connotes so many different things to different people. However, if competition begins to make things rough for some providers, or if it fails to contain costs, a large fraction of the procompetition camp will become embittered. The competition mind-set has one political advantage: If you go bankrupt,

Table 3.7

Leveraged Scenario: Three Hospitals Borrow $300,000 (8.5% Interest) and Develop a PPO, 1993–1997, for Sale at $250 per Enrollee in 1998–2000 (All Dollar Figures in Thousands)

	1993	1994	1995	1996	1997	1998	1999	2000
Income Statement								
Enrollment	5,000	8,000	10,000	12,000	14,000	16,000	18,000	18,000
Revenues	5,960	10,108	13,267	16,716	20,477	24,572	29,025	30,447
Expenses								
Operating	6,860	9,822	12,646	15,630	18,782	22,109	25,619	26,388
Interest	76	76	76	76	76	76	76	76
Earnings before taxes[a]	-976	210	545	1,010	1,619	2,387	3,330	3,983
Net income	-976	141	365	677	1,085	1,599	2,231	2,669
Cash flow[a] cumulative	-925	-733	-317	411	1,547	3,197	5,479	8,199
Current Liabilities								
Debt	900	900	900	900	900	900	900	900
Equity	0	0	0	0	0	0	0	0
Total	900	900	900	900	900	900	900	900
Potential Sale (at $250 per PPO enrollee)								
PPO sale price	1,250	2,000	2,500	3,000	3,500	4,000	4,500	4,500
Net	-5,652	-4,710	-3,794	-2,566	-931	1,220	4,002	6,722
Capital gains (22%)	0	0	0	0	0	951	3,121	5,243
Discount rate 8 percent:								
NPV (net present value) without capital gains								
NPV	-5,233	-4,038	-3,012	-1,887	-634	769	2,335	3,632
NPV with capital gains	-5,233	-4,038	-3,012	-1,887	-634	600	1,821	2,832
Discount rate 12 percent:								
NPV (net present value) without capital gains								
NPV	-5,046	-3,755	-2,701	-1,631	-528	618	1,810	2,715
NPV with capital gains	-5,046	-3,755	-2,701	-1,631	-528	482	1,412	2,118

[a]Tax rates 33 percent. Cash flow includes interest (1 - Tax), $51,000 each year.

Table 3.8

Equity-financed Scenario: Three Hospitals Contribute Equally to Develop a PPO, 1993–1997, for Sale at $250 per Enrollee in 1998–2000 (All Dollar Figures in Thousands)

	1993	1994	1995	1996	1997	1998	1999	2000
Income Statement								
Enrollment	5,000	8,000	10,000	12,000	14,000	16,000	18,000	18,000
Revenues	5,960	10,108	13,267	16,716	20,477	24,572	29,025	30,447
Expenses								
Operating	6,860	9,822	12,646	15,630	18,782	22,109	25,619	26,388
Interest	0	0	0	0	0	0	0	0
Earnings before taxes[a]	-900	286	621	1,086	1,695	2,463	3,406	4,059
Net income	-900	192	416	728	1,136	1,650	2,282	2,720
Cash flow[a] cumulative	-900	-708	-292	435	1,571	3,221	5,503	8,223
Current Liabilities								
Debt	0	0	0	0	0	0	0	0
Equity	900	900	900	900	900	900	900	900
Total	900	900	900	900	900	900	900	900
Potential Sale (at $250 per PPO enrollee)								
PPO sale price	1,250	2,000	2,500	3,000	3,500	4,000	4,500	4,500
Net	-6,510	-5,569	-4,652	-3,425	-1,789	361	3,143	5,863
Capital gains (22%)	0	0	0	0	0	282	2,452	4,573
Discount rate 8 percent:								
NPV (net present value) without capital gains								
NPV	-6,028	-4,774	-3,693	-2,517	-1,218	228	1,834	3,168
NPV with capital gains	-6,028	-4,774	-3,693	-2,517	-1,218	178	1,431	2,471
Discount rate 12 percent:NPV (net present value) without capital gains								
NPV	-5,813	-4,439	-3,312	-2,177	-1,015	183	1,422	2,368
NPV with capital gains	-5,813	-4,439	-3,312	-2,177	-1,015	143	1,109	1,843

[a]Tax rates 33 percent.

you cannot blame it on external regulations. Bankrupt service institutions in a purely competitive environment have only two scapegoats: poor management or poor provision of service.

REFERENCES

Abou, F., Falle, V., and Matsuwaka, R. (1991). "Hospice Care Can Yield Savings to HMOs, Patients." *Healthcare Financial Management* 45:8 (August), 84–86.

Abramowitz, H. (1988). *Bernstein Report on Health Care Growth Sectors of the Future.* New York: Sanford C. Bernstein and Company, New York Stock Exchange.

Aluise, J., Konrad, T., and Buckner, B. (1989). "IPAs and Fee-for-Service Medical Groups." *Health Care Management Review* 14:1 (Winter), 55–63.

American Hospital Association. (1990). *Physicians in the Management of Risk in Managed Care Contracts.* Chicago: AHA.

Anderson, G., Steinberg, E., Powe, N., Antebi, S., Whittle, J., and Horn, S. (1990a). "Setting Payment Rates for Capitated Systems: A Comparison of Various Alternatives." *Inquiry* 27:3 (Fall), 225–233.

Anderson, G., Steinberg, E., Whittle, J., Powe, N., and Antebi, S. (1990b). "Development of Clinical and Economic Prognoses from Medicare Data Claims." *Journal of the American Medical Association* 263:7 (February 11), 967–972.

Ash, A., Porell, F., Gruenberg, L., Sawitz, E., and Beiser, A. (1989). "Adjusting Medicare Capitation Payments Using Prior Hospitalization Data." *Health Care Financing Review* 10:4 (Summer), 17–29.

Atkinson, G., and Eastaugh, S. (1984). "Guaranteed Inpatient Revenue: Friend or Foe to PPOs and Alternative Delivery." *Maryland HFMA Quarterly* 18:5 (May), 1–4.

Baloff, N., and Griffith, M. (1982). "Managing Start-up Utilization in Ambulatory Care." *Journal of Ambulatory Care Management* 5:2 (February), 1–12.

Beebe, J., Lubitz, J., and Eggers, P. (1985). "Using Prior Utilization Information to Determine Payments for Medicare Enrollees in HMOs." *Health Care Financing Review* 6:3 (Spring), 31–49.

Berenson, R. (1991). "Payment Approaches and the Cost of Care." In J. Moreno, (ed.) *Paying the Doctor.* Westport, Conn.: Auburn House, 63–74.

Berenson, R. (1986). "Capitation and Conflict of Interest." *Health Affairs* 5:1 (Spring), 141–146.

Berwick, D., Godfrey, A., and Roessner, J. (1990). *Curing Health Care: New Strategies for Quality Improvement.* San Francisco: Jossey-Bass.

Boland, P. (1990). "Joining Forces to Make Managed Health Care Work." *Healthcare Financial Management* 44:12 (December), 21–25.

Bridges, J., and Jacobs, P. (1986). "Obtaining Estimates of Marginal Cost by DRG." *Healthcare Financial Management* 40:10 (October), 40–46.

Brody, B., Wray, N., and Bame, S. (1991). "Impact of Economic Considerations on Clinical Decisionmaking: The Case of Thrombolytic Therapy." *Medical Care* 29:9 (September) 899–910.

Cherkin, D., Grothaus, L., and Wagner, E. (1989). "Effect of Office Visit Copayments on Utilization in a HMO." *Medical Care* 27:11 (November), 1036–1045.

Clancy, G., and Hillner, B. (1989). "Physicians as Gatekeepers: The Impact of Financial Incentives." *Archives of Internal Medicine* 149:4 (April), 917–920.

Cohodes, D. (1985). "HMOs: What Goes Up Must Come Down." *Inquiry* 22:4 (Winter), 33–334.

Cook, J. (1983). "Hospital Prospective Rate Setting." *Healthcare Financial Management* 37:4 (December), 67–69.

Cunningham, F., and Williamson, J. (1980). "How Does the Quality of Health Care in HMOs Compare to Other Settings?" *Group Health Journal* 1:1 (Winter), 2–23.

Custer, W. (1991). "Employer Health Care Plan Design and Its Effect on Plan Costs" *Inquiry* 28:1 (Spring), 81–86.

Davis, A., Ware, J., Brook, R., Peterson, J., and Newhouse, J. (1986). "Consumer Attitudes toward Prepaid and Fee-for-Service Medical Care: Results from a Controlled Trial." *Health Services Research* 21:2 (July), 429–452.

Department of Health and Human Services. (1985). "Medicare Program: Payment to HMOs and CMPs—HCFA Final Rules and Comment Period." *Federal Register* 50:7 (January 10), 1314–1418.

Dolinsky, A., and Caputo, R. (1991). "Assessment of Employers' Experiences with HMOs." *Health Care Management Review* 16:1 (Winter), 25–31.

Eastaugh, S. (1986). "Differential Cost Analysis: Judging a PPO's Feasibility." *Healthcare Financial Management* 40:5 (May), 44–51.

——— (1985). "Improving Hospital Productivity under PPS: Managing Cost Reductions Without Quality and Service Reductions" *Hospital and Health Services Administration* 30:4 (July/August), 97–111.

——— (1984). "Hospital Diversification and Financial Management." *Medical Care* 22:8 (August), 704–723.

——— (1982). "The Ineffectiveness of Community-based Health Planning." *Applied Economics* 14:5 (October), 475–490.

Edelston, J., Valentine, S., and Ginoza, D. (1985). "PPO Contracting: A California Experience." *Hospitals* 59:19 (October 1), 81–83.

Egdahl, R., and Walsh, D. (1989). *Health Cost Management and Medical Practice Patterns*. Cambridge, Mass.: Ballinger.

Eisenberg, J., and Kabcenell, A. (1988). "Organized Practice and the Quality of Medical Care." *Inquiry* 25:1 (Spring), 78–89.

Enthoven, A. C. (1980). *Health Plan*. Reading, Mass.: Addison-Wesley.

Epstein, A., Begg, C., and McNeil, B. (1986). "Use of Ambulatory Testing in Prepaid and Fee-for-Service Group Practices: Relation to Perceived Profitability." *New England Journal of Medicine* 314:17 (April 24), 1089–1094.

——— (1983). "The Effects of Group Size on Test Ordering for Hypertensive Patients." *New England Journal of Medicine* 309:7 (August 16), 464–468.

Feldman, R., Chan, H., Kralewski, J., Dowd, B., and Shapiro, J. (1990). "Effects of HMOs on the Creation of Competitive Markets for Hospital Services." *Journal of Health Economics* 9:2 (September), 207–220.

Feldman, R., Finch, M., and Dowd, B. (1989). "The Role of Health Practices in HMO Selection Bias." *Inquiry* 26:3 (Fall), 381–387.

Fielding, J. (1985). "A Utilization Review Program in the Making." *Business and Health* 2:7 (June), 25–28.

Fox, P., and Anderson, M. (1986). "Hybrid HMOs and PPOs." *Business and Health* 3:4 (March), 20–27.

Gabel, J., and Ermann, D. (1985). "Preferred Provider Organizations: Performance, Problems, and Promise." *Health Affairs* 4:1 (Spring), 24–40.

General Accounting Office. (1989). *Medicare: Physician Incentive Payments by Prepaid Health Plans Could Lower Quality of Care*. GAO Report HRD–89–29 (January). Washington, D.C.: U.S. Government Printing Office.

Gifford, G., Feldman, R., Dowd, B., and Finch, M. (1991). "A Simultaneous equations model of employer strategies for controlling health benefit costs" *Inquiry* 28:1 (Spring), 56–66.

Ginsburg, P., and Hackbarth, G. (1986). "Alternative Delivery Systems and Medicare." *Health Affairs* 5:1 (Spring), 6–22.

Goldberg, L., and Greenberg, W. (1979). "The Competitive Response of Blue Cross and Blue Shield to the HMOs in Northern California and Hawaii." *Medical Care* 17:10 (October), 1019–1028.

Goldfield, N., and Goldsmith, S. (1989). *Financial Management of Ambulatory Care*. Rockville, Md.: Aspen.

Graham, J. (1986). "Insurers to Launch PPOs as a Way to Contain Costs, Protect Markets." *Modern Healthcare* 16:8 (April 11), 40.

Grossman, W. (1990). "Risk Contracting." *Topics in Health Care Financing* 16:4 (Summer), 24–30.

Group Health Association of America. (1991) *HMO Industry Profile*. Washington, D.C.: GHAA, annual book.

Gurnick, D. (1991). "HMO Survival: Determination of Optimal Size." Unpublished AUPHA paper, Medical College of Virginia, Richmond.

Harrington, C., and Newcomer, R. (1991). "Social HMOs Service Use and Cost." *Health Care Financing Review* 12:3 (Spring), 37–52.

Harvard Community Health Plan. (1991). *Annual Report, Harvard Community Health Plan*. Boston:

Health Insurance Plan of Greater New York. (1991). *HIP Annual Report*. New York: HIP.

Hillman, A., Pauly, M., and Kerstein, J. (1989). "How Do Financial Incentives Affect Physicians' Clinical Decisions and the Financial Performance of HMOs?" *New England Journal of Medicine* 321:2 (July 13), 86–92.

Homer, C. (1986). "Methods of Hospital Use Control in Health Maintenance Organizations." *Health Care Management Review* 11:2 (Spring), 15–24.

Hornbrook, M., and Berki, S. (1985). "Practice Mode and Payment Method." *Medical Care* 23:5 (May), 484–511.

Hreachmack, P., and Stannard, R. (1990). "The Managed Care Environment." *Employee Assistance* 11:6 (July), 12–14.

Interstudy. (1991). *The Interstudy Edge*. Vols. 1–2. Excelsior, Minn.: Interstudy.

Johns, L. (1989). "Selective Contracting in California: An Update." *Inquiry* 26:3 (Fall), 345–352.

Johnsson, J. (1990). "Budget Forecasting Key for Surviving Price Competition." *Hospitals* 64:4 (February 20), 81.

Kirkman-Liff, B., and van de Ven, W. (1989). "Improving Efficiency in the Dutch Health Care System: Current Innovations and Future Options." *Health Policy* 13:4 (October), 35–53.

Kralewski, J., Feldman, R., Dowd, B., and Shapiro, J. (1991). "Strategies Employed by HMOs to Achieve Discounts.'' *Health Care Management Review* 16:1 (Winter), 9–15.

Kuntz, E. (1985). "Hospitals' PPOs Face Hard Times." *Modern Healthcare* 15:3 (February 1), 60.

Langwell, K., and Hadley, J. (1990). "Insights from the Medicare HMO Demonstrations." *Health Affairs* 9:1 (Spring), 74–84.

Larkin, H. (1990). "HMO Ownership Pays Off for Systems That Stick with It." *Hospital* 64:3 (February 5), 56–60.

Lee, R. (1990). "The Economics of Group Practice: A Reassessment" In R. Scheffler (ed.), *Advances in Health Economics and Health Services Research*. Greenwich, Conn.: JAI Press, 111–129.

Lichtenstein, R., Thomas, W., Adams, J., and Lepkowski, J. (1991). "Selection Bias in TEFRA At-Risk HMOs." *Medical Care* 29:4 (April), 318–331.

Lubitz, J., Beebe, J., and Riley, G. (1985). "Improving the Medicare HMO Payment Formula to Deal with Biased Selection." In R. Scheffler and L. Rossiter (eds.), *Advances in Health Economics and Health Services Research*. Greenwich: JAI Press.

Luft, H. (1991). "Translating U.S. HMO Experience to Other Health Systems." *Health Affairs* 10:3 (Fall), 172–186.

Luft, H. (1981). *Health Maintenance Organizations: Dimensions of Performance*. New York: John Wiley.

Madlin, N. (1991). "EPO, Exclusive Provider Organizations: Stricter Controls Than a PPO, Cheaper to Administer Than an HMO." *Business and Health* 9:3 (March), 48–53.

Marion. (1991). *Marion Managed Care Digest on PPOs*. Kansas City: Marion Labs Inc.

McClain, J., and Eastaugh, S. (1983). "How to Forecast to Contain Your Variable Costs: Exponential Smoothing Techniques." *Hospital Topics* 61:6 (November/December), 4–9.

McClure, W. (1978). "On Broadening the Definition of and Removing Regulatory Barriers to a Competitive Health Care System." *Journal of Health Politics, Policy, and Law* 3:3 (July), 303–327.

McCurren, J. (1991). "Capitated Primary Physicians in Medicare HMOs." *Health Care Management Review* 16:2 (Spring), 49–53.

McGuire, T. (1981). "Price and Membership in a Prepaid Group Medical Practice." *Medical Care* 19:2 (February), 172–183.

McGuirk, M., and Porell, F. (1984). "Spatial Patterns of Hospital Utilization: The Impact of Distance and Time." *Inquiry* 21:1 (Spring), 84–89.

McNerney, W. (1980). "Control of Health Care Costs in the 1980's." *New England Journal of Medicine* 303:19 (November 6), 1088–1095.

Memel, S. (1986). "PPOs Spawn Maricopa-Phobia: Legal Issues." *Healthcare Executive* 2:2 (March–April), 51.

Moore, S. (1979). "Cost Containment through Risk-Sharing by Primary-Care Physicians." *New England Journal of Medicine* 300:24 (June 14), 1359–1362.

Moran, D., and Savela, T. (1986). "HMOs, Finance, and the Hereafter." *Health Affairs* 5:1 (Spring), 51–65.

Mott, P. (1986). "Hospital Utilization by HMOs: Separating Apples from Oranges." *Medical Care* 24:5 (May), 398–406.

Nelson, L., Swearingen, G., and Sing, M. (1991). ''Medigap PPOs: Issues, Implications and Experience'' *Health Care Financing Review* 12:4 (Summer), 87–97.

Nyberg, T. (1988). ''Maxicare Selling HMOs, Reworking Finances to Return to Profitability.'' *Managed Care Outlook*, May 27, 2–3.

Palsbo, S, and Gold, M. (1991). *HMO Industry Profile*: Washington, D.C.: Group Health Association of America.

Porell, F., and Turner, W. (1990). ''Biased Selection under the Senior Health Plan Prior Use Capitation Formula.'' *Inquiry* 27:1 (Spring), 39–50.

Reisler, M. (1985). ''Business in Richmond Attacks Health Care Costs.'' *Harvard Business Review* 63:1 (January–February), 145–155.

Riley, G., Rabey, E., and Kasper, J. (1989). ''Biased Selection and Regression to the Mean in Medicare HMO Demonstrations: A Survival Analysis of Enrollees and Disenrollees.'' *Medical Care* 27:4 (April), 337–350.

Robinson, J., Luft, H., Gardner, L., and Morrison, E. (1991). ''Method for Risk-adjusting Employer contributions to competing health insurance plans.'' *Inquiry* 28:2 (Spring), 107–16.

Rosko, M., Walker, L., McKenna, W., and DeVita, M. (1983). ''Measuring Consumer Preferences for Medical Care Arrangements.'' *Journal of Medical Systems* 7:6 (June), 545–554.

Sabatino, F. (1990). ''Survey: Managed Care Led Diversification.'' *Hospitals* 64:1 (January 5), 56–59.

Schlesinger, M., Blumenthal, D., and Schlesinger, E. (1986). ''Profits under Pressure: The Economic Performance of Investor-owned and Nonprofit HMOs.'' *Medical Care* 24:7 (July), 615–627.

Schmitz, V. (1990). ''Better Forecasting Ensures Profitability, Quality Care.'' *Healthcare Financial Management* 44:1 (January), 60–66.

Seaman, L. (1990). ''Preparation: The Key to Nursing Case Management.'' *Journal of Post-anesthesia Nursing* 5:3 (June), 177–181.

Shafer, E., and Gocke, M. (1988). *Going Prepaid*. Denver: Center for Research in Ambulatory Care.

Shouldice, R. (1987). ''Controlling HMO Operations.'' *Medical Group Management* 14:4 (July/August), 8–10.

Sloss, E., Keeler, E., and Brook, R. (1987). ''Effect of a Health Maintenance Organization on Physiologic Health: Results from a Randomized Trial.'' *Annals of Internal Medicine* 106:1 (January), 130–138.

Sorensen, A., Saward, E., and Wersinger, R. (1980). ''The Demise of an IPA: A Case Study of Health Watch.'' *Inquiry* 17:3 (Fall), 244–253.

Stein, J. (1986). ''How HMOs Adapt: A Perspective from the Inside.'' *Business and Health* 3:10 (October), 44–46.

Survey of Current Business. (1991). Monthly Report of the U.S. Department of Commerce 71:8, Bureau of Economic Analysis, Washington, D.C.

Sutton, H., and Sorbo, A. (1991). *Actuarial Issues in the Fee-for-Service/Prepaid Medical Group*. Denver: Medical Group Management Association.

Temkin, H., and Winchell, M. (1991). ''Medicaid Beneficiaries under Managed Care: Provider Choice and Satisfaction.'' *Health Services Research* 26:4 (October), 467–481.

Traska, M. (1986). ''HMOs: A Shake-up and Shake-out on the Horizon?'' *Hospitals* 60:3 (February 5), 42.

Trauner, J. (1986). "The Second Generation of Selective Contracting: Another Look at PPOs." *Journal of Ambulatory Care Management* 9:5 (May), 13–21.

Tresnowski, B. (1985). "PPOs: The Choice Isn't Always for the Least Expensive." *Inquiry* 22:4 (Winter), 331–332.

Vignola, M. (1986). "Health Maintenance Organizations: Performance in a Crowded Market." Report T–05 (February 28) of L. F. Rothschild, Unterberg, Towbin, New York.

Ware, J., et al. (1986). "Comparison of Health Outcomes at a HMO with Those of Fee-for-Service Care." *Lancet* 8488 (May 3), 1017–1022.

Welch, W. (1991). "Defining Geographic Areas to adjust payments to physicians, hospitals and HMOs" *Inquiry* 28:2 (Spring), 151–60.

———. (1989). "Improving Medicare Payments to HMOs: Urban Core versus Suburban Ring." *Inquiry* 26:1 (Spring), 62–70.

———. (1986). "The Elasticity of Demand for HMOs." *Journal of Human Resources* 21:2 (Spring), 252–266.

Welch, W., and Frank, R. (1986). "The Predictors of HMO Enrollee Populations: Results from a National Sample." *Inquiry* 23:1 (Spring), 16–22.

Welch, W., Hillman, A., and Pauly, M. (1990). "Toward New Typologies for HMOs." *Milbank Quarterly* 68:2 (Summer), 221–243.

Wells, K. Marquis, M., and Hosek, S. (1991). "Mental Health and Selection of PPOs: Experience in Three Employee Groups." *Medical Care* 29:9 (September), 911–924.

Wilensky, G., and Rossiter, L. (1986). "Patient Self-selection in HMOs." *Health Affairs* 5:1 (Spring), 66–80.

Williams, B., Mackay, S., and Torner, J. (1991). "Home Health Care: Comparison of Patients and Services among Three Types of Agencies." *Medical Care* 29:6 (June), 583–587.

Wrightson, C. (1990). *HMO Rate Setting and Financial Strategy*. Ann Arbor, Mich.: Health Administration Press.

Yelin, E., Hencke, C., Kramer, J., Nevitt, M., Shearn, M., and Epstein, W. (1985). "A Comparison of the Treatment of Rheumatoid Arthritis in HMOs and Fee-for-Service Practices." *New England Journal of Medicine* 312:15 (April 11), 962–967.

Zwanziger, J., and Auerbach, R. (1991). "Evaluating PPO Performance Using Prior Expenditure Data." *Medical Care* 29:2 (February), 142–151.

Chapter 4

Long-Term Care: Issues and Options

Those who care for the old partake of divinity, since to preserve and renew is almost as noble as to create.

—Voltaire

Palliative chronic care is as noble and necessary an undertaking as curative "make-a-save" heroic medicine for television. The "Cinderella services" as the British define them, may not get the budget or respect of high technology medicine at my Massachusetts General Hospital, but they are just as important for society.

—John Knowles, M.D.

The nursing home industry is the largest long-term-care market sector, spending almost $56 billion in 1991 (HCFA 1991). This chapter will outline some of the financial possibilities for the long-term-care sector. Because the nursing home sector has been extensively covered elsewhere, we shall place emphasis on six other, higher-growth segments of this industry: life-care facilities (LCFs), continuing health care communities (CHCCs), congregate housing, home health care, hospice facilities, and social HMOs (SHMOs).

The elderly are a growing segment of the population (Infante 1991). If elderly is defined as aged 65 and over, there were 20 million elderly in 1966; there will be 36 million by the end of 1992 and 60 million by the start of 2010. According to DHHS Secretary Louis Sullivan, if FY 1991 federal entitlement programs remain unchanged, with no new federal commitments, 67 percent of the entire federal budget will be devoted to the elderly. The Medicare trust fund will be solvent through the year 2008 and $639 billion in the red by 2010. Consequently, while there is definitely an expanding supply of elderly citizens, who will finance their care is a moot point. One obvious answer is that private funds will finance care for the elderly as $2,200 billion of pension funds are paid over the coming four decades (Laventhol and Horwath 1990). However, federal and state governments still represent the principal financing source for many of the elderly. In this chapter we shall survey the prospects for long-term-care insurance, which represents one sensible financial hedge that nonelderly workers could purchase against the possibility that sufficient public commitments to expand benefit programs will not be forthcoming.

Later in this chapter we shall survey the slow-growing market for long-term-care insurance coverage. McCall, Knickman, and Bauer (1991) have outlined a number of ways in which the Robert Wood Johnson Foundation is trying to promote long-term-care insurance for the elderly in eight states. In Oregon and California the minimum amount of insurance required in the program is two years or at least a $50,000 lifetime maximum benefit. Oregon is initiating state tax credits on the long-term-care premiums paid. New York State has expanded the minimum amount of insurance required to three years. Massachusetts has expanded its program to include 2,500 working-age citizens and 7,500 people aged 65 to 69. The Massachusetts program sets the minimum amount of insurance required to the amount purchased with a maximum of 5.0 percent of income (including annuitization of nonhousing assets). Five states offer a more liberal pilot program whereby policyholders are eligible for Medicaid after their private insurance is exhausted (Connecticut, California, Indiana, New Jersey, and Wisconsin). Massachusetts and New York do not link asset protection to the actual amount of private benefits paid out (Somers and Merrill 1991).

NURSING HOMES

Nursing home expenses were 44 percent financed by Medicaid in 1991, but state Medicaid payments represent a greater percentage of revenues for most nursing home chains. Beverly Enterprises, the nation's largest nursing home chain with 94,000 beds, receives 60 percent of patient revenues from Medicaid. Hillhaven Corporation of Tacoma, Washington, the second-largest nursing home chain with 45,000 beds, receives 56 percent of its revenues from Medicaid. While many nursing home chains complain about the low rate of payment from local Medicaid programs, Medicaid has financed the rapid growth in for-profit nursing home chains (McKay 1991).

The nursing home business divides into six basic market segments: 345,000 beds are in for-profit nursing home chains (Beverly, Hillhaven, Manor Care of Silver Spring, Maryland, and others), 47,000 beds are owned and operated by for-profit multihospital systems, 250,000 beds are operated by freestanding for-profit facilities, 32,000 beds are operated by nonprofit nursing home chains (Good Samaritan of Sioux Falls, South Dakota, owns 162 homes and contract-manages 13 facilities in 25 states), and 52,900 beds are operated by tax-exempt multihospital systems (23,000 Catholic beds, 11,000 other religious beds, 17,000 secular beds, and 1,900 public nursing home beds). Finally, 104,000 beds are in freestanding tax-exempt facilities. These totals represent 831,000 nursing home beds eligible to receive Medicaid and Medicare patients, but do not include the estimated 470,000 beds without accreditation to take federally funded patients (subacute care), hospice and rehabilitation beds, and beds controlled by LCFs, for a total long-term-care bed supply of 1.6 million beds (54 beds per 1,000 aged).

Nursing home spending increased from $39.7 billion in 1987 to an estimated $62 billion in 1992. Growth in nursing home spending from 1987 to 1991 was 41 percent attributable to general price inflation, 21 percent attributable to the aging of the population, and 38 percent attributable to changes in the amounts and mix of nursing home services and intensity. Despite the fact that the number of Americans purchasing long-term-care insurance has grown rapidly, from 1.1 million in mid-1989 to 2.7 million in 1991, private insurance only pays for 1.4 percent of nursing home expenditures. Nursing home expenditures are financed 44 percent by Medicaid, 1.8 percent by Medicare, 49.8 percent by out-of-pocket spending, and 2.9 percent from other sources (religious or public).

Patient volume in the nursing home industry doubled in the period 1974–1986, even as the number of operating nursing homes has declined 6 percent. A number of nursing homes (2,900) closed in the late 1970s following the scandals concerning the maltreatment of helpless elderly patients (Vladeck 1980). In 1991 the nation had 16,600 nursing homes; 77 percent were for-profit and served 1.4 million residents. This volume dwarfed the $3 billion in annual expenditures for life care. However, nursing homes have had trouble attracting good managers. The low esteem with which nursing homes are held by many health workers is largely a function of the frequent stories of inappropriate utilization and abuse (Johnson and Grant 1985; Smith 1990).

The nursing home industry has been pressured to serve more acutely ill post-hospital-discharge patients because of recent changes in Medicare hospital payment policies. A number of analysts have argued that DRG payments under PPS systematically undercompensate hospitals for treating the frail elderly (Berenson and Pawlson 1984). Hospitals have discharged the elderly at higher levels of need for care (severity) since 1984. Nursing homes were not prepared for the onslaught of early-discharge patients, but PPS has also produced some benefits. On the positive side, a Rip Van Winkle, ready to doze for nine years in 1982, could not wish for a better incentive system than DRGs to stimulate capital investment by hospitals in long-term care (Teschke 1991). Hospitals were not about to invest significantly in long-term care and purchase nursing homes and other facilities (e.g., home health centers) until it was in their best interest financially. According to the 1991 AHA annual survey, hospital-sponsored nursing facilities and home care programs have increased fivefold in number, and health promotion and hospice programs have tripled since 1983. Adult day care is another increasingly popular service (Hedrick, Rothman, and Chapko 1991).

The popular notion that nursing homes are used exclusively by terminal patients ignores the fact that 28.3 percent of cases are discharged to community settings (Weissert and Scanlon 1985). Good-quality nursing care can result in higher rates of discharge back to the community. The Institute of Medicine (1986) study report *Improving the Quality of Care in Nursing Homes,* concluded that government and the industry have failed to maintain adequate quality standards. Quality-assurance activities in skilled nursing facilities (SNFs) and intermediate-care facilities (ICFs) are almost nonexistent in most cases. The report did note that the scandals of the mid-1970s are not common now, but significant room for improvement still exists. The principal recommendation of the two-year study involved elimination of the regulatory distinction between SNFs and ICFs which was done in FY 1991.

Productivity and Payment Rates to Nursing Homes

Nursing home capital needs for the period 1992–2010 can be conservatively estimated at $210 to $230 billion for new beds, $70 billion for working capital, and $120 billion for replacement beds for the 33 percent of existing beds that were built prior to 1969. The facility has some endogenous control over profitability and productivity and can retain earnings to build new beds, but payment rates are exogenous and outside the control of the nursing home manager. Before we survey trends in reimbursement levels for capital expenses, we will summarize a review of productivity levels in the industry.

Any assessment of productivity, the ratio of output to unit of input, must be adjusted for case mix. The standard way to adjust for case mix in the nursing home industry involves measurement of activities of daily living (ADLs). The ADLs offer a time-tested measure of a nursing home resident's functional ability for eating, bathing, toileting, mobility, transferring from bed to chair, personal hygiene (continence), and dressing (Liu, McBride, and Coughlin 1990; Rowland et al. 1989). In the September 1990 federal HCFA census of 1.373 million nursing home residents, case mix was measured as ADLs applicable 60 percent of the time for the previous two weeks. Obviously, a nursing home workload with a higher ADL dependency score (sicker patients) would require a higher level of nursing home staffing. The case-mix-adjusted ADL levels for the 10 states with the highest levels of nursing home productivity are given in table 4.1. Such normative comparisons are important in two basic ways: (1) They tend to provide a yardstick for improvement of substandard homes, and (2) they demonstrate a correlation between high level of quality (fewer bedsores) and better (lower) levels of staffing. In addition to enhancing productivity and raising quality in the period 1980–90, many of these nursing homes also cut labor costs by increasing inflation-adjusted nurse-staff wages for productive nurses 10 to 15 percent to reduce the reliance on more costly nurse registries (costing two to three times as much per hour). As chapter 10 of this book indicates, productivity, cost reduction, and quality enhancement are correlated. States not listed in table 4.1 often have a HCFA-cited deficiency in infection control; for example, this is the case in 44 percent of the homes in Ohio and Arizona.

While not available on a national basis yet, an alternative case-mix measure is being utilized in payment programs in five states. This alternative measure of

Table 4.1
Staffing Ratio, Quality, and Nursing Home Beds per 1,000 Aged Population

State, Rank Ordered by Variable 1	1. Staff Ratio Nurse and Aide Hours per Diem Adjusted for Case-Mix ADL	2. Low Quality: Percentage Patients with Bedsores	3. Beds per 1,000 Aged
1. Texas	2.0	6.6	66.7
2. Oklahoma	2.2	5.6	82.6
3. Lousiana	2.2	4.9	79.1
4. Arkansas	2.25	5.7	71.2
5. Tennessee	2.35	5.7	55.5
6. Kentucky	2.4	6.8	49.2
7. South Dakota	2.4	4.1	79.8
8. Colorado	2.5	6.9	57.7
9. North Carolina	2.5	6.9	39.2
10. Virginia	2.5	7.0	44.4
National Average	2.9	6.8	53.7

case mix for long-term care, resource utilization groups (RUGs), involves 18 to 24 groups (clusters) of patient categories (Fries 1990). This analog to the acute-care DRGs has been used successfully in New York, Texas, and Massachusetts. The RUG system will have to go through a fourth version to sufficiently recognize heavy-care residents and their particular needs (Manton, Vertrees, and Woodbury 1990). The heavy-care patient is becoming more prevalent as the hospital payment system encourages earlier discharge of elderly patients (Shaughnessy and Kramer 1990; Fries and Cooney 1985).

A number of studies have been done of nursing home productivity. The study by Sexton et al. (1989) involved a small sample (52 nursing homes) and a lack of case-mix and quality variables. Since quality and case mix are output measures of a firm, any study of the output-to-input ratio (productivity) should measure these attributes. We know that quality is important to the consumers (Cryns et al. 1989) and to the government (Spector and Drugovich 1989). Since the passage of Pub. L. 100–203 for FY 1988, the regulators have increasingly tried to focus less on the potential of each facility to deliver care (checklists) and more on the outcome quality of care delivered (e.g., bed sores). (Starting in FY 1991 the distinction between SNFs [skilled nursing facilities] and ICFs [intermediate care facilities] was eliminated, and a single common term, nursing facility, was used; but the published literature uses the old terms.)

The best productivity study incorporating quality and case-mix measures involves an analysis of 296 homes (Nyman, Bricker, and Link 1990). The authors concluded that higher levels of productivity are found in for-profit homes and larger homes. They provided no evidence to suggest that Medicaid should raise the payment rates to cover the costs of hiring extra staff to create marginal improvements in patient quality of life and concluded that "the relationship between reimbursements and quality is complex and may be counterintuitive under excess demand conditions" (Nyman, Bricker, and Link 1990, 550). To borrow a theme from chapters 9 and 10: More is not better; better is better.

The basic issues underlying any nursing home rate program involve setting sufficient levels of payment to assure adequate quality of care, an adequate return on investment to owners, and, consequently, an adequate supply of beds for the aged population. Within a homogeneous cluster of patients any variation in profitability to the home under a fair payment system should be the result of efficient management and not the result of differences in patient characteristics between nursing homes. Setting fair rates is no easy task. A number of states have recognized the importance of case mix in designing a more appropriate higher level of payment for the severely ill patient groups. The preferred approach for the 1990s might be to adjust rates directly in proportion to the quality of care and resulting quality of life, for the residents. One intrinsic problem with the RUG system is that it relies on subjective staff estimates of patients' requirements for nursing care (Cameron 1985). Asking the worker to rate the workload utilizing a five-point scale can become a self-serving activity; that is, one works less hard on the unit if the patients are rated more acutely in need of nursing care.

To enhance nursing home quality through reform in the payment system, Nyman (1989) suggested that homes be paid a fixed percentage of the price they charge private patients and that this percentage be allowed to increase with the percentage of private patients in the home. Empirical results by Nyman (1989) suggested that quality is higher, and both average costs and the private price are lower, in homes with a larger percentage of private patients. If there are fewer private patients, more cost-shifting must occur onto them to compensate for low Medicaid payment rates. If the nursing home can attract a substantial proportion of private-pay patients, it need not overcharge each patient so much. One strategy that a few dozen homes have used to attract private patients and to sensitize the medical profession to special needs of the elderly is the teaching nursing home. However, the private nursing home buyer is a price-sensitive buyer. Therefore, the teaching nursing home may attract the elderly and their families on a quality basis, but remain financially unattractive if the price is too high. Teaching nursing homes must strive to keep their cost behavior in line with a price structure that a sufficient number of private patients can afford.

Payment to Nursing Homes: How Much for Capital?

In 44 states nursing home Medicaid payments are set on a prospective basis or some hybrid combination of prospective and retrospective systems. Considerable variation exists across states as to how to treat capital costs, ranging from a single payment to a three-way payment for interest, depreciation, and a return on equity for the investors. Industry representatives argue that nursing homes should have the opportunity to earn a return on Medicaid patients equal to the return earned on private-pay patients. Rate regulators counterargue that the charges paid by private-pay patients are excessive. A few Medicaid programs have progressively offered incentive "carrots" for efficiency. For example, in Maryland the difference between the Medicaid payment ceilings and the actual cost per diem is shared by the state and the facility 60/40; the home retains 40 percent of the differential. The Medicare hospital payment system under PPS is much more generous, allowing the hospital to keep 100 percent of the cost savings below the price line. Maryland officials should not be surprised that nursing home cost behavior clusters near the maximum ceilings for payment, given that a 40 percent "carrot" is not a sufficient stimulus to promote productivity and cost reductions among most home operators.

The effect of insufficient return-on-equity payment rates on nursing homes has long been controversial. Rate regulators argue that nursing homes are sufficiently profitable. Economists argue that nursing homes have the worst profitability and cash flow among 167 business sectors (Buchanan 1982). Regulators make a mistake when they comingle issues of operating profitability with return on equity invested in the nursing home business. A few states have faced up to the obvious problems with historic cost-accounting treatment for capital payments. The so-called "fair-rental" capital payment systems in West Virginia and Maryland explicitly recognize (1) the increasing value of nursing home assets over time, (2) that accounting values do not rise with inflation and thus erode (undervalue) assets over time, and (3) that no incentives should exist for property manipulation and resale merely to extract, in a "backdoor" fashion, a return on equity out of the payers. Under fair-rental systems, a simulated rent is paid based on the current value of assets, irrespective of the sales history or financing methods.

A cost-based or flat-rate-of-return payment system encourages frequent sales of nursing homes to revalue assets following sales at inflated prices and restart the depreciation "game." Depreciation payments improve as a result of each sale, and many homes have changed owners every few years. The industry has referred to this game as "trafficking," with many nursing home chains buying each other's homes in addition to investing in freestanding independent homes. However, the adoption of fair-rental payment systems encourages ownership for longer periods of time and, more importantly, stronger incentives to invest in the quality of the physical plant and the services within the institution. Without fair-rental capital payments, there is no incentive to invest in quality and upgrade the facility's reputation if the owners have to sell the facility every two to three years. According to Cohen and Holahan (1986), neither the West Virginia gross-rental approach or the Maryland net-rental approach need to increase aggregate payment levels to the industry over the life cycle of the assets, and both systems can provide acceptable (market) rates of return on equity. Fair-rental capital payments create incentives for owners to seek the most efficient financing arrangements because they reap the cost savings (and need not manipulate property ownership for maximization of reimbursement). Payers must not "rob" the homes by setting the rental rates too low, thus paying a return on equity that is below that of comparable investments elsewhere in the economy. If the payment rates are too low, capital will flee the nursing home industry.

A number of studies have suggested that operating risk is rising in the nursing home industry (Buchanan and Eastaugh 1991). We will test this hypothesis using Altman's (1983) discriminant Z'' model. The multivariate analysis can be retrospective (what financial ratios predict bankruptcy based on the past), diagnostic (what areas can be improved to avoid fiscal distress), or predictive (what the probability of distress or failure in the future is). The secondary research question is whether risk is different in different state rate-regulatory environments. Nursing homes with more than 100 beds were surveyed in a random sample of 20 states. Over 39 percent of the sample provided financial statements for the years 1982–90. The sample broke down into three basic regulatory climates for Medicaid payment of capital-related costs.

1. In tight rate-setting states, payment is based on historic cost or the cost of constructing the facility, which is the least costly basis for Medicaid payment. Change of ownership does not increase the home's value. The sample included 174 nursing homes in Washington, D.C., and 12 states: California, Connecticut, Florida, Iowa, Kansas, Kentucky, Louisiana, Pennsylvania, South Dakota, Utah, Vermont, and Washington.

2. In fair-rental systems, payment is based on an imputed rent for residential-related services to sufficiently pay the current value of the capital assets used in providing care, yet is not so generous as to reward frequent resale (trafficking) in nursing homes to create successively higher valuation of the home. Facility valuation is based on assessed value, inflating historic costs. The sample included 93 homes in 6 states: Colorado, Illinois, Maryland, Oklahoma, Oregon, and West Virginia.

3. Generous-payment systems establish the basis of payment on the market value of the facility, thus rewarding frequent resale (trafficking in nursing homes) at higher prices to create successively higher valuation of the home. Three homes in this group had four owners in the eight-year study period 1982–90. The sample included 17 homes in Alabama and Wyoming.

Background on Models Assessing Distress or Closure

The multiple-discriminant model (MDM) attempts to measure the importance (weights, coefficients) in detecting financial distress, establish a best-estimate equation (reduced form), and assess how the weights can be objectively validated. MDM is used to classify and make predictions where the dependent variable is yes/no (bankrupt/open) or good/questionable/bad (open/distressed/terminated). In this nursing home study MDM attempts to derive a linear combination of characteristics that best discriminates between the categories (Altman 1983). If the Z'' score is greater than 2.6, the nursing home is financially strong; if the Z'' score is less than or equal to 1.1, the nursing home is very distressed (it may be closing or already be closed); and if the Z'' score is between these two limits (1.1 and 2.6), the analyst is in a zone of ignorance.

In summary, MDM provides a single measure of the propensity of a nursing home to enter into severe financial distress within an eight-year time horizon. The reduced-form equation of unique independent variables is offered under the principle of Occam's razor: The simple model with optimal predictive accuracy should be preferred to a more complex model that includes multiple unnecessary ratios. The estimated reduced-form equation includes only four significant unique ratios:

$$Z'' = 4.41\,X_1 + 5.36\,X_2 + 5.09\,X_3 + 1.41\,X_4,$$

where X_1 = retained earnings/total assets, X_2 = working capital/total assets, X_3 = earnings before interest and taxes/total assets, and X_4 = book value of equity/ book value of total liabilities. A 39 percent sample of the nursing homes in the 20 states may not be great for population inferences, but the findings are suggestive. Bankruptcy rates and Z'' scores are presented over time in table 4.2 for each of the regulatory payment environments. The Z'' model for bankruptcy prediction had a successful classification probability of 94 percent one year prior to failure, 85 percent two years prior to failure, and an impressive 68 percent six years prior to failure. Two years prior to bankruptcy the 32 failures had a median Z'' score of 1.39, compared to median Z'' scores of 4.46 for going concerns (still nonbankrupt in December 1990). Other model specifications and functional forms, including a Zeta model and a quadratic (rather than linear) equation did not improve the results (Altman 1974; Zmijewski 1984).

The results in table 4.2 suggest a steady erosion in Z'' over time. The results for the 12 tight rate-setting states are particularly troubling since the 1990 Z'' score is only slightly above the 2.6 threshold level for financial strength. This trend bears watching because state governments, financing 48 percent of the nursing home care in the nation, may soon get more stringent. The macroeconomic incentives are clear to any state governor: Medicaid may only represent 17 percent of the average state budget, but it represents 60 percent of every incremental new dollar in the state budget. Medicaid is crowding out other social programs like education, so state budget directors are planning to reduce payment levels. The etiology of this fiscal problem is demographic: Medicaid is paying more nursing home care for the expanding number of medically indigent elderly.

The tight-payment states can be expected to get tougher, and the generous-payment states are currently studying the implementation of a fair-rental system

Table 4.2
Average Z″ Index, Probability of Distress in the Future, and Fraction Bankrupt
(N = 286 Nursing Homes in 1982, N = 254 Homes Still Open in 1990)

	Year	Z^a Mean	Probability of Distress	Cumulative Fraction Closed
Tight rate-setting states	1982	4.26	22.3%	0
	1984	4.03	22.9%	.04
	1986	3.95	23.4%	.06
	1988	3.62	29.5%	.09
	1990	2.89	40.4%	.14
Fair-rental-system states	1982	5.37	13.1%	0
	1984	5.28	13.8%	.03
	1986	5.02	14.4%	.04
	1988	4.90	13.9%	.04
	1990	4.15	19.8%	.075
Generous-payment states	1982	6.84	4.8%	0
	1984	6.97	4.6%	0
	1986	6.87	4.8%	0
	1988	6.21	8.9%	0
	1990	5.52	13.4%	.05

for capital payment. Future research may have to subdivide the fair-rental states into two categories as more states copy the Minnesota example (not included in this sample) by (1) capping the return on equity rates at a low level (5.66 percent) and (2) placing limits on overall debt. No state is currently considering making payment rates more generous (Buchanan, Madel, and Persons 1991). Some states (e.g., Michigan) are considering linking payment rates to process measures of the quality of care.

One potential problem with Z″ models is that they might be subject to type-two statistical errors, misclassifying certain firms as soon to be bankrupt. If a financial analyst claims that the nursing home deserves a going-concern exception, and suppliers of credit withhold funds based on a low Z″ score or other grading system, then the firm's demise may actually be partially caused by the receipt of a low score (poor grades create a self-fulfilling prophecy).

Prescriptive Action: Seeking a Turnaround

MDM analysis can be used as an early warning system to detect problems in advance and prescribe rehabilitative action. Just because the Z'' for nursing homes in a region indicates that widespread distress has not permeated the nursing home business does not mean that a facility is in great shape. One nursing home studied had a Z'' score of 1.9, resulting primarily from a recent productivity bleed (erosion) that in turn eroded retained earnings. Nursing productivity and task delegation are important acute problems in institutional management (chapter 9), and these results offered a wake-up call to the CEO with the low Z'' score. Z'' scores should not be seen as a steady prediction of doom, but rather as a management tool to recovery (Cleverley 1990). To paraphrase Alfred Sloan's dictum: Decay is not your predetermined destiny. Poor labor productivity and other underutilized assets are often the major causes of the deterioration of a nursing home's financial ratios. Altman (1983) was probably unfamiliar with the highly regulated nature of the health care industry when he stated that "in almost all cases the fundamental business failure problems lie within the firm itself." In a regulated industry like the nursing home sector, there can be payment levels so low that the firm cannot internalize control of its Z'' score (cannot make a turnaround). For this reason, having 32 nursing homes among a sample of 286 go bankrupt from 1982 to 1990 is a source of concern for public policy makers, especially as pressures to control health care costs rise.

Supply of Nursing Home Beds

Does the nation need a markedly higher supply of nursing home beds per 1,000 aged Americans? It may be true that certain states have an insufficient supply of nursing home beds, but we do not wish to treat health care problems of an aging population mainly by institutionalization. For example, it is better economics and leads to a better quality of life to channel patients into low-cost sites of service distribution (e.g., low-tech and high-tech home health care). High-tech home health care workers distribute drugs and intravenous (IV) treatments without "chaining" the patient to a nursing home bed. In 1992 the cost of home health care is predicted to exceed $7.1 billion (financed 45 percent from Medicare and 35 percent from Medicaid). More growth in care modalities will be needed to keep pace with the aging of the population. From 1971 to 1991 the nursing home bed supply increased at an annual rate of 2.26 percent, reaching an estimated 1.74 million nursing home beds by 1995. Bed supply has not kept pace with the aging of the population. Since 1971 the prime nursing home population cohort, the elderly 85 years of age or over, has increased in number by 4.22 percent annually, resulting in a 1.93 percent per year average decline in nursing home beds per 1,000 elderly aged. A number of states with less than three-fourths the national average of beds per 1,000 elderly aged are considering major expansion programs in nursing home construction (including Florida, Alabama, South Carolina, West Virginia, and New Jersey).

The American Association of Homes for the Aging (AAHA) predicts that by the year 2010 the nation will need 1.65 million additional nursing home beds to achieve the target ratio of 55 beds per 1,000 aged. Also by the year 2010 the nation will need 150,000 LCF beds, 200,000 other continuing-care retirement center (CCRC) beds, and 750,000 congregate housing beds to achieve a target ratio of 65 alternative-living-arrangement beds per 1,000 aged in 2010. There will probably be a disequilibrium between these estimates of ''need'' and bed supply created because of insufficient reimbursement rates, local health planners' restrictions on new building, poor financial planning, and insufficient external financing (debt and equity). However, a sufficient expansion of long-term-care beds would help reduce the discharge delays at hospitals located in areas with few such beds and in states with tight prospective Medicaid nursing home payment rates (Kenney and Holahan 1990; Nyman 1989). Technology may reduce the need for chronic services for certain demographic segments, such as those with Alzheimer's disease. Evans (1990) estimated that without any technological breakthrough the number of elderly Americans with ''probable Alzheimer's disease'' will increase from 3.8 million to 10.3 million in the year 2050.

HOME HEALTH CARE

That the home health care sector is a creature of public policy is undeniable. In some nations home health care is centuries old (China), whereas in other nations the home health care center is having difficulty surviving because the physicians refuse to allow competition (Korea). In the American context, as payment rates remain flat, so has business remained flat at $6.2 billion annually in the home health sector (1988–91). The only growth segment in the home care business is the high-tech home infusion-therapy market (Wagner 1990). Infusion-therapy firms grew from 330 in 1988 to 890 in 1991 because of advances in drugs, drug-delivery technology, and insurance coverage. It is obvious to health insurance companies that it is more cost-effective to shift patients from expensive hospital settings to home infusion therapy (Shaughnessy and Kramer 1990). AIDS patients are more cost-effectively treated at home ($188 per day for home infusion antibiotics and $160 per day for nursing care, compared to over $1,000 per day for an inpatient hospitalization; National Underwriter [NU] 1991). It is less obvious to federal public policy makers that national coverage of home health care would be cost-effective (Williams et al. 1990; HCFA 1991; Kemper 1990). The economies of scale are inconsequential for home health firms (Kass 1987). If the entitlement to home health care creates a demand-pull inflation of questionable home health care seekers (people wanting custodial care for the first time because its price is reduced by insurance), it may not be good public policy. The Pepper Commission's call for ''full social insurance'' was largely ignored because the price tag, $13 to $16 billion annually for additional home health and custodial care, was judged too costly by Congress (Rockefeller 1990). There is a wide level of agreement that families would be relieved of the burden of providing unreimbursed home care for relatives if the government could afford to pay for it. There is a less salient level of agreement as to the "crushing impoverishment" that long-term care represents to the frail elderly without family and friends. Some policy makers misinterpret a study like that of Burwell, Adams, and Meiners (1990) by jumping to the conclusion that Medicaid spend-down in nursing homes (impoverishment before eligibility for Medicaid) is not a substantial problem. The study by Burwell, Adams, and Meiners (1990) indicated that during a single nursing home episode only 10 percent of patients who entered as private payers received Medicaid at discharge. There is a need for a longitudinal study of multiple episodes tracking individuals over a long period of time to assess the fiscal burden of the Medicaid spend-down provision on elderly patients and their relatives.

Home health care grew from 1.6 percent of Medicaid expenditures in 1975 to 3.2 percent in 1985 and 3.9 percent in 1989–91. Medicare has also paid for $1.6 to $1.9 billion of home health care per year since 1984 (1.6 million people served and 24 visits per person per year, on average; HCFA 1991). Policy makers are currently considering prospective payment for the 5,500 home health care firms. In this era of DRGs for hospitals and RUGs for some nursing homes, it is inconsistent that home health care is still cost reimbursed. In the interest of containing home health care expenses, more payers will begin to replace cost reimbursement with prospective payment.

Some researchers refer to the subacute care that hospitals had traditionally provided but that is now provided on an ambulatory basis (in response to PPS or utilization review) as *transitional care*. Transitional care can be provided in a nursing facility, intermediate-care facility, at home (with the assistance of home health workers), and sometimes in hospital-based, subacute-care-bed sections. Some of the eliminated hospital days—168 million between 1983 and 1991—result in increased days of care in other transitional settings. Russell (1990) may have overstated the $17 billion in savings to the Medicare program. The savings from shorter stays and fewer admissions among public and private patients are partially offset by the costs incurred in transitional care. Medicare enrollees, other patients, and families are finding that some of the financial burden for this transitional care has shifted onto them. By definition, some cost shift has to occur because transitional care is less well insured (more consumer out-of-pocket cost sharing) than hospital care.

Much of the growth in transitional care has been in the home health care arena (table 4.3). The nature of home health service is changing. The 1986 survey of Area Agencies on Aging (AAAs) reported a fivefold increase in case management services, a threefold increase in home skilled nursing care, and a twofold increase in personal care services and housekeeping following the first three years of PPS (1983–86). In contrast, the 1991 survey suggested a fourfold increase in high-tech home health care since 1987.

Table 4.3
Medicare Beneficiaries' Usage of Home Health Care and Skilled Nursing Facilities by Age, 1970–1990

| | Utilization per 1,000 Medicare Enrollees | | | |
| | Home Health Agency | | Skilled Nursing Facility | |
Patient Age	1970	1990	1970	1990
65-69	5	39	5	6
70-74	7	65	10	6
75-79	9	88	19	11
80-84	12	106	36	21
85 and over	12	115	54	36
Total	8	74	16	12

Source: Health Care Financing Administration, 1991.

Data on the development of hospital-based subacute-care beds will become available from the American Hospital Association. HCFA officials fear that some hospitals may place financial concerns above the clinical concerns of the patients by moving some individuals prematurely so as to "game" the system and receive supplemental payments for rehabilitation or other transitional types of care. Unfortunately, it will be nearly impossible to judge how much of this is "gaming" versus a medically appropriate transfer or discharge to a lower-cost service setting. These lower-cost service settings not only represent an alternative source of revenue, they also help minimize losses that might have been incurred by a PPS patient sitting in an inpatient bed any longer than deemed necessary. However, when medically appropriate, transitional care is a good loss minimizer and revenue-generating strategy. If medically inappropriate, the transfer or early discharge may cause the PPS patient to relapse and be rehospitalized, much to the embarrassment (e.g., in PRO oversight) and financial loss of all concerned at the hospital.

Most ethical providers argue that transitional care is more properly and less expensively delivered in less resource-intensive settings. Officials at HCFA and in the HMO industry can observe (with some smugness) that this discovery of lower-cost alternative care settings was largely prompted by hospital prospective payment formulas and employer interest in prepaid care. The most critical policy question is whether this movement to transitional care will decrease total per capita costs. Three other key questions are (1) whether increasing severity-of-illness levels among transitional-care patients pose a threat to patient quality of care, (2) whether access to services is a problem for certain patient groups, and (3) whether theorized continuity-of-care benefits accrue if the patients receive all their transitional care from one institution. Future research may provide answers.

One major stimulus to the rapid growth in Medicare home health payments, in addition to the PPS hospital payment scheme, was Pub. L. 96–499 to liberalize home health benefits in 1980. This bill provided for the first time coverage for an unlimited number of home health visits and eliminated the three-day prior-hospitalization requirement as a condition for the receipt of home health services.

The policy debate concerning home care versus institutionalization has raged since precolonial Elizabethan poor laws. In the American context, pioneering hospitals developed home care "hospitals without walls" in the 1950s to compensate for the decline in the rate of physician house calls. Physicians in markets of oversupply have provided a modest rebirth of the home health care market, but home care is unlikely to become physician dominated. If anything, experts argue that physician involvement has been too minimal (Burton 1985; Koren 1986). House calls as a percentage of the 1.1 billion physician visits with non-institutionalized Americans increased from 0.6 percent in 1982 to 2.9 percent in 1991. Payment rates will limit the expansion in house calls. Rates set for a home visit by a physician will never be commensurate with those for other hospital or office visits.

HCFA is playing its part in curtailing the growth of a booming home health market (Department of Health and Human Services [DHHS] 1986). The rate increases fall substantially short of any inflation-adjustment levels, and the regulatory requirements are increasing (HCFA 1991). Still, many hospitals plan continued expansion into home health care, which led analysts at Kurt Salmon and Associates (1989) to predict a glut of home health care agencies in the future. Lower payment rates are the traditional payer response to any glut in supply.

The marketplace is littered with the wreckage of well-intentioned home health agencies and meals-on-wheels programs disbanded. On the other hand, high-tech home care has been rapidly promoted by manufacturers. Insurers, HMOs, and PPOs are eager to pay for these high-tech services if they substitute for higher-cost hospital care. Antibiotics, chemotherapy, central intravenous lines, peripheral lines, cardiac pressor agents, and parenteral nutrition have become major product lines in home health care since 1983. For example, some 260,000 Americans have digestive problems each year and require total parenteral nutrition (TPN). If TPN can be done for $5,000 per month at home, it is substantially more cost-effective than paying $12,000 to $14,000 per month for inpatient TPN.

Some 6.6 million elderly require help in the tasks of daily living. Approximately 80 percent of this help comes in the form of unpaid assistance from friends and relatives. Home health care assists all concerned in maintaining the activities of daily living, so that the elderly are not forced into an institution (Haug 1985). According to one survey, home health care patients are younger and less functionally disabled than nursing home patients (Kramer, Shaughnessy, and Pettigrew 1985). For years advocates of home health care had hoped that "low-tech" provision of services would prove cost-effective relative to inpatient care.

Hedrick and Inui (1986) surveyed 12 economic evaluations of home health services. Home health care had no impact on patient functioning, mortality, nursing home placements, and acute hospitalization (in three studies hospitalization actually increased with home care provision). The total cost of care was either not affected or actually increased by 15 percent. Poor organization and fragmentation of services could explain why home health care has yet to live up to its promise for cost-benefit. For example, Medicare-reimbursed home health care not only lacks homemaker/chore services, but also needs more stringent case management and referral services to prevent fragmentation. A new delivery style, managed care, allows the broker or case-managing agency to assess needs for care, develop a comprehensive care plan, refer the patient, and monitor the individual's situation so that the care plan can be readjusted if necessary.

Case management in home health care has typically been very poor. Medicare requires that a beneficiary be homebound and need skilled nursing, physical therapy, or speech therapy in accordance with a physician's treatment plan, but physician intervention is so minimal as to involve but a few minutes of time (Koren 1986). This is not to suggest that the case manager must be a physician, but cost-benefit is only achievable if the case manager takes the time to closely monitor the case. If the case manager does not get the appropriate services delivered on a consistent basis, very costly events will be forthcoming (hospitalization or nursing home placement). The challenge for home health care has been particularly strong since 1984. Because of the DRG payment system, home health care patients are sicker, and coordination of care is even more critical than before. Nurses or social workers, who may work for the organization to which they refer patients, have not been effective as case managers seeking to maximize either quality or cost-efficiency (Kemper 1990).

Our understanding of home health care agencies' shortcomings is equally matched by federal analysts' misunderstandings of the patient population. Very few patients who use home-based services would have become long stayers in nursing homes in any case (Weissert and Cready 1989). Long stayers tend to be older, more dependent, and poorer in social resources than those who use home care. Few patients who actually use home care have their institutional stay averted or shortened. Patients who use "high-touch, low-tech" home care are most often using it as an add-on (complement) to existing services, rather than as a substitute for institutional care. The sickest and most dependent cases may be less expensive to serve in a nursing home or a clinic than in the home, except in the case of a few high-tech home health conditions.

Public support for home health care might best focus on functionally dependent people rather than on the aged per se. Home health agencies might be able to market their services on a cost-benefit basis with better case management. However, "low-tech" home health care might still have to resort to intangible quality-of-life benefits for justification, like reduced feelings of isolation or improved cognitive functioning (Sheffler 1985).

SOCIAL HMOs FOR THE ELDERLY

Protection from catastrophically high health care costs is becoming an increasingly recognized public problem. One alternative delivery system, the social HMO (SHMO), attempts to efficiently coordinate care for older people who are most likely to have multiple health problems requiring the attention of multiple providers. SHMOs are prepaid managed-care systems for long-term care and medical care geared toward elderly enrollees. The sponsoring organization takes responsibility for integrating a wide range of services for a membership. Under the 1983–89 SHMO Demonstration Project with HCFA, members of a representative sample of the elderly, both disabled and able-bodied, were paid on a prepaid capitation basis at four SHMOs (Kaiser Portland, Elderplan Brooklyn, Ebenezer Minneapolis, and Senior Care Action Plan Long Beach). The SHMO is at risk for service costs, taking responsibility for operating within a budget and generating a profit (or loss) depending on how effectively costs are managed.

If the SHMOs are successful, it is hoped that they will interest employers, insurance carriers, and government to encourage greater prefunding of long-term care (McCall, Knickman, and Bauer 1991). We shall discuss long-term-care insurance in the next section, but HMOs face a number of the same generic problems (e.g., adverse selection). There are three basic methods by which a SHMO can protect itself from attracting a disproportionate share of the sicker elderly enrollees. First, the SHMO could provide less than full chronic-care benefits and charge a lower premium to attract the healthier elderly. Second, one could cheat the system by screening potential enrollees on the basis of health factors outside the HCFA adjusted average per capita cost (AAPCC) formula, but the demonstration prohibited such skimming behavior. Third, queuing, with a significant waiting period to join the SHMO, is one formal mechanism to minimize adverse selection, be fair to the payer, and collect a representative share of high-risk elderly.

Two of the SHMOs in the demonstration project did not achieve the projected financial break-even level of 4,000 enrollees by 1989. The SHMOs are enrolling Medicare-only beneficiaries and Medicare beneficiaries who receive Medicaid assistance and are designed to be budget neutral for both payer groups. Considering a study demonstrating how one long-standing HMO appears to have discounted quality for poor enrollees (Ware et al. 1986), government officials should continue to monitor the quality of care. The innovative impulse behind SHMOs resides in the integration of services and funding sources, so that the elderly are not shuffled from one provider to another. The business community should be attracted to the idea of "living within a budget," and consumer groups should like the idea of reduced fragmentation of services. The HMO incentive structure encourages the substitution of earlier, less expensive, "low-tech" services prior to the need for expensive inpatient services. Reducing hospital use is essential to the SHMOs' ability to support expanded long-term-care benefits. In addition to promoting increased use of community-based alternatives, SHMOs should (1) decrease inappropriate nursing home admissions and (2) slow the Medicaid "spend-down" rate at which elderly beneficiaries expend personal resources. To advise Congress on what levels of cost sharing are most appropriate for the elderly, the SHMO demonstration sites offered different cost-sharing packages (Leutz et al. 1990).

Gerontologists and psychologists will be interested in the degree to which the SHMO case management system strengthens or erodes the informal principle-care-person and family support system for the enrollee. In theory, as the difficulty of caring for frail elders increases due to the stress of precipitating events, the informal support network should be less likely to break down. Such a prediction assumes that the extensive SHMO case management placement system works well. However, the system could break down if the case manager is perceived as an enemy who is forcing a too severely ill patient to be treated at home by overworked family and friends. SHMOs have a clear financial incentive to shift more burdens to the family, even though their efficient placement services should be faster and more effective at final institutional placement. There comes a point where the sicker home care patients are better served in an institution, yet SHMOs have a financial incentive to underadmit.

If the SHMOs are not providing good service or overextend the patience of unpaid family and friends, one would predict that disenrollment levels would be high. If the demonstration proves a success, perhaps in the late 1990s Congress will enact a SHMO entitlement for Medicare enrollees that will do for long-term care what Pub. L. 97–248 did for hospice care. If we enact a national SHMO program, shoddy "fast-buck" operators may have less interest in ethics, equity, and service than the four model SHMOs.

After a slow start the four SHMOs are beginning to improve operating performance. Three of the first SHMOs reported substantial losses in their first three years, primarily because of slow enrollment and resultant high marketing and administrative costs (Leutz et al. 1990). After assuming full risk, two of the three showed surpluses in fiscal year 1989. Management and service costs for expanded long-term care were similar across the four sites and are affordable within the framework of Medicaid and Medicare payment rates (Birnbaum et al. 1991).

Case managers can help channel patients to cost-effective providers within the context of SHMOs and also in the context of more flexible organizations. For example, one report on the National Channeling Demonstration Project (Kemper 1990) suggested that case managers are not yet cost-effective at substituting home health care services for nursing home care. The reason the case managers were not successful at limiting costs is that they had no financial incentive to do so. Kemper and Murtaugh (1991) suggested giving the case managers more autonomy and incentive to channel home care services to the patients that will in turn be most likely to substitute this care for inpatient nursing home care. In theory, case managers can also assist in the quality-assurance process and help negotiate prices below the prevailing market rates. Case managers will begin to justify their 6 to 10 percent administrative expense when they have the monetary incentive to trim costs, make home care a substitute for bed care, and not simply make home care an extra add-on service (without economic benefit).

We need to provide case managers with the tools to predict nursing home admissions and length of stay (Liu, Coughlin, and McBride 1991; Short, Cunningham, and Mueller 1991) and to assess the quality of care (Ferris and Wyszewianski 1990). Greater reliance on geriatric nurse practitioners has some potential to reduce cost per case (Buchanan et al. 1990).

SLOW GROWTH FOR LONG-TERM CARE INSURANCE

The aging of the population clearly represents a major public policy challenge, and new public programs may have difficulty getting funded in an era of budget austerity. Therefore, increasing attention has turned to the development of private insurance funds for long-term care. The pioneer in the private long-term-care insurance business was Acsia Insurance Services. Acsia of California began issuing policies through Fireman's Fund Insurance in 1976. Fireman's will issue the policy to a person over age 79 if the spouse is under age 80 and insured for an equivalent or greater amount of indemnity (Phillips 1984). Applicants of all ages are carefully screened to determine that they are not an immediate risk for institutionalization. At prevailing prices a 65-year-old could pay $100 per month for a policy that would cover up to $700 per week in nursing home costs for up to four years.

Insurance to cover the costs of long-term care has failed to develop in the private sector for a number of reasons. While a total of 120 companies sell some form of long-term-care insurance for 2.7 million Americans, the market penetration in any given state was disappointingly small in 1991. Members of the group for which the premiums are the most reasonable, the middle-aged, have little incentive to purchase such insurance in our prevailing youth culture. They have numerous other pulls on their income, from the mortgage to their children's education. The insurance industry would have to structure premiums to reflect actual risk at a certain age, rather than the lifetime risk, in order to encourage greater participation by the population aged 45 to 69. Moreover, some public subsidy would be required to encourage significant market growth. The Heritage Institute has advocated an individual retirement medical account (IRMA) to encourage prefunding of long-term care. The investment return would be taxable and, although earmarked for health care, would be owned by consumers to do with as they choose.

Pricing of long-term-care insurance must be based on careful actuarial data.

Kemper and Murtaugh (1991) reported that the probability that a person had used a nursing home increased sharply with age at death: 17 percent for those aged 65 to 74, 36 percent for those aged 75 to 84, and 60 percent for those aged 85 to 94. Of those turning 65 in 1990, 43 percent are projected to need a nursing home at some time before they die. A surprising 21 percent of this 43 percent requiring a nursing home will have total lifetime use of five years or more. The expense of a five-year nursing home stay, discounted to 1992 dollars, should exceed $140,000. If these trends continue, some 200,000 Americans turning 65 during 1992 will spend more than $140,000 on nursing home stays exceeding five years. Who will pay the bills? Government? Private long-term-care insurance? Studies like these may prompt the middle-aged population to purchase long-term-care insurance (Kane and Kane 1991).

A private 1991 Gallup Poll indicated that 22 percent of Americans said that they expect to need a nursing home at some point. Over 62 percent of adults said that they would be willing to purchase long-term-care insurance, and the mean respondent would be willing to pay $42 per month in premiums, with 14 percent willing to pay $61 or more. Greater reliance on long-term care might benefit the general economy if it would free up informal caregivers (spouse, family) to do other productive activities (Stone and Short, 1990). However, documented cases of policyholders being denied benefit payments due to prior-hospitalization and prior-skilled-care clauses in the contract (Wilson and Weissert 1989) may limit the public interest in purchasing long-term-care insurance. Rice et al. (1991) emphasized the point that the premiums would be more affordable if they were purchased in the middle years, ages 40 to 64. However, many families have other consumption needs during that period (raising a family, education costs). Estimates of how much a federal subsidy program to purchase long-term-care insurance would cost annually range from $20 billion (HCFA 1991) to $4 billion (Wallack 1991, a study for the Health Insurance Association of America [HIAA]). The current restrictive clauses in long-term-care policies have done little to reduce uncertainty and financial risk (National Association of Insurance Commissioners [NAIC] 1991). Setting the inflation-protection clause and the duration of policy coverage are problematic (Rubin, Weiner, and Meiners 1989).

BET THE HOUSE ON LONG-TERM CARE

Home equity conversions are another possibility to finance long-term care. An elderly person could tap the equity accumulated in his or her residence to free up resources for long-term care. If home equity and other property are taken into account, 40 percent of the elderly have potential annual incomes of $30,000 or more. Moreover, reverse mortgages and leaseback sales could increase available funds. The "catch–22" paradox is that people of modest means may jeopardize Medicaid benefits, food stamps, and other income by converting their home equity into monthly income. The average elderly household had a net worth of $97,000 in 1991, but one-third of the elderly (10.8 million) do not own a home. Nearly 24 percent of the elderly have a net worth in excess of $150,000, but 7.3 million elderly do not own their homes outright. Elderly homeowners rode the inflation curve to higher property values. The average adult aged 25 to 35 paid more for his or her first new car than his or her parents paid for their first house. Even if 90 to 95 percent of the elderly are no longer "ill-clad, ill-housed and ill-nourished," to quote both Presidents Roosevelt and Kennedy, one still needs to worry about the poorest elderly. (One can utilize statistics to argue in many directions. The poverty rate for the elderly [10 percent] is lower than the poverty rate for those under 65 [12 percent]. Alternatively, if one considers the "near poor," those within 125 percent of the poverty line, the elderly have 2 percent more near poor [18 percent of the nonelderly versus 19.9 percent of the elderly].) For example, we have a "feminization" of elderly poverty, with almost one million women over age 70 living alone and in poverty. Isolation and depression were major problems among the 12 million elderly living alone in 1991 (80 percent female).

Belling (1989) documented the expanding popularity of home equity conversions for the elderly. Older homeowners can access the accumulated equity in their homes to pay current expenses. Small amounts of cash can be raised from deferred-payment loans, but larger amounts can be raised through reverse mortgages. Reverse mortgages provide monthly income, and the homeowner is not obligated to repay the funds until some specified future date (typically at death or within 3 to 12 years, depending on terms). In 1991 over 400,000 reverse mortgages had been written in 39 states. Providers of long-term care wish that more elderly would raise cash flow through reverse mortgages so that the elderly could consume more comprehensive (and expensive) home health services and support services. With a strategy of "coordinated risk" more elderly could self-finance home care and independent living with reverse mortgages and avoid the most expensive form of care (institutionalization). A second strategy of "offsetting risks" would involve utilizing the reverse-mortgage income to purchase long-term-care insurance (Pawlson 1990).

Advocates for the elderly are concerned with issues such as whether enough elderly have the purchasing power to afford such insurance and the willingness to pay for such coverage. Certain elderly individuals have the risk aversion to pay for such insurance. If one attends any public hearing on the topic, one is struck by the number of elderly that purchase 4 to 14 duplicative medigap policies "just to be sure." While these are atypical individuals, the elderly are obviously highly sensitized to long-term-care issues, and they have a financial reason to be sensitized. In 1991 it was estimated that the elderly population's out-of-pocket health care costs represented 16 percent of mean income and 24 percent of median income. The elderly were paying a much smaller share in 1979; 12.5 and 18.5 percent, respectively (American Association of Retired Persons [AARP]

1991). Medicare beneficiaries must pay the average first-day hospitalization costs as a deductible. Because PPS has restrained costs per admission, the government has substantially increased the cost per first day.

Long-term-care insurance is more of a product in search of a market than an emerging growth industry. If the nonelderly do not have the motivation to purchase long-term-care insurance, the elderly have a number of basic misconceptions concerning their current insurance. In a survey conducted by the American Association of Retired Persons, 80 percent of senior citizens incorrectly believed that Medicare fully covers nursing home care (Fackelmann 1985). In fact, Medicare covers less than 42 percent of the health care costs for the elderly. Medicare only provides 1.8 percent of nursing home revenues. The majority of the elderly erroneously believe that private medigap coverage includes nursing home care (Lane 1985; AARP 1991).

HOSPICE SERVICES

Hospice services for the terminally ill, emphasizing care in the home, were largely supported by charitable contributions until the 1982 passage of Pub. L. 97–248. Prior to this change in the law, hospice reimbursement for home care was insufficient because the visits required two to four times as long to complete as the average home visit. The hospice benefit is available to terminally ill Medicare patients who have been physician certified as having less than six months to live. This estimate of when a case is terminal is no easy task for physicians. The hospice will be reimbursed for two 90-day periods and one 30-day period during the patient's lifetime; this 210-day cap has recently been made flexible (Moinpour, Polissar, and Conrad 1990). The hospice faces a substantial financial risk if it admits terminal patients who stay longer. The patient may revoke the hospice benefit at any time and return to the previously waived standard Medicare benefits. In 1985 a cap of $6,500 per hospice patient was established, with the amount adjusted annually for inflation. The hospice faces an 80/20 minimum ratio of home to inpatient care and cannot discontinue care.

Religious sponsors and other advocates of hospice care have long argued that hospice care yields "obvious" cost savings by substituting for expensive hospital services (Paradis 1985). In the view of many, those who are to die benefit little from intensive inpatient interventions to save their lives when they suffer greatly in the process (Angell 1982). Unfortunately, physicians are afflicted with a tendency to "oversave" and overtreat the terminal case, as evidenced by the quote from John Knowles at the beginning of this chapter.

A number of third parties have followed Medicare's lead and are offering the hospice benefit. Many insurance plans also cover family bereavement counseling. Medicare regulations require the hospice to offer bereavement counseling for the family, but do not allow its reimbursement by Medicare. Such services can be paid by the family or other sources. Medicare cannot pay for such services because the Medicare trust fund is targeted to provide services for Medicare beneficiaries.

Almost two-thirds of all hospice programs in 1991 were hospital based or strongly hospital affiliated (the hospital invested in the hospice and sometimes acted as a junior partner). Seven percent of the estimated 1,380 hospices are proprietary. The number of purely hospital-based hospice programs increased from 487 in the fall of 1982 to over 900 in 1990. Not surprisingly, larger hospitals tend to have hospice programs (21 percent of the hospitals with over 400 beds, in contrast to only 6 percent of the hospitals with less than 200 beds). Hospice programs are dependent on volunteers to help contain their labor costs, both in the facility and at home. Hospices rely heavily on a primary-care person (PCP) to assist in all aspects of care for the patient. The PCP is typically a family member and must devote much of his or her time to care of the terminal patient. The opportunity cost of PCPs should be estimated (shadow priced) in any comprehensive cost-benefit analysis of hospice care.

Mor and Kidder (1985) reported results from a national hospice study of 5,853 terminal cancer patients in 25 hospices and 14 conventional oncology departments (the control group) over a 2.5-year period. As expected, the authors reported that hospice patients consistently cost less than conventional care during the last month of life, but the cost advantage declined over the months for longer-surviving patients. If the data are analyzed from a perspective of cost and utilization over the last 12 months of life, the findings differed for home versus hospital-based hospice programs. Cost savings compared to conventional care that accumulated in the first month for home care hospice patients persisted and even slightly increased over the last year of life, for a net savings of 20.6 percent ($2,221) in the last year of life. The initial savings observed in the hospital-based hospices were considerably reduced over the months, to the point where the cost advantage compared to conventional care ($12,700) was only 4.6 percent ($585).

These observed differences in cost for the two groups cannot unequivocally be attributed to the hospice, as hospice admission may reflect earlier patient choices made about the style of care desired. The patients in the hospice group, if they had been forced to receive conventional oncologists' care, might have been capable of forcing the providers to practice a style of medicine costing at least 4.6 percent less than $12,700 (1982 dollars) in the last year of life. However, the patient and family would not have received the same high-quality product, including, more bereavement counseling and painkillers, that a hospice provides. As with home health care, quality of life becomes a principle argument for the less conventional care setting. Mor and Kidder (1985) also questioned whether the home care hospice would not have been less than 20.6 percent cost-effective if such programs were not able to attract individuals prone to low inpatient utilization. Good case management and "inverse adverse selection" (selection of short-living cases) are potential keys to survival in the financially unstable hospice industry.

CCRCs AND LIFE CARE

Continuing-care retirement communities (CCRCs) increased in number from 286 in 1984 to 841 in 1991. CCRCs provide long-term contracts for lifetime health care, shelter, and widely varying degrees of social-service benefits. The elderly are attracted to the vintage-life-care-concept pairing of the twin ideas of security and independence in a campuslike CCRC facility. The elderly dislike frequent increases in fees and the introduction of new fees. However, CCRCs must operate under the same risk-sharing principles on which private medical insurance plans are based. If medical cost-inflation rates are unexpected, if mortality rates decline, or if morbidity rates increase, then the CCRC must raise fees to cover the increased expenses. Many CCRCs have fallen into financial distress because of inappropriate pricing schemes, insufficient rate hikes, and an insufficient volume of new members. The CCRCs that grow in the 1990s will price appropriately and offer cost-effective managed-care health services (rather than inflationary fee-for-service unrestricted medical services). The provision of preventive services will be as cost-effective for a CCRC as they are to a social HMO (SHMO).

CCRC users pay a life-care fee for health services and a housing fee. The 80 CCRCs that experimented with one-time life-care fees in the 1970s experienced severe financial distress. Only 45 religious CCRCs in 1991 still operated based on the outdated principle of asset turnover of all wealth in return for a lifetime of total life care. The other 796 CCRCs require some combination of a one-time entry fee and a monthly condo fee (sometimes including extra voluntary premiums for additional health insurance coverage). Some CCRCs have had to introduce patient cost-sharing provisions at the point of service to contain outpatient medical expenses. (Many HMOs never offering patient cost sharing prior to 1983 started requiring copayments per visit in the late 1980s.)

Risk analysis and planning for the "worst-case" scenario is the key to appropriate CCRC pricing. What is a worst case for the CCRC may be good news for the elderly; for example, lower mortality rates mean lower cash flow for the CCRC from the one-time entry fee. If CCRCs are a happy environment, and the quality of the medical care is above average, DHHS mortality tables may overstate the incidence of one-time entry fees. Apartment turnover rates would be lower than expected from DHHS data sources, even when the federal tables are adjusted for the higher income and lower number of chronic conditions preexisting in CCRC members compared to the larger population of elderly Americans. Therefore, CCRCs should pool data and engage in experience rating to more accurately forecast the financial risk involved in managing a life-care facility (Topolnicki 1985).

Actuarially based CCRC pricing must take into account (1) turnover rates, (2) a reserve fund for contract termination, (3) start-up costs for capital and marketing, (4) a reserve fund for capital replacement, and (5) a reserve fund for medical expenses. Apartment turnover rates generally range from 6 to 11 percent per year. The fraction of apartment turnover caused by death can range from two-thirds for a mature CCRC to as low as one-third for a new CCRC (the majority of the turnover is caused by voluntary disenrollment). Most managers understand the need to replace buildings and continuously market the CCRC, but the fifth factor, the need for reserves for future medical expenses, is more difficult to estimate. A young CCRC with less than 12 years' experience (lacking actuarial maturation) needs higher levels of medical reserves than the older, continuously operating CCRCs. The younger CCRCs require higher medical reserve funds, financed by a higher rate of growth in medical fees to residents, because health care utilization per capita is higher for a newer (less mature) disequilibrium population. By contrast, a CCRC that has reached a steady-state population, with the apartments 100 percent occupied, tends to utilize fewer medical services per capita (and experience lower rates of morbidity).

Pricing policies differ by ownership: for-profit, private nonprofit, and religious nonprofit. If the goal of a religious nonprofit CCRC is to operate with low end-of-year cash balances, it may charge an entry fee of $55,000 and a monthly fee of $500 for one-bedroom single entrants. If the goal of a private nonprofit CCRC is to contain costs yet maintain a slight steady growth in end-of-year cash balances that keeps pace with inflation, it may charge an entry fee of $90,000 and a monthly fee of $700 to $730 for one-bedroom single entrants, whereas a for-profit CCRC interested in turning a profit in the long run might keep the entry fee competitive with the private nonprofit CCRCs ($85,000–$95,000), but charge a higher monthly fee of $750 to $775 for a one-bedroom single entrant.

Prices should be set depending on client age (American Association of Homes for the Aging [AAHA] 1991). There is an obvious financial trade-off between entry fees and monthly fees: The higher the fixed fee, the lower the monthly fee needed. For example, a 75-year-old female might present a $186,512 actuarial liability, which could be financed by a $90,000 entry fee and $715 monthly fees. Alternatively, this same liability could be covered by a $115,000 entry fee (if no refunds were allowed) and $465 monthly fees. The entry fee would have to be $125,000 if the contract allowed the individual a prorated entry-fee refund over the initial five years of CCRC membership, implying that 20 percent of the entry fee is deducted annually.

The widest variation in fees exists among the 320 private nonprofit CCRCs. Those CCRCs with the highest levels of financial distress are new CCRCs utilizing the pay-as-you-go method (low prices). The best-managed new CCRCs offer closed-group pricing: maintenance of inflation-indexed monthly fees, group equity, and full funding of the contract-termination reserve fund. The fees in the early years for a new CCRC closed-group facility may be high for 12 years, but after 12 years this CCRC can charge lower prices than pay-as-you-go CCRCs. Pay-as-you-go CCRCs offer no reserve funds for contract termination and accumulate no equity. A middle-of-the-road pricing strategy between the two extremes of the closed-group and pay-as-you-go methods involves open-group stable prices, (1) partially funding 50 to 95 percent of a contract-termination reserve, (2) offering a retrospective lagged inflation-indexed adjustment to monthly fees, and (3) building a modest degree of group equity (Curran and Brecht 1985).

From the point of view of equity and financial stability, the conservative open-method pricing strategy is best. The fees of the open-method pricing strategy generate sufficient reserves to close out (liquidate) all future liabilities associated with current members. The closed-group method allows for the greatest accumulation of group equity by setting fees to cover expected future expenses for each new entrant cohort, thus preventing the need for any intergenerational taking of funds from other age groups, because each age group is self-supporting. The pay-as-you-go method saps the resources of new entrants to pay for the expenses of old entrants to the CCRC. In summary, because it is high-priced for a new CCRC, the closed-group method may limit the growth in occupancy of a CCRC, but it provides the most fiscal security for management and membership in the long run. Some CCRCs have employed the lower-priced pay-as-you-go method to build up a critical mass of occupants and have then shifted pricing methods after 3 to 6 years to the open-group or closed-group method. Pay-as-you-go pricing is the most expensive method for a mature CCRC (over age 12). Most mature large CCRCs with greater than 400 residents use the closed-group pricing strategy (Coopers and Lybrand 1991).

Projecting Future Demand for CCRCs

An individual CCRC can forecast a fixed deterministic projection of demand for services or an alternative stochastic estimation technique. The advantage of the stochastic method is that it allows management to analyze the risks connected with random deviations. For example, what if the next ten occupants are couples rather than single individuals plus one couple? What if old entrants have unexpected declines in health status, or new entrants have better than expected health status? Decision support systems utilizing stochastic models can help management deal with such "what if" situations.

Actuarial liabilities must be projected in the form of present value for medical expenses and present value for housing costs. Discounted at 9.0 percent, the present value of CCRC housing for a 90-year-old single male may be only $6,838, compared to $103,294 for a 75-year-old single female. The present value for the medical expenses of the 90-year-old male will be $24,162, and expenses for the 75-year-old single female will be $83,218.

In addition to age, marital status is another important demographic factor. The present value of future expenses for a couple is less than the expenses for one man and one woman. There are two basic reasons for this actuarial finding: couples share one apartment, and couples have better health status than singles. The actuarial liability (the present value of future expenses) for an 80-year-old male and a 75-year-old female are $281,116 for the couple, but the unrelated female would cost $186,512 and the unrelated male would cost $124,070 (two individuals cost $29,466 more than the equivalent-age couple). The couple is 9.5 percent less expensive than two single individuals of equal age. Medical expenses for the couple are 15.1 percent less than for the single individuals, and housing expenses for the couple are 6.8 percent less. Living as two is not that much less expensive when one considers the present value of future housing expenses because the last survivor of a couple is expected to occupy an apartment longer than a single resident. This example assumes that the survivor downsizes the apartment from a one-bedroom to a studio apartment one year after the death of the spouse.

Strategic Pricing Options

Pricing couples poses a unique problem for CCRCs. Some CCRCs make the mistake of charging only one entry fee for the couple, the same price as a single person's entry fee ($90,000), but charge the couple a $1,773 monthly fee (two and one-half times that of a single 75-year-old woman). CCRCs must optimize the mix of monthly versus entry fees with consideration for two basic risk factors: (1) If monthly fees are set too high, this increases the probability that this expense will exceed the clients' monthly income and exhaust their wealth while it misses the opportunity to collect a big entry fee (that the elderly will not be able to divest over time, because the money resides with the CCRC); (2) if entry fees are set too high, this slows the growth in CCRC occupancy rate; and less reliance on monthly fees exposes the CCRC to more risk of underestimated future inflation and morbidity and overestimated mortality.

As a rule of thumb, it might be best to set the entry fee at 35 to 50 percent of the present value of future expenses and to set the monthly fees according to changing demographic and economic conditions (with a profit margin incorporated into the monthly fees). For example, in the case of the couple (male aged 80, female aged 75), the CCRC could set their entry fee equal to 45 percent of the present value of future expenses, or $126,500, and the monthly fees at $1,450 to $1,470 for a one-bedroom unit. If this couple wanted a two-bedroom apartment, the entry fee could be set 21 percent higher, and the monthly fee would be 8 percent higher. The relative entry fees are largely preset by capital expenditures, and the relative monthly fees are preset by expected differential variable costs (e.g., labor and maintenance). Therefore, the capital expense on a two-bedroom apartment is 21 percent higher than on a one-bedroom apartment (which is 27 percent more expensive than a studio apartment). The annual variable cost for maintaining a two-bedroom apartment is 8 percent higher than for a one-bedroom apartment (which is 9 percent more expensive than a studio apartment).

In summary, pricing decisions depend on apartment size, resident age, marital status, competitive position (other CCRCs), occupancy rate, and the risk preferences of CCRC owners. Actuarially responsible prices assure that in the aggregate the CCRC community will be financially sound, but in certain highly competitive markets the CCRC may never survive to celebrate a 12th birthday of equilibrium stability if it does not price to attract a critical mass of initial residents. Entry fees as low as 25 to 30 percent of the present value of future expenses should be maintained for short periods (e.g., the initial two years of growth in the CCRC).

Resetting Monthly Fees

Forecasting the future is much more difficult than backcasting historical data. Therefore, annual shifts in medical expenses and smaller unexpected shifts in housing expenses require that monthly fees be reset on a regular basis. The well-run CCRC should use the same actuarial valuation methods that are used by pension plans to reset annual contributions that keep the plans financially sound (Winklevoss and Powell 1989). Small shifts in the asset/liability ratio can be countered by minor annual changes in the monthly fees (and the next year's entry fee for new members). However, if these regular price hikes are not made, and the problem is ignored for 5 to 10 years, the price shock can be so high that it demarkets the CCRC (residents disenroll in higher numbers than if the price hikes had occurred at regular annual intervals).

Actuarial valuations balance a facility's aggregate assets against its aggregate liabilities. Aggregate assets include the CCRC's physical plant, liquid assets (cash and securities), and the prospective asset of the present value of future fees. Most CCRCs generate sufficient liquid assets from an accounting perspective. The difficult question is from a financial perspective, how to calculate the stream of future prospective assets (fees) to fund the CCRC's future liabilities. There are two alternative methods of estimating future liabilities, open-group and closed-group. Under the less stringent open-group valuation method the CCRC's liability is based on both future and current residents over a fixed time period (15 to 20 years). An actuarially balanced financial position can be achieved with lower prices under the open-group method because the higher medical expenses for residents with a life span in excess of 15 to 20 years can be deferred to the entry fees of future generations of CCRC residents. The analogous valuation game is utilized by the American Social Security System to assume that huge tax rates paid by a smaller number of young people in the twenty-first century will finance $12 billion of expenses by the elderly from 2015 to 2050. The open-group method sets fees low in the present, "passing the buck" (fiscal burden) onto future generations.

The closed-group method of estimating future liabilities is the highest standard of fiduciary responsibility. It assumes that each new generation of entrants will pay its own way with break-even prices set at the time of entry. The higher liability calculation under the closed-group method takes into account only current residents, but suggests levels of funding to cover liabilities over their life span (e.g., 40 years). Under the closed-group approach the CCRC will have sufficient funds to pay all the obligations for existing residents without having to increase future fees by more than the rate of inflation. An analogy can again be drawn to Social Security, which overtaxes the young and the future generations, whereas a Japanese banker operating under closed-group valuation principles would have set Social Security payroll taxes at much higher rates in the mid-1900s. The older CCRCs can operate under the strict closed-group standard, whereas the younger CCRCs may have to operate under the "cosmetic" fiction of the open-group valuation philosophy. The adjective "cosmetic" may be harsh if it turns out that the future generations of elderly are very rich and can afford huge entry fees in the year 2015 (to subsidize the liability created by low fees for veteran entrants to the CCRC in the 1990s). This optimistic scenario appears unlikely if American wealth and productivity erode in competition with Japan and Germany, and our Social Security trust fund is utilized to finance the federal deficit.

Two Ways to Amortize Losses and Raise Fees

One mature CCRC with 400 current residents had a closed-group valuation of prospective liabilities equal to $59.4 million in present-value 1991 dollars. Under the open-group 20-year valuation method the prospective liabilities would have equaled $53.35 million, because this method excludes the 11.5 percent of present value of future liabilities that occurs after a 20-year life span. The CCRC continued to adhere to the strict closed-group valuation of future liabilities, under which it had a $1.1-million unamortized actuarial loss (rather than a $4.95-million unamortized actuarial gain under open-group valuation). The $1.1-million actuarial loss in 1991 could be passed onto the CCRC residents by a supplemental fee or through creation of a buffer fund. The CCRC buffer fund would represent a contingency reserve-fund account. This fund account would be adjusted up or down as annual changes in unamortized actuarial liabilities gained or declined. The CCRC decided to utilize the supplemental-fee method and spread the monthly fee adjustments over three to five years. Each year unamortized deviations are added to the sum of adjustments from past years. The supplemental-fee method smooths out the price hikes over the short run (three, four, or five years).

One of the advantages of a strict closed-group valuation of prospective liabilities is the strong level of financial ratios of the CCRC if the facility is sufficiently occupied. Long-term debt typically equals 20 to 35 percent of prospective liabilities. But leverage ratios, the ability to service the debt, tend to be much better in closed-group or mature large CCRCs. The debt-service-coverage ratio may improve to as high as 2 to 4 within a decade, and the ratio of cash to annual debt service may improve to as high as 15 to 25. Mature CCRCs with great financial ratios and no preference for raising supplemental fees may backslide to an open-group valuation methodology and reduce price hikes in the future. But if the CCRC's financial position erodes sufficiently, the owners should return to a closed-group valuation of future liabilities (justifying higher price increases). The closed-group method may be more expensive, but it is the only valuation method that fully covers the CCRC's contractual obligations to all existing contract holders.

CCRC Sponsors

The largest nonprofit owner of CCRCs, the Good Samaritan Society of South Dakota, operates 5,700 apartments with 3,700 nursing home beds attached. Proprietary operators of CCRCs include hospital chains and hotel corporations (Marriott and Hyatt operate a total of 31 CCRCs). The health care chain National Medical Enterprises operates 25 CCRCs with 2,800 apartments. The nonprofit Adventist Health System operates 1,350 CCRC apartments, and the Lutheran Health Care System operates 1,500 apartments. Growth has slowed for many CCRC builders in the 1990s, and one firm has retrenched. The giant nursing home chain Beverly reduced its number of CCRCs from 45 in 1988 to 33 in 1991.

With changes in sponsorship for CCRCs has come a change in the degree to which different facilities provide long-term-care services without an increase in fees. One should draw a distinction between centers that are ''principally life-care'' and those that are ''oriented towards nursing care.'' Those facilities that provide a nursing home bed for every two or more residents should be defined as primarily life-care, whereas those with a lower ratio of apartments to nursing home beds are more health-care-intensive. Since 1980 almost two-thirds of the centers constructed have been life-care oriented. Many of these facilities will need to add nursing home beds in the coming years as residents age and their health deteriorates, causing fixed expenses to rise. Life-care-oriented centers tend to have more proprietary sponsors. Though most still have a large entry fee, some of the newer ''rental adult congregate living'' centers require no entry fee at all (Tilson 1990).

Financial data on the CCRCs are limited. The one accounting firm that conducted an annual survey on this issue, Laventhol and Horwath (1990), has gone out of business. Ruchlin (1988) used ratio analysis to determine the financial health of a sample of continuing-care facilities for the years 1981, 1983, and 1985. Due to the relative newness of the industry, he stressed that it was difficult to have a good set of historical data with which to establish critical values for success or failure of a facility. A comparison of the median 1983 current ratio value for acute-care hospitals, 1.82, to that of CCRCs, 1.40, showed that CCRCs were probably in less healthy shape in terms of liquidity. The CCRC ratios were more comparable to the current ratios of personal-care homes (1.4), skilled nursing facilities (1.5), and room-and-board homes (1.2). More significant, however, were the equity ratios for net income and net worth, which indicate profitability. Forty of the 109 centers analyzed had negative values for at least one of the ratios, and 20 were negative for both. Many also had low asset-turnover ratios. Part of the low activity numbers may be explained by noting that CCRCs are much less capital-intensive than hospitals. Moreover, the centers in the worst financial shape appeared to be those covering the greatest amount of nursing home care services, while partial- and minimal-care groups fared better. Ruchlin was unable to conclude whether the problem was that fees were not set high enough initially to cover services, or whether residents were consuming more services than originally anticipated. The entry fees and monthly resident fees in the full nursing care facilities tended to be higher than the fees charged by the more socially oriented facilities, though their itemized charges of the nursing care portion per month were lower. Many CCRCs have problems setting the optimal refund policy (Wynd, Stewart, and Hunter 1991). Because the continuing-care industry is unregulated, Ruchlin concluded that it is important that unhealthy industry financial trends not destroy the savings of enrollees should the facility prove to be financially insolvent.

Hospital developers of CCRCs will emphasize continuity of care and the medical "campus" atmosphere, while real-estate developers will market a "country-club" spa and recreation atmosphere. Advocates of the medical model may be disappointed to find out that the spa life-style model sells much better in the marketplace. The image of the elderly is increasingly healthy and affluent; just ask Medicare enrollee actor Paul Newman. Illness is not the unvarying accompaniment of aging. Moreover, aging eliminates the capacity to live in the community for only 5 percent of those over age 65. The "graying" or "tinting" of America spells opportunity for developers who view CCRCs as a chance to capitalize on the "last-time home buyer." Many CCRCs will be built and operated as joint ventures, with the various parties placing a different emphasis in their marketing.

CCRCs are the Cadillacs of the long-term-care industry. Many individuals and families cannot afford such expensive housing and service-delivery settings. There are two more affordable alternatives to CCRCs. Continuing health care communities (CHCCs) are similar to CCRCs, but thrust more of the financial risk for finding and purchasing health insurance and support services onto the residents. The elderly in CHCCs act as a co-op, meeting most of their own needs by living together and helping each other. Publicly financed congregate housing (CH) is a more affordable alternative to CHCCs or CCRCs. The Department of Housing and Urban Development (HUD) offers rental subsidies through the Section 8 program to qualifying low-income citizens. Under this program the family pays a rent of 15 to 25 percent of its gross income after deductions for health and child-care expenses. Assets are not taken into account in the calculation of gross income.

SUMMARY

We have surveyed a number of alternative delivery modes and financing mechanisms for providing long-term care. If we continue our bankrupt policy toward the nonrich elderly, there is little doubt that continued reliance on fragmented programs and expensive institutional care will return to haunt us in the future. We shall be richer as a society if we commit resources to improve the quality of life in our "golden years," postponing morbidity and disability. We must still decide the parameters of our private and public investment in better health services for our elderly. Some analysts fear a demand-pull inflation and a flood of demand. Kane and Kane (1985) provided some evidence for this expectation in a study of the initiation of universal long-term-care benefits in Canada. Three Canadian provinces added long-term care to their package of benefits at different times, and the expenditures for such care increased substantially. Nursing home expenditures increased at double the rate of hospital expenditures (e.g., 14 percent for nursing homes versus 8 percent for hospitals in British Columbia in 1982). Home health care visits per capita increased threefold over the first three years, leveling off in 1982–84. Even with extensive usage of case workers to constrain cost increases, costs did increase substantially. However, the Canadian people proudly observe that they initiated universal coverage for long-term care because the role of a good society is to provide for those most in need.

The financing of long-term care is one area in which little progress has been made in the United States since 1966. American analysts often question the wisdom of enacting a national program to shift responsibility to a federal agency and away from what sociologists label "mediating structures" for private charity and joint undertakings involving the spouse, family, friends, and the church and other voluntary organizations. On the other hand, perhaps the voluntary support system cannot keep pace with the aging of the population and needs public funds or tax incentives to assure quality care for the elderly. Our geriatric demographic imperative seems capable of outstripping our capacity for voluntarism (Grannemann 1991). Certain methods of price control may prove counterproductive in the long-run (Schlenker 1991; Soumerai, Ross, and Avorn 1991).

REFERENCES

Abel, E. (1986). "The Hospice Movement: Institutionalizing Innovation." *International Journal of Health Services* 16:1 (January), 77–88.

Altman, E. (1983). *Corporate Financial Distress: A Complete Guide to Predicting, Avoiding, and Dealing with Bankruptcy.* New York: Wiley.

Altman, E. (1974). "Zeta Analysis: A New Model to Identify Bankruptcy Risk." *Journal of Banking and Finance* 1:1 (January) 29–54.

American Association of Homes for the Aging (AAHA) and Ernst and Young. (1991). *Continuing Care Retirement Communities: An Industry in Action.* Washington, D.C.: AAHA.

American Association of Retired Persons. (1991). *Aging America: Trends and Projections.* Washington, D.C.: AARP.

American Hospital Association. (1985). "Life Care Industry Grows Despite Costs." *Hospitals* 59:23 (December 1), 41.

Angell, M. (1982). "The Quality of Mercy." *New England Journal of Medicine* 306:2 (January 10), 98–99.

Arling, G., Zimmerman, D., and Updike, L. (1990). "Nursing Home Case Mix in Wisconsin." *Medical Care* 27:2 (February), 164–180.

Belling, B. (1989). "Home Equity Conversions: A Financing Option for Long-Term Care." *Caring* 8:4 (April), 30–32.

Berenson, R., and Pawlson, L. (1984). "The Medicare Prospective Payment System and the Care of the Frail Elderly." *Journal of the American Geriatrics Society* 32:11 (November), 843–848.

Birnbaum, H., Holland, S., and Lenhart, G. (1991). "Savings Estimate for a Medicare Insured Group." *Health Care Financing Review* 12:4 (Summer), 39–48.

Boerstler, H., Carlough, T., and Schlenker, R. (1991). "Analysis of Nursing Home Capital Reimbursement Systems." *Health Care Financing Review* 12:3 (Spring), 53–60.

Buchanan, J., Arnold, S., Bell, R., and Witsberger, C. (1990). *Financial Impact of Nursing Home-based Geriatric Nurse Practitioners.* Santa Monica, Calif.: Rand Corporation.

Buchanan, R. (1982). "The Financial Status of the New Medical-Industrial Complex." *Inquiry* 19:4 (Winter), 308–316.

Buchanan, R., and Eastaugh, S. (1991). "Financial Analysis of the Proprietary Long-Term Care Industry." Working paper, George Washington University.

Buchanan, R., Madel, R., and Persons, D. (1991). "Medicaid Coverage of Nursing Home Care: A National Survey of Reimbursement Policies." *Health Care Financing Review* 13:1 (Supplement), 55–72.

Burton, J. (1985). "The House-Call: An Important Service for the Frail Elderly." *Journal of the American Geriatrics Society* 33:3 (March), 291–293.

Burwell, B., Adams, E., and Meiners M. (1990). "Spend-down of Assets before Medicaid Eligibility among Elderly Nursing-Home Recipients." *Medical Care* 28:4 (April), 349–362.

Cafferata, G., and Stone, R. (1989). "The Caregiving Role: Dimensions of Burden and Benefits." *Comprehensive Gerontology* 3 (Supplement), 57–64.

Cameron, J. (1985). "Case-Mix and Resource Use in Long-Term Care." *Medical Care* 23:4 (April), 296–309.

Cleverley, W., ed. (1991). "Financing Long-Term Care: Selected Papers." *Topics in Health Care Financing* 17:4 (Summer), 1–77.

———. (1990). "After the Fall: Reasons behind 1989 Hospital Closings." *Healthcare Financial Management* 44:6 (July), 22–24.

Cohen, J., and Holahan, J. (1986). "An Evaluation of Current Approaches to Nursing Home Capital Reimbursement." *Inquiry* 23:1 (Spring), 23–39.

Coopers and Lybrand. (1991). "Continuing Care Retirement Communities: A Guide to Health Care Facilities." New York: Coopers and Lybrand.

Cryns, A., Nichols, R., Katz, L., and Calkins, E. (1989). "The Hierarchical Structure of Geriatric Patient Satisfaction." *Medical Care* 27:8 (August), 802–816.

Cunningham, P., and Bice, T. (1989). "Home Care in the National Medical Expenditure Survey." *Caring* 8:1 (January), 57–59.

Cunningham, R. (1985). "The Evolution of Hospice." *Hospitals* 59:8 (April 16), 124–126.

Curran, S., and Brecht, S. (1985). "A Perspective on Risks for Lifecare Projects." *Real Estate Financial Journal* 25:2 (Summer), 65–71.

Davidson, G., Moscovice, I., and McCaffrey, D. (1989). "Allocative Efficiency of Case Managers for the Elderly." *Health Services Research* 24:4 (October), 539–553.

Davis, M. (1991). "Nursing Home Quality: A Review and Analysis." *Medical Care Review* 48:2 (Summer), 129–65.

Deane, R. (1985). "Principles of Nursing Home Reimbursement." *Healthcare Strategic Management* 3:9 (August), 25–33.

Department of Health and Human Services. (1991). *Results of the 1990 National Nursing Home Survey.* NCHS advanced data. Hyattsville, Maryland.

———. (1986). "Limits on Home Health Agency Costs—Final Notice." *Federal Register* 51:104 (May 30), 19734–19741.

DesHarnais, S., Wroblewski, R., and Schumacher, D. (1990). "How Medicare Prospective Payment System Affects Psychiatric Patients." *Inquiry* 27:4 (Winter), 382–388.

Dranove, D. (1985). "An Empirical Study of a Hospital-based Home Care Program." *Inquiry* 22:1 (Spring), 59–66.

Evans, D. (1990). "Estimated Prevalence of Alzheimer's Disease in the United States." *Milbank Quarterly* 68:2 (Summer), 267–289.

Fackelmann, K. (1985). "Insurers Should Be Urged to Market Long-Term Care Policies." *Modern Healthcare* 15:1 (January 4), 62.

Fahs, M., Muller, C., and Schechter, M. (1989). "Primary Medical Care for Elderly Patients." *Journal of Community Health* 14:2 (Summer), 89–99.

Ferris, A., and Wyszewianski, L. (1990). "Quality of Ambulatory Care for the Elderly: Formulating Evaluation Criteria." *Health Care Financing Review* 12:1 (Fall), 31–38.

Freeborn, D., Pope, C., Mullooly, J., and McFarland, B. (1990). "Consistently High Users of Medical Care among the Elderly." *Medical Care* 28:6 (June), 527–539.

Fries, B. (1990). "Comparing Case-Mix Systems for Nursing Home Payment." *Health Care Financing Review* 11:4 (Summer), 103–119.

Fries, G., and Cooney, L. (1985). "Resource Utilization Groups: A Patient Classification System for Long-Term Care." *Medical Care* 23:2 (February), 110–122.

Getzen, T., and Elsenhans, V. (1986). "Insuring against Poverty from Long-Term Care." *Business and Health* 3:10 (October), 20–21.

Giardina, C., Fottler, M., Shewchuk, R., and Hill, D. (1990). "Hospital Diversification into Long-Term Care." *Health Care Management Review* 15:1 (Winter), 71–82.

Grannemann, T. (1991). "Priority Setting: A Sensible Approach to Medicaid Policy?" *Inquiry* 28:3 (Fall), 300–305.

Haug, M. (1985). "Home Care for the Ill Elderly—Who Benefits?" *American Journal of Public Health* 75:2 (February), 127–128.

Health Care Financing Administration (HCFA). (1991). "Trends in the Utilization of Medicare Home Health Agency Services." Washington, D.C.: DHHS.

Hedrick, S., and Inui, T. (1986). "The Effectiveness and Cost of Home Care: An Information Synthesis." *Health Services Research* 20:6 (part II, February), 851–880.

Hedrick, S., Rothman, M., and Chapko. M. (1991). "Adult Day Health Care Evaluation Study." *Health Services Research* 25:6 (February), 935–960.

Hiller, M., and Sugarman, D. (1984). "Private Nursing Homes in the U.S.: Effects of Ownership and Affiliation." Unpublished monograph, University of New Hampshire, Durham.

Hughes, S. (1992). "A Randomized Trial of the Cost Effectiveness of Home Care." *Health Services Research* 26:6, 844–855.

———. (1985). "Apples and Oranges? A Review of Evaluations of Community-Based Long-Term Care." *Health Services Research* 20:4 (October), 461–488.

Infante, M. (1991). Medicare Reimbursement. Baltimore: Health Professions Press.

Institute of Medicine. (1986). *Improving the Quality of Care in Nursing Homes*. Washington, D.C.: National Academy of Sciences.

Intergovernmental Health Policy Project of the National Governor's Association. (1989). "Recent and Proposed Changes in State Medicaid Programs: A 50-State Survey." Washington, D.C.: George Washington University (Fall).

Johnson, C., and Grant, L. (1985). *The Nursing Home in American Society*. Baltimore: Johns Hopkins University Press.

Kane, R., and Kane, R. (1991). "A Nursing Home in Your Future." *New England Journal of Medicine* 324:9 (February 28), 627–629.

———. (1985). "The Feasibility of Universal Long-Term Care Benefits." *New England Journal of Medicine* 312:21 (May 23), 1357–1364.

Kass, D. (1987). "Economies of Scale and Scope in the Provision of Home Health Services." *Journal of Health Economics* 6:1 (February), 130–146.

Kemper, P. (1990). "Case Management Agency Systems of Administering Long-Term Care: Evidence from the Channeling Demonstration." *Gerontologist* 30:6 (June), 817–824.

Kemper, P., and Murtaugh, C. (1991). "Lifetime Use of Nursing Home Care." *New England Journal of Medicine* 324:9 (February 28), 595–600.

Kenney, G. (1991). "Understanding the Effects of PPS on Medicare Home Health Use." *Inquiry* 28:2 (Spring), 129–39.

Kenney, G., and Holahan, J. (1990). "The Nursing Home Market and Hospital Discharge Delays." *Inquiry* 27:1 (Spring), 73–85.

Knowles, J. (1973). "The Hospital." *Scientific American* 229:3 (March), 128–137.

Koble, R., and Dwyer, F. (1986). "Diagnosing the Physician as Gatekeeper in Hospice Marketing." *Journal of Health Care Marketing* 6:1 (March), 23–24.

Koren, M. (1986). "Home Care—Who Cares?" *New England Journal of Medicine* 314:14 (April 3), 917–920.

Kornblatt, E., Fisher, M., and MacMillan, D. (1985). "Impact of DRGs on Home Health Nursing." *Quality Review Bulletin* 11:10 (October), 290–294.

Kramer, A., Shaughnessy, P., and Pettigrew, M. (1985). "Cost-Effectiveness Implications Based on a Comparison of Nursing Home and Home Health Case Mix." *Health Services Research* 20:4 (October), 387–405.

Kurt Salmon and Associates Survey of Home Health Care. (1989). "Could America Have a Home Care Glut?" *Home Health Journal* 6:3 (March), 5.

Lane, L. (1985). "The Potential of Long-Term Care Insurance." *Pride Institute Journal of Long-Term Home Health Care* 14:3 (Summer), 18.

Laventhol and Horwath (1990). "Annual Report on the Life Care Industry." National Health Practice Group, Philadelphia.

Legg, D., and Lamb, C. (1986). "The Role of Referral Agents in the Marketing of Home Health Services." *Journal of Health Care Marketing* 6:1 (March), 51–56.

Leutz, W., Malone, J., Kistner, M., O'Bar, T., and Ripley, J. (1990). "Financial Performance in the Social HMOs." *Health Care Financing Review* 12:1 (Fall), 9–18.

Lewis, M., Leake, B., Clark, V., and Leal, M. (1990). "Changes in Case Mix and Outcomes of Readmissions to Nursing Homes." *Health Services Research* 24:6 (February), 713–727.

Liu, K., Coughlin, T., and McBride, T. (1991). "Predicting Nursing Home Admission and Length of Stay." *Medical Care* 29:2 (February), 125–141.

Liu, K., McBride, T., and Coughlin, T. (1990). "Costs of Community Care for Disabled Elderly Persons: The Policy Implications." *Inquiry* 27:1 (Spring), 61–72.

Liu, K., and Perozek, M. (1991). "Effects of Multiple Admissions on Nursing Home Use: Implications for Front-end Policies." *Inquiry* 28:2 (Spring), 140–50.

Manton, K., Vertrees, J., and Woodbury, M. (1990). "Functionally and Medically Defined Subgroups of Nursing Home Populations." *Health Care Financing Review* 12:1 (Fall), 47–61.

McCall, N., Knickman, J., and Bauer, E. (1991). "A New Approach to Long-Term Care." *Health Affairs* 10:1 (Spring), 164–176.

McKay, N. (1991). "Effect of Chain Ownership on Nursing Home Costs." *Health Services Research* 26:1 (April), 109–124.

Meiners, M. (1983). "The Case for Long-Term Care Insurance." *Health Affairs* 2:2 (Summer), 55–79.

Moinpour, C., Polissar, L., and Conrad, D. (1990). "Factors Associated with Length of Stay in a Hospice." *Medical Care* 28:4 (April), 363–368.

Mor, V., and Kidder, D. (1985). "Cost Savings in Hospice: Final Results of the National Hospice Study." *Health Services Research* 20:4 (October), 407–422.

Moran, D., and Kennell, D. (1986). "The Developing Market for Long-Term Care Insurance." ICF Inc., Washington, D.C.

Moss, F., and Halamandaris, V. (1977). *Too Old, Too Sick, Too Bad: Nursing Homes in America*. Germantown, Md.: Aspen.

National Academy of Sciences. (1986). *For-Profit Enterprises in Health Care*. Washington, D.C.: NAS Press.

National Association for Home Care. (1991). *Public and Private Expenditures for Post-acute Care*. Washington, D.C.

National Association of Insurance Commissioners (NAIC). (1991). "Recommended Model Standards for the Sale of Long-Term Care Insurance Policies." Washington, D.C.

National Underwriter (NU). (1991). "Home Care." *National Underwriter* 4–4/88, 23–24.

Newcomer, R., Harrington, C., and Friedlob, A. (1990). "Social HMOs: Assessing Their Initial Experience." *Health Services Research* 25:3 (August), 425–452.

Nyman, J. (1989). "Analysis of Nursing Home Bed Supply." *Health Services Research* 24:4 (October), 511–537.

Nyman, J., Bricker, D., and Link, D. (1990). "Technical Efficiency in Nursing Homes." *Medical Care* 28:6 (June), 541–550.

Paradis, L. (1985). "Hospice: The First DRG." *Health Matrix* 2:4 (January), 32–34.

Pawlson, G. (1990). "Financing Long-Term Care: An Insurance Based Approach." *Journal of the American Geriatrics Society* 38:6 (June), 696–703.

Phillips, C., and Hawes, C. (1992). "Nursing Home Casemix Classification and RUGS-II in Texas." *Medical Care* 20:2 (February), 105–116.

Phillips, R. (1984). "The Fireman's Fund Experience." In P. Feinstein, M. Gornick, and J. Greenberg (eds.), *Long-Term Care Financing and Delivery Systems: Exploring Some Alternatives*, 37–44. Washington, D.C.: HCFA.

Rice, T., Thomas, K., and Weissert, W. (1991). "Effect of Owning Private Long-Term Care Insurance Policies on Out-of-Pocket Costs." *Health Services Research* 25:6 (February), 907–933.

Rockefeller, J. (1990). "The Pepper Commission Report on Comprehensive Health Care." *New England Journal of Medicine* 323:14 (October 4), 1005–1007.

Rowland, D., Lyons, B., Neuman, P., Salganicoff, A., and Taghavi, L. (1989). *Defining the Functionally Impaired Elderly Population*. Washington, D.C.: American Association of Retired Persons.

Rubin, R., Wiener, J., and Meiners, M. (1990). "Private Long-Term Care Insurance: Simulations of a Potential Market." *Medical Care* 27:2 (February), 182–192.

Ruchlin, H. (1988). "Continuing Care Retirement Communities: An Analysis of Financial Viability and Health Care Coverage." *The Gerontologist* 28:2 (February), 156–162.

Russell, L. (1990). *Medicare's New Hospital Payment System: Is It Working?* Washington, D.C.: Brookings.

Schlenker, R. (1991). "Nursing Home Costs, Medicaid Rates, and Profits under Alternative Medicaid Payment Systems." *Health Services Research* 26:5 (December), 606–626.

Sexton, T., Leiken, A., Sleeper, S., and Coburn, A. (1989). "Impact of Prospective Reimbursement on Nursing Home Efficiency." *Medical Care* 27:2 (February), 154–162.

Shapiro, E., and Tate, R. (1989). "Is Health Care Changing? A Comparison between Physician, Hospital, Nursing Home, and Home Care Use of Two Elderly Cohorts." *Medical Care* 27:11 (November), 1002–1013.

Shaughnessy, P., and Kramer, A. (1990). "Increased Needs of Patients in Nursing Homes and Patients Receiving Home Health Care." *New England Journal of Medicine* 322:1 (January 4), 21–27.

Shaughnessy, P., Schlenker, R., and Polesovsky, M. (1986). "Medicaid and Non-Medicaid Case Mix Differences in Colorado Nursing Homes." *Medical Care* 24:6 (June), 482–495.

Sheffler, R. (1985). "Mental Health Services: New Policies and Estimates." *Generations* 9:2 (Summer), 33–35.

Shnelle, J., Newman, D., and Fogarty, T. (1991). "Assessment and Quality Control of Incontinence." *Journal of the American Geriatrics Society* 39:2 (February), 165–171.

Short, P., Cunningham, P., and Mueller, C. (1991). "Standardizing Nursing-Home Admission Dates for Short-Term Hospital Stays." *Medical Care* 29:2 (February), 97–113.

Silverman, H. (1991). "Medicare Covered Home Health Services." *Health Care Financing Review* 12:2 (February), 113–125.

Skellie, F., Mobley, G., and Coan, R. (1982). "Cost-Effectiveness of Community-based Long-Term Care." *American Journal of Public Health* 72:4 (April), 353–358.

Smith, D. (1990). "Population Ecology and Integration of Hospitals and Nursing Homes." *Milbank Quarterly* 68:4 (December), 561–595.

Somers, S., and Merrill, J. (1991). "Supporting States' Efforts for Long-Term Care Insurance." *Health Affairs* 10:1 (Spring), 177–179.

Soumerai, S., Ross, D., and Avorn, J. (1991). "Effect of Medicaid Drug-payment Limits on Admission to Hospitals and Nursing Homes." *New England Journal of Medicine* 325:15 (October 10), 1072–1077.

Spector, W., and Drugovich, M. (1989). "Reforming Nursing Home Quality Regulation: Impact on Cited Deficiencies and Nursing Home Outcomes." *Medical Care* 27:8 (August), 789–801.

Stephens, S., and Christianson, J. (1986). *Informal Care of the Elderly.* Lexington, Mass.: Lexington Books.

Stone, R., and Short, P. (1990). "The Competing Demands of Employment and Informal Caregiving to Disabled Elders." *Medical Care* 28:6 (June), 513–526.

Sulvetta, M., and Holahan, J. (1986). "Cost and Case-Mix Differences between Hospital-based and Free-standing Nursing Homes." *Health Care Financing Review* 7:3 (Spring), 75–84.

Swan, J., and Benjamin, A. (1990). "Medicare Home Health Utilization as a Function of Nursing Home Market Factors." *Health Services Research* 25:3 (August), 479–498.

Swan, J., and Harrington, C. (1986). "Estimating Undersupply of Nursing Home Beds in States." *Health Services Research* 21:1 (April), 57–83.

Teschke, D. (1991). "Elder Program Promotes Patient Loyalty." *Healthcare Financial Management* 45:3 (March), 110.

Thorpe, K. (1991). "The RUG System: Its Effect on Nursing Home Case Mix and Costs." *Inquiry* 28:4 (Winter), 357–365.

Tilson, D. (1990). *Aging in Place: Supporting the Frail Elderly in Residential Environments.* Glenview, Ill.: Scott Foresman.

Topolnicki, D. (1985). "The Broken Promise of Life-Care Communities." *Money* (April), 150–157.

U.S. Congress. (1991). *Medicaid Source Book: Background Data and Analysis.* House Committee on Energy and Commerce, Subcommittee on Health. Washington, D.C.: U.S. Government Printing Office.

Vladeck, B. (1980). *Unloving Care.* New York: Basic Books.

Wagner, M. (1990). "Gains in Home Infusion Therapy." *Modern Healthcare* (May 21), 87.

Wallack, S. (1991). "LifePlans Study of Long-Term Care Insurance." Washington, D.C.: HIAA.

Ware, J., et al. (1986). "Comparison of Health Outcomes at a HMO with Those of Fee-for-Service Care." *Lancet* 8488 (May 3), 1017–1022.

Weissert, W. (1985). "Seven Reasons Why It Is So Difficult to Make Community-based Long-Term Care Cost-Effective." *Health Services Research* 20:4 (October), 423–433.

Weissert, W., and Cready, C. (1989). "Toward a Model for Improved Targeting of Aged at Risk of Institutionalization." *Health Services Research* 24:4 (October), 485–509.

Weissert, W., and Scanlon, W. (1985). "Determinants of Nursing Home Discharge Status." *Medical Care* 23:4 (April), 333–343.

Wieland, D., Rubenstein, L., Ouslander, J., and Martin, S. (1986). "Organizing an Academic Nursing Home: Impacts on Institutionalized Elderly." *Journal of the American Medical Association* 255:19 (May 16), 2622–2627.

Williams, B., Phillips, E., Torner, J., and Irvine, A. (1990). "Predicting Utilization of Home Health Resources." *Medical Care* 28:5 (May), 379–391.

Wilson, C., and Weissert, W. (1989). "Private Long-Term Care Insurance: After Coverage Restrictions Is There Anything Left?" *Inquiry* 26:4 (Winter), 493–506.

Winklevoss, H., and Powell, A. (1989). *Continuing Care Retirement Communities: An Empirical, Financial, and Legal Analysis*. Homewood, Ill.: Richard Irwin Inc.

Wynd, W., Stewart, M., and Hunter, H. (1991). "Marketing, Financial Goals Play into CCRC Refund Plan." *Healthcare Financial Management* 45:2 (February), 50–60.

Zmijewski, M. (1984). "Methodological Issues Related to the Estimation of Financial Distress Prediction Models." *Journal of Accounting Research* 22:1 (Supplement), 59–82.

Part Three

STRATEGY SELECTION, MARKET ANALYSIS, DIVERSIFICATION, AND PRICING

Chapter 5

Diversification for the Single Hospital

It is futile to attempt to eliminate risk, and questionable to try to minimize it. But it is essential that the diversification risks taken be the right risks.
—Peter F. Drucker

The art of roasting was discovered in a Chinese village that did not cook its food. A mischievous child accidentally set fire to a house with a pig inside, and the villagers poking discovered a new delicacy. This eventually led to a rash of house fires. The moral of the story is: when you do not understand how the pig gets cooked, you have to burn a whole house down every time.
—Rosabeth Moss Kanter

Just as the March of Dimes diversified out of the polio business, so should many hospitals diversify out of the hospital business.
—James L. Elrod

The most impressive organizational change in the health economy during the 1980s was the emergence of health systems where the hospital represented the financial center of the system. Many hospitals view diversification into health and nonhealth (unrelated) ventures as being their only chance for survival in the 1990s. The hospital sector is a good example of the old French couplet, "That's a very bad animal; when it's attacked, it defends itself." The good news about all this talk of "diversification for a fighting chance at survival" is that it is not true in the majority of cases. Indeed, many hospitals diversify because they are cash rich (Eastaugh, 1988, 1984). The bad news is that for some hospitals this rhetoric is appropriate and accurate. The terrible news is that many hospitals have yet to discover that one cannot simply relabel a number of unsystematic, disjointed ventures as the hospital's diversification plan (Harrigan 1991). A health facility's strength cannot be built through coalescing weaknesses and promoting a collection of uncoordinated joint ventures. Hospitals planning to diversify might consider the following three bits of advice:

1. Do not mess with structure before one has a comprehensive strategy.
2. Do not kill a new service line with insufficient initial capitalization and unreasonable expectations as to profitability.
3. When a mistake has been made, jettison the service line and "recommit the resources to the core business" (Eastaugh 1985).

In this chapter we analyze the diversification trend in the hospital sector from an economic point of view. The emphasis is on diversification into related lines of business. Historically, many economists had assumed that hospitals maximized their cash flow (net revenue plus depreciation) in order to continually expand their facility. This tendency was often called "empire building" (Coddington 1988). However, in the 1980s the empire-building imperative was directed away from building beds (Alexander 1990; Conrad and Mick 1987) and toward generating cash flow outside the inpatient arena. Successful diversification can (1) allow accumulation of equity capital to offset anticipated lower capital and operating payment rates, (2) provide a storehouse of liquid assets for feeding the mothership hospital, and (3) generate wealth sheltered from the malpractice attorneys and rate regulators (which can also be channeled back to the mothership to cover unexpected contingencies). Diversification can also generate operational efficiencies for the hospital—for example, if the hospital controls the capacity of its home health agency or nursing home, it can facilitate better inpatient discharge planning (Clement 1988).

DIVERSIFICATION: A CAUTIONARY NOTE

Diversification efforts expand beyond the inpatient context, often including nonhealth (unrelated) independent corporate ventures. One can only speculate whether all this diversification and corporate restructuring have increased profitability and reduced business risk for the core mothership. The logic is obvious: spin-off into some nonregulated or less regulated sources of revenue to underwrite the overregulated hospital. Clement (1987) offered a limited test of the two hypotheses concerning risk and profits with data from 200 California hospitals. Unfortunately, the data base cannot link each subsidiary to the parent hospital, and all diversification ventures need not report to the facility file.

Successful hospital diversification efforts would in almost every case not show up in Clement's data set, the California Health Facilities Commission (CHFC) annual hospital financial disclosure reports. Unless the subsidiary was reporting to CHFC as part of a given hospital, Clement could not connect the parent (hospital) to the child (subsidiary, arm, or independent firm). With the help of hospital counsel, the nonhospital corporations are set up by a parent holding company (or any of a number of other options), with nonoverlapping independent corporate boards, which in turn funnel the new ventures' profits through conduits (e.g., foundations) back into the mothership hospital. All this "shell game" of fund transfers is done with a wink and a nod, and nothing is put down on paper that requires the satellite ventures to help the mothership institution (the hospital). For example, a local hospital on the East Coast gave away $109 million in assets to capitalize over 100 new corporations that have no legal connection to the mothership hospital.

A well-planned diversification program can allow a hospital to create a network of for-profit subsidiaries and holding companies (Gilbert 1986; Sax 1986). While diversification can save a hospital from a "plodder" or negative-growth existence, poorly selected multiple diversification programs can result in loss of autonomy (takeover or closure). Hospitals have a vast range of technical abilities to analyze return on investment and operate as "active seekers" of emerging diversification options (Pegels and Rogers 1989). The best options for diversification are those not yet documented in any journal article. In the parlance of an economist or organizational theorist (Porter 1980), this is labeled the "advantage of being first" (or at least first in a hospital's market catchment area).

The statistical evidence concerning the advantage of being first is far from uniform. For example, Glazer (1985) reported that in large business firms first entrants are, on average, as likely to fail as second entrants. First entrants carry the risk of being at the early stage in the development of a service market, so that there is a greater danger that customer demand will not increase to the extent predicted. Business risk is not as easily quantifiable as pro forma income (Boles and Glenn 1986), but the analyst should study the three basic factors: (1) effect on revenue stability (revenue risk), (2) effect on debt dependency and capital structure (financial risk), and (3) effect on the variability of the cost structure (expense risk).

If the new market does not reach the achieved critical mass and exceed the break-even point within a reasonable time, the first entrant will usually label the venture a failure. In the health context, the message might be: Do not try significant investment in a capital-intensive new technology (e.g., plasma apheresis) until one observes a first entrant succeed somewhere in the nation. If the initial investment is not substantial, hospitals need not be so risk averse. However, if the investment at risk is substantial, a second entrant in the market can often experience the safety of diversification into a proven market, soon to reach appreciable size (market demand). On the other hand, the first entrant may still reap some intangible benefits of better knowledge of the market and consumer tastes (preferences) and remarket elsewhere (Rindler 1989).

Any hospital should ex ante (up front) calculate the expected break-even point and a judgment of reasonable time to expect results (e.g., achieve the break-even point). Such calculations will be open to ex post judgment (e.g., as to whether a second injection of capital is needed to get the new service off the ground; Urban and Hauser 1989). However, a good marketing survey of the external environment is probably the most critical determinant of successful diversification ventures. When a hospital seems to jump off a cliff, either through excessive diversification or total inaction, if the researcher inquires as to why, 99 percent of the time everything the individual managers did made perfect sense as a response to internal politics. In other words, the fatal mistake was to let internal pressures block out external reality concerning risk and payoff (Placella 1986; Leontiades 1988).

Freestanding Emergency Care (FEC) Centers

In the spirit of a "hospital without walls," many hospitals diversified into FECs in the mid-1980s. The FECs that have experienced the most financial success have typically specialized: imaging, surgery, birthing, cancer care, health promotion and health clubs, or psychiatric care. Some hospitals expect to receive 40 percent of their revenues from specialized FECs by the year 1999, and the number of such FECs is projected to reach 1,700 to 1,900. But if specialized FECs present an example of a market niche turning into a storybook source of cash flow, general FECs offering basic urgent care present a far different story. General FECs went through a period of boom and bust. The boom occurred when many FECs were financed by leases with physician investors in the period 1982–85, and the bust occurred after 1986 when investors discovered that federal tax laws had changed, and there was no strategic advantage to being first in a market (general FECs are easily replicated by the competition, and product differentiation and segmentation based on prestige or quality are difficult). The insurance market has also changed in a negative direction for general FECs, because their brand of episodic care is not reimbursed by HMOs and PPOs that discriminate against independent FECs. General FECs have reached a state of market saturation and have declined in numbers in recent years (American Hospital Association [AHA] 1991).

To test a model of market failure for general FECs, financial data were collected from 241 FECs for the period 1984–90. In this mature industry 52 FECs went bankrupt in the period 1987–90. Lease information was included in the notes to the FECs' financial statements, and lease payments were capitalized for each firm using the market rate of interest. Use of a multiple discriminant model (MDM), as described in chapter 4, yielded a ratio of capitalized leases to total assets of 0.486 in bankrupt FECs three years prior to closure, but a ratio of 0.129 for nonbankrupt FECs. These results strongly suggest that leasing contributes to the accuracy of this failure-prediction model, but the results need further validation. The coefficients in the MDM model are inherently biased upward because the same FECs used to construct the model are also the firms classified by the model. Employing the model drafted by Booth et al. (1989) and Gentry, Newbold and Whitford (1987), one estimates parameters using a subset of each of the two FEC groups and then makes predictions on the sample based on the parameters established as a validation sample test. Six different replications of this test were performed with 26 FECs in each group. A simple t-test applied to the results rejected the hypothesis that there was no difference between the groups and strongly supported the view that the model does have significant discriminating power. In the stepwise discriminant model the variable with the greatest F-value was the ratio of capitalized leases to total assets.

Pitfalls and Fads That Fail

One basic axiom in the business world is the "strategic advantage of being first," being the first entrant or the first to move into a new product line. This idea does not always work in the business world, and it sometimes does not work in the health field. Consider the example of urgent-care centers, which grew in number from 300 in 1982 to 1,380 in 1986. Very few urgent-care centers have been initiated since 1986 because the prospector advantage of being a first mover did not exist. Urgent-care centers are an idea that can be easily imitated at low cost by competitors. Therefore, unless the center can differentiate on the basis of quality and promote a product with a quality label (brand name), it is hard to retain market share and profit margins in the long run. Some hospitals produced redesigned emergency-department walk-in services that competed with the hospital's own urgent-care center. This sort of service cannibalism, competing with oneself, is a very poor strategy.

If entry cost is low, and skills and experience can be easily transferred to the competition by ex-employees or consultants, first-entrant advantages do not exist. But if a hospital can be one of only 80 hospitals in the country with a positron emission tomography (PET) machine, the strategic advantage of being a first mover into this product line was high in 1991 (even if it cost the facility $2.2 million). On the other hand, the strategic advantage of being the sixth entrant into the market with the single photon emission computed tomography (SPECT) machine, a faster and cheaper technology than a PET scanner, may be low. Over 1,300 SPECT machines existed in hospitals and physician offices in 1991. Reimbursement is another concern in adopting a new product line or keeping an existing service. If a hospital's market has too high a share of cheap payers that refuse to pay break-even prices of $510 for a SPECT brain scan or $820 for a heart study, the smart manager may act as a defender and avoid (or drop) this technology.

Charges, the prices set by the provider, are a less important concern for the most highly regulated health services with few patients paying price. But some services are more price sensitive and offer the consumer time to shop for a better price, like maternity care or sports medicine. For price-sensitive services, volume building on low prices (and package pricing including aftercare) can be a good strategy. Other services are more physician driven and receive biomedical research dollars, like AIDS care, oncology, and cardiology. Price deals for these services are not a good business strategy. In any case, if the product line is a major source of prestige to the hospital, the board can designate the department a center of excellence, for example, in AIDS, cancer care, heart surgery, cholesterol control and lipid research, family medicine, sports medicine, arthritis, or long-term care (vintage caring).

CCRCs should take advantage of what marketing professionals call double-loop learning and realize after a second look at the issue that the assumptions underpinning the projections are overoptimistic. For example, if one is building a CCRC in a community with too much spending power and too many rich elderly homeowners, then they have the financial capability to purchase full-service private care in their own homes. On a second loop in the learning process, the CCRC may wish to downsize the facility.

DIVERSIFICATION: THE UPSIDE

Diversification can produce a more adaptable, flexible health care system that offers the institution new avenues to equity markets (Herzlinger 1989; Mick 1988) and offers patients greater continuity of care. Internal, strategic, and competitive benefits can be gained through new ventures. What is viewed at one hospital as a "burden that saps management talent" is viewed by a more adaptable institution as an invigorating challenge for management and staff. A diversification effort, when carried out appropriately, can be a powerful mode of altering the institution's competitive position, especially as management gains sufficient experience with assessing business risk. Optimally, diversification is not a risk strategy but, rather, a syndication-of-risk strategy. New-venture strategies should be analyzed using the portfolio theory of business management, where multiple business concerns can dampen the extremes of variability in cash flow in any single business (Zelman and Parham 1990).

Diversification can be viewed as a strategic management issue in the development of a marketing plan. For example, the basic ways to build market share involve the development of (1) more markets for current services, (2) more services for current markets, (3) more use of current services by the current market, and (4) a mixed strategy of growth in the first three areas. Some argue that the hospital that fails to diversify will be relegated to a "plodder" or negative-growth existence in the 1990s. Those hospitals most frequently employing the diversification and consolidation strategy (investor-owned or contract-managed hospitals) doubled their market share of hospital beds in the early 1980s (Shortell 1989).

In a classic business marketing text, Kotler (1991) argued that marketing-posture decisions usually precede marketing-mix decisions. Hospital marketing efforts seldom get by the initial posture-decision stage. Hospitals make the choice about how broad or narrow a diversification effort should be made (posture decision) but, at least prior to 1983, they almost never considered the strategic decision about whether to use a market-penetration or a market-skimming pricing strategy (Joskow 1981; Eastaugh 1984). Hospital administrators frequently submit to tortuous, protracted debates concerning whether their posture decisions should be narrow (e.g., pediatric outpatient services) or broadly diversified (e.g., a pediatric inpatient special unit, a neonatal intensive-care unit, and an organized pediatric outpatient department).

Some types of diversification appear to be simple examples of imitative entry or "bandwagoning," such as the explosion of podiatric services or speech pathology services. Posture variables considered by administrators and trustees include whether the new proposed hospital-based service offers a favorable degree of product differentiation relative to the service offered by incumbents (physicians currently providing the service in private offices). For example, does the hospital offer better quality, better convenience to its intermediate consumers (doctors) to practice medicine more productively, better provision of consumer education to foster increased utilization of health services, or better access to the ultimate consumers (patients)? The hospital, as a centralized service-distribution innovator, has the potential to reduce the time cost to physicians and the travel time cost to patients in the provision of many acute-care medical services.

The "new lines of business" we shall consider in this chapter are all related ventures—that is, they expand existing medical product lines of service. The central problem in modeling hospital diversification and its impact on the operating ratio is that the relationship is interdependent. For example, diversification might improve the operating ratio in a causal fashion, but the baseline operating ratio might be inversely proportional to the hospital's self-perceived need to diversify. Conversely, a hospital might need a certain baseline operating ratio to afford to finance a diversification effort or to gamble. Diversification might also occur because of expectations as to change in the operating ratio. In other words, the level of diversification and the level of operating ratio are hypothesized to be jointly dependent or endogenous within the context of two simultaneous equations. Success varies as a function of the strategy selected (Eastaugh 1991; White 1990; Sabatino 1989).

STRATEGY SELECTION

Hospital strategy making can focus on two basic areas: operational management (productivity and economic efficiency to yield cost leadership) or strategic management of product lines (diversification, divestment, and differentiation). Strategy is especially important to institutions experiencing a decline in performance, since working harder on the current strategy is not likely to win the day. According to Shortell, Morrison, and Friedman (1990), Ginn (1990), Luke and Begun (1988), there are four archetypal strategies: defender, analyzer, prospector, and reactor. Defenders emphasize operational management, improving productivity, cutting excess variable costs, and achieving cost leadership (lower expenses, better profit margins). Defenders may perform some product-line diversification, but the main strategy involves productivity and cost leadership.

The paradox of the Shortell study (1990) is that the hospital CEOs that were labeled "defenders" gave the least emphasis to productivity and cost-containment strategies. Therefore, those CEOs might better be labeled reactors. Research question number one in this chapter involves development of a better typology of archetypes beyond the standard list of four developed by Miles and Snow (1978) and utilized by Shortell. The three archetypal strategies involving increasing reliance on diversification are the analyzer, prospector, and reactor approaches. In the Shortell, Morrison and Friedman (1990) study prospectors did two and one-half times as much diversification as defenders and had an operating profit margin as a percentage of net revenue that was 1.9 points higher in 1983 and 5.7 points higher at the end of 1987. These results are at odds with other studies that suggest less success with the prospector diversification strategy (Fox 1989; Eastaugh 1988). Perhaps Shortell's results were atypical because he surveyed members of decentralized multihospital systems and did not sample freestanding hospitals or highly centralized hospital systems like Humana. Research question number two involves measuring the financial success or failure of diversification for a wider universe of hospitals utilizing more recent data.

Professionals in organizational theory and behavior tend to prefer the prospector strategy. This generalization seems to hold for a number of industries, ranging from airlines to trucking, as well as the hospital industry. For example, Cheng and Kesner (1988) reported that airline prospectors responded more aggressively and successfully to deregulation than managers in the other three strategic archetypes. Unfortunately, the authors did not discuss the resulting financial performance. Given that financial success is a multiattribute idea, research question number three in this chapter will assess the success of alternative strategies using a variety of financial ratios (not just the operating profit margin as a percentage of operating revenue).

The Changing Payment Environment

Environment has an impact on institutional strategy. Hospitals have experienced four basic payment environments since 1966. The end of the 1960s can be characterized as a placid random environment of cost-plus reimbursement that was so munificent that hospitals did not need strategies. The period 1970–82 can be characterized as a placid clustered environment that was relatively static but less munificent, so some strategy was required to maximize reimbursement by gaming (falsifying) the cost reports given to payers. The benefits of gaming cost reports for Medicare had diminished to nothing by 1990 (Cowles 1991). The mid-1980s, with the growth in managed-care plans and Medicare DRGs, can be characterized as a disturbed reactive environment of new competitive forces and dynamic change. Since 1987 the environment has been turbulent, characterized by more competition, tougher payment policies, and more dynamic interest in spinning off less regulated forms of diversification (outpatient care and unrelated diversification; Eastaugh 1990).

The initial price discounts negotiated by managed-care plans with little leverage and market share and the initial three years of DRG prices through 1986 were not as difficult as they could have been. The DRG prices were set based on unaudited cost reports and were 4.4 percent higher than they should have been under the 1987 federal rules. The second reason why the mid-1980s should be labeled a reactive rather than a turbulent environment involves the slow mechanism by which the DRG price scheme was phased in. The initial price limits for the DRG prices were based on each hospital's historical cost for treating patients in its area and were thus not that difficult to live with. However, the current payment prices offered by the majority of payers are more stringent and could be labeled "barebones reimbursement" by some facilities.

There is general agreement that hospitals now operate in a turbulent environment of numerous opportunities and threats to diversify and also to enhance productivity. When Miles and Snow developed the four archetypes in 1978, they speculated that all strategies were equally viable, but under our current turbulent conditions certain strategies may turn out to be superior. To determine if this is the case, a random sample of 400 hospital CEOs was surveyed in the fall of 1990. The hospitals were short-term acute-care nongovernmental facilities with more than 75 beds in the AHA 1988 annual survey. The response rate of 232 CEOs, 58 percent, was considered good for surveys of this type (this sample was used in chapter 2). The respondents differed from the nonrespondents in two significant characteristics: responding facilities were larger (the median bed size was 236 beds), and fewer respondents were in centralized multihospital systems (e.g., only three Humana hospitals responded).

Validity of Self-reporting of Strategy

To check the validity of CEO self-reporting of a hospital's strategy, a follow-up conjoint measurement survey was undertaken of 192 of the 232 CEOs willing to invest an extra hour of their time. Conjoint measurement technique is a statistical approach to preference analysis borrowed from the marketing-science literature (Moore and Semenik 1988). The strategy alternatives that hospital CEOs must select from are multidimensional. In the language of economics, strategic choice is affected by the utility function (preference) of the CEO and the environment. Conjoint measurement technique is the technique of choice used by marketing professionals to sort out the relative importance of multidimensional attributes. The technique breaks down the CEOs' ordinal observations into separate and compatible utility scales by which the original sequences can be surmised (see the Appendix in chapter 2). To find out that an attribute is of concern is less informative than finding out the depth of concern in each of the six attribute areas listed in table 5.1.

Information was collected utilizing a standard full-profile approach (Conjoint Analyzer 1988) rather than the simplistic bivariate approach. A factorial design was constructed to offer descriptive profiles of the productivity improvement

Table 5.1

Results of Conjoint Measurement Technique Survey and Cluster Analysis Yielding Five Archetypes, 1990 (N = 192)

Attribute Concerns (at 3 levels)	Part-Worth OLS Regression Eqn. Coefficients					Attribute-Level Weights for the Clusters				
	G_1	G_2	G_3	G_4	G_5	G_1	G_2	G_3	G_4	G_5
1-A. Interest in productivity improvement:										
Low (keep it stable)	0	0	0	0	0	0	.28	.90	.91	.88
Moderate	.81	.96	.30	.26	.22	.14	.53	.08	.06	.12
High (target annual gains)	3.68	.43	.08	.11	0	.86	.19	.02	.03	0
1-B. Incentive compensation										
None	-	-	-	-	-	.41	.44	.89	.72	.87
Based on revenue gains	0	1.03	0	.42	.14	0	.56	.11	.28	.13
Based on annual productivity improvements	1.97	.12	0	0	0	0	0	0	0	0
2-A. Quantity of diversification (net after 5 years, 1986-90)										
None/low	0	0	0	0	0	.45	.17	.19	0	.69
Moderate	.79	1.15	.33	.21	.42	.55	.83	.11	.08	.31
High	0	0	3.87	4.92	0	0	0	.70	.92	0
2-B. Scope of diversification										
Hospital-based services	0	0	0	0	0	.68	.51	.26	.11	.16
Unrelated to hospital care	.73	1.08	.94	1.07	1.66	.32	.49	.35	.36	.84
Unrelated to health care	0	0	.71	1.84	0	0	0	.39	.53	0
3-A. Divestment (discontinue dept.)										
Will not do	0	0	0	0	0	0	.19	.13	0	0
Yes if quality profits are poor	.38	.06	.14	.20	.52	1.0	.81	.77	.84	.73
Yes, for fiscal reasons	0	0	.08	.11	.16	0	0	.10	.16	.27
3-B. Interest in information systems for strategic planning										
Low	0	0	0	0	0	.06	.24	0	.19	.48
High	.61	.50	.91	.63	0	.70	.51	.38	.50	.52
Very high priority	.29	.32	.82	.59	0	.24	.25	.62	.31	0
Sample N	56	47	42	40	7	56	47	42	40	7

Note: Underlined attributes discriminate a cluster grouping.

(goals, willingness to offer incentive pay), diversification (quantity and scope), and willingness to change (to divest a poorly performing product line or to enhance information systems with a strategic planning focus). Incentive pay is sometimes labeled an organizational hygiene factor: a necessary condition to motivate individuals to implement the plan or enhance productivity. With six attributes and three levels of concern (low, moderate, high) for each attribute, a main-effects model (no interactions) was estimated by standard techniques (table 5.1). Five stable, discrete, readily interpretable groups were identified by the Barr/Johnson procedure of weighted hierarchical cluster analysis. The part-worth regression coefficients for each of the five clusters are given in the first five columns of table 5.1. The attribute-level weights resulting from a transformation of the original unpooled regression coefficients, using a conditional logit model, are given in the last five columns of table 5.1. The most interesting finding was that the analyzer archetype subdivided into two distinct strategies (G_2 and G_3 in table 5.1), yielding a total of five revealed archetypes. Selective analyzers (type-one analyzers) focus on limited diversification into related (health) business ventures as their major corporate strategy and on productivity enhancement as the minor strategy. As table 5.1 suggests, selective analyzers place the highest part-worth weight on diversification in health care (outside the hospital) and the second-highest weight on incentive compensation for revenue gains in departments. Type-one (G_2) analyzer CEOs place the third-highest part-worth weight on improving productivity. Defenders pay incentive compensation based on department or work-group annual improvement in productivity levels.

Type-two analyzers (G_3) focus on diversification into related (health) business ventures and un-related diversification (outside of health care) as their major corporate strategy and on improving information systems as their dominant minor strategy (table 5.1). The five new archetypes are defined in table 5.2. Payment of incentive compensation in the 1990s is a complex human-resources issue not done by 81 percent of the facilities in archetypes 3, 4, and 5 (no payment for better productivity or gainsharing division of improved revenues earned).

New Dimensions

The central problem with the Miles and Snow model (1978) is that strategy is seen as one-dimensional: Move outward for new lines of business (prospect, analyze, diversify) or look inward and defend current product lines with cost-containment activities. The results of our conjoint measurement technique survey suggest that Shortell, Morrison, and Friedman (1990) and Miles and Snow (1978) missed two other dimensions of strategy emphasized by Harvard professor Michael Porter's (1985) more comprehensive model of market-power shifts among buyers and sellers. If the first dimension of strategy is "Do you move outward and diversify?" the second dimension of strategy is "In what direction does the institution move the portfolio of product lines: to related or unrelated (outside of health care) lines of business?" A third dimension of strategy involves the

Table 5.2
Five Basic Management Strategies

Group 1: Productivity defender specialist
   Major strategy: to improve productivity, improve managerial cost accounting, reduce excess variable costs, and achieve cost leadership of specialized quality products.
   Minor strategies: incentive compensation paid on productivity gainsharing, slow diversification following divestment of poor product lines (inferior quality and poor profitability).

Group 2: Selective analyzer type one
   Major strategy: limited diversification into related (health) services, and incentive compensation based on revenue gains.
   Minor strategies: moderate interest in improving productivity.

Group 3: Analyzer type two
   Major strategy: moderate diversification into unrelated lines of business (nonhealth) and related (health) services.
   Minor strategies: good information systems to assess synergies between clinical departments and outposts.

Group 4: Diversify/prospector
   Major strategy: strong diversification into unrelated lines of business (nonhealth) and related (health) services.
   Minor strategies: create opportunities in a constant search for new and better investment opportunities.

Group 5: Reactor
   Nonstrategy, reaction to local competition.

---

risk of productivity enhancement weighed against the risk of sticking with the status quo—that is, do you take the action to cut costs and expand the ratio of output to input, with the risk of harming morale in the short run, or do you wallow in current levels of inefficiency (Eastaugh 1990)? Strategy selection involves operational management (dimension 3), the direction of diversification and portfolio choice (dimension 2), and the outward/inward demands on the organization to prospect or defend and divest (dimension 1).

   Conjoint measurement techniques provide a reliability check on whether CEOs consistently self-report their strategy. When presented with two methods of strategy classification, self-reporting and investigator inference from conjoint measurement techniques, 188 of 192 hospital CEOs self-reported their strategy consistently with the cluster analysis in table 5.1 after being resurveyed and selecting a strategy from the five in table 5.2. Such a strong level of agreement suggests high reliability and convergent validity (one trusts the self-reported strategy responses from the CEOs).

Shifts in Strategy from 1986 to 1990

The number of hospital CEOs that felt that their 1986 strategy was appropriate in 1990 ranged from 20 of 20 productivity defenders to 36 of 48 selective (type-one) analyzers, 28 of 49 type-two analyzers, 42 of 86 prospectors, and 7 of 29 reactors (see the diagonal of table 5.3). To restate this trend, 100 percent of defenders stuck with that strategy during 1986 to 1990, whereas 25 percent of selective (type-one) analyzers dropped that strategy by 1990 (most became productivity defenders with limited diversification), and 43 percent of type-two analyzers dropped their 1986 strategy by 1990 (12 became defenders, 8 became more selective type-one analyzers, and one increased diversification and became a prospector). Of the 86 hospital CEOs with the prospector strategy in 1986, 51 percent dropped this strategy by 1990 (two-thirds of this 51 percent became analyzers and one-third became defenders). The largest transition shift was away from the reactor strategy; 17 percent of 1986 reactors became prospectors, 34 percent became defenders, and 24 percent became analyzers. The smallest declines in operating profit margins as a percentage of net revenues occurred in the productivity-defender group, whereas the biggest downturn in profit margins occurred in the aggressive prospector group, which exhibited the best profit margin in 1986 (6.0 percent) but the second-worst profit margin in 1990 (-1.0 percent). The worst profit margins in all years were turned in by the passive reactors in table 5.3.

These results in table 5.3 suggest a link between degree of diversification and profitability. The diversification measure utilized is the number of services on the left side of table 5.4. This hospital-diversification measure subdivides into three basic categories: low diversification (0.25 or less of listed services), moderate diversification (0.3–0.55), and high diversification. Figure 5.1 graphs the link between diversification and operating profit margin over the five years 1986 through 1990. The results suggest that the link between diversification and operating margin is nonlinear: too much or too little diversification results in a more rapid decline in operating margin. The middle-of-the-road strategy, moderate diversification (74 hospitals), yielded the best financial results. The moderate-diversification strategy included 39 selective (type-one) analyzers, 31 defenders, and only four type-two analyzers. Over 90 percent of prospectors reported high levels of diversification, and reactors reported low diversification. The median reactor diversified into five new services from 1986 to 1988, but divested four of the five new services within the 36 months of 1988 to 1990, for a net diversification of one service.

Divestment, listed on the right side of table 5.4, is not a significant variable in predicting profit margins or strategic choice, except in the fifth group, the reactors. In any one year the diversification variable was low for reactors, but

Table 5.3
Number of Hospitals with Each Management Strategy and Financial Performance in a Sample of 232 Hospitals, 1986 and 1990

1986 Strategy	The 1990 Management Strategy					Number of of Hospitals	Operating Profit Margin, 1986
	1. Defender	2. Analyzer Type One	3. Analyzer Type Two	4. Diversify/ Prospector	5. Reactor		
1. Defender	20	0	0	0	0	20	.052
2. Analyzer type one	11	36	1	0	0	48	.041
3. Analyzer type two	12	8	28	1	0	49	.042
4. Diversify/prospector	16	10	18	42	0	86	.060
5. Reactor	10	3	4	5	7	29	.023
Total hospitals in 1990	69	57	51	48	7	232	
Operating profit margin 1990[a]	.025	.016	.014	-.010	-.029		

[a] The average operating profit margin was 1.3 percent in 1990 and 4.7 percent in 1986.

Table 5.4
Operational Definitions of Diversification and Divestment by Service Product Line

Diversification[a]	Divestment[b]
1. MRI	1. Urgent-care centers
2. CT scanner	2. Family planning
3. Laser system	3. In-home skilled nursing
4. Fitness center	4. Hospice
5. Birthing center	5. Health screening
6. Geriatric assessment and case management	6. Industrial or executive health services
7. Digital subtraction analyzer	7. Crisis intervention
8. Extracorp. shock wave lithotripsy	8. Durable medical equipment
9. Open-heart surgery	9. Co-60 therapy
10. Ultrasonic Dx system	10. Pediatrics
11. In-home infusion therapy	11. Outpatient AIDS care
12. Freestanding nursing home	12. In-home physical therapy
13. Gamma camera	13. Sports medicine
14. Neonatal services	14. Immunizations
15. Megavoltage radiology	15. Emergency department
16. Organ transplant	16. Meals on wheels (home delivered)

Note: For the 232 hospitals diversification ranged from 2/16 to 15/16, and divestment ranged from 0/16 to 7/16. Low divestment in figure 5.1 is defined as 0.125-0.25; high divestment is above 0.5.

aAt a given hospital take the number of service departments added and divide by the maximum number (16), e.g. 2/16.

bAt a given hospital take the number of departments closed and divide by the maximum number (16), e.g. 4/16 if 4 of 16 possible closed.

that is because the divestment variable counterbalances any growth. In other words, reactors pulled out of as many services as they initiated, closing one every 16 months but starting a new service every 12 months. The reactors seem to lack patience and to try trial and error making a knee-jerk dip into diversification: "If it doesn't work right away, pull out and try something else, my board doesn't believe in a learning curve," to quote one reactor CEO. It is okay to be opportunistic, but a successful analyzer knows that some product lines are like weak-kneed quarterbacks and require time, redesign, recapitalization, and remarketing (Eastaugh and Eastaugh 1986).

Figure 5.1
Time Trend in Operating Profit Margin for Hospitals with Varying Levels of Diversification, 1986–1990

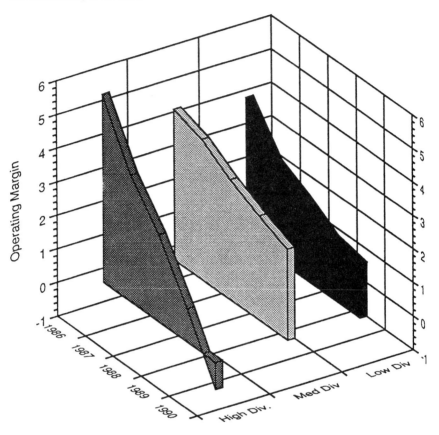

Profitability and Productivity

One should also test the link between goals and results to see whether productivity defenders were in fact successful in improving labor productivity. On average, small hospitals with only 74 to 199 beds have 10 percent lower labor productivity than larger hospitals. Therefore, table 5.5 divides the sample by bed size. The results indicate that the most rapid percentage growth was in the productivity-defender category, which should remain vigilant in continuing to improve. A 4.1-point gain in productivity over five years may seem impressive until one realizes that this is half the rate of gain in productivity of the general economy (Altman, Goldberger, and Crane 1990). Health and education are the two industries with the slowest productivity gains. The last two strategies listed

Table 5.5
Labor Productivity and Management Strategy for Small and Large Hospitals,
1986 and 1990 (Number of Hospitals in Parentheses)

1990 Management Strategy	Labor Productivity FTEs per Adjusted Occupied Bed[a]				Operating Profit Margin 1990	Percent Change in Prod. 1986-90
	75-199 Beds		200 + Beds			
	1986	1990	1986	1990		
1. Defender	3.47	3.31 (40)	3.82	3.69 (29)	.025	4.1
2. Analyzer type one	3.55	3.50 (37)	3.96	3.89 (20)	.016	1.5
3. Analyzer type two	3.53	3.55 (35)	3.99	3.97 (16)	.014	-.3
4. Diversify prospector	3.58	3.84 (26)	4.03	4.20 (22)	-.010	-5.9
5. Reactor	3.69	3.88 (5)	4.05	4.16 (2)	-.029	-4.2
Total hospitals	143	143	89	89	.013	0.2

[a]Full-time = equivalent employees per adjusted occupied bed includes ambulatory visit workload and is the American Hospital Association's standard measure for hospital productivity.

in table 5.5, prospector and reactor, have experienced substantial declines in productivity.

Figure 5.2 tracks the trends in operating profit margin for the five archetypal strategies over the period 1986–90. Operating profit margin is not the only measure of financial performance. Table 5.6 presents a number of alternative

Figure 5.2
Time Trend in Operating Profit Margin for Each of the Five New Archetype
Strategy Groups as Defined in Table 5.2, 1986–1990 (n = 232)

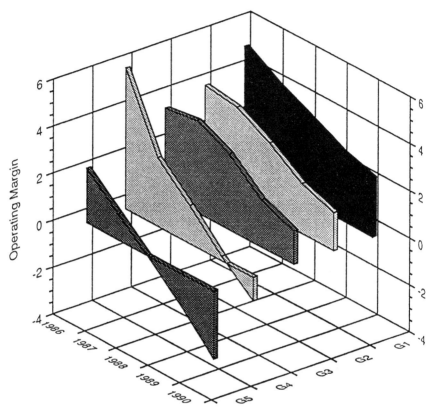

measures for profitability. It is disturbing that the return on investment is so low for archetypal strategies 3, 4, and 5. Cleverley (1990) suggested that the return on investment must exceed the cost of capital, and by this yardstick these last three strategies seem to be failures in the hospital economy. The first two strategies were more successful in the most recent period. The productivity-defender strategy and the selective analyzer strategy can be implemented with varying styles (ranging from active to passive) and varying levels of success. Two general propositions are suggested from the data. First, diversification has a limited band of success: Stick to health-care-related diversification, but avoid doing too much or too little. Second, hospitals have to foster a stronger productivity-enhancement focus. The rate at which managers enhance productivity, offer incentive pay immune to legal suits (because it is linked to productivity gains, not directly to revenue gains; chapter 10) and specialize rather than overdiversify offers a sus-

Table 5.6
Six Alternative Measures of Profitability, Group Medians, 1990

Group	G_1 Defender	G_2 Selective Analyzer	G_3 Analyzer Type Two	G_4 Prospector	G_5 Reactor
1. Operating margin (net oper. income/total oper. revenue)	2.5%	1.6%	1.4%	-1.0%	-2.9%
2. Return on total assets (rev. minus exp. as % of tot. assets)	4.0%	2.7%	2.3%	-1.6%	-3.4%
3. Return on equity (rev. minus exp. as % of fund balance)	7.6%	5.5%	5.1%	-2.9%	-6.4%
4. Return on investment, price-level adjusted ([cash flow + interest] as % of price-level-adj. investment)	9.2%	6.7%	6.5%	5.0%	2.4%
5. Operating margin, price-level adjusted ([profit before depreciation minus price-adjusted depreciation] as % of operating revenue)	.2%	-.6%	-.9%	-3.2%	-5.4%
6. Nonoperating revenue as a fraction of the excess of revenues over expenses	.38	.35	.34	-.29	-.15

tainable source of competitive advantage in the hospital industry. These results reinforce the advice of Tom Peters (1982) suggesting that health care organizations "stick to their knitting" rather than try to diversify into too many business lines. Just as the March of Dimes diversified out of the polio business, some limited diversification is necessary for hospitals to uncover less regulated revenue sources. Even productivity defenders take diversification risks, but they do less diversification and are more likely to take the right risks.

Future research should focus on which diversification strategies are most effectively tailored to which purchaser types (Zelman and McLaughlin 1990) and on the relationship of the control of diversification strategies to marketing and corporate decentralization. Selective diversification and strong productivity-improvement programs offer an optimal mixed strategy.

In contrast to previous research, the analyzer strategy is subdivided into two categories. The new type-one analyzer category balances the competing demands of both a productivity defender and the prospector strategy. The new Type-two analyzer is a limited version (50 percent) of the prospector strategy. The type-two analyzer strategy tends to yield more diversification and more focus on unrelated diversification (outside of health care) compared to type-one selective analyzers. Both types of analyzers are seldom the first new entrant into a market, whereas true prospectors are typically testing the strategic advantage of being the first to offer a new product or marketing concept.

Modeling financial performance is a complex issue that depends on a number of variables apart from the archetype strategy of the institution. Location, ownership and provider competition can interact with strategy selection to determine financial performance. A regression analysis standardizing for facility age, bed size, location (SMSA metropolitan, or rural), competition (number of HMOs in the county, hospital beds per 1,000 population, physicians per 1,000 population), ownership (for-profit), teaching status (major medical center or minor affiliation) was performed. All else equal, factoring out the influence of the above listed nine independent variables, exhibit 3 tracks the trends in operating margin for the five archetype strategies over the period 1986–1990. Regression analysis was utilized (Eastaugh 1992) to measure the unique impact of strategy on profitability, holding constant: facility age; bed size; location (SMSA metropolitan, or rural); competition (number of HMOs in the county, hospital beds per 1,000 population, physicians per 1,000 population), ownership (for-profit), teaching status (major medical center or minor affiliation). These nine variables were selected as a best fit for the data after examination of heteroscedasticity (Harvey and Breusch-Pagan tests), equation re-estimation using the heteroscedasticity-consistent covariance matrix estimator, and using the Ramsey specification error test. Rural location has an impact on profitability apart from strategy choice; e.g., 1990 rural hospitals had operating margins that were 3.6 points lower than urban hospitals, but rural G1 productivity defender hospitals had margins that were 2.3 points better than the average rural hospital.

STRATEGY EFFECTIVENESS

All five basic strategy archetypes do some degree of diversification. Prospectors do the most diversification; productivity defenders and selective analyzers do more profitable select health-related diversification. Diversification is like playing pool: Select your shots correctly and minimize distractions and inefficiency. But some aspects of diversification are like fishing: One needs to know when to make that "fish-or-cut-bait" decision to drop a product line, discontinue an activity, and retrench back to the base business. Limited diversification, focusing on related lines of business and prudent divestment behavior to close out a product line, seems to be the best market strategy. A poor diversification strategy is exhibited by (1) the prospector who will not pull his or her failing line in (and rebait the hook and try again) and (2) the reactor who does a lot of diversification but discontinues the product line too quickly (declaring it a failure). Knee-jerk reactors tend to lack stability and patience; they jump out of (discontinue) a product line as quickly as they jump into a new product line.

During any one year the diversification variable is low for reactors, but that is because the divestment variable is high only for reactors. The reactors' divestment is almost as quick as their diversification, and they never seem to learn from their mistakes. By contrast, analyzers and defenders launch a planned effort to influence the market, but reactors have no strategy and no persistence. Defenders, and to a lesser extent the selective analyzers, work their strategy in many dimensions, including cost leadership through better labor productivity. The best prospectors and analyzers also attempt to create synergy between product lines by linking their joint ventures. However, the prospectors as a group have poor productivity and thus diminished flexibility to set prices.

Some strategies are better than others, but each has some point of weakness. For example, defenders do some diversification, but do not sufficiently differentiate on quality-of-care dimensions compared to analyzers. Defenders should not market only a simple "no-frills" approach to quality. The type-two analyzers' weakness involves poor productivity; the prospectors have very poor productivity. Too much prospecting can exhaust capital availability, sap management time (and morale), and lead to deterioration, as in the decline of the MEDLANTIC health care system in Washington, D.C. Reactors have a weakness in all dimensions.

The primary strengths of defenders are labor productivity and the ability to trim variable costs in line with workload. Defenders also tend to specialize, and specialization breeds better quality and lower unit costs through higher volumes. According to Shortell, Morrison, and Friedman (1990), a strong defender becomes like a strong tree following the pruning of the deadwood to give light and air so that the healthy branches may grow stronger. Defenders divest or consolidate the deadwood in their portfolio of product lines, and they raise productivity by trimming deadwood employees.

Selective analyzers have a clear advantage in comparison to type-two analyzers or reactors: They try to convert middle managers to entrepreneurs by offering incentive compensation for revenue gains. Productivity defenders also offer incentive pay, but 56 of these hospitals tied incentive pay to productivity improvements through a gainsharing program. A surprisingly small number of prospector hospitals offered incentive pay (9 of the 48 hospitals). All prospectors try to be first entrants into new product lines, but the best prospectors have a strategic sense of who else is prospecting where and limit their scope of diversification. Prospectors have more persistence than reactors, so they allow their managers the time and opportunity to differentiate and mature a new product line. Even after a lengthy trial at a new product line, the good prospector is brave enough to divest some poor performers and recommit back to the core business. Every hospital needs a strong strategic planning process, but prospectors are most in need of comprehensive market data on consumers, employers, physicians, and the competition. Good managers know that the competition can counterpunch, and that one needs to stay one step ahead of the competing hospitals or physician groups (Howard 1988).

Some analysts have speculated (1) that small-scale gambles with diversification require less than average managerial patience to see the project to conclusion since the maximum regret (loss) is low and (2) that large-scale gambles may require less than average patience because the initial commitment has been so large that management fears the long-run consequences of timidly "cutting our losses" and pulling back on diversification (retrenching). Booth et al. (1989) reported that troubled banks continue to take more risks, thus contributing to the negative empirical association between risk and return. Ehrhardt (1991) provides a more theoretical discussion on risk and diversification.

ALTERNATIVE QUALITATIVE MODELS AND FUTURE RESEARCH

The quantitative results of the small study in this chapter must be regarded as tentative. However, the results for nonteaching hospitals suggest a potential interesting interaction between planning, diversification, and competition. The qualitative model presented in this section explains the quantitative and qualitative (anecdotal) information collected in this study with a life-cycle hypothesis for hospital behavior. The qualitative model we shall employ is a cusp catastrophe model (Chidley 1976), developed from the differential topology branch of pure mathematics. The word "catastrophe" implies sudden change and not necessarily a bad outcome. This theory has been applied in developmental biology. Harvard biology professor Stephen Gould argues that instead of changing gradually as one generation shades into the next, evolution proceeds with a discrete lurch or jump. Supporters of Darwin have to defend the past existence of hypothetical "missing links," but under Gould's new theory there are not any gradual transitional forms and thus no need to postulate "missing links." Species can either have a positive "catastrophe" or "leap" for the better and improve, or a negative catastrophe and become extinct. Gould labels this theory the "punctuated-equilibrium theory of evolution." Life cycles and lurches/jumps are topics of study for organizational theorists (Kimberly 1990). The strength of catastrophe models is that they explicitly recognize that hospital managers make interactive decisions, often with a jump (a quick change, adding two or three services), feedback, and imperfect incomplete information. Two organizations in approximately the same position on paper may experience two entirely different short-run futures: pervasive rapid change or none at all. Given the infancy of such qualitative models, the best we can do is generate a reasonable descriptive model, invoke limited tests for plausibility, and, as always, suggest avenues for future research.

The financial ability and desire of a hospital to diversify change suddenly, by fits and starts, in a fashion quite inconsistent with the typical linear regression analysis model. The qualitative pictorial catastrophe theory model for describing sudden change might better capture the interactions between competition, diversification, and external planning regulations. This model assumes that diversification behavior is controlled by two conflicting motivations, growth and retrenchment, as plotted in Figure 5.3 on the axes of the horizontal (control) surface. The behavior of the institution, which ranges from diversification to consolidation to contraction, is represented on the vertical axes. For any given point on the folded control surface (i.e., the surface $[P,CM]$ results from the combination of pressures to retrench and pressures to grow and compete), there is usually one point of most probable behavior.

The point of most probable behavior is located directly above the point on the control surface (P,CM) and at an elevation directly proportional to the degree of diversification on the y-axis. However, in the center of the figure, where pressures for competition and retrenchment are approximately in balance $(E,$ neutrality), there always exist two points of probable behavior (e.g., A and AA, also B and BB). A small prior change in P or CM can produce a large change in behavior D (diversification). The higher of these two points on the behavior surface (A) represents an aggressive institutional philosophy ("Let the planners be damned"), and the other point (AA) at a low value for diversification represents submissive inactivity ("Ignore the competition, please the regulators, and see what happens"). The intermediate point (A') represents the least likely of the three possible points, neutrality or status quo. This might be summarized in the homily, "It's hard to sit on a fence for long; things either have to fall right or left." In undertaking the diversification "catastrophe" to expand (jumping from B to BB), an institution faces the risk of having overdiversified and collapsing down through the contraction catastrophe (A to AA) in the future. Conversely, a facility that believes that "things must get worse before they can get better" and resides at point AA for a time may survive and have the opportunity to diversify into vacated markets at some future date (Urban and Hauser 1989).

If the hospital is pressured to compete but is not seriously hampered by the local certificate-of-need (CON) decision makers, then some aggressive action

Figure 5.3
Hypothesized Dynamic Interaction among Planning, Competition, and
Diversification Behavior

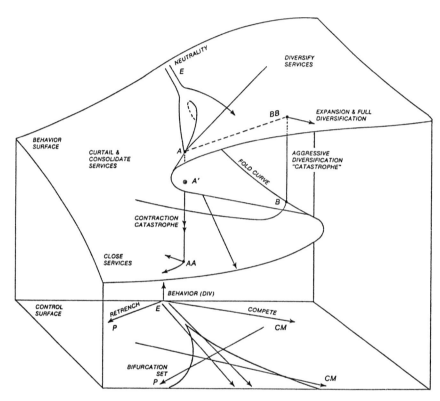

Note: The most diversified (aggressive) modes of behavior are assigned the highest values on the behavior axis (DIV) in this figure. For each point on the control surface (i.e., the surface (*P*, *CM*) equals the combination of pressures to retrench and pressures to compete) there is usually one point of most probable behavior. This point is located directly above the point on the control surface (*P*, *CM*) and at an elevation directly proportional to the degree of diversification. However, in the center of the figure, where pressures for competition and retrenchment are approximately in balance (*E*, neutrality), there always exist two points of probable behavior (e.g., *A* and *AA*, also *B* and *BB*). A small prior change in *P* or *CM* can produce a large change in behavior DIV (diversification). The word "catastrophe" implies sudden change and not necessarily a "bad" outcome.

such as diversification could be expected. If the hospital is not pressured to compete or expand market share but is faced by the frequent negative decisions of the CON decision makers, then passive inaction toward advocates of diversification, both internal and external (i.e., consultants), can be expected. The interesting question is, what if the institution were suddenly faced with a highly pressured environment to expand through diversification or to contract under the rate regulator's thumb? The two controlling factors, to compete or contract, are then in direct conflict. The regression models do not accommodate either discontinuity or the need to respond retroactively or proactively to these opposing pressures and thus predict (inaccurately) that the two pressures tend to cancel each other (Eastaugh 1984). In other words, the regression models tend to predict that the hospital will remain indifferent to countervailing forces and "stand pat" with the status quo. Such prediction of a neutral "canceling-out" effect is indicative of the inaccuracy of regression models, since standing with the status quo is in fact the least likely behavior. Competition always seems to prompt some diversification. The picture is most complex in the case of financial health, since a hospital with a good operating margin can, depending on whose anecdotes one believes, either (1) breed complacency because lack of necessity impedes innovation or (2) breed rapid diversification because the operating margin provides the venture capital for the hospital to experiment. However, the numerous anecdotes from northeastern and sunbelt states ignore the more plausible existence of a dynamic interaction by the decision makers. In a dynamic situation the first derivative of competition (increasing or decreasing) and financial health (improving or deteriorating) may be more crucial to the diversification issue than the absolute level of either competition or financial health.

THE CURRENT CONTEXT

Diversification is a delicate undertaking that involves many nonfinancial concerns. A rational portfolio framework must consider how to select new ventures, which internal and external partners are appropriate, and how much capital investment will be required. One should not oversimplify the situation and jump from a quick-and-dirty competitor analysis to decision. To paraphrase H. L. Mencken, for each complex alternative there is a simple explanation, and it is very often incorrect. The diversification plan can be accomplished through acquisitions, internal joint-venture spin-offs, partial-ownership joint ventures, contractual minority investments, or joint cooperative agreements (Anderson 1991). Every market situation is different, and generalizations about structure and process are often hazardous.

Changes in Medicare outpatient payment rates for 1992, outlined in chapter 7, will begin to shift the locus of outpatient care. The new fee schedule created incentives for hospital-physician outpatient joint ventures because the outpatient department payment rates were reduced. According to Anderson (1991), HCFA wanted to adjust the prices to shift more ambulatory care to doctors' offices rather than the more expensive hospital outpatient departments. HCFA reduced the payment to hospitals for the technical component of certain outpatient procedures that are linked to the relative-value fee schedules for similar services (e.g., outpatient radiology services). Earlier in 1991 HCFA also demanded that hospitals rebundle diagnostic services in the three-day ''DRG payment window'' prior to a hospital admission. Therefore, hospitals can no longer bill separately for these services, irrespective of whether these services were unrelated to the admission. Both of these changes in billing practices encourage more workups in the physician's office setting. Future research might explore whether the hospital-based physician community splits into two basic divisions: (1) the diagnostic division, containing equal numbers of prospectors and defenders, and (2) the therapeutic division, consisting of a multitude of defenders and a few entrepreneurial analysts willing to ''convince management to make that one large-scale bet.''

We have not exhausted the range of ventures into which hospitals may diversify (see figure 5.4). Increasingly, efforts are more specialized and targeted to a specific patient segment (e.g., eating-disorder units, diabetes fitness programs). Hospitals will find competition from a number of firms and institutions. For example, freestanding surgery centers are increasingly competing with hospitals (Lagoe 1991). The number of independent surgicenters grew from 41 in 1975 to 130 in 1981, 410 in 1985, 832 in 1990, and an estimated 900 in 1992 (with $1.4 billion in revenue). Hospitals may follow the example of U.S. Steel and drop inpatient care as their primary or core business. Due to a strong five-year diversification effort, in fiscal 1984 energy and chemicals replaced steel as U.S. Steel's primary profitable product.

The most substantial diversification activities that are likely to dampen the magnitude of revenue variability (e.g., from low DRG or HMO payments) are also the most fraught with risk. The trustees of each institution must counterbalance the risks against the rewards of improved financial autonomy. Initial and ongoing financial requirements of the diversification effort must be carefully assessed. In a highly regulated state like New York, most of the ventures are health related, but many might still carry a substantial risk. Just because a hospital is successful in heart surgery does not mean that it will be successful in mobile lithotripsy. Hospital managers should reflect on the fact that 50,000 to 85,000 businesses go bankrupt each year. The intangible benefit of experimenting with diversification in the 1980s involved the emergence of a risk-taking mentality to replace the superintendent caretaking mentality (Drucker 1989). Most of the diversification strategies discussed in this chapter involve significant capital budgets. However, some small-scale diversification strategies, when properly marketed to the physician community, can build referrals and volume, for example, starting an outpatient physical therapy department or diabetic maintenance and arthritis programs.

Diversification prior to federal tax reform in 1986 often involved tax-shelter benefits to physician investors. Now investment decisions are based on business

Figure 5.4
Two Roads for Diversification: The High Road, the Low Road, or Both Roads?

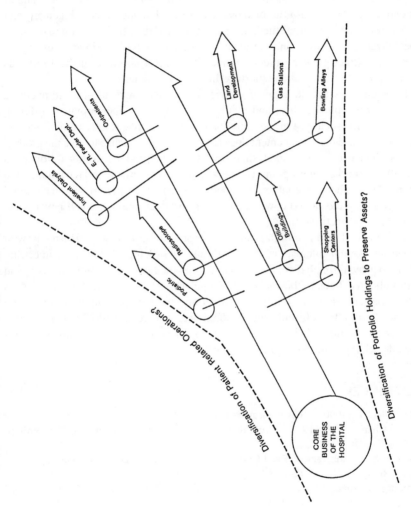

Diversification of Patient Related Operations?

Inpatient Dialysis

E. R. Feeder Dept.

Outpatients

Podiatric

Radioscope

CORE BUSINESS OF THE HOSPITAL

Land Development

Gas Stations

Bowling Alleys

Office Buildings

Shopping Centers

Diversification of Portfolio Holdings to Preserve Assets?

(Motto of the nonprofit hospital manager: We do not render new services or acquire a better portfolio of assets merely to collect money, but we must collect money in order to render future service.)

principles, with some concern for social dividends in the minds of certain investors. In the 1990s there is an increase in tribal warfare between various groups of physicians that invest in their facilities, rejected investors left out of the joint-venture deals, and the other members of the medical staff (Ginzberg 1991). Some hospital managers are considering charging user fees to join medical staffs, while physicians are following the professional tendency to redefine their jobs, and to extend their domain into the management arena (Umbdenstock, Hageman, and Amundson 1990). Internal-medicine physicians redefine their domain to do more specialized procedures, and surgeons relabel themselves ''primary-care physicians'' to attract greater patient volume. The doctor shortage of the 1960s has been replaced by the patient shortage in many physicians' offices.

Divestment is the strategy of choice for services with a weak competitive position, poor profitability, and a sufficient supply of other providers offering the service for society. On the other hand, certain services may be divested too quickly because the management does not have the persistence to give the product line a chance to gain market share and begin to produce profits following a redesigned marketing program, changes in the basic product, and recapitalization (if needed). The phaseout pricing option listed in chapter 6 will help timid managers slay the sacred cows, unnecessary product lines, that will never make it in these competitive times.

The hospital is an important civic enterprise in our society. Hospitals with broad and lateral interests in the health and well-being of their consumers are likely to grow through diversification into other medical arenas rather than expand into unrelated lines of business. The popularity of hospital restructuring plans has to be tempered by concern for direct and indirect administrative costs and the need to constantly enhance productivity. The forward-looking diversified institution should be better able to adapt to unforeseen, and many times unforeseeable, changes in the regulatory climate.

REFERENCES

Alexander, J. (1990). ''Diversification Behavior of Multihospital Systems: Patterns of Change, 1983–1985.'' *Hospital and Health Services Administration* 35:1 (Spring), 83–101.

Altman, S., Goldberger, S., and Crane, S. (1990). ''The Need for a Focus on Productivity.'' *Health Affairs* 9:1 (Spring), 107–113.

American Hospital Association. (1991). ''Trends in Outpatient Service Diversification.'' *Outreach* 4:4 (Fall), 1–3.

American Institute of Certified Public Accountants, Accounting Standards Division (1987). ''Statement of Position 81–2, Reporting Practices Concerning Hospital-related Organizations'' (August). New York: AICPA.

Anderson, H. (1991). ''RBRVS Creates Incentive for Hospital-Physician Outpatient Care Ventures.'' *Hospitals* 65:4 (February 20), 31.

Bayless, M., and Diltz, J. (1991) ''Relevance of Asymmetric Information to Financing Decisions,'' *Journal of Business Finance & Accounting* 18:3 (April), 331–334.

Boles, K., and Glenn, J. (1986). "What Accounting Leaves Out of Hospital Financial Management." *Hospital and Health Services Administration* 31:2 (March–April), 8–27.

Booth, D., Alam, S., Ankam, S., and Osyk, B. (1989). "A Robust Multivariate Procedure for the Identification of Problem S&L Institutions." *Decision Sciences* 20:3 (July), 320–333.

Cheng, J., and Kesner, I. (1988). "Responsiveness to Environmental Change: The Interactive Effects of Organizational Slack and Strategic Orientation." *Proceedings of the Academy of Management* (August 10), 165–169.

Chidley, J. (1976). "Catastrophe Theory in Consumer Attitudes Studies." *Journal of Marketing Resarch* 18:2 (April), 64–91.

Clement, J. (1988). "Vertical Integration and Diversification of Acute Care Hospitals: Conceptual Definitions." *Hospital and Health Services Administration* 33:1 (Spring), 99–110.

————. (1987). "Does Hospital Diversification Improve Financial Outcomes." *Medical Care* 25:10 (October), 988–1001.

Cleverley, W. (1990). "ROI: Its Role in Voluntary Hospital Planning." *Hospital and Health Services Administration* 35:1 (Spring), 71–82.

Coddington, D. (1988). "A Realistic Approach to Diversification." In *New Business Development in Ambulatory Care: Exploring Diversification Options*, 3–13. Chicago: American Hospital Publishing, Inc.

Coddington, D., and Pottle, J. (1984). "Hospital Diversification Strategies: Lessons from Other Industries." *Healthcare Financial Management* 38:12 (December), 19–24.

Conjoint Analyzer. (1988). Version 2.0. New York: Bretton-Clark.

Conrad, D., and Mick, S. (1987). "Management Education for Vertically Integrated Systems." *Journal of Health Administration Education* 5:3 (Summer), 441–448.

Cowles, C. (1991). "Review Effect on Cost Reports": impact smaller than expected", *Health Care Financing Review* 12:3 (Spring), 21–5.

Drucker, P. (1989). "What Business Can Learn from Nonprofits." *Harvard Business Review* 67:4 (July–August), 90–95.

Eastaugh, S. (1992) "Hospital Strategy and Financial Performance." *Health Care Management Review* 17:3 (Summer), forthcoming.

————. (1990). "Hospital Nursing Technical Efficiency: Nurse Extenders and Enhanced Productivity." *Hospital and Health Services Administration* 34:4 (Winter), 561–573.

————. (1988). "Hospital Diversification Revisited." *Medical Care* 26:12 (December), 1115–1117.

————. (1985). "Hospital Diversification and Business Risk." Keynote address to the Greater New York Hospital Association Annual Meeting (April 16).

————. (1984). "Hospital Diversification and Financial Management." *Medical Care* 22:8 (August), 704–723.

————. (1982). "The Effectiveness of Community-based Hospital Planning: Some Recent Evidence." *Applied Economics* 14:5 (October), 475–490.

Eastaugh, S., and Eastaugh, J. (1986). "Prospective Payment Systems: Further Steps to Enhance Quality, Efficiency, and Regionalization." *Health Care Management Review* 11:4 (Fall), 37–52.

Ehrhardt, M. (1991). "Diversification and Interest Rate Risk." *Journal of Business Finance & Accounting* 18:1 (January), 43–60.

Elrod, J. (1986). "Can Municipal Bond Futures Contracts Minimize Financial Risk?" *Healthcare Financial Management* 40:4 (April), 40–45.

Fox, W. (1989). "Vertical Integration Strategies: More Promising Than Diversification." *Health Care Management Review* 14:3 (Summer), 49–56.

General Accounting Office. (1988). "Hospital Links with Related Firms Can Conceal Unreasonable Costs." GAO/HRD 88–18 (January 19).

Gentry, J., Newbold, P., and Whitford, D. (1987). "Future Flow Components, Financial Ratios, and Bankruptcy." *Journal of Business Finance and Accounting* 14:4 (Winter), 595–606.

Gilbert, R. (1986). "Hospital Revenue Diversification: A Case Study in Joint Venturing." *Healthcare Financial Management* 40:4 (April), 46–53.

Ginn, G. (1990). "Strategic Change in Hospitals: An Examination of the Response of the Acute Care Hospital to the Turbulent Environment of the 1980s." *Health Services Research* 25:4 (October), 565–591.

Ginzberg, E. (1991). "Public-private Issues and Access." *Bulletin of the New York Academy of Medicine* 67:1 (January–February), 55–58.

Glazer, A. (1985). "The Advantages of Being First." *American Economic Review* 75:3 (June), 473–480.

Goldsmith, J. (1989). "A Radical Prescription for Hospitals." *Harvard Business Review* 67:2 (March–April), 95–103.

Harrigan, C. (1991). "Hospital/Physician Partnerships and Joint Ventures." Chicago: American Bar Association Division for Professional Education.

Herzlinger, R. (1992). *Creating New Health Care Ventures: The Role of Management.* Gaithersburg, Maryland: Aspen.

Herzlinger, R. (1989). "Failed Revolution in Health Care—The Role of Management." *Harvard Business Review* 67:2 (March–April), 99–103.

Howard, D. (1988). "Past Experiences and Future Directions in Ambulatory Care." In *New Business Development in Ambulatory Care: Exploring Diversification Options,* 15–24. Chicago: American Hospital Publishing, Inc.

Joskow, P. (1981). "The Effects of Competition and Regulation on Hospital Bed Supply and the Reservation Quality of the Hospital." *Bell Journal of Economics* 11:2 (Autumn), 421–447.

Kanter, R. (1989). *The Change Masters: Innovations and Entrepreneurship in the American Corporation,* New York: Simon and Schuster, 302.

Kimberly, J. (1990). *The Organizational Life Cycle: Issues in the Creation, Transformation, and Decline of Organizations.* San Francisco: Jossey-Bass.

Kotler, P. (1991). *Marketing Management Analysis Planning and Control.* 7th ed. Englewood Cliffs, N.J.: Prentice-Hall.

Kovner, A. (1991). "Case of the Unhealthy Hospital." *Harvard Business Review* 69:5 (September-October), 12–26.

Lagoe, R. (1991). "Comparison of Hospital-integrated and Freestanding Ambulatory Surgery." *Hospital Topics* 69:1 (Winter), 31–35.

Leontiades, M. (1988). *Strategies for Diversification and Change.* 2nd ed. Boston: Little, Brown.

Luke, R., and Begun, J. (1988). "The Management of Strategy." In S. Shortell and, A. Kaluzny (eds.), *Health Care Management: A Text in Organization Theory and Behavior,* 2d ed. New York: Wiley.

Mick, S. (1991). *Innovations in Health Care Delivery.* San Francisco: Jossey-Bass.

————. (1988). "The Decision to Integrate Vertically in Health Care Organizations." *Hospital and Health Services Administration* 33:3 (Fall), 345–360.

Miles, R., and Snow, C. (1978). *Organizational Strategy, Structure, and Process.* New York: McGraw-Hill.

Moore, W., and Semenik, R. (1988). "Measuring Preferences with Conjoint Analysis: Impact of a Different Number of Attributes in the Design." *Journal of Business Research* 16:2 (May), 261–274.

Pegels, C., and Rogers, K. (1989). *Strategic Management of Hospitals and Health Care Facilities.* Rockville, Md.: Aspen.

Peters, T., and Waterman, R. (1982). *In Search of Excellence.* New York: Harper and Row.

Placella, L. (1986). "Choosing a Growth Strategy: Diversification versus Vertical Integration." *Trustee* 39:11 (November), 26–28.

Porter, M. (1985). *Competitive Advantage.* New York: Free Press.

————. (1980). *Competitive Strategy: Techniques for Analyzing Industries and Competitors.* New York: Free Press.

Rindler, M. (1989). *Managing a Hospital Turnaround.* Chicago: Health Administration Press.

Sabatino, F. (1989). "The Diversification Success Story Continues." *Trustee* (January), 10–11.

Sabatino, F., and Grayson, M. (1988). "Survey Ranks 17 Most Successful Diversification Strategies." *Trustee* (March), 16–17.

Sax, B. (1986). "Joint Ventures and Illegal Remuneration: The Pressure Is Growing." *Healthcare Financial Management* 40:3 (March), 38–43.

Shortell, S. (1989). "The Keys to Successful Diversification: Lessons from Leading Hospital Systems." *Hospital and Health Services Administration* 34:4 (Winter), 471–490.

Shortell, S., Morrison, E., and Friedman, B. (1990). *Strategic Choices for America's Hospitals: Managing Change in Turbulent Times.* San Francisco: Jossey-Bass.

Umbdenstock, R., Hageman, W., and Amundson, B. (1990). "The Five Critical Areas for Effective Governance of Not-for-Profit Hospitals." *Hospital and Health Services Administration* 35:4 (Winter), 481–492.

Urban, C. (1991). "Market-driven Communication Strategy." *Healthcare Forum Journal* (January–February), 24–27, 50.

Urban, G., and Hauser, J. (1989) *Design and Marketing of New Products.* 2nd ed. Englewood Cliffs, N.J.: Prentice-Hall.

White, D. (1990). "Marketers Hone Their Skills to Reach Target Markets." *Hospitals* 64:15 (August 1), 62–66.

Zelman, W., and McLaughlin, C. (1990). "Product Lines in a Complex Marketplace: Matching Organizational Strategy to Buyer Behavior." *Health Care Management Review* 15:2 (Spring), 9–14.

Zelman, W., and Parham, D. (1990). "Strategic, Operational, and Marketing Concerns of Product-Line Management in Healthcare." *Health Care Management Review* 15:1 (Winter), 29–35.

Chapter 6

Marketing, Pricing, and Specialization

People do not care how much you know until they know how much you care. Quality work does not always mean quality service.
—David H. Maister

Marketing involves the identification and satisfaction of consumer needs. Marketing activity should not be regarded as an expensive, speculative drain on the resources, but rather as a planning process that can guide the allocation of these resources toward a more effective result.
—Philip Kotler

Marketing is not selling, rather marketing is improving consumer satisfaction. The AMA, American Marketing Association, recognizes this fact and has given its highest award to two studies that have resulted in socially desirable declines in sales of a very precious commodity: energy resources.
—Philip D. Cooper

Pressure on health-service providers to control costs and close facilities has stimulated interest in health marketing activities. Marketing consultants take the public stance that their activity can help the firm provide better service and be more responsive to consumers' demands. Marketing is defined operationally as the set of activities designed to satisfy consumer needs and wants, including delivery, advertising, selling, and pricing. In the past, providers seldom considered measuring and satisfying consumer preferences. During the mid–1980s consumer groups in a few states initiated programs for bland informational advertising in "Medical Yellow Pages," giving schedules, fees, and locations. In the late 1980s a few large urban hospitals, facing increased competition from suburban hospitals, bad debts, and the added responsibility of having their emergency rooms serve as the sole source of primary care for the poor, initiated competitive advertising schemes. The approach was usually linked to quality: "Buy our product (for example, open-heart surgery) or our service (for example, maternity and pediatrics) and you'll have a better chance of survival, thanks to our experienced staff and teaching hospital physicians.'' In one case the publication of differential survival-rate statistics at two institutions caused the closing of the higher-mortality suburban service and slight expansion of the previously underutilized urban hospital's service, much to the delight of the medical school officials who needed additional patients for the education of their students and residents. The slow/reactive administrators will continue to adopt a plodder strategy to pursue "quiet" competition—for example, to accept slight changes in customer mix as a fait accompli that should not result in open predatory reaction among hospitals, because no single competitor is strong enough to disturb the silence (Gronroos 1991).

Many health professionals balk at the term *marketing* because it runs counter to their feelings that health care is "special"—not to be treated like a marketable commodity or service. The nonprofit hospital industry has been criticized by Carlson (1975) and by other advocates of holistic medicine for having a static, limited-scope, product orientation that does not provide the consumer with the necessary information concerning the product (health services). Goldsmith (1989) and the National Research Corporation (NRC) (1991) argued for giving the public more ambulatory services they can afford. Marketing is seldom understood by large segments of the health care profession. Marketing need not involve superfluous treatments and promotional gimmicks or a legion of medical Hula Hoops, Pet Rocks, and Cabbage Patch dolls. Real health marketing involves consumer-preference evaluation and better service delivery, with advertising playing a minor role. If health marketing is viewed in this light, the medical staff can become the hospital's service-line development group, and HMOs or PPOs should be viewed as wholesale buyers. A professional can still remain a professional and adopt some of the techniques of the common merchant. No egregious harm will be done to the professional practice of medicine if we trade a philosophy of paternalism for consumer sensitivity. The president of the Wisconsin Medical Society summarized this obvious point during his inaugural address: "Marketing is an admonition to do right by your patient; virtue is a companion of competition" (Scott 1985). Hospital advertising frequently does not work because choice is limited by managed-care systems (Thompson and Rao 1990) or physician opinion (Fisher and Anderson 1990).

CONFLICTS BETWEEN MARKETING AND THE NONPROFIT ETHOS

Some nonprofit managers have the misconception that marketing is simply selling a fixed given product. Selling is only one aspect of the marketing process. Marketing is a process of assessing consumer wants by changing the product and/or the distribution channels. Marketing is not always a process designed to increase demand. Marketing is meeting the needs of people (Ventres and Gordon 1990). Marketing involves managing demand and improving consumer satisfaction. For example, a public utility may decide to decrease (demarket) demand for its product in the name of energy conservation. In the case of health care, a given institution or business coalition may wish to demarket nursing home care while promoting home care, or demarket inpatient surgical or psychiatric care in order to promote the substitute product—ambulatory care. One could postulate that the invisible hand and competitive pressures might induce a given firm (for example, a nursing home) to demarket its product to some extent and to promote substitute products (home health care). However, due to institutional inertia, the invisible hand often turns out to be all thumbs; nursing homes might prefer to maintain the status quo rather than to face charges of predatory marketing behavior that pulls demand away from their neighbors. Nursing homes, hospitals, and HMOs need to observe the marketplace, experiment, and generate tangible outcomes that help them discover what is occurring, what needs to be explained, and what should be done next (Weick 1987).

Marketing activities that are designed to communicate with the public and to motivate it to consume health care services have some unique problems in health-services delivery. First, the consumption of health services is frequently remembered in negative terms; pain is often a deterrent to seeking medical care. Second, even if the physicians make the major consumption decisions, health managers should increasingly treat patients as customers and potential sources of return business or word-of-mouth advertising. If the emphasis of the marketing program is to redirect the locus of care to less costly sites and to improve patient education and compliance, society will benefit (Singh 1990).

Hospital marketing rose steadily in popularity during the 1980s. The fraction of facilities with marketing departments in 1991 increased to over 89 percent of hospitals and 50 percent of CCRCs and rehabilitation facilities (NRC 1991). The average hospital's marketing budget doubled in the 1984–85 period. Recent rates of increase have approximately kept pace with inflation, leveling off with a marketing budget equal to 3.3 percent of total revenue or 14.8 percent of profit in 1990. Are these figures high in normative terms? Computer stores and department stores spend a little bit more, and hotels and women's apparel shops spend a little bit less (American Marketing Association [AMA] 1991). The more relevant question is what the investment is buying. Any marketing cycle should end with an evaluation phase (what worked and what was the cost benefit or return on investment).

Forthman (1990) suggested a better way to analyze market-share statistics. Good hospitals have reanalyzed their exclusive focus on bed days filled or inpatient market share. Hospitals are now in the health business, not just the inpatient, high-tech business. It may be only a minor victory for a hospital to attain a higher inpatient market share while the competition achieves a dominant position in ambulatory-, chronic-, and long-term-care services. No market segment is too small to overlook in this current financial recession for many hospitals. For example, one Miami hospital closed 16 beds and opened a "Sniffles and Sneezes" center—day care for sick children. Working parents can leave their children for 12 hours at a cost of $20 and receive a staff pediatrician's exam for an additional $10. To minimize nursing staff reductions, nurses in the 224-bed hospital have been making "missionary marketing calls" on day-care centers and schools. Marketing is giving the public a better service at more flexible hours and a lower cost. Alternatively, the superior or best hospitals can try the differentiation strategy of Nordstrom and, like the Mayo Clinic, sell premium quality at a premium (high) price.

Hospital marketing is not simply the maximization of hospital admission rates or patient census. Marketing tailored to this industry, often called "social marketing," implies a service orientation (better health)—not a product orientation (more patient bed days). The smart administrator need not decrease firm size or net revenues by diversification away from inpatient care to other services. The three major rationales for diversification are (1) to acquire profit-making services (such as laboratory, radiology, alcohol rehabilitation care, and inhalation therapy); (2) to increase production volume and consequently decrease unit costs by contracting with other firms to supply services (such as laboratory, laundry, and food services); and (3) to develop a feeder system into the hospital. Although under the new HCFA payment rates ambulatory-care clinics are loss leaders, most institutions operate clinics as a feeder system into the hospital. Further, the product portfolio of the hospital can be diversified to include health promotion and health education activities designed to improve patient compliance. The problem of patient compliance and health education is a major growth area in our health care system. Problems with patient compliance to medical regimen were a contributing factor in 21 percent of the hospitalizations in one study (Mason et al. 1980). One unquestioned benefit of health marketing activities is the resulting increased sensitivity to consumer needs for amenities, information, and emotional support. Some fear that marketing health care as a commodity will ultimately demean it. In transplanting marketing techniques from the business sector, one must be careful to avoid hucksterism while pursuing competitive consumerism (Herzlinger 1989).

Marketing activities aimed at potential health care consumers are necessary for a number of reasons. First, people concerned with day-to-day living often underestimate the value of early diagnosis and preventive medicine and have to be reminded of the potential benefits of screening activities. Second, the daily news accounts of malpractice suits and second-opinion surgery studies have shaken the public faith in the medical establishment. While some skepticism is in order, unbridled skepticism can keep some people away from the health care system for too long a period. Some of the health care providers can regain public trust through customer-preference analysis and integrated market planning. For example, Humana Corporation performed a market survey of patient preferences and concluded that (1) people want to see a triage nurse or physician within minutes of their arrival at the emergency room, and (2) people resent being hassled for financial and insurance-coverage information upon arrival. Consequently, the 84 Humana hospitals guarantee that a triage nurse will see the patient within 60 seconds after arrival at the emergency room and that the financial information will be collected in due time (10, 20, or 60 minutes later).

Health care institutions might borrow their marketing principles from the following three basic points in the "Penney idea," adopted by J. C. Penney in 1913:

1. To serve the public, as nearly as we can, to its complete satisfaction
2. To expect for the service we render a fair remuneration
3. To do all in our power to pack the customer's dollar full of value, quality, and satisfaction

MARKET ANALYSIS

Marketing is a multistage process with many potential audiences. A hospital's marketing audience might include patients as consumers, physicians as direct customers of the institution, and physicians as middlemen. The first step in any marketing program is the assessment of market structure. One needs to assess the distinctive role the facility plays in meeting consumer demand in various market segments (market positioning). The existing and potential catchment area and service mix should be identified. The attractiveness and specificity of the service or product line must also be defined (market definition). The analyst should also partition the market into fairly homogeneous segments, any one of which can be expanded as a primary target market with a marketing strategy tailored to the situation. This concept of market segmentation may imply multiple marketing efforts or marketing to only one segment area. For example, mental health has six market segments (Stone, Warren, and Stevens 1990).

The second step in the typical marketing effort involves an analysis of consumer tastes and attributes. The provider of service should assess the intensity of demand for various products, perceptions of specific services and the entire facility, and the causal link between consumer behavior and image. Consumer satisfaction and multiattribute consumer preferences should be determined through conjoint measurement techniques (Reidesel 1985; Wind and Spitz 1976). The next three steps in building a marketing approach involve assessment of the product line, presentation of differential advantages relative to the competition, and development of the initial marketing program design (integrated market plan).

Management must consider the following seven stages in evaluation and periodic reexamination before making decisions about promotion, pricing, product, and place (location):

1. Market catchment area definition—demographic and geographic areas that are served or could be served.
2. Physician customer-preference analysis—what physicians require and desire for a health care facility.

3. Patient customer-preference analysis—what potential patients seek in a health facility.

4. Product-definition objectives—assessment of the present and future product lines of the health facility.

5. Differential advantages marketing—definition of what services and reputation are marketable to advance facility prestige in the eyes of customers (doctors and potential patients), including providing different messages to different customers or regulatory agencies to best project the facility image.

6. Integrated market planning and promotion—coordination of actions resulting from assessment in steps 1–5. For example, we might conclude that integration between uncoordinated hospital departments is necessary to achieve a reliable and more efficient organization. The forthcoming management ideas are often quite simple—for example, placing nuclear medicine next to the X-ray department so that patient transporters in each department can assist the other during peak demand periods. Efficient transportation and scheduling can significantly contain costs and increase consumer perception of the quality of the institution. The marketing program promotes the message to the two basic customer groups: consumers and physicians.

7. Market activity evaluation—assessment of the costs and benefits of marketing activities and making timely corrective action. Management and trustees must ultimately decide whether the long-run intangible benefits and discounted cash flows justify reorganizing priorities.

The first stage, market catchment area definition, is a familiar process for most health care facilities. Hospitals have been performing this element of the marketing process under the title of needs assessment for over 20 years. However, certain elements of the marketing function, such as informing the public of the availability of new services and departments, are tasks that most administrators fail to perform effectively.

In performing a physician customer market survey (stage 2), the hospital must make basic decisions as to which preferences it should weight highest. If the objective function of the hospital is to maximize the patient census, then it should give highest priority to the preferences of physicians who admit the largest number of patients—general surgeons and family practitioners. If the objective function is to operate the hospital as a feeder system for the hospital-based specialists, then general surgeons who require less assistance from these specialists would have a lower priority relative to internists and other specialists.

Historically, market research of consumer preferences (stage 3) has been done by the health planners. While the old-style health planners of the 1950s and 1960s did not use marketing jargon, their mission was to assess consumer needs, promulgate new product lines, and open new service points. Planners utilized the jargon of needs assessment and increased accessibility, but the approach was vintage health marketing (Eastaugh 1982). Consumers value access, but they also value amenities such as well-decorated rooms, better food, and friendly personnel. Ease of exit can also help provide the patient with an overall positive impression of the institution. A courtesy discharge policy that avoids stops at the accounts receivable department on the final day of hospitalization is one potential approach.

Physician Bonding: Don't Stop in Stage 3

Some analysts tailor the marketing approach to the physician as the ultimate client, while others emphasize studying the preferences of consumers. A dual approach of studying both groups is probably warranted. The Humana Corporation applied a two-pronged approach in Louisville, Kentucky. Initially, it performed a market survey of consumer preferences by telephone and interview. After discovering that over one-third of the families did not have a physician, Humana published an ad in the paper stating: "If you need help finding a doctor, fill out this coupon." The consumers' referral coupons were provided only to the doctors affiliated with Humana. As a result of the coupon referral program, the patient census increased 8.1 percent. In the second prong of its market survey, Humana assessed physician preferences by asking existing Humana-affiliated physicians and potential new physicians how Humana might satisfy the physicians' needs.

Physician bonding in the 1990s, making medical staff more connected to their institution (hospital, HMO), goes well beyond the old simple strategy of having an annual physician recognition dinner (Valentine 1991). Programs to enhance physician bonding to their hospital are of four basic types: (1) physician income production (joint ventures, leasing companies); (2) referral production (consumer phone referrals, appointment tracking, patient-transportation systems, and voice mail systems between doctors); (3) patient retention (patient satisfaction tracking, market research); and (4) office support systems (practice management, computer networks, bill-collection services, malpractice coverage, fax machines, and subsidized office space). Certain physicians will return the favor by acting as "product champions" and will force a reluctant board to finance their product lines. The product champion can also assist in the formalized relationships necessary to build a referral system (D'Amaro and Pahwa 1990).

Do physician bonding efforts by hospitals have a sufficient return on investment to justify such programs? Each hospital should perform its own calculus on this issue, but there is some evidence in the aggregate to suggest that hospital-physician relations are shifting. If one considers hospital production efficiencies based on the 1985 American Medical Association's Professional Practice Activities census, primary staff physicians had marginal products of 82 admissions per year. However, if the analysis is updated to the 1990 AMA census, primary staff physicians had marginal products of 122 admissions per year for their hospital. Given that there has been no large upswing in admissions, these results suggest that physicians are committing more of their patient load to the hospital of their primary affiliation.

Product-Line Thinking: Stages 4 and 5

A facility should look at the product-market competencies of neighboring facilities in the process of assessing internal product-definition objectives (stage 4). Some product lines may need to be expanded, contracted, or phased out of existence (MacStravic 1989). The decisions are seldom simple—for example, the maternity or emergency-room services are seldom cost-beneficial unless one includes offsetting revenue from estimated return business and ancillary services. If diversification of the product line seems in order, the decision should be made in consultation with the four internal publics (trustees, physicians, volunteers, and employees) and the numerous external publics (bankers, unaffiliated physicians, philanthropists, suppliers, consumers, regulators, and competitors). Depending on the service-area demographics, new product lines for consideration might include rheumatology, multiphasic annual physicals, alcoholism treatment, prenatal clinics, nuclear medicine, nephrology, and mental health services (Zelman and McLaughlin 1990; NRC 1991).

Targeting more resources to certain segments of the market where one has a differential advantage (stage 5) and contracting resources from other segments can reap a larger market share for facilities that previously provided a whole range of services. In the recent era of more stringent forms of reimbursement, to ignore market segmentation increases the risk of falling behind in the purchase of state-of-the-art equipment. In other words, the rate regulators may allow a facility the slack to purchase expensive updated replacement equipment in three to five departments but not in all areas. Rate-regulation programs provide incentives for increased specialization in the hospital industry, as observed in chapter 2.

Stage 5, differential advantages marketing, should involve an honest self-assessment of the institution. One must carefully differentiate poor-quality "centers of nonexcellence" from the ego requirements of some physicians and managers to "offer all things for all DRGs"—even if services are done poorly. For a hospital to underspecialize is to renege on any commitment to quality and economy. To discard certain services does not renege on the principle of patient access when other hospitals already offer those services (Anderson and Lomas 1989). The resistance of hospitals to participate in regionalization plans has retarded both the quality and efficiency of care. The increasingly market-driven hospital sector will soon make the price system the "planner," and regionalization dreams of public health officials 30 to 40 years ago will rapidly become a reality. Petty ego-turf considerations among medical staff, managers, and trustees will slow the rate at which service-line specialization occurs. Some faculty members may suggest that medical education cannot be as efficiently accomplished in a world with fewer teaching beds and more specialization across hospitals. As we shall observe in chapter 8, finance will soon drive function and organization in many academic centers. The style of the $8-billion medical education system must adapt to a hospital economy fast approaching $300 billion, and not vice versa. Excess capacity and substantial fixed-cost investments in underutilized product lines make hospital underspecialization an irresponsible market strategy.

Stage 6, integrated market planning, includes more than tactical within-institution decisions. After the hospital has decided on a course of action, it must inform both the public and the physician community via a promotional campaign. The health care institution must extol the virtues of its new market-position plan in terms of optimum cost, service, and quality patient care. The promotional campaign should not tell consumers things that they already know—for example, "Our emergency room is open 24 hours a day." Promotion should establish in the consumer's mind a point of difference between the institution and the competition (White 1990). The desired target audience plus the message will determine the media of choice (magazines, newspapers, billboards, radio, television, directories). Teaching hospitals would do well to inform potential patients that they do not have to be referred in order to receive services. The marketing plan should also be consumer directed. For example, patients at the Cleveland Clinic are informed that if their physician is more than 15 minutes late, the bill gets cut in half. The message to the public is clear: We run an efficient system that respects consumers' time and money. The quality of amenities in a good hospital should not be different from the quality of amenities at a good hotel—you do not have to serve poorly prepared food to be called a hospital.

Prior to the 1980s marketing was viewed as "image" advertising or glorified public relations. The hospital's public-relations director would put forth a general image of institutional caring and compassion. This timid approach was characterized by the generalization that physicians drive the consumers to "need" services and that all demands are professionally defined. The current strategy is more aggressive and tailored to appeal to the informed consumer—that is, find out what consumers want and offer it at the right place and the right price and with the right style. If the institution continues to promote only general messages about "quality caring care," its consumer image will become indistinguishable from that of the competition. Hospitals that promote certain special areas of excellence often improve utilization across a number of service lines. These hospitals, by distinguishing their institutional comparative advantages in the minds of the consumers, benefit from a "halo effect" across a wider range of departments.

Consumers increasingly choose to select a new hospital or physician rather than return to the same provider. Patients also exercise more power in selecting which services will be "purchased" (Miaoulis 1985; Inguanzo and Harju 1985). The market-promotion campaign should communicate to all employees as well as to consumers. Many hospitals educate employees in better guest relations. Promises are made to all concerned—for example, that the nurses will respond to the call bell within 30 seconds, that the food will be served hot, and that people will knock before entering a patient's room. All these concerns are merely an application of the Golden Rule: Treat the patient as you would wish to be treated. Comparison shoppers may represent a minor fraction of the institution's potential patient mix, but one needs every possible patient. The most irrational management decision would be to invest millions to develop a new program and then to cut the promotional campaign designed to tell the community what has been done for it. Some administrators may wince at investing $130,000 per 100 beds per year on marketing activities, but the greater danger comes from underinvestment. If one was promoting a leisure good rather than a necessary service, the marketing budget could well run 20 to 50 times higher.

Promotional activities can also be organized by product line (Ruffner 1986). Most hospitals with over 200 beds could benefit from a product-line manager who wears two hats: one in operations and one as a marketer. If the potential job applicant thinks that marketing is "selling and advertising," you know that you have a "dud" job candidate. Product-line management is a critical function that requires some degree of marketing background. The good product-line manager will continue to evaluate the effectiveness of promotional campaigns, will suggest new and creative ways to communicate with the various market segments (including physicians), and will cross organizational lines informally to assess all activities that affect the product or service (Wixon 1985; Zelman and Parham 1990). Employees can better promote their institution if they have a uniform positive service vision, empowerment of the employees (Ulrich and Lake 1991).

Linking Declining Admission Rates to Product-Line Planning

Much of the decline in admission rates has to be explained by factors other than a simple substitution of inpatient care for ambulatory care. Many analysts predicted that admission rates would increase with PPS, but the opposite effect has been observed for all age groups. Is the decline in admission rates a perverse result of PPS? Indeed, if there existed only one DRG, and payment were on a per case basis, one would expect the admissions for that condition to increase. However, when there are hundreds of DRGs with varying degrees of hospital-specific profitability depending on product-line volume, price, and cost behavior, some profitable DRGs will have higher admission rates and some unprofitable DRGs will have declining rates. The net effect on admissions is hard to predict in the short run. Decisions in 1983–84 to trim or close product lines based on ex ante cost analysis may have produced the net decline in admission rates under PPS. This product-line profitability issue has been discussed for years among academics (Neuhauser 1972), but until PPS the incentive to actually change behavior and trim departments was buried under the comfortable blanket of cost reimbursement.

Two hypotheses may explain hospital decisions to shrink, divest (close), initiate (open), or expand a service line. One hypothesis is that hospital managers exhibit an asymmetry in confidence in their cost-accounting information in that they trust the information much more when it suggests that the facility is losing money on the service. For example, managers have only a 60 percent confidence in the information if the experimental cost-accounting system reports that money is being made on the product line, and thus they are slow to act. But if the cost analysis reports product-line losses, managers have 95 percent confidence in the information out of fear for financial survival, and they will definitely act on the information by trimming or closing the service. This asymmetrical concern in favor of the downside is best captured in one physician/manager's observation: "Dump those big money-losing services. That way you don't need to dump individual patients; you can just say you do not offer services in those areas." Such a policy would be good for the patients and good for the institution. To balance service and solvency, hospitals must eliminate their low-volume, low-quality services.

Consider the following example. A hypothetical hospital had three types of cases in 1991: 10,000 profitable cases, 10,000 money losers (unprofitable cases), and 20,000 break-even cases. In 1992, if the hospital expanded profitable service volume by 4 percent and cut back unprofitable service volume by 20 percent, the net impact on admissions could be a 4 percent decline. The portfolio of profitable/neutral/unprofitable admissions would have changed from 10,000/20,000/10,000 in 1991 to 10,400/20,000/8,000 in 1992, for a net decline of 1,600 admissions. Profitability is influenced by volume, operating costs, utilization review, and payment rates. Profitability is dynamic, so a service that is labeled a "loser" based on historic data could turn out to be highly profitable if neighboring hospitals drop that service or only pick up enough volume to achieve scale economies. For example, single DRG product lines like DRGs 88, 132, and 294 could be highly unprofitable at 60 percent of all hospitals, but could prove to be profitable due to the achievement of sufficient volume, resulting in scale economies, at 15 percent of the hospitals. Conversely, single DRG product lines like DRGs 148, 174, 209, and 336 could be profitable at 65 percent of hospitals, but unprofitable due to insufficient volume and consequent higher unit costs at 10 percent of hospitals.

The second hypothesis is that pressure to preserve market share and stabilize operating profit margins varies by organizational type (e.g., freestanding hospital versus multihospital system; Tucker and Zaremba 1991) and by the CEO's capacity to distinguish between controllable and uncontrollable strategic issues (Thomas McDaniel and Anderson 1990). Any CEO who thinks that quality is an uncontrollable issue in the "full control of the physicians" should consider a career change. Product-line decisions are dynamic and in turn affect quality care (Eastaugh 1991; Hughes et al. 1988; Eastaugh and Eastaugh 1986). Moreover, a number of studies have demonstrated that product-line management has proved effective in cutting costs, capacity, and duplication of service (Nackel and Kues 1986; Fackelman 1985; Goodrich and Hastings 1985; MacStravic 1986).

Quality and Unit Cost by Service Product Line

Two findings that economists and physicians accept as valid lead to a third supposition of interest to both groups. First, economies of scale exist, and unit cost falls as volume increases. Second, quality increases with scale—that is, it improves as volume of a product line increases. This second finding has been confirmed in numerous studies tracking posthospital and hospital mortality and morbidity (Flood, Scott, and Ewy 1984a, 1984b; Wolfe et al. 1983; Farber, Kaiser, and Wenzel 1981; Shortell and LoGerfo 1981; Luft 1980; Luft, Bunker, and Enthoven 1979; Smith and Larsson 1989; Maerki, Luft, and Hunt 1986; Hughes, Hunt, and Luft 1987). To paraphrase Peterson et al. (1956), in-practice, high-volume providers do the best-quality work, and low-volume, out-of-practice providers do poorly. The causal effect might be a two-way street: low-volume providers perform poorly, and poor-quality providers receive fewer referrals and therefore cannot increase volume. Both laws of scale—efficiency and quality enhancement—are outlined in figure 6.1. Figure 6.1.A is the well-known law of economies of scale; unit cost (U) declines with a larger scale of output. In figure 6.1.B open-heart surgery provides a classic example of curve A, chole-cystectomy provides an example of curve B, and transurethral prostate resections provide an example of curve C. These operations (curve C) flatten out at a scale of 100 to 200 (V') annual cases, whereas hip replacements flatten out at a relatively low scale of 30 to 50 cases (Luft, Bunker, and Enthoven 1979). These scale effects will shift with time and technology, but it is important to note that Peterson's original work was in primary care (Peterson et al. 1956). Hence the scale effect is not exclusive to surgery.

The supposition in figure 6.1.C is that good medicine is also good economics, with higher volume yielding better quality and lower unit costs. It may seem counterintuitive that facilities with lower unit costs (exclusive of their other special missions such as teaching or indigent care) also have higher-quality outcomes, but "economies running in hand with quality" are prevalent in the market for most ordinary consumer goods. One does not need to own a Porsche 928 or an American television to know that higher initial expense often buys higher rates of malfunction. For example, Whirlpool washing machines are substantially cheaper and of higher quality than General Electric. *Consumer Reports* labels the higher-cost GE product as the lower-quality product.

The impact of increases in volume on mortality is difficult to assess. For example, in the context of surgical studies, limiting the sample framework to in-hospital mortality may be a problem. Following patients for 60 days after surgery removes any possible confounding effects of length of stay, patient transfers, and other factors. Riley and Lubitz (1985) examined the relationship between volume and mortality 60 days after surgery and found a mortality decline with increased volume for coronary bypass, transurethral resection of the prostate, hip arthroplasty, and resection of the intestine. Their analysis was repeated using only inpatient deaths as the dependent variable, and the results indicated

Figure 6.1
Three Potential Relationships between Hospital Service Quality, Volume, and Unit Cost

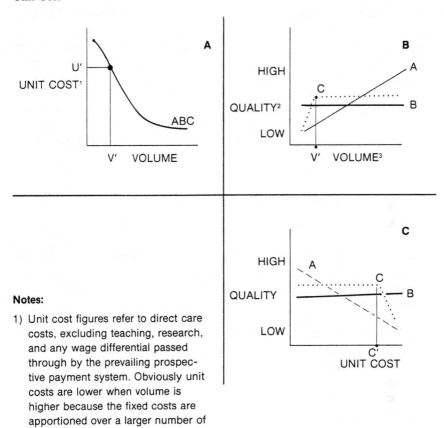

Notes:

1) Unit cost figures refer to direct care costs, excluding teaching, research, and any wage differential passed through by the prevailing prospective payment system. Obviously unit costs are lower when volume is higher because the fixed costs are apportioned over a larger number of patients.

2) Quality index would include outcome measures such as mortality rates correcting for case severity, morbidity rates, and serious adverse patient occurrence rates.

3) Point V' is the point along hypothetical curve C at which volume increases no longer improve the quality of service.

a considerably stronger association between increased volume and lower mortality. The complex volume-quality correlation has been reaffirmed by Luft et al. (1990).

If hospitals desire to maximize quality more institutions might consider specialization; yielding fewer departments with more volume per department (and hopefully more quality per product-line. Specialization of product-lines does not always occur, especially in two-hospitals towns with equal financial strength and with equally matched medical staffs. For example, no product-lines have been dropped in the two-hospital city of Kalamazoo, Michigan. The 462-bed Catholic hospital Borgess Medical Center is in a medical arms race with the 478-bed Bronson Methodist Hospital. Each tries to maintain a prenatal center and cardiovascular team; while the local newspaper editor argues for consolidation of the duplicated $5.1 million helicopter service and specialization of certain product-lines. One hospital is better in prenatal care, while the second hospital is better in cardiovascular surgery. Dysfunctional competition prevents cost control and quality enhancement. Consequently, C. Everett Koop, in his public television series, is correct in his assertion that two-hospital towns have 30 percent higher cost than one-hospital towns.

Doubts about Cost and Quality Scale Effects

Economies of scope have been postulated as a countervailing force to consider before trimming product lines in the name of specialization. Economies of scope, the efficiencies of joint production of a wide variety of product lines, have been found in other industries. However, if such benefits do exist among physician areas of specialization, the evidence is not statistically significant (Bays 1986; Conrad and Strauss 1983; Cowing and Holtman 1983). Some analysts have suggested that the causal direction between high volume and better quality has been reversed and that volume does not breed quality. Alternatively, quality attracts volume, and facilities do more surgery because they have lower mortality rates (Dranove 1984). This speculation might become more accurate in the late 1990s, as consumers receive more information on quality (Eastaugh and Eastaugh 1986). (Quality will be considered in chapters 11 and 15.) However, there is currently no evidence that patients or their physicians select hospitals based on their low mortality rates for specific conditions (Flood, Scott, and Ewy 1984a; Eraker and Sox 1981). The results of Flood, Scott, and Ewy's analysis concerning the volume effects on quality were strengthened, not weakened, by inclusion of teaching status and size into the analysis (Flood, Scott, and Ewy 1984a). This suggests that consumers and their physicians do not shop effectively on the basis of quality for the better hospitals. Perhaps with more physician competition, comparison shopping, and information disclosure, consumers will be able to shop more effectively for quality and value (Luft et al. 1990).

One should note that scale is measured by volume of the product-line output, not by capacity of the total institution. Thus a large hospital with many product lines may not have enough volume to achieve sufficient scale economies, while each line in a smaller, more specialized hospital may achieve a good scale volume. For instance, an 800-bed hospital offering 460 DRGs and 90 basic product lines with a net volume of 900 admissions per week would have an average scale of 10 admissions per product line. A 400-bed hospital offering

250 DRGs and 25 basic product lines might have a net volume of 500 admissions per week, or an average scale of 20 admissions per product line. The smaller hospital has double the scale per product line compared to the 800-bed facility. Scale by product line, not scale of the hospital, is the key to good medicine and good economics.

Hughes et al. (1988) raised the issue of whether high-volume providers make for better provider performance (the practice-makes-perfect hypothesis), or whether the better providers get more referrals and thus more volume (the best-get-more-business hypothesis). The mix of both explanations depends on the clinical condition. For some conditions the explanation that practice makes one better dominates (cholecystectomy, stomach surgery, acute myocardial infarction), while for other conditions the explanation of selective referral is more important (cardiac bypass grafts, prostatectomy, femur fracture). Cause and effect on the quality issue are difficult to establish, given two alternative explanations: volume is too low to maintain sufficient quality (i.e., if some hospitals closed the service, market share and volume would increase for those keeping this product line), or low-quality providers discourage referrals and keep the volume low (Eastaugh and Eastaugh 1986). Irrespective of the cause-and-effect dynamic, specialization is associated with maintaining or enhancing the quality of patient care. Hughes, Hunt, and Luft (1987) indicated that specialization allows nurses and physicians to develop more expertise with respect to a specific category of patients.

CLUSTERING DRGS INTO STRATEGIC PRODUCT-LINE GROUPINGS (SPGS)

Hospitals are in need of two forms of increased management control. First, line managers strive for better efficiency management in the production of intermediate services, such as nursing care or lab tests. The second crucial stage of management control is effectiveness management, including utilization review and quality assurance. The goal is to enhance quality and avoid the overtreatment of patients with costly intermediate services. From an ethical and economic viewpoint, what ultimately counts is the final product: a patient treated and returned to good health. It does little good to focus only on the intermediate components of the hospital-service production function (figure 6.2). What matters from an analytical viewpoint is effectiveness and efficiency within clusters of "peer" (like) final products or strategic product-line groupings (SPGs). It is important to know what it costs to start, expand, contract, or close an SPG in a hospital.

A SPG is defined as a clustering of similar DRGs performed by an identified subset of the medical staff. Trustees and managers have a responsibility to ask what it costs to open, expand, trim, or close a given SPG. Consequently, profitability and growth opportunity must be determined periodically. Unlike the business world, a hospital's service product line cannot sponsor its own auton-

Figure 6.2
Vertical Cost Accounting of Final Products and Strategic Product-Line Groupings of DRGs

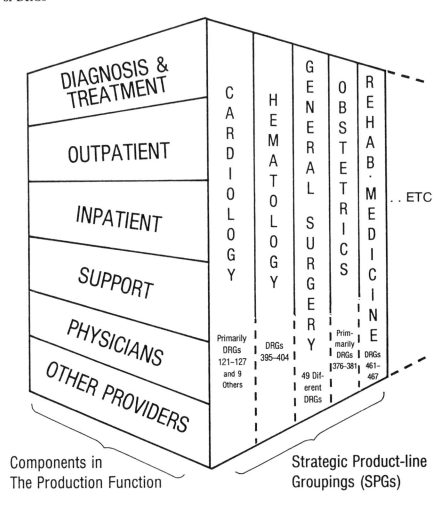

Components in The Production Function

Strategic Product-line Groupings (SPGs)

omous marketing division. Service lines in the hospital sector are clearly more jointly interconnected and interdependent in the provision of inpatient care. Insufficient realization of this interdependency is what caused zero-based budgeting to fail.

The definition of SPGs should be institutionally specific and should involve strong input from medical staff. Allowing each hospital's medical staff to "reinvent the wheel" offers the following three advantages: (1) identifying SPGs would be a first step toward effecting change in the organization; (2) physician partners in strategic financial planning must contribute in defining the unit of analysis if they are to gain some sense of "ownership" and defend the plan; and (3) medical practice habits vary considerably across regions. For a given SPG, the relevant type of physician to include in the process may vary. For example, in one northeastern city the service line of endoscopy is 85 percent controlled (performed) by gastroenterologists. However, in one southern city the market share of endoscopy is evenly divided 35/35/30 percent between general surgery, internal medicine, and gastroenterology, respectively. In the case of one western hospital, endoscopy is 75 percent controlled by internal medicine. Suggested changes in the medical-staff composition or marketing of an SPG will have to take account of local habits and physician supply characteristics.

SPGs are based on physician peer-grouping criteria for two reasons. First, SPGs have interconnected referral patterns that require a "critical mass" of certain cases to make the line economically viable for all parties concerned. Second, doctors are the most important input in the delivery of patient care. SPGs are operationally useful in making physician recruitment and retention decisions. If the hospital is aggressively growing in a given area, either because the market potential is good or because profitability is high, it could experience a high return on investment in attracting or keeping clinicians in that SPG. Medical-staff revenue projections by area are critical in staff development planning (Shortell 1985). If DRGs are the new language of rate setting, SPGs will soon follow as the new language of marketing, budgeting, and mission statements. Judging by the reports that trustees are the single most important factor in hospital price setting (Bauerschmidt and Jacobs 1985), trustees may often be averse to closing an SPG.

In evaluating profitability versus market opportunity potential, as shown in figures 6.3 and 6.4, decision making often becomes more of an art than a management science. The language can often get quite crass, especially in the area of marketing. For example, a CEO with a short-run focus might be reluctant to jettison two mediocre clinicians if they currently have fair to average profitability, even if they are "maxed out" (lack volume growth potential). To use the language of the other AMA, the American Marketing Association, these two doctors offering the SPG would be given the label "cash cow," because of their short-term profitability. The better hospital CEO would take the long-run perspective, consider life-cycle costing, and concentrate on safeguarding the reputation of the institution. If one factors in the malpractice expense of mediocre performers, a big loss in the courts could more than wipe out 10 years of "cash-cow" profits. Profitability should include some life-cycle costing adjustment for malpractice risk and facility reputation risk (impacting census across all SPGs).

Closing a SPG will not be a politically easy task. There are the problems of pride and ego: Clinicians invest three to nine years of their lives in graduate medical training to specialize in an SPG. Even if the market for the service is saturated, they still feel justified in prompting the hospital to continue offering the uneconomical SPG. However, why should the hospital be run down because

Figure 6.3
Hospitals Organize by Strategic Product-Line Groupings (SPGs) According to
Clusters of DRGs (20 are shown in this hypothetical hospital for FY 1985)

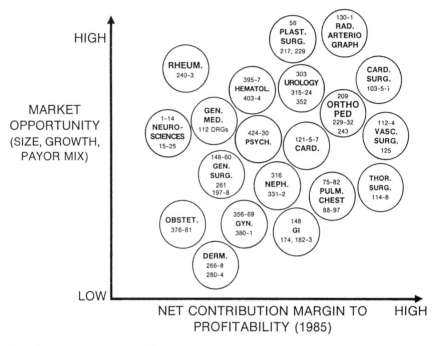

Note: Numbers refer to DRGs. The top 50 DRGs account for 94% of Medicare days and 90% of total patient days.

the supply of specialists has run up? Currently, many underutilized SPGs are incapable of achieving economies of scale or volumes sufficient to support quality care. Hiring more health care planners is not a solution for hospitals. Duplication, the oversupply of hospitals offering a SPG, is a problem not cured by external, community-based health care planning (Eastaugh, 1982).

Internal facility planning, under the pressure of tighter payment schedules, will reduce duplication and prompt regionalization. Both efficiency and effectiveness impart net profitability, as does the payer mix. Physicians must realize their part in the process. If they wish to save a SPG, they must do a better job of effectiveness management. It is impossible to run a hospital if too many SPGs lose money. Hospitals will have to pick and choose among SPGs rather than choose between high- and low-cost patients.

Specialization and Regionalization

Hospital trustees and managers are socially responsible individuals. One would predict, therefore, that they would choose to drop services (SPGs) rather than

Figure 6.4
PPS Stimulates Specialization and Regionalization over the Life Cycle of the
Institution, 1985–1987

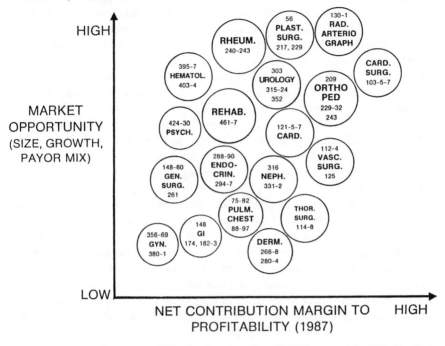

Note: Medicare declines to only 35% of patient days. Top 50 DRGs account for 98% of patient days.

lower the quality of service. The most unprofitable patients will not be left out in the cold. Instead, they will be better served at regional facilities that specialize in their SPG. Patients will have longer average travel time, but unit costs will be lower and quality will be higher. Insurance plans might consider covering travel costs for patients referred to a regional center, as is done in Canada (Luft 1985; Anderson and Lomas, 1989). This utopian summary of the possible effects of PPS-induced regionalization is all fine in theory, but the impact on access must be closely watched. One should not expect too much from the price system.

One important public policy question involves the degree to which patients would have to be concentrated in select hospitals to achieve significant reductions in preventable deaths. If society selects a realistic target, such as a 50 percent mortality reduction, the disruption in the hospital marketplace might be small (and consumer travel cost minimal). A study by Maerki, Luft, and Hunt (1986) showed that averting half the preventable deaths would require varying degrees of patient dislocation for different conditions. Patient shifts from low-volume to high-volume hospitals would involve 15 percent of the cirrhosis patients, 27 percent of the cases of fracture of the femur, 35 percent of the respiratory distress syndrome patients, 35 percent of the cardiac bypass cases, 23 percent of the gastric surgery cases, 22 percent of the appendectomies, and 15 percent of the transurethral prostatectomies. For other conditions a more realistic goal might involve only a 25 percent reduction in preventable deaths through shifting of patients (42 percent of peptic ulcer cases, 38 percent of hernia repair cases, 37 percent of total hip replacements, 33 percent of hysterectomies, 27 percent of catheterizations and angiography cases, and 18 percent of cholecystectomies) in Maerki, Luft, and Hunt's national sample. Maximal regionalization that would minimize mortality yet neglect time and travel costs for the patient and visiting relatives would suggest that patients be treated at only 10 percent of hospitals.

The burden is on the HCFA to set the price so that the last institution to offer a SPG in a local market does not drop that product line because the price is too low. Prices should be set so that access does not suffer, travel and time costs do not prove too onerous, and quality is not negatively affected. PPS prices will be most effective in stimulating specialization in nonemergency SPGs. However, the prices should not constrain emergency care, such as that for abdominal aortic aneurysms. For much of medicine, the price system can be used to close out low-volume, low-quality, high-cost SPGs. Will access be harmed under payment-system-induced regionalization? It will not if the regionalization is for non-emergency conditions, judging from the Canadian experience. Roos and Lyttle (1985) reported that in the case of hip replacements, there may be some minor differential access based on distance to the closest regional facility. However, in the cases they studied, the access differential disappeared rapidly, and the only patients who were temporarily denied service had controversial indications for surgery.

Comparisons can be made to other sectors in which competition has bred higher quality, efficiency, and access. Hospital specialization may breed regionalization similar to the airline industry's hub-and-spoke concept. A dominant medical center may have pruned a small percentage of its SPGs to act as a keystone for inpatient care in the area, with affiliations to smaller, highly specialized, few-frills, low-cost hospitals. On occasion, the hospitals that are "spokes" may pick up SPGs that the hub hospital cannot provide as efficiently or as effectively. Two hub hospitals might implicitly trade SPG areas of specialization while avoiding antitrust litigation. This concept has been carried out in the airline sector, where maintenance and cost per mile are substantially cheaper if companies "swap" SPGs and service fewer product lines. For example, in 1989 Pan Am traded 15 DC-10s to American Airlines for 8 747s.

Specialization brings lower costs and fewer mistakes. As small hospitals back out of the SPGs they never should have initiated, medical centers will inherit most intensive care unit (ICU) cases, to the benefit of quality care. Indeed, medical centers could become large ICUs. The ego-turf concerns of the professionals, whether they be physicians or pilots, will be emphasized under regionalization. For example, the "poor" 747 pilot now has to settle for flying a DC-10. What of the ego concerns of managers and providers who have to work in hospitals on a financial diet of staff reductions and lowered number of SPGs? To address this problem, incentive compensation—both financial and nonmonetary—has been proposed.

Deregulation and price competition do indeed have a habit of raising service quality and driving costly excess capacity out of the market—witness the airline, trucking, banking, and railroad industries. Judging by the over 300,000 empty hospital beds, short-term acute-care hospitals are plagued by excess capacity. Hospitals are further plagued by reregulation in the form of DRG-administered prices, but we cannot achieve "pure" competition by taking every citizen's insurance coverage away. The term "market competition" may sound to some as if philistine commercialism is being introduced to our medical system. All that is really advocated in the name of competition is to stop running hospitals like "gentlemen's clubs," immune to management science and lacking concern for productivity, efficiency, and effectiveness.

No longer will many hospitals be able to function as full-service institutions offering almost every DRG. Within the context of business history, an analogy can be drawn between hospitals and urban department stores 15 years ago. Those stores that offered a full scope of services ranging from high fashion to toasters, from soda drinks to yarn, and from hardware to silk went bankrupt. Stores that identified and specialized in their most productive product lines prospered. Stores that maintained 500 product lines and poor outpost satellite locations fell prey to the vicissitudes of the market.

Outpost clinic managers should take advantage of double-loop learning and realize after a second look at the issue that the assumptions underpinning the volume projections are overoptimistic. For example, if one builds an urgent-care center in a wealthy neighborhood, where everyone has a private physician, low prices and urgent care may not be a winning combination. On a second loop in the learning process, the clinic may be located in a middle-class neighborhood, where the clientele require the service and can pay their bills. However, productivity must be kept high to keep services affordable and profitable.

Farming provides another useful analogy to the hospital sector. Farmers who shunned excessive diversification in favor of productivity enhancement have prospered. They realize that maximum portfolio scope does little if all product lines are inefficient or experience declining utilization. Farms saddled with debt and diversified product lines have gone under. Hospitals saddled with 50 SPGs, serving over 400 DRGs, will soon discover that broadness and facility size do not ensure survival. In the jargon of economics, moving up the learning curve because of higher volumes in areas of specialization not only will increase productivity and cut costs, but also will improve service quality (Eastaugh and Eastaugh 1986).

Pitfalls of Underspecialization and Overspecialization

Hospitals on the vanguard of product-line planning have gone through one of two basic stages of misadventure: under- or overspecialization. Both groups fall prey to what Alfred North Whitehead (1932) termed the "fallacy of misplaced concreteness." Members of the first group, occupancy-maximization caretakers, place excessive faith in the slogan "Anything beats cold sheets." They will develop any SPG and underspecialize, believing that higher occupancy rates are more important than profitability. Members of the second group, short-run profit-maximizing risk takers, place excessive faith in specialization, marketing, and the ability to attract new demand to compensate for closing other SPGs. They overtrim SPGs based on short-run profitability without careful analysis of what this does for long-run profitability. It is possible, however, to balance the two approaches.

The practitioners of underspecialization and occupancy maximization in group 1 have a false sense of security in reasoning a posteriori that hospitals are like airlines in that if the hospital is filled to capacity, everything will be fine. Hospital beds are somewhat like airline seats in that they cannot be stocked as inventory, so if they are not sold today, the revenue is forgone. However, should the strategy be to offer an indiscriminately high number of SPGs in hopes of filling beds? That idea is too clever by half. Actually, a hospital can offer so many SPGs that the majority are utilized well below capacity and the net profitability contribution is negative. Hence increased volume does not prevent bankruptcy and may actually hasten closure. In finance, the ratio of volume to capacity by SPG is a critical concern. One should avoid the mania of declaring that all is well if census rises.

Members of group 2, profit maximizers through overspecialization, find false security in believing that dropping all the unprofitable SPGs improves the long-run bottom line. These short-run managers are unimpressed with the argument that profitability of the facility next year can be damaged by excessive concern for retrospective product-line profit reports. They are misled by a shallow reading of the business literature. Hospitals are more interdependent than most organizations, whereas business divisions can jettison a line without much concern for the core corporation's fixed-cost burden. Unfortunately, those forgone patients in SPGs that are closed no longer make a contribution to cover fixed costs. The remaining product lines must pick up more of a burden of the fixed costs and thus may become less profitable or unprofitable. For example, a "star" product line with fixed costs of $2,400 and profits of $275 per case can suddenly have fixed costs of $2,700 and a $25 net loss per case. The crucial task is getting compensated through increased volume in remaining SPGs after closing last year's unprofitable SPGs. In other words, enough patients must be pulled from the competition to fully compensate for the empty beds caused by discontinued SPGs.

Good marketing can go only so far in improving volume. As a general proposition, managers in group 2 would do well to trim SPGs in a slow, phased manner and to come to understand their market better over time. Hospitals face a morass of problems, of which self-induced rapid declines in occupancy rates are both an outcome and a contributing cause. Long-run profitability should be the focus of financial managers. A hospital may close some unprofitable SPGs but not so many that the patient census erodes to the point of harming the financial health of the institution. Moreover, certain slow-developing SPGs may be misidentified as poor long-run performers. Such slow-starter SPGs can be like weak-kneed quarterbacks: they may eventually save the franchise (Eastaugh and Eastaugh 1986).

Excessive pruning of SPGs in pursuit of overspecialization can cause as many financial problems as underspecialization. Overspecialization can decrease patient census and impact negatively on long-run profitability. Classic cases of occupancy reductions being a self-induced problem are found among three investor-owned chains that finished 1985 with 38 to 43 percent occupancy rates. Hospitals that succumb to the "big-picture" paralysis of underspecialization invite either closure or a takeover.

STRATEGIC PRICE SETTING

Although price elasticity of demand for hospital care is low, price decisions are still important to consumers. Consumers might be attracted by a more liberal credit policy, health education programs, or single-priced "packages" for underinsured services (for example, maternity care). One major threat to the success of hospitalization package pricing is the possibility of excessive variation in resource costs across patients. For example, the facility could unwittingly attract a biased sample of admissions that represent the more complex and costly cases because they perceive the price as a bargain.

Marketing strategy involves a number of basic questions: what services to offer (product); where to serve (place); whom to serve and how to communicate to buyers and providers (promotion); and what to charge (price). These four P's of marketing strategy were often softened by health marketers: service selection (product-mix decision), access (place), public information (promotion), and "service consideration" (price). In this section we discuss objective functions in selecting prices in the medical context and avoid renaming well-known constructs with euphemisms such as "service consideration." Hospital market planning was formerly inpatient oriented: getting the right patient in the right bed at the right time following the right promotion and sometimes following communication of a right price. Marketing activities are increasingly concerned with pricing decisions—not merely for inpatient care but for ambulatory and alternative care. Currently, there is less reliance on bed filling and more reliance on getting the patient to the most appropriate cost-effective channel of service distribution (including home care) so that society and the individual both get the most value for the investments. This trend is often labeled "social demarketing" (less institutional care), which should be contrasted with its antithesis, "negative demarketing" (a sleazy attempt to discourage the poor or underinsured patients from coming to the facility).

A review of Porter's (1980) seminal book on competitive strategy unveils six basic categories of competitive forces. In the context of pricing hospital products, those forces include the following:

1. Rivalry among existing competitors
2. Potential new entrants to the market (e.g., ambulatory surgery)
3. Bargaining power of buyers (e.g., bulk buyers eliciting PPO price discounts)
4. Bargaining power of physician/suppliers
5. Bargaining power of other suppliers
6. Rivalry from substitute products or services (these may include self-care)

In pricing hospital products, the first three factors are most critical. For each service product line, the institution should consider developing a tactical implementation plan. The hospital may undertake nine different pricing strategies for nine product lines, depending on existing competitive conditions, the possibility of new entrants, and forecasted buyer response to price changes (price elasticity). The nine strategic pricing options are the following:

1. Predatory penetration pricing is short-run pricing to gain market share, with no change in the product.
2. Slash pricing involves long-run lower prices and changing the product to make the price slashes supportable in the long run.
3. Follower pricing is not much of a strategy; it simply sets prices relative to the market leader (i.e., it avoids initiating a price war).
4. Phaseout pricing involves setting prices high, which may only be at true cost, to eliminate a seldom-utilized, often poor-quality service product line from the institution.
5. Preemptive pricing is lowering the price to make the service less attractive to potential new entrants.
6. Skim pricing is setting the price high for a unique service (unique because quality is outstanding) or for a service for which the probability of short-run declines in market share is low.
7. Segment pricing is charging higher prices when so-called ''snob effects'' exist, that is, charging a vastly different rate for a slightly different service like VIP suites.
8. Slide-down pricing is traditional price discrimination of moving down the pricing policy to tap successive layers of consumer demand when the service is highly price sensitive and/or significant economies of scale exist.
9. Loss-leader pricing is setting prices low relative to the average profit margin, but hopefully not below cost, to attract customer flow to the service or to complementary services.

Some mixture of these nine strategic pricing strategies is superior to the old-fashioned policy of hospital wide pricing rules. For example, old-style cross-subsidization through public-enterprise pricing was never statistically defensible (policies of markdowns for maternity care or markups for radiology or elective surgery were passed down through the generations of hospital superintendents on stone tablets). Likewise, public-utility pricing at marginal cost always made such charitable institutions appear capital-consuming, wasteful, and inefficient to the taxpayers who had to underwrite their operations by picking up all the other costs associated with the facility. Last, fair-share average-cost pricing with an equal percentage markup across all products suffers from two defects. First, it disallows the marketplace the opportunity to dictate a buyer-driven cross-subsidization policy—for example, accepting a higher profit markup in cosmetic surgery to support preventive medicine (e.g., mammography screening of high-risk groups). Second, it takes away all the requisite flexibility needed by management to initiate, expand, or close a service line through prudent use of different pricing strategies over time.

A specific example of how these pricing strategies might be used in a sequential fashion over the life cycle can be offered. If the hospital has no market share in starting a new product (table 6.1), it may wish to attempt the most aggressive pricing strategy, especially if this is a high-growth service. Strategy 1, predatory pricing, is a short-run, price-slashing strategy to gain initial market entry and hopefully gain significant market share. The new firm on the block should not expect the dominant firms always to react. For example, IBM seldom reacts to a price-cutting campaign from smaller firms because it would rather take a wait-and-see attitude to observe if the new entrant (1) can survive, (2) can pick up a significant market share, and (3) can equilibrate back to a higher price level that still might beat IBM's prices but does not threaten to take much more market share away. Any hospital should raise its prices after short-run experimentation with predatory pricing in order to solidify its market position. If weaker rivals in the marketplace decide to stop offering a given service, one can charge substantially higher prices (and perhaps even reap monopolists' profits). If existing firms maintain this service line but do not counterpunch or appear as potential losers in a price war after the new firm's successful entry into the market, one may wish to attempt strategy 2: slash pricing in the longer run.

Slash pricing invites a price war. In almost every case slash pricing should involve a change in the product in order for the price structure to prove sustainable over time. For example, People's Express and Southwest Airlines changed the product called air travel by making the public pay for certain à la carte services (food, a checked bag) and through nonmonetary mechanisms (e.g., the time costs of flying through Newark). However, the quality of the basic product, air travel, was in no sense discounted. Indeed, the slash-pricing strategy can result in a social good by opening up the product to new users, including first-time users.

Southwest Air survives, but People's Express went bankrupt. People's Express underestimated the ability of other existing competitors to employ strategy 5, preemptive pricing. For example, United Airlines could sharply reduce the prices on 11 new routes that People's moved into or was about to move into. Preemptive pricing is a strategy to preserve market share by preventing competitive entry

Table 6.1
Seven Basic Strategic Pricing Methods

Market Growth Potential	Market Share			
	Zero	*Low*	*Moderate*	*High*
A. High	1. Predatory penetration pricing (no change in product) 2. Slash pricing, and change the product 2. Slash pricing 3. Follower pricing	2. Slash pricing 1. Predatory penetration pricing 3. Follower pricing	5. Preemptive pricing 3. Follower pricing 6. Skim pricing	5. Preemptive pricing 7. Segment pricing 6. Skim pricing
B. Moderate	1. Predatory penetration pricing 3. Follower pricing	1. Predatory penetration pricing	3. Follower pricing 6. Skim pricing	5. Preemptive pricing 6. Skim pricing
C. Low	3. Follower pricing 2. Slash pricing	4. Phaseout pricing 3. Follower pricing	6. Skim pricing 7. Segment pricing	6. Skim pricing 7. Segment pricing

Note: The strategies are listed within each box according to strategic preference; the numbers refer only to order of listing in the text. Two other pricing methods are discussed in the text: 8. slide-down pricing and 9. loss-leader pricing.

or expansion. Preemptive pricing is typically used by firms with above-average market share for services with above-average market-growth potential. For example, if the People's Express of the local health market catchment area is attempting to open a nearby urgent-care center or expand into coronary angioplasty, one can preempt the firm's plans with pricing strategy 5. To maintain preemptive price levels that make market expansion into the specific service line seem unattractive, the firm would have to trim its cost behavior in line with the reduced prices and/or make money elsewhere in the organization to cross-subsidize the discounted prices. With sufficient economies of scale, the firm may still make a profit at a price that would be unprofitable for new entrants.

Not to have a strategy is itself a strategy. Consequently, pricing strategy 3, follower pricing, is the easiest alternative. If the service offers little potential for product differentiation and it proposes to offer a "me-too" or "copycat" entry (e.g., endoscopy), a facility can simply price relative to the industry leader. Needless to say, this is a timid strategy that invites and almost guarantees low growth. For example, one cannot name a single company that exists by offering copies of IBM products at IBM prices (under those circumstances consumers would rather buy from IBM). To paraphrase a basketball college coach, follower pricing is a "chill-out" strategy, allowing time to mend and heal before deciding on a new strategy.

If all else fails and the service line has proven a financial failure, the best strategy to close out a product is strategy 4: phaseout pricing. This strategy should never be employed if any harm would come to the health of the community, perhaps because only one hospital is offering the service. However, phaseout pricing can quickly allow the price-sensitive patients to close an existing service when flat-out withdrawal of the service would result in a negative reaction from certain trustees, physicians, or local citizens. For example, if the hospital offers poor-quality cardiac surgery once every three weeks at an actual cost that is 200 percent higher than that of the local teaching hospital, one can phaseout price the service at actual cost. So few customers will come to visit the hospital for poor-quality cardiac surgery at a premium high cost that the hospital will have to close the service. The results of phaseout pricing are both good medicine and good economics. (A more detailed discussion of quality of care is contained in chapter 11.)

For certain providers unaccustomed to the business-strategy literature, the talk of closing services or engaging in price wars seems unprofessional. However, the public will avidly support the price wars among health care providers in the 1990s the way they supported aggressive competition among airlines and banks. The public benefits from such activity. Managers and providers must recognize the dynamic quality of health care markets. All the constant change and competitive action and reaction will make any pricing strategy out-of-date very rapidly. Failure to grasp this point and to readjust the pricing (and promotion) plan every four, six, or eight months will contribute to the closing of a number of hospitals.

Strategy 6, skim pricing, offers the institution an opportunity to reap profits by attracting "cream buyers" to a unique-quality product. The product has to have consumer perception of high value for the money, and marketing researchers have uncovered this image in everything from lithotripsy (kidney-stone treatment) to Maytag washing machines. Skim pricing is most effective for the hospital if the price elasticity of demand is low (e.g., consumers care little about price in avoiding chest pain or kidney-stone pain). The market barriers to entry are usually high because of the substantial fixed costs associated with acquiring the service. However, skim-pricing policies will be hard to maintain if competitors enter and achieve a comparable high-quality unique reputation in the eyes of the consumer. However, if one's brand-name reputation is so firm that one can continue to skim price indefinitely, the institution should continue to price high (e.g., the Cleveland Clinic in cardiac surgery). Analogously, Maytag washing machines continue to sell at a very high price because their breakdown (quality) rate is substantially better than that of the competition. Pricing strategy 7, segment pricing, is a mechanism to sell prestige "Yuppie snob suites" to those with the ability to pay cash for additional amenities.

Pricing strategy 8, slide-down pricing, is a mechanism by which the facility can tap successive layers of demand at different price levels. For example, one may wish to sell mobile mammography screening to high-risk women at $111 in the three wealthy neigborhoods in Washington, but in the poor neighborhoods the van can change the list price to $39. This strategy makes sense when there is a substantial price and income elasticity of demand. Moreover, the investment has a better net present value if the van is utilized to scale. In addition, this pricing policy does substantial social good if it brings a necessary service to new customers. Insurance plans often prevent the practice of price discrimination, but the strategy can be pursued if the service is not insured or if the provider wishes to forgo aggressive collections of cost-sharing payments from poor or elderly patients. As with any form of price discrimination, the rich can beat the system by driving to the lower-cost point of service, but few if any do so.

Finally, strategy 9, loss-leader pricing, has two basic variations. Some hospitals sell loss leaders at below actual costs, which is a less than prudent strategy in an increasingly competitive marketplace. Other hospitals charge "loss-leader" prices in the sense that they charge 50 to 100 percent less than their average hospitalwide profit margin, but they never price at less than average cost for the service. The loss-leader approach is often rationalized as a marketing tool to pick up complementary demand. For example, one can sell baby care as a loss leader to attract the parents to have adult care at the facility. Alternatively, a dentist or optometrist could sell the initial-visit charge as a loss leader in hopes of making a substantial profit on the follow-up care.

In a service industry such as health care, consumption and production typically occur in the same location. Consequently, vertical pricing decisions within distribution channels are seldom relevant except in the case of independent practice associations or other contract-service situations. Horizontal pricing decisions are made at the retail level by commercial insurance plans or Blue Cross plans paying negotiated charges. Governmental payers and half of the Blue Cross plans simply pay cost or the health industry equivalent of wholesale prices.

ADVERTISING AND DEMAND CREATION

In principle, to inform the public is the essence of advertising. The most frequently misunderstood concept concerning the marketing process is the belief that consumers are so ignorant and gullible in the health care business that they can be duped into asking for services they do not in fact need. No study has demonstrated that advertising merely stimulates medically unnecessary utilization. A number of 1991 surveys suggested that Americans are well informed about health and hygiene matters but believe that modern medicine has the miracle techniques and spare parts to fix them no matter how they live their lives. Future research should consider the question of whether the excessive faith the public has in technology makes it susceptible to misleading advertising campaigns or whether public faith is on the wane. Malpractice stories in the media might be eroding the public faith in medical technology.

One should not suggest that advertising will induce consumers to suddenly shop for health plans and providers as methodically as they shop for automobiles. It is clear that many individuals will opt for the protection and security of the status quo and will not shop among competing health plans. Most consumers will not immediately abandon their current providers, even after being convinced that a new health-delivery option will save the family a few dollars per week. However, over time, if the family has a ''bad'' experience with its doctor or hospital, it will be more likely to upgrade the importance of cost considerations in its future annual enrollment decisions and move to the plan that provides the best buy with all factors considered. Consumer tastes concerning what is valuable in health care service delivery will vary widely in American society. Not all individuals will agree with the average group consensus concerning medical care, because care is in many ways an ''experience good''—that is, a good that must be experienced in order to value its intangible and tangible attributes.

Expanded services or new inclusive pricing packages should be promoted in a well-managed institution. The perceived style of advertising is important in the health arena. Noncompetitive ''natural'' advertising, sometimes labeled ''social marketing,'' is generally more acceptable to health providers than competitive advertising (''buy our product''). Hospitals should go beyond the product orientation of selling inpatient or hospital-based services and realize that their one chance for expansion may reside in taking a broader market orientation. The hospital could then better serve the latent demands of the community with independent ambulatory surgicenters, home health care services, and health education and promotion (Eastaugh 1984). The target market segments might best be reached by interpersonal media (Gombeski, Carroll, and Lester 1990) or be drawn to the facility by a basic change in the product—an augmented product with supplemental activities provided (e.g., in maternity care; Panitz 1990).

Five basic rationales for advertising include (1) public education about health care, (2) information on service availability, (3) accounting to the community, (4) seeking support, and (5) employee recruitment. The industry also lists guidelines for acceptable advertising content: truth and accuracy, "fairness" in avoiding any quality comparisons with the competition, and avoiding "claims of prominence." The hospital industry has been rather slow in recognizing the need for differential advantages marketing. In the minds of the authors of the advertising code, the public has no right to know if a competitor has less modern facilities, a less well trained staff, or inferior quality of care. Most hospital marketing campaigns should be more consumer oriented and less physician oriented.

Physician-induced investment, leading to overcapitalization, is a frequently mentioned problem of the hospital industry. Granfield (1975) was the first to suggest that the hospital industry is subject to the Averch-Johnson (1962) hypothesis: Hospitals are regulated, protected from competition, and consequently overcapitalized. As was observed in chapter 2, from the standpoint of physician utility preferences, overcapitalization in the hospital sector is helpful if it increases slack capacity (and thus the certainty that physicians can get their patients admitted) and technology availability. Having an excess capacity of diagnostic and therapeutic equipment is "efficient" for physician utility maximization because it increases income from interpretation of test results and decreases waiting time for information to be acquired. Physicians have an incentive to keep their retailer—the local hospital—afloat and well equipped. Many physicians view their relationship with the hospital as analogous to the relationship of a freelance mechanic to a garage, except that the clinical setting must be substantially cleaner. The medical staff, like the mechanic, is not required to pay rent for user privileges. In this context, we shall review three basic models for describing the patient service-production process.

If one assumes that the physicians control the medical-hospital producer-retailer channel, the clinician can achieve maximum profits by forcing the retailer (hospital) to purchase inputs and produce services that just cover the hospital's costs. The physician as the producer (manufacturer) controls the supply in the distribution channel and can largely dictate the price for nonphysician providers in the channel. It is in the physicians' interest to have the retailers (hospitals) provide a very expensive, technologically intensive style of service. The professional fees of the physicians are proportionally higher when they are interpreting and performing the more technologically intensive tests and procedures. Prevailing fee-for-service medical care involves a one-level distribution channel (where the number of intermediaries determines the length of the channel) consisting of the physician (manufacturer) and the hospital (retailer) providing care to the consumer. Medical care provided in the inner city is typically a two-level channel of physician (manufacturer), teaching hospital (wholesaler intermedi-

Figure 6.5
Potential Equilibrium in the Doctor-Hospital Producer-Retailer Production
Channel for Hospital Services

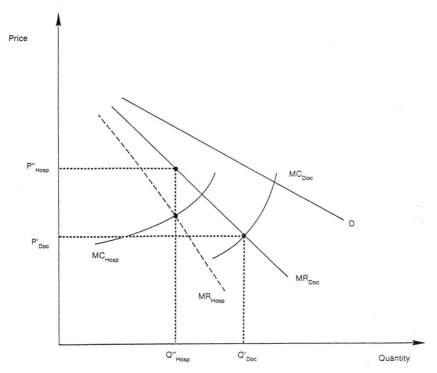

ary), and satellite clinic (retailer) providing the product to the consumer. The physician must set prices in reference to the demand function for professional plus hospital services combined, since physician and hospital services are complements. Consequently, making maximum use of hospital resources, collecting maximum possible fees for test interpretation, and supporting profit minimization in the hospital support profit maximization for individual physicians.

Alternatively, if one assumes that the retailer controls the production channel, as in the case of a HMO, the plan can achieve maximum profits by hiring physician services at below-market prices. A third alternative is to assume that the physicians and hospitals or HMO plans pursue profit maximization while allowing a "necessary" profit margin to the other party. Such a compromise may result in an inefficient equilibrium at a price between P' and P'' producing a quantity of service ranging between Q' and Q'' in figure 6.5. To maximize profits, physicians set marginal physician revenue equal to their marginal costs, implying a transaction with the hospital involving Q' units of care at price P'. To maximize hospital revenues in excess of costs, hospitals would prefer a transaction with the physicians involving fewer units of service (Q'') at a higher level of reimbursement (P'').

Prepaid group health plans are one of the few markets where health facility managers and physicians are on a relatively equivalent bargaining basis. The management of new HMOs must frequently report to the private risk bearers who supplied the venture capital. The HMO sponsors are always putting on the pressure and searching the market for better managers. The market for HMOs is less stable than the hospital industry, in that there is a higher chance of exit (going out of business). However, the opportunity for growth is very large. Consequently, the owner-sponsors of the HMO search for the best-quality managers to deal with the potential growth opportunities in the market for prepaid group health care (Dolinsky and Caputo, 1990).

MARKET SURVEYS

For the hospital initiating a program, one natural place to begin a marketing research effort is in the patient-representative department. The institution will benefit more from a survey of the needs and values of its consumers than from listening to planners or consultants speculate on what they think market preferences should be.

HMOs that have taken heed and listened to potential new enrollee preferences have grown substantially. Historically, innovation in the area of health marketing for HMOs has been retarded for fear of retaliation by organized medicine. For example, in the mid-1970s the HMOs in Boston and New York would promote only the physician perception of what consumers value: good, comprehensive care. Beginning in 1982, these same HMOs ran ads mentioning the major advantage of their product from a consumer viewpoint: cost savings, reduced out-of-pocket premiums, and less paperwork than fee-for-service billing procedures. The advertising had a positive effect on consumer response; that is, the HMOs had an increased enrollment.

For customer-preference surveys to be usable to management, some aggregation of individual responses has to be made. The customers can be algorithmically clustered according to similarity in benefits preferred. Alternatively, they can be a priori clustered according to observable demographic or utilization characteristics—for example, urban versus rural, high-user versus low-user, or physician-referral versus self-referred.

Physician preferences also need to be aggregated into clusters. Physicians could be partitioned into four basic groups: clinicians who are hospital based, clinicians who frequently utilize their privileges at hospital X, clinicians who seldom utilize their privileges at hospital X, and area physicians who have never sought treatment privileges at hospital X. The hospital can organize a marketing program after identification of the sources of physician dissatisfaction. Some physician complaints may not be easily resolved: unacceptable nursing care, demands for additional equipment, or unpredictable availability of same-day surgery. Frequently the hospital attracts new physicians with a capital project: satellite clinics, inclusion of a family-practice department, provision of part-time office space, and ambulatory surgicenters. The marketing ideas need not involve capital acquisitions; marketing the hospital with coupons in the newspapers for families can act as a practice-building source for the physicians.

Marketing in a traditionally nonprofit industry will be fraught with a number of technical and political pitfalls. Some critics may argue that the academic advocates of marketing and competition have substituted benevolent descriptions of success stories for critical analysis. Future health marketing evaluation studies may conclude that the assumptions that were basic to the competition health plan argument fail to hold in all smaller communities and many larger communities. The process of doing market surveys on a national scale may help to convince providers that we should aggressively market caring services and demarket or decrease the marginal curing services that seldom "cure"—for example, heart transplants or heroic medical procedures that prolong for months suffering in a hospital bed (Eddy 1991; Caper 1988).

PHYSICIANS AS CUSTOMERS AND MIDDLEMEN

The hospital can meet the needs of its office-based physician customers in a number of ways. The oldest physician-marketing technique is to provide low-rent office space next to or within the hospital grounds. A more recent technique is to set up a loan fund from philanthropic funds to attract physicians. The monies from the loan fund are "loaned" to fill the gap between the actual annual income of the physician and the individual's targeted yearly income. In highly competitive areas, hospitals and hospital chains are even going so far as to purchase physicians' practices—that is, have doctors work for the hospital. Young physicians are the best targets for loans or equipment gifts, because they work the longest hours and can provide a steady, high flow of patients to the hospital over the coming years. These "perks" or inducements for physicians are seldom formalized in a written agreement, since such behavior would be considered unethical and sometimes illegal in most states. This situation leaves physicians in the enviable position of being able to request new equipment and take advantage of underutilized facilities, while retaining the flexibility to break the unwritten agreement with the hospital if they get a better deal elsewhere. With the increasing cost of new equipment and medical education, physicians can be expected to make decisions among competing offers on a financial basis. Most physicians cannot be expected to stay with a poorly equipped and poorly staffed neighborhood clinic for altruistic reasons, and some of those who do stay end up doubting the marginal value of their services.

Clinics should be considered in market terms as middlemen or facilitating intermediaries. Satellite clinics seldom have a written agreement with the individual hospital that financed much of their development. However, in providing money and management expertise, the hospital would be foolhardy not to demand a return on its investment. Typically, the clinic is managed by an individual who represents the hospital by informing physicians whenever the occupancy level is low and by providing information regarding which types of beds are most underutilized. In some cases the clinics are not placed where the patient need is higher, such as a poorly insured neighborhood of the working poor (too wealthy to qualify for Medicaid and too poor to afford commercial insurance). Instead, the clinics are placed where the population has the best insurance coverage for hospital reimbursement or in a location near a competitor's clinic to prevent potential hospitalization cases from straying to another facility. There is legitimate skepticism in the nonprofit sector as to whether location decisions should be made in a fashion that dumps unprofitable poorly insured patients on the facilities with an open-door policy.

Some representatives of organized medicine claim that younger physicians are too flexible and cooperative with the "hospital bureaucracy." Increasing numbers of physicians are becoming "employees," and by 1993, 36,000 will be members of unions. According to the American Medical Association, the percentage of practicing physicians working as employees increased from 23 percent in 1983 to 35 percent in 1991. However, a sense of individuality and independence, combined with a measure of arrogance, still exists in the physician community under age 50. Contacts with medical staff would be less interesting if this were not the case. Entrepreneurialism is still alive within the younger cohort of clinicians, but the avenue for expression has changed. Physician entrepreneurs sell utilization review and quality-assurance activities, initiate PPOs and HMOs, and enter joint-venture investment opportunities. The tendency of some older solo practitioners to balk at terms like "customer," "provider," and "marketing" indicates an inability to adjust to the times. Society has made a number of commitments to provide access to mainstream medicine for all. Medical care has become readily accessible to 90 percent of the population, and physicians are now working according to schedules convenient for the patients. Consumers are increasingly receiving more information on where to shop. Even the "hotel side" of hospital services production improved in the 1980s.

Respect for the patient/consumer/customer was a marketing revolution. The revolution was bloodless; doctors Marcus Welby and Ben Casey lost. During two decades of cost reimbursement, with little pressure to market, the cost "crisis" was a by-product of the system and the incentive structure and not of cost per se. One could ignore consumers, run up a big bill, and get paid dollar for dollar. What a great deal! However, competition, with emphasis on purchasing on an economic basis, had to rear its head. We all like competition in what we buy, not in what we sell, and health care providers were no different. With the rise of competition came a rising interest in customer satisfaction, marketing, discovering what the patients wanted, cutting excess costs, and offering the service at a favorable price. Innovation occurred on five major fronts:

1. Competitive pricing and contracting (HMOs, PPOs, managed care)
2. Staffing in proportion to workload (dumping unproductive staff)

3. Financial disincentives against overhospitalizing and testing
4. Incentives to invest in aftercare and long-term care
5. Sufficient supply of both doctors and empty hospital beds

This new competitive world is not without risks—for example, dumping patients, eroding the professional ethic, and a myriad of other problems (Colombotos and Kirchner 1986). However, one can work as a salaried physician and even join a union without losing one's professional ethic and interest in safety. The prototype for physician groups in the next century may well be the airline-pilot unions. Health care costs may decline since doctors will earn less individually and as a group. Airline pilots have experienced a drop in earnings, but their workweek is shorter, is less hectic, and allows more time for family life. The pilot unions have done an admirable job in the areas of quality assurance, statistical quality control, and customer safety. Quality improvements lead to increased volume, potential economies of scale, and competitive advantage (Brown 1991). Enhanced quality will diminish both internal and external quality-maintenance costs. Internal costs include such things as rework of faulty documents, wasted materials, and loss of morale. External costs affect customers and include losses through malpractice judgment and negative word-of-mouth advertising. Last, quality gains reduce the pressures from JCAHO and the public recommending tighter oversight. The increase in the quality-maintenance budget may prove that poor-quality care is the most costly care (Heskett, Sasser, and Hart 1991).

STATISTICAL TECHNIQUES IN MARKETING

Statistical techniques are increasingly directed at causal modeling of consumer behavior. For example, how long is a consumer willing to wait at a clinic without seeing a contact person of any sort before deciding not to return or to repeat elective service? Path analysis is one technique that might be applied to such consumer behavior problems. The technique of path analysis allows the analyst to decompose the correlation between any two relevant factors into a sum of compound and simple paths (Wright 1960). The decomposition of the correlation has three basic components: direct effects, indirect effects, and spurious effects from compound paths that are not interpretable but are mathematically part of the decomposition. For example, the finding that more liberal maternity benefit packages attract more enrollees to an HMO (Hudes et al. 1980) may or may not be a spurious relationship. However, if one had built a path model, the efficacy of liberalizing maternity benefits might be found to be spurious if the correlation between benefits and number of enrollees vanished when the effects of income and other socioeconomic variables were controlled (Singh 1990).

Customers' preferences and objectives are multifaceted and consequently require very sophisticated methods of analysis. Customers providing preference judgments about a set of hypothetical questions may produce errors in the responses provided. In considering the percentage of error variance in the criterion variable, one would expect an inverse relationship between errors and individual involvement in the process of providing preference judgments. One would expect lower degrees of error if the choice is among alternatives of substantial importance to the individual, for example, among potential customers for open-heart surgery or among radiologists concerning preferences toward purchasing CAT scanners. High rates of error probably result from situations where the decisions have minimal impact, such as patients' decisions concerning vaccinations or pediatricians' preferences concerning whether the hospital should have a CAT scanner (Kotler and Roberto 1991).

No single technique is appropriate for all marketing problems. One technique, conjoint measurement, is probably the most underutilized and promising technique in the health services marketing arena. Conjoint analysis is a major technique used to assess what combination of service or product attributes the users, consumers, or providers most prefer. It summarizes the preference-ranking information as an index that is easily understood by nonquantitative decision makers. Wind and Spitz (1976) were the first to utilize conjoint measurement techniques in a health-services market to analyze the effect of a number of independent variables on a single (response) dependent variable: "consumers' hospital selection decision." The authors cited the previous work of Green and Rao (1971) concerning conjoint techniques for quantifying judgmental data. In a conjoint measurement study the respondent (hypothetical consumer) is presented with a set of multiattribute alternatives and is asked to rank or rate combinations of attributes on the basis of some desired dependent variable (intention to buy, preference to utilize). Contrary to traditional attitude-measurement approaches in psychology, the respondent is asked to provide an overall evaluation of a product basket or combination of various attributes, rather than simply providing only the relative rating on each individual attribute. The resulting internal trade-offs that each respondent makes among the various attributes can be decomposed into internal, scale-derived utility judgments of given attributes and reconstructed to impute the consumer's predicted preference for new combinations of attributes.

The early applications of conjoint measurement techniques in the health sector (Wind and Spitz 1976) provided insight into what consumers value. The consumers' three most important factors in evaluating a hospital were, in order of importance, proximity to home, prestige of the physician(s), and physical appearance of the hospital. It may be surprising to some that the least important factor was whether the hospital was a teaching hospital or had some affiliation with a major university. This corroborates the anecdotal testimony of many multihospital-system managers that consumers place a slightly positive minuscule value on whether or not a hospital is a teaching facility (Gombeski, Carroll, and Lester 1990).

Conjoint analysis has been applied to a number of HMO market research protects (Akaah and Becherer 1983; Carroll and Gagon 1983). Irrespective of what institutional market segment is under study, ignoring health marketing is an increasingly hazardous style of management that frequently leads to retrenchment of services or fiscal insolvency. However, refinements will be required to sell the industry on marketing techniques. As increasing numbers of health-services-administration students are being introduced to marketing, these activities will increase, and the public and the managers will be better able to assess needs and improve efficiency. As with any management-science technique, poorly applied marketing can be a disaster for the institution (Reidesel 1985). The reasons why health marketing is underdeveloped range from a lack of adequately trained manpower to the hesitancy of trustees to support marketing efforts due to pejorative "business-world" connotations. The health institutions that grow in the 1990s will be forward-looking and market-wise; these institutions will not be simply reacting to the immediate demands of regulators and local physicians. A good marketing program can increase consumer satisfaction, improve efficiency, and deliver better-quality health services.

REFERENCES

Adams, E., Houchens, R., Wright, G., and Robbins, J. (1991). "Predicting Hospital Choice: Role of Severity of Illness." *Health Services Research* 26:5 (December), 566–584.

Akaah, I., and Becherer, R. (1983). "Integrating a Consumer Orientation into Planning of HMO Programs: An Application of Conjoint Segmentation." *Journal of Health Care Marketing* 3:2 (Spring), 9–18.

American Marketing Association. (1991). "AMA Survey on Marketing Expenditures in The Service Sector." Chicago: American Marketing Association.

Anderson, G., and Lomas, J. (1989). "Regionalization of Coronary Artery Bypass Surgery: Effects on Access." *Medical Care* 27:3 (March), 288–296.

Averch, H., and Johnson, L. (1962). "The Firm under Regulatory Constraint." *American Economic Review* 52:4 (December), 1052–1069.

Bauerschmidt, A., and Jacobs, P. (1985). "Pricing Objectives in Nonprofit Hospitals." *Health Services Research* 20:2 (June), 153–162.

Bays, C. (1986). "The Determinants of Hospital Size: A Survivor Analysis." *Applied Economics* 18:4 (April), 359–377.

Blattberg, R., and Deighton, J. (1991). "Interactive Marketing: Exploiting the Age of Addressability." *Sloan Management Review* 33:1 (Fall), 5–14.

Brown, S. (1991). *Service Quality*. Lexington, Mass.: Lexington Books.

Caper, P. (1988). "Solving the Medical Care Dilemma". *New England Journal of Medicine* 318:23 (June 11), 1535–1536.

Carlson, R. J. (1975) *The End of Medicine*. New York: John Wiley.

Carroll, N., and Gagon, J. (1983). "Identifying Consumer Segments in Health Services Markets: An Application of Conjoint and Cluster Analysis." *Journal of Healthcare Marketing* 3:3 (Summer), 22–34.

Clarke, R., and Shyavitz, L. (1983). "Strategies for a Crowded Marketplace." *Health Care Management Review* 8:3 (Summer), 45–52.

Colombotos, J., and Kirchner, C. (1986). *Physicians and Social Change*. New York: Oxford University Press.

Conrad, R., and Strauss, R. (1983). "Multiple-Output Multiple-Input Model of the Hospital Industry in North Carolina." *Applied Economics* 15:3 (June), 341–352.

Cowing, T., and Holtmann, A. (1983). "Multiproduct Short-Run Hospital Cost Functions: Empirical Evidence and Policy Implications from Cross-sectional Data." *Southern Economic Journal* 49:3 (January), 637–653.

D'Amaro, R., and Pahwa, S. (1990). "Developing Referral Systems: A Key to Survival." *Journal of Health Care Marketing* 10:1 (March), 62–64.

Dolinsky, A., and Caputo, R. (1990). "Role of Health Care Attributes and Demographic Characteristics in the Determination of Health Care Satisfaction." *Journal of Health Care Marketing* 10:4 (December), 31–39.

Dranove, D. (1984). "A Comment On: Does Practice Make Perfect?" *Medical Care* 22:10 (October), 967.

Eddy, D. (1991). "Oregon's Methods: Did Cost-effectiveness Analysis Fail?" *Journal of the American Medical Association* 266:15 (October 16), 2135–2141.

Eastaugh, S. (1991). "Sharing the Burden: Containing the Health Care Bill for American Industry." *Business Forum* 15:4 (Winter), 25–28.

———. (1984). "Hospital Diversification and Financial Management." *Medical Care* 22:8 (August), 704–723.

———. (1982). "Effectiveness of Community-based Hospital Planning: Some Recent Evidence." *Applied Economics* 14:5 (October), 475–490.

Eastaugh, S., and Eastaugh, J. (1986). "Prospective Payment Systems: Further Steps to Enhance Quality, Efficiency, and Regionalization." *Health Care Management Review* 11:4 (Fall), 37–52.

Eraker, S., and Sox, H. (1981). "Assessment of Patients' Preferences for Therapeutic Outcomes." *Medical Decision Making* 1:1 (January), 29–39.

Fackelman, K. (1985). "Cleveland Hospital on the Road to Product-Line Management." *Modern Healthcare* 15:24 (November 22), 70–71.

Farber, B., Kaiser, D., and Wenzel, R. (1981). "Relation between Surgical Volume and Incidence of Postoperative Wound Infection." *New England Journal of Medicine* 305:4 (July 23), 200–204.

Feldman, R., and Begun, J. (1980). "Does Advertising of Prices Reduce the Mean and Variance of Prices?" *Economic Inquiry* 18:3 (July), 484–492.

Fisher, C., and Anderson, C. (1990). "Hospital Advertising: Does It Influence Consumers?" *Journal of Health Care Marketing* 10:4 (December), 40–46.

Flood, A., Scott, W., and Ewy, W. (1984a). "Does Practice Make Perfect? Part I: The Relation between Hospital Volume and Outcome for Selected Diagnostic Categories." *Medical Care* 22:2 (February), 98–125.

———. (1984b). "Reply to the Dranove Comment." *Medical Care* 22:10 (October), 967–969.

Forthman, L. (1990). "Achieving Competitive Advantage through Information Management." *Computers in Healthcare* 5:1 (January), 40–43.

Gallagher, K., and Weinberg, C. (1991). "Coping with Success: New Challenges for Nonprofit Marketing." *Sloan Management Review* 33:1 (Fall), 27–42.

Goldsmith, J. (1989). "A Radical Prescription for Hospitals." *Harvard Business Review* 67:2 (March–April), 95–103.

Gombeski, W., Carroll, P., and Lester, J. (1990). "Influencing Decision Making of

Referring Physicians.'' *Journal of Health Care Marketing* 10:4 (December), 56–60.

Goodrich, R., and Hastings, G. (1985). ''St. Luke's Hospital Reaps Benefits by Using Product-Line Management.'' *Modern Healthcare* 15:4 (February 15), 157–158.

Granfield, M. (1975). ''Resource Allocation within Hospitals: An Unambiguous Analytical Test of the A-J Hypothesis.'' *Applied Economics* 7:4 (December), 241–249.

Green, P., and Schaffer, C. (1991). ''Importance of Weight Effects on Self-explicated Preference Models: Some Empirical Findings.'' *Advances in Consumer Research* 18:1 (Spring), 476–482.

Green, R., and Rao, V. (1971). ''Conjoint Measurement for Quantifying Judgment Data.'' *Journal of Marketing Research* 8:3 (July), 355–363.

Gronroos, C. (1991). *Service Management and Marketing*. Lexington, Mass.: Lexington Books.

Hanemann, W. (1991). ''Willingness to Pay and Willingness to Accept: how much can they differ?'', *American Economic Review* 81:3 (June), 635–647.

Herzlinger, R. (1989). ''Failed Revolution in Health Care—The Role of Management.'' *Harvard Business Review* 67:2 (March–April), 99–103.

Heskett, J., Sasser, W., and Hart, W. (1991). *Service Breakthroughs*. New York: Free Press.

Hillestad, S., and Berkowitz, E. (1991). *Health Care Marketing Plans: From Strategy to Action*. 2d ed. Homewood, Ill.: Dow-Jones-Irwin.

Holleman, M., Loe, H., Selwyn, B. (1991). ''Uncompensated Outpatient Medical Care by Physicians.'' *Medical Care* 29:7 (July), 654–660.

Hudes, J., Young, C., Sohrab, L., and Trinh, C. (1980). ''Are HMO Enrollers Being Attracted by a Liberal Maternity Benefit?'' *Medical Care* 18:6 (June), 635–648.

Hughes, R., Garnick, D., Luft, H., McPhee, S., and Hunt, S. (1988). ''Hospital Volume and Patient Outcomes: The Case of Hip Fracture.'' *Medical Care* 26:11 (November), 1057–1067.

Hughes, R., Hunt, S., and Luft, H. (1987). ''Effects of Surgeon Volume and Hospital Volume on Quality of Care in Hospitals.'' *Medical Care* 25:6 (June), 489–503.

Inguanzo, J., and Harju, M. (1985). ''Affluent Customers Most Discriminating.'' *Hospitals* 59:19 (October 1), 84–86.

Kaufman, N. (1984). ''Product Integrity: The Missing Unit in a Hospital's Marketing Process.'' *Health Marketing Quarterly* 2:1 (Spring), 29–32.

Keith, J. (1984). ''Personalized Care Helps Facilities Compete.'' *Health Progress* 65:10 (October), 36–61.

Kelly, J., and Hellinger, F. (1986). ''Physician and Hospital Factors Associated with Mortality.'' *Medical Care* 24:9 (September), 785–800.

Klinkman, M. (1991). ''Process of Choice of Health Care Plan and Provider: Development of an Integrated Analytical Framework.'' *Medical Care Review* 48:3 (Fall), 295–329.

Koch, C., and Cunningham, L. (1986). ''Physicians in Product-Line Marketing.'' *Healthcare Executive* 1:2 (January–February), 41–43.

Kotler, P. (1991). *Marketing Management: Analysis, Planning, and Control*. 7th ed. Englewood Cliffs, N.J.: Prentice-Hall.

Kotler, P., and Roberto, E. (1991). *Social Marketing: Strategies for Changing Public Behavior*. New York: Free Press.

Linder, J. (1991). "Outcomes Measurement: Compliance Tool or Strategic Initiative." *Health Care Management Review* 16:4 (Fall), 21–33.

Luft, H. (1985). "Regionalization of Medical Care." *American Journal of Public Health* 75:2 (February), 125–126.

———. (1980). "The Relation between Surgical Volume and Mortality: An Exploration of Causal Factor and Alternative Models." *Medical Care* 18:9 (September), 940–959.

Luft, H., Bunker, J., and Enthoven, A. (1979). "Should Operations Be Regionalized? The Empirical Relation between Surgical Volume and Mortality." *New England Journal of Medicine* 301:25 (December 20), 1364–1369.

Luft, H., Garnick, D., Mark, D., and McPhee, S. (1990). *Hospital Volume, Physician Volume, and Patient Outcome: Assessing the Evidence.* Ann Arbor, Mich.: Health Administration Press.

MacStravic, R. (1991). *Beyond Patient Satisfaction: Building Patient Loyalty.* Ann Arbor, Mich.: Health Administration Press.

MacStravic, S. (1989). "Market Administration in Health Care Delivery." *Health Care Management Review* 14:1 (Winter), 41–48.

MacStravic, S. (1986). "Product-Line Administration in Hospitals." *Health Care Management Review* 11:2 (Spring), 35–44.

Maerki, S., Luft, H., and Hunt, S. (1986). "Selecting Categories of Patients for Regionalization." *Medical Care* 24:2 (February), 148–158.

Mason, W., Bedwell, C., Zwaag, R, and Runyan, J. (1980). "Why People Are Hospitalized." *Medical Care* 18:2 (February), 147–163.

Miaoulis, G. (1985). "A Model for Hospital Marketing Decision Processes and Relationships." *Journal of Healthcare Marketing* 5:2 (Spring), 37–45.

Nackel, J., and Kues, I. (1986). "Product-Line Management: Systems and Strategies." *Hospital and Health Services Administration* 31:2 (March–April), 109–123.

National Research Corporation. (1991). *Healthcare Market Guide.* Denver: National Research Corporation.

Neuhauser, D. (1972). "The Hospital as a Matrix Organization." *Hospital Administration* 17:4 (Fall), 8–25.

Panitz, E. (1990). "Developing Supplemental Activities for Primary Care Maternity Services." *Journal of Health Care Marketing* 10:4 (December), 61–66.

Parry, M., Parry, A., and Farris, P. (1991). "Marketing Budget in Nonprofit Hospitals." *Journal of Health Care Marketing* 11:2 (June), 2–13.

Peters, G. (1991). "Fixing the Quick Fixes to Physician Relations." *Healthcare Financial Management* 45:11 (November), 36–50.

Peterson, O., Andrews, L., Spain, R., and Greenberg, B. (1956). "An Analytic Study of North Carolina General Practice." *Journal of Medical Education* 31:12 (Part 2) (December), 12–20.

Porter, M. (1980). *Competitive Strategy: Techniques for Analyzing Industries and Competitors.* New York: Free Press.

Reidesel, P. (1985). "Conjoint Analysis Is Worthwhile Tool, But Be Sure the Data Are Valid." *Marketing News* 19:37 (September 19), 41–42.

Riley, G., and Lubitz, J. (1985). "Outcomes of Surgery in the Medicare Aged Population: Surgical Volume and Mortality." *Health Care Financing Review* 7:1 (Fall), 37–60.

Roos, P., and Lyttle, D. (1985). "The Centralization of Operations and Access to

Treatment: Total Hip Replacement in Manitoba." *American Journal of Public Health* 75:2 (February), 130–133.

Rosko, M., and Broyles, R. (1984). "Unintended Consequences of Prospective Payment: Erosion of Hospital Financial Position." *Health Care Management Review* 9:3 (Summer), 35–43.

Ruffner, J. (1986). "Product-Line Management." *Healthcare Forum* 29:5 (September–October), 11–14.

Samuels, S., Cunningham, and Choi, C. (1991). "Impact of Hospital closures on travel time to hospitals." *Inquiry* 28:2 (Spring), 194–199.

Scott, J. (1985). "Virtue a Companion of Competition." *American Medical News* (August 16), 4.

Shortell, S. (1985). "The Medical Staff of the Future: Replanting the Garden." *Frontiers of Health Services Management* 1:3 (February), 3–48.

Shortell, S., and LoGerfo, J. (1981). "Hospital Medical Staff Organization and the Quality of Care: Results for Myocardial Infraction and Appendectomy." *Medical Care* 19:10 (October), 1041–1055.

Singh, J. (1990). "Multifacet Typology of Patient Satisfaction with a Hospital." *Journal of Health Care Marketing* 10:4 (December), 8–20.

Smith, D., and Larsson, J. (1989). "Impact of the Learning Curve on Costs: The Case of Heart Transplantation." *Hospital and Health Services Administration* 34:1 (Spring), 85–97.

Stone, T., Warren, W., and Stevens, R. (1990). "Segmenting the Mental Health Care Market." *Journal of Health Care Marketing* 10:1 (March), 65–69.

Thomas, J., McDaniel, R., and Anderson, R. (1990). "Hospitals as Interpretation Systems." *Health Services Research* 25:6 (February), 859–880.

Thompson, A., and Rao, C. (1990). "Who Is Likely to Join a Prepaid Health Care Plan?" *Journal of Health Care Marketing* 10:1 (March), 16–25.

Tucker, L., and Zaremba, R. (1991). "Organizational Control and Marketing in Multihospital Systems." *Health Care Management Review* 16:1 (Winter), 41–56.

Ulrich, D., and Lake, D. (1991). "Organizational Capability: Creating Competitive Advantage." *Academy of Management Executive* 5:1 (February), 77–92.

Valentine, S. (1991). *Physician Bonding: Developing a Successful Hospital Program.* Rockville, Md.: Aspen.

VanDoren, D., and Spielman, A. (1989). "Hospital Marketing: Strategy Reassessment in a Declining Market." *Journal of Health Care Marketing* 9:1 (March), 15–24.

Ventres, W., and Gordon, P. (1990). "Communication Strategies in Caring." *Journal of Health Care for The Poor* 1:3 (Winter), 305–314.

Weber, D. (1988). "Alta Bates-Herrick Hospital Implements Service Line Management Model." *Healthcare Organization Report* 1:1 (Spring), 1–9.

Weick, K. (1987). "Substitutes for Corporate Strategy." In D. Teece (ed.), *The Competitive Challenge.* Cambridge, Mass.: Ballinger.

White, D. (1990). "Marketers Hone Their Skills to Reach Target Markets." *Hospitals* 64:15 (August 1), 62–66.

Whitehead, A. (1932). *Science and the Modern World.* London: Collier Macmillan.

Wilson, A., and West, C. (1980). "The Marketing of Unmentionables." *Harvard Business Review* 59:1 (January–February), 91–102.

Wind, Y., and Spitz, L. (1976). "Analytical Approach to Marketing Decisions in Health Care Organization." *Operations Research* 24:5 (September–October), 973–990.

Wixon, D. (1985). "Product-Line Management Requires a Full-Time Worrier." *Hospitals* 59:21 (November 1), 46–47.

Wolfe, R., Roi, L., Flora, J., Feller, I., and Cornell, R. (1983). "Mortality Differences and Speed of Wound Closure." *Journal of the American Medical Association* 250:6 (August 12), 763–766.

Wright, S. (1960). "Path Coefficients and Path Regressions: Alternative or Complementary Concepts?" *Biometrics* 16:5 (June), 189–202.

Zeithaml, V., Parasuraman, A., and Berry, L. (1985). "Problems and Strategies in Services Marketing." *Journal of Marketing* 49:1 (Spring), 33–46.

Zelman, W., and McLaughlin, C. (1990). "Product Lines in a Complex Marketplace: Matching Organizational Strategy to Buyer Behavior." *Health Care Management Review* 15:2 (Spring), 9–14.

Zelman, W., and Parham, D. (1990). "Strategic, Operational and Marketing Concerns of Product-Line Management in Healthcare." *Health Care Management Review* 15:1 (Winter), 29–35.

Part Four

MANAGING PHYSICIANS, MEDICAL SCHOOLS, AND TEACHING HOSPITALS

Chapter 7

Paying the Doctor

Concerning the coming surplus of 60,000 physicians, I use "surplus" with caution because I do not believe the United States will ever see a surplus such as exists in some Western European countries, where trained physicians have taken jobs as taxicab drivers and have applied for welfare.
—Alvin Tarlov, M.D., Chairman of the 1980 Graduate Medical Education National Advisory Committee

In analyzing physicians a useful mnemonic is TUMS: tantalized by technology, uncomfortable with uncertainty, motivated by money, scared by suit.
—Richard Riegelman, M.D.

To the general public, physicians are like cops: The aggregate supply appears to be adequate, but there is never one around when you need one. The growing supply of physicians is important because they add to the medical cost-inflation problem. Grumbach and Lee (1991) reported that depending on whether expenditures per physician grow at the historical 1980s rate or at the projected rate of the consumer price index, the rising supply of doctors could add between $40 and $21 billion (in 1986 dollars) to national health expenditures in the year 2000. Physician supply is an interesting manpower issue because physicians have some control over the volume of patient demand and, as Christensen (1990) pointed out, can partially offset the impact of fee freezes (price controls) by expanding volume. Christensen studied 1,000 internists and general practitioners in Colorado and reported a volume offset of approximately 50 percent. Mitchell, Wedig, and Cromwell (1989) studied the 1984–86 Medicare fee freeze and reported that expenses per capita increased 30 percent while fees were frozen. Volume increased most rapidly for radiological procedures and diagnostic surgery. In addition to the quantity and adaptability of the physician community, the composition of doctors by specialty distribution is a major issue for public policy because specialists are more expensive than generalists (Baumgardner and Marder 1991). These same physician manpower issues are being faced by our neighbors in Canada (Barer 1991).

Since the publication of the Tarlov Graduate Medical Education National Advisory Committee (GMENAC) American study in 1980, the concept of a doctor glut (oversupply) has become part of the conventional wisdom. In the context of the 1990s the term "glut" might be a misnomer, like the term "doctor shortage" in the 1960s. In Rashi Fein's classic book *The Doctor Shortage* (1967) Fein pointed to the two real problems: maldistributions of physician supply by geographic location and specialty choice (too many specialists). As a number of economists from the Rand Corporation have pointed out, these maldistribution problems have diminished as the supply of physicians per capita has increased. However, perception of a "glut" of doctors is still the conventional wisdom among policy makers regardless of the data.

A number of so-called procompetition measures were initiated in the 1980s to stimulate cost-decreasing behavior. In reaction to regulations and payer-driven fee negotiations, the physician community has been more willing to accept utilization review programs and discount pricing because of the so-called doctor glut (Schloss 1988). Consequently, the perceived doctor glut has served as a primary catalyst for change in payment policies even if the projected oversupply of 60,000 physicians in 10 to 20 years never becomes a reality. The GMENAC (1980) study overestimated supply, as fewer doctors are being trained and clinicians are working shorter hours each month doing patient care. A study by Schwartz, Sloan, and Mendelson (1988) suggested that a slight shortage of physicians might exist by the year 2000 if the capitated health plans (HMOs, PPOs, and other managed-care plans) do not achieve a 28 percent market share of the American population. Such predictions of a shortage of 30,000 physicians due to AIDS and inefficient fee-for-service medical-staffing ratios are highly suspect, as Schwartz, Sloan, and Mendelson conceded. Demand-expanding and demand-constraining forces flow like a tide over a medical community hardly conscious of economic forces. Technological change could increase patient demand beyond all projections, whereas corporate and federal attempts to ration services could decrease the demand for physician services. Whether society has an under- or oversupply of doctors depends on two factors: demand (highly unpredictable) and supply (stable in the 1990s compared to the rapid growth in the period 1965–82; Moore and Priebe 1991).

RECENT TRENDS IN PHYSICIAN SUPPLY

In 1978 medical schools received over 45,000 applications. By 1988 the number of applications for 16,400 medical school slots had declined to under 24,000, and many of the applicants were multiple reapplicants. The demand for medical education had declined by 50 percent in one decade. The reasons that fewer students are applying to medical school are complex. Physicians are fighting to maintain their authority and their incomes. Third-party payers wish to constrain prices and volume levels. Payers implement peer review programs to affect the style of medical care and have some sentinel effect in determining unnecessary or inappropriate medical care (Eisenberg 1989). It is ironic that doctors in countries where doctors have economic freedom (e.g., where they are not salaried employees of a public system) practice medicine with less clinical freedom (Reinhardt 1987). Cost containment has replaced the cost-is-no-concern view of medical practice in America.

The data from the American Medical Association and the Health Resources and Services Administration of the Department of Health and Human Services (HRSA, DHHS) in table 7.1 review recent trends in physician supply. One can observe in line 2 the steady climb in the supply of physicians per capita. A geographic maldistribution of physicians still exists beyond what can be expected from trends in urban group practice and the need to create citadels for medical education in urban centers. New York State is still 44 percent above the national average of physicians per capita, and Mississippi is 37 percent below average physician supply. Some of the growth in the physician supply ratio is necessary due to the aging of the population, but some of the additional physicians specialize in quality-of-life subspecialty care (e.g., plastic surgery; Eastaugh 1991). A very slight tendency toward more primary-care physicians has been observed. In the 1980s the supply of primary-care physicians grew faster than that of all non-primary-care physicians (30 percent compared to 23 percent). The primary locus for physician activity seems to change at a glacial pace toward more administration and research activity and less office-based fee-for-service self-employment. Those who think that office-based practitioners will decline at a faster pace in the future should reflect on the 1910 Flexner Report. Those who predicted the demise of the private practitioner following publication of the 1910 report were grossly inaccurate (Starr 1982).

One last trend that is apparent in table 7.1 is the decline in foreign medical graduates (FMGs) since the mid–1980s. Congress took action to restrict the flow of immigrant physicians during the 1980s. Public hospitals and small marginal teaching hospitals are still highly dependent on a FMG work force to deliver patient care (Ginzberg 1990). One educational response to the perceived doctor glut in the 1980s was to lengthen the period of graduate medical education. For example, plastic-surgery residents spent 50 percent more time in graduate training in 1989 than they did in 1981. The elder senior medical staff may lengthen the apprenticeship to enhance quality of care and also may keep their competition in the educational pipeline for as long as possible. On a national average, 38 percent of the physicians who will be in practice in 1999 were in training in 1990. Some of the younger doctors in training wish that their elders would listen to Hippocrates and reflect that "life is so short and the craft so long to learn." Lucky Hippocrates never faced a $50,000 debt service from his medical education.

A career in medicine is being viewed as increasingly regulated and less prof-

Table 7.1
Supply of Allopathic M.D.s and M.D. Characteristics, 1963–2000[a]

	1963	1970	1980	1985	1990[b]	2000[b]
Number of active M.D.s[a]	258,958	314,217	440,357	512,849	568,000	664,000
M.D.s per 100,000 population[c]	135	151	189	211	227	248
M.D.s per 100,000 population:						
General and family practice		27.8	26.0	27.6	28.7	26
Internal medicine		20.1	30.9	37.2	42.4	49
Other medical specialty		17.0	23.5	28.5	34.3	38
Surgical specialties		41.3	47.9	52.8	58.6	69
Anesthesiology		5.2	6.9	9.1	11.0	13
Psychiatry[d]		11.2	13.4	14.9	16.0	19
Radiology		6.4	8.8	10.4	10.2	10
Other specialties		21.6	31.1	30.1	26.2	24
Major locus of activity as a percentage of active M.D.s:						
Office-based		57.6%	58.2%	59.7%	58.9%	57%
Hospital-based		25.8	22.3	21.5	20.2	19
Teaching/research/admin.		9.7	8.2	8.7	9.3	12
Other activities		6.8	11.2	10.1	11.5	12
Percentage of foreign medical graduates 9FMGs)	13%	20%	23%	22%	21%	18%
FMGs as a percentage of residents	28%	33%	25%	16%	13%	11%

[a]These figures do not include osteopathic doctors (D.O.s): 12,000 in 1970; 17,100 in 1980; 22,000 in 1985; 28,000 in 1990; 40,000 in 2000.
[b]1990 and 2000 estimates by Eastaugh (1991).
[c]Inactive M.D.s vary from 19,000 to 39,000 depending on the AMA survey year for *Physician Characteristics and Distribution*.
[d]Psychiatry includes child psychiatry.

itable than in prior decades. According to the AMA survey of socioeconomic characteristics of medical practice, physician incomes after inflation increased a total of only 5.4 percent from 1979 to 1988. However, the cost of a medical education markedly outpaced inflation. Average tuitions at medical schools outpaced inflation by 194 percent over the decade. Those without substantial wealth have to incur a substantial debt before graduation day. Nearly one in every four graduates was more than $50,000 in debt by graduation. Because of the rise in bureaucratic paperwork and the increasing competition within the profession, some doctors are steering young people away from a career in medicine.

Clearly, nonfinancial factors such as loss of autonomy or prestige contribute to the downward trend in applications to medical schools. Medicine is not a poverty profession. As an index of physicians' economic status within a society, one can consider the ratio of physicians' net income to gross domestic product per capita within a nation. In 1988 by that yardstick the West German physician (BASYS 1989) outpaced the general public in Germany by a ratio of 7.2 to 1, closely followed by American and Japanese physicians in their countries (6.6 to 1). However, these pretax medical-practice figures understate the economic advantage among Japanese physicians. The Japanese physicians have such high status that by law they pay no income taxes. In contrast, the physicians in most of Western Europe outpace the general public by 3.9 to 4.2. Because of the high tax rates in these countries with national health insurance, it is futile to negotiate higher salaries, so the clinicians negotiate about working hours and working conditions (Iglehart 1991).

While American physicians fear the idea of government-negotiated salaries, the cost-escalation problem is driving Congress to consider broad systemic reforms in the payment of physicians. In 1989 physicians' income represented 23 percent of personal health expenditures and 2.24 percent of the gross national product. Unconstrained, physician expenses will rise to $1,400 per capita by the year 2000. This chapter cannot survey all physician manpower issues, but many analysts believe that there is a maldistribution of types of physician (too many surgeons and subspecialists and not enough primary-care or internal-medicine specialists). However, some economic analysis suggests that even in the year 2000 some large cities will have a deficit of most types of subspecialists (Schwartz et al. 1989). Before surveying the payment options, one should survey the incentives implicit in the three basic methods of paying the doctor.

PRINCIPAL METHODS FOR PAYING THE DOCTOR

The three basic methods for compensating clinicians are salary, capitation, and fee-for-service. Each method has relative strengths and weaknesses. (For a more extended discussion of these methods, see Berenson 1991.) The primary advantages of a salaried system are cost control and a controlled workweek (many young doctors like the life-style advantage of working a salaried shift and going home). If a doctor is salaried (paid per unit of time), the organizational risk involves poor productivity and the potential underprovision of care. The salaried individual can try to come late, leave early, and do a minimum amount of work per hour. Because of this obvious moral hazard to underprovide service, salaried contracts increasingly come with an incentive compensation provision to pay more for enhanced productivity. Clever salaried contracts try to promote the carrot (additional pay for additional work above the average) rather than to emphasize the stick (sanctions if one fails to meet a quota for workload per month).

The second method for paying physicians involves capitation. Pure capitation pays the doctor a fixed payment per person joining his or her panel of potential patients. The incentives are to keep the patients happy and healthy (happy so they do not disenroll and healthy so they do not overutilize expensive health care resources). Capitation offers no incentive to overprovide expensive care, and it offers the long-run incentive to provide preventive care (thus saving money in future years). In our mobile American society this last incentive is probably overstated because subscribers change jobs and health plans often. Thus the capitated system providing the preventive care accrues only a small fraction of the financial benefits. Capitated managed-care systems make the doctor a gate-keeper with the dual responsibility to do no harm to the patient while acting as an explicit guardian of the health plan's financial welfare. Capitated systems run the risk of undercare, so quality must be closely monitored. Capitated systems also run the risk of overreferral, in that gatekeepers may minimize their workload by shunting too many patients to specialists elsewhere in the health plan (this can be controlled through the process of utilization review and reinforced through financial incentives by providing less holdout pay at year's end). A number of managed-care systems have demonstrated that physicians can practice excellent and cost-effective medicine under a capitated contract. Unnecessary admissions and routine tests (e.g., chest roentgenograms) can be reduced without detriment to the patient. Consequently, capitated payment was the most rapidly growing method of paying physicians in the 1980s. A study by Pauly et al. (1990) suggested that HMO for-profit ownership does enhance the power (or the need) of management to offer effective rewards for parsimonious use of resources.

The predominant, but declining, method for paying the doctor is fee-for-service (AMA 1991). Under fee-for-service payment per unit of work the clinician's income is directly related to work ethic and business acumen. However, just as capitation runs the potential risk of conflict of interest for financial reasons, fee-for-service offers the conflict of interest to steer patients to tests or facilities in which the doctor reaps financial returns (e.g., the doctor owns the equipment that does the test or receives kickback incentive pay for referrals). For example, it looks greedy to the public if the clinician is a business partner with the laboratory and the radiology imaging center. Congress is increasingly wary of the argument that the physician is unconcerned with cash flow and only owns such facilities to ensure the quality of patient care. Fee-for-service doctors get paid more if they provide more services, but they also get paid more (1) if they are paid as owners of the equipment that does the test or procedure and paid again to interpret the results, and (2) if they are paid for upcoding (upgrading) the coded work done to receive higher payment rates. The fee-for-service system has been very inflationary because all the incentives stimulate overprovision of inappropriate or unnecessary care. In contrast, salaried or capitated physicians have no incentive to own health care facilities or upcode the patient record in current procedural terminology (CPT) coding. For example, a total hysterectomy (58150) might be coded as exploration of the abdomen (49000), removal of ovaries and tubes (58720), appendectomy (44955), and lysis of adhesions (58740). According to the CPT manual, this coding is incorrect because all of these procedures are bundled together as total hysterectomy (58150), and the moral hazard exists to select the code that maximizes payment.

WANTED: SOME EFFECTIVE CONTROLS ON QUANTITY AND QUALITY

Capitation systems are growing in popularity because governments and insurance companies want to negotiate with bundles of services, fewer sellers, and risk-contracting care organizations (e.g., a few hundred plans willing to take an annual per person check as payment in full). Both in terms of cost control and administrative simplicity, capitated plans are superior to dealing separately with 500,000 physicians and each and every ancillary service provider and their unbundled pile of bills. However, organized medicine fears declining professional autonomy and loss of the prerogative to exceed the employers' norms for standard care if clinicians are only salaried or capitated employees of some faceless corporation. An emerging change in physician attitudes may result over the 1990s as guidelines and models are developed for plans that have excellent quality as well as excellent cost-efficiency. Billions of dollars could be saved each year if physicians practiced in the same style as those at Stanford, the Mayo Clinic, or Case Western Reserve (Caper 1988). Such facilities are what Jack Ott (1991) referred to as competitive medical organizations (CMOs), acting as islands for 5 to 20 percent of the physicians in an area, enhancing quality, taking responsibility for patient needs, and making prudent decisions concerning discretionary care.

Naive policy makers question the concept of discretionary care, saying that the world is black or white, that care is either unnecessary or necessary and there is no middle category. One could expand Ott's concept of the CMO one step further and suggest that such organizations represent pathway guidelines for better medical practice at a reasonable cost in the community. Pathway guidelines serve as yardsticks for cost-effective clinical decision making and as a standard to demonstrate that good medicine and good economics can coexist. Too much attention has been focused on a second type of guideline: boundary guidelines for payers to define the range of medical practice beyond which a clinician incurs the wrath of the payers. If the practitioner exceeds the boundary, the computer suggests an administrative sanction, and after a number of due-process hearings a monetary penalty may result. This second type of guideline gives the topic a bad reputation and has led to the phrase "cookbook medicine." Physicians are not ignorant or venal, but many clinicians need help with the positive, proactive type of pathway guideline. If physicians wish to preserve their autonomy, they should actively participate in the development of pathway guidelines. Case management can remain a caring art and not a cold cookbook formula if beacons are established to assist experienced practitioners in developing pathway guidelines. The guidelines are suggestions, and the microcomputer is more of an educational tool than an enemy to be consorted with as a part of standard federal operating procedure (Derzon 1988). In summary, boundary guidelines clamp down on "bad" physicians, whereas pathway guidelines assist the profession.

What constitutes appropriate care and an optimal pathway can be established in three basic ways: the implicit ad hoc method, the risk-benefit method, and the cost-benefit method. Decision trees in academic settings focus on the cost-benefit method (an action is appropriate if the marginal benefit exceeds the marginal cost, with the intangible benefits shadow priced). The risk-benefit approach suffers because this method only includes traditional medical risks and excludes monetary costs. The implicit approach used in hospital utilization review is hard to export to other settings and has questionable validity, given that we know little of what the reviewer had in mind during the ad hoc process of making judgments (Wennberg 1988; Chassin et al. 1987; Eastaugh 1991).

CONTROLLING THE VOLUME OF SERVICES

The great equation in medical economics involves the control of expenditures (E), which are equal to price (P) times quantity (Q). All payers desire to control their expenditures by trimming P and constraining Q (the volume of services). The health care system is a very adaptable balloon, where squeezing down on only one factor (e.g., P) can cause a bulge in another area (increased volume). Medicare Part B services, which pay for physician services, averaged an 18.7 percent annual increase from 1975 to 1984 until Congress imposed a price freeze in 1984. During the first year of the freeze the growth rate declined to 8.3 percent per year, but it rebounded to 16.2 percent in 1985 and 14.3 percent in 1986. The price freeze was co-opted by an obvious expansion in volume. Congress lifted the freeze as part of the October 1986 Consolidated Omnibus Reconciliation Act (Mitchell, Wedig, and Cromwell 1989). However, in the 30 months following the lifting of the fee freeze, the Part B expenditures per capita increased at 17 percent per annum, while prices only rose at 2.4 percent on average. Price controls without volume controls yield little in the way of cost control. Service volume per capita is clearly out of control. Physicians can expand volume by a stepped-up quantity of procedures, operations, and provider-initiated follow-up visits. Moreover, with 7,200 codes available to label physician services, including six subjective codes for the basic office visit, code creep (upcoding) becomes prevalent. The fine detail of the codes allows the smart physician to unbundle the patient experience or upcode individual items (e.g., the minimal visit is upcoded as brief, and the extended visit is upcoded as a comprehensive office visit). Hospitals played the same game in the 1980s with DRG creeping of patient classifications to the better-paying higher-code groups.

Some of the added volume and intensity might represent real health benefits to patients, but some of the increase has been clearly labeled unnecessary and inappropriate by the federal Health Care Financing Administration (HCFA; Roper 1988). The number one physician reimbursement issue seems to involve controlling the growth in per capita service volume. The most effective single solution is capitation. Capitation decentralizes decisions about which patient receives what and how much while heightening the need for quality assurance and minimizing the chance of underprovision of care. Capitation will not be the voluntary choice of all Americans, as evidenced by the fact that capitated Medicare only covers 1.4 million Americans. Since 1988 HCFA has pilot tested in six HMOs an improved average adjusted per capita cost (AAPCC) formula by adding a health-status adjustment factor based on demographic data to place individuals in diagnostic cost groups (DCGs; Ash and Ellis 1989). A ratebook has been established in which enrollees will be classified in a particular cost-weight category based on age, sex, welfare status, and the highest number of eight possible DCGs associated with a hospitalization in the previous 15 months (DCG 0 equals no hospitalization or a discretionary one- to two-day hospitalization). Ash and Ellis's (1989) DCGs may eliminate any incentive that exists for discouraging sick enrollees from joining a capitated plan. Capitation cures the incentive to game the payment system through increased volume of unnecessary services and will leave the plan with the discretion to divide the annual payments among the various physicians and facilities.

The number two physician reimbursement issue involves selecting a fair workload scale for equitable payment among physician specialties. Hsiao (1989) worked for five years to develop a resource-based relative-value scale (RBRVS) as an alternative to the current charge-based system. Resource inputs by physicians include (1) total work input performed by the physician for each service, (2) practice costs (including office overhead and malpractice premiums), and (3) the cost of specialty training (e.g., the opportunity costs for spending 13 years going to medical school and training to become a cardiac surgeon). The Hsiao study, with the help of the AMA and a number of specialty societies, presented fairly valid and reliable estimates of physicians' work according to four dimensions: time, psychological stress, mental effort and judgment, and technical skill plus physical effort.

The Hsiao et al. (1988) study has been subject to one minor and one major criticism. The minor point revolves around the heavy emphasis on time measurement. Other professionals (e.g., lawyers) do not have their charges related so fully to their work time expended. This minor point is easily dismissed: (1)

In the name of scientific accuracy Resource Based Relative Value Units (RBRVUs) are better than perpetuating tradition, (2) time orientation may stimulate physicians to enhance productivity, and (3) other professions make less use of government funds or insurance dollars (e.g., if we had government paying half the legal fees, then RBRVUs would be necessary for that profession). On a more important point, the RBRVS study methodology could be improved if a refined estimate for health-status improvement to the patient could become a major measure of workload. Hsiao could only equate physician activity with workload. If activity were replaced by health-status improvement as the purists' measure for effective workload, the providers who offer better care could be paid better. In the business world this mechanism would be labeled pay for performance (chapter 10). Obviously, not all activity proves to be beneficial, given that the real output in an ideal study would be health-status improvement. If we had a refined health-status measure, the clinicians who produce higher-quality patient outcomes could get paid more for their effort and skill (Shortell 1990).

The basic research question the Hsiao study answers is how much to pay for cognitive services relative to procedures. The payment system is biased toward paying for procedures done to the patient, rather than for talking to or thinking about the patient. The specialist who spends 25 minutes inserting a Swan-Ganz catheter into a patient who has heart failure receives $275, but the doctor who spends 60 minutes doing a history and physical on the same patient arrives at the diagnosis and is only paid $70. Under the Hsiao scheme, physicians would be paid more equitably per unit of work (there would not be a tenfold variation in the last column of table 7.2). If the gains and losses among physicians had been redistributed in a zero-sum fashion among the various specialties, $140,000 of income would have been carved out of the average thoracic surgeon's $350,000 in 1988. Most surgeons would lose money, but urologists and otolaryngologists would lose only a fraction. Primary-care fees would rise by more than 60 percent, which might (1) cause physicians to spend more time talking with their patients and (2) reenergize the declining supply of filled residency positions in internal medicine (many medicine programs have gone begging for residents since 1986).

THE HSIAO RELATIVE-VALUE APPROACH IN ACTION

The Hsiao resource-based relative-value units will be the basis for the new Medicare fee schedule in 1992. In the short run, primary-care doctors may be energized by the higher fee schedules. However, critics argue that in the long run, government fee schedules may eventually lose all receptivity to market signals from consumers (Pauly 1988; Glasser 1990). Under a worst-case scenario competition among physicians may decrease, and they may channel their energies to political negotiation with government for higher pay (which is what British physicians have done since the 1950s and what South Korean doctors have done since the passage of national health insurance in 1989). Physicians may spend more

Table 7.2
Physicians' Charges and Workload under a Resource-based Relative-Value Scale

Service Workload	Charge (1987)	Work Units	Charge per Work Unit
Follow-up visit of family physician to nursing home patient, with extended service	$37	159	$0.23
Diagnostic proctosigmoidoscopy examination of colon	53	118	0.45
Simple repair of superficial wound, 2.5 to 7.5 cm	66	75	0.88
Delivery of child (vaginal)	481	407	1.18
Repair of inguinal hernia (in the groin)	732	476	1.54
Triple coronary artery bypass	4,663	2,871	1.62
Insertion of permanent pacemaker (ventricular)	1,440	620	2.32

time in unionization activities to negotiate with the government, managed-care systems, and insurance companies (Eastaugh 1991). Other payers should be expected to copy the Medicare approach as the list of RVUs expands (Becker et al. 1990). These payers need only change the conversion factor ($32 for Medicare in FY 1993).

In the period 1988–90 Hsiao developed vignettes describing a typical patient for the service to be provided for a representative sample of services for each physician specialty. Each vignette was intended to represent the average service for its corresponding current procedural terminology (CPT) code. Data from both the Hsiao study and the Visit Survey suggest that physicians responding to vignettes may have overestimated the share of time they spend in pre/post activities in actual practice. According to the Physician Payment Reform Commission (PPRC 1991), the Visit Survey demonstrated that physicians spend most of the encounter performing the history, physical examination, and counseling. By contrast, most pre/post time is spent in activities that would be expected to be less intense, such as scheduling, reviewing records, and contacting other providers. Hsiao and the PPRC will continue working on the Medicare adjuster. They will need to determine whether intraservice work is different when certain surgical global services are performed on elderly and all-age populations. PPRC will also need to obtain information about age-related differences in intraservice work and pre/post work for nonoperative technical procedures (such as endoscopy or angioplasty).

Hsiao (1989) and the PPRC (1991) utilized the human-capital concept that resources devoted to increasing an individual's skills or knowledge, such as education, can be thought of as investment in future income. Income is not limited to monetary compensation, but includes the psychic benefits from any undertaking. For example, most people derive monetary income from their jobs and psychic income from leisure activities. Most theoretical discussions of human capital include all forms of income as the result of the stock of human capital that individuals are endowed with at birth and any subsequent investment in human capital (medical school education, varying lengths of time in residency, and fellowship programs). An individual's pool of skills and knowledge is the input he or she can use to create a product, whether a good or service or leisure activity, that will generate monetary or psychic income. Economic studies with regard to human capital have led to many estimates of the implicit return in earnings from investments in different levels of education. The weakness of these analyses is that they cannot include the psychic income that people derive from their work and leisure activities. Conservative physicians will continue to protest "comparable-worth" attempts to set fair payment levels, given different levels of education. To determine fair payments, it is also necessary to determine what rate of return nonphysician practitioners should realize on their investment in education. One measure that could be used is the rate of return to education realized by all professionals, including nonphysician providers.

Ginsburg, LeRoy, and Hammons (1990) and Lasker et al. (1990) have projected the impact of the new RBRVUs. Recent projections by the AMA suggest that Medicare payments to family practitioners may rise only half as much (28 percent) in 1992, and thoracic surgeons may anticipate a dip in Medicare prices of only half as much (23 percent). Some analysts have worried that Medicare may attract fewer physicians in the long run (Kay 1990; Pauly 1990). The PPRC (1991) supported the concept of prospective payment for ambulatory procedures (surgery, medical services, and tests) done in outpatient settings, including physicians' offices. Prospective payment by DRG for most physicians' services may not be far behind in the late 1990s. The HCFA is already studying a system of 400 ambulatory patient groups (APGs) based on the outpatient principal diagnosis, treatment (CPT codes), age, sex, and status as a new or established patient. To collapse the current 7,000 CPT codes and 1,900 lab codes into 400 APG groups will not be easy. Physicians also face a number of new legal and paperwork limits on medical practice.

Congressman Pete Stark's (Democrat of California) Ethics in Patient Referrals

Act 1992 is one attempt to constrain physician income-generating options. Such proposed bills are reactions to studies suggesting a conflict of interest in the physician-patient relationship. Hillman (1990) reported that diagnostic imaging involving self-referring physicians (having the equipment) resulted in 4.5 times as many films and average charges 4.4 to 7.5 times as expensive as episodes involving imaging done by referrals. A self-referral pattern has the obvious moral hazard of conflict of interest. The problem may exist beyond films and lab tests done in private offices. Referral patterns, friendships, and complex factors bind providers into a network of mutual obligations and courtesies. Even the Joint Commission on Accreditation of Healthcare Organizations (JCAHO 1991) is looking into the possibility that the quality of care could be regrettably compromised by informal arrangements and conflict-of-interest relationships.

Perceived equity implicit in the new payment system will affect physician reaction to the Hsiao approach. Zuckerman, Welch, and Pope (1990) have developed an improved geographic index of physician practice costs using relative prices for four practice inputs: physician time, employee wages, office rents, and malpractice insurance. In this Laspeyres index each input price is weighted by the share of physicians' gross revenues spent on that input. The index is useful in explaining geographic variation in physician fees.

The federal government recognizes 12 classes of visits: new and established patient office visits, initial and subsequent hospital visits, initial and follow-up consultations, initial and subsequent nursing facility visits, initial and subsequent rest home visits, and new and established patient home visits. This allows payment per level of service to vary, reflecting differences in effort (work per unit time) and practice costs for different types of visits and for visits in different sites. The following terminological definitions are used:

New patient (ambulatory settings): A visit with a patient who is new to the physician's practice or who has not been seen within the past three years. The transfer of care from one physician to another constitutes a new patient visit.

Established patient (ambulatory settings): A visit with a patient who has been seen by the physician's practice within the past three years. Concurrent care constitutes an established patient visit.

Initial care (inpatient settings): The initial visit by the admitting physician in which the medical record is established for an admission. The transfer of care from one physician to another constitutes initial care.

Subsequent care (inpatient settings): Follow-up visits in an institution during an inpatient stay. Concurrent care constitutes subsequent care.

Initial consultation (all settings): A visit in which a physician, at the request of another health care provider, renders an initial opinion regarding a specific problem. The consultant must document the need for the consultation, his or her opinion, and any services that have been ordered or performed. In addition, the consultant must document that this information has been communicated to the health care provider who requested the consultation.

A number of medical reporters gave rather imperfect examples of the Hsiao study; for example, "The specialist who spends 45 minutes inserting a tube and a catheter into a patient with a stomach ulcer receives $550, but the cognitive doctor who spends 60 minutes talking to the patient arrives at the same diagnosis at a price of only $70." This example is imperfect, because the gastroscopy procedure is a better diagnostic tool for gastrointestinal bleeding than history with physical; one needs to know the area and the specific pathology of the stomach ulcer. Table 7.3 offers a simple example of how Medicare fees will be set in 1992. Table 7.4 provides an example of the variation in expenses for different physician specialties.

Surgeons and other specialty groups most affected by the Hsiao study suggest that redistribution of physician fees could worsen the volume of services (e.g., more discretionary operations might be performed and might not be detected by peer review or second-opinion surgery programs). In a pessimistic worst-case scenario the RBRVS would not stimulate many more primary-care doctors to accept assignment under Medicare and the government check as payment, but a massive number of surgeons already on assignment with Medicare (because surgical fees are difficult to collect) would either drop assignment (and charge more) or drop out of the Medicare program. This scare scenario seems unlikely because surgeons are in need of the cash flow. From 1979 to 1991 the number of surgeons increased from 8,514 to above 13,000, but the average number of operations per surgeon declined 28 percent, thus proving that supply and demand are alive and well in the surgical marketplace. Surgeons need Medicare business too much to drop out of the Medicare program. Moreover, the HCFA never hoped that a RBRVS scheme would induce a flood of demand for primary care by the elderly, given the tight budgets. Physicians may find it increasingly difficult to join a hospital medical staff in the 1990s (Morrisey and Jensen 1990).

The importance of the Hsiao study is not simply in its proposal of a cost-control mechanism to keep the FY 1992 Medicare budget from exceeding $124 billion. The RBRVS will give all payers the device to implement a type of aggressive price competition unknown to physicians. Each insurance company could go to the medical community and ask for a single number, on a sealed bid, for its minimum contract price relative-value multiplier. Insurance companies will then have a simple device and one confidential number on a piece of paper to force physicians to bid down their prices (and incomes) each year.

ALTERNATIVES TO "OVERHAUL GRADUALLY"

The phrase "overhaul gradually" is a classic oxymoron, two words that do not go together. Yet we know that the physician community will resist major changes in payment policies, even as we know that the policy must be dramatic to curtail a 16 percent inflation rate in Medicare Part B expenditures (PPRC 1991). A number of alternatives, not all mutually exclusive, have been suggested. One could simply reform the existing system to prevent upcoding by reducing

Table 7.3
Medicare Fees for an Intermediate-Length Office Visit with a New Patient in Three Locations, 1992

	Work		Overhead		Malpractice		Conversion Factor		Payment
	RVU^a	GCI^b 1.009	RVU	GCI 1.031	RVU	GCI 1.140			
Ithaca, N.Y.									$38.95
New York, N.Y.	20.6 x	1.059	+ 15.4 x	1.255	+ 2.0 x	1.865	x	$1 =	$44.88
Paris, Texas		0.961		0.825		0.447			$33.41

Note: Starting in 1992, Medicare fees will be set by Meshing Seven Components, including geography, variation in overhead, malpractice, and work.
[a]RVU = Relative value units (Hsiao et al., 1988).
[b]GCI = Geographic cost index.

Table 7.4
Variation in Expenses as a Percentage of Practice Revenue for Six Types of Physicians

	Practice Costs as Percentage of Revenue	Salaries and Fringes	Administration	Malpractice
Family practice	52	42	3	12
Gen'l surgery	45	38	3	29
Internal medicine	48	43	3	10
Ophthalmology	48	41	3	8
Orthopedics	51	45	3	20
Urology	44	41	5	17

Source: PPRC (1991).

the number of available billing codes. This idea worked in the Canadian context with Quebec physicians, but may not prove as effective with American doctors who see their incomes protected by code creeping into better-paying classification categories (Fuchs and Hahn 1990). The second reform idea, fee schedules, involves implementing the Hsiao RBRVS concept such that a uniform price list pays the same rate for similar services (in marked contrast to uniform customary rates that have wide variability). A third reform idea, payment for packages of services, sets a prospective rate that puts doctors at financial risk for the use and cost of those services (Mitchell 1985; Culler and Ehrenfried 1986). For example, the DRG prices could be expanded to include physician fees (e.g., if the care is done more efficiently, the physician receives a higher residual share of the check, and the payer provides extra outlier payments for severely ill patients). Ambulatory care could be reimbursed through an analogous DRG mechanism of ambulatory visit groups (AVGs; Lion et al. 1989). The problem with the third reform idea is that it may fall prey to the law of small numbers. Consider the use of DRGs to pay hospitals. Hospitals are partly protected from undue financial risk by the effect of large numbers if each DRG has over 75 or 100 cases. But individual physicians may have only 1 to 2 patients in each category and may experience a poverty wage if their patient mix is more severely ill than the average. AVG payments would unfairly redistribute payments from those clinicians with genuinely more complex and costly cases for a given AVG to their peers who have less complex cases.

The fourth reform idea, capitation, is currently the most popular initiative. Whether the nation moves to capitation or tougher fee schedules, specialists left out in the cold are headed for two possible fates: serious financial trouble and/ or membership in a union. As the payers get tougher with doctors, they must respond with a countervailing force that acts as a bargaining unit (Ginzberg 1990).

JOIN TOGETHER OR SUFFER ALONE

As the formation of the AMA was an event to combat the cults in the nineteenth century, aggressive specialty unions may form in the future to defend specialists' declining incomes and strike for better-quality patient care. Unionization, once a dirty word in the medical world, is spreading. The California-based Union of American Physicians and Dentists has 29 state chapters. Politically conservative physicians may have to face two economic truths: (1) Unions are not always bad, and (2) clinicians in overdoctored locations can properly go broke. Going broke is a major cost-containment agenda for those who pay for medical services. Payers report with joy that economic failure of excess doctors and hospitals will eject the pathology from the system and drive costs down. Physicians require better productivity and a voice to negotiate on their behalf (Koska 1991). If the profession does not act together as a group and continues to pursue only individual business interests, medicine will be no more protected or respected than a used-car dealership. Likewise, those who disrespect business skills, productivity, marketing to the public, and patients' shifting tastes will also face an early retirement.

A NEW ERA OF FEDERAL PRICE SETTING

HCFA administrator Gail R. Wilensky has characterized the RBRVS payment system initiated for Medicare in 1992 as the dawn of government-administered pricing in medicine. If our goal is to contain the growth in expenditures, a product of price times volume, a simple system of price controls can be ineffective because of expansion in volume. Global based budgets (GBB) that constrain expenditures, with so called behavioral offsets (for volume expansion), have proved successful in countries like Germany, Sweden and South Korea. Annual social arbitration over spending caps could set incomes for all sectors of the health economy: physicians, hospitals, home health care, and long-term care. If the volume growth outpaces the global budget by 4.5 percent, prices are subsequently deflated by 4.5 percent. In the decentralized German system, fee negotiations between hospitals and sickness funds require final approval from state governments, but the overall management of policy is typified by compromise and consensus building. Federal and state governments, sickness funds, labor unions, hospitals and physician groups (geographic-based councils known as the Arztekammern, with an average membership of 7,000 doctors) annually agree on fees, and annual expenses in each sector of the health economy. If physician fees exceed their target in one time period, they are subsequently reduced in future periods to penalize providers for cost overruns due to unplanned volume shifts. In the jargon of accounting, this political process is described as variance analysis under a limited budget (the global pie of dollars for local health care). If the budget variance is unfavorable (overbudget), the fees are deflated in proportion to the "unnecessary part of the increase in volume."

A recent article by Iglehart (1991a) suggests the policy question: could passage of a German Style GBB promote social cooperation and aid the eventual passage of an American national health plan? Is GBB a *quid pro quo* for reducing administrative expense incurred by providers? With one payment process nationally there will be less administrative expense. Is GBB expected to make national health care affordable? Can GBB discern the public interest and promote good economic and good quality health care? In the spirit of democracy and pluralism the GBB will subject each interest group to public scrutiny. Four years of experience with the Physician Payment Review Commission (Eastaugh 1992) suggests the potential benefits of public scrutiny. The hope is that this process will yield a more efficient, effective, and equitable health care system.

One final caveat should be considered. The consensus building for GBB is a bit more difficult in the American context of separation of powers. By contrast, GBB is more easily created in parliamentary systems with inherent consensus between legislative and executive branches. However, just because a GBB is more difficult to initiate does not mean that the GBB will be any less effective at cost control once created. All nations with GBB spend one-third less a proportion of GNP on health care than the United States. Moreover, creation of a GBB might be the catalyst that breaks the gridlock against national health care reform for the 34 million uninsured Americans and those otherwise squeezed by the current approaches. Implementation of GBB will not cause the United States to spend 4.0 percent of Gross National Product (GNP) less on health care (Eastaugh 1992) but it will free up the resources necessary to make health care coverage more affordable. GBB can reduce the need for explicit rationing (e.g., the Oregon Medicaid program; Eddy 1991). The distributional impact of GBB may yield more funding for long-term care.

It is difficult to forecast the impact of the new Medicare physician fee schedule (Lee and Ginsburg 1991). By law the new fee schedule was to be implemented in a "budget-neutral way." Therefore, all four federal estimates agree that physicians were scheduled to receive $191 billion over the five budget years FY1992–96. However, the AMA and other physician groups lobbied against the expense-neutral interpretation of the law, and suggested that physicians receive $211 billion over the five years. HCFA argued in 1991 that the prices be downadjusted 6.4 percent (or $7.5 billion over 1992–96) to exactly compensate for the predicted 6.4 percent upsurge in volume ($7.5 billion) so that no more than $191 billion is spent on Medicare physician fees 1992–96. The initial spring 1991 HCFA estimate of 16.3 upsurge in volume over the period 1992–96 was rejected for political reasons to appease physician groups.

Is a 16.3 percent upsurge in volume over five years possible? Not only is it possible, but it is half the historic rate of physician volume inflation. The AMA's spokesman on the Physician Payment Review Commission (PPRC), Thomas Reardon, reports that historically volumes have gone up 7.0 percent a year and not 3.1 or 1.1 percent (Iglehart, 1991b). The average number of services provided per Medicare beneficiary has increased from 12 in 1978 to 28 in 1991. The Medicare fees are also asymmetric in transition: increased fees for undervalued services will be more rapid than the decreases in fees for surgeons. For example, in 1992 family practice and general practice physicians will see their Medicare fees enhanced by 14 percent, while thoracic surgeons will have their fees deflated by only 5.6 percent. However, by 1996 thoracic surgeons will experience a nearly 30 percent five-year deflation in Medicare fees, while family and general practice fees will be inflated by a five-year total of 15.5 percent. The net impact on physician income is harder to predict. Two policy questions remain. Is HCFA correct that physicians who lose income will only offset half their losses with a volume shift (above 1.1 percent), and the physicians who gain income (price hikes) will not also increase their volume? If every physician lets their volume go up 4.5 percent per year, the profession will earn a windfall profit of $23.9 billion (over and above $191 billion) over the five years 1992–96. Physicians are smart people, and like any profession they can adapt to the new game in order to make more money (unless the PROs are successful in curtailing unnecessary service volume). Shifts in physician income may be insufficient to convince many (or any) young doctors to work in a rural area or choose a primary care specialty.

The Medicare fee schedule differentials between specialties must be more substantial to affect new physicians, unless we go to an all-payer global budgeting system for setting prices and expense targets for all patients and providers. Will the Hsiao (1992) methodology lead to a better (more equitable) distribution of incomes and services? Germany has tried this broad approach with a major revision of physician fees in 1987. The impact was minimal in that: (i) no substantial substitution effect occurred between technical procedures and patient-centered communication, and (ii) income rankings of the top specialties did not change by more than two points (Brenner and Rublee 1991). However, average income at the lowest end of the physician scale, gynecology and pediatrics, did increase substantially. The German context for global budgeting and rate setting is discussed further in chapter 15.

HOSPITAL PRACTICE PRIVILEGES

Fewer than 1,000 physicians had their licenses suspended or revoked for inappropriate or unnecessary practice behavior in 1990. The federal professional review organizations (PROs) took sanction actions against fewer than 200 physicians during 1990–91. However, as hospitals win court cases related to staff-privilege decisions based on quality or efficiency concerns, hospital managers and medical staff are getting more selective about which physicians they allow admitting privileges. Self-serving members of the medical staff may want to close the doors on their hospital's medical staff in a crowded marketplace and force the institution to cease taking new applications from potential competitors. In negotiating compensation agreements with hospital-based physicians, management clearly likes the leverage to negotiate from a large pool of potential replacement clinicians. All types of physicians have potential anticompetitive reasons for closing their segment of the medical staff (raising antitrust legal concerns), but hospital managers and trustees are more interested in the composition of their medical staff and their cost behavior relative to levels of payment.

Institutions may no longer allow physicians who erode the financial standing of the institution through imprudent, wasteful use of hospital resources to admit patients. Hospitals that allow inefficient doctors to admit patients may go so heavily into debt that their survival is unlikely. In 1990–91 almost one-third of all hospital clinical departments were closed to new medical staff appointments; most of these were internally reviewing whether certain clinicians should not have their privileges renewed (legally it is easier not to renew privileges than actually to revoke privileges). The percentage of physicians with admitting privileges at any hospital has been declining each year since 1982, according to AMA survey statistics. Almost half of the physicians only have privileges at one hospital. Any physicians losing their practice privileges at one hospital will have a tough time establishing a relationship with other local hospitals. Inefficient ordering and treatment habits are a liability for the individual doctor in a market in which fees increasingly are paid prospectively (i.e., inefficiency is not reimbursed by a pass-through of costs for the hospital) and in which hospital privileges are in short supply. The practice-profile cost per case experience of a doctor should be appropriately adjusted for DRG mix and case severity to make any data-based credentialing process fair (i.e., for medical-staff membership). Physicians can be analyzed on whether they are inefficient on two basic dimensions: length of stay and ancillary cost per case (figure 7.1). (The third dimension, appropriate admissions, was discussed in chapter 3. See Wennberg 1989. Siu, Manning, and Benjamin [1990] suggested that 24 percent of admissions are inappropriate.)

If the individual physician is ''double trouble'' on both dimensions, the total cost per case (adjusted for case mix) will be high. Many midwestern hospitals have been particularly effective at trimming lengths of stay relative to the national average since 1983. By point of contrast, West Coast hospitals historically tend to be very efficient on length of stay. However, West Coast investor-owned hospitals have tended to generate particularly high ancillary costs per case. Such behavior was rewarded in an era of cost reimbursement or full-charge payment, when the profit margins were highest in the area of ancillary tests. The hospital CFOs' best physicians were the ones who ordered the most ancillary tests per case (earning the hospital more money). Now, however, the medical staffs have had to unlearn all the lessons of the 1969–83 ''maximization of reimbursement'' period (outlined in chapters 1 and 2) and become more efficient (Eastaugh 1990).

Figure 7.1
Two Dimensions of Utilization Review before and after the Initiation of
Prospective Payment

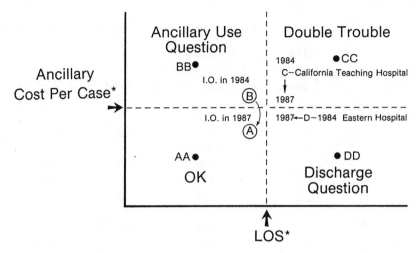

*Corrected for case-mix differences between institutions. A third dimension of utilization review
  would monitor physician billings.

The medical staff is sometimes provided a break-even-point analysis by product
line to serve as a yardstick for target areas to trim cost behavior.

The concept of strategic product-line groupings (SPGs) was discussed in Eastaugh (1991). The intent of table 7.5 is to provide the medical staff with sensitivity
estimates as to how much one has to trim in the other three areas if, for example,
the clinicians running SPG 7 decide that they cannot improve length of stay
(options 8 or 9) or adjust behavior in radiology (options 1–3 and 5). Such
estimates are highly dependent on the blend of variable and fixed costs for the
specific hospital under study. Therefore, the analysis must be done at each
hospital every one to three months. In studying two of the hospitals sampled in
chapter 2, McNeil (1985, 18) indicated that there was

enormous variability in the fixed-variable cost ratios of tests done in chemistry labs,
ranging from under 20 percent variable cost for some to over 90 percent for others.
Information on the distribution of tests in the ''highly fixed'' cost category compared to
those in the ''highly variable'' cost category should be useful in the design of educational
programs for cost containment.

The challenge for physicians and managers is not to break even on every product
line. There will always be some cross-subsidization in the hospital sector. The
real challenge is to have all parties work toward common goals: quality care,
institutional financial health, and enough retained earnings to keep the hospital/
doctor workshop state-of-the-art. One must balance this last goal against the

Table 7.5
Options for Achieving a Break-even Cost-Behavior Profile for Strategic Product-line Grouping 7 (SPG 7 Consists of 16 DRGs Produced by 13 Attending Physicians)

Option	LOSa Length of Stay	Inhalation Therapyb, IVs, and Misc. Therapy	Labc	Radiology
1	-15%	0	0	0
2	-10%	-27%	0	0
3	-10%	-10%	-23%	0
4	-10%d	-10%	-10%	-18%
5	-5%	-20%	-24%	0
6	-5%	-20%	-10%	-19%
7	-5%	-16.8%	-16.8%	-16.8%
8	0	-27%	-22%	-39.7%
9	0	-29.8%	-29.8%	-29.8%

aThe semivariable and variable cost savings from reduction in LOS are distributed as follows: 45.0 percent in forgone "hotel" costs, 27.1 percent in forgone nursing services, 13.3 percent in forgone therapy (inhalation therapy, IVs, medications, recovery room, OR, anesthesia, etc.), 8.5 percent in forgone lab tests, and 6.1 percent in forgone radiologic services.

bFor this hospital and this strategic product-line grouping 7, the example is only atypical to the extent that overutilization of inhalation therapy was a major problem identified in peer review audits. Requiring a 27 percent aggregate reduction in inhalation therapy could be easily accomplished by a 75 percent reduction in usage by 4 of the 13 doctors offering this SPG, with no change in behavior required of the other 9 doctors (who were already utilizing 24 to 32 percent less inhalation therapy than the group average).

cUtilization per diem.

dThe cost savings from a 5 percent drop in LOS equal a 27 percent drop in therapy per diem (for the reduced number of per diems remaining after the LOS reduction), which is equivalent to a 43 percent drop in lab tests per diem and a 59 percent drop in radiology usage per diem.

broader social goal of not having too much wasteful excess capacity or excess patient admissions (Wennberg 1990, 1989). Federally developed clinical guidelines will help reduce wasteful habits (Field and Lohr 1991; Frech 1991).

Supplier induced demand (SID) offers the obvious possibility of a conflict of interest: the physician provides extra service to generate income. The evidence is usually indirect by nature. For example, Broward County Florida has 19 doctor-owned Magnetic Resonance Imaging (MRI) machines and 41 MRI procedures per 1,000 population. Baltimore County Maryland has one doctor-owned MRI and two medical schools, but only 12 MRI procedures per 1,000 in 1991. Are the physicians at Johns Hopkins and University of Maryland underserving their patients, or is it more likely that the Florida physicians are generating unnecessary patient volume to cost-justify (break-even) or profit from their MRI business ventures? Is the Florida number for utilization per 1,000 citizens too low in Baltimore or too high in Florida? Classical economic theory would predict that competition would keep the price of an MRI scan down in Florida. However, the charge in Broward County is nearly double the Baltimore price, and all the extra utilization is performed on nonpoor insured patients. Under the new 1992 regulations, in order to avoid prosecution under the anti-kickback law, a physician who has invested in an outside MRI facility or lab must meet the following six tests: (1) dividends must be related to the amount of capital contributed (not to the number of patients referred), (2) ownership does not impose a requirement on the physician to refer patients, (3) the equity and price of shares in the outside facility must be the same for referring physicians and all other investors, (4) the facility must not give loans to the physician, (5) no more than 40 percent of the revenue received by the outside facility can come from those who have investments in it, and (6) no more than 40 percent of the investors can be physicians (Eastaugh 1992).

REFERENCES

Alhaider, A., and Wan, T., (1991). "Modeling Organizational Determinants of Hospital Mortality." *Health Services Research* 26:3 (August), 303–324.

American Hospital Association. (1991). *The Emerging Roles of Physicians*. Chicago: AHA.

American Medical Association. (1991). *Physician Characteristics and Distribution in the United States*. Chicago: AMA.

Ash, A., and Ellis, R. (1989). "Diagnostic Cost Groups DCG Methodology." Boston University Working Paper.

Association of American Medical Colleges. (1992). *Supplying Physicians for Future Needs: Report of the Task Force on Physician Supply*. Washington, DC: AAMC.

Barer, M. (1991). "Controlling Medical Care Costs in Canada." *Journal of the American Medical Association* 265:18 (May 8), 2393–2394.

BASYS. (1989). "Wirkungen von Verguetungsystemen auf die Einkommen der Aerzte, die Preise, und auf die Struktur aerzlicher Leistungen im Internationalen Ergleich." Augsburg, Bavaria, Germany: BASYS GmbH, mimeo.

Baumgardner, J., and Marder, W. (1991). "Specialization among Obstetrics Gynecologists: Another Dimension of Physician Supply." *Medical Care* 29:3 (March), 272–281.

Becker, E., Dunn, D., Braun, P., and Hsiao, W. (1990). "Refinement and Expansion of the Harvard Resource-based Relative Value Scale." *American Journal of Public Health* 80:7 (July), 799–803.

Berenson, B., and Holahan, J. (1992). "Medicare Physician Expenditures." *JAMA* 267:5 (February 5), 687–691.

Berenson, R. (1991). "Payment Approaches and the Cost of Care." In J. Moreno (ed.), *Paying the Doctor*, 63–74. Westport, Conn.: Auburn House.

Brenner, G., and Rublee, D. (1991). "The 1987 Revision of Physician Fees in Germany." *Health Affairs* 10:3 (Fall), 147–156.

Caper, P. (1988). "Solving the Medical Care Dilemma." *New England Journal of Medicine* 318:23 (June 11), 1535–1536.

Chassin, M., Kosecoff, J., Park, R., and Brook, R. (1987). "Does Inappropriate Use Explain Geographic Variations in the Use of Health Care Services? A Study of Three Procedures." *Journal of the American Medical Association* 258:26 (December 27), 2533–2537.

Chilingerian, J., and Sherman, D. (1990). "Managing Physician Efficiency and Effectiveness in Providing Hospital Services." *Health Services Management Research* 3:1 (March), 3–14.

Christensen, S. (1990). "Estimate of Behavioral Responses." In Congressional Budget Office, *Physician Payment Reform under Medicare*. Appendix B. Washington, D.C.: Congressional Budget Office.

Cohen, A., Cantor, J., Barker, D., and Hughes, R. (1990). "Young Physicians and the Medical Profession." *Health Affairs* 9:4 (Winter), 138–147.

Crane, M. (1991). "Annual Fee Survey." *Medical Economics* 68:19 (October 7), 124–142.

Culler, S., and Ehrenfried, D. (1986). "On the Feasibility and Usefulness of Physician DRGs." *Inquiry* 23:1 (Spring), 40–55.

Derzon, R. (1988). "The Odd Couple in Distress: Hospitals and Physicians Face the 1990s." *Frontiers of Health Services Management* 4:3 (Spring), 4–18.

Eastaugh, S. (1992). *Health Economics: Efficiency, Quality, and Equity.* Westport, Conn.: Auburn House.

———. (1991). "Financial Methods for Paying the Doctor: Issues and Options." in J. Moreno (ed.), *Paying the Doctor.* 49–62. Westport, Conn.: Auburn House.

———. (1990). "Financing the Correct Rate of Growth of Medical Technology." *Quarterly Review of Economics and Business* 30:4 (Winter), 54–60.

Eddy, D. (1991). "What Care Is 'Essential'? What Services Are 'Basic'?" *Journal of the American Medical Association* 265:6 (February 13), 782–788.

Eisenberg, J. (1989). *Doctors' Decisions and the Cost of Medical Practice Patterns and Ways to Change Them.* Ann Arbor, Mich.: Health Administration Press.

Fein, R. (1967). *The Doctor Shortage.* Washington, D.C.: Brookings Institution.

Field, M., and Lohr, K. (1991). *Clinical Practice Guidelines: Directions for a New Program.* Washington, D.C.: National Academy Press.

Frech, H. (1991). *Regulating Doctors' Fees: Competition, Benefits and Controls under Medicare,* Washington, D.C.: American Enterprise Institute Press.

Freeland, M., Chulis, G., and Arnett, R. (1991), "Measuring Input Prices for Physicians: MEI" *Health Care Financing Review* 12:4 (Summer), 61–74.

Fuchs, V., and Hahn, J. (1990). "How Does Canada Do It? A Comparison of Expenditures for Physician Services in the U.S. and Canada." *New England Journal of Medicine* 323:13 (September 27), 884–890.

Ginsburg, P., LeRoy, L., and Hammons, G. (1990). "Medicare Physician Payment Reform." *Health Affairs* 9:1 (Spring), 178–188.

Ginzberg, E. (1990). *The Medical Triangle: Physicians, Politicians, and the Public.* Cambridge, Mass.: Harvard University Press.

Glasser, W. (1990). "Designing Fee Schedules by Formula, Politics, and Negotiation." *American Journal of Public Health* 80:7 (July), 804–809.

Glenn, J. (1989). "Hospitals and the Ecology of Primary Care." *Hospital and Health Services Administration* 34:3 (Fall), 371–384.

Graduate Medical Education National Advisory Committee (GMENAC). (1980). *Graduate Medical Education National Advisory Committee Report to the Secretary of DHHS.* Washington, D.C.: PHS:HRA.

Grimaldi, P. (1992). "Medicare Physician Fees Overhauled." *Health Progress* 73:1, 33–36.

Grumbach, K., and Lee, P. (1991). "How Many Physicians Can We Afford?" *Journal of the American Medical Association* 265:18 (May 8), 2369–2372.

Herger, T. (1990). "Two-Part Pricing and the Mark-ups Charged by Primary Care Physicians for New and Established Patient Visits." *Journal of Health Economics* 8:4 (February) 399–414.

Hillman, A. (1990). "Frequency and Costs of Diagnostic Imaging in Office Practice: A Comparison of Self-referring and Radiologist-referring Physicians." *New England Journal of Medicine* 323:23 (December 6), 1604–1608.

Hsiao, W., Braun, P., and Becker, E. (1992). *Managing Reimbursement in the 1990s: Physician's Reference to Resource-based RVS.* New York: McGraw-Hill.

Hsiao, W. (1989). "Potential Effects of an RBRVS-based Payment System on Health Care Costs and Hospitals." *Frontiers of Health Services Management* 6:1 (Fall), 40–43.

Hsiao, W., Braun, P., Yntema, D., and Becker, E. (1988). "Estimating Physicians' Work for a Resource-based Relative-Value Scale." *New England Journal of Medicine* 319:13 (September 29), 834–841.

Hu, T., and Yang, B. (1988). "Demand for and Supply of Physician Services in the U.S.: A Disequilibrium Analysis." *Applied Economics* 20:8 (August), 995–1006.

Hughes, R., Barker, D., and Reynolds, R. (1991). "Are We Mortgaging the Medical Profession?" *New England Journal of Medicine* 325:6 (August 8), 404–408.

Iglehart, J. (1991a). "Germany's Health Care System." *New England Journal of Medicine* 324:7 (February 14), 503–508.

———. (1991b). "The Struggle over Physician-payment Reform." *New England Journal of Medicine* 325:11 (September 12), 823–28.

———. (1990). "The New Law on Medicare's Payments to Physicians." *New England Journal of Medicine* 322:17 (April 26), 1247–1252.

Ikegami, N. (1991). "Japanese Health Care: Low Cost through Regulated Fees." *Health Affairs* 10:3 (Fall), 87–108.

Joint Commission on Accreditation of Healthcare Organizations (JCAHO). (1991). *Report of the Joint Commissions Survey.* Chicago: Joint Commission on Accreditation of Healthcare Organizations.

Kay, T. (1990). "Volume and Intensity of Medicare Physicians' Services." *Health Care Financing Review* 11:4 (Summer), 133–146.

Koska, M. (1991). "RBRVS and Hospitals: The Physician Payment Revolution." *Hospitals* 65:4 (February 20), 24–30.

Lasker, R., Mongoven, A., Colby, D., and Ginsburg, P. (1990). "Medicare Surgical

Global Fees: The Relationship between Included Services and Payment.'' *Inquiry* 27:3 (Fall), 255–262.

Lee, P., and Ginsburg, P. (1991). ''The Trials of Medicare Physician Pay Reform.'' *Journal of the American Medical Association* 266:11 (September 18), 1562–1565.

Lion, J., Henderson, M., Malbon, A., and Noble, J. (1989). ''Ambulatory Visit Groups AVGs: A Prospective System for Outpatient Care.'' In N. Goldfield and S. Goldsmith (eds.), *Financial Management of Ambulatory Care*, 3–18. Rockville, Md.: Aspen.

McMahon, L. (1990). ''A Critique of the Harvard Resource-based Relative Value Scale.'' *American Journal of Public Health* 80:7 (July), 793–798.

McNeil, B. (1985). ''Hospital Response to DRG-based Prospective Payment.'' *Medical Decision Making* 5:1 (January), 15–21.

Mitchell, J. (1991). ''Physician Participation in Medicaid Revisited.'' *Medical Care* 29:7 (July), 645–653.

Mitchell, J. (1985). ''Physician DRGs.'' *New England Journal of Medicine* 313:11 (September 12), 670–675.

Mitchell, J., Wedig, G., and Cromwell, J. (1989). ''The Medicare Physician Fee Freeze: What Really Happened?'' *Health Affairs* 8:1 (Spring), 21–33.

Moore, F., and Priebe, C. (1991). ''Board-certified Physicians in the United States, 1971–1986.'' *New England Journal of Medicine* 324:8 (February 21), 536–543.

Morrisey, M., and Jensen, G. (1990). ''Hospital Demand for Physicians.'' *Quarterly Review of Economics and Business* 30:1 (Spring), 16–25.

Newhouse, J. (1988). ''Has the Erosion of the Medical Marketplace Ended?'' *Journal of Health Politics, Policy, and Law* 13:2 (Summer), 263–278.

Orsund-Gassiot, C., and Lindsey, S. (1991). *Handbook of Medical Staff Management.* Rockville, Md.: Aspen.

Ott, J. (1991). ''Competitive Medical Organizations: A View of the Future.'' In J. Moreno (ed.), *Paying the Doctor*, 83–92. Westport, Conn.: Auburn House.

Pauly, M. (1990). ''Objectives for Changing Physician Payment.'' *Frontiers of Health Services Management* 6:1 (Fall), 44–47.

Pauly, M., Hillman, A., and Kerstein, J. (1990). ''Managing Physician Incentives in Managed Care: The Role of For-Profit Ownership.'' *Medical Care* 28:11 (November), 1013–1024.

Petersdorf, R. (1992). ''Primary Care Applicants.'' *New England Journal of Medicine* 326:6 (February 6), 408–409.

Politzer, R., Harris, D., and Gaston, M. (1991). ''Primary Care Physician Supply and the Medically Underserved.'' *Journal of the American Medical Association* 266:1 (July 3), 104–108.

Physician Payment Reform Commission (PPRC). (1991). *Annual Report to Congress.* Washington, D.C.: PPRC.

Pope, G. (1990). ''Physician Inputs, Outputs, and Productivity.'' *Inquiry* 27:2 (Summer), 151–160.

Reinhardt, U. (1987). ''Resource Allocation in Health Care: The Allocation of Lifestyles to Providers.'' *Milbank Quarterly* 65:2 (Summer), 153–176.

Riegelman, R. (1991). ''Taming Medical Technology.'' In J. Moreno (ed.), *Paying the Doctor*, 75–82. Westport, Conn.: Auburn House.

Rizzo, J., and Zeckhauser, R. (1991). ''Advertising and Entry: Physician Services.'' *Journal of Political Economy* 89:3 (May), 436–454.

Roper, W. (1988). "Perspectives on Physician Payment Reform: The RBRVS in Context." *New England Journal of Medicine* 319:13 (September 29), 865–867.

Rosenbach, M., and Stone, A. (1990). "Malpractice Insurance Costs." *Health Affairs* 9:4 (Winter), 176–185.

Schloss, E. (1988). "Beyond GMENAC—Another Physician Shortage from 2010–2030?" *New England Journal of Medicine* 318:14 (April 7), 920–922.

Schwartz, W., Sloan, F., and Mendelson, D. (1988). "Why There Will Be Little or No Physician Surplus between Now and the Year 2000." *New England Journal of Medicine* 318:14 (April 7), 892–896.

Schwartz, W., Williams, A., Newhouse, J., and Witsberger, C. (1989). "Are We Training Too Many Medical Subspecialists?" *Journal of the American Medical Association* 259:2 (January 8), 233–239.

Shortell, S. (1990). "Revisiting the Garden: Medicine and Management in the 1990s." *Frontiers of Health Services Management* 7:1 (Fall), 3–31.

Shroder, M., and Weisbrod, B. (1990). "Medical Malpractice, Technological Change, and Learning-by-Doing," in R. Scheffler, *Advances in Health Economics and Health Services Research*, 185–199. Greenwich, Conn.: JAI Press,

Siu, A., Manning, W., and Benjamin, B. (1990). "Patient, Provider, and Hospital Characteristics Associated with Inappropriate Hospitalization." *American Journal of Public Health* 80:10 (October), 1253–1256.

Starr, P. (1982). *The Social Transformation of American Medicine*. New York: Basic Books.

Steinbrook, R., and Lo, B. (1992). "Oregon Medicaid: Will It Provide Adequate Medical Care?" *New England Journal of Medicine* 326:5 (January 30), 340–344.

Tarlov, A. (1990). "How Many Physicians Is Enough?" *Journal of the American Medical Association* 263:4 (January 26), 571–572.

Weiner, J. (1989). "Forecasting Physician Supply: Recent Developments." *Health Affairs* 8:4 (Winter), 173–182.

Wennberg, J. (1990). "Outcomes Research, Cost Containment, and the Fear of Health Care Rationing." *New England Journal of Medicine* 323:17 (October 25), 1202–1204.

———. (1989). "Hospital Use and Mortality among Medicare Beneficiaries in Boston and New Haven." *New England Journal of Medicine* 321:17 (October 26), 1168–1173.

———. (1988). "Improving the Medical Decision-making Process." *Health Affairs* 7:2 (Summer), 99–106.

Zuckerman, S., Welch, W., and Pope, G. (1990). "Index for Physician Fees." *Journal of Health Economics* 9:1 (June), 39–69.

Chapter 8

Graduate Medical Education and the Teaching Hospital

Changes in the availability of federal funds have already led to some dramatic changes in the way medical schools support themselves. To survive and to prosper in the decade to come, medical academe must adjust to a period of no growth and change imaginatively to allow progress to continue.

—David E. Rogers

He who pays the piper can call the tune.

—Old English proverb

Future research that explicitly recognizes variations in medical staff characteristics and organizations may be fruitful in discovering reasons underlying variations in hospital performance in response to regulation. Put another way, is "control" of medical staff a necessary condition for containment of hospital costs?

—Frank A. Sloan

Stressed by the continued emphasis on cost containment, teaching hospitals appear to be facing serious problems in financing traditional levels of patient care, education, and biomedical research (Custer and Willke 1991; Eastaugh 1990). The problems have different etiology in all three areas—for example, declines in Medicare payments for graduate medical education (residents and interns)—but they are all described in the language of revenue shortfalls (Petersdorf 1985; Chin et al. 1985; Foley and Mulhausen 1986). In order to preserve their mission, teaching hospitals increasingly need to streamline their activities so as to price their services competitively through promotion of cost consciousness to their residents, attending physicians, and employees. Some teaching hospitals appear to be adjusting to the new competitive era better than others. A number of well-known teaching hospitals with annual gifts and grants in excess of $100 million have had to reduce staffing by 700 to 1,300 full-time-equivalent employees.

In the first half of this chapter we attempt to disaggregate the full cost of graduate medical education (GME) and discuss the impact of patient severity on cost per case. In the second half of the chapter we survey the health-services research literature to discern how much of the extra patient care in certain hospitals in excessive, inappropriate, or unnecessary and outline medical school finances. A reduction in optional or redundant hospital workups and elimination of nonsystematic usage of unproven procedures (those not tested in a legitimate clinical trial) not only will save money but also will increase patient satisfaction.

Teaching hospitals will always offer somewhat different treatment protocols than nonteaching facilities because of differences in patient severity, research trials, innovative techniques, and, sometimes, better quality of care. Teaching will always require some legitimate extra costs, such as (1) the surgical resident spending an extra 20 to 90 minutes in the operating room learning to do a technique from the more experienced mentor attending surgeon or (2) the apprentice resident ordering a liberal large number of tests to avoid making a mistake or missing a rare interesting condition (that is, before learning how to better balance risk aversion and wasted effort and not to follow every "wild-goose chase"; Eeckhoudt, LeBrun, and Sailly 1985; Eastaugh 1979). These so-called learning effects are legitimate costs of training the next generation of competent, high-quality clinicians. The indirect cost of education requires more than simply an additional increment of variable patient-care costs. Teaching hospitals require additional fixed costs beyond the additional space required to house biomedical research projects. For example, because the teaching function requires additional space in the patient's room for groups of residents and medical students, builders typically allocate 30 to 50 percent more square feet of space per bed to accommodate the traffic.

THE GME QUANDARY: WHO SHOULD PAY AND HOW MUCH?

The educational component of medical care costs is frequently given adequate earmarked support via funds from departments of education in Canada and Europe (Relman 1984; Eastaugh 1980a). The American tradition is to subsidize such costs indirectly through the "back door" of patient hospital bills. For example, the 1991 survey of the Association of American Medical Colleges (AAMC) reported that 85 percent of residents' stipends and fringe benefits were derived from hospital patient revenues. The Commonwealth Task Force on Academic Health Centers report (1985), a two-year project by a 16-member national task force of teaching hospital professors and managers, suggested that a tax on all hospital admissions should be collected to reimburse hospitals for doing graduate medical education. This is a rather attractive payment "solution" for teaching hospitals because it involves minimum disruption of business as usual ("don't look at what we do, just pay us"). Such a proposed tax on hospital admissions, a sort of "sick tax" for education, has the administrative advantage of distributing the costs of teaching hospitals across all inpatients without disaggregating how much of this cash flow underwrites (1) appropriate treatment of a more severely ill case mix (Newhouse 1983), (2) charity care for the poor (Epstein 1986; Rieselbach and Jackson 1986), or (3) inappropriate high-cost care (Keeler 1990).

In fairness to the Commonwealth Task Force report (1985), Congress also has not had much success in weighting the relative importance of the various reasons for the higher costs observed in teaching hospitals. The U.S. Senate Finance Committee report (1983) on Medicare reform explicitly included a lump-sum payment for graduate medical education in recognition of teaching hospitals' higher burden of charity-care cases and the inability of the DRG classification system to account fully for patient severity of illness. The largest group of teaching hospitals, the Council of Teaching Hospitals (COTH), accounted for 6 percent of the hospitals, 18 percent of the admissions, and 52 percent of the charity care in 1983 (Iglehart 1986). Anecdotal reports suggested that teaching hospitals had more severity of illness within each DRG category, and this assertion was confirmed by a number of studies (Horn et al. 1985; Horn, Horn, and Moses 1986).

The initial DHHS adjustment formula for the indirect cost of graduate medical education was based on a multiple regression analysis by two researchers at HCFA. Pettengill and Vertrees (1982) analyzed 1980 Medicare cost reports from 5,071 hospitals and concluded that costs rose 5.795 percent for each increase of 0.1 in the ratio of residents to beds after adjusting for DRG mix and local wage levels. Pressure from the Council of Teaching Hospitals led Congress to double this adjustment rate to 11.59 percent. The stated reason was that this extra payment factor would help underwrite uncompensated care and increased severity of illness not captured by the DRG categories (U.S. Senate Finance Committee 1983). Nonteaching hospitals in the shadow of major teaching hospitals with 0.8 residents per bed would receive half the Medicare payment for the same DRG case treated. Because this payment formula was excessively generous to the 136 hospitals that provide 55 percent of the residency slots in the nation, payment rates for the indirect cost of graduate medical education were reduced in 1986. As part of the Consolidated Omnibus Budget Reconciliation Act (COBRA) effective April 7, 1986, the indirect teaching adjustment was reduced to 8.1 percent for FY 1986 and FY 1987. This reduction was made in part because the DRG rates would recognize, for the first time, hospitals serving a disproportionate share of poor patients. The Bush administration has proposed cutting the indirect teaching adjustment to 4.4 percent ($2.5 billion) by 1993.

Medicare reimbursement for residents stimulated more hospitals to initiate residency programs. The number of residency programs accredited by the Council for Graduate Medical Education increased by 21 percent from 1983 to 1991. But while the number of programs increased, the number of residents declined to below 85,000 in 1991 because of a decline in the number of graduates from

American medical schools. The residents are distributed unevenly: 74.9 percent work for the 330 largest COTH programs, and 25.1 percent work in 925 other teaching hospitals.

State hospitals are most dependent on residents to provide patient care. Forty COTH state hospitals have 47.3 residents per 100 beds, whereas the 20 non-COTH state teaching hospitals have 12.55 residents per bed. The 33 COTH county or municipal hospitals have 34.4 residents per bed, while the 119 non-COTH county or municipal hospitals have 7.3 residents per bed. The 277 private tax-exempt COTH hospitals have 21.3 residents per bed, whereas non-COTH tax-exempt private hospitals have 3.2 residents per bed. In 1991 an estimated 54,000 residents and interns received $2.6 billion in salary and $468 million in fringe benefits (AAMC 1991).

Anderson and Lave (1986) presented a good explanation of why resource costs increase at a slower rate as teaching programs get larger. A curvilinear formula takes into account the basic fact that teaching costs less than double as R doubles (e.g., R increases from 0.3 to 0.6). For example, under the old linear formula, two teaching hospitals in the same location were receiving quite different payment rates if they had different levels of R—even though they were both experiencing approximately the same factor markets, comparable severity of illness and elderly case loads, and equivalent amounts of charity care.

In addition to the Medicare payment rate adjustments for graduate medical education, many teaching hospitals benefit from the disproportionate-share adjustment. The disproportionate-share adjustment was designed in 1985 to compensate hospitals that serve a very high fraction of low-income patients. According to the Congressional Budget Office (CBO 1991), this disproportionate-share adjustment accounts for $1.6 billion of the estimated $51.7 billion in Medicare prospective payments. The 42 teaching hospitals with disproportionate-share indexes of 55 percent or more receive an average adjustment of $1,190 per patient, representing 20 percent of their payments from Medicare.

MEDICARE PAYMENT FOR TEACHING

The original Medicare payment bonus of 11.59 percent for each 0.1 increment in the resident-per-bed ratio was considered biased (prejudiced) in favor of teaching hospitals because the coefficient was set at twice the level of the regression coefficient (Pettengill and Vertrees 1982). The overpayment for teaching has been confirmed by Custer and Willke (1991). Many rural hospitals were paid by Medicare half the price that some local teaching hospitals received for the same patient DRG in the mid-1980s. In America, if one group gets a great deal under the system of price controls, the losers scream. The corollary of the regulatory squawk theory (Hilton 1972) is that the losers seek parity. Rural hospitals won their point with Congress in the late 1980s. The indirect graduate medical education teaching adjustment was decreased from 11.59 percent to 7.7 percent, and the urban-rural payment gap was scheduled to be closed by 1995 (ProPAC 1991). This is a textbook example of the reaction of a countervailing power, the rural hospitals winning one back from the big urban teaching hospitals.

One is still left with the more basic question of what the teaching-adjustment payment factor should be. Some of the extra cost might be unnecessary or inappropriate (Eastaugh 1987). Thorpe (1988) redid the regression analysis with more recent data and concluded that the fair payment rate might be 3.15 percent for each 0.1 increment of the resident-to-bed ratio. In the current cost-cutting climate Medicare will probably trim the indirect graduate medical education adjustment. ProPAC (1991) has proposed trimming the adjustment to 5.5 percent in 1992 and lowering it steadily to 3.2 percent in 1996. Congress is also narrowing the urban-rural gap, to the benefit of many financially distressed rural hospitals. If teaching hospitals enjoyed a prejudiced position in their favor during the mid-1980s, the prejudice of the Medicare payment formula may be against them in the 1990s.

Managers of residency programs will be under pressure to provide residents a superior educational experience based on a reasonable workload supervised by senior attending physicians. Continued requests for more federal aid could lead to massive intervention in medical education. The federal government would want more control over the quantity, quality, and type of residency slots (e.g., more primary-care and fewer surgical residency positions). This trend has already been noted by Petersdorf (1985), Iglehart (1986), and a number of politicians. Faculty and hospital managers may have to face the trade-off of some loss of autonomy for stabilization of revenue sources. Nonfederal payers of inpatient care seem less willing to generously underwrite residency training; therefore, teaching hospitals' revenue may decline without an expansion in competitive-bidding schemes. Manpower-training-program decisions may increasingly be made by federal or state governments rather than by institutional decision makers. Smaller and leaner teaching programs may soon be mandated by legislation (Ginzberg 1990).

The need for better cost analysis in an era of fluctuating payment policies should be obvious to all managers and providers in teaching settings. One of the basic problems with the aforementioned cost studies is that true cost-accounting systems at the institutional level are lacking. The Arthur Young and Policy Analysis, Inc. (1986), study offered the analytical advantages of a good cost-accounting framework, uniform accounting across 36 teaching hospitals and 9 control (nonteaching) hospitals, and uniform measurement of severity of illness, disease stage, and quality of care. The next four sections will survey joint production activities, standard costing, results of the Arthur Young study, and the role of severity-of-illness measures.

JOINT PRODUCTS AND TOTAL COST PER CASE

Lave and Frank (1990) and Pfordresher (1985) reported that it is very difficult to partition joint activities such as teaching, research, and patient care. *Joint activity* is a phrase used to describe the simultaneous production of multiple outputs during a given activity. Joint activity is most obvious when multiple individuals are involved in multiple tasks at the patient's bedside. However, joint activity also occurs in instances in which a single individual is involved in multiple tasks or activities. Here a joint product may be indicated by comparative amounts of time taken to perform a task. If an attending physician acting alone, for example, performs a patient-care task in an average of 12 minutes and a second-year resident takes an average of 18 minutes, then the resident's time may be attributed in part to patient care and in part to education. The attending physician's average time in this example is presumed to have no educational content. Thus, if the task is performed in that given period of time, whether by attending physicians or second-year residents, it is taken entirely as an input to patient care. But if the time taken is greater, then a portion becomes an input to education, on the normative premise that the individuals performing the task are not yet as skilled, on average, as the attending physicians and therefore must still be learning.

The most basic question to consider is, why joint-production institutions exist. Joint production most often derives from economies of simultaneous production. Joint production may also arise from joint factor supply, especially in a profession like medicine. For example, if a factor required to produce instructional outputs, like faculty members, is to be made available only if allowed to produce research, a phenomenon labeled joint factor supply exists. One should see the folly in postulating the existence of a godlike dean who is capable of determining the minimum amount of research time to buy if the only objective is hiring a teaching faculty.

Fortunately, deans in the real world are concerned with the quality and quantity of patient care, research, and education. Deans must consider issues such as how much additional faculty practice-plan effort on patient care must be requested to restrain tuition rate increases, secure adequate faculty resources, optimize the prestige of the research program, and still produce the level of educational output that the residency program is committed to produce.

Two caveats are in order. First, the sum of pure time spent on each of the three activities has to be less than total time effort, and the sum of pure and joint time has to be more than total hours worked. Second, one could optimize the production of one activity and erode the quality of the other two activities. It is obviously not desirable to reduce research and patient care to the minimum levels actually required for educational purposes. Consequently, we shall include measures of the quality of patient care in the cost functions for teaching hospitals.

MEASURING TOTAL COST PER CASE

Unbiased cost analysis of teaching hospitals must focus on total costs: physician costs plus inpatient costs per illness episode. It has often been stated that residents and interns save money on their patients' physician fees even as they raise hospital costs (Cameron 1985). In teaching hospitals these salaried residents and interns are paid by the hospital and provide many services that could otherwise be performed and billed separately by an attending senior physician. On the other hand, services are sometimes largely performed by the resident and also billed by the attending physician, so the payer is stuck with the problem of "paying twice" (Garg et al. 1982). If net total cost per patient episode is higher among teaching hospitals, this higher price might in turn purchase an added benefit. Perhaps patients receive better-quality care through continuous 24-hour availability of residents and the immediacy of their responses to patient-care problems. Irrespective of whether any quality-enhancing activities turn out to be cost-saving or cost-increasing, regulatory forces and business will continue their vigilant attempts to minimize double billing.

Some evidence points to greater utilization of ancillary services at teaching hospitals without any obvious improvement in quality of care (Frick, Martin, and Schwartz 1985; Garg et al. 1982; Eastaugh 1987). It has also been argued that graduate medical education programs introduce operational inefficiencies into the activities of senior attending physicians. The teaching hospital as a complex organization may exhibit cost-decreasing or cost-increasing behavior. On the positive side, teaching facilities may be the first to question "tenet-of-faith" habits— for example, the evening-before-surgery shave has proven to be harmful and costly (Brown, Ehrlich, and Stehman 1984). On the downside, Beck (1986) has suggested that teaching hospitals have a cost-increasing bias to employ overly expensive nonclinicians, wasting millions of dollars by using highly trained, expensive labor to perform tasks that require only moderate or minimal skill.

Determining the costs (and benefits) of graduate medical education is complicated by all these confounding factors. Moreover, our sample of 36 hospitals selected from a national sample of four strata of teaching facilities and 9 nonteaching hospitals (rather than only 9) would have substantially more statistical power. However, the Arthur Young analysis has the advantage over Cameron (1985) of measuring hospital costs as accurately as possible. In contrast, previous studies from Salkever (1970) to Cameron (1985) have had to create "costs" from patient-charge-claim data for each case. Charges are not an accurate approximation of costs (see chapter 2). In addition, our sample was not restricted to Medicare and Medicaid patients only. Our analysis also collected severity-of-illness and cost information for a population sample of patients (Eastaugh chapter 2 in Arthur Young, 1986).

ARTHUR YOUNG GME RESULTS

Our focus was on average unit cost per episode: hospital plus physician costs. We were not concerned with the typical HCFA specification for how inpatient total costs of production vary among hospitals. The dependent variable in our regressions was total cost per case. Average cost was measured as a function of nine independent variables (Arthur Young 1986): R (resident and intern full-time equivalents per bed); DRG cost weight (1.0 national average); Horn et al.'s (1985) severity-of-illness index; other case variables (length of stay and whether the individual was covered by Medicaid or was self-paying); a department-level quality index (using percentage of adverse patient outcomes divided by at-risk potential adverse patient occurrence opportunities [the APO rate done by the same raters across the sample hospitals]; and three input price wage indexes for physicians, nurses, and technicians. To avoid problems of multicollinearity in our cost-estimation procedure, we did not include resident wage rates (because they were already captured through the 0.91 correlation with nurse wage rates), and we excluded capital prices (because they had a 0.8 correlation with technician wage rates).

The last three variables were included in the analysis to separate the cost-of-education effect from input-price effects driving up the costs of care. Better quality of care could be cost-increasing or cost-decreasing. For example, Haley, Schaberg, and Crossley (1981) reported that the surgical department saves the hospital seven days of variable cost for every wound-infection APO avoided. Length of stay was included in the analysis because patients within a DRG category have a wide variation in length of stay (Lave and Frank 1990; U.S. Senate Finance Committee 1983) not captured by the DRGs, case severity, or acuity. DRG conditions that have higher cost weights are by definition more complex and expensive to treat than those with lower weights (e.g., bypass surgery has a weight thirteen times as high as that of lens procedure DRG 39). The Medicaid/self-pay variable was included in the analysis because poor people often have inadequate prior medical care, deficient nutritional status, more complications, and secondary health problems (i.e., a net level of additional acuity not captured by severity of illness or length of stay).

To capture at least part of the effect that the teaching function has on case costs, independent variable R, interns and residents per bed, was included. To improve the econometric fit of this variable in the regression model, we multiplied the observed value in each facility by 1,000. Table 8.1, column 1, presents the regression results for a random sample of 300 to 375 patients at each of the 45 hospitals. Columns 2 through 9 in table 8.1 present the results from patients in the eight tracer diagnoses under study. The maximum tracer sample size within each group was 25 cases per hospital (e.g., if only 14 cases of tracer 2 could be found at a given hospital in the year 1984, then only 14 cases would be included for analysis). The impact on average cost of increasing residents per bed by 0.1 ranged from 4.1 percent for benign prostatic hypertrophy to 10.5 percent for nonsurgical treatment of acute myocardial infarction. The value for the random sample was a 7.2 percent increase in cost.

Quality of care had a negative, but statistically insignificant, impact on patient costs. One would not want to read too much into this finding, but perhaps the net cost to society of investing in quality-enhancing activities is self-financing. Superior-quality care may cost a little bit more, but it avoids the costly consequences of fixing poor-quality care through prolonged duration of stay. The cost

Table 8.1

Cost per Case Regressions for a Random and Tracer Sample at 45 Hospitals (Arthur Young Study, 1986)

	Random Sample	1. Acute Myocardial Infarction	2. Upper G.I. Hemorrhage	3. Asthma	4. Gastroenteritis Acute Colitis	5. Complicated Delivery	6. Gallbladder	7. Hysterectomy[a]	8. Benign Prostatic Hypertrophy[a]
# Patients	n = 13,436	n = 857	n = 827	n = 821	n = 704	n = 793	n = 951	n = 833	n = 848
Average Cost	$4,150	$8,407	$5,633	$2,040	$1,693	$4,001	$7,890	$6,329	$6,818
Variable (units of measurement)									
Residents per bed (1 per 10 beds)	7.2	10.5	5.7	2.5	0[ns]	0[ns]	5.4	4.2	4.1
Severity (.1 change in 4 point SOI)	3.2	4.0	3.6	2.5	2.4	2.7	5.2	3.3	3.2
DRG Cost Weight (.1 change)	7.7	11.7	6.2	1.5[b]	4.9	8.4	1.7	-3.4[b]	3.7
Length of stay (1 Day)	5.0	21.1	22.2	8.9	24.2	4.5	14.1	20.0	17.3
Medicaid or self-pay patients	.1[ns]	.41	-.2[ns]	.43	.89	1.7	-.02[ns]	.21[ns]	-.16[ns]
Quality of care (APO actual/at risk)	-.01[ns]	—	—	—	—	—	—	—	—
RN wage (1% change)	1.1[ns]	18.2	5.6	4.2	2.3[ns]	-8.3[b]	-4.4[b]	5.6[b]	1.5[ns]
Physician wage (1% change)	5.1	7.6	3.7	1.9[b]	-1.1[ns]	10.0	7.4	.6[ns]	2.4
Technician wage (1% change)	12.0	31.3	-.5[ns]	5.7[ns]	14.6	52.1	35.3	10.1	11.2
R-squared (fraction of variance explained)	.541	.523	.585	.438	.735	.628	.606	.508	.680

NOTES: Coefficients are mean elasticity estimates. APO = Adverse Patient Occurrence 15-item inventory. All variables significant at the .01 level, except those marked b and c.

[a]Surgical cases; b = .05 level of significance; c = not significant at 0.1 level.

of treating Medicaid and self-pay patients was only 1 to 2 percent higher, given that the equation already included a measure of severity of illness. This could best be described as a proxy measure of "social acuity."

The Horn et al. (1985) severity-of-illness index had the expected positive and significant impact on average cost. A 0.1 unit increase in the index was associated with a 2 to 5 percent higher cost per case. If severity of illness has a case-mix and cost effect within DRGs, rather than across DRGs, this suggests that Horn et al.'s measure may be a fine-tuning mechanism to add onto or supplement the DRGs. In the context of an inventory-control problem, DRGs may capture broad-based product lines, but severity measures a second dimension (degree or amount). We will survey some competing measures of patient severity in the next section. We will not be able to answer the critical question of how much the reduction in variance of unexplained cost has to be to justify the data collection. However, by 1991 Horn had already marketed a less expensive alternative measure, the computerized severity index (CSI), to over 100 hospitals.

SEVERITY-OF-ILLNESS MEASURES

The concept of severity of illness encompasses many dimensions. For the purposes of payment, the fundamental concept underlying each system is translated into resource demand. But each severity system originated as an attempt to classify cases according to a particular notion of severity or to measure a particular parameter chosen to serve as a proxy for resource demand. Attempting to distinguish between several concepts related to severity serves to illustrate the subtleties:

1. *Severity*, in the strictest sense, has usually been used to describe extent of disease (deviation from normal physiology, extent of organ failure) or risk of death or morbidity.

2. *Acuity* describes the urgency with which intervention is required.

3. *Complexity* describes effects due to interaction of multiple diseases or conditions.

4. *Intensity* is associated with the level of care required and is the term most consistently associated with (legitimate) demand for hospital services.

5. *Treatment difficulty* is associated with the extent and rate of the patient's response to therapy.

In case-mix systems designed to span the spectrum of cases in acute-care hospitals, the link between the underlying concept on which a severity system is founded and resource demand may be inconsistent across disease categories. Moreover, advanced clinical stages of disease are not always associated with increased resource consumption, for example, admission of a cancer or AIDS patient for terminal care. While well justified by the intensity of supportive care required, this admission may still impose far less resource burden than would an admission at an earlier stage of the same disease, when aggressive experimental intervention was indicated.

A fundamental objective is to base the classification on characteristics of the patient rather than on the services that were provided, in an attempt to reflect legitimate resource demand rather than to include excessive or inappropriate resource consumption. Typically this is done by focusing on physiologic parameters, objective clinical findings, or the final diagnosis, combined with patient characteristics such as age and sex. In many systems, including DRGs, the quantum jump in resource demand associated with the need for an operating-room procedure is reflected by considering surgical procedures in the classification scheme, relying on PRO utilization controls to ensure that procedures performed were necessary.

As a result of this attempt to avoid defining resource categories in a circular fashion, most systems are unable to indicate the degree of diagnostic challenge that some patients pose. No classification scheme based on the final diagnosis can possibly reflect the resources required by a "complex rule-out," an uncommon manifestation of a disease (a "Zebra") whose diagnosis and treatment are usually straightforward. A high prevalence of Zebra cases has a significant impact on teaching hospitals specializing in tertiary services, who see a disproportionate number of Zebra patients requiring extensive workups due to unusual presentations of common diseases.

Tulane University researchers have done an independent evaluation of the five severity systems and have concluded that the Johns Hopkins computerized severity index (CSI; Horn, Horn, and Moses 1986) was the most accurate for predicting survival of medical patients following a myocardial infarction. Other studies have shown that for intensive-care patients, APACHE II works best for predicting survival (Knaus, Draper, and Wagner 1985). However, the payers do not seem ready to pay in proportion to patient severity, but any large hospital should engage the services of one or two severity systems to do workload-driven staffing (chapter 9), quality assurance, and utilization review.

Will a severity system ever exist that answers all doubts among members of the medical staff? The easy answer to that question is no. Many physicians will assume that the majority of any unexplained event is associated with patient factors: The severity measure is imperfect and the adjustments for comorbidity and complications are not adequate to prove that the patient is the reason for elevated mortality rates, infection rates, or higher costs (Wennberg 1990; Malenka et al. 1990). Perfect measures for severity will never exist, and most systems have misclassification rates of 12 to 17 percent. More research needs to be done on the nonlinear relationship between severity and resource use, because as severity is increased from low levels (type 1), resource use continues to increase at a decreasing rate, reaching diminishing returns (plateau or flat of the curve) before declining for the highest-level patients (those about to die; see Rapoport et al. 1990).

A suitable severity adjustment to the DRGs would provide all hospitals with an equitable incentive to become more efficient (Eastaugh 1990; Steinwald and Dummit 1989). Currently, hospitals that admit an atypically high proportion of high-severity patients and are paid the DRG average have an "excessive" incentive to become more efficient. However, they might never be able to lower costs to the DRG average payment levels without harming the quality of care. Consequently, teaching hospitals with a higher severity of illness might be faced with the choice of eroding either their financial health or the quality of care provided. Conversely, hospitals that presently admit an atypically high proportion of low-severity patients and are paid the DRG average have little incentive to become more efficient.

There are a number of systems in use, based on discharge abstract data, that provide hospitals with measures of case mix and severity, including DRGs and the PAS-A list from the Commission on Professional and Hospital Activities (CPHA). In the PAS-A list system, severity is quantified by the existence of secondary diagnoses (the complications and comorbidity conditions) that are thought to cluster isoresource cases. Moreover, DRGs differentiate types of operating-room procedures in different DRGs, rather than just noting the existence or nonexistence of an operating room procedure.

Two newer systems are analyzed here: disease staging and the manual severity-of-illness (SOI) index (Horn et al. 1985). The key attribute of the manual SOI system is that it attempts to capture how ill a patient is within a specific disease condition—not just that the patient has the specific condition. As a result, it predicts resource use somewhat better than DRGs alone (Horn, Horn, and Moses 1986). The SOI index is a more complex measure and captures more patient information than disease staging. Advocates of the disease-staging approach would disagree (Gonnella, Hornbrook, and Louis 1984). The only inputs to disease staging are ICD–9-CM diagnosis and procedure codes, whereas the SOI system uses information based on laboratory values, radiologic findings, vital signs, and other data found in the medical record but not captured in the current five-digit discharge abstract data base. In addition, disease staging has no mechanism to combine all of a patient's diseases together to form a single overall stage for a patient. Disease staging as a case-mix measure has been found to be substantially less predictive of resource utilization per case than DRGs. Even when combined with DRGs, disease staging has added little predictive power (Coffey and Goldfarb 1986).

Several new severity measurement systems have appeared in recent years, including the computerized severity index six-digit coding system (CSI; Horn 1986), Western Pennsylvania Blue Cross PMCs (patient management 800 categories; Young 1986), and MEDISGRPS (Brewster et al. 1985). Brewster et al.'s MEDISGRPS system goes beyond traditional five-digit discharge abstract data. This parallels the two Horn systems (SOI, CSI) and PMCs. It uses about 500 "key clinical findings" to designate the severity of a patient on a scale of 0 to 4. These key clinical findings are recorded by trained hospital personnel on the third day of hospitalization (the MEDISGRPS authors refer to this as "on admission''), and the information is processed by a computer program that determines the severity of the patient on admission to the hospital. The MED-ISGRPS system designates one rating for the severity of the patient on admission and another with data collected at ten days if the patient is still in the hospital. In this section we shall examine the relative ability of SOI and disease staging to enhance the resource-consumption predictive power of DRGs, but no assessment will be made of the MEDISGRPS, PMC, or CSI systems.

The Horn SOI Measure

The severity-of-illness (SOI) measure was developed by a panel of physicians and nurses who were asked to define patient severity and develop the requisite list of parameters that would be necessary to implement the definition. The panel suggested 32 variables, which were ultimately reviewed and collapsed into seven dimensions, each having four levels of increasing severity. The decision to include certain parameters was based on the relationship of the parameter to patient severity. Parameters not directly related to the patient, such as those related to the skill or experience of the physician, were excluded. Four levels of severity were chosen for each variable and for the overall severity index (rather than five or some other odd number) to avoid the problem of having most responses fall naturally at the middle level. An even number of levels forces the rater to chose decisively between two middle points and hence provides more distinction among patients. Raters require careful initial training (and periodic follow-up) to become proficient in coding SOI. Horn, Horn, and Moses (1986) reported that almost all raters scored 90 percent or greater agreement with blind reratings of the same records, with an average agreement of 93.5 percent across 90 raters in 18 hospitals. The seven SOI dimensions are the following:

1. The stage of the principal diagnosis at admission, including the greatest extent of organ involvement.

2. Complications that developed during the hospital stay due to the principal disease or as a direct result of the therapy or hospitalization.

3. Preexisting problems other than the principal diagnosis and its complications (e.g., diabetes in a patient admitted with acute myocardial infarction).

4. The degree to which the patient requires more than the minimal level of direct care expected for the principal diagnosis. A dependency score above level 1 indicates that the stage of illness, complications, or preexisting diseases require extra monitoring or care.

5. Diagnostic and therapeutic procedures performed outside of the operating room. The highest level of procedure, such as those required for life support, rather than the total number of procedures performed, determines the score for this dimension. The need for such a procedure also should be reflected in one or more of the first three dimensions (stage, complications, and/or preexisting problems).

6. The patient's response to hospital treatment for the principal diagnosis, complications,

and interactions. This relates to treatments for acute illness or acute manifestations of chronic illness that one expects to manage during a hospital stay. It does not relate to improvement in underlying chronic conditions for which there is no expectation of either cure or significant progress during the hospitalization.

7. The extent to which a patient shows residual evidence of the acute injury or illness at the time of discharge.

Disease Staging

The SOI measure uses a generic instrument that can be applied to all cases and generates a four-level measure of severity. In contrast, disease staging covers most cases in our sample but not all conditions. SysteMetrics (Louis et al. 1983), under contract to the National Center for Health Services Research, developed stages for 480 specific disease conditions. The recent efforts by SysteMetrics include the development of the staging process using not only data drawn from the medical records, but also ICDA codes from computerized discharge data sets. Staging is a system of categorizing patients into one of four levels of severity based on pathophysiological parameters primarily obtained from the medical record abstract (computer software has been developed to enable staging to be done using discharge abstract data). Disease staging has three basic limitations in the context of the Arthur Young study:

1. Stage-one conditions are by definition patients with a single uncomplicated diagnosis, and often the hospitalization is questionable. Since teaching hospitals might only rarely deal with such patients, the remaining levels of staging may be inadequate for measuring severity for a particular condition.

2. Garg et al. (1978) suggests that the construct validity of staging is supported because an increased stage correlates with increased cost. However, there is little evidence to determine whether the various stages have statistically significant differential charges and whether these differences would remain when charges are adjusted to costs.

3. While the method is sensitive to complications of the principal diagnosis, it is insensitive to patients in whom multiple diseases (not related to the principal diagnosis) interact in an additive, multiplicative, or other way.

One central conceptual strength of disease staging is that the severity measure is independent of provider behavior (e.g., treating a condition medically or surgically). By utilizing only diagnostic information to define stages of specific diseases and neglecting procedure classification, disease staging does not confound treatment preference with case-mix severity. In only three situations are procedures used to form stage classifications, and only because this identifies the diagnoses more precisely (e.g., cesarean deliveries). This conceptual strength of the disease-staging process, however, leads to a practical problem. Because the technique does not distinguish surgical from nonsurgical patients, costs within the same diagnosis and stage vary widely.

We shall limit our literature review to the familiar DRGs. The new 486 DRGs, like the old DRGs, utilize length of stay as the primary dependent variable to reflect resource use. DRGs as a case-mix measure differentiate surgical from nonsurgical cases and consequently exhibit significant differences in case complexity between teaching and nonteaching hospitals. The Goldfarb and Coffey (1987) retrospective regression study of 144 teaching hospitals and 226 nonteaching hospitals reported that teaching institutions admitted 1.4 times as many surgical candidates as nonteaching hospitals after differences in disease staging between hospitals were controlled. A more extensive commitment to teaching (e.g., membership in COTH or a medical-school-based hospital) did not significantly increase surgical intensity (.46 versus .33 of cases). The intent of the calculation was to get away from the surgery/nonsurgery distinction embedded in the DRGs and to standardize for disease stage of the patient population. Goldfarb and Coffey also reported no differences between hospital types in case-mix-standardized fatality rates, despite the greater use of resources in teaching hospitals. This result concerning patient outcomes is surprising given the conventional wisdom that the continuous all-day availability of residents and the immediacy of their responses to problems should result in increased quality of service. One could speculate that a more sensitive measure, such as an inventory of adverse patient occurrences (APOs), would better detect differences in the quality of care than a crude measure (fatality). APO items include iatrogenic adverse reactions, complications, incomplete clinical management, unexpected cardiac or respiratory arrest, unplanned return to the operating room, nosocomial infection, iatrogenic neurological deficit, death, and other dysquality events, infections and so on (Panniers and Newlander 1986). In our study we collected APO data on the random case sample to provide a measure of quality of care at the case level. The APO measure will be used in the following analysis due to the unavailability of the disease-specific (tracer-sample) quality-of-care measures assessed by the Rand Corporation.

Methodological Concerns

One of the basic conceptual problems with the SOI index is the inclusion of treatment decisions in the measure—that is, if more is done, the case must be more severe. Some components of the severity score reflect higher ancillary utilization by providers, and the researcher cannot tell how much of this is independent of the medical status of the patient. The SOI index is less effective than disease staging in providing a case-mix measure attributable purely to patient differences and independent of provider practices due to the treatment standards of the hospital's medical staff. Medical staff selects the workload, draws on hospital inputs to provide care consistent with peer standards, and generates positive outputs (live discharges, education, research, and so on). One difficulty in analyzing the effects of the SOI index is that it comingles the case mix and the provider practice behavior into one measure (labeling it "severity"), confounding the separation of patient-driven treatment actions from medical-staff-driven decisions about the treatment process that might be affected by demand for graduate medical education (Goldfarb and Coffey 1987; Eastaugh, 1990).

It would be difficult to collapse the seven-dimension SOI measure into a scale that is independent of treatment preferences of attending physicians, residents, and interns. For example, dimension 4, the dependency score, is a measure of illness requiring extra monitoring or care. We have no independent verification of whether that extra care is medically appropriate if assessed by some unbiased peer reviewer. One study suggested that teaching hospitals do not have a more severe case mix if the severity measure is itself independent of resource consumption (Goldfarb and Coffey 1987). Using 1977 data, the authors reported that severity was no higher in teaching hospitals in a national sample of 9 medical-school-based hospitals, 44 other COTH member hospitals, 91 community teaching hospitals, and 226 nonteaching hospitals. While the sample size is impressive, the data were more limited than in our study (they were based on eight-year-old discharge record abstracts), and the measure of severity was crude. The health-services researcher is firmly placed on the horns of a dilemma: The measure of severity must by definition be increasingly crude as it is made unbiased for provider practices (independent of physician resource decisions driven by GME needs or by the idiosyncratic preferences of the medical staff unrelated to GME). In a multiple analysis of variance, the SOI measure has a clear identification of the patient's idiosyncratic factor (individual response to therapy), but how much of the residual behavior is the provider's idiosyncratic behavior and not truly patient severity?

There is ample evidence that provider taste can dominate treatment behavior patterns (Brook et al. 1984; Wennberg, Freeman, and Culp 1987). For example, if a patient resides in a community teaching hospital ICU, does that prove that the patient is more severely ill? If the Medicare PPS has created a tendency to treat more cases in less costly channels of service distribution (outside the ICU or even outside the hospital), does that mean that these patients are suddenly less severely ill because they command fewer resources relative to habits under pre–1984 treatment practices? One should note that a nonteaching hospital might have wide latitude to eschew a more conservative style of medicine and so be able to report a more severe case mix. In the Horn et al. (1985) study, contrary to expectations, the one nonteaching hospital had severity scores that exceeded those of the two community teaching hospitals. It is difficult to state how much of the extra severity was attributable to (1) poor medical practices; (2) physician preferences to avoid the new and untried, without harm to quality-of-care outcomes; or (3) differences in actual patient severity.

Regression analysis was used to examine the relative power of the three case-mix measures available to the study (DRGs, SOI, and disease staging) in explaining variation in total (combined hospital and physician) cost. The results of the regression analysis showed that DRGs as a case-mix measure were more effective in explaining variation in cost than either of the other measures alone.

In the random case sample of all hospitals in the study, DRGs explained approximately 15 percent of total cost per case, versus 4.7 percent for SOI and 2.0 percent for disease staging. One might suggest that DRGs and disease staging are measuring much the same construct (product-line categories), whereas the SOI measure offers a more substantial improvement in explained variation in costs (i.e., it measures a second construct—acuity amount of illness within a product line).

Further analysis of DRGs showed a marked difference in explanatory power by hospital department. Table 8.2 presents a summary of the reduction in unexplained variance in cost for DRGs as a case-mix measure and for the two severity measures in combination with DRGs. The result if surgical cases are compared to nonsurgical cases is pronounced. For surgical cases (all cases in the random sample assigned to the department of surgery), the DRG accounted for more than 25 percent of the total variation in cost, but it explained only 2.1 percent for the nonsurgical cases. (The difference in explanatory power of the DRGs between any of the four nonsurgical departments was minimal. For this reason, the results are presented as surgical versus nonsurgical cases, rather than by department.) While this result is not surprising, given the inputs to the algorithm used to construct DRGs, it does support the findings of previous studies that suggest that DRGs might not be an effective measure for differentiating resource utilization and, by extension, cost for cases that do not involve extensive surgical intervention.

RECENT DEVELOPMENTS IN SEVERITY SYSTEMS

The early 1990s have been a time of steady improvement and competitive testing of severity systems (Miller, Cuddleback, and Gallo 1991). Eight new or refined severity systems will be surveyed in this section. Some abstract-based systems using elements of the Uniform Hospital Discharge Data Set (UHDDS) have not performed well, for example, the CPHA Body Systems Count, and therefore are not surveyed here. Other abstract-based systems like refined diagnosis related groups (RDRGs), acuity index method (AIM), and Patient Management Categories (PMC) are surveyed. The systems that are chart based, requiring additional data collection (CSI, APACHE III) tend to do a better job in explaining outcome or quality variations between providers.

The free (no license fee) system of refined diagnosis related groups (RDRGs) was developed by the Health Systems Management Group of Yale University in the 1980s for HCFA. It was designed to account for severity within existing DRGs by differentiating patients on the basis of complications and comorbidities specific to the principal diagnosis or procedure. A patient is first assigned to a major diagnostic category (MDC) on the basis of principal diagnosis; the MDCs are identical to the 23 MDCs used in the current DRG system. Patients with temporary tracheostomies and early deaths (within two days of admission) are assigned to separate groups. All other patients are assigned to one of 317 cat-

Table 8.2

Percentage Improvement in Explained Variation of Cost per Case, Random Sample of 300–375 Cases per Hospital (Arthur Young Study, 1986)

(% listed are R^2, percent variance explained)

Sample		DRGs	DRGs and Severity of Illness	DRGs and Disease Staging	DRGs Severity of Illness and Disease Staging
45 hospitals	- all cases	15.3%	18.9%	16.9%	19.8%
	- surgical cases	28.7%	32.9%	30.9%	34.6%
	- non-surgical cases	2.1%	6.0%	3.3%	6.7%
Nonteaching hospitals ($n = 9$)	- surgical cases	36.8%	45.1%	37.2%	45.8%
	- non-surgical cases	4.4%	8.8%	5.7%	9.6%
Minor teaching ($n = 3$)	- surgical cases	28.0%	34.5%	32.7%	35.9%
	- non-surgical cases	2.9%	4.8%	5.9%	6.9%
Moderate teaching ($n = 4$)	- surgical cases	34.5%	37.1%	40.0%	41.1%
	- non-surgical cases	.1%	5.9%	1.5%	6.9%
Major teaching hospitals ($n = 16$)	- surgical cases	26.7%	31.5%	31.2%	35.0%
	- non-surgical cases	1.9%	4.9%	2.8%	5.5%
COTH medical centers ($n = 12$)	- surgical cases	22.8%	27.4%	25.7%	29.2%
	- non-surgical cases	2.8%	6.7%	4.2%	7.8%

egories referred to as adjacent DRGs (ADRGs), based on their principal diagnosis or surgical procedure. Within these categories the patient's secondary diagnoses determine the appropriate RDRG. The RDRG system classifies secondary diagnoses as major, moderate, or minor, according to their effect on resource demand. Ohio has mandated the use of RDRGs since 1989. Except for MDC 15, neonates, for whom a separate grouping methodology was developed, RDRGs were derived on the basis of data from adult populations. As a first step in creating the RDRGs, all possible principal diagnoses (those diagnoses that describe the chief reason for a patient's hospitalization) were divided into 23 mutually exclusive categories known as major diagnostic categories or MDCs. Generally, all diagnoses within a MDC correspond to a single organ system (e.g., respiratory system, circulatory system, digestive system) and are associated with a particular medical specialty. Because not all diagnoses are organ-system based, a number of residual MDCs were created (e.g., systematic infectious diseases, myeloproliferative diseases, and poorly differentiated neoplasms). The system has not been thoroughly evaluated on pediatric and adolescent populations. In this study, RDRGs were tested both with and without an age split. First, all patients were considered together to develop one set of resource-consumption weights. Then patients aged 18 and over were considered separately from those under 18 to develop a second set of weights. Excluding MDC 15, there are a total of 1,126 RDRGs (Fetter and Freeman 1991). HCFA uses a simplified list of 430 basic RDRGs pilot tested in New York State. The RDRG system was developed from analysis of more than four million discharges in Maryland and California. An important goal of this effort was to ensure that RDRGs would be applicable to all types of patients, not just Medicare patients. Thus the discharges analyzed included all payer data, including pediatric cases.

 ·RDRGs utilize specific sets or classes of comorbid conditions (CCs, secondary diagnoses) for each ADRG rather than a list of substantial CCs for all DRGs. By utilizing specific CC classes, the RDRGs are better able to predict hospital costs and are able to accomplish a 50 percent improvement in the R-squared (over DRGs alone) from 0.28 to 0.42 without costly additional data collection from the medical chart. The medical ADRGs have three severity ratings (refinement classifications): baseline (class 0, e.g., otitis media), moderate (class 1, e.g., diabetes, gastrointestinal [GI] obstruction), and major (class 2, e.g., meningitis). The surgical RDRGs have a fourth class (class 3, e.g., stroke myocardial infarction). ADRGs try to capture the complexity of care, which may be more relevant than the medical severity of illness in explaining cost per patient. Using a chart-based severity system typically rates coronary bypass surgery patients as modestly ill (level 1 or 2) at admission; but RDRGs place over 55 percent of the bypass patients into the most complex ADRG class.

 Patient management categories (PMCs, developed by the Pittsburgh Research Institute) were initially designed as a basis for comparative hospital cost analyses and hospital payment systems. The categories were defined to represent clinically specific groups of patients, each requiring a distinct diagnostic and treatment strategy for effective care. Patient categories were initially identified by physician panels, independent of patient data. The resulting classification scheme comprises more than 880 PMCs, encompassing all patients in general, acute-care hospitals, including psychiatric patients and neonates. The categories defined by physicians were mapped onto ICD–9-CM codes. Assignment of patients to PMCs is accomplished using UHDDS data (diagnoses, procedures, age, and sex). Related PMCs are grouped into "modules" and considered together. Patients with comorbid conditions may be assigned to a maximum of five PMCs. In addition to the clinical classification scheme, the system includes weights based on the relative cost of the diagnostic and therapeutic services typically required for each patient type, as defined by physician panels. This contrasts with the empirical methods of deriving category weights used by other systems, which rely primarily on hospital charges for services actually provided to particular patients. The software that assigns cost weights includes adjustments for patients who fall into multiple PMCs.

The acuity index method (AIM, developed by Iameter) severity score is derived from information contained in the UHDDS. Each DRG is subdivided, based on secondary diagnoses and operating-room procedures related to the principal diagnosis and procedure. The patient's age and sex are also considered. The clinical judgment of medical and surgical subspecialists was used to assign "comparative severity" rankings to pathologic and therapeutic processes represented by ICD–9-CM codes. Each DRG has its own unique algorithm, with an acuity rating from 1 (least sick) to 5 (most sick). Severity-adjusted norms for length-of-stay charges and mortality rates may then be compared with actual case experience.

APACHE III (APACHE Medical Systems): The original APACHE system (the acronym stands for acute physiology and chronic health evaluation) was designed to predict the intensity of services required and the risk of death for intensive-care patients. It was also designed to provide a basis for evaluating the quality of care provided. The system requires 12 physiologic values that are routinely collected within a patient's initial 24 hours in an intensive-care unit (e.g., heart rate, mean blood pressure, temperature, hematocrit, white blood cell count, serum creatinine, arterial blood gases, and Glasgow coma scale). The values are derived through weights, adjusted for age and chronic disease, that are designed to reflect the degree of physiological variance from a norm. APACHE III and II-b scores are independent of physician practice patterns, therapeutic choices, and invasive diagnostic procedures. This George Washington University Hospital system does not attempt to distinguish complications and comorbidities from the underlying (acute) disease. The developers of APACHE argued for limiting the scope of the system to those clinical areas where physiologic hypotheses relating clinical indicators to outcome or resource demand can be formulated and tested. To the extent that these clinical areas are responsible for a significant proportion of the overall variance, this more limited strategy would not necessarily compromise the overall result. APACHE II–6 is a hospitalwide evaluation system that builds on APACHE II, reflecting severity of illness in four specific disease classes—stroke, congestive heart failure, pneumonia, and acute myocardial infarction. Additional clinical data elements are required, depending on the 16 disease groups. APACHE III is utilized for intensive-care patients (Knaus, Wagner, and Draper 1991).

The computerized severity index (CSI, developed by Health Systems International) is designed to be used together with DRGs to explain differences in resource use among patients. The system attempts to quantify the patient's total burden of illness by incorporating the clinical problem (severity of the principal diagnosis) and the clinical environment (severity of the complications and co-morbidities) the patient experiences during hospitalization. The severity measures are based on the patient's laboratory test results, vital signs, and history and physical findings abstracted from the medical record. The severity of individual diseases is measured on a scale ranging from 1 (normality or mild disease) to 5 (death). Relying on standard five-digit ICD-9-CM codes to indicate the presence of disease, CSI generates a sixth digit that reflects the severity of the principal and most severe secondary diagnoses. The vendor makes the system's logic available to clients, and Susan Horn seeks input on potential refinement. The individual disease severity scores identify the complications or comorbidities that make the greatest contributions to the patient's overall severity. An overall severity score is generated by considering the interaction of the principal diagnosis with the patient's secondary diagnoses, as well as the severity of each secondary diagnosis. CSI's severity score can be computed at any time during the hospital stay, but it is generally determined within the first and/or last 48 hours. A unique feature of the implementation of CSI is interactive abstracting. Beginning with the ICD–9-CM codes for diagnoses and procedures, the system requests only the specific additional data needed to make relevant distinctions. This helps keep CSI 50 percent less expensive than disease staging.

MedisGroups (medical illness severity grouping system) (MediQual) classifies patients into one of four severity groups based on clinical data. The system employs approximately 260 key clinical findings (KCFs) that are abstracted from the medical record. A proprietary classification scheme assigns patients to severity groups, independent of diagnosis or procedure data (except insofar as the KCFs are obtained as results of diagnostic procedures). The four severity groups are designed to reflect increasing levels of physiologic instability or risk of organ failure. Three states mandate the usage of MedisGroups—Pennsylvania (1987), Iowa (1991), and Colorado (1992). An admission severity score is assigned within the first 48 hours of an inpatient stay. The classification is repeated by separately abstracting current values of KCFs on the eighth day of the hospital stay or on the sixth postoperative day. In addition to computing empirical measures of resource consumption by admission severity score, MedisGroups is unique in its emphasis on the change in severity score over the course of the patient's hospitalization as an indicator of the effectiveness of therapy or the presence of complications of care. Patients who fall into the two highest severity categories upon the second evaluation are characterized as "major morbidity."

MediQual has encouraged the use of rates of major morbidity, alone or in combination with rates of in-hospital mortality, as an indicator of quality of care (Iezzoni, Schwartz, and Restuccira 1991). The system is marketed as a clinical management information system, rather than just a patient classification system or a method of measuring the severity of patients' illnesses. UHDDS and UB-82 data are also collected and incorporated into the MedisGroups data base.

The fundamental concept behind illness outcome groups (IOGs), developed since 1987 by Medi Qual, is to create groups of clinically related DRGs or RDRGs that have been shown, in a large data base created by combining the experience of 102 MedisGroups client hospitals, to present similar risk of mortality or major morbidity. By aggregating DRGs or RDRGs with similar clinical behavior, it may be possible to achieve almost the same explanatory power with a much smaller number of categories, while avoiding the statistical problems associated with small numbers of cases in low-volume DRGs.

CURTAILING INAPPROPRIATE UTILIZATION

One of the conceptual problems that economists have had in the area of utilization in hospitals is understanding the wide range of heterogeneous products that physicians identify in the teaching hospital setting. In teaching hospitals physicians simultaneously produce the joint products of education, research, and patient care. Even within the category of patient care, the care "produced" is quite diverse, due to the great variance in the complexity of cases handled. Thus physicians have largely ignored medical economics studies because they do not capture the diversity of patient care within hospitals or across different hospital types. For example, the product of a hospital cannot be captured with just four figures: inpatient days, operative cases, outpatient visits, and number of residents on staff.

Payment incentives can have a downward impact on hospital utilization and cost (Kassebaum 1986). New Jersey was the first state to experiment with a DRG payment system and the first all-payer DRG system (1980–87). In 1991 some 19 state Medicaid programs operated a prospective case-mix system, and Connecticut was the only state to drop use of the DRG approach within the 19 programs. Since New Jersey has the longest duration of experience with DRGs over the widest possible population cohort, the impact of its DRGs on hospital utilization has been widely studied. Broyles (1990) reported that the New Jersey DRG system reduced length of stay and cut radiological procedures per diem (and per case). On the other hand, the DRG system was associated with an increase in laboratory procedures per diem and a slight rise in laboratory use per case. This last result is a surprise, because it was thought that DRGs offered the incentive to trim utilization per case, but perhaps would collapse most of the same care (90 to 95 percent of the same work) into a shorter period of hospitalization (so utilization per diem would rise).

Carter and Melnick's (1990) study of 300,000 Medicare patients concluded

Table 8.3
Trends in Average Expense per Admission, Staff Productivity, and Labor Cost per Day in 28 Large Teaching Hospitals, 1976–1990

	Expense per Adjusted Inpatient Stay	FTE Staff Adjusted Inpatient Day	Expense for Personnel per Adjusted Inpatient Day
1976	$2,476.61	4.04	$204.47
1978	3,239.09	4.34	250.29
1980	4,286.84	4.57	314.02
1982	5,975.21	4.86	423.51
1984	7,650.78	5.23	532.14
1986	9,464.82	5.97	651.32
1988	11,476.59	6.29	765.19
1990	13,824.90	6.56	857.84
Total % Growth, 1976-1990	458.2	62.4	319.5

that to the extent that cost per admission is greater in major teaching hospitals, length of stay is the primary cause, not intensity of service provided per day. This result may not hold for other patient age groups, but there is some anecdotal evidence that this generalization may prove true. This author has tracked expenses in 28 large nonfederal teaching hospitals since 1976 as cohorts in a National Research Council (1977) study. The expenses per case and per day, utilizing the standard American Hospital Association adjustment process for workload, are displayed in table 8.3. Whereas the inflation per diem is nearly double the consumer price index cited in chapter 1, the cost per case is inflating at triple the rate of the general economy. This suggests that teaching hospitals need to trim length of stay to contain cost per case.

In this context, Finkler, Brooten, and Brown (1988) studied neonatal care for a group of patients not subject to reimbursement and concluded that strong reductions in length of stay can save money without harming quality. They indicated that proportional reductions in service utilization were even greater than declines in length of stay, with no detrimental patient outcomes. In length of stay, more is not necessarily better, especially when the hospital is a dangerous and costly place for a prolonged visit. The 25 percent lowest-cost teaching hospitals in table 8.3 have seen their average length of stay for myocardial infarction cases decline from 15.7 days in 1976 to 8.6 days in 1987 and 3.2

days in 1991, and no member of the medical staff would suggest that the quality of care has declined.

Excessively long lengths of stay are a source of public concern not only because they are costly, but also because such care is often unnecessary. It has even been suggested that reduction of unnecessary or excessive amounts of care could raise the general health status of the population by decreasing the likelihood of iatrogenic complications. Reducing the length of stay minimizes the chance of exposure to antibiotic-resistant bacteria peculiar to hospitals; thus the number of difficult-to-treat infections may be lessened. Shortened lengths of stay are a morale builder for adult patients; and in the case of children, the trauma of separation from their parents is minimized, even when there are liberal visiting privileges (Innes, Grant, and Beinfield 1968). One study suggested that the marginal benefit of excessive days of hospitalization is negative, with 20 percent of the patients being exposed to some hazardous episode (Schimmel 1974). Clearly, the problems of cost and iatrogenic disease played a major part in the congressional commitment to the Professional Standards Review Organization PSRO program enacted in 1972 and the PRO program of the 1980s and 1990s.

Brown, Ehrlich, and Stehman (1984) demonstrated that significant cost savings can be obtained by reducing the time involved in preoperative skin preparation. Beck (1986) suggested an annual variable cost savings of $700,000 per 10,000 surgeries per year. He went on to critique a number of aseptic "fetishes that continue to be used despite repeated proof of their lack of value."

Utilization patterns are not merely a function of patient characteristics and the requirement of "good medicine." Medical care requirements can be met with different amounts of resources and lengths of hospitalization. How these requirements of good medicine are met depends in some part on the physician characteristics and the hospital environment. Surgical utilization is affected by hospital characteristics such as the laboratory turnaround time, the availability of hospital beds, the availability of a surgical suite, and the type of hospital ownership (federal, voluntary, municipal) (Eastaugh 1987).

If utilization review has not trimmed the lengths of stay of teaching hospitals as substantially as nationwide declines in length of stay (National Center for Health Statistics [NCHS] 1991), at least certain insurance companies are reaping the benefits of utilization review. Wickizer, Wheeler, and Feldstein (1990) studied 223 insured groups and found that utilization review in the two-year period reduced inpatient days 11 percent, routine inpatient services by 7.0 percent, and ancillary services by 9.0 percent. Medical staff should work at trimming unnecessary admissions, tests, and procedures (Chulis 1991; Harrison and Payne 1991; Oleske et al. 1991; Relman 1991). In an attempt to assess the impact of chart reviews, feedback, and lectures on residents' ordering behavior, Manheim et al. (1990) randomized residents into two groups: the cost-conscious program-review group and a control group. The authors concluded that a reduction of $391 in charges per patient resulted from lower lengths of stay, and charges were $106 lower in radiology (both statistically significant at the 0.01 level).

The lower-cost experimental group's style of care achieved lower patient impairment ratings at discharge, indicating that more efficient care may be quality-enhancing at the one university hospital.

ALTERNATIVE MEASURES OF THE TEACHING HOSPITAL DEPENDENCY LINK

One additional question is whether there are not more relevant behavior variables involving the hospital and the sources of education (residency directors, deans) that better measure graduate medical education. These more complex variables might not be as administratively simple or appropriate as a single scalar measure (resident-to-bed ratio), but they may be more indicative of the mutual dependency between the hospital and the education program. A number of studies used the following measure of teaching-staff characteristics (National Research Council 1977; Eastaugh 1980b, 1979):

1. Fraction of the attending physicians on the surgical service with actual teaching faculty appointments at the local medical school who receive salary from the school (intended as an index of the hospital's dependence on the medical school for physicians)
2. Fraction of the affiliated medical school's students who did their required core clinical clerkship on the hospital surgical service (intended as an index of the school's dependence on the hospital as a training ground)
3. Fraction of surgeons (excluding anesthesiologists) at the facility who are foreign medical graduates (FMGs)

The fraction of the medical school's students depending on the individual hospital as a source of clinical education is intended as a proxy measure of the school's dependency on the hospital. One might suggest that if the school is highly dependent on a hospital for teaching cases, the students, interns, residents, and attending physicians, acting as agents of the school's interest, would have added reason to increase length of stay or tests ordered in order to maximize the number of teaching days available and to maximize tests and cost per case in order to serve a technological interest in maximizing revenues for new equipment (Eastaugh 1987).

The basic premise of the economic model emerging from cost analysis is that physicians are influenced in patient-management decisions by the economic advantage of actions to them or their hospital, or perhaps to their medical school. We should guard against overutilization that results from physician pursuit of less explicit forms of economic advantage than income-maximization tendencies under a fee-for-service system of reimbursement. The subtle incentives to overutilize are much more insidious and affect salaried and private entrepreneur physicians equally.

Physician background characteristics are determinants of physician behavior. The duration of stay and number of tests per patient are likely to be affected by the educational background of the surgeon and the strength of the affiliation with the local medical school (Eastaugh 1979). The process outlined in figure 8.1 implies a causal sequence. Differing combinations of physician and hospital characteristics lead to different styles of medicine, which in turn lead to different utilization patterns (Twaddle and Sweet 1970). For example, one might presuppose that medical school faculty members involved in patient care have a professional interest in curtailing inappropriate prescriptions, but it might not always be in the faculty members' interests to curtail all types of excessive utilization. Faculty members and attending physicians might have an interest in maximizing their revenues.

Hospital-based specialists are interested in maintaining distribution channels that ensure an "interesting" product assortment, efficiency (whenever possible), and progressiveness (including the ability to foster technological change). Elimination of a service or department should be analyzed in light of risks and benefits, response from the competition, and alienation of internal hospital-based vested interests. The hospital-based physicians frequently lobby for revitalization rather than elimination.

If we presume that the surgeon wishes to maximize prestige or popularity within the profession, rather than overutilize for the sake of overutilization, then the problem for policy makers becomes one of framing a set of incentives that makes prestige maximization incompatible with overutilization. Underutilization that has a detrimental effect on quality would injure the physician's prestige and image among his or her peers.

Future research might consider whether physicians operate under the norms hypothesis (Wennberg 1990), making length-of-stay decisions based on the average or modal staff characteristics within their hospital and their region, rather than handling these decisions on an individual basis. In particular, a fair test of the norms hypothesis would be to take a sample from teaching and nonteaching hospitals and compare staff characteristics for one surgeon to characteristics of everyone who made decisions about a given patient. From there, the study would proceed to characteristics of surgeons in the surgical service of a given hospital and to characteristics of all surgeons in the health-service area for a sample of both teaching and nonteaching hospitals.

NATIONAL PRICES ARE NOT YET HARMING QUALITY

Goodall (1990) and Pope (1990) both argued that the transition from hospital-specific Medicare costs to adjusted national DRG Medicare prices since 1988 has been inequitable. Both of these health economists argued that Medicare should return to a blend of hospital-specific costs and national prices, as was done in the prospective payment system phase in the period from 1984 to 1988. There is a wide variety of cost per case, but the question is what proportion of the cost differences is justified (and what is due to inefficiency, excess length of stay, and so on). Keeler (1990) took the position of the ethical regulator and

Figure 8.1
Interdependence of the Medical School, the Physician Staff, and the Hospital Staff in the Production of Patient Care

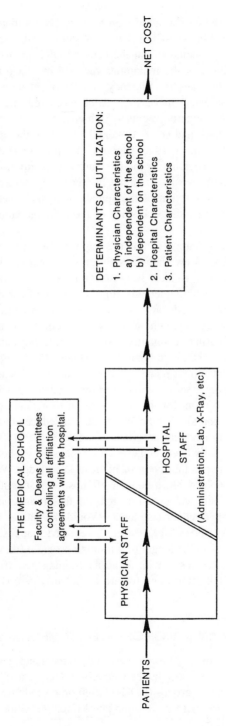

The same conceptual framework could be used to describe the relationship between a hospital's medical service and the medical school, or the affiliation of a psychiatric service with the medical school, or a hospital's department of radiology or pathology affiliation with the medical school. Each department or service within a hospital could have a different degree of affiliation with the medical school.

identified cost due to sickness at admission as a clearly justifiable expense. He measured severity using the APACHE II acute physiological score variables (see Knaus et al. 1985) and concluded that the national DRG prices are adequately connected to costs. Some of the remaining variance in cost per case is noise, some comes from differences in efficiency and treatment intensity, and some comes from justifiable factors that are yet to be measured in a severity index. There is no evidence that underpayments to high-cost hospitals and profits earned by low-cost hospitals have had any detrimental impact on the quality of patient care. Witsberger and Kominski (1990) supported the position that less utilization may not harm quality, especially for the five surgical conditions with the fastest annual declines in length of stay (inguinal hernia repair, transurethral prostatectomy, mastectomy, exploration of the spinal canal, and knee and ankle arthroplasty). They also concluded that some of the extra outpatient surgery may not be appropriate care.

Payment system changes are affecting the way we educate future doctors. The Harvard Medical School New Pathways Program, pioneered in a number of places from New Mexico to Boston, suggests a number of innovative case-study and computer-driven teaching methods for the 1990s (Tosteson 1990). It is difficult for medical school educators to allocate sufficient time to procedural skills, medical technology, and general knowledge acquisition and save enough time for respect and caring (Humanity 101). Younger physicians seem more receptive to computers, economic analysis (Eastaugh 1987) and consumerism. Patient utility judgments count more in the modern world because patients are rightfully becoming more assertive about their own bodies. Certain subjects have to be trimmed to make room for the new material (e.g., cuts in microbiology or pharmacology lab hours). A number of medical educators have called for fundamental changes in teaching programs (Cator et al. 1991; Tosteson 1991).

Some medical educators have suggested an expansion of the training period to absorb the rapidly expanding body of medical knowledge. While these suggestions are made in good faith, a number of subspecialists outside of the university environment would welcome a decrease in the production of competitors for all the reasons suggested in chapter 7. Would the future residents put up with longer training periods? McKay (1990) reported that residents are quite unresponsive to changes in the length of a training program (they will stick with it and not switch to a residency with a shorter training period). The locus for residency education is shifting more toward ambulatory care (Kirz and Larsen 1986).

AMBULATORY CARE: IN SEARCH OF CASE-MIX MEASURES

Gold (1988) outlined the need for prospective payment and case-mix measures in the field of ambulatory care. James Cameron's UCLA team has developed 216 emergency-department groups (EDGs) based on a subdivision of nine medically diagnostic categories (e.g., trauma/poisoning; see Gildea 1988). These

EDGs are based on four variables: diagnosis, patient age, type of injury or procedure performed, and patient disposition (admitted, discharged, transferred). A second, older, more comprehensive approach is the 571 ambulatory visit groups (AVGs) developed by the Yale team that invented inpatient DRGs in the 1960s. The AVGs are clinically comprehensive, with less than 1.0 percent of the clinic or emergency-department patients failing to fall into one of the 571 categories (Lion, Malbon, and Bergman 1987). As with all of the ambulatory case-mix systems, AVGs do not reflect the resource needs to treat an episode of illness requiring several visits. Paying for ambulatory care on a prospective case-mix system may encourage shortened visit length and increased visit frequency.

Whereas AVGs and EDGs do not incorporate severity of illness per case, a new system tested for five years does address stages of illness and complications. The 24 PACs (products of ambulatory care) and the 19 PASs (products of ambulatory surgery) crudely measure severity and utilization of technology by classifying the episode as being either for diagnostic or patient-management purposes. This New York State demonstration project suffers from too small a number of categories (allowing for too much heterogeneity within each PAC or PAS group). The statistical variability within groups is lower for a larger number of groups. More research is needed in the area of ambulatory-care case-mix groups and clinical severity. Two research teams at Johns Hopkins University are working on better systems that go beyond these visit-based approaches. Johns Hopkins ambulatory cost groups (ACGs), developed by Barbara Starfield et al. (1991), represent a person-based system for application to capitated and insured populations. Other researchers at Johns Hopkins have developed an ambulatory severity index (ASI) for tracking clinical severity. The topic is increasingly important as more medical schools seek ambulatory-care revenues.

MEDICAL SCHOOL FINANCES

The peak year for new enrollment in American medical schools was 1981 (16,757 first-year students). For eight consecutive years medical schools experienced a decline in enrollment, until a slight up-turn in enrollments began in 1990 (AAMC 1991). Financial pressures on medical schools have been outlined in a number of areas (Tosteson 1990; Eastaugh 1987; Iglehart 1986). The intent of this section is to provide an outline of the financial position of the different types of medical schools and their need to plan for further reductions in state and federal financial support and research funding. One first might ask how the medical schools got so dependent on government funding. As the supply of physicians per capita more than doubled between 1962 and 1979, there was no longer a justification for the federal medical school capitation program. This form of subsidy, paid to the school per head (per student enrolled), created an obvious incentive to expand class size. The public believed that more doctors were needed and that more of any trained professional group in society must be good for society (Ginzberg 1990). In this section we question the value of a uniform program of financial assistance to medical education and research. Medical schools have an uneven ability to compensate for declining federal capitation and research grants. We also utilize financial ratio analysis and cluster analysis for the period 1979 to 1990 and suggest three adaptive responses to future financial pressures. The four potential avenues of response involve reducing faculty size, expanding faculty involvement in medical-practice plans, and raising tuition. Medical schools will also have to strive for better financial management if the 29 schools revealed to be in poor financial health are to survive.

The federal government predicted since 1980 that the enrollment expansion already achieved is sufficient to meet the national demand for physicians. It has withdrawn its 1970s level of support for medical education by cutting general institutional operating subsidies. Reduced funding in the 1990s will require some reaction on the part of the medical schools and university medical centers. Grants that induced changes in academic health centers presumably increased reliance of those institutions on the federal government. Grants now are targeted to applied research like AIDS (Eastaugh 1992). It has been said that with grants, a cut in revenues means an equal cut in expenditures, but this does not follow. Grants pay for many of the indirect costs of running an institution. When grants are reduced or eliminated, funds must come from some other source to cover these indirect costs (Eastaugh 1990). Action can come in the form of changes in programs or shifts to greater reliance on alternative sources. One source is the student on whom the federal government explicitly wishes to place more of the burden of financing medical education.

The Historic Policy Context

Behn and Sperduto (1979) reviewed the growth of a medical school "entitlement ethic" since passage of the first health manpower bill in 1963. In response to the national perception of a doctor shortage, the 1965 amendments to the 1963 Health Professions Education Assistance Act required only that the school expand enrollments by 2.5 percent per annum. In the following years Fein (1967) questioned the validity of the assumption that a doctor shortage existed regionally or nationally. However, Congress was predisposed to respond to the 1970 Carnegie Commission assertion that the nation had a shortage of 50,000 doctors. The 1971 Health Manpower Act replaced the basic improvement grants of the 1960s with a program of capitation grants to stimulate rapid growth in class size. The capitation grant program stipulated that small schools with fewer than 100 students per class expand the class by 10 students and that larger schools expand class size by 5 percent.

These financial incentives to expand class size were a smashing success story. By 1968 the nation had already exceeded the American Medical Association's declared appropriate supply ratio of 154 physicians per 100,000 population (Carnegie Commission 1970). By 1975 the national supply of physicians exceeded the Carnegie Commission's (1970) most optimistic projection of 171.3 physicians per 100,000 population for 1982. In renewing the capitation program in 1976, Congress expressed concern over the doctor surplus in the preamble and concluded that the nation had a maldistribution, but not a shortage, of physicians. Stevens (1971) and Reinhardt (1975) had argued that productivity, and not supply ratios, was the more salient public policy issue. Stevens went so far as to suggest that the physician supply could be reduced 12.5 percent if all U.S. physicians had the same level of productivity as physicians in the Kaiser Health Plan, or reduced 42.5 percent if U.S. physicians had Kaiser productivity and patient utilization rates.

Medical education policy was formulated in various statements to the effect that medical schools were a precious national resource in need of federal aid. From 1971 to 1980 Congress ignored the arguments of economists and accountants to terminate capitation grants and followed the advice of social activists to address the specialty maldistribution problem and the advice of medical lobbyists to perpetuate the entitlement ethic and foster increased government funding. Paradoxically, federal support had not kept pace with the inflation in medical school expenditures. From 1966 to 1976 federal research support declined from 34.1 percent of revenues to 19.6 percent, and federal grants for teaching and recovery of indirect costs declined from 18.5 percent of revenues to 17.5 percent. Social activists' concerns for the overproduction of specialists were placated by the 1976 Capitation Bill provision that specified annual national targets for percentage of filled residencies in primary care. If the targets of at least 35 percent primary-care residencies by 1977, 40 percent by 1978, and 50 percent for 1979 were not met in any given year, then each school had to meet the target in succeeding years as a mandatory condition for capitation supports.

One important policy question concerns how medical schools can cope with the anticipated substantial reduction of the research funds in the 1990s (Relman 1991; Doolittle 1991). Protecting the public interest requires that the resulting short-run financial problems of the schools be managed in ways that have the fewest adverse long-run effects on medical education. To accomplish this, the schools must devote more systematic attention to financial ratio assessment. It is equally important for school administrators and federal officials to realize that different clusters or categories of medical schools must be treated differently. The uneven ability of medical schools to compensate for declining federal support cannot be overemphasized (Schwartz, Newhouse, and Williams 1985).

Most private schools began to charge five-digit tuition fees per year by 1983. The impact of rapidly escalating tuition figures on the finances and attitudes of students is unclear. Loans are always available to students, but the thought of being $80,000 in debt upon graduation may frighten some of them away from private schools. Private schools may find that they have a student body composed of a few scholarship students from lower-class backgrounds, many students from upper-middle-class backgrounds, and no one in between (AAMC 1991). Perhaps the greater danger lies in the probability that some new physicians who might otherwise have chosen family practice or a practice in an underserved area may opt for a specialty practice that promises a better cash return on their investment.

Medical schools are not structured to be managed. Future organizational theorists doing a postmortem on financially troubled schools (e.g., South Dakota) may well conclude that a medical faculty represents the ''bumblebee of organizations'' (e.g., no rule can be written without a dozen exceptions) and that no engineer can ever figure out how they fly. Less flattering analogies might characterize medical schools as the dinosaur of educational organizations. In any case, medical schools will have to diversify their portfolio of ventures (e.g., start health-administration programs or develop severity systems). Given the federal deficit morass, medical schools will have to rely on their own ventures for survival. One can pose this basic question: Will the welfare of the medical school and its programs take precedence over the financial well-being of individual faculty members? First we shall consider basic financial issues.

Financial Ratio Analysis

Financial ratio analysis is suggested as a tool that would enable medical school deans to assess their financial position in absolute and normative terms. The appropriate ratios, calculated from data reported in balance sheets and income statements, may be used to determine an organization's profitability, liquidity (ability to meet short-term obligations), and leverage (ability to meet debt obligations). Any institution can monitor its performance by comparing financial ratios over time or by comparing its ratios against industry norms. Ratios that change significantly or are markedly different from the industry norms serve as warning signs, indicating that an evaluation of the institution's financial position is warranted (Cleverley 1986). For example, a school that is already capital-intensive and reports a high fixed-assets/total-assets ratio might achieve greater efficiency with better use of short-term funds (working capital).

Until now, no attempt has been made to establish national norms to facilitate ratio analysis of medical schools. At a time when many medical schools are facing fiscal crises, it is important that deans and financial officers have the data base to enable them to assess their school's financial position. A comparison of ratios over time or between schools might prove helpful in understanding why some medical schools are being forced to erode their endowment in order to survive.

Financial Data

Financial data utilized in the ratio analysis were obtained from an Association of American Medical Colleges (AAMC) annual questionnaire. Included in the questionnaire were data items from the financial statements. These cash-flow items indicated the schools' sources and uses of funds. No balance-sheet information, however, was provided about fund balances, assets, and liabilities. The

AAMC provided the author with data for the following ten ratios in the years 1979, 1984 and 1990, expressed in percentages:

1. *Profitability:* total revenues minus expenses as a percentage of total revenues.

2. *Tuition and fees:* total student tuition and fees, including undergraduate medical programs as well as other degree programs, as a percentage of total revenues.

3. *Restricted revenues:* current revenues that are designated to be spent for specific projects as a percentage of total revenues. Since very little federal money is unrestricted, this classification covers virtually all federal sources of revenue.

4. *Government appropriations:* unrestricted revenues made available to the school by legislative act or local taxing authorities and restricted revenues from the same sources used for general operations.

5. *Federal appropriations:* federal revenue as a percentage of total revenues.

6. *Private gifts, grants, and contracts:* all unrestricted and restricted gifts from non-governmental sources, as well as contracts for the furnishing of goods and services of an instructional, research, or public service nature, as a percentage of total revenues.

7. *Medical practice plan:* patient care reimbursement for faculty service to the medical practice plan (MPP) as a percentage of total revenues (also called faculty practice plans).

8. *Instruction and departmental research:* expenditures for all activities that are part of the school's instructional program and departmental research expenditures that are not separately budgeted as a percentage of total expenses.

9. *Sponsored research:* all expenditures for research activities that are externally commissioned or separately budgeted as a percentage of total expenses.

10. *Administration and general expenditures:* academic and institutional support and funds for student support services as a percentage of total expenses.

Table 8.4 presents the average values of these ten basic ratios for the years 1979, 1984, and 1990 for public and private medical schools. In 1979 the income margins of public and private schools had fallen precipitously from 1977 levels to 1.2 percent and 0.7 percent, respectively. The percentage of schools with a net margin of 2 percent or higher declined from 44 percent to 8 percent. The income margins of private schools rebounded in 1984, before all schools declined in 1990. Fewer and fewer schools, therefore, have any margin for inefficiency before they operate in the red. The conclusion from these data is that all medical schools are facing increasing fiscal pressures, but private medical schools are in far greater fiscal danger than public medical schools.

Moreover, there has been an observable decline in sponsored research support over the past five years. This may be due to a change in priorities among both big business and government. The benefits of medical research are often not realized for dozens of years. In a period of fiscal belt-tightening, medical research has been assigned a low priority.

Table 8.4
Medical School Ratios (Percentages)

	1979		1984a		1990	
	Public	*Private*	*Public*	*Private*	*Public*	*Private*
Profitability	1.2	0.7	1.1	1.9	0.0	0.3
Tuition and fees	2.7	10.1	3.3	9.5	2.6	5.9
Restricted revenues	33.8	47.1	31.5	42.4	22.8	26.9
Government appropriations	43.2	7.8	32.4	4.4	23.9	1.6
Federal appropriations, grants, and contracts	22.9	28.2	19.9	28.2	12.5	13.8
Private gifts, grants, and contracts	5.6	9.3	4.1	6.9	7.9	11.0
Medical practice plan	10.3	15.5	17.6	23.2	32.1	36.4
Instruction and departmental research	37.9	23.7	34.9	21.5	30.5	20.4
Research	17.8	24.5	17.5	21.9	14.9	16.4
Administrative and general expenses	13.0	12.3	14.4	13.1	14.7	13.8

aIn 1984 the sample included 75 public schools and 50 private schools.

Private schools have always relied heavily on sponsored research projects for the bulk of their revenues. These revenues pay faculty salaries and support new technologies for tertiary-care medicine and basic research. The rapidly escalating costs of biomedical research leave little room for an excess of revenues over expenditures (profit). As these sponsored programs are cut back, as they were from 1979 to 1991, and the machinery and personnel remain, the financial squeeze begins. A gap is created between funds available and funds necessary for operation of the school. This hits most private schools harder than public schools, but it is felt everywhere.

Appropriations from state and local governments and grants and appropriations from the federal government have also fallen off sharply since 1979. These items accounted for 72 percent of public schools' revenues and 36 percent of private schools' revenues in 1979. Federal funds as a fraction of medical school revenues were cut in half by 1990.

Profits were almost zero for medical schools in 1990 (table 8.4, line 1). While the average medical student has nearly $50,000 of debt (Jolly 1991), tuition was only 5.9 percent of the 53 private medical schools' total revenue in 1990 and only 2.6 percent of the 74 state medical schools' revenue. One of the more interesting trends is the convergence of the gap between public and private schools in table 8.4, line 3. This line includes federal grants and contracts in line 5, a figure that has declined by almost 60 percent as a fraction of school revenue for the private schools since 1984. While revenues and expenses grew at 15 to 22 percent per year, the volume of federal grants grew very little for the private schools, yielding the reductions in both lines 3 and 5 of table 8.4. The two pieces of good news for both types of medical schools are the rise in private funds and contracts (line 6) to compensate for the freeze in real dollar growth of federal support and the massive rise in medical practice plan income in line 7 of table 8.4. In 1990 both public and private medical schools were one-third financed through the hard work of their faculty MPPs. There may be a slight statistical bias in the data, due to a change in the questionnaire by the late 1980s to correct a questionnaire design that underreported 15 percent of MPP funds in 1979–85. The decline in research support (table 8.4, line 9) and the rise in administrative and general overhead should be a long-run concern for medical school managers. For example, in 1990 medical schools spent over $770 million for operation and maintenance of plant.

Filling the financial gap between funds available and funds required is a major problem for medical school deans and budget officers. The tactics used have been partially successful but often create additional problems. One tactic that has gained virtually universal acceptance is the expansion of medical practice plans (MPPs). In private schools, especially, often 35 to 45 percent of the schools' revenues come from patient services rendered by the faculty. At first these MPPs were justified to the physicians as a way of keeping up-to-date with new techniques. Now most faculty involved realize that these MPPs are a critical source of funds to the medical school and that some schools could not survive without them.

Another issue, as yet unresolved, is whether medical researchers become better researchers and/or teachers when exposed to a few hours of clinical medicine daily. It is clear that medical school faculty now must wear three hats—the traditional ones of teacher and researcher and now the additional one of practitioner. Salaries are not necessarily commensurate with the job responsibilities. The time available for research is reduced, and individuals interested purely in biomedical research have much to consider before agreeing to a medical school staff appointment. Thus it is conceivable that the explosion of MPPs may adversely affect the quality of biomedical research at medical schools. As MPPs grow, it will be interesting to see from where the faculty's work time in these plans is taken. In less prestigious schools that no longer can attract as much research funding, the faculty may discover that hours previously spent on research need to be dedicated to clinical work if the school is to improve.

The financial figure with which the public is most familiar—tuition—has skyrocketed as well. As expenses have gone up, all medical schools have raised tuition to meet them. State appropriations to public schools are mainly tuition subsidies. Nationwide, tuition in 1990 accounted for only 4.0 percent of school revenues and an estimated 6.6 percent of the actual cost of instruction.

The Eight Types of School Clusters

Cluster analysis is a technique that groups firms or subjects together according to shared characteristics. The Department of Health, Education, and Welfare (McShane 1977) performed a cluster analysis of medical schools and devised eight clusters for 1978, grouped according to six factors. These clusters were redeveloped from AAMC data and characterize different kinds of medical schools (Eastaugh 1980b). The groupings were not developed on the basis of any of the financial ratios. The specific objective of this section is to study the shifts in financial ratios across clusters and time periods.

Schools were divided into eight clusters based on the following six shared characteristics:

1. *Emphasis on graduate medical education program.* Schools that are strong in this area have high ratios of interns and residents to undergraduates, a high proportion of faculty with M.D. degrees, and a low ratio of undergraduates to faculty. A disproportionately small number of graduates of these schools go into general practice.

2. *Size and age of school.* This factor includes the rate of growth of the school, with low growth being considered a sign of age.

3. *Control.* Public schools rate low and private schools high on this factor. Included is the proportion of in-state students in the school.

4. *Research funding success.* This is proxied by the approval rates for grants from the National Institutes of Health.

5. *Developmental stage of school.* This is a better measure of maturity than size and age.

6. *Research emphasis.* This is the level of sponsored research activity.

The eight clusters contain schools that are roughly similar in these six factors. Several schools were excluded from this analysis because of lack of data. Descriptions of the eight clusters are as follows:

1. Cluster 1 contains 19 public medical schools. These are all established schools with few other distinguishing characteristics. They have below-average emphasis on graduate medical programs and research and are below average in research funding success.

2. The 8 schools in cluster 2 are the oldest and largest medical schools. Six are public, with average total enrollments of around 800 undergraduate medical students. These schools do not place much emphasis on research or graduate medical education.

3. The 17 public schools in cluster 3 have a high degree of emphasis on research and have good research funding success. There is less emphasis on graduate medical education. They are of moderate size with little growth, except in research funding.

4. Cluster 4 has 15 large well-established medical schools with strong education programs at all levels.

5. Cluster 5 contains the 11 newest schools. It should be interesting to examine how their finances differ from those of the rest of the medical schools.

6. Relatively new public schools experiencing rapid growth are in cluster 6. Research support is not a substantial fraction of revenues but is growing rapidly for these 15 schools.

7. Cluster 7 contains mainly older private schools with low emphasis on research and graduate education. These 21 schools have the highest tuition but the lowest annual revenues.

8. The 19 schools, mostly private, in cluster 8 have strong research and graduate medical education programs. They are smaller than average and have the highest ratio of house staff to students of any cluster. They rely on federal support more than any other cluster.

Table 8.5 presents the values of various ratios for each cluster in the years 1979, 1984, and 1990. The data presented are only for the 77 medical schools in 1979 that subscribed to the uniform financial reporting practices of the AAMC. It can be readily observed that the decline in profit margin present in all medical schools as a whole is present in most of the clusters. Only one group of schools, cluster 2, experienced a substantial increase in profit margin from 1979 to 1984. Apparently, the inertia present in these older, larger schools gives them a unique fiscal stability. With this exception, the decline in net profit margin is a broad-based phenomenon; profits in cluster 2 also declined by 1990.

The percentage of expenditures for restricted purposes, such as sponsored research programs, declined significantly in all clusters. Sponsored revenues declined in all clusters in the period. This cutback in research funding is perhaps the biggest cause of medical schools' fiscal problems and has not struck medical schools selectively.

The prestige schools (clusters 4 and 8) do not attract much state or local money, but they still attract their share of state and federal research funds. Most of these schools continue to run in the black. The schools with the deepest trouble are the less prestigious private schools. Reduced government appropriations coupled with major cutbacks in sponsored programs are the chief culprits for the fiscal decline of 23 public hospitals in clusters 1 and 3. State political leaders may have to increase funding to financially troubled state schools. The future is also uncertain for 6 of the newest schools in cluster 5.

Potential Adaptive Responses by the Schools

Given the elimination of federal capitation grants (1983–84) and the reduction in research grant support, it appears probable that most schools will face difficulties in meeting increasing direct costs. Expanded graduate medical education and continuing-education programs have not contributed significantly to the medical school financial picture. Rogers (1980) and Rabkin (1986) pointed out that the academic medical center is becoming a stressed institution that cannot find

Table 8.5
Cluster Analysis of Medical School Finances for Nine Financial Ratios, Expressed in Percentages, 1979, 1984, and 1990

Item	I	II	III	IV	V	VI	VII	VIII
			Mean 1979 Cluster Values[a]					
			III	*IV*	*V*	*VI*	*VII*	*VIII*
Revenue ratios[b]	*I*	*II*						
Profitability ratio (percent)	0.5	1.4	0.79	1.0	0.75	2.1	-0.17	1.0
Tuition ratio	4	6	2	5	19	2	15	6
Restricted revenue ratio	34	39	36	49	17	26	44	51
State government ratio	41	38	33	18	54	51	9	3
Federal government ratio	21	20	27	26	28	19	29	31
Medical practice plan ratio	11	6	18	10	9	12	16	16
Expense ratios[c]								
Instruction and departmental research	40	36	35	22	69	42	25	21
Sponsored research	15	17	23	27	13	17	22	32
Administration and general expense	10	12	9	10	20	17	14	9
			Mean 1984 Cluster Values					
Revenue ratios[b]								
Profitability ratio (percent)	0.4	1.6	0.6	2.6	2.2	1.8	0.5	2.4
Tuition ratio	6	6	3	4	16	3	16	5
Restricted revenue ratio	27	34	32	41	15	22	37	42
State government ratio	35	28	28	6	36	40	4	1

				Mean 1990 Cluster Values[a]			
Federal government ratio	16	16	20	18	21	14	27	30
Medical practice plan ratio	16	13	22	16	14	16	25	24
Expense ratios[c]								
Instruction and departmental research	38	34	34	21	54	38	24	21
Sponsored research	13	14	23	23	11	14	20	29
Administration and general expense	12	13	11	11	17	17	14	10
Revenue ratios[b]								
Profitability ratio (percent)	-0.1	0.3	-0.1	0.2	0.2	0.5	0.4	0.7
Tuition ratio	3	4	2	3	8	2	10	3
Restricted revenue ratio	20	26	19	28	13	19	25	30
State government ratio	27	23	22	4	27	31	2	1
Federal government ratio	11	11	16	13	12	8	16	19
Medical practice plan ratio	31	30	39	32	26	32	39	40
Expense ratios[c]								
Instruction and departmental research	35	31	30	20	48	31	20	18
Sponsored research	12	12	19	16	11	13	17	21
Administration and general expense	13	15	12	11	18	17	15	11

[a]Definitions of the 8 clusters appear in the text.

[b]Expressed as a percentage of total revenues.

[c]Expressed as a percentage of total expenditures.

relief from any of the financial pressures it is facing. Given that hospital-rate regulators will not allow teaching hospitals to bail out medical schools, the schools have three potential avenues of response: raise tuition, induce faculty to devote more time to reimbursable patient services in MPPs, or reduce faculty size.

The first possible response in the minds of many school administrators is to raise medical school tuition. Schools could pursue a policy of three-tiered tuition pricing for poor ($2,000), middle-class ($8,000), and rich students ($30,000 per annum). The growing numbers of rich students willing to pay exorbitant tuitions and the existence of large pools of qualified rejected medical school applicants and students willing to undertake the expensive task of attending a foreign medical school suggest that schools can raise tuition substantially.

One potential problem of increasing the tuition burden is that newly graduated physicians may charge excessively higher fees to compensate for unmanageable debt burdens. Raising the debt burden of students exacerbates two existing problems for the medical schools. University-sponsored loans typically subsidize medical education by not requiring interest payments or repayment of principal until completion of a postgraduate residency or entrance into practice. Second, many university officials have observed that even following payment of the debt principal, the debtor is less likely to donate to the medical school than the average alumnus.

Two other potential responses to declining federal financial support involve changing the composition or size of the faculty. Medical school faculties are divided into three major categories: (1) full-time teaching and research, (2) part-time, and (3) geographic full-time (faculty members allowed to have private practices). One response would involve inducing faculty members to devote more time to MPP activities and to spend less time in research activities or independent private practice. Rather than raise revenues, a third response would be to decrease costs by reducing faculty size. The number of full-time clinical faculty in the United States increased over 536 percent from 1966 to 1990 according to unpublished AAMC statistics. The prime candidates for elimination are full-time faculty members who do not contribute substantially to the medical practice plan and part-time faculty members who receive a school salary out of line with their limited teaching activities. Faculty members in "soft-money" areas that lack a solid base of political support in negotiating with the dean are most likely to be eliminated. Unless the federal government is willing to provide increased targeted financial support, a number of new programs and faculty may be eliminated.

PROBLEMS FOR THE FUTURE

The federal government has effectively resisted pressure to bail out medical schools despite the fact that they are a precious national resource. The basic dilemma faced by the medical schools is whether they can acquire renewed federal support and maintain their current degree of autonomy from government bureaucrats. Congress's problem is how to allocate resources effectively among many competing high-priority national needs in the face of limited discretionary funds. The presence of financial exigencies felt by government and the schools means that careful attention must be paid to find a solution that is cost-effective. A segmented approach for different categories of schools may be better than the traditional uniform approach to federal financing of medical school operations.

Many adaptive response tactics have not been explored in this chapter. For example, increasing the number of non-M.D. graduate degrees and offering more continuing-education programs could increase school revenues. Most analysts assume that medical schools' primary response will be to increase revenues by raising tuition charges. But the schools should not ignore the importance of reducing costs. The Carnegie Commission on Higher Education (1970) made a number of recommendations for program changes that would lead to reduced costs, including making fuller use of facilities by having year-round programs and entering two classes each year. A number of medical schools did institute the three-year curriculum but found it unsatisfactory and have reverted to the four-year program (Beran 1979).

Most medical schools will find it difficult to preserve their financial position through the 1990s. In the 1980s the schools tended to erode their limited endowments, withdrawing funds for operations and capital projects. Many poor capital-expansion and stock-investment decisions were made, and there were large investments in new facilities. As the endowments began to shrink, they became increasingly harder to rebuild, and the resultant income from investments declined. Drucker (1973) was one of the first to point out that diagnosing schools as "inefficient" because they operate on the basis of a service ethic rather than a business-management ethic is overly simplistic. Nevertheless, there is an obvious need for more medical school managers with business training. However, such individuals would have to be sensitive to the health-service ethic so as not to put considerations for revenue maximization and cost minimization ahead of quality education. Talented management personnel might compel schools to respond to the public cry for more primary-care services. However, their real challenge would be to trim the fat from tertiary-care medicine without harming the basic research and development functions of medical schools.

As medical schools become increasingly reliant on patient-care revenues, corporate strategic planning must be utilized. Academic medical centers have already had a tough time adjusting to increasingly competitive markets (Ginzberg 1990; Kassebaum 1986). Competition has segmented the medical marketplace into a number of managed-care systems that explicitly target nonemergency-patient demand to specific hospitals and physician groups. HMOs and PPOs will increasingly restrict referrals. Medical centers that wish to remain state-of-the-art and cost competitive will have to redouble their efforts in the areas of strategic planning, departmental coordination, and ambulatory-care diversification (Ott 1991). Given that patients seem to like the cost savings of care systems that preselect their referral options, few teaching hospitals can survive by attracting the shrinking number of unenfranchised patients.

The message is clear: If you want enough patient volume to fill your teaching beds, the medical center must enroll enough people in its own managed-care health plan. This will require more teaching and patient care in the area of ambulatory care. Therefore, if the financial future of the medical center and medical school is increasingly dependent on their emergency and family-practice programs, the whole power structure of medical school faculties may undergo a revolution in the coming decade. Those "low-status" ambulatory care types may save the franchise and feed sufficient cash flow to underwrite capital-intensive inpatient-care programs. Ambulatory teaching faculty and staff should also demand high pay and fringe benefits. This is the natural economic response in any profession. For example, in football, when passing (ambulatory care) became more important than running (inpatient care), we began to pay quarterbacks (ambulatory-care faculty) more than running backs (hospital inpatient-care specialists).

REFERENCES

Alemi, F., Rice, J., and Hankins, R. (1990). "Predicting In-Hospital Survival of Myocardial Infarction: A Comparative Study of Various Severity Measures." *Medical Care* 28:9 (September), 762–775.

Ament, R., Breachslin, J., Kobrinski, E., and Wood, W. (1982). "The Case Type Classifications: Suitability for Use in Reimbursing Hospitals." *Medical Care* 20:5 (May), 460–467.

Anderson, G., and Lave, J. (1986). "Financing Graduate Medical Education Using Multiple Regression to Set Payment Rates." *Inquiry* 23:2 (Summer), 191–199.

Arthur Young and Policy Analysis, Inc. (1986). *A Study of the Financing of Graduate Medical Education: Final Report.* 3-volume study of 45 hospitals, DHHS 100–86–0155 (October). Washington, D.C.: U.S. Government Printing Office.

Association of American Medical Colleges (AAMC). (1991). Data on Medical Students and Medical School Finances. Washington, D.C.: AAMC.

———. (1986). *Association of American Medical Colleges Final Report: Financing Graduate Medical Education* (April). Washington, D.C.: AAMC.

Beck, W. (1986). "Asepsis and DRGs." *Infections in Surgery* 8 (August), 425, 448.

Behn, R. D., and Sperduto, K. (1979). "Medical Schools and the 'Entitlement Ethic.' " *Public Interest* 14:57 (Fall), 48–68.

Beran, R. L. (1979). "The Rise and Fall of Three-Year Medical School Programs." *Journal of Medical Education* 54:3 (March), 248–249.

Brewster, A., Karlin, B., Jacobs, C., Hyde, L., Bradbury, R., and Chae, Y. (1985). "MEDISGRPS: A Clinically Based Approach to Classifying Hospital Patients at Admission." *Inquiry* 22:4 (Winter), 377–387.

Brook, R., Lohr, K., Chassin, M., Kosecoff, J., Fink, A., and Solomon, D. (1984). "Geographic Variations in the Use of Services: Do They Have Any Clinical Significance?" *Health Affairs* 3:2 (Summer), 63–73.

Brown, T., Ehrlich, C., and Stehman, F. (1984). "A Clinical Evaluation of Chlorhexidine

Spray as Compared with Iodophor Scrub for Preoperative Skin Preparation.'' *Surgery, Gynecology, and Obstetrics* 158:4 (April), 363–366.

Broyles, R. (1990). ''Efficiency, Costs, and Quality: The New Jersey Experience Revisited.'' *Inquiry* 27:1 (Spring), 86–96.

Cameron, J. (1985). ''The Indirect Costs of Graduate Medical Education.'' *New England Journal of Medicine* 312:19 (May 9), 1233–1238.

Carnegie Commission on Higher Education (1970). *Priorities for Action: Report of the Carnegie Commission on Higher Education.* Los Angeles: Maple Press.

Carter, G., and Melnick, G. (1990). *How Services and Costs Vary by Day of Stay for Medicare Hospital Stays.* Washington, D.C.: ProPAC.

Cator, J., Cohen, A., Baker, D., and Shuster, A. (1991). ''Medical Educators' Views on Medical Education Reform.'' *Journal of the American Medical Association* 265:8 (February 27), 1002–1006.

Chulis, G. (1991). ''Assessing Medicare's Prospective Payment System Hospitals.'' *Medical Care Review* 48:2 (Summer), 167–206.

Chin, D., Hopkins, D., Melmon, K., and Holman, H. (1985). ''The Relation of Faculty Academic Activity to Financing Sources in a Department of Medicine.'' *New England Journal of Medicine* 312:16 (April 18), 1029–1034.

Cleary, P., Greenfield, S., and Mulley, A. (1991). ''Variation in Length of Stay and Outcomes for Six Medical and Surgical Conditions.'' *JAMA* 266:1 (July 3), 73–79.

Cleverley, W. (1986). *Essentials of Hospital Finance.* Germantown, Md.: Aspen Systems, 53–80.

Coffey, R., and Goldfarb, M. (1986). ''DRG's and Disease Staging for Reimbursing Medicare Patients.'' *Medical Care* 24:9 (September), 814–829.

Commonwealth Task Force on Academic Health Centers. (1985). *Future Financing of Teaching Hospitals: A Framework for Public Policy* (October). New York: Commonwealth Fund.

Congressional Budget Office (CBO). (1991). *Medicare's Disproportionate Share Adjustment.* Washington, D.C.: CBO.

Custer, W., and Willke, R. (1991). ''Teaching Hospital Costs: The Effects of Medical Staff Characteristics.'' *Health Services Research* 25:6 (February), 831–857.

Detsky, A., McLaughlin, J., Abrams, H., Labbe, K., and Markel, F. (1986). ''Do Interns and Residents Order More Tests Than Attending Staff?'' *Medical Care* 24:6 (June), 526–534.

Doolittle, R. (1991). ''Biotechnology: The Enormous Cost of Success.'' *New England Journal of Medicine* 324:19 (May 9) 1360–1362.

Drucker, P. (1973). ''Managing the Public Service Institution.'' *Public Interest* 9:33 (Fall), 43–60.

Eastaugh, S. (1992). ''Economic Issues in Defining Stable Funding Levels for AIDS Research.'' *Journal of Health Administration Education* 10:1 (Winter), 68–87.

Eastaugh, S. (1990). ''Financing the Correct Rate of Growth of Medical Technology.'' *Quarterly Review of Economics and Business* 30:4 (Winter), 34–60.

———. (1987). *Financing Health Care.* Dover, Mass.: Auburn House, 323–377.

———. (1981). *Medical Economics and Health Finance.* Dover, Mass.: Auburn House.

———. (1980a). ''Organizational Determination of Surgical Lengths of Stay.'' *Inquiry* 17:2 (Spring), 85–96.

————. (1980b). "Financial Ratio Analysis and Medical School Management." *Journal of Medical Education* 55:12 (December), 983–992.

————. (1979). "Cost of Elective Surgery and Utilization of Ancillary Services in Teaching Hospitals." *Health Services Research* 14:4 (Winter), 290–308.

Eeckhoudt, L., LeBrun, T., and Sailly, J. (1985). "Risk-Aversion and Physicians' Medical Decision-Making." *Journal of Health Economics* 4:3 (September), 273–281.

Epstein, A. (1986). "Socioeconomic Characteristics and Utilization for Hospitalized Patients: Do Poor People Cost More?" *Clinical Research* 84:1 (January), 360–373.

Fein, R. (1967). *The Doctor Shortage*. Washington, D.C.: Brookings Institution.

Fein, R., and Weber, G. (1971). *Financing Medical Education: An Analysis of Alternative Policies and Mechanisms*. New York: McGraw-Hill.

Feinglass, J., Martin, G., and Sen, A., "Financial Effect of Physician Practice Style on Hospital Resource Use." *Health Services Research* 26:2 (June), 183–205.

Fetter, R., and Freeman, J. (1991). *DRG Refinement with Diagnostic Specific Comorbidities and Complications: A Synthesis of Current Approaches to Patient Classification*. Washington, D.C.: Health Care Financing Administration.

Finkler, S., Brooten, D., and Brown, L. (1988). "Utilization of Inpatient Services under Shortened Lengths of Stay: A Neonatal Care Example." *Inquiry* 25:2 (Summer), 271–280.

Foley, J., and Mulhausen, R. (1986). "The Cost of Complexity: The Teaching Hospital." *Hospital and Health Services Administration* 31:5 (September/October), 96–109.

Fossett, J., Choi, C., and Peterson, J. (1991). "Hospital Outpatient Services and Medicaid Patients' Access to Care." *Medical Care* 29:10 (October), 964–976.

Frick, A., Martin, S., and Schwartz, M. (1985). "Case-Mix and Cost Differences between Teaching and Nonteaching Hospitals." *Medical Care* 23:4 (April), 283–295.

Garg, M., Elkhatib, M., Kleinberg, W., and Mulligan, W. (1982). "Reimbursing for Residency Training: How Many Times?" *Medical Care* 20:7 (July), 719–726.

Garg, M., Louis, D., Gleibe, W., Spirka, C., Skipper, J., and Parekh, R. (1978). "Evaluating Inpatient Costs." *Medical Care* 16:3 (March), 191–201.

Gildea, J. (1988). "Toil and Trouble over Outpatient Prospective Payment." *Health Care Management* 5:1 (January), 1–10.

Ginzberg, E. (1990). *The Medical Triangle: Physicians, Politicians, and the Public*. Cambridge, Mass.: Harvard University Press.

Gold, M. (1988). "Common Sense on Extending DRG Concepts to Pay for Ambulatory Care." *Inquiry* 25:2 (Summer), 281–289.

Goldfarb, M., and Coffey, R. (1987). "Case-Mix Differences between Teaching and Nonteaching Hospitals." *Inquiry* 24:1 (Spring), 68–84.

Gonnella, J., Hornbrook, M., and Louis, D. (1984). "Staging of Disease: A Case-Mix Measurement." *Journal of the American Medical Association* 251:5 (February 3), 637–641.

Gonnella, J., Louis, D., and Zelenik, C. (1990). "The Problem of Late Hospitalization." *Academic Medicine* 65:5 (May), 314–319.

Goodall, C. (1990). "A Simple Objective Method for Determining a Percent Standard in Mixed Reimbursement Systems." *Journal of Health Economics* 9:3 (November), 253–271.

Goodman, L., Brueschke, E., and Bone, R. (1991). "An Experiment in Medical Education: A Critical Analysis.'' *Journal of the American Medical Association* 265:18 (May 8), 2373–2376.

Haley, R., Schaberg, D., and Crossley, K. (1981). ''Extra Charges and Prolongation of Stay Attributable to Nosocomial Infection.'' *American Journal of Medicine* 70:1 (January), 51–58.

Harrison, R., and Payne, B. (1991). ''Developing Criteria for Ordering Common Ancillary Services,'' *Medical Care* 29:9 (September), 853–877.

Hilton, G. W. (1972). ''The Basic Behavior of Regulatory Commissions.'' *American Economic Review* 62:2 (May), 47–54.

Horn, S. (1986). ''Measuring Severity: How Sick Is Sick? How Well Is Well?'' *Healthcare Financial Management* 40:10 (October), 21–32.

Horn, S., Buckley, G., Sharkey, P., Chambers, A., Horn, R., and Schramm, C. (1985). ''Inter-Hospital Differences in Patient Severity: Problems for Prospective Payment Based on DRGs.'' *New England Journal of Medicine* 313:1 (July 4), 20–24.

Horn, S., Horn, R., and Moses, H. (1986). ''Profiles of Physician Practice and Patient Severity of Illness.'' *American Journal of Public Health* 76:5 (May), 532–535.

Hough, D., and Bazzoli, G. (1985). ''The Economic Environment of Resident Physicians.'' *Journal of the American Medical Association* 253:12 (March 22), 1758–1762.

Hsia, D., Krushaat, W., Fagan, A., Febbutt, J., and Kusserow, R. (1988). ''Accuracy of Diagnostic Coding for Medicare Patients under the Prospective-Payment System.'' *New England Journal of Medicine* 318:4 (January 22), 352–355.

Iezzoni, L., Schwartz, M., and Restuccia, J. (1991). ''Role of Severity Information in Health Policy Debates: A Survey of State and Regional Concerns.'' *Inquiry* 28:2 (Spring), 117–28.

Iglehart, J. (1986). ''Federal Support of Health Manpower Education.'' *New England Journal of Medicine* 314:5 (January 30), 324–328.

Innes, A., Grant, A., and Beinfield, M. (1968). ''Experience with Shortened Hospital Stay for Postsurgical Patients.'' *Journal of the American Medical Association* 204:8 (May 20), 647–652.

Jolly, P., and AAMC staff (1991) ''U. S. Medical School Finances.'' *Journal of the American Medical Association* 266:7 (August 21), 985–991.

Kassebaum, D. (1986). ''Adjustments and Opportunities for Academic Medical Centers under Health Care Competition and Cost Containment.'' *Journal of Medical Education* 61:5 (May), 421–423.

Keeler, E. (1990). ''What Proportion of Hospital Cost Differences Is Justifiable?'' *Journal of Health Economics* 9:3 (November), 359–365.

Kenney, G., and Holahan, J. (1991), ''Nursing Home Transfers and Mean Length of Stay in the Prospective Payment Era.'' *Medical Care* 29:7 (July), 589–609.

Kirz, H., and Larsen, C. (1986). ''Costs and Benefits of Medical Student Training to an HMO.'' *Journal of the American Medical Association* 256:6 (August 8), 734–739.

Knaus, W., Draper E., and Wagner, D. (1985). ''APACHE II: A Severity of Disease Classification System.'' *Critical Care Medicine* 13:12 (December), 818–827.

Knaus, W., Wagnor, D., Draper, E., Zimmerman, J. (1991). ''APACHE III Prognostic System: Risk Predictor of Hospital Mortality.'' *Chest* 100:6 (December), 1501–1565.

Lave, J., and Frank, R. (1990). "Effect of the Structure of Hospital Payment on Length of Stay." *Health Services Research* 25:2 (June), 325–347.

Lion, J., Malbon, A., and Bergman, A. (1987). "AVGs: Implications for Hospital Outpatient Departments." *Journal of Ambulatory Care Management* 10:1 (February), 56–69.

Louis, D., Barnes, C., Jordan, N., Moynihan, C., Pepitone, T., Spirka, C., Sredl, K., and Westnedge, J. (1983). *Disease Staging: A Clinically Based Approach to Measurement of Disease Severity.* Final Report to DHHS (NCHSR 233–78–3001), Rockville, Maryland (August). Washington, D.C.: U.S. Government Printing Office, NTIS-PB83–254649.

Louis, D., and Gonnella, J. (1991). *Q-Stage: Q-Scale.* New York: SysteMetrics/McGraw-Hill.

Malenka, D., Roos, N., Fisher, S., and Wennberg, J. (1990). "Further Study of the Increased Mortality Following Transurethral Prostatectomy." *Journal of Urology* 144:8 (August), 224–228.

Manheim, L., Feinglas, J., Hughes, R., Martin, G., Conrad, K., and Hughes, R. (1990). "Training House Officers to Be Cost Conscious: Effects of an Educational Intervention on Charges and Length of Stay." *Medical Care* 28:1 (January), 29–41.

McGuire, T. (1991), "An evaluation of Diagnosis-related group severity & complexity refinement." *Health Care Financing Review* 12:4 (Summer), 49–60.

McKay, N. (1990). "Economic Determinants of Specialty Choice by Medical Residents." *Journal of Health Economics* 9:3 (November), 335–357.

McMahon, L., Wolfe, R., and Tedeschi, P. (1989). "Variation in Hospital Admissions among Small Areas: A Comparison of Maine and Michigan." *Medical Care* 27:6 (June), 623–631.

McShane, M. (1977). *An Empirical Classification of United States Medical Schools by Institutional Dimensions.* Final Report of the Association of American Medical Colleges to the Department of Health, Education and Welfare, Publication HRA 77–55. Washington, D.C.: Health Resources Administration, Bureau of Health Manpower.

Mennemeyer, S. (1978). "Really Great Returns to Medical Education?" *Journal of Medical Education* 13 (January) 73–90.

Miller, M., Cuddleback, J., and Gallo, J. (1991). *Severity of Illness Measures for Hospitals.* Tallahassee, Fla.: Florida Health Care Cost Containment Board.

National Center for Health Statistics. (1991). Vital and Health Statistics: Data from the National Health Interview Survey. Hyattsville, Md.: DHHS.

National Research Council. (1977), *Health Care for American Veterans.* Washington, D.C.: National Academy of Sciences.

New York State. (1991). *Products of Ambulatory Care (PACs) and Products of Ambulatory Surgery (PAS) Reimbursement Project.* New York: New York State Ambulatory Care Case Mix Demonstration Project.

Newhouse, J. (1983). "Two Prospective Difficulties with PPS of Hospitals, or, " 'It's Better to Be a Resident Than a Patient with a Complex Problem.' " *Journal of Health Economics* 2:3 (September), 269–274.

Oleske, D., Glandon, G., Giacomelli, G., and Hohmann, S. (1991). "Cesarean Birth Rate: Influence of Hospital Teaching Status." *Health Services Research* 26:3 (August), 325–338.

Ott, J. (1991) "Competitive Medical Organizations." In Moreno, J. (ed.) *Paying The Doctor*, 83–90 Westport, Conn: Greenwood.

Panniers, T., and Newlander, J. (1986). "Adverse Patient Occurrences (APO) Inventory: Validity, Reliability, and Implications." *Quality Review Bulletin* 12:9 (September), 311–315.

Perry, D., and Challoner, D. (1979). "A Rationale for Continued Federal Support of Medical Education." *New England Journal of Medicine* 300:22 (January), 66–71.

Petersdorf, R. (1985). "A Proposal for Financing Graduate Medical Education." *New England Journal of Medicine* 312:20 (May 16), 1322–1324.

Pettengill, J., and Vertrees, J. (1982). "Reliability and Validity in Hospital Case-Mix Measurement." *Health Care Financing Review* 4:2 (December), 101–128.

Pfordresher, K. (1985). "Clinical Research and Prospective Payment." Report of the Council of Teaching Hospitals, monograph (January). Washington, D.C.: American Association of Medical Colleges.

Pope, G. (1990). "Using Hospital-specific Costs to Improve the Fairness of Prospective Reimbursement." *Journal of Health Economics* 9:3 (November), 237–251.

Prospective Payment Assessment Commission (ProPac). (1991). *Medicare Prospective Payment and the American Health Care System: Report to Congress*. Washington, D.C.: ProPAC.

Rabkin, M. (1986). "Reducing the Cost of Medical Education." *Health Affairs* 5:3 (Fall), 97–104.

Rapoport, J., Teres, D., Lemeshow, S., Avrunin, J., and Haber, R. (1990). "Explaining Variability of Cost Using a Severity of Illness Measure for ICU Patients." *Medical Care* 28:4 (April), 338–348.

Reinhardt, U. (1975). *Physician Productivity and the Demand for Health Manpower*. Cambridge, Mass.: Ballinger.

Relman, A. (1991). "The Health Care Industry: where is it taking us?" *New England Journal of Medicine* 325:12 (September 19), 854–59.

Relman, A. (1984). "Who Will Pay for Medical Education in Our Teaching Hospitals?" *Science* 226:1 (October 5), 20–23.

Rieselbach, R., and Jackson, T. (1986). "In Support of a Linkage between the Funding of Graduate Medical Education and Care of the Indigent." *New England Journal of Medicine* 314:1 (January 2), 32–35.

Rogers, D. (1980). "On Preparing Academic Health Centers for the Very Different 1980's." *Journal of Medical Education* 55:1 (January), 1–12.

Rosko, M. (1988). "DRGs and the Severity of Illness Measures: An Analysis of Patient Classification Systems." *Journal of Medical Systems* 12:2 (Spring) 257–266.

Salkever, D. (1970). "Studies in the Economics of Hospital Costs." Ph.D. diss., Economics Department, Harvard University.

Scheffler, R., Sullivan, S., Haochung, T. (1991), "Impact of Blue Cross and Blue Shield plan utilization management programs", *Inquiry* 28:3 (Fall), 263–75.

Schimmel, E. (1974). "Hazards of Hospitalization." *Annals of Internal Medicine* 60:1 (January), 100–110.

Schwartz, W., Newhouse, J., and Williams, A. (1985). "Is the Teaching Hospital an Endangered Species?" *New England Journal of Medicine* 313:3 (July 18), 157–162.

Shortliffe, E. (1991). "Medical Informatics and Clinical Decision Making." *Medical Decision Making* 11:4 (October-December), S4-S14.

Sloan, F. (1976). "A Microanalysis of Physicians' Hours of Work Decisions." In M. Perlman (ed.), *Economics of Health and Medical Care*, 302–325. New York: John Wiley.

Starfield, B., Weiner, J., Mumford, L., and Steinwachs, D. (1991). "Ambulatory Care Groupings." *Health Services Research* 26:1 (April), 53–74.

Steinwald, B., and Dummit, L. (1989). "Hospital Case-Mix Change: Sicker Patients or DRG Creep?" *Health Affairs* 8:2 (Summer), 35–47.

Stevens, C. (1971). "Physicians Supply and the National Health Care Goals." *Industrial Relations* 10:5 (May), 119–144.

Stoskopf, C., and Horn, S. (1992). "Predicting Length of Stay." *Health Services Research* 26:6, 749–765.

Thomas, J., and Ashcraft, M. (1991). "Measuring Severity of Illness: Six Severity Systems and Ability to Explain Cost." *Inquiry* 28:1 (Spring), 39–55.

Thorpe, K. (1988). "Use of Regression Analysis to Determine Hospital Payment: The Case of Medicare's Indirect Teaching Adjustment." *Inquiry* 25:2 (Summer), 219–231.

Tosteson, D. (1991). "New Pathways for Medical Education." *Journal of the American Medical Association* 265:8 (February 27), 1022–1023.

———. (1990). "New Pathways in General Medical Education." *New England Journal of Medicine* 322:4 (January 25), 234–238.

Twaddle, A., and Sweet, R. (1970). "Characteristics and Experiences of Patients with Preventable Hospital Admissions." *Social Science and Medicine* 4:1 (July), 141–145.

United States Senate Finance Committee. (1983). *Social Security Amendments of 1983*. Report 98–23 (March 11), 52.

Weiner, J., Starfield, B., Steinwachs, D., and Mumford, L. (1991). "Development and application of a Population-oriented Measure of Ambulatory Care Case-mix." *Medical Care* 29:5 (May), 452–472.

Wennberg, J. (1990). "Status of the Prostate Disease Assessment Team." *Health Services Research* 25:5 (December), 709–716.

Wennberg, J., Freeman, J., and Culp, W. (1987). "Are Hospital Services Rationed in New Haven or Over-utilized in Boston?" *Lancet* 1:8543, 1185–1187.

Wickizer, T., Wheeler, J., and Feldstein, P. (1991). "Have Hospital Inpatient Cost Containment Programs Contributed to the Growth in Outpatient Expenditures?" *Medical Care* 29:5 (May), 442–451.

Wickizer, T., Wheeler, J., and Feldstein, P. (1989). "Does Utilization Review Reduce Unnecessary Hospital Care and Contain Costs?" *Medical Care* 27:6 (June), 632–647.

Witsberger, C., and Kominski, G. (1990). *Recent Trends in Length of Stay for Medicare Surgical Patients*. Washington, D.C.: HCFA, R-3940.

Wong, D., Knaus, W. (1991). "Predicted Outcome in Critical Care: APACHE." *Canadian Journal of Anesthesiology* 38:3 (April), 374–383.

Young, W. (1986). *Measuring the Cost of Care Using Patient Management Categories*. HCFA Publication Number 86–03228 (June). Washington, D.C.: U.S. Government Printing Office.

Part Five

QUALITY ASSURANCE AND PRODUCTIVITY CONTROL

Hospital Productivity: Managing Cost Reductions without Harm to Quality or Access

> Do not confuse bad management with destiny. You can improve your position with the right management and incentives.
>
> —Alfred Sloan

> Thinking that the facility cannot improve productivity substantially is the principal affliction of the health care industry. Productivity is the first test of management's competence. One should get the greatest output for the least input effort, better balancing all factors of service delivery to achieve the most with the smallest resource effort.
>
> —Peter F. Drucker

> When you are through improving, you are through.
>
> —Bo Schembechler

In this chapter we will explore a number of "tenets of faith" concerning hospital productivity improvement—for example, "Cutting staff harms service quality" (Mullaney 1989), "More staff buys more quality," "Reducing staff translates into reduced employee morale," and "Performance gains accrue only to those who work harder." Alternative mechanisms by which the organization may work smarter rather than harder are also advanced. The implementation of efficient scheduling systems and work-unit reorganization, especially when reinforced by an incentive-pay plan, has led to significant cost reductions. We shall discuss the topic of incentive pay in the next chapter.

The hospital sector's incentive structure has been revolutionized by Medicare's switch from payment based on recovery of costs to payment based on a fixed price per diagnosis related group (DRG). In the future, productivity will not be just a minor part of the management job or simply an area for added emphasis; it is, to quote Karl Bays (1984), "the whole job for hospital managers". Hospitals have been thrown into a new game with new rules. Before the enactment of the prospective payment system (PPS), rational managers emphasized revenue enhancement, maximization of reimbursement, and, often, negative productivity shifts. If the choice was either to improve the productivity of 22 employees or to hire 4 more, the response was typically to hire, because the added cost was a pass-through under cost reimbursement. In the future, however, the "only game in town" will be cost reduction through productivity improvement, not old-style growth and revenue maximization.

Productivity, in its simplest form, equals output divided by resource inputs. Productivity can be improved either by expanding output or by contracting inputs, or by having the rate of change in output volume outperform the rate of change in input resources. For example, the ratio of output to input improves (that is, we do more with fewer resources) if volume increases 8 percent and staff hours increase by less than 8 percent. Alternatively, if staff hours decline by 10 percent and volume decreases by less than 10 percent, productivity is increased. Thus productivity can be improved either by reducing costs or by increasing output, or by doing both.

But hospital services are a special kind of output. Producing more services than are medically necessary, even if they are produced at a lower unit cost, has little to do with real increase in productivity. A hospital's production of unnecessary services is inefficient, and the institution will not be compensated for them under PPS. The federal government and other third-party payers will be cooperating with professional review organizations (PROs) to curtail the production of unnecessary services. Cost reduction, not output expansion, is the key to future productivity improvement in most hospital markets. For example, in 1991 Northwestern saved $1.9 million by trimming 220 FTEs, Full-Time Equivalent employees in the hospital.

One measure of hospital output, patient days, is currently declining at a rather alarming rate. The "recession" in patient days may represent a permanent shift in provider behavior, rather than a cyclical recurring problem. With fewer patients in bed one obviously needs less staff, although some of these "extra" employees can be trained to work in ambulatory care or other settings. In the past, hospital managers have tried to soften the impact of sudden cuts and rehires (Wood 1984). However, the future may not allow much rehiring. Even after hospitals net out the shift in employees to other settings, much of the staff reductions of the mid–1980s will be permanent. For all but the most efficient hospitals, some unpleasant staff reductions are lamentably inescapable if hospitals are to avoid closure.

AREN'T OUR PRESENT PRODUCTIVITY MEASURES GOOD ENOUGH?

It was curious to hear a hospital manager recently exclaim: "So what if patient census dropped 10 per cent last year? All departments are reporting more units of activity, so productivity is up and staff should be increased, not decreased!'' On the contrary, the efficiency of activity production is essentially irrelevant. Another service industry, police protection, affords an interesting comparison: The important variable for the public is crimes prevented and solved, not staff hours of internal office activity generated, tabulated, or filed. It is easy to get lost in a mass of numbers, producing measures of insignificant activity that turn out to have no meaning. The reporting and analyzing process saps endless hours of management time throughout various departments, and such productivity information systems do not by themselves bring about real cost reductions (Sumeren 1986).

In the new world of PPS, the basic unit of productivity is the DRG case treated, not the activity units accumulated. There has long been a need for a final-product perspective in health care. Counting relative value units (RVUs) misses the target completely. It is largely irrelevant to measure ''the product'' with nurse relative intensity measure (RIM) points (Grimaldi and Michelètte 1982), GRASP points (Meyers 1981), or laboratory standardized unit value College of American Pathologists (CAP) points accumulated (Eastaugh 1985a). Although RVUs are an improvement over simple procedure counts and tallies, the appearance of high levels of activity can result from inefficient allocation of responsibilities rather than from the group being understaffed or ''overproductive.'' When productivity experts talk in terms of RVUs, they lapse into a jargon that is an industrial engineer's version of the secret lodge handshake. Even the most technically savvy senior managers are likely to doze off when they are bombarded with indecipherable RVU trends dear only to the heart of the management engineer. Who cares if RVU workload is improving because overreporting is on the increase? What matters to the CEO is that patient census has declined 10 percent, cash flow is down 11 percent, and the hospital will be running a big deficit. We in academia lecture on pristine systems development, but the analyses of RVUs and other activity measures are largely unproductive contributions to the management process in times of stress.

The compilation of activity measures is of little use in setting staffing levels and even less useful for cost accounting. Perhaps more dangerous, management has been lulled into believing that ''productivity must be sufficient if we reside in the happy middle range of Monitrend normative standards.'' Under PPS incentives to ''meet or beat'' the DRG prices, many hospitals will find the ''happy middle'' staffing levels fostered by cost reimbursement severely inflated for an institution that wants to survive after 1992.

Productivity is not easy to measure in all departments (Reuschel and Earle (1991). Overemphasis of small activity measures is the principal weakness of traditional productivity analysis, and the normative staffing study is not very useful in getting cost-saving results. But if these traditional means of dealing with the issue of productivity are not going to work in hospitals' new environment, what can we do to ensure that services are provided at the lowest cost?

WHAT MUST BE DONE TO IMPROVE PRODUCTIVITY?

The basic requirement of a successful productivity program is that the senior managers and trustees must really want cost reduction. They cannot follow the path of least resistance. As the noted physician and administrator Richard Egdahl remarked in the *Harvard Business Review* (1984), a cost-reduction program will likely result in reducing the number of employees and may involve reducing facility capital stock (beds and equipment). If it is true, as Peter Drucker has often said, that productivity is the first test of management's competence, we should reward managers who do more with less, those who reduce staff rather than those who increase staff each year.

Move rapidly. The best productivity programs are rapid, are large in scale, are cost-beneficial, and provide benchmarks for assessing future performance. Productivity-improvement studies do not need to be multiyear and very costly. The first stage of operational assessment can be rapid (three to five months) and quite cost-beneficial. Substantial cost reductions can be obtained in the short run, while second and third stages of more refined improvements (scheduling systems, for example) and incentives are put in place for permanent, long-run cost containment. Timing depends on the size and scope of the facility and the areas under study, but rapid plan development and implementation is essential for both financial and nonfinancial reasons. Allowing the assessment to go beyond a few months would create undue uncertainties among anxious employees.

Start big. The departments under study should be large if the gains are to be large. For example, a 5 percent improvement in nurse productivity would dwarf a 30 percent improvement in labor productivity of central supply, pharmacy, housekeeping, laundry, plant, and maintenance. The frequent management complaint, "We have the best laundry costs and the worst hospital cost increases," illustrates a major point. Significant cuts in the big cost areas in a hospital cannot be avoided in the vain hope that cost containment can either be easy or confined to cosmetic reductions in staff. Merely conducting an overhead variance analysis and cutting the number of housekeepers, administrative residents, and summer interns will not get to the heart of a hospital's problems in managing productivity improvements.

Ask the right questions. Trustees and senior management should ask critical questions like these: What staffing ratio do we really need? How did other hospitals get expanded output with much lower growth in staff? What new equipment and organizational changes can be used to reduce staff and make the work force more effective? Examples from other institutions convince management that new methods of organizing and scheduling can be made to work. Normative comparison of "best actors" among peer hospitals (those exhibiting the best levels of productivity) can also be useful in making ballpark guesstimates of the potential for staff reductions.

Use a conceptual approach. The program that produces lasting, significant change, however, must be based on a conceptual rather than a consensus approach. First, the simplistic percentile ''peer'' comparison approach of productivity by department has little impact on management unless the facility is a severely overstaffed or understaffed outlier (everyone reports being close enough to the ''happy middle''). Second, the hospital's unique employee skill mix and patient case mix is seldom captured by the phrase ''peers of the same size.'' Third, the consensus method assumes that other hospitals have approximately the right staff organization and staffing levels for emulation. Fourth, the ''quick-and-dirty'' consensus approach typically prescribes motivating individual employees to work harder or faster to produce more units of activity (Eastaugh 1986).

Programs that focus on the activities of individual workers ignore the two greatest keys to productivity improvement: organization and work-team scheduling. Much can be achieved by examining what is being done and how employees are being organized into work teams (stage one), and how middle-level managers can schedule more efficiently (stage two).

Stage One: Operational Assessment

The conceptual approach argues that it is possible to determine rather precisely the number and types of employees a given hospital needs to supply quality patient care and meet its other objectives (teaching and research, for example). Exceeding this number does not increase quality; it simply creates unnecessary costs. Stage one, the initial operational assessment, involves finding answers to two basic questions: How many people should really be working here? What is the best mix of staff and other resources? Four basic actions make up the formal operational assessment:

1. Review historical, current, and budgeted staffing levels.
2. Evaluate facility layout, equipment, intraunit functional relationships, and interdepartmental coordination.
3. Identify operational deficiencies and recommend improvements.
4. Analyze all current forms and management reports for appropriateness and timeliness of the information.

It is the hospital management's ability to focus on those actions and ideas that highlight unnecessary costs that determines the real usefulness of the assessment.

Focus on basic problems. The study should be based on these principles:

1. Don't organize for what is done only 5 per cent of the time.
2. Streamline overlapping functions and excessive layers of supervisions.
3. Reduce those departments that exhibit excess capacity.

The efficiency of standing orders and standard operating procedures (SOPs), such as letting nurses restart IVs, needs to be assessed. Nurse activities that need increased delegation to other staff, such as patient transport, running errands, or making beds, should be evaluated. Situations worsened by rigid specialization (for example, a small water spill that takes less time for a nurse to clean up herself than to make three calls to housekeeping) also should be identified (Eastaugh 1985b).

Reorganize and retrain for improved productivity. Nursing and ancillary departments should reorganize and retrain for improved productivity. Flexibility in staffing is the key to adjusting to the flux in demands during peak periods while keeping staffing levels down. For example, the OR workers from nurses to housekeeping can be pulled together into one team so that housekeeping can assist in pulling supplies for the next case, thus enhancing productivity. If the ancillary department is having an easy level of volume on the night shift, let it work on the setups for the next day. The key to better productivity is to smooth out the work flows and minimize idle time associated with the work. Japanese hospitals use the "utility infielder" approach; they cross-train all staff in two areas, so that other departments can be cross-covered within the same day or within the same month. Staffing can be reduced 20 percent by using this approach; at the same time, workers with two roles to play experience improved job satisfaction and morale.

Define the necessary staff qualifications. A good operational assessment of any work unit should study each task and determine the actual level of staff qualifications required. Aggregate numbers of recommended FTEs are not the principal output of stage-one analysis. Let us return to nursing as an example. Equally as important as the staffing ratio of nurses per patient is an optimal mix of nurses employed for the given tasks assigned. An excess number of RNs in the name of quality enhancement is the biggest problem in nursing cost containment. Nurse administrators who think that "quality" depends on how many of their nurses have bachelor of science in nursing (BSN) degrees are as mistaken as college presidents who judge "quality" by the number of faculty members with Ph.D.'s. It is the organization of the work to be done and the skill mix of the employees doing it that are the crucial issues in staffing (Shukla 1985). Although the emergency room needs critical-care nurses, for example, delegation of more tasks to aides and clerks helps to control payroll expenses.

Use an adequate reporting system. Functional procedural flow-chart analysis and task evaluation are two key tools in operational assessment. Nursing productivity studies, in particular, are often hampered by poor information systems and support systems. Although some facilities allocate float nurses' work effort back to the home department, rather than to the understaffed units or subspecialty areas (like the operating room), other facilities draw all float-pool personnel from an outside registry and define float time as a cost center, with no information concerning where the work effort should actually have been allocated. Useful operational assessment depends on accurate, comparable information. The essential elements in stage one of a productivity-improvement program are summarized in the top half of figure 9.1.

Figure 9.1
Three-Stage Approach to Productivity Improvement

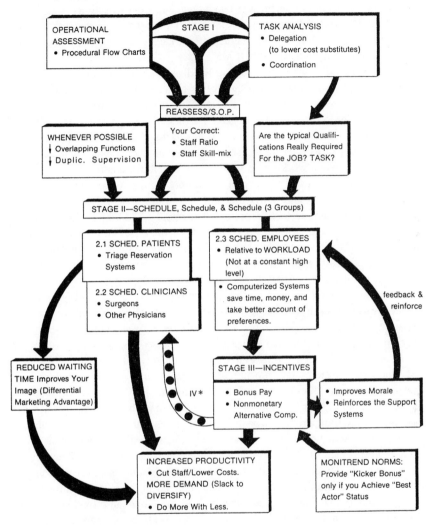

Note: *Potential stage four: either form of incentive compensation can be paid to physicians with appropriate attention to IRS restrictions (link it to a productivity index and not to ''profits,'' ''gross,'' or ''net income'' if your institution is tax-exempt).

Stage Two: Who Can Be Scheduled Better?

Stage one, operational assessment, yields better work assignments, identifies ''lost resources'' and unnecessary activities, and suggests ways to foster efficient interdepartmental coordination. Major productivity improvement, however, depends on one basic element: scheduling. Three critical actors—the patient, the employee, and the physician—must be scheduled for improved productivity. Better scheduling of all three groups can reduce unnecessary activity flow, reduce unit costs, improve patient satisfaction, and reduce waiting time for both providers and patients (Shorr 1991; Sahney 1982; Deguchi, Inui, and Martin 1984; Martin, Dahlstrom, and Johnston 1985).

Forecast actual workloads. Staffing-level assessment in stage one refers to the numbers of personnel; scheduling refers to when the personnel are working and when patients are expected to arrive. Obviously, the staffing ratios should be set in proportion to forecast workloads. In scheduling nurses, for example, if the workload on day shifts is three times as high as that on night shifts, it would be illogical to provide the same number of nurses over all three shifts. Similarly, even when workload is unscheduled, as in the emergency room, there are predictable patterns of utilization. A sample survey over a few months will demonstrate the days and shifts that have the highest workload, and staffing should be proportionate to this predicted demand. Additional adjustments for seasonal changes and case-mix severity can be made, of course (McClain and Eastaugh 1983). The result will be that the emergency room will not be staffed so that the day shift experiences 12 visits per nurse per shift and the night shift experiences only 4 visits per nurse.

Preserve employee morale. A basic requirement of a scheduling system is that it preserve morale and meet the personal needs of employees for days off, vacations, birthdays, and holidays. In addition, employees must believe that the scheduling process is fair and that it is carried out competently.

Use an automated scheduling system. Unfortunately, many hospitals use manual scheduling systems that are unresponsive to subtle shifts in workload and that are perceived as being unfair. It is amazing that personnel are still manually scheduled in an industry that spends over $3 billion each week and that has such complex scheduling problems. For example, if 12 nurses are being scheduled over a month so that each nurse works 22 days, disregarding all other constraints, there would be 1.5 million possible schedules. It is hard to imagine any human being, even under no other constraints, who could find the best schedule. A computerized scheduling system, however, can select the best schedule without hours of paperwork, hassles, and appeals. The computer can provide convincing documentation of fairness, demonstrating that weekend assignments and shift changes (A.M. to P.M. to nights) have been equalized. Frequently one finds capable employees being promoted to "scheduler" without ever having been taught the importance of, or techniques for, efficient scheduling. Computer-generated schedules are guided by efficiency and equality and not by who is the individual "pet" friend of the scheduler.

One needs to allocate nurses by a methodology that accounts for acuity or the level of care a patient needs. The goal is acuity-driven workload staffing, not merely census-driven staffing (Eastaugh 1985b). However, even the most refined industrial engineering methodology can be undercut if management eschews flexibility in favor of a fixed decision rule—for example, each nurse is allowed every other weekend off. Such a rule results in overstaffing on the weekend and on one or two of the weekdays. One can reduce nursing costs and improve morale by fostering nontraditional staffing arrangements. Flexible use of part-time staff and a combination of two 12-hour shifts and two 8-hour shifts for some full-time nurses can assure a better match between workload and FTEs. The worst of all possible worlds exists when one forces nurses to overstaff a facility on weekends and some weekdays and runs short of staff on the busy weekdays.

Shukla (1985) has demonstrated at the Medical College of Virginia that a computerized nurse-scheduling system achieves a far superior match between workload and staffing levels, thus improving the quality of patient care. Nursing costs are reduced, peak periods of overstaffing are smoothed out, and staffing levels can be reduced. Further, morale improves because the shift changes can be reduced by 75 percent or more, and minimal staffing levels are achieved 10 to 50 percent more often. With regard to possible changes in quality of service, a tight ship is usually a quality ship, that is, we should not be surprised at the report that quality improves in more productive units or departments.

Schedule physicians better. Scheduling systems for physicians can also reduce costs through a reduction in the downtime (wasted time). When an operating room mishandles scheduling of cases, cost overruns result from either under-utilization and/or overtime wages. Sahney has instituted highly successful scheduling systems in the operating room and in a number of other settings. One can easily implement a triage reservation system for ambulatory clinics by scheduling 25 percent more patients per hour (five per hour, instead of one every 15 minutes) at staggered times (easy cases at 10 and 10:05, two cases at 10:20 and 10:25, respectively, and the hardest case served from 10:40 to 11:00), with varying duration of forecast necessary visiting time with the physician (Sahney 1982). The organization works smarter, but no individual experiences a perceptible shift toward working harder. Slack periods or downtime simply decline in frequency and duration (Eastaugh 1986).

The University of Michigan Medical Center has been a pioneer since 1986 in operating-room (OR) scheduling. Operating-room scheduling efficiency is improved by scheduling on the basis of patient DRG, severity level, and surgeon (speed based on past experience). Scheduling policies were made uniform across all departments in 1988, and a service-specific scheduler was assigned in each area (one person for cardiac surgery, one for ophthalmology, one for general surgery). The specialist in scheduling knows how to collect information, stagger schedule time blocks, minimize misscheduled cases, call surgeons if necessary, and collectively make optimal use of the 33 OR suites (only 19 percent downtime in 1991).

Develop an accurate system of productivity measurement and a workload-driven staff-scheduling system. Responsive daily adjustment of the scheduling system is necessary, such as having department managers report labor hours and scheduled workload to the CEO by 8:15 A.M. and distribute data to vice presidents by 9:15 A.M. while vice presidents have until 11 A.M. to investigate and correct variances (are we overstaffing or understaffing at this time?). Overstaffing should lead to adjustment in future schedules, and if possible, personnel can be asked to take time off.

Understaffing should not be "solved" simply by paying more overtime (although paying a little overtime is preferred to full-time overstaffing). Instead, understaffing should be treated by reallocation of labor and cross-utilization of staff. To help cross-utilization and avoid balkanized job descriptions and poor attitude (e.g., "That's not my job"), employees should be cross-trained in multiple jobs. This Japanese "utility infielder" approach to cross-training requires the facility to pay for education programs and certification tests in multiple disciplines, but the organization benefits from (1) a more engaged and challenged work force, (2) lower employee turnover, (3) better daily staffing flexibility to move idle workers to overworked departments, and (4) monthly flexibility to plan vacation slots and cross-utilize staff. Technicians can learn EKGs, nurses and nurse extenders (NEs) can be cross-trained in ancillary skills, and RNs can be cross-trained in nursing specialties.

The all-RN nursing staff, created in the name of "pure" primary-care nursing, had the best intentions but the worst results in terms of productivity. Despite RNs putting forth their best effort, each little increment of activity done in the name of "primary-care tradition" does little for quality and may erode productivity substantially. The better way to go in the spirit of the Deming method is to increase task delegation from RNs to lower-cost NEs and have NEs do clerical and simple administrative tasks, thus increasing the percentage of the RN's shift spent at the bedside. Some RNs still dislike the NE concept because they miss being the patients' sole caregiver, but as Mary Walton (1990) observed, the yielding of trust to the NE enhances both productivity and service response time (one attribute of service quality).

Trim bureaucracy. Many cost-conscious hospitals have recently worked to reduce management layers of supervision and limit the number of vice presidents to a select few (rather than three per 100 beds, the median peak level in the "good old days of 1988"). One hospital's nursing department had seven layers of supervisory staff trimmed to two (department director and vice president for patient care); 8 vice presidents were eliminated in 1991, and 28 managerial support staff were fired. Hospitals should also try to minimize the number of departments with under 8 to 9 FTEs by consolidating departments with similar skill requirements and functions. Hospitals, like HMOs, need to reduce bureaucracy as a semifixed cost of business. Hospitals should not utilize census-driven staffing. A staffing and scheduling system based on monitoring case-mix complexity, such as the one at Riverside Hospital, is a better alternative (Shukla 1985; Eastaugh 1985b). To be output driven (workload based) in setting staff levels is superior to simply linking staffing to the census.

Stage Three: When Can Incentives Be Provided?

It is a relatively easy task to cut costs by cutting services or service quality. We have outlined a two-stage strategy that undertakes the hard tasks of managing cost reductions without service reduction or quality reduction. Little attention, however, has been paid to the use of motivational tools. Incentives can improve employee attitudes concerning the innovations implemented under the first two stages. Monetary incentives involve the provision of alternative compensation to individual employees or to departments (the bonus pool is divided up among specific individuals). Stage three, the provision of incentives, will reinforce the new scheduling systems and new modes of work units. Adherence to reorganization into efficient work units (stage one) and compliance with scheduling systems (stage two) have been very successfully reinforced through the payment of incentive compensation.

Put incentives in context. In the hospital industry there are many jobs where individuals have considerable discretion over how they manage their work. Employees and medical staff have control over their personal commitment and their productivity. They can withhold it, or they can give it in exchange for something they value (cash, vacation time, nonmonetary rewards). Management needs carefully to present a philosophical and financial context for the announcement of incentive programs. Employee perception is critical. A system of perceived "bribes" will not change behavior, but "incentive pay" as a substitute for even more belt-tightening does improve productivity and morale.

Communicate the benefits of cost reduction. Many hospital administrators believe that reducing staff results in working harder and translates into lower employee morale. Indeed, it is true that if the staff cuts appear abrupt and arbitrary and offer no incentive "carrot" to maintain performance, morale may decline and the most outstanding workers may look elsewhere for job security. Staff cuts can improve morale, however, if employees share in the benefits of cost reduction and understand the new incentives and why things must change. For example, the institution and the employees can both be in a better financial position following a 15 percent reduction in employees and an average 9 percent increase in compensation per employee.

Help employees "work smarter." Management should explain to the employees why fiscal realities make net cost and employee reductions an imperative rather than an elective course of action. If the remaining employees receive significant incentive bonuses, they are less likely to unionize and/or strike. Incentive pay offers substantial benefits beyond the reductions in rates of absenteeism. One study at Henry Ford Hospital outlined how incentive compensation formulas can be provided to the three critical actors: employees, medical staff, and managers (Eastaugh 1985a). The keys are to provide bonus incentive pay by work subunits, thus reinforcing friendly acceptance of the efficient work and scheduling system, and to work smarter, not harder, thanks to these systems.

In the case of Henry Ford Hospital's incentive program, over 80 percent of the gross improvement in efficiency was returned to employees (including physicians), and only about 18 to 19 percent was retained by the hospital. In industry the facility or firm would generally retain 50 to 75 percent of the savings (Eastaugh, Sahney, and Steinhaver 1983). One could speculate that the spirit of a greater sharing of the benefits is more customary in nonprofit hospitals, and that professional and support staff in nonprofit institutions need large incentive rewards to alter existing patterns of behavior. Perhaps hospitals need to be more generous than industry to change the psychology engendered by cost reimbursement.

Henry Ford Hospital's alternative compensation plan has four important features. First, it is department based (not individual-specific until the department divides the bonus pool). Reliance on a department or work-subunit level of incentive reward encourages teamwork, relaxes central control, and encourages initiative and autonomy. Second, the program involves no "downside" risk of reduced salary, although business analysts fantasize that poor productivity performance should be rewarded with reduced wages. However, in the hospital context, the no-wage-reductions "riskless" approach was utilized to maximize acceptance of these new incentive-payment concepts.

Third, the bonus pay plan was originally operated for clinicians and employees before being expanded to include managers. Not surprisingly, incentive pay is equally as powerful a motivator of performance for managers as it is for employees. Although often overlooked, manager morale is just as important as employee morale. One encounters many managers who seek new opportunities because their employees received consecutive 9 or 11 percent wage increases while management wages had been frozen or constrained to increases of under 5 percent per annum. One should not simply align employee and firm interest under incentive-pay schemes and avoid aligning the financial status of the manager with the productivity performance of the organization. Managers who do more with less should be paid more. Inferior managers should have to face the economic consequences of their extravagance or inefficiency.

The fourth feature of the plan is that if the department or division achieves a target level of very high efficiency relative to carefully controlled HAS Monitrend peer comparisons, a special bonus should be provided each year or each quarter, whether or not it continues to improve. The rationale for such a special "kicker bonus" is that it will maintain the incentive to economize. The alternative— paying no additional bonus after a group has reached a certain maximum or optimal level of performance—implies that the benefits of the incentive plan fade when the incentive pay is no longer provided. If improvement has been made, why should a department or division maintain such high performance standards? Why not just let performance slide for two or three years, establish a new baseline, and earn a bonus relative to improvements on this new yardstick? This problem was addressed at Henry Ford Hospital by providing a "kicker bonus" for achieving a target level of efficiency—that is, giving a bonus for maintaining great performance. The approach avoids long-run motivation problems of constantly "chasing your own tail" in trying to forever reduce staff to earn a bonus. We shall discuss other incentive systems in the next chapter.

Use incentives to improve quality of care. Incentives are quite effective at stimulating the best employees to push the existing standard operating procedure (SOP) to the limits of efficiency without harming service quality. Who are the best employees? They are those innovative employees who exhibit episodic rule breaking under the SOP, not merely to add variety to their work life, but to demonstrate that SOP or JCAHO standards do little to foster efficiency or quality. Implementation of incentives, following a conceptual study on task requirements, common skills, job training, flexible staffing, and scheduling, causes the total organization to focus on making a given line of work most productive. With the help of incentives, a hospital can establish and maintain a dedication to high levels of productivity, craft excellence, and quality service (Eastaugh 1990; Deming 1986).

PHYSICIANS AND PRODUCTIVITY IMPROVEMENT

Physicians must be a part of the new drive for productivity under PPS. When physicians order unnecessary RVUs of activity that provide no marginal information gain in diagnosis or treatment decisions, real productivity declines. If the hospital's product is now a DRG case treated, and if the total payment and clinical outcome are the same whether 1,000 or 7,000 RVUs of activity are ordered, the extra marginal resources drive up costs without any benefit to the patient or the hospital. Having employees work harder in ancillary departments will not be useful unless the extra information resulting from that work is valuable. Some unnecessary RVUs will always be produced because of the uncertainties implicit in medical practice. The drive to contain hospital costs, however, will increasingly influence the judgment concerning what is acceptable slack versus what is waste. As the president of the AMA, Frank Jirka (1984) said: "We can find ways to eliminate the frill, the waste, the excessive treatments and tests, the unnecessary surgery, and the expensive extras of medical care. We have an obligation to do it, because we cannot put ourselves above or beyond the needs for more economy and efficiency."

Innovative physicians and other care providers are coming to realize that both efficiency and quality can coexist. Unfortunately, most labor-intensive institutions such as hospitals often believe that one cannot cut staff without harming quality. The corollary is the belief that more staff buy more quality service. But quality does not improve merely by increasing the number of staff available. Poor response time to a patient's call bell, slow transport time, and slow lab turnaround time are almost never resolved by adding more staff. Continual management oversight is needed to balance all the factors of service delivery if the greatest output for the smallest resource effort is to be achieved. Previously, the unequivocal message by society to hospitals was to expand access and technology. The equally unequivocal mandate in the 1990s is to cut costs by improved productivity management. One is hard pressed to cite a single example of a decline in staff that caused a real increase in adverse patient occurrence (APO) rates or mortality rates (InterQual 1991). Moreover, the one basic lesson that Japanese management should have taught American managers is that you can rapidly improve productivity and enhance quality simultaneously (Eastaugh 1985a).

THE SEARCH FOR PRODUCTIVE PRODUCT LINES

One handicap for hospital productivity analysis is that we do not know the resources per product line that go into our operations. Hospital administrators are very familiar with cost reimbursement and per diem averaging, but the PPS market dictates increased concern for true cost accounting and productivity resource-consumption controls. Consider two analogous service industries. One could not manage a rent-a-car operation by charging $110 per diem regardless of whether the vehicle being rented was a compact car or a 30-foot truck. One could not manage a restaurant by charging $14 per meal irrespective of whether the consumer ordered toast or steak and lobster. However, in hospital finance we have been uniformly allocating more than 30 percent of inpatient costs as per diem nursing, room and board, and routine daily services. With the advent of DRGs, such a per diem catchall costing method assumes that all patients utilize equal amounts of nursing time, whether the case is simple or complex. Each patient utilizes a near-uniform amount of laundry and linen, but a crude costing system that has more than one-fourth of costs in per diems is nearing invalidity. Managers and clinicians need to know how much hospitals are wasting resources in the production of intermediate products (radiology, lab tests, and so on) and how this waste might be reduced. Since hospital care is becoming more competitive and businesslike, it will reassure nonprofit managers to know that every dollar invested in good control systems can be paid back many times annually in reduced waste. In other words, it is cost-beneficial to take the time to perform true cost accounting, whether one deals in compacts or trucks, toast or lobster, or, in the case of hospital managers, LPNs and aides or RNs, or lab equipment versus personnel time, in the selection of production-mix input decisions (Wood 1984).

EXPAND OUTPUT OR CUT INPUTS?

PPS has provided strong incentives to expand alternative delivery system (ADS) activities, including surgicenters, PPOs, and freestanding emergency centers. Productivity improves if equal numbers of employees can provide increased output by shifting staff out of the inpatient-care business and into ADS activities. However, nonhospital-based providers of ADS services, including physicians, may rapidly saturate this course of output expansion.

The Medicare PPS system offers ample incentive to expand volume. The PPS system implicitly assigns a 100 percent variable cost factor—that is, hospitals receive 100 percent of the payment for each additional case and, conversely, lose 100 percent of the payment for each case lost. This provides a clear incentive for individual hospitals to increase admissions, since the additional revenue they will receive for the extra cases will greatly exceed the additional costs incurred to treat the extra cases. To make this point clear, consider two hypothetical low-cost firms, hospital A and hospital Z.

If hospital A experiences a 1 percent increase in annual volume, its costs may only increase slightly, probably by the costs of the supplies used per extra patient. Additional revenue may exceed additional cost by a ratio of 10 to 1, and an economist studying the firm might conclude that the short-run variable costs are 10 percent of average costs in this one year at A. Next consider hospital Z. It has experienced a 20 percent increase in volume over three years. The hospital may have to increase staff (depending on the situation, staff may increase, for example, by 5 to 15 percent), probably increase its administrative capacity (say, 2 to 10 percent), and increase supplies plus square feet of space available pro rata. Additional revenues at Z may exceed additional costs by a ratio of anywhere between 2 to 1 and 5 to 4. An economist studying the firm might conclude that the medium-run (three-year) variable costs are 50 to 80 percent of average costs (McClain and Eastaugh, 1983). The essential three points are that variable costs depend on the size of the volume change, management's resolve to improve productivity, and the time frame. With regard to the second point, doing more with less cannot be achieved with a CEO acting as a "superintendent" by saying: "If volume increases 7.5 percent, I expand my staff by over 9.5 percent, but when volume declines 10 percent in a year, I do not reduce my staff."

One of the basic tenets of good management is that deferring action, especially painful action, often makes the situation worse over the long run. For example, one director of nursing involved in the Minneapolis nursing strike of 1984 stated that "the wimpy CEO could not lay off 80 nurses in January, so he waited five months and was forced to announce layoffs for 140. This proves that hospital managers do not manage effectively." Needless to say, a good labor representative might call for the "CEO's head" if the layoffs were for 80, or 140, or even 20. However, in implementing the productivity-improvement program, senior management will have to fully communicate their concerns to department managers if they desire lasting cost reductions. Each specific action must be placed in a framework of what should be done, by whom, and when. To some extent, department managers should assist in developing the action plan. Too frequently, the department managers are perceived as not really part of hospital management for three reasons. First, they have problems identifying with the management group and instead identify and socialize with the people with whom they work. Second, they therefore resist staff reductions or job/task reorganization in the name of protecting their people. Third, they believe that the larger the department's FTEs, the higher their prestige within the organization. It is not uncommon for a department manager to proclaim with pride that the number of employees in his or her area has doubled in five years. This phenomenon is typical of nonprofit organizations. Again, we should reward managers who do more with less rather than inflate the number of employees each year (Eastaugh 1990, 1986).

DOING MORE WITH LESS

The productivity-improvement issue has been around for two decades, but until now the will to act has been buried under the comfortable blanket of cost reimbursement. The economic shock to hospitals of prospective price payment may produce a flurry of petty, short-sighted cost reductions. Hiring freezes may prevent facilities from acquiring talented people who have the requisite management-science skills to save the institution. Morale will decline if continuing-education programs are sharply reduced, anticipated raises are chopped, and marketing and reorganization plans are canceled. Fruitful cost reduction should not be so short-run, superficial, and spasmodic as to "cut a little fat" or so ruthless and indiscriminate as to impair the hospital's ability to survive in the long run (Suver, Oppermann, and Helmer 1984; Sumeren 1986). Any significant cost-reduction effort must involve a significant reduction in the number of employees. Touting the snake oil of cost containment without pain and staff cuts is a very poor guide to survival under PPS.

Because hospitals are a labor-intensive service industry, we have emphasized labor productivity. However, productivity has a capital-management and materials-management component. For example, one should care about the hundreds of years of "reduced available equipment life" in poorly managed hospitals with inferior maintenance programs. Under PPS the hospital industry cannot afford to perform as poorly as the Department of Defense in the area of capital maintenance.

There is little question that it is more difficult to be a hospital manager today than ever before. That difficulty is going to be compounded many times over by the PPS pressure to downsize and "downstaff" hospital operations. We now have a system for closing out excess beds, and it is called "prospective poverty system" DRG prices. Cost reimbursement and health planning prevented bed closures, which kept the pathology in the system and inflated hospital costs. In the future, hospitals can trim costs through productivity programs and/or contract their scope of product lines by closing the less productive elements in their DRG portfolio. If a hospital does not do a good job in either of these areas, it may have to close. Closure would be tragic to all concerned, for as we know, a closed hospital does nobody any good. Without doubt, employee incentive systems are our best tool to trim costs and maintain morale.

HOSPITAL NURSING PRODUCTIVITY

The hospital nursing profession is undergoing a major transformation. Task delegation and the allocation of nurses within the hospital have become major medical economics issues for the 1990s (Aiken 1990). Nursing-department employees represent 62 percent of the hospital employees and 36 percent of hospital expenses (Eastaugh 1987). Hospitals increased their employment of full-time registered nurses (RNs) per 100 patient days by 56 percent in the period 1982–88. The report of the Secretary's Commission on Nursing (1988) indicated that the hospitals reporting the most severe RN shortages have been the leaders in replacing licensed practical nurses (LPNs) with more expensive RNs. Alternative labor input in the form of the technician nurse extender (NE) is an increasingly popular approach to alleviating the problem of inadequate nurse staffing levels (Klein 1989). While a careful empirical study has not yet been done to assess the degree to which employment of NEs and efficient task delegation to clerks or LPNs can enhance department productivity and free nurses to perform their unique clinical activities, in theory, NEs can intensify the marginal value product of the most educated nurses when RNs are able to concentrate their workday around the most severely ill patients.

Hospital nursing has undergone a number of major organizational shifts, from functional nursing in the 1940s to team nursing in the 1960s and primary nursing in the 1970s. The 1960s' innovation of team nursing set the experienced RN as the team leader, working with nursing aides and LPNs. The team leader delegated much of the patient care to the team members and planned the care for each patient during that specific shift (Shukla 1983b). Team nursing had the financial benefits of cost-effectiveness and the positive and negative aspects of any task-oriented system. Hospital administrators liked team nursing's focus on centralization of control while nurse educators desired a new system that would focus on the autonomy of the BSN-trained RN (and would maximize reliance on RNs while decreasing employment of LPNs).

Primary nursing became popular in the 1970s as nursing focused on the need for autonomy and the evolution of a knowledge-based professional practice (Aiken and Mullinix 1987). Primary nursing involves decentralization of the nursing unit and the establishment of a responsibility relationship between a nurse and the patient. The primary nurse writes a 24-hour-care plan for each patient, and the associate nurse implements the plan when the primary nurse is not working. Primary nursing has the advantage of improved continuity of care but carries the cost of a smaller number of patients per RN (Shukla 1983b).

The nurse extender concept, as a substitute or complement to primary-care nursing, has become increasingly popular since 1985 (Eastaugh and Regan 1990). The NE technologist label is an attempt to rid the profession of any sexist bent and recruit men (NEs are typically two-thirds male and earn 20 to 45 percent less per hour than RNs).

Nurse extender technicians became popular because the hospital sector experienced difficulty in finding a sufficient supply of RNs for primary nursing staffs (Eastaugh 1985a). Some nursing groups were not receptive to the NE concept because of fears that it represented a return to team nursing and under-trained LPNs with a new job title (Lenehan 1988). However, task delegation to

NEs by itself does not undermine the standardization of nurse education. In fact, the realization that the nation needed more caregivers and that NEs would still be under the control of the nursing department prompted the nursing literature to become less militant. Now the NE is referred to in the literature as a "technical assistant to an experienced RN in a primary partnership" or an "executive administrative assistant assisting the executive nurse" (Manthey 1989; McCarthy 1989). Such glowing titles may seem unimportant to economists, but in the workplace it is important for job retention that NEs not be labeled reborn LPNs who do "scutwork" or "menial tasks." One profession's menial task is another profession's vital activity, so NEs spend most of their workday performing a "noninterpretive" collection of vital signs, EKGs, lab slips, and paperwork.

The Production Function Approach

Production-function studies of technical efficiency (productivity) have been done by economists since the 1930s. Production functions are useful to understand how resources are combined by the department or firm (hospital) to produce some particular level of output and to ascertain how these resources complement or substitute for one another in the service-production process. (Arthur Young and Policy Analysis Inc. 1987).

A number of studies have analyzed production functions in business and in the hospital sector (Arthur Young and Policy Analysis Inc. 1986; Kalirajan and Shand 1989). The first major study of American hospital production functions involved a sample of 60 Ohio nonteaching hospitals in 1975. Hellinger (1975) utilized a translog (transcendental logarithmic) production function, which attenuates or eliminates restrictions on the functional form, thereby leaving as much generality and flexibility as possible in the service-production-estimation process (in contrast to the traditional Cobb-Douglas model). The translog form used in this study involves two basic assumptions. First, managers monitor nursing costs when deciding the appropriate staff mix and range or level of hospital output and nurse workload. This assumption does not mean that nurse managers are perfect cost minimizers operating at the production possibility frontier of 100 percent technical efficiency. The second assumption is that nursing departments exhibit constant returns to scale in producing their output; that is, a fourfold increase in inputs leads to a fourfold increase in output. Consequently, there is no reason to presuppose that nurses are any more productive in a 1,022-bed hospital than in a 260-bed hospital. (Previous hospital cost studies, not focused on the nursing department, reported very shallow economies of scale of only 11 percent. These studies are surveyed in chapter 1, table 1.5).

In comparing isoquants—curves producing the same output for different quantities of inputs—two extreme situations can exist. Under perfect complementary production between inputs, no substitution at all is possible between inputs A and B, and inputs A and B must always be used in fixed proportions (isoquants are straight downward-sloping lines) (Feldstein 1989). Under the opposite extreme, perfect substitutability between inputs defines the isoquants as perfect right angles. In the first step in the data analysis to follow, a translog production function will be estimated from data at 29 hospitals. The second step measures the curvature of the nursing isoquants and thereby the substitution among inputs (the elasticity of substitution).

Since nursing is a complex production process, we will be assessing a production process with five inputs and thus five-dimensional isoquants. Between each pair of inputs partial elasticities of substitution will be measured (e.g., NE substitution for RNs). The five basic inputs studied include (1) NEs (nurse extenders), (2) RNs, (3) H (house-staff residents and interns performing some nursing activities while nursing is understaffed), (4) A (clerks, LPNs, and nurse aides), and (5) E (capital).

Sample Framework and Data Analysis

Collection of data on labor inputs is straightforward and has been done in a number of previous studies. Nursing output is specified by a point-scoring system sold by the largest proprietary vendor of nurse workload and nurse-scheduling systems. (Medicus System Corporation 1989). This same system tracks work hours to measure the contribution of nonphysician inputs (input factors 1, 2, and 4). House-staff resident and intern input was measured not on an annual basis, but only on a one-shot, two-month sampling basis in one year, 1985. However, we have no reason to presuppose that house-staff input to nursing activities should exhibit any major change in 1986–88. Filled residency slots have been largely time-invariant for the 14 sample teaching hospitals, and physician labor in nursing activities only ranges from 0.1 to 1.2 percent of nursing activities. To omit this measured work input in the analysis would slightly overstate the productivity of nursing departments in certain hospitals.

One last caveat must be presented concerning measurement error in this study: Measurement of capital inputs must avoid the pitfalls of using depreciation charges to more accurately reflect differences in the age and productivity of the capital stock. I have used the same index I employed in the Arthur Young study (1987) to adjust the capital expenses for differences across the 29 sample hospitals in the average age of their capital stocks. For each hospital the ratio of accumulated depreciation to total assets is taken as a measure of age. Age-adjusted capital input was calculated as follows:

$$E = UA \times \mathrm{Exp}\,(M - R) \tag{9.1}$$

where UA is the unadjusted capital expenses, R is the ratio of accumulated depreciation to total assets, M is the mean value of R for the sample, and Exp is the inverse natural logarithm.

The sample is a convenience sample of hospitals with active nursing-activity-research programs: 15 of 17 hospitals in a study by Eastaugh and Regan (1990) and 14 of 45 hospitals in an earlier study (Arthur Young and Policy Analysis Inc. 1987). Obviously, the sample is not generalizable to all American hospitals. The more progressive hospitals, with active support for health-services research, may have production technologies (scheduling and staff education; Eastaugh 1985b) that are ten years more advanced than those of the average American hospital. Each of the sample hospitals had subscribed to the same nurse-workload system since 1985, and the hospitals ranged in size from 194 to 1,092 beds. The hypothetical frontier production function can be expressed as

$$y_{ij} = \Pi_k (X_{ijk})^{\beta}_k \, e^{u}_{ij}, \tag{9.2}$$

where Y_{ij} is the nurse output of the jth hospital in the ith period for periods 1–4 (1985, . . . , 1988) and x_{ijk} is the kth input applied by the jth hospital in the ith period. If the jth hospital realizes its full technical efficiency at 100 percent, then inefficiency μ_j takes the value zero, and if not, μ_j takes a value less than zero depending on the extent of the lost productivity. The e^{uij} term provides a measure of hospital-specific productivity, and improvement in e^{uij} will be reflected in higher mean productivity over time. Inefficiency can be expressed as

$$\mu_j = \ln y_{ij} - (\Sigma \, \beta_k \ln x_{ijk} + v_{ij}). \tag{9.3}$$

Estimation of μ_j and then E^{uj} is possible once density functions for μ and v are assumed. Let μ follow a half-normal distribution and v follow the full normal distribution. (The validity of the half-normal distribution was verified at the end of the analysis by plotting the combined residual $(\mu + v)$, the hospital's technical efficiency and the output levels.) Equation (9.2) can be rewritten as

$$y_{ij} = \Pi_k (x_{ijk})^{\beta k} \, e^{\epsilon ij}, \tag{9.4}$$

where $\epsilon_{ij} = \mu_j + v_{ij}$.

The estimation of the maximum possible stochastic output, had the hospital realized its full technical efficiency, is carried out by applying maximum-likelihood methods (Johnston 1989) to equation (9.4). With this model one can estimate individual hospital technical efficiencies together with the mean technical efficiency using four years of panel data (dummy variable D [0,1] for each of the last three years 1986, 1987, 1988). One can hopefully also target some factors causing variation in technical efficiencies in nursing among the 29 sample hospitals.

Maximum-likelihood methods of estimation were applied to equation (9.4), and the parameter estimates of the translog model are presented in table 9.1. The ratio of hospital-specific variability in productivity was significant at the 0.01 level, indicating that productivity dominates in explaining the total variability of nurse output produced. Judging by the significance of the four dummy variables, we can reject the hypothesis that productivity was time-invariant over

Table 9.1
Translog Production Function for Medical/Surgical Nursing Service Delivery in a Sample of 29 Hospitals, 1985–1988

Variable[a]	Parameter Estimate[b] (Maximum Likelihood)
D_1, 1986	0.002 (9.4)
D_2, 1987	0.013 (28.1)
D_3, 1988	0.022 (50.4)
ßNE,E	0.082 (7.5)
ßH,E	0.098 (18.2)
ßH,NE	0.137 (29.3)
ßRN,H	-0.059 (9.6)
ßRN,E	0.102 (19.4)
ßRN,NE	-0.098 (24.1)
ßA,NE	0.089 (17.0)
ßA,H	-.006 (1.4)
ßA,RN	-0.047 (8.3)
ßA,E	0.119 (16.8)
Constant χ	0.038 (7.7)

Source: Eastaugh (1990)

[a]NE = nurse extenders, RNs, H = house-staff residents and interns doing some nursing activities while understaffed, A = clerks, LPNs, and nurse aides, E = capital.

[b]T-values in parentheses. Log likelihood = 42.075.

Table 9.2

Allen Partial Elasticities of Substitution for the Input Factors of Medical/Surgical Nursing Productivity

Lines 1-5: own price partial elasticities negative (as expected).

1.	NE/NE[a]	-0.234	Complements
2.	RN/RN	-0.157	Complements
3.	H/H	-0.140	Complements
4.	A/A	-0.079	Complements
5.	E/E	-0.388	Complements
6.	NE/E	0.353	Substitutes
7.	H/E	0.796	Substitutes
8.	H/NE	0.907	Substitutes
9.	RN/H	-0.231	Complements
10.	RN/E	0.519	Substitutes
11.	RN/NE	-0.448	Complements
12.	A/NE	0.586	Substitutes
13.	A/H	-0.026	Complements
14.	A/RN	-0.230	Complements
15.	A/E	0.372	Substitutes

Source: Eastaugh (1990).

[a]NE = nurse extenders, RNs, H = house-staff residents and interns doing some nursing activities while understaffed, A = clerks, LPNs, and nurse aides, E = capital.

the four years. Most of the parameters not involving the two weakest variables (*H* and *E*) are significant at the 0.05 level.

A second alternative partial elasticity can also be derived. The Allen elasticity of substitution holds constant the quantities of all other inputs in addition to the level of nurse output. The Allen elasticities are related econometrically to the cross-price elasticity of demand for factor inputs (Johnston 1989), for example, the demand for input 1 (nurse extenders) to change in the price of input 2 (RNs). The sign of a cross-price elasticity of demand (column 3 of table 9.2) by itself is an indicator of gross substitution—a negative sign indicating complementary factors, a positive sign indicating substitution. As line 11 of table 9.2 reveals, a negative sign on the elasticity of demand for NE labor with respect to the price of RN labor indicates that as RN labor becomes more costly, the labor of NEs is used less extensively in place of RNs. On the positive side, this suggests that NEs and RNs are complementary team members, not in competition with each other. On the other hand, this suggests that a rapidly inflating costly all-RN nursing staff trades away efficiency by avoiding the opportunity for NE-induced productivity gains. Moreover, using nonemployee RNs, the temporary agency nurses, can cost many urban hospitals as much as $55 to $75 per hour.

The NEs substitute fairly well and fluidly for clerks and LPNs (line 12) while complementing RNs. A positive sign in line 8 on the elasticity of demand for NE labor with respect to the price of house-staff (resident) labor indicates that as house-staff labor (H) becomes more costly per hour, the labor of NEs is used more extensively in place of residents. As some state regulators and hospital managers have moved to restrict the house-staff workweek—fewer hours at the same fixed annual wage—this raises the hourly wage of the house staff and raises the employment level of NEs. However, the negative sign in line 9 of table 9.2 reveals that no increase in RN employment can be expected as New York and other states implement a maximum hourly workweek for residents and interns.

Lines 6, 7, 10, and 15 in table 9.2 have the expected positive signs, indicating that labor can substitute for capital (0.01 level of significance). Line 7 has the highest observed elasticity, suggesting that the highly skilled M.D. members of house staff, with their technical diagnostic skill as doctors, partially substitute for more equipment and physical capital. This generalization may be increasingly true in the future as more residents benefit from economic grand rounds, think-before-testing education programs, and the cost-effective clinical decision-making ethic.

Improving Nurse Productivity

The three dummy variables at the top of table 9.1 indicate that nurse productivity for this sample of 29 hospitals was not time-invariant over the four-year period. Mean nurse productivity for each cross-sectional equation improved from 0.696 in 1985 to 0.741 in 1988, but in 1988 nursing departments were still realizing only 74.1 percent of their technical efficiency (productivity). While averages are interesting, distributions are more policy relevant. Table 9.3 lists the average productivity level across the 29 nursing departments and the factor input (nurse extenders) with the two highest t-values (from table 9.1). Individual nurse productivity ratings ranged from 0.56 to 0.89. Table 9.3 suggests discrete differences in production technologies as well as differences in input mix. This wide range could in theory reflect differences in organizational efficiency (Kalirajan and Shand 1989) or differences in the availability and use of factor inputs (e.g., a shortage of nurses; Eastaugh 1987). However, the 7 hospitals with the worst nursing productivity at the top of table 9.3 employed no nurse extender technicians, operated a 100 percent RN primary-care nursing organization, and exhibited productivity 9 to 16 percent below average. The 5 hospitals in table 9.3 with the highest levels of nurse productivity made heavy use of nurse extenders: 2 used the team-nursing organizational concept, but 3 employed primary-care nursing with a 57 to 62 percent BSN RN staff.

In summary, the results suggest that (1) primary-care nursing can be either highly productive or inefficient; (2) the all-RN nursing staff, used in only 8 of

Table 9.3
Frequency Distribution of Nursing Departments' Productivity and Nurse Extender Staffing Mix

Productivity Level (Range)	Number of Hospitals	Percentage of Hospitals	Ratio of NEs to RNs
0.55-0.60	3	10.34	0.0
0.60-0.65	4	13.79	0.0
0.66-0.70	4	13.79	0.16
0.71-0.75	8	27.59	0.37
0.76-0.80	5	17.24	0.54
0.81-0.85	3	10.34	0.79
0.86-0.90	2	6.90	0.71
Total	29	100.00	mean = 0.35

0.72 = mean productivity

Source: Eastaugh (1990).

the 29 hospitals, reported the worst productivity performance; (3) a shortage of nurses did not drag down productivity levels in table 9.3, as the four cities with the tightest nursing markets contained the 5 hospitals with the highest levels of productivity; and (4) employment of nurse extenders reduces wasted labor and enhances productivity.

The last of these four conclusions indicates a number of avenues for future research. For example, the results at the end of the last column in table 9.3 weakly indicate that nurse extenders, as with any labor input, may approach a level of diminishing returns. Does having 8 to 10 NEs per 10 RNs constitute a zone of diminishing returns? Does a primary-care nursing staff with greater than 80 percent BSN RNs constitute an inefficient staff mix of diminishing returns? Does deploying 5 to 8 NEs per 10 RNs harm patient-care quality? Judging from the deployment of NEs at prestigious hospitals (e.g., Johns Hopkins Hospital; Eastaugh and Regan 1990), task delegation can enhance the quality of patient care.

Last, what additional tasks can be delegated to NEs beyond obtaining vital signs and EKG results, patient transport, procuring supplies and equipment, procedural assistance, and paperwork (e.g., lab slips)? Some of the 21 hospitals utilizing NEs have begun to utilize specialist technicians to dress wounds and do other nursing functions. Other activities performed by nurse extenders are outlined in table 9.4. Progressive nurse managers will participate in careful

Table 9.4
Selective Examples of Nonnursing Menial Tasks versus Important Nursing Tasks

Nonnursing Tasks to Delegate to Nurse Extenders (NE)a	Important Nursing Tasks
1. Obtaining vital signs	Interpreting vital signs
2. Patient transport	Physical assessment and condition monitoring
3. Housekeeping and bedmaking	Technological monitoring, infusion pumps, Swan-Ganz catheters
4. Meal trays	Tube and IV feedings
5. Physician procedural assistance (pelvic exam)	IV therapy: nitroglycerine, Insulin, TPA drips
6. Venipuncture	Evaluation/outcome documentation
7. Getting supplies and equipment	Discharge planning
8. Secretarial (e.g., lab slips)	Special tube placements: NGs, foleys, oxygen therapy
9. Obtaining EKGs	Narcotic count

Source: Eastaugh (1990).

aNonnursing tasks, often called "scutwork," are activities easily delegated to NEs in a high-productivity unit.

studies to set standards, study task-delegation feasibility, and circumscribe the job descriptions for two to three levels of NE technicians (Powers 1990; Bennett and Hylton 1990). With future funding limitations, barebones reimbursement dictates that the recent tradition of 100 percent RN primary-care nursing must be abandoned. Development of an efficient staff-mix criterion in nursing should enhance nursing's rising sense of professionalism. In this regard Manthey (1988, 1970), one of the initial founders of primary-care nursing, has recently subscribed to the idea that the 100 percent RN concept is not a necessary component for primary-care nursing. Maximizing RN hospital employment levels is hardly a desirable or economical goal unless America has a gross oversupply of nurses. Since no such oversupply exists, increased reliance on nurse extenders is good economics, good nursing, and good medicine. The validity of this assertion will be retested, utilizing 1991 data, in the next section.

Alternatives to Production Functions

The production functions in the previous section are helpful in assessing nurse productivity. For line managers there is a simpler technique called data-

Table 9.5

A Data-Envelopment Analysis of the Relationship between Productivity and Nursing Organization

(N = 39 Hospital Inpatient Nursing Departments, 1991)

	Efficient Departments	Inefficient Departments
Primary-care nursing (all-RN staff)	0	7
Team nursing (limited use of nurse extendersa)	3	9
Primary-care nursing (limited use of nurse extendersa)	3	6
Heavy reliance on 0.56-0.8 nurse extenders per RN	11	0
	—	—
	17	22

aRatio of nurse extenders to RNs in the 0.17 to 0.41 range.

envelopment analysis (DEA) for considering relative labor productivity between hospitals. DEA is a mathematical programming technique that optimizes the relative technical efficiency (productivity) ratio of current inputs over current outputs for each nursing department. DEA has the advantage of neatly dividing departments into two classes (efficient and inefficient) and producing a summary scalar efficiency ratio for each nursing department. DEA has been used in the health care field since publication of the Charns, Cooper, and Rhodes (1981) study. The data are for 1991, and the sample has been expanded from 29 to 39 hospitals (with the inclusion of 2 public hospitals, 6 voluntary tax-exempt hospitals, and 2 for-profit hospitals).

The data-envelopment analysis sums up all nursing services and takes RN, NE, and other-nurse (e.g. LPN) labor input into account separately, assessing the overall performance of the inpatient nursing department. The DEA model generates a scalar efficiency categorization using nonparametric deterministic mathematical programming to optimize the technical efficiency ratio in each department. One generic advantage of DEA analysis is that each input and each output variable can be measured independently in a useful unit without being transformed into a single metric. One advantage of the DEA analysis in tables 9.5, 9.6 and 9.7 is that in contrast to previous DEA studies of nursing (Nunamaker 1983), output measures are not simply inpatient days, but rather the DRG-adjusted Medicus-standardized nurse workload (Medicus 1989; Eastaugh 1990).

The sample of 39 hospitals divides into two categories in table 9.5. The 17

Table 9.6
Logistic Regression Analysis of the Relationship between Nursing Organization, Nurse Extenders, and Efficiency
(N = 39 Hospital Inpatient Nursing Departments, 1991)

Independent Variables[a]	Beta	Standard Error	R
Nurse extenders high[b]	3.16*	1.37	.291
Nurse extenders low[c]	1.43*	1.14	.128
Primary nursing	-.89	1.03	-.006
Team nursing	-.92	1.01	-.004

[a]Dependent variable efficiency classification of DEA (Table 9.5). Only 2 of the 3 variables
 need be included in each category.
[b]Ratio of nurse extenders to RNs in the 0.56 to 0.80 range.
[c]Ratio of nurse extenders to RNs in the 0.17 to 0.41 range.
*Chi-square test significant at 0.05 level.

efficient nursing departments are not necessarily efficient in the absolute sense (compared to an updated production function like that in table 9.3, their productivity is 9 to 21 percent less than perfect), but in the DEA analysis they represent "best-performance" departments compared to the 22 inefficient departments. The inefficient departments have productivity levels that are 28 to 44 percent less than perfect. The chi-squared value of table 9.5 is significant at the 0.05 level with two degrees of freedom. It is interesting to note that 3 of 16 primary-care nursing departments achieved the DEA label of efficient by employing a staffing ratio of NEs to RNs in the 0.30–0.41 range, whereas all 100 percent RN nursing departments were found to be inefficient. The 11 departments with heavy reliance on NEs were all judged efficient by 1991.

To validate the DEA results, a logistic regression equation was run, and the results are reported in table 9.6. Primary-care nursing in itself was not a statistically significant drag on productivity, given that by 1991, 9 of 16 primary-care nursing departments had begun to make use of task delegation to nurse extenders. The more interesting question is what the 22 inefficient hospitals can do differently to improve productivity. The DEA output of the average inefficient department divided by the guidepost value if efficient in 1991 is presented in table 9.7. The values-if-efficient denominators (bottom of the fractions in the last column of table 9.7) are obtained by multiplying the peak technical efficiency ratio of 0.91 by the current values, then subtracting the slack (Grosskopf and Valdmanis 1987). Nursing departments should work to trim the inefficiency

Table 9.7
A Data-Envelopment Analysis of Average Inefficiency
(N = 39 Hospitals, 1991)

Factor (Workload/Input)	Current Value Value If Efficient in 1991
•Workload per Case-Mix-Adjusted Admission	
1. General nursing administration	18.6% inefficient
2. Assessing and monitoring physical condition	17.4% inefficient
3. Planning for patient discharge	14.9% inefficient
4. Completing evaluation/outcome documentation	14.8% inefficient
5. Administering tube or IV feedings	9.5% inefficient
6. Placing special tubes (NGs, Foleys, O_2)	8.2% inefficient
7. Monitoring tech equipment (Swan-Ganz catheter)	7.9% inefficient
•Labor Input	
1. Nursing administration	21.3% oversupply
2. Nurse extender (technicians)	24.7% undersupply
•Uncontrollable (Ownership)	
1. Hospital is for-profit (N = 2)	output/input 2.4% above mean
2. Hospital is public facility (N = 2)	output/input 4.9% above mean

associated with the seven top tasks in table 9.7 and should especially target ways to trim unneeded bureaucratic tasks. Judging by the results for labor inputs, the 22 inefficient nursing departments could trim administrative activities by 21.3 percent and expand the supply of NE employees by 24.7 percent. The one uncontrollable variable in table 9.7 is hospital ownership type (not under the control of the nursing department). One would not want to generalize much from a sample of only two for-profit hospitals and two public hospitals, but it is interesting to note that the efficiency levels were 2.4 percent better for ''inefficient for-profit'' hospitals than for peer hospitals and 4.9 percent lower for the two public hospitals. In the Valdmanis (1990) study Michigan public hospitals in 1982 had slightly higher levels of productivity than tax-exempt voluntary hospitals.

Task delegation to nurse extenders, a leaner nursing administration bureaucracy, and nurse-scheduling systems using optimizer linear programming software (Shorr 1991) appear to be the three keys to enhancing nursing productivity. Nurse productivity is important because nurses represent over 60 percent of hospital employees. However, other departments have need for productivity

Table 9.8
Productivity Standards for Performance in Select Departments, 1991

Department	Performance (Target Standards per Unit of Service (UOS)	
	Good. 70th Percentile	*Very Good* 90th Percentile
Radiation oncology	1.16	0.73
Respiratory therapy (RT)	0.25	0.20
Pulmonary (in dept. RT)	0.57	0.46
EEG (in dept. RT)	1.42	1.25
ECG (in Heart Center, HC)	0.60	0.51
Echocardiology (in dept. HC)	1.63	1.47
Emergency Department (ED)	1.77	1.50
Behavioral Services (M.H.& S.W.)	7.3	6.4
Laundry (linen per diem)a	16 lbs/patient day	14 lbs/patient day

Source: Eastaugh Consulting Services, N = 199 hospitals.

aProductivity enhancement can also involve decreasing unnecessary units of activity or unneeded output, for example, minimizing linen consumption per patient per day.

improvement. Better scheduling systems for staff and patients can enhance productivity in radiology, respiratory therapy, and a number of other departments. Staffing standards for efficient (good, 70th percentile) hospital departments and very good (top 10 percent) departments are given in table 9.8. Data-envelopment analysis can also be used on smaller-scale health care facilities, like rural primary-care centers and community health centers (Huang and McLaughlin 1989).

A total quality-management program should focus on both external customers (patients, employers) and internal customers. Frequently one department does not understand how its work product is utilized by the next department; for example, quality and productivity may be enhanced if a hospital lab stops skimping on hiring a $7.50 per hour technician without which the talents of a $75 per hour emergency-room doctor are being wasted waiting for lab results. The concept of internal customers (Deming 1986), fostering respect and efficient interdependency between departments, can help morale in the total organization. Doctors are a "customer" of the nursing department, the medical floor is a "customer" of the recovery room, and the recovery room is a "customer" of the operating room. Sometimes certain departments can be inappropriate or excessive customers of another department. In the typical hospital the patient-transport department should have its work done by nurses for 0.3 to 0.4 percent of the workweek. For example, in one hospital the nurses were spending 8.1 percent of their time doing patient transport. Was the patient-transport department understaffed (so it needed nurses to do its work)? No. Patient transport was overstaffed 90 percent and would typically fill up its day by creating unnecessary meetings and calling up nurses to transport patients to radiology (where three or four idle patient-transport employees would talk to the nurse on line). Over-staffing is seldom a self-diagnosing problem. Departments fill up the idle time with makework activity while other departments go understaffed.

Consider an example of doctors as customers of the nursing department. Attending physicians at one hospital often complained that they seldom saw the same faces twice. A team was formed to study the problem and provide solutions. The problem was caused by an insufficient supply of RNs to recruit and a nursing department that believed in 100 percent RN primary-care nursing. Rather than continue the expensive habit of hiring agency nurses that were new to the de-partment and unknown to the doctors, the solution involved maximizing use of existing RNs' clinical skills by employing NEs to do the 43 percent of nurses' work that the law dictated that a nonnurse could perform. Morale among nurses improved because their time was no longer wasted doing menial work. Morale among attending physicians improved because they could identify specific RNs in connection with their individual patients. A good hospital does not need a sign Our Nurses Care; the RNs, NEs, managers, and physicians just know it.

EVOLVING A LEANER ORGANIZATION

Hospitals should annually reevaluate their workload-driven staffing ratio in line with fiscal goals and shifts in payment rates. Managers should use ''best-cost'' standards from engineering studies. Staff need to realize that downstaffing usually correlates with better-quality care (Walton 1990) and that staff-to-patient ratios can be cut by over 15 percent in many cases (e.g., Emanuel Hospital in Portland in 1990 and Beloit Hospital in Wisconsin in 1987). White Memorial Medical Center in East Los Angeles reduced nursing hours per patient day from 10 in 1988 to 7.1 by September 1990, while total FTEs per adjusted patient day declined from 4.94 to 4.0. Redundant staffing in a fat organization leads to low-quality care (Ahmadi 1989; Caldwell, McEachern, and Davis 1990).

In direct-patient-care departments bureaucracy, paperwork, and other useless units of activity should be eliminated. One hospital had six patient charting forms until this process was replaced by a single flow sheet in 1991. Lab results should be reported to the floor and the emergency department by computer, and med-ication orders should be either faxed to the pharmacy or sent by computer systems to eliminate the need to transcribe orders. The modern hospital should realize that its employees are increasingly members of the MTV television generation and should communicate productivity messages and Deming-method teamwork results to staff through interactive visual communication. Changes can be added to the disk each month, and employees can run their disks at home or in the hospital.

REFERENCES

Ahmadi, M. (1989). "Traditional versus Nontraditional Work Schedules." *Industrial Management* 31:2 (March–April), 20–23.

Aiken, L. (1990). "Charting the Future of Hospital Nursing." *Image: The Journal of Nursing Scholarship* 22:2 (February), 72–77.

Aiken, L., and Mullinix, C. (1987). "The Nurse Shortage—Myth or Reality." *New England Journal of Medicine* 317:10 (October 18), 641–651.

Arthur Young and Policy Analysis Inc. (1987). *Study of the Financing of Graduate Medical Education.* 2 vols. Report DHHS 100–87–0155. Washington, D.C.: DHHS (January).

Bays, K. (1984). "A Common Sense Approach to Productivity." *Trustee* 37:5 (May), 29–32.

Begun, J., and Feldman, R. (1990). "Policy and Research on Health Manpower Regulation: Never Too Late to Deregulate?" in *Advances in Health Economics and Health Services Research*, ed. by Scheffler, R., Greenwich, Conn.: JAI Press, 79–109.

Behner, K., Fogg, L., Fournier, L., and Frankenbach, J. (1990) "Nursing Resource Management." *Health Care Management Review* 15:4 (Fall), 63–71.

Bennett, M., and Hylton, J. (1990). "Modular Nursing: Partners in Professional Practice." *Nursing Management* 21:3 (March), 20–24.

Bodegraven, A. (1989). "Developing and Using Standards for Work Performance." *Topics in Health Care Financing* 15:3 (Spring), 13–25.

Caldwell, C., McEachern, J., and Davis, V. (1990). "Measurement Tools Eliminate Guesswork." *Healthcare Forum Journal* 11:4 (July/August), 23–28.

Charns, A., Cooper, W., and Rhodes, R. (1981). "Evaluating Program and Managerial Efficiency: Application of DEA Analysis." *Management Science* 27:6 (June), 668–697.

Chase, R., and Hayes, R. (1991). "Beefing Up Operations in Service Firms." *Sloan Management Review* 33:1 (Fall), 15–26.

Deguchi, J., Inui, T., and Martin, D. (1984). "Measuring Provider Productivity in Ambulatory Care." *Journal of Ambulatory Management* 7:2 (May), 29–38.

Deming, W. (1986). *Out of the Crisis.* Cambridge, Mass.: Massachusetts Institute of Technology Press, Center for Advanced Engineering.

Drucker, P. (1976). *The Unseen Revolution.* New York: Harper and Row.

———. (1970). *Technology, Management, and Society.* New York: Harper and Row.

Eastaugh, S. (1990). "Hospital Nursing Technical Efficiency: Nurse Extenders and Enhanced Productivity." *Hospital and Health Services Administration* 35:4 (Winter), 561–573.

———. (1987). *Financing Health Care: Economic Efficiency and Equity.* Dover, Mass.: Auburn House.

———. (1986). "Work Smarter, Not Harder." *Healthcare Executive* 1:2 (March–April), 56.

———. (1985a). "Improving Hospital Productivity under PPS: Managing Cost Reductions without Harming Service Quality or Access." *Hospital and Health Services Administration* 30:4 (July/August), 97–111.

———. (1985b). "Organization, Scheduling Are Main Keys to Improving Productivity in Hospitals." *FAH Review* 18:6 (November/December), 61–63.

———. (1985c). "Impact of the Nurse Training Act on the Supply of Nurses, 1974–1983." *Inquiry*, 22:4 (Winter), 404–417.

Eastaugh, S., and Regan Donovan, M. (1990). "Nurse Extenders Offer a Way to Trim Staff Expenses." *Healthcare Financial Management* 44:4 (April), 58–62.

Eastaugh, S., Sahney, V., and Steinhauer, B. (1983). "Alternative Compensation Incentives for Stimulating Improved Productivity." *Journal of Health Administration Education* 1:2 (Spring), 117–137.

Egdahl, R. (1984). "Should We Shrink the Health Care System?" *Harvard Business Review* 62:1 (January–February), 125–132.

Feldstein, P. (1989). *Health Care Economics*. 3d ed. New York: Wiley Medical.

Fera, M., and Finnegan, G. (1986). "Building a Productivity Improvement Team through MIS Leadership." *Hospital and Health Services Administration* 31:4 (July/August), 7–17.

Grimaldi, P., and Michelette, J. (1982). "RIMs and the Cost of Nursing Care." *Nursing Management* 13:12 (December), 19–20.

Grosskopf, S., and Valdmanis, V. (1987). "Measuring Hospital Performance: A Nonparametric Approach." *Journal of Health Economics* 6:2 (September), 89–107.

Hellinger, F. (1975). "Specification of a Hospital Production Function." *Applied Economics* 7:2 (March), 149–160.

Huang, Y., and McLaughlin, C. (1989). "Relative Efficiency in Rural Primary Health Care: Application of Data Envelopment Analysis." *Health Services Research* 24:2 (June), 143–157.

Hurdle, S., and Pope, G. (1989). "Physician Productivity: Trends and Determinants." *Inquiry* 26:1 (Spring), 110–115.

InterQual. (1991). *Hospital Risk Management and Malpractice Liability*. Westborough, Mass.: MediQual and InterQual, Inc.

Jirka, F. (1984). "Three Major Challenges: Quality, Cost, and Balance." *Journal of the American Medical Association* 251:14 (April 13), 1867–1868.

Johnston, J. (1989). *Econometric Methods*. 4th ed. London: McGraw-Hill.

Kalirajan, K., and Shand, R. (1989). "A Generalized Measure of Technical Efficiency." *Applied Economics* 21:1 (January), 25–34.

Klein, L. (1989). "Experimental Nursing Tech Program Strengthens Staff." *Federation of American Health Systems Review* 22:4 (July–August), 27–30.

Lenehan, G. (1988). "The AMA's Registered Care Technologist Proposal: Old Wine in New Bottles." *Journal of Emergency Nursing* 14:5 (May), 268–271.

Manthey, M. (1989). "Practice Partnerships: The Newest Concept in Care Delivery." *Journal of Nursing Administration* 19:2 (February), 33–35.

———. (1988). "Primary Practice Partners: A Nurse Extender System." *Nursing Management* 19:6 (June), 58–59.

———. (1970). "A Dialogue on Primary Nursing." *Nursing Forum* 9:4 (April), 356–379.

Martin, J., Dahlstrom, G., and Johnston, C. (1985). "Impact of Administrative Technology on Acute Care Bed Need." *Health Services Research* 20:1 (April), 63–81.

McCarthy, S. (1989). "The Future of Nursing Practice and Implications for Nurse Education." *Journal of Professional Nursing* 5:3 (March), 121–168.

McClain, J., and Eastaugh, S. (1983). "How to Forecast to Contain Your Variable Costs." *Hospital Topics* 61:6 (November/December), 4–9.

Medicus System Corporation. (1989). *Inpatient Nursing Productivity and Quality System (NPAQ)*. Evanston, Ill.: Medicus (and *Nursing Management* 20 [May 1989], 30–33).

Meyers, D. (1981). *Grasp Two*. Morgantown, N.C.: MCS.

Mullaney, A. (1989). "Downsizing: Response to Decreasing Demand." *Health Care Management Review* 14:3 (Summer), 41–47.

Nunamaker, T. (1983). "Measuring Routine Nursing Service Efficiency: A Comparison of Cost per Patient Day and Data Envelopment Analysis Models." *Health Services Research* 18:2 (Summer), 183–205.

Palasco, P. and Eastaugh, N. (1986). "Effective Utilization of Operating Room Services." *Health Matrix* 4:3 (Fall), 29–32.

Pink, G. (1991). "Are Managers Compensated for Hospital Financial Performance?" *Health Care Management Review* 16:3 (Summer), 37–46.

Reuschel, J., and Earle, D. (1991). "Measuring Productivity in the Academic Setting." *Medical Group Management Journal* 38:5 (September/October), 52–5.

Sahney, V. (1982). "Managing Variability in Demand: A Strategy for Productivity Improvement." *Health Care Management Review* 7:2 (Spring), 37–42.

Secretary's Commission on Nursing. (1988). *Final Report to DHHS*. Vol. 2. Washington, D.C.: DHHS (December).

Shorr, A. (1991) *The Optimizer: Productivity Evaluation Methodology for Scheduling Staff with Linear Programming*. Tarzana, Calif.: Shorr Associates.

Shukla, R. (1985). "Admissions Monitoring and Scheduling to Improve Work Flow in Hospitals." *Inquiry* 22:1 (Spring), 92–101.

———. (1983a). "All RN Model of Nursing Care Delivery: A Cost-Benefit Evaluation." *Inquiry* 20:2 (Summer), 173–184.

Shukla, R. (1983b). "Technical and Structural Support Systems and Nurse Utilization." *Inquiry* 20:4 (Winter), 381–389.

Shukla, R., and O'Hallaron, R. (1986). "AM Admissions/PM Discharges Can Reduce Length of Stay." *Hospital and Health Services Administration* 31:4 (July/August), 74–81.

Sorkin, A. (1986). *Health Care and the Changing Economic Environment*. Lexington, Mass.: Lexington Books.

Sumeren, M. (1986). "Organizational Downsizing: Streamlining the Healthcare Organization." *Healthcare Financial Management* 40:1 (January), 35–39.

Suver, J., and Neumann, B. (1986). "Resource Measurement by Health Care Providers." *Hospital and Health Services Administration* 31:5 (September/October), 44–52.

Suver, J., Oppermann, E., and Helmer, F. (1984). "Using Standards to Predict Nurse Staffing Patterns." *Healthcare Financial Management* 38:9 (September), 48–50.

Valdmanis, V. (1990). "Ownership and Technical Efficiency of Hospitals." *Medical Care* 28:6 (June), 552–561.

Wagstaff, A. (1991). ''QALYs and the equity-efficiency trade-off'', *Journal of Health Economics* 10:1 (May), 43–64.

Walton, M. (1990). *Deming Management at Work*. New York: G. P. Putnam's, 99.

Wood, C. (1984). ''Productivity in Health Care.'' In J. Wood (ed.), *Health Care: An International Perspective*, chap. 12. New York/Geneva: International Economics and Management Institute.

Chapter 10

Incentives for
Productivity Improvement

Incentive programs can hold together a productivity program and make it
work better. If the employee compensation incentives are sufficient, the
employee will work smarter. . . . One has to assume that the individual human
being at work knows better than anyone else what makes him or her more
productive. Even in routine work the only true expert is the person who
does the job.

—Peter F. Drucker

PPS is the flag of the army of cost containers. Whether we will welcome
these changes will depend on the ability of the institutional managers and
physicians to safeguard the humane values of this most human of human
service organizations.

—Sye Berki

Implementing a successful employee incentive system requires that the health
institution already have a strong value system. Senior managers should express
in their work the values of trust, excellence, open communication, participation,
consistency, recognition, personal fulfillment, innovation, and financial responsibility. Some hospitals and clinics are overmanaged, but very few have an
excess of leaders skilled at enhancing both morale and efficiency (Barczewski
and Michelson 1991; Mick 1990). As an industry, hospitals need less of the
style and more of the substance of being businesslike. On the positive side,
many businesses have much to learn from excellent health care institutions in
implementing employee incentive programs. Innovation in incentive compensation has been rapid. Wyatt Company (1991), benefit consultants, reported that
55 percent of health care organizations responding in 1991 had incentive-pay or
gainsharing plans, as compared to only 7.1 percent in 1985. Herzberg (1987)
labeled the offering of incentive pay a "hygiene factor" that is a necessary but
not sufficient condition for motivating employees to work more efficiently and

effectively. Incentive pay is often misunderstood by workers and physicians. Incentive pay is not a bribe, but "carrot" incentives do produce results. It is misleading to think of incentive pay as contemporaneously causing higher productivity and profitability, because the three are determined simultaneously (Carruth and Oswald 1990).

According to one federal study, Congress may wish to ban arrangements that closely link financial rewards with individual treatment decisions and to limit profits earned by selective referral patterns for diagnosis or treatment (General Accounting Office [GAO] 1989). However, the incentive-pay mechanisms described in this chapter do not link pay to individual treatment decisions but to improvements in group productivity.

Although most incentive-pay texts focus on senior executive compensation (Williams and Coolidge 1991; Hay Group 1991), it is the average health care worker who can help the productivity of hospitals and clinics (Eastaugh 1990). Akerlof (1982) suggested in a seminal article that the organization can gain loyalty and productivity through the offering of extra gainsharing pay to employees. Productivity has been improved in hospitals utilizing the Deming method (Walton 1990) and in more traditional productivity-enhancement programs (Gilbert 1990). The gainsharing incentive-pay approach has also worked in medical-group clinics (Holets 1990).

One basic question is at what level the incentive pay should be offered: to individuals, to physician groups, to a single medical-staff group, or to physician-nonphysician teams. Another critical question is whether morale is adversely affected if the incentive-pay potential is most generous for the individual doctors with the most preexisting room for improvement, or, conversely, whether it is fair to have little incentive available to those already doing a good job, working efficiently and effectively. These criticisms are partly eliminated by offering the incentive contract between the institution and the departments, with bonus payments offered to the group and not to specific individuals. Internal group pressure to earn a quarterly or annual bonus reward will compensate for the fact that each individual does not derive 100 percent of the benefits for his individual actions. Moreover, the above-average performers will have the incentive to assist those not doing as well, because the net monetary benefit is shared by all. The sum total of shifts in doctor-specific practice habits and improvements in department productivity will determine the amount of incentive compensation earned.

One final concern is whether the group, at the department or subdepartment level, should include only the "top dogs," senior managers and physicians. What is at stake if the hospital does not include a wide spectrum of employees in the incentive scheme? Five basic things are at risk: middle-manager morale, other employees' morale, institutional market image, scheduling efficiency, and the resulting downtime from inefficient scheduling. While incentives can be the glue that holds an efficiency and effectiveness program together (working smarter on productivity improvement and utilization review), to exclude those who are paid less than $50,000 per annum would undermine the best of plans. The so-called little people can sabotage the process and throw a monkey wrench into a program from which they derive no benefits. The incompetent receptionist or scheduler can go along with the good ideas of the entrepreneur thinkers or can continue to mismanage provider and patient time. For example, the quality of the first contact link in the employee-patient-physician interaction will partially determine whether the institution receives repeat business. In an era of low occupancy rates, repeat business is an important issue for all concerned. Moreover, all of the problem areas are interrelated: Poor morale can yield decreased scheduling efficiency, longer patient waiting time, increased consumer dissatisfaction, decreased efficiency, consequently higher costs, and reduced business from cost-conscious payers. In summary, an incentive plan open to the majority of employees seems the best compromise to support harmony and efficiency while trading off the administrative costs of offering the plan to everyone.

THE DO'S AND DON'TS OF STRUCTURING AN INCENTIVE PLAN

One of the great unanticipated benefits of a well-designed incentive compensation program is the potential for enhanced physician and employee loyalty. Hospital employees are an important implicit component of the marketing program, because word-of-mouth advertising is important in any service industry. If employees are jealous of an incentive plan that excludes them, they may act in a more abrupt or uncaring manner. Likewise, if employees believe that pay has no relation to performance, they will bad-mouth the institution. But if employees are offered incentives, morale typically improves and all concerned get about "doing the things that really need doing." This action includes minimizing unnecessary activity, working smarter, and, in the process, cooperating to reduce levels of staffing to more closely approximate case-mix-adjusted workload. Physicians are traditionally an important element of marketing, and if offering an incentive plan enhances physician loyalty, that translates into more patients for the hospital. As a general rule, for every physician who believes that incentive plans are a mistake and threatens to admit patients elsewhere, there are many other physicians who will actually take the initiative and refer more patients to the hospital with the better incentive plan.

As mentioned earlier, the incentive plan should be groupwide and not individual-specific. An individual-specific plan, especially if it is so short-run as to also be patient-specific, can rapidly erode medical-staff support for the incentive plan. A classic example of what not to do is the 1985–88 Paracelsus Healthcare Corporation physician incentive plan. The program had two basic faults: (1) Compensation was physician-specific and (2) bonus pay was short-run (monthly). Paracelsus, a 14-hospital proprietary chain of California and Nevada hospitals, was highly criticized by the December 1985 American Medical Association House of Delegates for creating "monetary temptation" to generate unnecessary admissions. Ron Messenger, president of the West German–owned Paracelsus chain, argued that the payment to the physician for each individual patient was so small that clinicians would not want to jeopardize their reputations from a malpractice or peer review standpoint. While the California Board of Medical Quality Assurance concluded that the incentive plan did not violate tough state restrictions prohibiting rebates or kickbacks for patient referrals, the public-relations damage was immense.

The Paracelsus plan beat the letter of the law by not explicitly connecting payment to the referral of individual patients. The plan paid an individual physician a defined amount each month if all of the physician's admissions during that month exceeded 75 percent of the hospital's charges. For AMA physicians, including James Sammons (executive vice president), the plan co-opted the existing DRG system by creating incentives for physicians to channel (cream-skim) DRG "winners" to Paracelsus hospitals. Moreover, a physician acting as a perfect economic actor would not admit DRG "losers" to Paracelsus facilities so as not to pull the monthly average profit profile down. Paracelsus's financial managers had calculated that prior to the 1986 Gramm-Rudman budget cuts, on average, Medicare prospective payments ran at about 75 percent of charges (list price). For example, for a case in which the Medicare payment equaled 85 percent of the patient's charges, the hospital would pay the physician an incentive bonus of 0.1 of the amount over the trigger point [$0.1 \times (85 - 75) = 1$ percent]. In the 85 to 95 percent patient charge range, the hospital would pay 0.15, and over 95 percent, the hospital would pay 0.2 of the hospital's financial benefit.

Consider a hypothetical patient with a DRG payment of $6,000 from Medicare and actual retail charges of $6,000 in a Paracelsus facility, contrary to historical expectation of charges being generated for that condition equaling $8,000. If PPS paid the hospital $6,000, then $1,500 of that figure would go into computing the incentive payment. The individual admitting physician would receive 10 percent of the first $600 ($4,501 to $5,100), plus 15 percent of the next $600 ($5,101 to $5,700), and 20 percent of the next $300 ($5,701 to $6,000). Consequently, the physician would pocket $210 and the hospital would pocket $1,290.

The traditional AMA perspective is that "ethical physicians" do not need financial inducements to manage the treatment of their patients efficiently. However, physicians are not immune from incentives. A good incentive compensation plan is good for the institution, the individuals involved, and society as a whole. The Paracelsus plan suffered in this third regard, especially if money-losing DRGs were simply dumped to hospitals not in the Paracelsus chain and net efficiency across all patients was not affected positively. Reducing detrimental or nonbeneficial excess utilization is the major goal of the physician component of a total incentive compensation plan. However, curtailed utilization is a necessary but not sufficient condition to improve the institution's financial position. If the hospital does not cut its cost function (paid hours, FTEs, supplies) as the utilization rates decline, no economic benefit is generated from which to pay out an incentive bonus to the critical actors. Bringing key actors on stage is never easy, but the challenge is even greater when the actors represent physicians, financial officers, management engineers, and personnel. The three themes of the play are productivity improvement, cost reduction, and enhancement of service quality. Therefore, each group must reduce costs and improve efficiency to underwrite bonus compensation.

Insufficient understanding of the incentive structure and uncertainty concerning the benefits are the two principal impediments to successful compensation-plan innovation. There is an intrinsic dichotomy of economic incentives between a hospital and the medical staff. Three basic situations exist, depending on the patient's payment methodology. If the physicians are reimbursed fee-for-service (FFS), and the hospital is not (e.g., Medicare DRGs), doctors have an incentive to inflate the amount of chargeable services, even if this harms the financial status of the hospital. Second, in the case of prepaid per capita care, both the physician and the institution have an incentive to curtail the amount of service offered. Third, if both the hospital and the doctors are paid FFS, all parties have an incentive to inflate services within the constraint that the charts may be red flagged for retrospective denial of payment by a utilization review audit.

From a financial standpoint, should the hospital design an incentive compensation program that sends two conflicting messages to the medical staff: to generate more chargeable services when it helps the hospital but to curtail chargeable services per case when the hospital is paid a fixed price per episode? Ignoring such concerns as public-relations impact, the message serves to confuse the medical staff. The majority of clinicians from 1984 to 1987 appear to have operated in one direction: to curtail duration of patient stay and also admission rates across a wide range of payer groups, even if some would actually make the hospital money if clinicians would inflate admission rates and non-Medicare patient days. The physician community is responding to pressure from Medicare PPS and PRO programs (Fielding 1984) and from private utilization review efforts (ProPAC 1991).

Some hospitals have offered a way of obfuscating the idea of a differential style of medicine by payer class. In this type of incentive compensation plan, the hospital calculates three target lists of high-volume DRGs, ignores low-volume DRGs, and claims to pay bonus compensation independent of payer source. For high-volume DRGs, the hospital generates a Medicare-intensive (e.g., more than 45 percent of the patient days serve Medicare patients) list of DRGs, offers a "carrot" (positive) incentive to bring in more DRGs on this specific list, and at the same time offers a disincentive to generate more cost per case. The hospital also generates a second list of prepaid-intensive DRGs (disproportionate share of capitated patient cases) and offers an incentive to minimize costs per case (and perhaps admissions) for the DRGs on this list (within the constraint of not producing such consumer dissatisfaction as to reduce per capita payer-source income). For the third list, the hospital generates a list of DRGs with a high proportion of fee-for-service patients and offers positive incentives to generate more chargeable services, more admissions, and more services per admission.

Rather than sending conflicting signals to the medical staff through three-tiered differential incentives by type of DRG or payer type, a more simple and honest incentive plan pegs bonus pay to economic efficiency for labor. Such a plan has been developed in a number of contexts (Eastaugh 1985a). The plan is based on an improvement (decline) in a unit's compensation ratio (CR), equal to the unit's total staff compensation divided by adjusted gross revenue (a fraction typically between 0.35 and 0.85). The work unit in question can equal a clinic, a department, or a strategic product-line grouping (SPG) of jointly produced DRGs. An SPG cluster is identified as a clearly defined list of DRGs performed by a defined subset of the providers and staff. In order to avoid risking loss of the tax-exempt status of an institution, one has to avoid paying a bonus based on "profits" or "cost savings relative to income" (Eastaugh, Sahney, and Steinhauer 1983; Eastaugh 1985b) and instead pay a bonus for improvements in the CR relative to an external target.

Allocation of Incentive Pay to a Work Unit

The external target is the desirable compensation ratio (DCR) or lowest ratio (best economic efficiency) for peer work units across peer institutions (e.g., compare the Cleveland Clinic to the Mayo Clinic, the Lovelace Clinic, and Henry Ford Hospital clinics). This DCR ratio is equal to total labor compensation in the "best-actor" (lowest CR) unit nationally or locally divided by adjusted gross revenue (Eastaugh, Sahney, and Steinhauer, 1983). Adjusted gross revenue equals actual collected revenue—that is, gross revenue less contractual allowances, bad debt, or retrospective denial of payment from the utilization reviewers. The DCR is set on a prospective annual basis by the policy, planning, and finance committees, based on the recommendation of a compensation committee that utilizes historic department/unit/clinic performance data and comparative data on other "efficient" peer institutions to set up targets.

These three committees work on the basis of monthly or quarterly mutual feedback. An incentive-pay share (fraction) is paid for any percentage improvement in lowering the DCR ratio, and a "kicker bonus" is paid for merely achieving the DCR ratio. If the compensation committee has set a DCR ratio that is too easily achieved, the finance committee may consider reducing the slope of the incentive payment if necessary (so as not to "give away the store" and pay more compensation than is warranted by the economic gain). If the compensation committee has set the DCRs in certain areas very high, the finance committee may calculate a more generous incentive-pay slope for any percentage improvement in CR performance, even when performance falls short of (excess costs are above) the given DCR target. For example, if actual CR is 0.77 and the DCR at two efficient "peer" hospitals is 0.48, the benefits of any lowering in CR could be shared between the hospital and those involved in that area (including physicians). The share of the benefits going to individuals might have to be higher (70 to 80 percent) to get inefficient departments that exceed the DCR by more than 20 percent to improve their behavior. However, if a department or clinic lowers its CR to within 0.096 of 0.48, the benefits should be shared equally between the hospital and those employees and clinicians involved.

In setting the targets across hospitals, one can find a tight range of DCR variability, such as 0.45 to 0.50, for certain strategic product-line groupings (SPGs): colon and rectal surgery, vascular surgery, or obstetrics and gynecology (Eastaugh, Sahney, and Steinhauer 1983). However, the range of DCR variability for an SPG can be from 0.45 to 0.70 for pediatrics or pediatric surgery and from 0.55 to 0.80 for internal medicine. This approach has been tried in a wide range of facilities (Eastaugh 1986, 1985a). If the SPG group achieves its DCR target, there should be a small (3 to 5 percent) additional "kicker" bonus (expressed as a percentage of adjusted gross revenue). If a SPG group improves its DCR to below the target, it will generate an additional bonus payment (the slope is set by the finance committee, with approval by the board of trustees). One might ask: Why pay a "kicker bonus"? One long-term problem for departments that serve as the industry standard for efficiency (DCR in department X) is that the best performers will have a diminished motive for improving efficiency in the future. Without any incentive the best departments or clinics will not have any motivation to take risks or innovate when the opportunity arises. Efficient SPGs should generate some incentive pay whether or not they continue to improve. Moreover, without a "kicker bonus" there is a clear incentive to "game" the system—that is, let the department or clinic have a bad year and then "clean up" the next year by reachieving the DCR target.

Allocation of Incentive Pay within the Work Unit

Whereas the decision as to how much incentive pay to allocate to a work unit should be based on performance-outcome criteria, the division of incentive pay within the group typically involves process criteria. Employee criteria are usually developed with a weighting scheme in four basic areas: (1) attendance (e.g., score two performance-criteria points for the year if unplanned absences are 0–3, one point if 4–7), (2) quantity of work per hour, (3) quality of work, and (4) team effort (e.g., score two criteria points if the employee willingly accepts new processes and team methods; subtract one criteria point if the employee passively resists new directions or changing work methods). All criteria points should be scaled relative to the work-unit minimum level of performance—that is, zero points are earned if the employee just does the minimum. The performance appraisal should be numerically scaled so as to avoid words that carry pejorative meanings that might anger employees (e.g., poor, fair, good, so outstanding as to be administrative material). The rater will always encounter negative reactions in telling the employee, "You have achieved minimum standards; congratulations, you are slightly below average.' '' Consequently, the scoring form should list numbers only, not words.

Too wide an array of possible ratings should also be avoided, as this only invites excessive subjectivity into the performance-appraisal process. The form should be kept short, so that performance appraisal is viewed as a management tool and not a management burden. In addition, the form should be somewhat task-specific, so that individual employees know where to improve their performance. Finally, as the hospital allows departments to earn a "kicker bonus," so department managers should allow good performance by employees on the top end of the pay and performance scale to receive a "kicker" bonus. As a hypothetical example, a department might receive $176,000 of bonus pay, and the pay might be allocated at the rate of 2 percent of base salary paid to an individual per criteria point earned; in addition, two exceptional employees might receive a $1,200 "kicker" bonus. The performance-criteria point system will always need to incorporate a significant degree of subjectivity. For example, the number of research articles produced might be a subcomponent of team effort that adds to the output of the department but has nothing to do with the improved economic performance (the $176,000 earned).

Managers should be evaluated with four analogous criteria: (1) department planning, direction, and marketing; (2) budget management and control per quarter; (3) personal professional development; and (4) human-resources development. Managers do react to incentives, which is why incentive compensation has become so popular in the health sector since the enactment of PPS. The weights for various measures should be provided ex ante (up front). For example, a senior manager's performance could be based 30 percent on improvements in the operating margin, 20 percent on improved market share, 10 percent on improved inventory turnover, and so on. Does incentive pay yield improved market share or financial performance? The CEO of Beverly Hospital outside of Boston attributed his 14 percent increase in admissions and 5 percent decline in FTEs over 30 months (1984–1986) to just such an incentive-pay scheme. Incentive pay can act as a countervailing force to competitive pressures (e.g., when seven HMOs and PPOs entered the Beverly Hospital market). Managers, other employees, and physicians are much more likely to evolve, proact, improve standard operating procedures, and initiate joint ventures if they receive direct compensation. Hospitals without incentive plans experience an erosion in morale and market share.

The Spirit of Teamwork

Incentive plans are often a response to competition between organizations that in turn creates more productive cooperation within the organization. Superior output (quantity and quality of care) does not require dog-eat-dog competition, but incentive plans can reward cooperative and productive behavior. Antiproductive employees may view all incentive plans as "yuppie victory behavior," but the institution is better off without such individuals on the staff. Team-specific incentive plans establish the ethic that (1) others are depending on you and (2) your lazy behavior will adversely affect other members of the team. Incentive compensation should reinforce the love of doing both greater quantity and better quality of work. Competition between departments or hospitals may increase, but incentive plans typically enhance cooperation between team members (Richer and Weiss 1988). It is pop-sociology nonsense to suggest that incentive plans produce anticooperative or antiproductive "vying behavior" between workers. However, incentive plans can reward what Peters and Austin (1985) referred to as "skunks" or "disruptive champions of innovation" (the entrepreneurs referred to in chapter 9 are in effect salaried "skunks" attempting to do things more productively and promote better forms of efficient cooperation). Experiments in hospital gainsharing incentive pay abound in a number of locations from Sutter Health Systems in California to Sisters of Charity Health Care System in Cincinnati and Rhode Island Hospital in Providence (AHA 1991).

One could consider nonmonetary incentive programs, but they typically have little impact on behavior. The one exception to that generality is religious hospitals. In the case of religious hospitals, the incentive might be educational (e.g., extended management-development programs). If the nonmonetary incentive is too trivial, it will do more harm than good. The classic example is offering pins on nurse appreciation day while the competition offers incentive pay at the local nonprofit hospitals. On one such occasion, a nurse stood up and said, "They don't have a doctor's appreciation day—those people get money—and my spouse in the factory gets a semiannual bonus check, so why not us?" Financial incentives are quite new in the tax-exempt hospital industry, as are the forces that make them increasingly necessary. These forces include unilateral price payments (e.g., Medicare PPS) and aggressive price discounters (e.g., PPOs). Titles of incentive programs are often sugarcoated with phrases like "gainsharing" and "global hospitalwide incentive sharing," as if certain segments of the hospital could not improve efficiency with autonomy. In contrast, most business executives are quite aggressive about the use of incentives. Many business executives receive half of their total compensation from incentive provisions. Having the firm, the hospital, keep 20 to 50 percent of the economic gain may seem overly generous by industrial standards. Judson (1982) reported on business incentive programs that retained at least 66 percent of the gross economic benefits for the company. One could argue that professionals and support staff in tax-exempt hospitals need a larger incentive reward to alter inefficient patterns of behavior. Alternatively, the spirit of a greater sharing of benefits is more customary among health care institutions, in which case the institution should accrue a minority share of any labor-productivity gains.

Incentive Plans of the Future

In the 1990s tax-exempt managers may increasingly have to mimic investor-owned motivational plans and issue not only bonus compensation, but also stock options. Conveying a "sense of ownership" may evolve increasingly into giving an equity share in the organization. Managers, employees, and doctors may come to own stock in their core business (the hospital itself), or some co-op subchapter T corporation of the hospital, or a for-profit subsidiary of the hospital. Defenders of the status quo in nonprofit hospital administration will resist this trend in the 1990s, just as they resisted pay increases for hospital employees in the 1960s and resisted calling administrators "managers" in the 1970s and "executives" in the 1980s. These archaic individuals are often wrong, thus demonstrating a remarkable degree of consistency. Times change, and economic efficiency must improve, but this need not result in any erosion of the hospital mission.

The challenge for senior management and trustees is to find a means whereby all parties are motivated to work toward a common goal. Counterproductive workers might be weeded out, so that creative entrepreneurs can do much more. Reductions in salary expenses by firing nonproductive employees would provide the resources for offering incentive compensation and, more important, the resources for institutional survival and better-quality care in an era of total revenue controls. The incentive plan outlined has four crucial features:

1. Departments requesting more financial support will have to face some of the economic consequences of their extravagance (inefficiency is no longer a reimbursable expense).
2. The plan should involve no downside risk of reduced salary.
3. The plan should offer a "kicker bonus" for those who achieve the target (DCR) level of performance in order to maintain the incentive to economize.
4. The plan should be group-specific until the department divides the compensation pool among individuals.

The department-level director in charge of the compensation pool can also reward excellent noneconomic performance, such as for research and teaching. This builds a spirit of harmony in the teaching hospital context (Eastaugh, Sahney, and Steinhauer 1983) and helps to underwrite improvements in graduate medical education and to encourage biomedical research. The incentive compensation system should be viewed as a means of relaxing central control and encouraging local department initiative and autonomy. Management must be vigilant, however, to prevent departmental "turfing" behavior—that is, shifting work to others to appear more efficient on paper.

Fairness and Efficiency

If some clinical areas are viewed as intrinsically lucrative, one could consider pooling 10 to 20 percent of the net institutional bonus compensation pool and distributing it equally to all employees. This would add to an institutional feeling of cohesion and teamwork and make the program de facto 10 to 20 percent "gainsharing" and 80 to 90 percent department sharing. Innovation in cost control may be quantum, that is, in leaps and spurts (Eastaugh 1986). For example, if an individual department does not perform well in 1992 but earned a great bonus payment in 1991, at least it shares in some small bonus in 1992 under a limited gainsharing program.

Many old-line administrators might fear that clinicians and/or managers might be tempted to understaff their departments in order to minimize the compensation ratio, thus maximizing their incentive-plan income. There are a number of arguments against these fears, apart from the fact that this behavior has not been observed (Eastaugh 1985a, 1985b; Shyavitz, Rosenbloom, and Conover 1985). One can explain this finding within the context of economic utility theory or Herzberg's (1974) construct of two motivating factors: satisfiers and dissatisfiers. If one really does understaff—the classic dissatisfier—an erosion in the quality of the workplace will come into play. For an educated professional, the hassles associated with running an understaffed department or clinic far outweigh the potential gain in income. Satisfiers include income, local and national peer status, recognition, and reputation.

Cutbacks on the compensation ratio to the detriment of the quality of service would have a terrible impact on prestige and reputation. Insensitive practitioners of the "cowboy school of management," irrespective of quality concerns, fortunately do not last long in the health field. Concern solely for short-run income would have a negative impact on long-run income and reputation. It appears from recent trends in staffing FTEs and workload that in the jargon of economics there is enough X-efficiency (slack) to improve productivity closer to the level of an efficient "peer" facility without harming quality (e.g., Pink 1991; Shukla 1990; Shukla and O'Hallaron 1986). Departments and institutions in any industry attempt to optimize slack in order not to work too hard, but the health care industry has grown a high degree of slack under the safe blanket of cost reimbursement. For most, reputation is more important than a few extra dollars, but the few extra dollars in bonus compensation reinforce the decision to trim excess costs and initiate productivity innovations, all without harm to one's reputation. Therefore, until most slack X-efficiency is exhausted, we have in the health sector a number of effective, related incentives that act as checks against domination from purely monetary concerns. Tax-exempt hospitals that ignore incentive reward systems will find productivity and the financing of quality-enhancing programs as elusive as the golden fleece. Moreover, health facilities that do not reward their managers and effective employees sufficiently will find their best employees going to other facilities. When one considers the joint costs of the search process (for a replacement) and training, incentive pay is typically more cost-beneficial in the 1990s than having a high turnover rate. Proprietary health care facilities have realized for decades that they "get what they pay for" in terms of the correlation between pay and performance.

OTHER INCENTIVE COMPENSATION PLANS

The DCR incentive plan outlined in this chapter offers a blend of four traditional gain-sharing incentive plans: Scanlon, Improshare, Rucker, and profit sharing. These gainsharing plans engender bottom-to-top employee involvement and are considered a component part of a total compensation plan (table 10.1, lines 1–5). However, an alternative innovative reward system can be run independently of the compensation program (table 10.1, lines 6 and 7). Performance management systems (PMSs) offer equal payout to work-unit members for achievement of various financial or physical corporate objectives. PMS programs typically result in a modest 4 to 6 percent across-the-board improvement in manager incomes. Second, team suggestion programs (table 10.1, line 7) pay out a fixed percentage (20 to 25 percent) of work units' successfully implemented cost savings or business-expansion ideas. In contrast to monthly PPS programs, team suggestion programs are paid out as earned. (For the interested reader, Laliberty and Christopher [1984] and Bodegraven [1989] provide good introductory surveys to employee-work-study methods and incentive plans.) The team suggestion payout is typically made with merchandise, not cash, as the employee earns "recognition credits" redeemable for items in the Green Stamp award book. While human-resources personnel point to the "cute reaction" of employees who bring their gifts to the workplace to "show them off," such merchandise incentive plans have a number of drawbacks. Operating the gift plan has significant administrative costs, and employees come to resent the limited lists of available items. One New Jersey hospital reported good long-run financial and employee performance from a suggestion program. The 550-bed Raritan Bay Medical Center improved productivity 10 percent (1983–86), generated a net savings of $4 million, and paid out $1.1 million in merchandise to employees.

Cash is a much less paternalistic form of incentive. However, one of the disadvantages of cash as a motivator is that the bonus checks are perceived to be too modest in size if they are delivered weekly (Improshare) or monthly. The DCR plan and traditional profit-sharing plans avoid this problem by offering annual payouts and quarterly accounting reports of bonus earnings. A number of other plans overemphasize timing—that is, the need to have the payout within weeks of the performance improvement (Scanlon, Rucker, Improshare). The concerned individual can keep a tally of how much bonus pay he or she has earned and directly realize the connection between actions and benefits without having the cash in pocket under the DCR plan.

One of the central strengths of the Improshare gainsharing plan, like the DCR plan, is that the incentive payout is work-unit specific (those who earn it receive it). The Scanlon and Rucker plans suffer from being hospitalwide in focus. Improshare incentive programs do have their downside. Improshare managers report that their employees are doing departmental functions that they "never had time to do." However, in the documentation of more relative value units (RVUs) of activity, these employees can generate more useless activity that does not improve actual productivity. The DCR incentive plan offers incentive pay to streamline and eliminate useless departmental functions and free up more productive hours of nonadministrative activity. The DCR plan offers a less generous payout sharing with employees than the Rucker plan (100 percent to

Table 10.1
Seven Alternative Incentive Compensation or Reward Systems

Reward Plan	Formula Basis	Goals (type of situation)	Level (timing)	Sharing Split of Benefits	Reserves
1-5 Gainsharing Incentive Compensation Plans					
1. Scanlon	Labor costs: Sales	A. Reduce labor expenses B. Suggestion committee C. Common-fate atmosphere (crisis situation)	Firmwide (quarterly)	75% to labor	10% set aside
2. Desirable compensation ratio (Henry Ford Hospital)	Total labor costs: Net revenue (kicker bonus—if this DCR ratio equals the best, lowest, among peers)	A. Reduce labor input expense or expand rev. B. Merit-based pay for performance (ongoing situation)	Work group (annual)	60-80% to labor & MDs	10% distributed hospitalwide the following year
3. Improshare (J.F.K. Hospital, Edison, N.J.)	Nonfinancial base productive hours factor (BSF)	A. Improve productivity B. Reduce nonproductive hours (ongoing situation)	Work group (weekly)	50% to labor	10-25% rolling average
4. Rucker	Labor costs: Sales-allowances-materials-supplies	A. Reduce costs fast B. Suggestion committee C. "Open books" spirit of trust (short-run crisis)	Firmwide (monthly)	100% to labor	25%
5. Profit sharing (Humana)	Bottom-line profits	A. Control cost behavior B. Expand operating profits (ongoing situation)	Work group (quarterly)	10-40% to labor	50/50 deferred income available
6-7 Innovative Reward Systems (Independent of the Compensation System)					
6. Team suggestion (Raritan Bay Med. Center, N.J.)	5-20% split of the savings among team members	A. Suggestion system B. Earn points to purchase merchandise (ongoing situation)	Work group (payout as earned)	15-20% to labor	Possible
7. Performance management system (NME)	% share of the value of improvements (sales, cost)	A. Highly customized for a big firm/chain B. Driven by senior management objectives	Strategic business units	10-30% to labor	Possible

the employees, but usually for only 6 to 12 months). The team suggestion and PMS plans offer only 10 to 20 percent of the benefits to those who earn them, which suggests that the incentive "carrot" might not be sufficient as a long-run motivator. The DCR plan offers a more generous payout to the employees, while retaining a 10 percent hospitalwide reserve fund to be shared by all employees.

As a thought experiment, one could hypothesize that the simplest method of offering direct incentives for better performance would be for those involved to divide up the proceeds every time $25,000 in cost reduction were achieved or 5 to 10 extra patients were brought in (cost variance and volume variance, respectively) compared to the forecasts. Unfortunately, the Internal Revenue Service would question the inurement provisions that no private individual (employee, physician) benefit from the tax-exempt status of the institution under section 501(c)(3) of the tax code. According to a number of IRS rulings, tax-exempt institutions may not have an incentive plan involving the distribution of "profits," "net income," "gross receipts," or "cost savings" (Groner 1977; Eastaugh, Sahney, and Steinhauer 1983). However, the plan can pay for performance relative to technical efficiency (productivity) or a desirable compensation ratio (a proxy variable for labor productivity). One merely needs to demonstrate to the IRS that the plan does no financial harm to the institution by paying out too much incentive compensation ("giving away the store"). In preparing a report on the incentive plan, the institution should be able to demonstrate that the plan contains maximums for salary improvement each year (e.g., 33 to 40 percent) and that the institution will always benefit under the compensation plan. The actual payment of the bonus may be offered in a number of ways, ranging from a check to payment into each employee's tax-sheltered annuity account.

INCENTIVES AND PERFORMANCE REVIEW

Incentives are an important third stage in any comprehensive productivity-improvement plan. A successful plan must attract the enthusiastic support of the employees and the physicians. Behavior will not change if the plan is viewed as merely a short-run management gimmick. One critical requirement of any good productivity program is that the facility have comprehensive and timely management information systems (Fera and Finnegan 1986). Moreover, the program should build on a pre-existing strong human-resources program and involve strong support from senior management (Dailey 1988).

There are two inherent difficulties in the emerging application of the Deming (1986) method in the American hospital industry. Deming has lived in the Japanese context for five decades and so understated the positive impacts of microeconomic fiscal incentives to employees and the cultural context of the American worker. Deming was incorrect in his assertion that incentive pay creates suboptimal competition between people. Incentive pay that is broad based (distributed equitably across the group without nitpicking over merit-appraisal annual reports on each worker) produces good results: higher productivity and morale (Eastaugh 1986, 1985a). Deming was correct that incentive pay provided only to "top dogs" (senior managers) or bonus pay based on performance appraisal is counter-productive. But if the incentive pay is offered with minimal paperwork by the human-resources department—for example, if department productivity improves 15 percent, then each worker gets 15 days of extra pay or extra vacation time—then the group works better to achieve the goal of enhanced performance. In other words, Deming was right that gainsharing bonus pay should not be based on performance reviews that rank people and reward them according to rank. But Deming was wrong to state that incentive pay cannot exist without performance reviews of employees.

Deming stated in his seminal book *Out of the Crisis* (1986) that performance ratings nourish rivalry and politics and leave people battered and bruised. However, in the competitive American workplace, incentive pay that is group based and linked to productivity gains (without any input from human-resources types that like to rank people), the pre-specified gains that can be earned offer idea people (entrepreneurs) an opportunity to improve the department. Such productivity-enhancement actions get the full support of other workers, who have no incentive to sabotage an idea that might earn them more pay or make their product higher in quality or their workday more productive and less stressful. Incentive pay that is group based nourishes the incentive to bring forth good ideas and test them, while avoiding counterproductive rivalry. Benefit is linked to performance improvement for the entire group, not faster work by one single individual earning more pay for only his or her own paycheck. Individual incentive pay based on merit ratings is unfair because differences may be caused totally by the system that the individual works in. There is nothing ineffective about distributing annual gains earned by a group (department or subdepartment) to the individuals and voting two or three times as much incentive pay to the one entrepreneur who came up with an idea that worked. It is insulting to give hospital workers no gainsharing pay for improving performance when they see others earning bonus pay elsewhere in the general economy. Two summary points need emphasis: (1) Not to offer incentive pay to health care workers is equivalent to telling them that they are undervalued or better served by quitting the business, and (2) to allow the human-resources department to operate a merit ranking system for employees is a waste of money and human capital (no worker in Japan is given such a "rating"). Implicit in the Deming concept of continuous improvement is the capacity to improve all people and move the entire distribution of worker productivity in a better direction rather than identifying and penalizing the bad performers.

PAY FOR PERFORMANCE FOR SENIOR MANAGERS

Some hospital trustees have suggested that chief executive officers be paid up to 50 percent incentive pay. Hospitals have begun to write contracts to improve market share or profitability (Gandossy and Jonassen 1989; Hay Group 1991). Gibbons and Murphy (1990) developed a model for assessing the relationship between CEO compensation and financial performance. If their results are typical, business tends to be three times as generous as the hospital industry in rewarding a financial turnaround (improvement) in profitability. Perhaps the ideal contract for hospital CEOs has the form pay (P, C), where P is a fraction of operating profit in excess of the peer-group average (like hospitals in the same reimbursement climate) and C is charity care (a social dividend to the community). C is necessary to assess the CEO's unobservable capability to enhance P by dumping some of the charity burden. If ethical improvements in P through better productivity improvements and trimming of variable costs (Eastaugh and Regan 1990) were indexed to peer hospitals, the incentive pay-for-performance gain to the CEO could be nonlinear: (1) If cost reduction improved productivity by 2.0 percent versus the peer-group hospitals, then the CEO might receive 5.0 percent of the incremental improvement (and middle managers might divide up 20 percent of the gain according to relative effectiveness), but (2) if cost reduction improved productivity by 4.0 percent versus the peer-group hospitals, then the CEO might receive 15.0 percent of the incremental improvement for doing such a superior job (and middle managers might divide up 50 percent of the gain).

Pink (1991) studied the average compensation of the senior executive team rather than the CEO compensation alone and reported that for a sample of 223 Canadian hospitals, management was better paid in the hospitals with superior profit margins and larger bed size. Industry is more generous than the hospital industry, in that in a cross-sectional elasticity of compensation to sales is about 0.31; that is, a 100 percent larger firm will pay its managers an average of 31 percent more. Pink (1991) found that for equal-sized hospitals earning equal profit margins, teaching hospitals paid their management 7.7 percent more in salary and 8.6 percent more in perquisite benefits (perks). Pink also reported that a 100 percent larger hospital paid its management 6.7 percent more in salary and 5.7 percent more in perquisite benefits. If the complexity of managerial responsibilities is greater for larger hospitals and for teaching hospitals, then trustees should reward managers accordingly. But all workers from the bottom up should receive some share of the benefit for any successful productivity-enhancement cost-reduction program.

FINAL COMMENTS

A 1991 AHA survey revealed that 70 percent of nonsmall hospitals are utilizing or plan to utilize incentive compensation plans. One should infer from this chapter that a well-designed plan should have five E-Q-U-I-P attributes:

1. Establish a merit-based performance climate with pay for performance rewards for superior workers and idea makers (entrepreneurs).
2. Quality should be emphasized by making the incentive bonus pay significant in size

(and linked to a quality-enhancing customer orientation) to overcome the antiproductive orientation that "if you try, if you come to work, you should all get the same pay."

3. Unproductive workers should face sanctions and no pay increases, so hopefully they will leave the facility (and go to the competition).

4. Incentives should be offered in the spirit of a "cut of the action" or, in less entrepreneurial rhetoric, a common-fate atmosphere that requires change and continuous improvement if the institution is to survive.

5. Promote a spirit of job security and trust, built upon the preexisting compensation system and performance-appraisal framework.

Further research is needed to analyze how these incentive reward programs affect the total institution. Organizational theorists have developed a number of competing hypotheses to explain explicit and implicit contractual relationships between senior managers, middle managers, employees, and independent contractors (Murphy 1986; Coughlan and Schmidt 1985). Response to incentives can be analyzed under two alternative hypotheses: (1) Productivity depends on efforts that are difficult to observe, or (2) ability is unknown and is revealed (learned) over time. If the preexisting productivity measurement system is crude or continues to remain highly imperfect (e.g., due to the nature of the job), past performance may remain irrelevant in predicting current or future performance. Under the second hypothesis, incentive compensation could merely unlock the door of innate managerial ability, which is initially unknown but revealed over time. The two hypotheses are not mutually exclusive, and individual incentive-payment profiles should reflect some mix of both incentives and learning (Olson 1989).

A number of noted members of the economics profession have written extensively on the relationship between progress and the "law of comparative advantage": If each good or service is supplied by the most productive producer, all in society will be richer. To be against productivity is to be against medical progress. Productivity gains will help underwrite our future improvements in service delivery and technology. These programs will provide the linchpin to ensure that we continue to deliver a quality service at an affordable cost for all concerned (Sahney 1991).

REFERENCES

Akerlof, G. (1982). "Labor Contracts as Partial Gift Exchange." *Quarterly Journal of Economics* 97:4 (November), 543–569.

American Hospital Association (AHA). (1991). "Human Resources: Gainsharing." *Hospitals* 65:1 (January 5), 46.

Barczewski, R., and Michelson, L. (1991). "Motivating Employees: An Incentive Program." *Medical Group Management Journal* 38:5 (September/October), 24–28.

Berki, S. (1985). "DRGs, Incentives, Hospitals, and Physicians." *Health Affairs* 4:4 (Winter), 70–76.

Bodegraven, A. (1989). "Developing and Using Standards for Work Performance." *Topics in Health Care Financing* 15:3 (Spring), 13–25.

Carruth, A., and Oswald, A. (1990). *Pay Determination and Industrial Prosperity*. Oxford, England: Clarendon Press, 124

Coughlan, A., and Schmidt, R. (1985). "Executive Compensation, Management Turnover, and Firm Performance." *Journal of Accounting and Economics* 7:1 (January), 43–66.

Dailey, R. (1988). "Productivity Monitoring Systems in Hospitals: A Work Group Focus." *Hospital and Health Services Administration* 33:1 (Spring), 75–88.

Deming, W. (1986). *Out of the Crisis*. Cambridge, Mass.: Massachusetts Institute of Technology Press, Center for Advanced Engineering.

Drucker, P. (1979). *Adventures of a Bystander*. New York: Harper and Row.

———. (1964). *Managing for Results*. New York: Harper and Row.

Eastaugh, S. (1992). "Healthy Management Alternatives for Better Productivity." *Harvard Business Review* 70:1 (January–February), 161–162.

———. (1990). "Hospital Nursing Technical Efficiency: Nurse Extenders and Enhanced Productivity." *Hospital and Health Services Administration* 35:4 (Winter), 561–573.

———. (1986). "Work Smarter, Not Harder." *Healthcare Executive* 1:2 (March—April), 56.

———. (1985a). "Improving Hospital Productivity under PPS: Managing Cost Reductions without Harming Service Quality or Access." *Hospitals and Health Services Administration* 30:4 (July/August), 97–111.

———. (1985b). "Organization, Scheduling Are Main Keys to Improving Productivity in Hospitals." *FAH Review* 18:6 (November/December), 61–63.

Eastaugh, S., and Regan, M. (1990). "Nurse Extenders Offer a Way to Trim Staff Expenses." *Healthcare Financial Management* 44:4 (April), 58–62.

Eastaugh, S., Sahney, V., and Steinhauer, B. (1983). "Alternative Compensation Incentives for Stimulating Improved Productivity." *Journal of Health Administration Education* 1:2 (Spring), 117–137.

Fera, M., and Finnegan, G. (1986). "Building a Productivity Improvement Team through MIS Leadership." *Hospital and Health Services Administration* 31:4 (July/August), 7–17.

Fielding, J. (1984). *Corporate Health Management*. Reading, Mass.: Addison-Wesley.

Fralic, M., Kowalski, P., and Llewellyn, F. (1991). "The Staff Nurse as a Quality Monitor." *American Journal of Nursing* 91:4 (April), 40–43.

Gandossy, R., and Jonassen, P. (1989). "Bucks for Behavior: Hospitals Get Innovative." *Hospitals* 63:8 (April 20), 50–51.

General Accounting Office. (1989). *Medicare: Physician Incentive Payments by Prepaid Health Plans Could Lower Quality of Care*. GAO Report HRD–89–29 (January). Washington, D.C.: U.S. Government Printing Office.

Gibbons, R., and Murphy, K. (1990). "Relative Performance Evaluation for CEOs." *Industrial and Labor Relations* 43:1 (February), 30S–51S.

Gilbert, J. (1990). *Productivity Management: A Step-by-Step Guide for Health Care Professionals*. Chicago: American Hospital Association.

Groner, P. (1977). *Cost Containment through Employee Incentive Programs*. Germantown, Md.: Aspen Systems.

Hay Group. (1991). *The Hay Group Guide to Executive Compensation: How to Meet* the Complicated and Sensitive Challenge of Rewarding Key Executives in Health Care. Walnut Creek, Calif.: Pluribus Press.

Hepner, J. (1989). Hospital Labor Relations. Ann Arbor, Mich.: Health Administration Press.

Herzberg, F. (1987). "One More Time: How Do You Motivate Employees?" Harvard Business Review 65:5 (September–October), 109–120.

———. (1974). "The Wise Old Turk." Harvard Business Review 52:2 (March–April), 70–80.

Herzberg, F., Mausner, B., and Synderman, B. (1959). The Motivation to Work. New York: John Wiley.

Holets, T. (1990). "Productivity Enhancement: Implications for Medical Group Management." College Review of the American Medical Group Administrators 7:2 (Fall), 22–35.

Hranchak, W. (1985). "Incentive Compensation and Benefits of Profit Sharing Plans." Topics in Health Care Financing 13:1 (Fall), 33–40.

Judson, A. (1982). "The Awkward Truth about Productivity." Harvard Business Review 60:1 (January/February), 93–97.

Laliberty, R., and Christopher, W. (1984). Enhancing Productivity in Health Care Facilities. Owings Mills, Md.: National Health Publishing.

Mick, S. (1990). Innovations in Health Care Delivery: Insights for Organization Theory. San Francisco: Jossey-Bass.

Milkovich, G., and Newman, J. (1984). Compensation. Plano, Tex.: Business Publications.

Murphy, K. (1986). "Incentives, Learning, and Compensation: A Theoretical and Empirical Investigation of Managerial Labor Contracts." Rand Journal of Economics 17:1 (Spring), 59–76.

Nutt, P. (1992). "Contract Management and Institutional Cost Control." Hospital and Health Services Administration 37:1 (Spring), 115–130.

Olson, G. (1989). "The Point Rating Incentive Plan for Health Care Managers." Health Care Supervisor 8:3 (October), 42–44.

Peters, T., and Austin, N. (1985). A Passion for Excellence: The Leadership Difference. New York: Random House.

Pink, G. (1991). "Relative Performance Evaluation of Nonprofit Hospitals." Health Services Management Review 4:3(November), 181–192.

Prospective Payment Assessment Commission (ProPAC). (1991). Medicare Prospective Payment System and the American Health Care System: Report to the Congress. Washington, D.C.: ProPAC.

Richer, S., and Weiss, D. (1988). "Employee Suggestion Programs." Health Care Management Review 13:3 (Summer), 59–66.

Rogerson, W. (1985). "The First-Order Approach to Principal-Agent Problems." Econometrica 53:11 (November), 1357–1367.

Sahney, V. (1991). "Quest for Quality and Productivity in Health Services." Frontiers of Health Services Management 7:4 (Summer), 3–22.

Shukla, R. (1990). "Effect of an Admission Monitoring and Scheduling System on Productivity and Employee Satisfaction." Hospital and Health Services Administration 35:3 (Fall), 429–441.

Shukla, R., and O'Hallaron, R. (1986). "AM Admissions/PM Discharges Can Reduce

Length of Stay.'' *Hospital and Health Services Administration* 31:4 (July/August), 74–81.

Shyavitz, L., Rosenbloom, D., and Conover, L. (1985). ''Financial Incentives for Middle Managers.'' *Health Care Management Review* 10:3 (Summer), 37–44.

Smith, H., Ottensmeyer, D., and Pasternak, D. (1984). ''Physician Incentive Compensation.'' *Health Care Management Review* 9:1 (Winter), 41–50.

Vergara, G., and Bourke, J. (1985). ''Reward Employees, Achieve Goals, with Incentive Compensation.'' *Healthcare Financial Management* 15:8 (August), 50–53.

Walton, M. (1990). *Deming Management at Work*. New York: G. P. Putnam's, 99.

Welch, W. (1991). ''Giving Physicians Incentives to Contain Costs under Medicaid.'' *Health Care Financing Review* 12:2 (February), 103–111.

Whitted, G., and Ewell, C. (1984). ''Survey of Hospital Management Incentive Programs: What Will Motivate the Motivators?'' *Hospitals* 58:5 (March 1), 90–94.

Williams, J., and Coolidge, R. (1991). ''Annual Hay Compensation Survey: Incentive Plans on the Upswing.'' *Trustee* 44:10 (October), 7–10.

Williams, J., and King, M. (1985). ''Executive Compensation Trends.'' *Hospitals* 59:19 (October 1), M14–M16.

Wyatt Company. (1991). *Survey of Benefit Trends in Health Care Facilities*. Boston: Wyatt Company.

Chapter 11

Quality Measurement, Value Shopping, and the Deming Method

Quality is a matter of survival. Sometimes people get caught up with all kinds of fuzzy, abstract "quality is a warm puppy" notions. That is wrong. Quality is profit and productivity and market share. And that's no warm puppy.

—John Guaspari

Physicians doing unnecessary care for reasons of added income is not the problem. We are startled to find how poor the level of medical knowledge is oftentimes. There are a lot of doctors out there who really need help.

—John Davis, M.D.

The state medical society is essentially a trade union. They have a very narrow outlook, viewing utilization profiles or quality reports as information that should be kept from the public.

—Benjamin Barnes, M.D.

The quality-of-care issue can be approached from a supplier's point of view (e.g., using the Deming method for improvement; Veney and Kaluzny 1991; Lynn and Osborn 1991) and from a consumerist point of view (the quality-disclosure method; Health Care Financing Administration [HCFA] 1991). A number of issues remain moot. Should the health sector place more emphasis on physician reeducation, credentials, PRO review, or public disclosure of quality scorecards? Quality is a difficult-to-measure attribute that has only recently pushed itself into the public eye. In 1981 the Public Citizen Health Research Group issued a policy statement calling on the federal government to assist Medicare beneficiaries in avoiding high-priced physicians. Consumerism should extend beyond simple price-disclosure activities to include expanded information on quality and availability of care. The libertarian conservatives in the Bush administration should be supportive of any efforts designed to promote informational equality between providers and patients. Improved informational equality is a necessary condition for stimulating competitive markets. However, the traditional conservatives in organized medicine may resist any efforts to supply patients with more information concerning cost, quality, and access (Morley 1991).

On April 17, 1985, the Health Care Financing Administration (HCFA 1985), controlling almost $100 billion in medical expenditures, announced that the 54 local professional review organizations (PROs) would be required to release data on hospital quality by DRG and department to the public. Confidentiality would be maintained as to the identity of specific doctors and patients. PROs and hospitals could provide their own interpretations concerning the quality of care. From a political perspective this is a unique issue, in which strange bedfellows like Ralph Nader and Milton Friedman (1965) are in agreement that consumers must be provided with information as a basis for shopping for health care. For both liberals and conservatives, if the data are collected with public funds, they must be made available to consumers, employers, and insurance companies. Consumer information is the fuel that fosters cost-decreasing competition, quality enhancement, and innovation in the marketplace. Improving quality and productivity through improved information to the multiple buyers, especially in a local service market (e.g., health care), puts into practice the economic theory concerning the benefits of a better buyer's knowledge of the supplier (Stigler 1961). For consumerists, the battle cry is "Select your providers on facts, not just hopes."

Provider concern for quality is not new (Sahney 1991). However, the type of systematic inquiry that characterizes the contemporary quality-assurance field has evolved within the health-services research community over the past two decades. Donabedian (1967) and Roemer, Moustafa, and Hopkins (1968) laid the groundwork for quality-measurement and quality-control activities. Donabedian outlined three basic approaches to quality assessment: structure (credentials, accreditation, licensure, and certification), process (what is done for patients, checklists, or criteria-mapping protocol, including the coordination and sequence of the activities), and outcomes (fatality, infection, and other adverse events or positive results, assessed from medical records or interviews). As a number of Rand Corporation researchers in the quality arena attest, measures of care by outcome are the best yardstick because they reflect net changes that occur in the patient's health status (Brook and Lohr 1985). Milton Roemer, as a strong advocate of both outcome measures and consumerism, proposed in 1968 a hospital quality index based on fatality rates crudely adjusted for case severity. A more refined version of that index by hospital product lines may soon be published on a regular basis in local community newspapers (Eastaugh 1986).

INJECTING QUALITY INTO THE COST-CONTAINMENT EQUATION

Are consumers smart enough to interpret quality statistics? The most basic answer to that question is yes, if we make the summary statistics comprehensible to the nontechnical reader. Just as buyers weigh a multitude of attributes in complex purchases, from televisions to cars, so payers and patients can shop for providers with better information at their fingertips. Many hospital visits cost as much as luxury cars, and some outpatient visits cost as much as televisions. Sensitivity to quality is even more acute in the case of health care. Consequently, buyer awareness is high, and the resources invested are not trivial.

A comprehensive review of the entire range of quality-measurement techniques is beyond the scope of this chapter. We shall briefly review methodological issues first and then examine the federal role in information data collection and dissemination. The danger if employers utilize Medicare PRO quality measures is that they may represent inappropriate tracers for overall facility quality. Employer groups may privately contract with the PROs to gather information on younger patient populations. The Commission on Professional and Hospital Activities (CPHA) offers normative quality data on 29 million nonelderly patients.

The prevalence of empty beds across the board has destroyed a low-cost (easy-to-get) signal of quality, the degree of empty beds in a facility. Many hospitals, regardless of quality, currently have low occupancy rates much of the year. Consumers may close inferior-quality hospitals and reward high-quality facilities. A high level of unnecessary and inappropriate care has contributed to the litigious atmosphere in our medical care system. Redoubling our efforts in the area of quality control is not only consumerist, but assists in reducing the headaches and prestige deterioration implicit in a high-malpractice volume. Future research should attempt to measure whether there is any significant correlation between malpractice volume and outcome measures of the quality of care. The relative merits of more direct regulation of quality (e.g., minimum standards) versus the market philosophy of providing information only (i.e., "let the buyer beware") will be surveyed in this chapter. The basic data sources for quality and access studies are outlined in table 11.1 (Eastaugh 1986; Siu et al. 1991).

There is some evidence that the HCFA (1991) report continued to identify too many high-mortality outlier hospitals. Green, Passman, and Wintfeld (1991) reported that the number of outlier hospitals declined by half (to 101) if the following four proxy measures for case severity were added to the regression analysis: share of patients aged 85 or over, percentages of patients with pneumonia and with urinary-tract infections, and discharges to a nursing home (as opposed to HCFA's less accurate variable "transfers from a nursing home"). The HCFA (1991) report was superior to earlier federal lists because mortality was shown for 30, 90, and 180 days after admission (rather than only for 30 days after admission). The 1991 HCFA list also adjusted the rates for new subdiagnoses not used in previous reports.

QUALITY STATISTICS: LARGE STATISTICAL PROBLEMS

Quality measures that are inaccurate, either because the case is one of a hundred conditions that require a severity adjustment in the analysis or because the sample is too small, can yield an unjustified slur against, or recommendation for, a

Table 11.1
Three Data Sources for Obtaining Information on Quality, Utilization, and Access to Health Care

	Patient Report	Administrative Data	Medical Record
1. Outcomes of care	Richest source of data on patient function.	Useful for assessing mortality and other selected outcomes likely to be recorded on claims.	Useful for some outcomes, but data on many outcomes are frequently missing, and functional status is missing.
2. Technical aspects of care	Patients may be good reporters, but recall of past visits is untested.	Not useful.	Data may be available only on most important processes.
3. Diagnostic tests	Patients recall testing in general terms but may not know details.	If available, may be best source of data, although test results will not be available	Good source, particularly for abnormal test results, but hospital records may miss data on outpatient tests.
4. Medications	Fair source of information on current medications.	If available, may be good source for certain types of medications.	Good source for important drugs; other drugs may not be recorded.
5. Symptoms	May be best source of information.	Not useful.	Limited data, generally on most important symptoms.
6. Access to care	May be best source of information.	Data on frequency of visits only.	Data on frequency of visits only.

Sources: Eastaugh 1986; Siu et al. 1991.

Table 11.2
Hypothetical Difference between Quality Scoring Report Cards, DRG Adjusted,
But with and without Appropriate Adjustments for Severity

Hospital	Quality Score without Severity Adjustment			Quality Score with Severity Adjustment		
	Fatality Rate per 10,000 Cases	*Morbidity Rate per 100 Cases*	*Total Score[a] FR&MR*	*Fatality Rate per 10,000 Cases*	*Morbidity Rate per 100 Cases*	*Total Score[a] FR&MR*
1	13	20	33 (B-)	6	12	18 (A-)
2	7	8	15 (A)	9	12	21 (B+)
3	10	18	28 (B)	12	40	52 (C-)
4	21	54	75 (F)	15	48	63 (D+)

[a]As in golf, the lower the score the better (combined fatality rate [FR] and morbidity rate [MR] score). As with golfers, providers also have handicaps.

given hospital (Daley and Kellie 1991). For example, the March 1986 DHHS Health Standards and Quality Bureau report on 269 ''atypical'' hospitals nationwide (Krakauer 1986) identified providers with abnormal fatality rates. The *New York Times* coverage of this story focused on two cases: (1) inferior hospital A, having a mortality rate of 6.0 percent when the predicted DRG-adjusted national average rate should have been 2.7 percent, and (2) good hospital B, having a 4.4 percent mortality rate, compared to the national standard rate of 6.2 percent (if the average hospital treated the same mix of DRGs) (Sullivan 1986). However, these statistical estimates were based on a 5 percent sample of Medicare patients. The lower limit of the 95 percent confidence interval for hospital A was a 1.9 percent fatality rate, and the upper limit for hospital B was a 7.3 percent fatality rate. In other words, hospital A may not have been worse than the national average, hospital B may not have been better than average, and there was a small chance that hospital A might be better than hospital B. For instance, two very severely ill heart-attack or gastrointestinal-hemorrhage cases could have made hospital A look bad. In summary, one should not be quick to generalize from 5 to 20 percent samples; analysts and consumer groups need the full data tape. Moreover, the performances of small hospitals may have to be analyzed with two to three years of compiled data to make statistically significant statements about the 10 to 20 most popular DRGs treated.

A brief example will highlight the shortcomings of a quality report-card rating system that does not adjust for both case mix and severity. Consider a simplified

2 × 2 contingency situation (table 11.2) where the first dimension consists of case-mix severity dichotomously labeled easy or hard, hospitalwide. Dimension two consists of the "true" quality of care as measured by the perfect study (a Rand report, circa 2020 A.D.), labeled good or bad, hospitalwide. God has provided the true quality ratings of the four hospitals, letter graded, as A −, B +, C −, D + (God, being forgiving, seldom gives grades below D +). The local PRO has ignored recent research and offers only severity-insensitive, but DRG-adjusted, quality grades for the four hospitals of B −, A, B, and F, respectively. Hospital 1 (table 11.2) resides in the severe (difficult) case-mix category, with very good (A −) true underlying quality. However, due to the insensitivity of the DRG system at capturing severity, hospital 1 appears to have mediocre quality (B −) when in fact it is doing a great job, considering the severity of its patient mix (error 1: understating the teaching/referral hospital's quality).

Hospital 2 resides in the low-severity category with high underlying (true) quality (B + rating by God). However, the imperfect PRO gives this hospital a quality score of A, largely because it has such an easy patient mix that it incorrectly appears to be superior to hospital 1 (error 2: overstating the good community hospital's quality of care). Hospital 3 is an example of a low-severity patient mix with truly low underlying quality (C −). This hospital receives a respectable quality grade from the PRO of B only because its patient mix is so easy to treat without complications and high fatality rates (error 3: labeling a poor-quality hospital as fair/good). Last, hospital 4 has a difficult severity level, given its DRG case mix, and low true underlying quality (D +), so it receives an abominable quality grade of F from the PRO. A poor grade is reported at an even lower level of performance because the difficult cases compound its already poor performance (error 4: labeling a poor hospital as being of lower quality than it deserves).

Error 4 is not a major problem for public policy, but the other three cases are cause for concern. Error 1 risks doing real harm to the patient census and financial viability of some of the 447 members of the Council of Teaching Hospitals. Error 2 falsely directs patients to vote with their feet to be cared for at suburban hospitals with a less severe case mix. Error 3 may cause some potential "shoppers" in the market for quality care not to shop because their local familiar grade-B hospital is good enough for most DRGs, when in fact this is a C- facility. Table 11.2 makes these points clear with a hypothetical aggregate scoring system. The March 1986 federal report highlighted three other possible scenarios: hospitals without any fatality because their case mix is easy and/or their sample size is so small, and specialized hospices or hospitals with enormous fatality rates.

The quality yardstick should focus on comparisons between acute short-term medical and surgical hospitals, not terminal-case treatment. There is an eighth possible case: the teaching hospital with a great quality score and complex case mix. For example, in the March 1986 report the predicted death rate for Georgetown Hospital Medicare patients, if equal to national average performance, was

5.4 percent (Krakauer 1986). The actual death rate was 1.9 percent, making this facility one of the fifty hospitals rated best. However, these ratings only considered case fatality rates, DRGs, and patient demographics. In reality, hospitals would have differing scores and severity ratings across departments and from year to year. The challenge for researchers is to make the rankings meaningful both statistically and for consumers trying to choose a hospital.

We have surveyed a number of severity-of-illness measures in chapter 8, including the Horn et al. (1985) severity-of-illness (SOI) index and her computerized severity index (CSI), Brewster et al. (1985) key clinical findings (KCFs), Gonnella's et al. (1984) disease staging, and Young's (1984) patient-management categories. The KCF system (Medis Groups) has the widest application, being used by over 600 hospitals (Iezzoni 1991). A fifth severity measure, the APACHE index (acute physiology and chronic health evaluation), done by Knaus et al. (1986), has been validated on intensive-care patients (Zimmerman 1989). This APACHE index is the only severity-of-illness measure that has been validated using clinical outcomes such as mortality and morbidity (Keeler et al. 1990). The streamlined second version of APACHE requires only 12 routine physiologic measurements, patient age, and chronic health status. The Knaus et al. (1986) study contained 10 teaching and 3 nonteaching hospitals. The best hospital had 41 percent fewer deaths among ICU patients than predicted utilizing the physiologic severity index. This particular teaching hospital had 69 predicted fatalities, but only 41 observed deaths, statistically significant at the 0.0001 level. In contrast, the worst-rated teaching hospital in the sample had 27 percent more deaths than expected (44 predicted, 56 observed). The worst nonteaching hospital in the sample had 58 percent more deaths than expected (33 predicted, 52 observed). There is much room for improvement in refining severity systems (Stearns 1991; and chapter 8) and DRGs (MacKenzie, Steinwachs, and Ramzy 1991).

Pine et al. (1990) explored the limited effectiveness of quality-assurance screening using large but imperfect data bases. A number of studies have suggested that the federal approach at HCFA still has imperfections (HCFA 1991; Hartz et al. 1989). State government officials have been equally cautious in drawing conclusions. For example, the New York State Cardiac Surgery Reporting System labeled only 4 of 28 hospitals as having significantly low-quality mortality rates (Hannan et al. 1990). While there is no evidence in the October 1990 Rand Corporation study that Medicare quality of care has been harmed by the DRG system of payment (Kahn et al. 1990), more states need to fund Medicaid quality-assurance programs.

A Harvard University evaluation team (Leape et al. 1991) identified 27,179 adverse events involving negligence in New York hospitals during one year. Some adverse events may result from limited medical knowledge, and a large percentage result from simple management errors that are preventable. The Deming (1986) or Juran (1964) approaches to statistical quality control are two approaches to identifying causes and developing systems to prevent error or reduce its harmful impact on the patient. Quality-assurance (QA) programs are slowly improving in this direction (Casanova 1990; Neuhauser 1991; Kuperman et al. 1991; Kritchevsky and Simmons 1991).

SEVERITY MUST BE BALANCED WITH APPROPRIATENESS REVIEW

Quality scorecards without severity measures may lead to needless apprehension among patients for the one-third of DRGs that are severity sensitive. Brook et al. (1990) reported that being treated by a surgeon who performed a high volume of carotid endarterectomies decreased the likelihood of an appropriate operation by 35 percent. This type of severity-adjusted appropriateness review can attempt to document the additional increments of severity caused by bad-quality medicine or poor medical judgment (e.g., doing an elective operation on a terminal cancer case). For example, one teaching hospital defended its high fatality rates on the HCFA outlier list (Krakauer 1986) as being the result of seven unfortunate (fatal) operations on six terminal cancer cases and one total hip replacement operation on a wheelchair-bound patient with above-knee amputations. The fact that these cases were more severe explains why the fatality rates were high, but why were the operations done at all? Was the hernia operation going to cure the cancer? Was the hip operation going to make the patient walk? All concerned agreed that the answer to these questions was no. However, provider motivation to do inappropriate care had two aspects: Senior attending physicians desired the additional income, and residents desired the extra patient volume since the teaching hospital occupancy rate had declined rapidly.

Such ethical problems, producing needless pain and suffering, can be addressed with more aggressive appropriateness review. The more basic question is whether we run our medical care system for doctors or for patients. The question is raised not so much to nettle as to alert teaching hospitals that attempt to misuse severity as a defense for their high fatality rates. Such hospitals will discover that the defense that their patients are more severely ill may get the hospital into more hot water if the public discovers that the elderly were overtreated.

Each year, according to the Centers for Disease Control (1991), 20,000 Americans die because of nosocomial infections. One-third of the hospital-acquired infections could easily be prevented with better quality-control techniques, saving society an estimated $2 billion in direct hospital care costs (not counting the billions of dollars of other costs, forgone earnings, and pain and suffering). The very nature of Medicare PPS payments has fueled renewed interest in investing in quality control (Keeler et al. 1990). Fewer hospital-caused complications translate into a shorter patient stay at lower cost, more in line with the prospective payment price for the case. Consider one simple example, the common "catheter fever" nosocomial infection. One should take a catheterized patient's urine specimen out of the plastic bag with a syringe, rather than unhooking the bag and draining the urine into a specimen cup. This example also highlights the fact that quality is a function of both medical-staff and hospital employee behavior (Eastaugh 1986).

The Federal Role

Federally financed PROs are surveying a wide array of quality measures, including (1) department fatality rates for cases with length of stay in excess of one day (given that some hospitals receive a disproportionate share of critically ill patients who cannot be immediately stabilized); (2) abnormally high rates of inpatient admission following outpatient surgery; (3) abnormally high readmission rates 30 to 60 days following discharge; (4) abnormally high rates of transfer for medical complications after the hospital treated the patient for more than two days; and (5) excessively high rates of adverse patient occurrences (APO morbidity events, i.e., an infection not present on admission, unexpected cardiac or respiratory arrest, unexpected deterioration leading to transfer into a critical-care unit, unplanned return to the operating room, or pathology tissue diagnosis not matching the patient diagnosis). If all these alternative measures of quality agree, then they provide independent confirmation of the validity of labeling a hospital good or bad.

Consumers also have their foibles. Just as individual doctors have a practice-style pattern or "clinician signature," so certain consumers have a consumption pattern or "demander signature" (e.g., to get the inappropriate drug prescribed or procedure done). Increased consumer education is warranted. If the federal government cannot afford it, employers may have to finance the effort (Eastaugh 1986; McClure 1985). If consumers are to reap the benefits of information disclosure on quality, they could assist the effort through personal word-of-mouth advertising and alert value shopping for the best providers to meet their needs.

Shifting Concerns in Consumer Behavior

Health care consumers are beginning to learn that "what you don't know can hurt you." Current questioning of the traditional model of the physician acting as the patient's agent, called agency theory, offers a number of challenges to the medical profession. If doctors do not send their patients to the best hospitals, but in fact make decisions for reasons of income maximization or travel minimization, as suggested by a number of studies (Luft et al. 1990; Flood, Scott, and Ewy 1984), one should bury the idea that "doctor knows best." Hospital quality does vary widely, and the public would benefit from reading a valid summary scorecard on quality, disaggregated by logical groupings of similar elective conditions (high, moderate, or low risk; probable surgical versus nonsurgical). Information on nonelective conditions would be less valuable for shopping considerations, especially for trauma cases. Consumers are increasingly coming to realize that it would be desirable to have the facts before choosing a hospital and, in turn, a doctor. This is a reversal of past tendencies to select the doctor first and let the doctor make the subsequent decisions. Surveys by the American Hospital Association suggested that physicians made only 39 percent of all nonemergency hospital selection in 1983 (Professional Research Consultants 1984). Consumers have become even more involved in selecting the hospital where they are to be treated over the last four years. Consequently, this figure now may be well below 25 percent. Consumers often make the de facto selection of a hospital by selecting certain HMOs or managed-care options.

Consumers select providers on the basis of imperfect information, and the extent of their rational (and semirational) search behavior suggests an ongoing process in which they seek their own balance between technical quality (e.g., outcome statistics), personal care-giving quality, and out-of-pocket price (Bolton and Drew 1991). If their perceptions of these three attributes become, on balance, sufficiently unattractive, they will search for new providers. Shock waves would resonate through the provider community if only 10 to 20 percent of patients comparison shopped. The health care delivery system has always been controlled by the element in short supply: previously the doctors, currently the patients. A lack of response from the majority of consumers can be predicted if two basic conditions occur: (1) information overload from too many conflicting and divergent sources, and (2) information "underload" because the informational content of the data is low. Information disclosure will be most effective when the data are packaged in nontechnical simplified ratings and reported for a list of possible local providers. The data presentation could be popularized in a convincing manner with a five-star rating system for a number of inpatient service lines. Five stars imply excellent quality, one star implies poor quality, and no star implies dangerously insufficient quality. Currently, the Joint Commission on Accreditation of Healthcare Organizations (JCAHO) provides a crude dichotomous estimate of the hospitals with no star (nonaccredited) versus those with some stars (accredited).

The statistical power of the estimates may not be capable of differentiating between a three-star and a two- or four-star hospital. Consequently, the ratings could be summarized by excellent quality (five stars), moderate quality (four, three, or two stars), low quality (one star), and poor quality (no star). For hospitals with more than 100 beds, a different rating might be presented for six broad-scope popular service lines: (1) high-mortality surgical (valve, coronary bypass, bowel; DRGs 104–7, 148); (2) low-mortality surgical (DRGs 161–62, 195–96, 336); (3) high-mortality nonsurgical (cancer cases, stroke, pneumonia, heart failure, and shock; DRGs 82 and 296, 14, 89, 127); (4) moderate-mortality (2 to 5 percent national average) nonsurgical (chronic pulmonary obstruction, gastrointestinal hemorrhage, renal failure, arrhythmia, diabetes; DRGs 88, 174, 320, 138, 294); (5) low-mortality nonsurgical (bronchitis, transient ischemic attacks, and angina; DRGs 96, 15, 140, 182); and (6) negligible-mortality conditions (DRGs 39, 121, 243) where morbidity, infection, and complication rates would be the only available quality yardsticks.

Provider Reaction

This six-category, five-star rating system can be improved over time. However, the biggest intangible benefit of any rating system may be the degree to which it stimulates patients to ask questions. The more questions, the fewer mistakes, and the higher the pressure on the hospital sector to invest in quality-enhancing systems and procedures. Patients who ask assertive questions avoid unnecessary procedures and reduce needlessly long waits (Hadorn and Hays 1991; SHS 1991; Eastaugh 1986). The hospital is not a healthy place to wait, as the iatrogenic risks are substantial. The pressure might become so powerful among the medical staff and trustees that they would develop the courage to throw the "rascals" (inferior-quality doctors) off the medical staff. For example, when the *Washington Post* newspaper published fatality rates among area hospitals doing heart surgery in 1981, two major teaching hospitals with poor ratings refused to renew admitting privileges for six low-quality surgeons.

Quality disclosure appears to have two basic supply-side effects: improving the medical-staff composition and providing quality-control muscle to a quality-assurance program that previously existed in name only. Quality assurance, in contrast to quality assessment, involves systematic identification of shortcomings in quality service delivery and designing activities to overcome the problems. One must implement follow-up evaluation to guarantee that no new problems have been introduced and that corrective activities have improved patient-care outcomes. Quality research is often slow to lead to quality-enhancing action plans unless the reaction to quality disclosure by the public makes inaction a costly strategy for the hospital (Williamson 1988).

Health care organizations justifiably fear that quality report cards might further undermine public confidence in providers. Sensationalized press accounts of malpractice or misconduct cases have heightened the public appetite to read quality report cards, question their current choice of providers, and question alternative methods of treatment. In highly competitive markets, hospitals may publish quality statistics as part of their marketing ad copy. In two-hospital towns where both facilities are half-full, one could expect the better-quality facility to advertise such statistics on a monthly basis. If nearly 1,000 hospitals will not survive the coming decade, why not make it the low-quality hospitals that fail? Public policy should be concerned with sufficient points of access to service, including access for the indigent. However, a large number of hospitals can close in a market with 300,000 empty acute-care hospital beds.

The Deming Method for Quality Improvement

Dr. Donald Berwick, a pediatrician and executive with the Harvard Community Health Plan, was the director of the 1987 National Demonstration Project on Industrial Quality Control and Health Care Quality. This demonstration project paired up 21 hospitals with Deming-method quality-control managers at Xerox, Ford Motor Company, Corning Glass, and Hewlett-Packard. The industrial experts taught the hospital managers statistical quality control, including productivity-enhancement techniques and some methods to enhance the clinical quality of care. Berwick continues to be a strong advocate for continuous improvement and the Deming method as an ideal in health care. Berwick (1989) argued in favor of going beyond the traditional Joint Commission on Accreditation of Healthcare Organizations (JCAHO) concept of accreditation or the regulatory concept of certification that "simply establishes thresholds for acceptability, just as the inspector at the end of an assembly line decided whether to accept or reject finished goods."

The Joint Commission on Accreditation of Healthcare Organizations reviews mainly hospitals. Hospitals are reviewed every three years. In 1991, 81 percent of hospitals had applied for accreditation and passed, and 8.1 percent were conditionally accredited by JCAHO (these facilities must correct problems cited in the review or lose approval). Each hospital is given an overall "confidential" grade, ranging from 33 to 98, but the JCAHO reports are in the public domain in 14 states and are often made public by individual hospitals. To its credit, under the leadership of former George Washington University faculty member Dr. Dennis O'Leary, the JCAHO has moved to support outcome measures of quality and some elements of the Deming concept of continuous quality improvement.

The Deming (1982) method strongly criticizes external standards, arguing that a facility that seeks merely to meet standards cannot achieve excellence. However, in health care we do need external standard setters from government and from the private sector (JCAHO). We also cannot assume that all workers will get better, but we must try retraining, and if all else fails we must fire the truly deficient health care workers. However, we must also strive to achieve the ideal of the Deming method by minimizing inflexible targets, documenting and defining critical processes (for quality control and cost control), creating an organizational culture in which people are not afraid to report problems, and having senior management commit to tiny improvements in hundreds of places to yield increased quality, productivity, and efficiency. Deming is fond of quoting Shewart (1925) that quality is not best achieved by discovering bad apples and removing them from the lot. In health care we must improve the distribution of performance levels, "make everyone a little better," and improve the work flow through better scheduling. Improvements are often reversible. Procedural changes, like distributing new criteria for doing something, are reversible (and require effort to maintain the new high levels of performance). Technical change through introduction of a new technology typically produces irreversible gains. The goal is to achieve a world of better quality through better economics, the engineering and operations-research approach to productivity and statistical quality control.

One Quality Improvement Program: Hospital Corporation of America

Quality-improvement programs cannot be done on a shoestring budget. Consequently, most of the initial quality-control programs were sponsored by large organizations, for example, Harvard Community Health Plan, the 1987 National Demonstration Project on Industrial Quality Control and Health Care Quality, or the example given in this section, the Hospital Corporation of America (HCA). HCA employs the Deming method of quality transformation (1986) and continual improvement in over 200 owned and contract-managed hospitals. The HCA effort was initiated by the president, cardiac surgeon Tommy Frist, and directed by pediatrician Paul Batalden, the HCA vice president for medical care since 1986. The Deming method was a new way of looking at the workplace from an egalitarian team perspective.

To work, the Deming method has to be performed as a regular part of the organizational culture. HCA had the resources and the motivation to begin experimenting with interdisciplinary quality-improvement teams in 1986. One aggravating external source of pressure came from nonprofit hospital managers claiming that for-profit firms like HCA operate with lower than average quality of care. To counteract these charges and to promote quality in the face of barebones reimbursement, Tommy Frist studied the Deming method as applied at Ford Motor Company and Xerox and observed the mixed results that General Motors experienced with the Deming approach. In HCA's pilot-test phase Paul Batalden tested the Deming concept at eight HCA hospitals in 1987. Since the original pilot test, any Deming-method HCA facility has been required to have part of the course taught by the CEO of the local hospital. The 14 basic points of the Deming approach (1986) are the following:

1. Create constancy of purpose for improvement of service from the CEO down through the organization.
2. Adopt the new philosophy that quality is a religion (not a slogan).
3. Cease dependence on inspection because quality comes from improvement in the process.
4. Do not overemphasize input prices.
5. Improve constantly the system of service production.
6. Institute training so all employees understand statistical quality control and the reality that all decisions will be data driven.
7. Institute leadership (HCA has a Quality Improvement Council at each hospital to charter and monitor multiple teams within the hospital).

8. Drive out fear so employees ask questions.

9. Break down ego barriers between professionals or departments.

10. Eliminate slogan exhortations (e.g., "Work harder").

11. Eliminate numerical quotas.

12. Remove barriers to communication to build pride and motivation (e.g., all team members are equal, physicians do not dominate).

13. Continually retrain and cross-train.

14. Have a bias to action that transforms the organization.

Deming (1986) also outlined some deadly diseases that get in the way of the process, including the annual performance review (merit rating) that undermines teamwork and discourages people from taking risks. Teamwork in the Deming process is not a process without some level of conflict. Teams will have both skeptics and quality champions. The skeptics help bring the champions back to reality (Walton 1990).

CEO Chip Caldwell et al. (1990) at HCA West Paces Ferry Hospital outside Atlanta documented some impressive success stories resulting from Deming-method teamwork. Sometimes the solutions are as simple as changing the time of day a process is done. To trim the needless waste of antibiotic IV preparations by 45 percent, the team studying this process simply changed the time of day in which IV admixtures were performed so that "discontinue" orders would come to the pharmacy before the admixture was performed. The team's next step was to modify the salvage process so that less antibiotic was thrown away. A second team worked on the problem of reducing the delay on stat medications in half by trimming the number of unnecessary trips (sending orders one at a time was too inefficient and caused a queue to form; Walton 1990). Another team increased preadmission testing from 17 percent of admissions in August 1988 to 73 percent by July 1989 by simplifying the paperwork process and educating patients. Increasing the rate of preadmission testing helped to reduce length of stay and to improve the gap between revenues and expenses.

HCA has a simple acronym to summarize its Deming-method cycle. The HCA quality-improvement method is called FOCUS-PDCA:

1. Find a process to improve.

2. Organize a team that knows the process.

3. Clarify current knowledge of the process.

4. Understand causes of process variation.

5. Select the process-improvement approach.

6. Plan the improvement and continue data collection.

7. Do the improvement, data collection, and analysis.

8. Check the results and lessons learned from the team effort.

9. Act to hold the gain and to continue to improve the process.

The final four steps are the standard Deming-method (1986) PDCA evaluation cycle. Never-ending continuous improvement by definition requires a circular PDCA cycle.

In summary, the Deming approach emphasizes identification of problem areas, team building, implementing successful remedies, and holding and extending performance gains. The job of quality control never ends because improvements are often reversible. Procedural changes, like distributing new criteria, require effort to maintain the new high levels of performance and productivity. By avoiding mistakes and useless units of activity, gains in productivity occur as quality improves (Neuhauser 1988).

IS BETTER QUALITY WORTH THE COST?

The buy-right movement, purchasing value for the money among a number of business groups, has some limited experience in Cleveland and Pennsylvania (Herrmann 1990). The more basic question from a hospital manager's perspective involves whether the incremental improvements in quality are worth the effort. Casalou (1991) provided a number of examples in which quality enhancement yielded a higher market share and improved productivity. Many stressed hospital managers face a number of quality problems: high infection rates, admitting time over three hours, and a high third-party claims-rejection rate. However, unless linked to tough productivity-enhancement scheduling systems as outlined in chapter 9, so-called "breakthrough" Deming quality-enhancement methods will produce no measurable benefits. A quality-improvement program that works will earn strong support from the finance department because (1) quantifiable benefits produced mean that the quality-assurance program is self-funding and (2) quality goals will be quantifiable to be motivational (Deming 1986). Little gains in trimming length of stay (Poses et al. 1990) or using statistical quality control in a clinic (Re and Krousel-Wood 1990) are examples of self-funding. In a four-week tour of Japanese hospitals I observed frequent usage of the Juran (1962) handbook and Ishikawa (1989).

The Deming method employs cause-and-effect fishbone diagrams (as used in the quality-circles approach) to depict and categorize causes of a specified problem. The solution to a problem usually involves changing the process. A process is a series of actions that repeatedly come together to transform inputs of a supplier into outputs received by a customer. Process-flow diagrams or flow charts are especially useful in service industries to identify all the unseen steps in a work process. Trend charts offer graphs of the clinical outcomes, productivity shifts, or fiscal changes as a result of the work process plotted over time. Control charts are the most advanced of the Deming-method techniques for plotting the range of variation in a system between the 10 and the 90 percent confidence intervals. When used for internal management purposes, they are run charts with statistically determined lower and upper limits for performance. As long as the process variable under study falls within these limits, the system is labeled "in control,'' and variation therein stems from common causes (seasonality, typical shifts in work force on July 1, and so on). To attempt to correct individual shifts within the system leads to overcorrection (tampering), thus causing more variation in performance (not less). The goal of the Deming method is to narrow the range between the upper and lower limits by seeking to eliminate the common causes of inefficiency that occur day in and day out. There is nothing sacred about the 10/90 confidence intervals. Studies have been done for patient-transport departments with 5/95 confidence limits and for labs with 20/80 confidence limits. How much variation can and should be accepted is a management decision. When a point falls outside the confidence interval, it is a special case that the department team should investigate. Common causes of variation may include a flu epidemic or the necessity to train new recruits to the department; a special cause would be equipment breakdown or information-system breakdown.

MORTALITY: ONE INDEX OF QUALITY

In December 1989 an article by Hartz confirmed the conventional wisdom of a link between hospital mortality rates and the quality of care. The Hartz et al. (1989) study linked an outcome measure (mortality, severity adjusted to some degree) with peer review judgments of quality of care in PRO panels. These results may apply only to inpatient elderly Medicare cases, but other researchers are studying data bases for all ages (Lohr 1990).

External users of quality-control information utilize the 10 and 90 percentile confidence interval in a different way. The regulatory emphasis is on tagging bad performers annually, rather than plotting performance at one facility over a number of days or weeks and trying to improve it. Consumers should try to vote with their feet to avoid the hospital in table 11.3, where actual death rates fall at the high end of the predicted range for half the most prevalent DRGs. The opposite situation applies in table 11.4, where the hospital is better than 9 in 10 hospitals for two-thirds of the DRGs listed. The risk-adjusted mortality rates presented in these tables employ different statistical techniques depending on the frequency of mortality. For most DRGs, representing 84 percent of patient admissions, a contingency-table model must be employed because the mortality rate is less than 5.0 percent (DesHarnais 1990). Low-mortality DRGs are not reported in the tables. However, a more detailed logistic model can be employed for the 65 DRGs, representing 74 percent of deaths and 16 percent of discharges, where the mortality rate is 5.0 percent or higher. These logistic regressions should include items like patient-severity comorbid conditions (Medical Technology and Practice Patterns Institute [MTPPI] 1991). Earlier work with smaller sample sizes (e.g., Greenfield, et al. 1988) revealed wide variations among hospitals in patient age, severity, and the burden of comorbid conditions. The teaching hospitals with high crude-mortality rates may also have the highest comorbidity burden, and this must be corrected for in any valid risk-adjusted mortality index (RAMI). The hospital listed in table 11.4 was a below-average

Table 11.3
Confidence Intervals of 90 Percent for Binomial Distributions of 1991 Death Counts and Severity-adjusted Mortality at Hospital Z

DRG	Number of Patients	Severity-adjusted Expected Dead	Actual Dead at Z	Upper 90 Percent Confidence Interval
127	986	92.39	151*a	127
14	571	74.84	82	97
89	549	63.92	90*	83
82	173	40.53	59*	53
87	168	38.20	55*	50
416	140	31.89	32	41
79	104	24.15	31	31
296	393	19.85	18	26
299	368	19.70	25	26
110	152	17.68	24*	23
239	156	13.29	20*	18
138	393	11.92	14	17
130	195	11.48	19*	16
403	99	10.96	15	16
132	150	9.03	11	14
182	853	8.87	13	14
209	348	6.99	6	10
15	349	3.65	4	6
243	396	3.64	7*	6

aThe asterisk denotes mortality rates in excess of the 90 percent confidence interval.

performer in mortality-rate terms in the federal HCFA statistics, but the results from the RAMI demonstrate that the facility is in fact better (fewer deaths) than 90 percent of hospitals when patient severity is factored into the analysis.

All great hospitals are not equally great across all departments. Moreover, effectiveness for certain services like ambulatory care cannot be measured by mortality rates or morbidity rates (Taulbee 1991). A certain teaching hospital may be in the 99th percentile for mortality rates, morbidity rates, or consumer satisfaction in some departments and rated between the 40th and 80th percentiles in other departments. In some cases the best hospitals in certain service product lines may be small or moderate-sized facilities. Consumers should inquire about quality ratings of specific departments where possible.

Table 11.4

Confidence Intervals of 90 Percent for Binomial Distributions of 1991 Death Counts and Severity-adjusted Mortality at Hospital A

DRG	Number of Patients	Severity-adjusted Expected Dead	Actual Dead at A	Lower 90 Percent Confidence Interval
127	2,071	205.41	126*a	137
14	1,319	186.72	109*	125
89	1,235	155.96	101*	104
82	414	104.84	72	70
87	369	89.38	51*	60
416	266	64.72	39*	43
79	211	50.31	29	34
296	917	48.63	39	33
299	718	40.58	22*	27
110	280	35.18	29	24
239	359	31.89	18*	21
138	882	28.25	11*	19
130	394	23.72	14*	16
403	181	20.95	10*	13
132	266	16.93	12	10
182	1,442	15.07	8*	9
209	678	14.21	11	8
15	802	8.51	1*	3
243	733	6.94	3	2

aThe asterisk denotes mortality rates better (lower) than the 90 percent confidence interval.

Cancer patients might look to the 57-bed Dana-Farber Cancer Institute in Boston or larger hospitals like Johns Hopkins, Stanford University, or Memorial Sloan-Kettering Cancer Center in New York. Ophthalmology patients might look to Johns Hopkins Hospital, the 100-bed Bascom Palmer Eye Institute in Miami, the 120-bed Wills Eye Hospital in Philadelphia, or the 113-bed Massachusetts Eye and Ear Infirmary (MEEI). Patients suffering from allergies, ear problems, or sinus conditions might look to the otolaryngology services at MEEI in Boston or to UCLA Medical Center, the University of Michigan Medical Center, Barnes Hospital in St. Louis, or the Mayo Clinic in Rochester, Minnesota. Patients seeking rheumatology services for arthritic joints might go to the Mayo Clinic, UCLA Medical Center, or Brigham and Women's Hospital in Boston. The best-quality rehabilitation services might be found at the 160-bed National Rehabilitation Hospital in the nation's capital, the Mayo Clinic, New York University Medical Center, Ohio State University Hospital, or the 176-bed Rehabilitation Institute of Chicago. The best urology care might be found at New York Hospital–Cornell Medical Center, the Mayo Clinic, Johns Hopkins, UCLA Medical Center, or the Cleveland Clinic. The best cardiology and cardiac surgery might be found at the Cleveland Clinic, Massachusetts General Hospital, the Mayo Clinic, or Duke University Hospital. The best gastroenterology care might be found at the 270-bed Lahey Clinic outside Boston, the Massachusetts General Hospital, the Mayo Clinic, Johns Hopkins, or the Ochsner Foundation Hospital in New Orleans. The best neurology care might be found at the Massachusetts General Hospital, the Mayo Clinic, the University of Michigan, Shands Hospital in Gainesville, or Columbia-Presbyterian Medical Center in New York. The best specialized pediatrics care might be found at Johns Hopkins Hospital, the 328-bed Texas Children's Hospital in Houston, the 294-bed Children's Hospital of Philadelphia, the 335-bed Children's Hospital in Boston, or the 279-bed Children's Hospital National Medical Center in the nation's capital. The best AIDS services may be found at George Washington University Hospital, San Francisco General Hospital, Duke University Hospital, or St. Vincent's Hospital in New York. This list is not exhaustive (it does not include every top hospital in each category).

Two parting caveats are in order. First, every patient cannot go to the best places (but a standard of excellence is important). Second, this analysis concerns technical quality of care, which may differ from the ex-patient's self-report of the total quality of care (bedside compassion, amenities, long-run results).

Hospital mortality is a relatively uncommon event and, as such, a rather limited measure of quality. Rehospitalization and patients' return to function may be more sensitive indicators, although they are costly to measure with accuracy. Anderson, Bush, and Berry (1986) suggested a quality-of-well-being (QWB) scale. Unfortunately, the costly interviewer-administered instrument, using question algorithms, is necessary if health-status quality-of-life data are to have sufficient reliability and validity.

PATIENT-CENTERED SELF-REPORTING OF QUALITY

A consumers' utility function in weighing the multiattribute dimension they label as "quality care" may vary widely according to education of the rater, experience, and the clinical disease in question (Lehr and Strosberg 1991; Sahney, Dutkewych, and Schramm 1989). Technological sophistication may be highly important to the educated cardiology consumer, but less relevant in selecting a rheumatology provider. Participation in clinical trials may be a positive attribute for cancer and AIDS patients, but irrelevant to the average consumer seeking neurology, ear, or eye care. The quality of nursing services may be highly important for AIDS care or rehabilitation, but less important for ophthalmology care. The crude RN-to-patient staffing ratio is a poor predictor of nursing quality; for example, San Francisco General Hospital with 0.8 RNs per patient can give better-rated nursing care than facilities with 50 percent more RNs and very few nurse extender technicians. The foregoing results are from a proprietary conjoint measurement technique (see chapters 2 and 6) survey of consumer preference.

The 1990 Institute of Medicine study, *A Strategy for Quality Assurance*, was groundbreaking for a National Academy of Sciences study team because it went beyond using the model of expert/professional dominance to suggest that consumers have a right to assess quality. The Institute of Medicine study team suggested that perhaps in a restructured PRO program some patient-centered perspectives on quality might be studied. The report cited the Picker/Commonwealth patient-centered project of Dr. Thomas Delbanco at Beth Israel Hospital in Boston. He will publish in 1992 a book on patient-centered care, patient education, and patient satisfaction, based on surveys of 6,500 patients at 62 hospitals. With patient satisfaction come better patient compliance and higher-quality long-run clinical outcomes. Medicine and surgery have to become more patient focused if the quality of our health care system is to improve. This viewpoint is also endorsed by DHHS Secretary Dr. Louis Sullivan, who often states that consumers and physicians must work together to enhance quality and solve the corrosive problems that cloud our future as a leading nation and as a strong, yet compassionate people.

ORGANIZED MEDICINE AND REGULATORY PHILOSOPHY

In practice, hospitals will trim low-quality, low-volume departments before they consider closing the entire hospital. For these low-volume, poor-quality, high-cost departments, the best solution may well be competition through information disclosure. Patients can break the habit of going to such a facility, whereas professional groups often try to hide the problem. For lack of competition and information, low-quality operators have been able to avoid bankruptcy; cost reimbursement underwrote their unit costs, no matter how high. If one in six hospitals goes out of business, how will this affect the careers of physicians?

Organized medicine has offered a festoon of arguments for not releasing report cards on provider quality. Analysts are correct in pointing out that without a severity adjustment per patient, one may not be able to discriminate between a 38th percentile two-star hospital and a 62d percentile four-star hospital. In such cases where the measurable differences in quality may be small and may fluctuate up and down from year to year, the differences in cost may be more relevant to the purchaser of care. Consequently, one could advise employees and employers to utilize economic criteria, access, and other criteria to differentiate two- to four-star hospitals. Users of the ratings should be confident that a one-star hospital is in fact a below-average hospital. Likewise, a five-star hospital is in fact an above-average hospital. What will happen if we do not tout the good news about five-star hospitals? Patient flow to such hospitals may decline in a price-competitive marketplace. One business executive of a large Fortune 500 company had a chilling rejoinder: "I don't care if 900 to 1,000 hospitals close over the coming five years, just as long as 100 of those Council of Teaching Hospitals members close. They are too expensive in the states we do business." Valid quality report cards, and not economics, may well be the trump card for survival among the expensive five-star hospitals.

WANTED: QUALITY ENHANCEMENT

Five-star hospitals might gain more patients than they can, or wish to, accommodate. However, higher volume will allow the hospital departments to, in the jargon of economics, slide down their average cost curves and take advantage of economies of scale (Eastaugh and Eastaugh 1986). Because consumers are constrained by travel costs, time costs, and out-of-pocket care costs, the problem of too many patients going to good hospitals seems a minor problem in the current low-occupancy marketplace. On the other end of the scale, perhaps the low-quality hospitals will be disciplined by the marketplace to go out of business. Those patients who shop deserve and receive better value for their money. Conservatives would suggest that those who remain with their inferior-quality providers deserve whatever they receive. Regulators would argue that the government should close some low-quality hospitals. If the medical profession gets more serious about its own independent investigations and fulfills the paradigm of the self-policing professional, licensing groups will give out more sanctions, expulsions, punishments, and mandatory exams and education.

If the medical profession does not police itself, and protect the public from low quality doctors, government review programs will expand. Market philosophy views technical quality as being simply another attribute, taken together with price, place (access), bedside manner, and hospital religious orientation, on which customers may or may not choose. Government's role is limited to breaking the information asymmetry between providers and consumers by providing PRO statistics and data for private reanalysis on care quality.

One of the difficult problems for researchers is that it will be hard to discriminate between a hospital that has two or three unethical senior attending physicians and a facility where the majority of physicians and nurses could benefit from a substantial upgrade in performance quality. A retrospective data base may never be capable of pinpointing whether quality is a problem with 3 or 40 people in the organization. Researchers may have to expose the quality shortfalls and leave it up to the hospital to develop an effective remedial quality-control program. The hospital can then decide whether it desires to be ranked poor or excellent in the eyes of its public, in which case many hospitals may finally get tough with providers of inappropriate care who in the past produced appropriate revenue for the hospital and infrequent reprimand.

One could ask, especially if we have a doctor surplus, how many doctors should be disciplined by the marketplace and whether the discipline should end careers. Some substantial fraction of physicians suffer from problems that significantly impair their functioning at some point in their careers. The number so impaired at any one time may remain small, perhaps under 5 percent. Who do we have to monitor competence? As one "60 Minutes" television segment documented in November 1985, the state of Massachusetts had two medical licensure investigators, in contrast to eight hairdresser investigators. In comparison to the hairdressing profession, health-service consumer awareness is higher, and the dollar amounts are more significant. Physicians tend to be dedicated, hardworking individuals, subject to human foibles and fearful that quality disclosure will further erode the patient-physician relationship.

One could ask if there is a way to obtain consumer attention without resorting to overstatement? Politicians often sensationalize issues such as "premature discharges" and hospital deception concerning "what day your Medicare benefits run out under DRGs." Senator John Heinz (R., Pa.), chairman of the Senate Special Committee on Aging, claimed frequently during 1985–86 that "seriously ill Medicare patients are catapulted out of hospital doors prematurely." However, in the vast majority of these "documented abuse cases," physicians kept their patients in the "facility" until it seemed safe to discharge them (Ray, Griffin, and Baugh 1990).

The definition of what is included in the "facility" has substantially changed as hospitals diversify, initiate less expensive and more appropriate settings for patient care, and "unbundle" the patient episode. For example, hospitals increasingly transfer patients to "swing beds" (lower-cost nursing beds), thus maintaining the elderly patient within a more appropriate setting, yet preserving continuity of care across the hospital/campus (Shaughnessy 1992). When appropriate, providers often discharge the patient with follow-up home health care services (often owned and marketed by the hospital). In the marketing literature this situation is often summarized by the rather unattractive word "demarketing"—that is, directing the patient to more appropriate channels of cost-effective service distribution. If the measures of quality for the individual patient do not erode under this demarketing/diversification strategy, then no harm is done. Customers would be left to decide whether a differential advantage, or shortfall, in comparing providers is substantial enough to change their behavior. For some Americans a small differential on fatality or infection rates may be substantial, but to other customers this difference is insignificant, even if it is statistically significant at the 5 percent level.

DIRECT REGULATION OR BUYER BEWARE

The chief failing of the proregulatory school is in defining a "significant" national or local cutoff point beyond which the quality of care is judged so substandard as to justify closing the provider. The issues are more complex in medical care because the quality measures are more complex and subject to future refinements than in truck safety or meat safety. In the 1986 case of naval heart surgeon Donal Billig, a fatality rate 1.24 times the national average was judged "terrible." If 18 fatal cases among 240 is terrible because the national average performance is 5.9 percent (or 14 cases in 240), should the regulatory protectors of the quality of care be charged with finding those four bad results? Billig was tried on five cases (five of 65 died) and convicted on three. In some sense a 7.3 percent fatality rate was surprising, considering that Billig was legally blind with vision of 20/400, certainly a handicap for a member of the surgical profession.

Reactionary providers lobbying against consumer disclosure argue that patients should be interested in two attributes: access and continuity of service. They refuse even to call patients "consumers." In other words, consumers should know as much about the quality of health providers as they know about the quality of electricity. One might recall the ad copy "All you need to know about electricity is that it is there when you need it." Considering the highly personal and potentially final (critical, life-threatening) nature of health care, most of the population would desire more comprehensive information concerning provider quality. Everyone likes competitive information about what we buy, not about what we sell or provide.

Ultimately it is a question of regulatory philosophy as to whether one makes normative or absolute judgments about quality of care. The liberal proregulatory school of thought suggests that the national PRO should make absolute judgments as to what a minimum standard of care is and should close those 5 to 20 percent of hospitals that do not meet this standard. However, any imposed national standard is by definition arbitrary; for example, should we set it such that it closes 8 or 16 percent of hospitals? On the other side, the conservative market-oriented school would suggest that we simply publish the information, promote consumer awareness, and let the customers vote with their feet to close poor-quality hospitals. Customers would be left to decide whether a differential advantage or shortfall in comparing providers is substantial enough to change their behavior. For some Americans a small differential on fatality or infection rates may be substantial, but to other customers this difference may be insignificant, even if it is statistically significant at the 5 percent level.

Advocates of more regulation ask whether market mechanisms and the courts will close providers fast enough. Regulators, while having problems defining minimum standards or "fast enough," do have a point. Low-quality providers will be harmed by consumer disclosure in two ways (business volume and further quality erosion), but will not close if enough patients continue to visit. With more information, low-quality providers will lose even the patient volume necessary to maintain their substandard level of performance and will decline further in quality rating (if they can stay in business). At this point Peterson et al.'s (1956) "out-of-practice" (negative impact on quality) effects come into play, and it may be in the best interest of society to close the provider. However, most economists would counterargue that the press and the provider's financial state could close the business quicker than the courts.

CONSUMERISM AND RATIONING

Are hospitals to be more like restaurants, in which the public servant assures us against food poisoning and the PRO critic provides a zero-to-five-star rating of the quality before the discriminating consumer decides to trust the kitchen? Or do we leave the decision totally up to government regulators, as with taxicabs, to save us from making personal calculations on car safety and cost before consuming the service? Considering this mixed metaphor, physicians and hospital managers should weigh which hassle they dislike less: (1) answering the critics and improving the kitchen or (2) being rationed like taxi cabs and burdened with substantially more paperwork. The facts seem to suggest that medical care providers are more like restaurants than taxi cabs: The variability in quality is substantial, and taste is highly personalized. Sorting single-handedly through a barrage of restaurant or hospital ad copy is an onerous task. But having a five-star hospital guide available seems prudent. The guide would have a brief summary section for 6 to 12 basic hospital case types, followed by what would be a seldom-used lengthy appendix listing actual numerical quality scores on a number of measures by hospital department for popular DRGs.

People spend more time shopping for restaurants than selecting health care providers. Good information concerning quality has heretofore not attracted much attention. Customs will change over time. As the population listens to friends who summarize or share information from *Consumer Reports* on health care provider quality, behavior will change. To utilize the very frank term, "excess deaths" will decline. If providers attempt to falsely discredit *Consumer Reports* on quality, they will experience the lament of deregulated bankers and airline executives: Information talks, people walk (to those with the better numbers). Doctors can either steer patients to the best-quality hospitals for which they have admitting privileges or try to gain privileges at better hospitals.

The cash flow now channeled to low-quality hospitals and doctors is destined to decline because of better consumer information. If society lets the low-quality providers fail, closing out their fixed costs, the average quality-of-care level improves. This method would cost less than any regulatory method of rationing through price controls done by Medicare DRGs or alternative delivery systems. If we trust consumers with an array of quality ratings, the public will have the ability to directly insist on better-quality care. The surviving providers would function in a better-equipped and less tightly reimbursed environment. Resources dedicated to health care would certainly be better spent, which is good economics and good medicine (Epstein 1990).

PAYERS SHOPPING FOR QUALITY PROVIDERS

HCFA has tried to improve the predictive ability of the statistical model used in the 1991 release of "Medicare Hospital Mortality Information." This latest model included information on patient characteristics such as: principal diagnosis (grouped into 17 analytical risk categories), age, sex, previous hospital admissions within the prior six months, admission source (e.g., physician reference, skilled nursing facility reference), admission type (e.g., elective or emergency), and the presence of up to four comorbid conditions—cancer, chronic cardiovascular disease, chronic renal disease, and chronic liver disease. Two additional adjustments for patient risks were also carried out. First, account was taken of the effect of the specific reason for admission—the principal diagnosis within each analytic category—on the probability of patient death. Second, additional information was carried by the grouping of patients into clinically informative categories. This last adjustment proved particularly important in the case of the surgical categories.

JCAHO and HCFA must come to the realization that to recognize true hospital quality (the signal) one must be able to adjust for differences in case-mix (bias) and account for random variation (random noise). Although adjustment for case mix differences has been discussed extensively in the literature, the effect of random variation has not been adequately addressed. Predictive error rates with respect to "quality" for both "outlier" and "non-outlier" hospitals show that death rates are not yet a good indicator of underlying quality. HCFA and the PROs must continue to improve the predictive error rates of their quality measures. Large hospitals with large sample sizes that are high fatality rate outliers for several years in a row may be, with high probability, hospitals with low quality of care. However, it is likely that only a small number of hospitals would be identified this way. As the number of patients served by the hospital increases, because more years of data are included in the analysis, classification may grow more reliable. JCAHO and regulators will have difficulty in their efforts to recognize low quality hospitals by looking at (case-mix adjusted) mortality rates because random variation appears to swamp the quality signal. Mortality rates will not be our only measure of quality. DesHarnais, McMahon and Wroblewski (1991) report that some hospitals that rank well when compared with mortality rates do not do as well on quality measures such as readmission rates or complication rates.

Some employers should be uneasy with the idea of utilizing Medicare patient quality statistics (even if they represent one-third of all hospital cases) as tracer "proxy" indicators of hospital quality. If the patient sample were expanded to include nonelderly patients, the resulting quality report cards could change significantly. From the hospital perspective, the "good news" is that large employers are paying state PROs to expand their review functions to nonelderly cases under private contract. Under federal contract, the PROs review only inpatient Medicare cases, but the sponsoring firms offer their utilization review services fee-for-service to employers, insurers, HMOs, and PPOs. However, for hospitals with bad quality ratings, the "bad news" is that employers will shop aggressively, ask for larger discounts, or exclude the bad performers from their selective contract listing. Employees will also be strongly encouraged to shop on cost and quality (Herrman 1990). Large employers are already setting up advisory offices where employees can obtain advice on the "best" providers to utilize (McClure 1985). As bulk purchasers attempt to teach individual purchasers to "buy right," they should also invest in PRO research and development of better-quality assessment tools. Experts in quality assessment lament that their measures are imperfect and that investment in this area is insufficient. However, in this era of reduced public spending, private-sector investment must finance the bulk of new basic research (Couch 1991; Fleming 1991).

If researchers overcriticize the potential uses for quality-of-care-measurement systems, private purchasers of health services will become totally preoccupied with cost concerns. Some large employers have argued that the provider selection process can focus either on price or quality attributes, and attempting to achieve a balance of both concerns would lead to strategic mediocrity. The rejoinder reads: Tell us you cannot measure quality, and we shall ignore it. Discounting quality-measurement efforts may lead to government takeover of the accreditation and licensure business from health professionals and to a mandate of a federal minimum standard of care. Future increases in consumer comparison shopping and public disclosure of valid quality ratings are better than further government intrusion into health care. Luft, Garnick and Mark (1990) reported that hospitals with poorer than expected outcomes attracted fewer admissions than other hospitals. Consumers are increasingly concerned with, and confused by, undigested quality comparisons. The more valid (severity-adjusted), careful studies will target fewer low-quality places (e.g., they will tag four bad hospitals in the area rather than eight). Why? Two properties explain why a severity measure that is significant at the patient level of analysis may not be significant at the aggregate hospitalwide level of analysis: restriction in range and the law of averages. Restriction of range harms predictive possibilities; for example, the Scholastic Aptitude Test (SAT) scores are very helpful in predicting who will be the successful Stanford undergraduates if the entire population of high-school seniors is the range studied, but if the range of students is restricted to only Stanford and Harvard undergraduates, SAT scores are of no value in predicting successful students. In the fatality studies, samples with a restricted range, such as Medicare surgery patients or pediatric Medicaid patients, and the further restriction of range implicit in the DRG system for categorizing similar patients dampen or reduce the predictive impact of clinical severity. Physicians may be correct in asserting the understated impact of severity on resource consumption per patient. More research needs to be done on severity measures and patient values. Hall, Epstein, and McNeil (1989) and Ware and Berwick (1990) provided strong support for the development of wider multidimensional patient-centered quality measures. Tarlov et al. (1989) utilized this approach with a five-choice excellent-to-poor patient response scale to measure quality, rather than the "warm puppy" called "satisfaction."

CONCLUSIONS

Relman (1988) labeled the rising outcomes/quality-measurement movement as the "third great revolution in medical care." If this dream is to come true, more research should be financed in the area of national practice standards. Perhaps Robert Brook was correct in stating that national practice standards will make better doctors, because a good cook always starts with a cookbook.

Aggressive use of information on quality and cost has always been the principal advantage of any competitive industry (Dunlop 1980; Stigler 1961). Valid quality measures that provide easily understandable rankings for public consumption will prove eye-opening for patients, payers, and physicians. Hospitals and physicians will have to exist in a world of more aggressive comparison shoppers, including individuals, employers, and insurance companies. The major weakness that researchers perceive in the current vision of scorecards and directories is a failure to adjust for patient severity of illness within DRGs. Consumer power, from the provider viewpoint (more irritating, but better informed), will force institutions to invest more in quality-enhancing efforts.

In a quality-competitive marketplace, it becomes even more important for clinicians to ally themselves with good-quality hospitals and more strongly support the Deming approach. Until recently a simple doctrine existed that said that competition would not work in health care, patients would not shop, and all "credentialed" doctors and hospitals offered approximately the same quality of care. The simple doctrine has died. Consider the popular joke among medical school students concerning what they should call the lowest-quality graduate in their class. Answer: doctor. A quality physician is as unhappy as anybody else about incompetent clinicians who give physicians a bad name. Future research should consider how accurately performance in residency programs and medical school predict postgraduate quality of care in practice. A number of studies have suggested a link between the quality and quantity of care provided. Medicine is far from monolithic in style, and therefore preferred practice pattern (PPP) efficiency profiles vary widely across the country. For example, Burns and Wholey (1991), in a study of 55,000 discharges, reported that the medical school attended by the physician influences the patient's length of stay. Perhaps a future quality-of-care study in 10 years could rate medical schools according to the quality of their graduates. Economists and physicians are concerned that all the additional care paid for may not be medically necessary.

One should not assume that poor-quality care is a predetermined destiny for certain urban medical centers. One hospital used its severity-adjusted fatality data to convince the medical staff to standardize orders for antibiotics and blood cultures in the emergency department (where 92 percent of pneumonia fatality cases originated). Within three months the severity-adjusted fatality rates had declined 45 percent to the average level for teaching hospitals in that city. Two advantages of enhancing quality of care include image improvement and saving resources. Bad-quality care is expensive because it is costly to "fix" the mistakes (e.g., prolonged length of stay, malpractice suits).

REFERENCES

American Hospital Association. (1992). *Quality Measurement and Management*. Chicago: HRET Report, AHA.

Anderson, J., Bush, J., and Berry, C. (1986). "Classifying Function for Health Outcome and Quality of Life Evaluation." *Medical Care* 24:5 (May), 454–470.

Benson, D., and Townes, P. (1991) *Excellence in Ambulatory Care*, San Francisco: Jossey-Bass.

Berwick, D. (1989). "Continuous Improvement as an Ideal in Health Care." *New England Journal of Medicine* 320:1 (January 5), 53–56.

Bodendorf, F., and Mackey, F. (1986). "Evaluating a Hospital's IQ: Indicators of Quality." *Medical Benefits* 3:9 (May 15), 1–3.

Bolton, R., and Drew, J. (1991). "Multistage Model of Customers' assessments of service quality and value", *Journal of Consumer Research* 17:4 (March), 375–384.

Brewster, A., et al. (1985). "MEDISGRPS: A Clinically Based Approach to Classifying Hospital Patients at Admission." *Inquiry* 22:4 (Winter), 377–387.

Brewster, J. (1986). "Prevalence of Alcohol and Other Drug Problems among Physicians." *Journal of the American Medical Association* 225:14 (April 11), 1913–1920.

Brook, R., and Lohr, K. (1985). "Efficacy, Effectiveness Variations, and Quality: Boundary-crossing Research." *Medical Care* 23:5 (May), 710–722.

Brook, R., Park, R., Chassin, M., and Solomon, D. (1990). "Predicting Appropriate Use of Carotid Endarterectomy, Upper Gastrointestinal Endoscopy, and Coronary Angiography." *New England Journal of Medicine* 323:17 (October 25), 1173–1177.

Burns, L., and Wholey, D. (1991). "Effects of Patient, Hospital, and Physician Characteristics on Length of Stay and Mortality." *Medical Care* 29:3 (March), 251–271.

Caldwell, C., McEachern, J., and Davis, V. (1990). "Measurement Tools Eliminate Guesswork." *Healthcare Forum Journal* 11:4 (July/August), 23–28.

Casalou, R. (1991). "Total Quality Management in Health Care." *Hospital and Health Services Administration* 36:1 (Spring), 134–146.

Casanova, J. (1990). "Status of Quality Assurance Programs in American Hospitals." *Medical Care* 28:11 (November), 1104–1109.

Centers for Disease Control. (1991). *Study on the Efficacy of Nosocomial Infection Control*. Washington, D.C.: DHHS.

Cleary, P., Epstein, A., Oster, G., and Morrissey, G. (1991). "Health-related Quality of Life among Patients Undergoing Percutaneous Coronary Angioplasty." *Medical Care* 29:10 (October), 939–950.

Couch, J. (1991). *Health Care Quality Management for the 21st Century*. Tampa: American College of Physician Executives.

Cunningham, L. (1991). *The Quality Connection in Health Care*. San Francisco: Jossey-Bass.

Daley, J., and Kellie, S. (1991). *Guidebook on Uses of Mortality Data: Applications in Hospital Quality Assurance Activities*. Chicago: AMA.

Dans, P., Weiner, J., and Otter, S. (1985). "Peer Review Organizations: Promises and Potential Pitfalls." *New England Journal of Medicine* 313:18 (October 31), 1131–1137.

Deming, W. (1986). *Out of the Crisis*. Cambridge, Mass.: Massachusetts Institute of Technology Press, Center for Advanced Engineering.

———. (1982). *Quality, Productivity, and Competitive Position*. Cambridge, Mass.: Massachusetts Institute of Technology Press, Center for Advanced Engineering.

DesHarnais, S. (1990). "Current Uses of Large Data Sets to Assess the Quality of Providers: Construction of Risk-adjusted Indexes of Hospital Performance." *International Journal of Technology Assessment in Health Care* 6:2 (Spring), 229–238.

DesHarnais, S., McMahon, L., and Wroblewski, R. (1991). "Measuring Outcomes of Hospital Care using Risk-adjusted Indexes." *Health Services Research* 26:4 (October), 425–466.

Donabedian, A. (1968). "Promoting Quality through Evaluating Patient Care." *Medical Care* 6:1 (January), 181–202.

Dubois, R. (1990). "Inherent Limitations of Hospital Death Rates to Assess Quality." *International Journal of Technology Assessment in Health Care* 6:2 (Spring), 220–227.

Dunlop, J. (1980). *Business and Public Policy*. Cambridge, Mass.: Harvard University Press.

Eastaugh, S. (1986). "Hospital Quality Scorecards: The role of The Informed Consumer" *Hospital and Health Services Administration* 31:6 (November/December), 85–102.

———. (1983). "Placing a Value on Life and Limb: The Role of the Informed Consumer." *Health Matrix* 1:1 (Winter), 5–21.

Eastaugh, S., and Eastaugh, J. (1986). "Prospective Payment Systems: Further Steps to Enhance Quality, Efficiency, and Regionalization." *Health Care Management Review* 11:4 (Fall), 37–52.

Epstein, A. (1990). "The Outcomes Movement—Will It Get Us Where We Want to Go?" *New England Journal of Medicine* 323:4 (July 26), 266–270.

Finkler, M., and Wirtschafter, D. (1991). "Cost-effectiveness and Obstetrics Services." *Medical Care* 29:10 (October), 951–963.

Fleming, S. (1991), "The Relationship between Quality and Cost: pure and simple" *Inquiry* 28:1 (Spring), 29–38.

Fleming, S., McMahon, L., and DesHarnais, S. (1991). "The Measurement of Mortality: Risk-adjusted Variable Time Window Approach." *Medical Care* 29:9 (September), 815–822.

Flood, A., Scott, W., and Ewy, W. (1984). "Does Practice Make Perfect?" *Medical Care* 22:2 (February), 98–125.

Friedman, M. (1965). *Capitalism and Freedom*. Chicago: University of Chicago Press.

Gonnella, J., Hornbrook, M., and Louis, D. (1984). "Staging of Disease: A Case-Mix Measurement." *Journal of the American Medical Association* 251:5 (February 3), 637–644.

Green, J., Passman, L., and Wintfeld, N. (1991). "Analyzing Hospital Mortality: The Consequences of Diversity in Patient Mix." *Journal of the American Medical Association* 265:14 (April 10), 1849–1853.

Greenfield, S., Aronow, H., Elashoff, R., and Watanabe, D. (1988). "Flaws in Mortality Data: The Hazards of Ignoring Comorbid Disease." *Journal of the American Medical Association* 260:15 (October 21), 2253–2255.

Guaspari, J. (1989). *I Know It When I See It: A Modern Fable about Quality*. New York: AMACOM.

Hadorn, D., and Hays, R. (1991). "Multitrait-multimethod Analysis of Health-related Quality-of-life Measures." *Medical Care* 29:9 (September), 829–840.

Hall, J., Epstein, A., and McNeil, B. (1989). "Multidimensionality of Health Status in an Elderly Population." *Medical Care* 27:3 (March), 168S–177S.

Hannan, E., Kilburn, H., O'Donnell, J., Lukacik, G., and Shields, E. (1990). "Adult Open Heart Surgery in New York State: Analysis of Risk Factors and Hospital Mortality Rates." *Journal of the American Medical Association* 264:21 (December 5), 2768–2774.

Hartz, A., Krakauer, H., Kuhn, E., Young, M., and Jacobsen, S. (1989). "Hospital Characteristics and Mortality Rates." *New England Journal of Medicine* 321:25 (December 21), 1720–1725.

Hass, D., and Savoca, E. (1990). "Quality and Provider Choice: A Multinomial Logit-Least-Squares Model with Selectivity." *Health Services Research* 24:6 (February), 791–809.

Health Care Financing Administration (HCFA). (1991). *Medicare Hospital Mortality Information: Summary Information and Methodology.* Washington, D.C.: HCFA, DHHS.

———. (1985). *Federal Register* 50:12 (April 17), 312–322.

Herrmann, J. (1990). "Buying Health Services from a List of the Highest Quality: The Cleveland Initiative." *Federation of American Health Systems Review* 23:6 (November–December), 26–31.

Horn, S., and Horn, R. (1986). "The Computerized Severity Index: A New Tool for Case-Mix Management." *Journal of Medical Systems* 10:1, 73–79.

Horn, S., et al. (1985). "Interhospital Differences in Severity of Illness: Problems for Prospective Payment Based on DRGs." *New England Journal of Medicine* 313:1 (July 4), 20–24.

Iezzoni, L., Ash, A., and Coffman, G. (1991). "Admission and Mid-Stay MEDISGRPs Scores as Predictors of Death." *American Journal of Public Health* 81:1 (January) 74–78.

Institute of Medicine. (1990). *A Strategy for Quality Assurance.* Washington, D.C.: National Academy of Sciences Press.

Ishikawa, K. (1989). *Guide to Quality Control.* Tokyo: Asian Productivity Organization.

Joint Commission on Accreditation of Healthcare Organizations (JCAHO). (1991). *Report of the Joint Commissions Survey.* Chicago: Joint Commission on Accreditation of Healthcare Organizations.

Juran, J. (1964). *Managerial Breakthrough.* New York: McGraw-Hill.

———. (1962). *Quality Control Handbook.* New York: McGraw-Hill.

Kahn, K., Rubenstein, L., Draper, D., Kosecoff, J., Keeler, E., and Brook, R. (1990). "Effects of the DRG-based PPS on Quality of Care for Hospitalized Medicare Patients." *Journal of the American Medical Association* 264:15 (October 17), 1953–1961.

Keeler, E., Kahn, K., Draper, D., and Sherwood, M. (1990). "Changes in Sickness at Admission Following the Introduction of PPS." *Journal of the American Medical Association* 264:15 (October 17), 1962–1968.

Knaus, W., Draper, E., Wagner, D., and Zimmerman, J. (1986). "An Evaluation of Outcome from Intensive Care in Major Medical Centers." *Annals of Internal Medicine* 104:3 (March), 410–418.

Knaus, W., Wagner, D., and Joanne, L. (1991). "Short-term Hospital Prediction for Critically Ill Hospital Patients." *Science* 254:18 (October 18), 389–394.

Krakauer, H. (1986). "The Prediction of Statistical Outliers Based on Medicare Fatality

Rates, Report (March), Office of Medical Care Review.'' Health Standards and Quality Bureau, Health Care Financing Administration, DHHS.

Kritchevsky, S., and Simmons, B. (1991). ''Continuous Quality Improvement.'' *Journal of the American Medical Association* 266:13 (October 2), 1817–1823.

Kuhn, E., Hartz, A., Gottlieb, M., Rimm, A. (1991). ''Relationship of Hospital Characteristics and Peer Review in Six Large States.'' *Medical Care* 29:10 (October), 1028–1038.

Kuperman, G., James, B., Jacobsen, J., and Gardner, R. (1991). ''Continuous Quality Improvement Applied to Medical Care.'' *Medical Decision Making* 11:4 (October-December) S60-S64.

Leape, L., Brennan, T., Laird, N., Lawthers, A., Newhouse, J., Weiler, P., and Hiatt, H. (1991). ''The Nature of Adverse Events in Hospitalized Patients.'' *New England Journal of Medicine* 324:6 (February 7), 377–384.

Lehr, H, and Strosberg, M. (1991). ''Quality Improvement in Health Care: Is the Patient Still Left Out?'' *Quality Review Bulletin* 17:10 (October), 326–330.

Lohr, K. (1990). ''Use of Insurance Claims Data in Measuring Quality of Care.'' *International Journal of Technology Assessment in Health Care* 6:2 (Spring), 263–270.

Luft, H., Garnick, D., and Mark, D. (1990). ''Does Quality Influence Choice of Hospital?'' *Journal of the American Medical Association* 263:21 (June 6), 2899–2906.

Luft, H., Garnick, D., Mark, D., and McPhee, S. (1990). *Hospital Volume, Physician Volume, and Patient Outcome: Assessing the Evidence*. Ann Arbor, Mich.: Health Administration Press.

Luft, H., and Hunt, S. (1986). ''Evaluating Individual Hospital Quality through Outcome Statistics.'' *Journal of the American Medical Association* 255:20 (May 30), 2780–2784.

Lynn, M., and Osborn, D. (1991). ''Deming's Quality Principles: A Health Care Application.'' *Hospital and Health Services Administration* 36:1 (Spring), 111–119.

MacKenzie, E., Steinwachs, D., and Ramzy, A. (1991). ''Trauma Casemix and Hospital Payment: Refining DRGs.'' *Health Services Research* 26:1 (April), 3–22.

McClure, W. (1985). ''Buying Right: The Consequences of Glut.'' *Business and Health* 2:9 (September), 43–46.

Medical Technology and Practice Patterns Institute (MTPPI). (1991). ''Report on Medicare Hospital Mortality Statistics: A Detailed Analysis of the Mortality Profile.'' Medical Technology and Practice Patterns Institute, Washington, D.C.

Milakovich, M. (1991). ''Creating a Total Quality Environment.'' *HealthCare Management Review* 16:2 (Spring), 9–20.

Morley, J. (1991). ''Cleveland Health Quality Choice Program.'' *Federation of American Health Systems Review* 24:1 (January–February), 40.

Neuhauser, D. (1991). ''Parallel Providers, Ongoing Randomization, and continuous improvement'', *Medical Care* 29:7 (July Supplement), JS5-JS9.

Neuhauser, D. (1988). ''The Quality of Medical Care and the 14 Points of Edwards Deming.'' *Health Matrix* 6:2 (Summer), 7–10.

O'Leary, D. (1986). ''JCAH New Series of Quality Indicators Based on Outcome, Clinical Standards.'' *Federation of American Health Systems* 19:3 (May/June), 26–27.

Peterson, O., et al. (1956). ''An Analytic Study of North Carolina Medical Practice, 1953–54.'' *Journal of Medical Education* 31:12 (December), 1–165.

Pine, M., Rogers, D., Morgan, D., and Beller, R. (1990). ''Potential Effectiveness of

Quality Assurance Screening Using Large But Imperfect Databases.'' *Medical Decision Making* 10:2 (April–June), 126–134.

Poses, R., Bekes, C., Copare, F., and Scott, W. (1990). ''What Difference Do Two Days Make? Inertia of Physicians' Sequential Prognostic Judgements.'' *Medical Decision Making* 10:1 (January–March), 6–14.

Professional Research Consultants, Inc. (1984). ''Marketing Surge Tied to Consumers.'' *Hospitals* 58:12 (June 16), 33–35.

Ray, W., Griffin, M., and Baugh, D. (1990). ''Mortality Following Hip Fracture before and after Implementation of the Prospective Payment System.'' *Archives of Internal Medicine* 150:10 (October), 2109–2114.

Re, R., and Krousel-Wood, M. (1990). ''How to Use Continuous Quality Improvement Theory and Statistical Quality Control Tools in a Multispecialty Clinic.'' *Quality Review Bulletin* 16:11 (November), 391–397.

Relman, A. (1988). ''Assessment and Accountability: The Third Revolution in Medical Care.'' *New England Journal of Medicine* 319:23 (December), 1220–1222.

Riley, G., Lubitz, J., and Rabey, E., ''Enrollee Health Status under Medicare Risk Contracts: Analysis of Mortality Rates.'' *Health Services Research* 26:2 (June), 137–163.

Roemer, M., Moustafa, A., and Hopkins, C. (1968). ''A Proposed Hospital Quality Index: Hospital Death Rates Adjusted for Case Severity.'' *Health Services Research* 3:2 (Summer), 96–118.

Sahney, V. (1991). ''Quest for Quality and Productivity in Health Services.'' *Frontiers of Health Services Management* 7:4 (Summer), 2–41.

Sahney, V., Dutkewych, J., and Schramm, W. (1989). ''Quality Improvement Process: Foundation for Excellence in Health Care.'' *Journal of the Society for Health Systems* 1:1 (January), 17–30.

Shaughnessy, P. (1992). *Shaping Policy for Long-term Care: Learning from the Effectiveness of Hospital Swing Beds*, Ann Arbor, Mich.: Health Administration Press.

Shewhart, W. (1925). ''The Application of Statistics as an Aid in Maintaining Quality of a Product.'' *Journal of the American Statistical Association* 20:8, 546–548.

Siu, A., McGlynn, E., Morgenstern, H., and Brook, R. (1991). ''A Fair Approach to the Quality of Care.'' *Health Affairs* 10:1 (Spring), 62–75.

Sloan, F., Perrin, J., and Valvona, J. (1986). ''In-Hospital Mortality of Surgical Patients: Is There an Empirical Basis for Standard-Setting?'' *Surgery* 99:4 (April), 446–454.

Sloan, F., Valvona, J., Perrin, J., and Adamache, K. (1986). ''Diffusion of Surgical Technology: An Exploratory Study.'' *Journal of Health Economics* 5:1 (March), 31–62.

Society for Health Systems (SHS). (1991). *Proceedings of the Quest for Quality Conference*. Norcross, Georgia: Industrial Engineering & Management Press.

Stearns, S. (1991). ''Hospital Discharge Decisions, Outcomes, and the Use of Unobserved Information on Casemix Severity.'' *Health Services Research* 26:1 (April), 27–51.

Stigler, G. (1961). ''The Economics of Information.'' *Journal of Political Economy* 69:3 (May), 213–225.

Sullivan, R. (1986). ''Leading Hospital Accused of Poor Care.'' *New York Times*, March 4, B-3.

Tarlov, A., Ware, J., Greenfield, S., Nelson, E., Perrin, E., and Zubkoff, M. (1989).

"The Medical Outcomes Study: Application of Methods for Monitoring the Results of Medical Care." *Journal of the American Medical Association* 262:6 (August 18), 925–930.

Taulbee, P. (1991). "Outcomes Management: Buying Value and Cutting Costs." *Business and Health* 9:3 (March), 28–39.

U.S. Congress. (1986). Health Care Quality Improvement Act, title IV of Public Law 99–660.

Veney, J., and Kaluzny, A. (1991). *Evaluation and Decision Making for Health Services.* 2d ed. Ann Arbor, Mich.: Health Administration Press.

Walton, M. (1990). *Deming Management at Work.* New York: G. P. Putnam's, 99.

Ware, J., and Berwick, D. (1990). "Patient Judgements of Hospital Quality: Report of a Pilot Study." *Medical Care* 28:9 (September), S39-S48.

Webber, A. (1986). "Status of the PRO Program." *Federation of American Health Systems Review* 19:3 (May/June), 28–29.

Williamson, J. (1988). "Future Policy Directions for Quality Assurance: Lessons from Health Accounting Experience." *Inquiry* 25:1 (Spring), 67–77.

———. (1978). *Assessing and Improving Outcomes in Health Care: The Theory and Practice of Health Accounting.* Cambridge, Mass.: Ballinger.

Wolfe, S. (1986). "Consumer Information on Hospital Quality." *Public Citizen Health Letter* 2:4 (September/October), 1.

Young, W. (1984). "Incorporating Severity and Comorbidity in Case-Mix Measurement." *Health Care Financing Review* 5:4 (Supp.), 23–32.

Zabakus, E., and Mangold, W. (1992) "Adapting the SERVQUAL Scale to Hospital Services." *Health Services Research* 26:6 (February), 766–778.

Zimmerman, J. (1989). "APACHE III Study Design: Selected Articles." *Critical Care Medicine* 17:12 (December Supplement), S169–S221.

Part Six

INVESTMENT, FINANCING, AND CAPITAL-STRUCTURE DECISIONS

Chapter 12

Tax-exempt and For-Profit Multihospital Systems

The medical entrepreneurs are risking more than money. They may be risking the security and effectiveness of institutions people depend on to provide services. There is a moral as well as a business judgment involved in taking such risks. Corporations give us a strong national defense against the danger of a noncompetitive health system in which obsolete care is not replaced by modern medicine because public funds are unavailable and private capital is unappreciated.

—Michael Bromberg

We should not manage capital or labor any different in the nonprofit sector. Everybody used to think there was a great difference between business and universities because one is profit and one tax-exempt. As president of Carnegie-Mellon University I am as interested in the bottom line as any business.

—Richard Cyert

He profits most who serves the best.

—Adam Smith

Multihospital systems have experienced a rough ride in strategic planning. Hospital chains' flirtation with vertical integration and selling insurance products in the 1980s proved unsuccessful for most (Ginzberg 1990; Carlsen 1988). In theory, vertical integration could allow the for-profit company to make profits selling insurance to consumers and hospital care to patients and to raise occupancy rates by channeling patients to their hospitals. Humana was the first chain to sell an insurance product (1983) and it took 6.5 years to make this theoretical dream come true. The other chains were 2 to 3 years behind Humana in developing their insurance products (1985), and they divested out of the business within 3 to 5 years. For example, HCA's venture into the insurance business was derailed in 1986 when 20 Blue Cross plans threatened to drop HCA facilities from local PPOs. Humana was the only chain still heavily into the insurance business after 1991. Other chains have limited involvement in a few small HMOs or PPOs (Shortell, Morrison, and Friedman 1990).

Many analysts have marked the trend away from individual independent hospital governance toward membership in investor-owned chains or tax-exempt multihospital systems. The fraction of community hospitals in multihospital systems increased from 20 percent in 1977 to 34 percent in 1984 and an estimated 60 percent by 1991 (*Modern Healthcare* 1991; Brown and Klosterman 1986). The hospital chains of the 1980s are the health care corporations of today. The 1,284 for-profit nonpsychiatric hospitals comprise 24.2 percent of the beds and 18 percent of the hospitals (table 12.1). Relman's (1986) fears of a massive industry takeover were grossly overstated. The biggest continuing trend seems to be the growth of nonprofit hospital chains, ranging from tightly knit centralized secular chains to alliances such as Voluntary Hospitals of America (VHA) or American Healthcare Systems (AHS). By the end of 1992 such nonprofit systems may well represent 41 percent of the hospitals and 47 percent of the hospital beds in the nation.

The rhetorical passion of the debate over corporate control reflects the fact that proponents of chains focus only on the desirable implications (e.g., better access to capital for modernization; Bromberg 1984), while critics fanatically denounce handing the health care system over to an "army of promotors and financial speculators." Just as it is not informative to compare for-profit chains with a nonexistent ideal nonprofit hospital, it is equally silly to suggest that for-profit firms are perfect entrepreneurs.

There is little definitive research into the advantages of decentralized versus centralized multihospital systems. The conventional wisdom seems to suggest that the best middle-of-the-road strategy is guided autonomy for the member hospitals, whereby the local manager selects the best market strategy, tests the marketplace, and takes responsibility for profitability and productivity, but does so within the guidelines of the central office's strategic planning style. The central office can help in procurement and in purchasing high-priced consulting advice, but all decisions are ultimately local in nature. Overly centralized systems often foist a turnkey (standardized and inflexible) information system and marketing checklist on their member hospitals, which erodes morale, effectiveness, and the ability to innovate (customize strategies to local market conditions). Fiscal audits and debt-capacity policies rightfully remain at the central office.

Tax-exempt multihospital systems increasingly avoid centralizing authority at the corporate-office level. The exceptions are most Catholic multihospital systems, which continue to remain centralized. The downside of a centralized plan is that it can (1) ignore local market conditions and (2) be overly ambitious in trying to do so many things that it leads to strategic mediocrity. The downside of decentralized tax-exempt systems often involves poor communication and goal-displacement conflicts with the systemwide mission statement.

Table 12.1

Investor-owned Capacity, Number of Beds, Facilities, Occupancy Rate, and Market Share of Total Nonfederal Short-Term General Hospitals, 1946–1991

Year	Investor-owned (For-Profit)			Total Nonfederal Short-Term General[a]			Investor-owned Market Share	
	Number of Hospitals	Beds	Occupancy Rate	Number of Hospitals	Beds	Occupancy Rate	% of Hospitals	% of Beds
1946	1,076	39,000	64.1	4,444	473,000	72.1	24.2	8.2
1951	1,190	41,000	61.6	5,050	520,000	73.3	23.6	7.9
1956	990	37,000	60.0	5,270	583,000	72.0	18.8	6.3
1961	856	38,000	65.5	5,477	655,000	75.0	15.6	5.8
1966	852	48,000	69.0	5,812	768,000	76.5	14.7	6.3
1971	750	54,000	71.0	5,865	867,000	76.7	12.8	6.2
1976	752	76,000	64.8	5,956	961,000	74.4	12.6	7.9
1981[b]	729	88,000	66.4	5,879	1,007,000	75.9	12.4	8.7
1986	1,102[c]	123,000	48.0	5,720	944,000	63.4	19.3	13.0
1991	1,284	155,000	51.4	5,312	862,000	66.2	24.2	18.0

[a]Does not include psychiatric facilities in either column (the investor-owned sector owns, leases, or contract manages 180 psychiatric facilities).

[b]Between 1961 and 1981, 75 percent of the investor-owned acquisitions were solo freestanding investor-owned doctors' hospitals being bought by chains (no change in AHA control; investor-owned before and after). However, in the period 1981-91, 63 percent of the acquisitions by investor-owned chains were tax-exempt (nonprofit) facilities, including only 18 teaching hospitals.

[c]Figures include 139 independent proprietary hospitals (8,000 beds) that are not members of investor-owned chains.

MULTIHOSPITAL-SYSTEM EVOLUTION

There is an evolving organizational-theory literature on hybrid organizations where the "hub" lead firm (the "parent") dominates the strategic behavior of the multi-institutional spokes (the member firms that follow the hub's direction; Borys and Jemison 1989). The parent in this organization may often be benevolent, for example, Hospital Corporation of America, with its Deming method of quality improvement (see chapter 11). Some analysts were surprised to report that HCA's corporate influence actually softened DRG payment incentives to intervene in medical practice by providing a generous supply of capital and by fostering a corporate culture conducive to cooperative relationships between physicians and managers (Campbell and Kane 1990).

What are the effects of being a "spoke," that is, being acquired by the hub of a multihospital system? Most of the literature in this area has concerned large multihospital systems, primarily located in southern states. One recent study of for-profit multihospital systems reported that the parent improved the financial and operating performance of acquired facilities (Lynch and McCue 1990). The authors found that in comparison to independent nonprofit hospitals, acquired hospitals increased access to long-term debt, made improvements in profitability, and improved plant and equipment. However, these results were for the period up to 1985, before the severe shakeout in the multihospital marketplace during 1987–90. Further research is warranted (Salmon 1991).

Too little research has focused on small multihospital systems. One exception is a study by Luke, Ozcan, and Begun (1990) of the strategy selection process, birth order, and growth patterns of small multihospital systems. The authors identified three basic model types of systems. The historical model, based on a religious or community-service purpose, tends to acquire or build similar nonprofit hospitals in cities spatially distant from the parent. The investment model tends to be for-profit and to acquire hospitals for a purely financial purpose per se, earning a return on equity. The third form, the market model, tends to emerge out of the initiative of a large parent hospital acquiring hospitals geographically proximate. A number of these regional market models have grown while investor-owned large corporate systems have retrenched, for example, Henry Ford Hospital or Johns Hopkins Health Care System are tax-exempt regional systems. The benefits and risks of these market "minisystems" have been reviewed elsewhere (Luke 1991; Shultz 1991; Eastaugh 1990), and we will return to this topic again in chapter 15. One basic social benefit is that the strong parent hospital acquiring local hospitals could represent the regionalized system concept envisioned by American Regional Medical Program planners in the 1960s, resulting in less duplication of equipment in an area and less repeat testing as the medical record moves with the patient through the rational system. The risk of minisystems is that they reduce competition in the long run, leading to antitrust litigation and charges of monopoly pricing.

Luke, Ozcan, and Begun (1990) reported that under the market model the sequence of acquisitions tended to involve picking up smaller, less complex community hospitals at increasingly greater distances from the parent hospital. The investment-model systems tend to have been initiated by entrepreneurs or nonhospital firms and typically involve no single hub parent hospital. This study should be replicated in the future to confirm the validity of the three models, any predictable pattern of systems evolution, and any differences between small and large systems.

FOR-PROFIT SYSTEMS IN SEARCH OF STABILITY

The number of for-profit hospitals in systems increased from 729 in 1981 to 1,284 in 1991. Most of the growth occurred between 1982 and 1986 through acquisitions of 610 hospitals (50 percent were proprietary local freestanding doctors' hospitals) and 14 teaching hospitals. This acquisitions boom was financed through $14.2 billion of debt. Consequently, each of the big six for-profit systems has listed "utilization of cash to reduce interest expense and retire long-term debt" as a major corporate goal since 1987.

The 1980s were unstable for the for-profit hospital chains. Hospital Corporation of America is the largest system, with 439 hospitals at its peak size (1987). HCA was smart to divest its insurance product in 1987 and to divest 22 Beverly nursing homes in 1988 (HCA did not know either industry sufficiently well). For three decades HCA had a physician as CEO/president, promoted local autonomy and high-quality care, and entered into management contracts in 27 states. HCA also owned or leased 197 hospitals before selling off a number of rural hospitals and channeling off 104 poorly performing hospitals onto its employee stock ownership plan (ESOP) in October 1987. The average bed size for HCA-owned/leased hospitals increased from 155 beds in 1986 to 235 beds in 1990. The ESOP, "HealthTrust the Hospital Company," had downsized from 104 to only 90 hospitals as of 1991. ESOPs have been tried in a number of industries (Millbank, Tweed, Hadley, and McCloy 1991). HCA as a management-led investor group took the company private from 1989–1992, downsized to 128 hospitals and reduced debt from $6.5 to 3.1 billion. HCA again became a publicly traded company selling stock in March 1992.

In stark contrast to American Medical International (AMI) and Humana, HCA since 1985 has staffed central-office positions with experienced hospital managers with HCA field experience. This move has been only partially successful in reducing the distance (and friction) between local hospitals and the corporate office. HCA stopped offering common stock by becoming a private company in the March 1989 $3.61-billion leveraged buyout. Once the giant of the multihospital business, run as a father-son business by two surgeons, HCA consists of three systems: HealthTrust (90 hospitals), the old HCA contract management company (dropping the label HCA in 1991 to avoid antagonism from local rate regulators) consisting of 172 contract-managed hospitals, and the private company, Hospital Corporation of America, with $6.1 billion in assets and owning

55 psychiatric hospitals (6,400 beds) and 75 acute-care hospitals (17,700 beds). The management company only had $59 million in assets in 1991.

American Medical International (AMI) represented the most decentralized proprietary system from an operations point of view, but AMI, like HCA, was highly centralized for strategic planning. AMI's formerly cavalier 1980s attitude that MBA-style "managing is managing" led to a failed acquisition strategy. This generic approach to managing did not work well. After AMI lost $97 million in 1986, it divested all nonhospital subsidiaries (except psychiatric services), including its two-year-old insurance product. In the period 1987–89 AMI reduced the number of hospitals by 50 percent by spinning off international facilities and copying the HCA ESOP strategy (Southwick 1988; Cleverley 1988) by giving its employees 37 hospitals in the fall of 1988 (a very good exchange for AMI, as it picked up the cash in the pension fund). AMI was willing and able to finance its ESOP, not because the plan was economic (it was not), but because 50 percent of the interest collected will be exempt from federal income tax (Teitelman 1988). AMI stopped trying to buy teaching hospitals and began to emphasize medical-staff relations and quality-of-care issues (items new to an MBA vision of the world; Maturi 1989). In 1991 AMI had 10 psychiatric hospitals (855 beds), 47 acute-care hospitals (11,000 beds), and $3.6 billion in assets. AMI's clinical indicator standards and patient-satisfaction surveys are copied by a number of smaller hospital chains.

National Medical Enterprises (NME) has the most diversified portfolio of investments: acute-care hospitals declined from 82 percent of revenues in 1981 to 29 percent forecast for 1992. Based in Santa Monica, California, NME has $5.16 billion in assets, including 63 psychiatric hospitals (5,400 beds), 28 rehabilitation hospitals (2,400 beds), and 36 acute-care hospitals (6,500 beds). NME was smart to avoid acquiring teaching hospitals in the mid–1980s and to divest its 362 nursing homes with 44,673 beds in 1990 by spinning off through a stock-distribution plan its Hillhaven Corporation as an independent division. NME still retains a 14 percent equity interest in Hillhaven, and if nursing homes become more profitable, NME can exercise the warrants to hold up to 33 percent of Hillhaven's common stock. NME has focused on the decentralized-management approach for two decades and has the leanest corporate staff and low overhead. In other systems administrative overhead expenses are typically 30 to 40 percent higher. NME's growth has emphasized specialty hospitals, rehabilitation hospitals, psychiatric facilities, and facilities for treatment of substance abuse. NME dabbled in HMO joint ventures for 18 months in the mid-1980s, but quickly pulled out of this line of business. Both NME and AMI have some experience with the health-campus concept of a total package of specialty services available in a small geographic area.

Humana, based in Louisville, Kentucky, was the first multihospital system in the insurance business (1983) and the only system to make insurance a profitable product line. For the last quarter in FY 1989 Humana made pretax profits of $6.3 million on its two health insurance products and averaged $13.5 million in annual profits in 1990 and 1991. To minimize the administrative costs of running an insurance product of PPOs and HMOs (Humana Gold Plus has 194,000 Medicare enrollees) for 1.1 million citizens, Humana has concentrated on geographic specialization (five southern cities and two midwestern cities). Humana bought an HMO with 80,000 enrollees in Kansas City in 1990. By divesting 36 urgent-care centers, Humana has made ambulatory care a money maker since 1990. Humana has 78 owned or leased acute-care hospitals, 16,500 beds, and $4.2 billion in assets. It has no contract-managed hospitals. Humana diversification ventures have been increasingly limited in scope, minimizing psychiatric care (HCA's and AMI's major market segment) and avoiding rehabilitation hospitals (NME's specialty).

Humana is the most centralized and most specialized multihospital system. However, in contrast to centralized nonprofit hospital systems that offer broad idealistic strategic plans that their memberships cannot sustain, Humana tries to offer specialized advice and a clear strategic focus (e.g., do 2 things well; do not try to do 11 things with mediocre degrees of success). The managers at Humana strive for tough industrial engineering standards for labor productivity and capital productivity (e.g., equipment maintenance). Humana even has guidelines for nurse response times following a call bell from a patient's room. Humana is the only chain to successfully nurture the insurance business and to fulfill the dream of former Vice President Hank Weronen to fill beds by operating in the insurance business. Humana's insurance plans accounted for 11 percent of patient days in 1988, rising to 20 percent in 1990 and 23 percent in 1991.

In summary, the most successful for-profit systems emphasize productivity and specialize (Humana specializes in insurance plans and hospital efficiency; NME specializes in rehabilitation and psychiatric hospitals). For-profit chains have less bad debt, but they compensate for this by paying $362 billion in federal income taxes. The 20 for-profit chains averaged 4.1 percent bad debt (charity care and uncollectibles), compared to 5.6 percent at 43 Catholic systems and 5.2 percent at 20 secular tax-exempt systems.

NONPROFIT MULTIHOSPITAL SYSTEMS

Tax-exempt systems do not pay federal income tax, but they often pay local property taxes on non-health-related property (parking lots and cafeterias). These local property taxes are often equivalent in size to the operating profits of the core business, the mothership nonprofit hospital. Tax-exempt systems have gone through recent cycles of corporate reorganization, expanding the number of divisions and reducing marketing and productivity reporting to the distant corporate office. Decentralization is the typical trend for most secular systems and some Catholic systems. The largest secular tax-exempt systems are Kaiser Foundation with 30 hospitals and 7,100 beds, Health One Corporation with 16 hospitals and 3,000 beds, and Intermountain Health Care with 25 hospitals and 2,800 beds.

Intermountain experienced a typical nonprofit-systems decline in operating margin from 7.1 percent in 1986 to 2.2 percent in 1989. Intermountain's experience mirrored the Humana strategy of geographic retrenchment, but instead of pulling back to offer services in five major state markets, Intermountain retrenched to two states and discontinued urgent-care centers and other free-standing facilities outside of Utah. Intermountain also began to emphasize stronger medical-staff relations, offering board positions to physicians at local hospitals and adding three physicians to the parent corporate board.

Both tax-exempt and for-profit systems allow the central office to exhibit more centralized control over owned/leased hospitals, giving less attention to the contract-managed hospitals. This tendency is certainly true of the way Health One's corporate office in Minneapolis manages its 10 owned hospitals in comparison to its 6 contract-managed hospitals. Health One merged with Health Central in 1987, downsized the number of facilities in the system by 33 percent, and divested the dental clinics and most urgent-care centers. Health One reacted to the criticism of Shortell, Morrison and Friedman (1990) that its system gave the least effort to contain costs and improve productivity by launching an aggressive program primarily for improving efficiency of the owned hospitals in 1991. The 6 contract-managed hospitals continue to be decentralized, experiencing either autonomy and innovation or a lack of direction, poor vertical integration of product lines, and weak, slow collective decision making. Diversification ventures have been increasingly limited in scope, and Health One has divested (discontinued) service delivery outside its home state (Minnesota).

The only seminational hospital chains still trying to cover the American landscape are HCA and the 67-hospital Adventist Health System. The Adventist system is an 11,000-bed religious system with $3.2 billion in assets in 1991. Its flagship medical center is the 1,100-bed Florida hospital in Orlando. The Adventist system has tried to find a middle road between centralization and decentralization, called guided autonomy. Since the management skills are better at the larger hospitals, they tend to have better productivity-improvement systems and proficiency in managerial cost accounting.

Of the 43 Catholic multihospital systems, the two largest have tried to move in the direction of strategic planning by guided autonomy. The largest, Daughters of Charity National Health System, based in St. Louis, has 45 hospitals, 14,000 beds, and $4.3 billion in assets. The second largest, Mercy Health Services of Farmington Hills, Michigan, has 37 hospitals, 7,300 beds, and $1.5 billion in assets. Both systems were highly centralized in 1987 and demanded that their hospitals plan for too many things, exceeding their fiscal capabilities and spreading their management talent too thin. By allowing guided autonomy to replace strict centralization at each system, the corporate parent is in effect saying, "You will be given less prescriptive rules from us; just give us good outcomes that are consistent with our Catholic mission statement." Intermountain also has followed this directing model of guided autonomy in strategic planning since 1989. All three nonprofit systems have tried to trim corporate overhead following the abandonment of the running model of strict centralization. If the corporate staff is doing less, less staff is needed. (Two for-profit chains, HCA and AMI, have evolved past this directing model of guided autonomy to a more decentralized model, but they still lack the lean cost-efficient low levels of corporate staff at NME.)

Multifacility systems need a central financial planning and auditing mechanism, a formal budget variance analysis process, a uniform human-resources policy, and a central quality-assurance system. Productivity-improvement programs and medical-staff relationships should be done largely at the local level. Memo writing at the corporate level never improved either of these two activities. After dealing with a bureaucratic central office, dissatisfaction among members of the medical staff increasingly becomes a problem ("What right do those corporate types in a distant office have in directing our patient care?"). However, with the shifting JCAHO and federal requirements, quality-assurance activities run by a physician at the corporate medical affairs office have been acceptable to local physicians.

Mercy Health Services and Daughters of Charity have each targeted services for the aging as their primary market for the twenty-first century. They realize that the drain implicit in getting increasingly into long-term care and home health care will require more fiscal discipline and a better productivity orientation. To achieve the vision of a campuslike integrated total community health care system for aging Americans, each system may have to retrench into a smaller number of geographic markets in the late 1990s.

In summary, multihospital systems have become smaller in size and in scope (more specialized) over the last five years. Many managers have expressed a mea culpa, a personal acknowledgment of fault, by stating that (1) it was dumb to spread administrative talent and capital on diversification into too many new business ventures, and (2) centralization offers an excessively broad and idealistic agenda for most member facilities in nonprofit hospital systems. Specialization on a limited agenda, with fewer product lines, is better than strategic mediocrity in pursuit of an idealistic agenda.

EXTERNAL PRESSURES

Analysis of investor confidence is an imperfect science, especially when the general market position has been so upbeat and the sector under study (health care) has experienced severe downbeat shocks (discussion of PPS, implementation of PPS, the severe downturn in earnings trends, and the announced withdrawal of return-on-equity payments). In a downbeat period the investors will favor firms that divest holdings in inpatient medical/surgical care and diversify into more profitable product lines. Many chains announced that while 50 to 65 percent of their revenues may have been hospital based, in seven years (1984–91) this "dependence" declined to 30 to 40 percent. The figures for the cost-of-equity contribution differ across the chains because of differences in perceived business risk (McCue, Pawlukiewicz, and Eastaugh, 1992). For the time-series analysis a pooled market index (NYSE, AMEX, and NASDAQ indexes) will be employed to broadly represent changes in American equity markets.

Beta is the standard measure for the risk of a security for which investors must be compensated with sufficient rate of return. Financial forecasters never project the rate of return with perfect accuracy (Klein and Rosenfeld 1991; Harrington 1983); therefore, one must consider the difference between actual and forecast values, labeled the "abnormal rate of return." In the parlance of finance, the abnormal rate of return reflects the arrival of new information (e.g., the bad news that for-profits lost their Medicare return-on-equity payments) during the investment period (one week), which causes a change in next week's price as investors revise expectations of future rates of return. If the period is marked by no new information, the abnormal rate of return will most likely take a "random walk," moving up and down with no clear trend. All rates of return in the time-series analysis were adjusted for stock splits and stock dividends and were converted to standard natural logarithm form (McCue, Pawlukiewicz, and Eastaugh 1991).

Now that for-profit hospitals receive no Medicare return-on-equity (ROE) payments; financial pressures have blurred the distinction between for-profit and tax-exempt facilities. Nevertheless, we shall survey the structural differences between the two sectors. Tax-exempt hospitals are generally responsible to a voluntary board of trustees (typically unpaid prior to 1984, often paid trustees in today's market). The managers who operate the tax-exempt facility have no claim on the assets; but since 1984 they are increasingly paid with incentive compensation plans that closely mirror those of the proprietary sector (see chapter 10). Managers of for-profit firms often receive compensation in terms of preferred stock and a claim on certain assets. It is a moot point whether stock ownership provides for-profit managers significantly more incentive than tax-exempt facility managers (with incentive pay) to take action based on mainly economic grounds. Tax-exempt hospital boards are struggling to make their organizations as market driven, businesslike, and incentive based as possible. As the two quotes by Bromberg and Cyert at the beginning of this chapter suggest, the drive for a surplus of revenues over expenses has become an essential goal of both for-profit and nonprofit institutions. To paraphrase Fallon (1991) not-for-profit should not be no profit.

As befits the academic controversy regarding for-profit health care and corporate organization (chains and nonprofit or proprietary status), this chapter examines a wide array of facts, perceptions, and opinions. The demise of the nonprofit, nonbusinesslike hospital correlates with, but was not largely determined by, the rise of for-profit hospital chains in the early 1980s. One problem with the literature in this area is that the authors often falsely equate correlation with causality—that is, if for-profit medicine increased at a time when government retrenchment exacerbated the problem of uncompensated care, then some analysts lay the blame for "dumping" nonpaying patients on the corporate chains (irrespective of any direct evidence). Rising interest in institutional financial position, product-line planning, and the so-called monetarization of medicine (Ginzberg 1984) seem to occur independently of whether the for-profit chains have a 0 to 50 percent market share (Institute of Medicine 1986). One should obviously entertain alternative hypotheses. If a home radio fails to operate, you do not reject the hypothesis that radio waves still exist; you check the radio and the fuse.

If the academics who exhibit a distaste of for-profit institutions fail to separate correlation from causality, the advocates for investor-owned hospital systems also fail to test their assertions (Frank et al. 1990; Friedman et al. 1990; Saywell 1989). Although standard economic theory was raised as an a priori fact to prove that for-profit concerns must have greater efficiency and lower patient costs, the opposite turned out to be the case (under cost-reimbursement payment conditions in 1975–83; Institute of Medicine 1986). Much of the overstated inflammatory rhetoric against investor-owned firms was the by-product of (1) false claims concerning cost efficiency and (2) claims that tax obligations serve as payment in full for all social and moral obligations (e.g., uncompensated care). On this second point, the Institute of Medicine study (1986, 203) cited the following Humana certificate-of-need application:

As a taxpayer, Humana contributes to the provision of indigent care through payment of property taxes, sales taxes, income taxes, franchise taxes, and other taxes. As a result of public policy and their status as taxpayers, Humana hospitals do not have the responsibility to provide hospital care for the indigent except in emergencies or in those situations where reimbursement for indigent patients is provided.

Although the public-finance argument that hospital chains pay taxes can be utilized to defend paying, say, 3.9 percent of gross patient revenues for charity care and bad debt, rather than 4.4 percent (as in the nonprofit sector), chains would benefit from demonstrating how sensitive their admitting policies are toward local market conditions. (The Institute of Medicine 1986 study cited 1983 figures of 3.1 percent for investor-owned chains and 4.2 percent for tax-exempt facilities.) In the case of Hospital Corporation of America, Vraciu and Virgil (1986) reported that uncompensated care amounted to 3.0 percent of revenues in areas of Kentucky where public hospitals existed, but was 4.8 percent of revenues in areas where HCA was the sole provider. For-profit chains may vary widely in their tendency to condone economically motivated transfers or admitting decisions.

CRITICS OF "COMMERCIAL" HEALTH CARE

Relman (1983, 1980), Ginzberg (1984), and Fein (1986) decried entrepreneurialism in investor-owned hospitals, as they decried such commercialism by physicians and nonprofit hospitals. It is feared that something essential and compassionate but not well defined will be lost if the service ethos is corrupted by a business ethic or conflict-of-interest situation (e.g., ownership of the facilities to which the provider refers patients). These concerns should be viewed in the context of a two-century-old active debate about whether market self-interest can replace charity and compassion as the basis of a society, and whether important social values are eroded by industrialization and commercialization. Neoliberals and Marxists have argued that for-profit activity fundamentally undermines the moral foundations of society (obligation, trust, and open access). The radical critics do not view frontline health workers as intrinsically any less ethical in corporate health systems, but they do postulate the existence of a corrupt business ethic in boardroom decisions as to what services should be offered in the community. According to these critics, the general interest of society and the local community becomes subservient to a distant corporate headquarters that views health care as merely a mechanism to generate profits and please stockholders. Ironically, such charges are seldom backed up with any supporting evidence. If the corporate chain does anything for the public good (e.g., American Medical International starting an 80-bed AIDS-only hospital in Texas), this action is dismissed by critics of for-profit medicine as being pure "public relations."

Advocates of for-profit medicine would counterargue that most of the big investors in health care are individuals with a career commitment to health care. Such investors, if they were merely interested in making money, would invest in something other than health care. Given that 80 percent of American industry groups earned higher profits and paid higher dividends than for-profit hospital chains in 1986, this explanation seems plausible. One could argue that 1986 was an atypically bad year for the investor-owned sector, with earnings declining 20 to 60 percent below 1985 levels. However, according to Value Line Investment Survey statistics, even in a good year for the investor-owned sector (1991), the profits of 82 percent of American businesses exceeded the performance of the hospital chains. While we can reject the myth of excess profitability in the for-profit hospital sector relative to the rest of the economy, one might postulate that investors may derive some nonmonetary "social dividend" in investing in health care. Any such social dividend must be small, declining, and insufficient for multihospital systems to rely on for future capital financing. The social dividend in the minds of owner/employees of the for-profit chains might well be described as "downward sticky" (slow to decline), given that they do not wish to sell their stock too quickly and drive down the price, or they hope that alternative strategies will improve future company returns (dividend yield, capital gains).

Cleverley (1990) confirmed the normative observation that hospital profits are low. Such a normative viewpoint of profitability relative to other for-profit concerns in the economy is not germane for critics of profits in health care (Buchanan 1982). Critics of the for-profit sector question whether it is legitimate to make any profits from the misfortunes of the ill. Such a standpoint is particularly ironic when it comes from a physician, because doctors have always benefited from billing the ill. Moreover, nonsalaried physicians have always faced a conflict of interest because they earn more profits if they overtreat their patients. Critics are wise to be worried over whether for-profit firms will corrupt fee-for-service clinicians into both overadmitting patients and, when prospectively paid (e.g., in accord with DRGs), undertreating the patient so as to maximize hospital profits (Eastaugh 1990). However, from the survey of incentive plans in chapter 10, only one investor-owned firm, based in West Germany, currently appears to be attempting such manipulations (Paracelsus). The rise of a market-driven competitive medical economy has certainly raised financial concerns to a primary goal for all types of hospitals. For some radical analysts, living in the shadows of the 10 best-endowed teaching hospitals offers a ''let them eat cake'' conde-scension. It is much easier to be charitable and above mundane financial concerns when one has an endowment that exceeds $100 million (and covers the inflation-adjusted replacement value of the institution). Unfortunately, many recent studies have demonstrated that the vast majority of hospitals must be concerned with survival (Hultman 1991; Young 1991).

In a sellers' market, with rapidly inflating prices and few empty beds, hospital executives could act as if profit was a subordinate goal (Eastaugh 1984). Rein-hardt (1986) applied the same logic to physicians, arguing that with rapidly rising physician fees and fewer doctors, physicians could act as if income were a subordinate goal. Relman's (1986) response to Reinhardt argued that medical care has a crucial moral component that outweighs such crass commercial con-cerns. Private practitioners, as a group, are not ardent supporters of Relman's philosophy, largely because many individuals view medicine as an entrepreneu-rial activity (in addition to answering a professional ''calling'' to do good). Many physicians have invested in clinics, imaging centers, and hospital chains as a hedge to protect their financial futures against anticipated tightening in the pay-ment system.

There are some interesting points of comparison between physician and hos-pital behavior. Physicians and hospitals are willing to provide some amount of uncompensated care as their social obligation. However, the two sectors have different reactions to a decline in consumer demand and growing oversupply. For-profit physicians seem willing to be saddled with more indigent patients in a market with unfilled appointment slots. In the jargon of economics, they will do more free care if the opportunity cost is lowered (Culler and Ohsfeldt 1986)— they do not have a paying patient waiting to make room for indigent patients. However, a for-profit hospital may feel less sanguine about treating a charity patient and absorbing the unreimbursed variable costs, or treating a Medicaid patient under a program payment scheme that barely covers the marginal cost of such an effort. Only an ideologue could deny the danger of an insensitive for-profit ethos (Ginzberg 1990). However, the good news is that most health care providers in for-profit settings still appear to have a sense of ethics. The bad news for Relman's argument, according to Reinhardt (1986), is that excision

of all for-profit enterprises from our health care system would not lead to restoration of the old social contract. Sear (1991) suggested that in Florida for-
profits have better profit margins because of the use of fewer man-hours per
adjusted patient day.

DEFINING TERMS AND THE SEARCH FOR BALANCE

Balanced presentation is an approach seldom offered by those engaged in a
crusade for or against profit-seeking multihospital systems. The term "investor-
owned" will be used in this chapter to connote companies with a large number
of stockholders. The word "proprietary" will connote the solo, owner-operated
institution with a relatively small number of shareholders (e.g., the traditional
doctor's hospital, 410 of which have been absorbed by investor-owned chains
since 1971). The term "for-profit" encompasses both investor-owned and proprietary facilities. The for-profit hospitals pay income taxes and property taxes.
The property taxes are roughly 22 to 25 percent of income taxes according to
Sam Mitchell of the Federation of American Healthcare Systems. The term "tax-
exempt" is used to connote institutions that do not pay taxes but may retain
earnings. The term "nonprofit" insufficiently describes institutions that
"should" have no surplus of revenues over expenses. Less than 28 percent of
tax-exempt hospitals were nonprofit in 1989. In a bad financial year, like 1991–
92, the term "nonprofit" can describe either a tax-exempt or a for-profit
institution.

The concept of profitless health care is moribund. A tax-exempt hospital must
earn a profit to render future patient service and stay modern. The Catholic
Hospital Association was the first to recognize the financial imperative in 1984
with the poignant slogan: No (profit) margin, no mission. An example of the
old-style paternalistic view that deplores both finance and marketing was provided
by Dr. Cecil Shepps at the November 1985 annual meeting of the American
Public Health Association. Shepps stated that "nonprofit hospitals should be in
the business of doing good, expanding a money-losing department because it is
the right thing to do; not breaking the rules, paying the fines, and making big
profits." There are a number of potential areas for argument with those who are
(1) quick to label all business concerns corrupt and unethical, (2) quick to treat
patients as supplicants rather than valued customers, and (3) quick to reject the
hypothesis that departments often lose money because consumers and local physicians steer clear of low-quality facilities (which in turn become unprofitable
because they are empty, not because they are providing any better social good).

Shepps, Relman, and Ginzburg would be surprised to learn the degree of
convergence among for-profit and tax-exempt hospitals in their board meetings
and annual conventions (having attended dozens since 1988, the author is hard
pressed to recall a major fiscal point of difference between firms). Even tax-
exempt institutions discuss tax issues, because their quasi-independent for-profit
subsidiaries have to pay taxes. Managers in both sectors are equally anxious

about generating capital to secure a better future for their institutions, like university president Richard Cyert, quoted at the start of this chapter. Managers and clinicians view capital as the lifeblood for rebuilding, modernizing, and remaining state-of-the-art as an institution. Indeed, it seems realistic to view private capital as a better bet than national health insurance or a second federal Hill-Burton program to revitalize the nation's hospitals.

There are still unique features in the investor-owned sector. Such hospital chains have to pay dividends to their shareholders from profits. They have more of a growth imperative to satisfy stockholders' desire for a long-term capital gain. Students unfamiliar with finance are often surprised to learn that investor-owned capital is also more expensive than tax-exempt revenue bonds (about twice as expensive, on average). Consider two hospitals, each producing $1 million in retained earnings after one fiscal year. The tax-exempt hospital can translate this $1 million of current earnings into $2 to $3 million of additional financing (depending on its credit rating), making a total of $3 to $4 million available to improve the capital position of the facility. An overoptimistic spokesperson for the investor-owned chains cited in the Institute of Medicine study (1986, 61) claimed that a chain could "easily" translate this $1 million in current annual earnings into $25 million of additional financing. In fact, the so-called multiplier effect may be half this amount. The future deals, not made with "ease," will be made at substantial cost (in terms of future expected earnings by the capital suppliers).

There are three basic problems with the logic of a multiplier effect of 25. First, a portion of the $1 million in current earnings must be paid to shareholders as a dividend (the median value was 20 percent in 1985 among the ten largest investor-owned chains). Therefore, only $800,000 of the current earnings will be available for leveraging additional capital financing. Second, with regard to additional equity financing through the sale of stock, price-to-earnings (P/E) ratios in 1989 declined to the 8 to 10 level (from the high-flying 15 to 25 P/E ratios of a few years earlier). Therefore, the chain will not have nearly the equity-financing multiplier of the "heyday era" of hospital chains, circa 1982–84. The minimally required return to investors is the chain's cost of equity capital (a "low" 16 percent in our hypothetical example in table 12.2).

One should also consider the obvious fact that owning stock can be a risky venture. Under a debt-financing contract the investor payback stream is prospectively fixed, enforceable, and relatively certain. In contrast, because of the risk inherent in being a shareholder, the cost of equity financing is typically double the cost of taxable debt financing (16 percent versus 7.25 percent in our example in table 12.2). The 16 percent figure could be understated if investors rapidly become dissatisfied with their net yield (annual dividends plus capital gains). Investor-owned chains will differ widely in their messages to the marketplace. Some chains will soon claim that they are paying declining dividends because they have implicitly shifted to greater reliance on long-run capital gains (typically promised for nonhospital operations). Other chains may be forced to

Table 12.2

Superior Capital Multiplier of Investor-owned Hospitals Requires Compensation for Borrowers and Shareholders: Hypothetical Example (33 Percent Corporate Tax Rate, 28 Percent Capital Gains, 16 Percent Rate of Return Acceptable to Investors) (Dollar Figures in Thousands)

	Day 1 1993	Day 2 1993	Day 3 1993	Day 4 1993	Years 1-14 1994-2007
1. Retained earnings from past 365 days	$1,000	800 (RE-retained earnings)	800		
2. Dividend paid by chain Z to shareholders (a "rental" for investing their $)		200			
3. Z sells stock on day 3 at a price/RE ratio of 9.0			7,200		
4. Z issues on day 4 long-term debt at 7.25% per year on $7.2 million in additional debt				7,200	
5. Capital available				15,200	
• Future earnings required to underwrite the $8 million of additional equity financing (lines 1 + 3, day 3), assuming investors receive 16 percent rate of return					
- Returns 100 percent in the form of dividends					$1,870 per year
- Returns 100 percent through capital gains in year 15					$2,530 per year
• Future earnings required to underwrite the $7.2 million of additional debt financing (line 4)					$541.3 per year
6. Additional pretax firm income required to pay shareholders and lenders (line 5 - taxes)					$2,400 to $3000
Additional revenues required to generate this much profit assuming an 8 percent profit margin assuming a 10 percent profit margin					$20-$25 million $16-$20 million

pay a higher dividend yield because the investment community is not gullible enough to believe in unrealistic capital-gains estimates.

In our case example in table 12.2, the shareholders would at minimum (if they were willing to accept a low 16 percent rate of return) require the chain to earn an additional $1.25 million per annum of after-tax earnings to keep them, as owners, financially secure. The firm would have issued at maximum $7.2 million in additional stock (given P/E ratios of 9 and current retained earnings of $800,000). Given an effective corporate tax rate of 33 percent, providing an annual $1.25 million return to shareholders, totally as a dividend yield, would require additional pretax profits of $1.87 million (table 12.2 line 5). If the firm anticipated paying the investors through capital gains (taxed at 28 percent), then the future dividends would have to be 1.4 times as high.

In addition to this $7.2 million of additional stock sold, the firm may be able to issue $7.2 million of additional long-term debt, given ample unused debt capacity. (Many chains do not have a debt-to-equity rate as low as 50 percent and are fighting to convert much of their long-term debt to equity shares.) The $7.2 million in new debt at 7.25 percent interest demands additional coupon interest of $541,300. This debt burden would have to be covered by additional after-tax earnings. On the date of maturity (2007 in table 12.2), the principal would have to be repaid. The additional $15.2 million ($7.2 million plus $7.2 million plus $0.8 million) of financing, hopefully utilized to transform or acquire at least $15.2 million of income-yielding assets, will require additional annual pretax net income of $2.4 to $3.0 million per annum. In summary, the multiplier effect currently appears to be closer to 15 than 25. More critically, given an 8 percent profit margin, the investor-owned hospital would have to find an additional $20 to $25 million in annual revenues to pay shareholders and lenders for the use of $7.2 million in each case.

Investor-owned firms have the mixed blessing of access to a unique and flexible, but more costly, source of capital (investor equity). In the best case, the chain may utilize $1 million in current earnings to attract an extra $14.4 million in financing, but at an average cost of capital of 12 percent (16 plus 7.25). If the investor-owned chain were to breach its past promises to shareholders, the cost of equity capital (16 percent) and cost of debt (7.25 percent) could rise significantly. Indeed, broken promises to institutional investors could do more to reverse the growth of for-profit hospitals than anything else on the policy front. In contrast, a tax-exempt hospital with a modest to good credit rating will be capable of parlaying $1 million in current earnings into $3 to $4 million in financing (by borrowing $2 to $3 million at 5.5 to 7.5 percent interest rates and receiving tax-exempt philanthropy).

WHO HAS LOWER COSTS?

The biggest question among economic analysts is whether investor-owned hospitals can begin to produce patient care at lower costs than tax-exempt providers. It is no longer a smart strategy to cost more per diem or per admission, as it was when payment methods were dominated by cost-reimbursement principles (Grimaldi 1991). Members of the Institute of Medicine (1986) study team should not have been surprised that investor-owned care cost 2 to 10 percent more per case based on pre–1984 data. For-profit hospitals achieved the standard of profit maximization simply through "maximization of reimbursement" by generating more costs. Pauly (1986) viewed this 2 to 10 percent cost-performance differential as "not of overwhelming practical significance, given the wide variations in costs and prices." For example, in the Watt et al. (1986) study, the initial statistically significant 17 percent difference in net patient-service revenue per day fell to less than 10 percent difference (1982 data) once the taxes and contributions were netted out. If investor-owned hospitals prior to PPS had expenses that were 2 to 4 percent higher per admission, adjusting for DRG mix, the differential was inconsequential (as small as the "air turbulence caused by a butterfly in a hurricane"; Pauly 1986). Table 12.3 surveys the major cost studies of investor-owned-hospital expenses per case. Future researchers can test 1987 data to ascertain whether for-profit hospitals have started to cost less, relative to tax-exempt hospitals, by medical and surgical condition, after the rapid erosion of cost reimbursement (Eastaugh 1991). The DRG price payment system for Medicare has certainly severed the link between cost and revenues, thus providing incentives to cut costs.

One of the surprising findings of the Pattison and Katz (1983) study of California hospitals was that for-profit chain hospitals' costs per case were 5.1 percent higher than solo proprietary hospitals' costs, primarily due to higher corporate administrative and fiscal-services expenses. On the face of it, this finding is inconsistent with the claims of multihospital-system executives that dollars and time will be saved (net) at the local-hospital level by having the functions of highly specialized corporate experts delegated from headquarters. In theory, spreading the costs of expensive high-quality experts among a large number of hospitals could be more cost-effective than each hospital employing its own experts (Gray 1987). One is left with two possible conclusions: Either the central office is not such a cost-effective bargain or these cost comparisons are mere statistical artifacts of the "maximization of reimbursement" games of the 1980s (whereby the corporate overhead was distributed on paper to those hospitals with the highest cost-paying-patient volumes—e.g., to "reap a high dollar yield from your Medicare cost report").

One might speculate that the health of Americans in certain communities might decline due to the unplanned closure of certain for-profit facilities. Society must continue to reinvest in the health care system to keep it going and to keep the population healthy. Although capital overinvestment is a problem in many states, for-profit facilities would also be sorely missed in 12 to 18 states. To ask whether profit or service is the primary objective of the firm is an interesting but not highly practical question in a capitalist economy. Many neoliberals still believe that all forms of profit in health care are inherently exploitive. On the other

Table 12.3
Investor-owned Hospital Expenses Relative to Those of Tax-exempt Freestanding Community Hospitals

Study	Higher Hospital Cost per Admit in Investor-owned Facilities	Sample Frame
Lewin, Derzon, and Margulies (1981)	Chains 4% higher, not statistically significant	1978 data, 53 matched pairs of hospitals (California, Florida, Texas)
Pattison and Katz (1983)	Chains 2% higher	1980 data, 280 California hospitals
Becker and Sloan (1985)a	Chains 8% higher per adjusted admit	1979 data, 2,231 AHA survey hospitals
Pattison (1986)	Chains 4-7% higher per adjusted admit	1977-81 data, 230 small (under 250 beds) California hospitals
Watt et al. (1986)	Chains 5% higher, not statistically significant	1980 data, 53 Lewin, Derzon, and Margulies pairs, plus 27 pairs from 5 other states
Watt (1986)	Chains 4% higher, not statistically significant	1980 data, 561 AHA survey hospitals
Coelen (1986)	Chains 4% higher, nonchain proprietary hospitals; were 2-3% lower per admission	1975-81, Medicare cost reports and AHA survey

Source: Institute of Medicine (1986).

aSloan and Vraciu (1983) reported 4% lower costs per case in 44 chain hospitals in Florida (1979 data, nonteaching hospitals with under 400 beds).

hand, it is a nightmare for many to imagine that America's doctors would become "slavish" devotees of remote corporate officers whose prime responsibility is to their shareholders. People need services, and for-profit concerns can supply what is needed if they remain decentralized and attuned to local consumer tastes and habits.

After a period of restructuring the balance sheet, taking write-offs on unproductive assets, and selling selected facilities, some of the investor-owned chains should bounce back in the near future. What will distinguish the winners from the losers are their abilities to promote productivity, encourage physician partnerships, integrate strategies, and recognize health care as a regionally consumed service (with widely varying market tastes).

Those who argue that the marketplace has made all hospitals, irrespective of ownership class, more profit oriented must also consider the question of cause and effect. Those who argue that financial concerns should take a back seat to the professional dominance tradition of old may in fact be reactionary, but they have a clear villain in mind. For-profit chains are that clear villain, because in their rapid-growth period (1981–84) they presumably became the dominant leaders in the world of health care administrators (Longsdorf 1985). To paraphrase Relman (1983), the rest of the market will be molded to the business ethos of that high-growth group, the for-profit manager. However, it is less likely that the "business ethic" was some sort of endogenous source of pollution harming the health care system than that exogenous pressure was applied by the troika of industry, government, and the insurance industry on health care providers to contain costs. In other words, the payers undermined such antibusiness pedestals as "cost is no object" and "resources are limitless." The tax-exempt managers discovered the for-profit efficiency ethos without any help from the for-profit chains. Scholars such as Relman (1983) and Starr (1982) might consider the problem of bias and whether they have an untested distrust of corporate culture.

TAX-EXEMPT HOSPITALS GO FOR PROFITS

Chapter 5 highlighted the rapid diversification into for-profit ventures by tax-exempt firms. To the extent that the tax-exempt hospital is, in reality, a profit-seeking firm, there is no reason to expect behavior that varies significantly from the proprietary norm. The for-profit corporations of a fully diversified tax-exempt hospital in 1992 were like tentacle feeders for the "nonprofit" (or lower-profit) mothership hospital. The hospital may be a member of a tax-exempt multihospital system, alliance, consortium, or group purchasing arrangement. Members of this corporate culture, relatively new to the health care industry, are in a position analogous to that of Odysseus. Managers of this new breed are caught between (1) the Charybdis of the consumerist's fears that they are as "greedy" and profit oriented as the investor-owned chains and (2) the Scylla of the medical staff's noble hope that the hospital's original mission remains unaffected by structure. Most managers tend to side with their physicians and justify this massive restructuring of the hospital organization as a vehicle to maximize financial stability and insulate the myriad of facilities from future anticipated reimbursement reductions. Consumerists counterargue that charity care might be reduced to meet a financial bottom-line target. Odysseus could sail away to another land, but the health care manager will be perpetually attacked by physicians, consumers, and trustees for having insufficient capital, plant, and equipment, and/or excessive profitability.

One intangible benefit of the proliferation of off-site nonhospital-based diversification is that many consumers reap the benefits of greater convenience. Reductions in patient travel time are often bolstered by the added benefit of a reduced price per unit of service. However, if not properly structured, these corporate spin-offs can threaten the tax-exempt status of the mothership hospital. One tax-exempt multihospital system (Intermountain Health Care, Inc., of Salt Lake City) has had problems in this regard. In June 1985 the Utah Supreme Court (no. 17699) denied the tax-exempt status of a community hospital on the basis of its having evolved into a business that no longer satisfied the constitutional requirements for a charitable institution. Tax-exempt organizations are chartered under specific limited-purpose provisions (benevolent, educational, scientific, or religious) for which their assets and income must be used. However, the vast majority of tax-exempt hospitals have restructured so as to minimize this threat to their tax-exempt status and still act as more of a multiproduct, multiservice business concern. Nevertheless, if the courts begin to mirror the attitudes of most economists, there will be increasing irrelevance in the distinction between for-profit and "nonprofit" hospitals.

A number of hospitals have sacrificed varying degrees of autonomy in pursuit of improved efficiency. Alexander and Rundall (1985) studied 80 hospitals under contract management and one to two years prior to contract management and observed a number of positive financial impacts. From an equity and access perspective, the hypothesis that contract-managed hospitals would cut back Medicaid and Medicare program participation received no empirical support. However, the data predated implementation of the PPS program and reduction in Medicaid benefits in many states. A wide variety of lease contracts have also been tried by some hospitals. For example, an arrangement can exist under a lease where a 20- to 40-year contract is made with a chain or company to provide full management without ownership (or offering partial ownership through joint-venture capital projects). One should be careful to note that management does not imply the same economic incentives and behavior as management plus ownership. Joint ventures can also exist outside the context of a lease contract. For example, NME and Massachusetts General Hospital developed a 340-apartment-unit continuing-care retirement community and a 60-bed skilled nursing facility for $38 million.

In two studies using pre-1984 data, for-profit hospitals were labeled more efficient than nonprofit hospitals (Arrington and Haddock 1990; Lynch and McCue 1990). However, Arrington and Haddock (1990) went further to suggest that nonprofits return more social benefit to the community than for-profits, especially in the areas of professional education and community access to care. This finding is in stark contrast to the Herzlinger and Krasker (1987) finding that nonprofits do not return more benefit to society than for-profits. Herzlinger and Krasker argued that there is no basis for the social subsidization of nonprofits and the tax preference for nonprofit hospitals. This last assertion is controversial as more local governments try to remove nonprofit hospitals' property-tax exemption (O'Donnell and Taylor 1990; Loebs 1989). In six states hospitals' charitability is something to be proved each year; for example, one Utah hospital was tax-exempt in 1990, but taxable in 1989 and 1991. This approach seems unfair to the hospital industry, because the fraction of revenues or expenses going to charity care is partially outside the hospitals' control (e.g., charity volume rises as local unemployment increases). Despite the antidumping laws passed by Congress, both for-profit and nonprofit hospitals seem to increasingly avoid nonpaying patients (Laddaga and Haynes 1991; Eastaugh and Eastaugh 1990; Valdmanis 1990).

PROBLEMS OF EACH SECTOR WITH THE TAX COLLECTORS

Increasingly, to retain their tax-exempt status, nonprofit firms are going to have to justify their charitability and demonstrate the social importance of medical education and other professional education programs within the hospital (e.g., with social benefits like enhanced quality). Tax-exempt hospitals must also defend their status to maintain access to tax-exempt bonds, a form of debt that has interest rates 2 to 3 points lower than taxable debt (Wheeler and Clement 1990). Nonprofit hospitals may have a difficult time convincing revenue-seeking politicians in Pennsylvania and Texas of the social worth of their collective goods: patient care, research, and education (Weisbrod 1988; Rammell and Parson 1989).

Herzlinger and Krasker (1987) offered the valid criticism that Relman (1986) and other physicians untrained in public finance and economics miss one very important social benefit of for-profit hospitals: They pay taxes that help finance social programs. However, the Arrington and Haddock (1990) reanalysis of the 1982 Herzlinger and Krasker (1987) data appears to be the superior study because Arrington and Haddock sampled a wider universe (both system and nonsystem hospitals) and because they used a better statistical technique (multiple-discriminant analysis; see chapter 4). One should also say that tax policy and social policy in the 1990s should be based on more recent data (Smith, Wheeler, and Clement 1991).

For-profits have a different set of problems in defining taxable income. Rules vary widely, depending on year and location, concerning the accounting treatment of discounts and allowances in cost-based contracts with Blue Cross, Medicare, and Medicaid. Revenue rulings issued by the Treasury would indicate that a discount is allowed in the year that revenues are accrued, but that net revenues cannot be less than reimbursable amounts reported on the cost report. IRS auditors have informed certain health care organizations that the IRS will determine the appropriateness of their discounts using this rule of thumb. The dilemma here is that revenues reported net of discounts for financial purposes are often much less than amounts requested in the cost report. This is because of the ''loading factor'' (i.e., the report will be aggressively loaded with controversial costs in hopes that some of them will be accepted by the third-party payer). While the hospital could argue that the formulas used for the book accrual are more accurate than the filed cost report (and history would probably confirm this argument), such a contention would probably be thrown out by the courts since the cost report represents the vehicle for which payment is requested. Thus the hospital should have to suffer the consequences of higher tax liabilities as a result of a frivolous cost report.

Categories of costs that have no hope for acceptance (Bentivegna 1991) should be eliminated, and those possessing only a small probability of approval should be identified on the face of the report as ''protested items.'' These protested items would not have to be included in taxable income since they are clearly identified as improbable occurrences. If a more accurate cost report is filed, ''phantom'' tax liabilities can be avoided. One local east coast firm experienced a $31.6 million 1991 difference between net-of-discount cost-based revenues reported for financial purposes and amounts requested per the cost report. The company's marginal tax rate is 38 percent. Thus, assuming a dubious cost report, the company paid approximately $12 million of taxes on revenues it can reasonably expect never to realize. While the company will be able to take a deduction when the cost report is settled and recoup the tax formerly paid, this will generally take three years. In terms of present value (assuming a conservative 6 percent discount rate), the company will lose approximately $1.9 million as a result of its artificially inflated tax liability.

MERGERS, COMPETITION, AND COST CONTROL

Recent evaluations of mergers suggest that cost control for society, in terms of lower costs for the community, will not be a primary benefit of the organizational marriage. Greene (1990) surveyed the result of a Health Care Investment Analysts (HCIA) study of financial results two years before and after mergers. The results suggest that mergers slightly improved profitability by reducing expenses and increasing gross and net patient revenues. The results contradict any claim that mergers save patients money, because the rise in billed charges more than makes up for any cost cuts; that is, cost reductions are not partially passed on to consumers through reduced patient expenses. Most of the 36 merging facilities realized that one cannot merge a little bit; a merger is all or nothing. Some hospitals also experience marginal cost increases in overhead due to the Noah's ark effect, the urge to keep two of everything, such as two department heads in too many areas of each hospital after the merger. Such lack of cost cutting does not make sense, unless one thinks that the hospital exists as an employment program for hospital employees. In a competitive world, cost control and product enhancement (quality) are keys to success. Merger participants must also consider Department of Justice antitrust concerns (Guthrie 1990).

One alternative to joining a multihospital system is merging with a neighboring hospital. Starkweather (1981) offered an overview of the potential benefits of mergers. Some hospitals may prefer to stand alone (Kazemek 1989). The remaining investor-owned freestanding hospitals may offer a fiscal example of economic Darwinism–one has to be very strong to avoid being absorbed by the for-profit chains. From 1988 to 1990 the median total profit margins of free-standing investor-owned hospitals improved from 0.15 percent to 1.14 percent, while the profit margins of system-affiliated hospitals eroded by 4 full percentage points (HCIA 1991). For-profit systems have problems with high overhead and a high ratio of debt to total assets. Half the big chains have action plans to cut overhead. Since 1989 HCA has done a better job trying to keep a leaner corporate staff. Two layers of administration were taken off the top, so that individual hospital CEOs now report directly to a group president who reports to the HCA president, Dr. Tommy Frist. Four regional group presidents replaced 12 regional division heads. HCA-owned hospitals are now more geographically concentrated; 77 percent reside in five southern states (Tennessee, Texas, Florida, Virginia, and Georgia). If for-profit systems do not cut their overhead, the 1990s trend of nonprofit hospitals acquiring single for-profit hospitals and nonprofit systems buying parts of for-profit systems (Nemes 1991a) will continue.

For the traditional economist, nonprice competition is to competition what noncontact sex is to sex, a poor approximation at best. Friedman and Shortell (1988) reported that price competition for HMO business kicked in during the early 1980s. Robinson and Luft (1988) did a good job of studying nonprice competition or rivalry behavior to maximize prestige and acquisition of hospital technology. Noneconomic competition for prestige creates higher costs. Robinson and Luft also reported from a sample of 5,490 hospitals in 1986 that investor-owned hospitals experienced rates of cost increase 11.6 percent higher than those of tax-exempt private hospitals and 15 percent higher than those of public hospitals. They indicated that in the period 1983–85 the average inflation-adjusted cost per nonelderly patient declined 0.71 percent in high-competition markets and increased 2.82 percent in low-competition markets. Market failure may be prevalent in the hospital industry, but competition does have the expected impact on hospital costs (contrary to the results of their previous studies in 1982 in an era of cost reimbursement).

HYBRIDIZATION AND JOINT VENTURES

The treacherous and complex payment climate demands creative joint venturing between chains, autonomous hospitals, insurance companies, HMOs, and consortia groups. We shall survey in chapter 15 how some of this competitive activity may lead to very noncompetitive monopoly or oligopoly markets. In-patient providers must soon realize that they are not facing a minor recession but rather an old-fashioned dog-eat-dog shakeout. For-profit firms are considering a number of strategies for improving their attractiveness to investors. Interdependent strategies range from tighter operations (reduced overhead, better productivity) to converting long-term debt and improving earnings per share by trading existing shares for a (REIT) (real-estate investment trust) on company property. The real-estate investment trust is a business organization that combines two concepts. First, it is an investment vehicle whereby individual and institutional investors can pool their resources and participate in a professionally managed real-estate portfolio. Second, a qualified REIT is exempted from any corporate income taxes, provided it complies with certain Internal Revenue Code requirements. The ability of a qualified REIT to distribute its income to shareholders in the form of dividends free of corporate income taxes obviously enhances its ability to generate an attractive yield to its outside investors (Press and Sherwin 1989; Jaffe 1991). This strategy was followed by Universal during fiscal year 1987. Earnings per share will become more attractive because the number of shares outstanding will be cut in half, but the balance sheet erodes. Investors in the REIT own the bricks and mortar on 26 hospitals, and Universal continues to own the equipment.

Ultimately, with the emphasis on cost control and debt reduction, investor-owned firms will shrink or expand according to their price competitiveness (especially as they enter more price-competitive markets like psychiatric care). Continued attempts to offer a capitation product, like Humana's CARE PLUS, present a two-edged sword: the risk of financial failure but the possible benefit of revitalization of this mature industry. Hybridization is becoming a two-way street. Tax-exempt firms were the first to travel the road to multiple for-profit taxable subsidiaries, and investor-owned firms may donate failed ventures to the tax-exempt (if one cannot make a business profit or a tax profit from a failure, one might as well label it a "nonprofit" concern).

Hospital chains will continue to reduce exposure to the declining inpatient sector and reduce corporate overhead. But if they fail to raise earnings, they will become ripe takeover candidates. In theory, the pooling of complementary strengths represents the hope behind the hybridization and joint-venture trend. Many weaker chains, insurance firms, and hospitals may be swallowed up by the large surviving chains. Restraints on autonomy will be especially difficult for the acquired firm if the parent firm instinctively overmanages its new "teammate" (Starkweather 1981).

While this chapter has been operations oriented, it appears most appropriate to end with a few observations concerning business ethics. The pursuit of a nonmonetary ethos has been paradoxical: The more it is pursued, the more elusive it becomes. An obsession with the ownership issue produces a narrowness of vision and ignores basic issues such as survival and access to sufficient capital to promote quality care. Our search for capital and joint ventures may reap some unfortunate results (given imperfect payment formulas) if socially irresponsible firms do harm to community access to the poor. The solution is to not kill the "golden goose" and rail against nonphysician profit taking; rather, the solution is to enforce a social contract to force all concerned to bear their fair share of the burden of charity care. Firms that did their fair share in the 1980s will have a tougher time handling the equivalent volume of charity patients in the 1990s; however, they must.

REFERENCES

Alexander, J., and Rundall, T. (1985). "Public Hospitals under Contract Management: An Assessment of Operating Performance." *Medical Care* 23:3 (March), 209–219.

Anderson, G., Schramm, C., Rapoza, C., Renn, S., and Pillari, G. (1985). "Investor-owned Chains and Teaching Hospitals: Implications of Acquisitions." *New England Journal of Medicine* 313:3 (July 18), 201–204.

Arrington, B., and Haddock, C. (1990). "Who Really Profits from Not-for-Profits?" *Health Services Research* 25:2 (June), 291–304.

Arzac, E. (1986). "Do Your Business Units Create Shareholder Value?" *Harvard Business Review* 64:1 (January–February), 121–126.

Becker, E., and Sloan, F. (1985). "Hospital Ownership and Performance." *Economic Inquiry* 23:1 (January), 21–36.

Bentivegna, P. (1991). "Facilities Planning under the New HCFA Capital Regs." *Health Systems Review* 24:5 (September/October), 41–50.

Borys, B., and Jemison, D. (1989). "Hybrid Arrangements as Strategic Alliances: Theoretical Issues." *Academy of Management Review* 14:2, 234–239.

Bromberg, M. (1984). "The Medical-Industrial Complex: Our National Defense." *New England Journal of Medicine* 309:21 (November 24), 1314–1315.

Brown, K., and Klosterman, R. (1986). "Hospital Acquisitions and Their Effects: Florida, 1979–1982." In Institute of Medicine, *For-Profit Enterprise in Health Care*. Washington, D.C.: National Academy of Sciences.

Buchanan, R. (1982). "The Financial Status of the New Medical-Industrial Complex." *Inquiry* 19:4 (Winter), 308–316.

Campbell, P., and Kane, N. (1990). "Physician-Management Relationships at HCA." *Journal of Health Politics, Policy, and Law* 15:3 (Fall), 591–605.

Carlsen, A. (1988). "HCA vs. Shareholders." *Health Week* 10:3 (January 22) 1–2.

Chang, C., and Tuckman, H. (1991). "The Single-hospital County: Is Its Hospital at Risk?" *Health Services Research* 26:2 (June), 207–21.

Cleverley, W. (1990). "Profitability: Comparing Hospital Results with Other Industries." *Healthcare Financial Management* 44:3 (March), 42–52.

———. (1988). "Is a Leveraged ESOP a Possibility for the Voluntary Hospital?" *Hospital and Health Services Administration* 33:3 (Fall), 386–406.

Coady, S. (1985). "Not-For-Profits, Beware—Foundation Formed by Sale Could Be Short-lived." *Modern Healthcare* 15:7 (March 29), 138–140.

Coelen, C. (1986). "Hospital Ownership and Comparative Hospital Costs." In Institute of Medicine, *For-Profit Enterprise in Health Care*, Appendix. Washington, D.C.: National Academy of Sciences.

Congressional Budget Office. (1991). *Trends in Health Expenditures by Medicare and the Nation.* Washington, D.C.: CBO.

Culler, S., and Ohsfeldt, R. (1986). "The Determinates of the Provision of Charity Medical Care by Physicians." *Journal of Human Resources* 21:1 (Winter), 138–156.

Eastaugh, S. (1991). "Sharing the Burden: Containing the Health Care Bill for American Industry." *Business Forum* 16:1 (Winter), 25–28.

———. (1990). "Financing the Correct Rate of Growth of Medical Technology." *Quarterly Review of Economics and Business* 30:4 (Winter), 54–60.

———. (1984). "Hospital Diversification and Financial Management." *Medical Care* 22:8 (August), 704–723.

Eastaugh, S., and Eastaugh, J. (1990). "Putting the Squeeze on Emergency Medicine: Pressures on the Emergency Department." *Hospital Topics* 68:4 (Fall), 21–26.

Fallon, R. (1991). "Not-for-profit Is Not No Profit: Profitability Planning in Not-for-profit Organizations." *Health Care Management Review* 16:3 (Summer), 47–61.

Ermann, D., and Gabel, J. (1985). "Changing Face of American Health Care: Multihospital Systems, Emergency Centers, and Surgery Centers." *Medical Care* 23:5 (May), 401–420.

Fama, E. (1976). *Foundations of Finance.* New York: Basic Books.

Federation of American Health Systems. (1991). *Directory of Investor Owned Hospitals and Health Care Management Companies.* Little Rock, Ark.: FAHS.

Fein, R. (1986). *Medical Care, Medical Costs: The Search for a Health Insurance Policy.* Cambridge, Mass.: Harvard University Press.

Finkler, S. (1991). *Hospital Cost Management and Accounting.* Rockville, Md.: Aspen.

Frank, R., Salkever, D., and Mitchell, J. (1990), "Market Forces and the public good: competition among hospitals and provision of indigent care", in *Advances in Health Economics and Health Services Research,* ed. by Scheffler, R., Greenwich, Conn.: JAI Press, 159–83.

Friedman, B., Hattis, P., and Bogue, R. (1990). "Tax Exemption and Community Benefits of Not-for-profit Hospitals", in *Advances in Health Economics and Health Services Research,* ed. by Scheffler, R., Greenwich, Conn.: JAI Press, 131–57.

Friedman, B., and Shortell, S. (1988). "Financial Performance of Selected Investor-owned and Not-for-Profit Systems." *Health Services Research* 23:2 (June), 188–211.

Garner, M. (1992). "Reporting Charity Care: New Accounting Rules." *Health progress* 73:1 (January-February), 58–63.

Ginzberg, E. (1990). *The Medical Triangle: Physicians, Politicians, and the Public.* Cambridge, Mass.: Harvard University Press.

———. (1984). "The Monetarization of Medical Care." *New England Journal of Medicine* 310:18 (May 3), 1162–1165.

Gray, B. (1987). "Shaky Basis for Report's Sweeping Recommendation on For-profits." *Health Progress* 68:3 (March), 38–41.

Greene, J. (1990). "Do Mergers Work?" *Modern Healthcare* 20:11 (March 19), 24–36.

Grimaldi, P. (1991). "Capital PPS: Trekking through the Labyrinth." *Healthcare Financial Management* 45:11 (November), 72–87.

Guthrie, M. (1990). "Mergers in Health Care." *Journal of Healthcare Marketing* 10:1 (March), 47–52.

Harrington, D. (1983). "Stock Prices, Beta, and Strategic Planning." *Harvard Business Review* 61:3 (May–June), 157–164.

Health Care Investment Analysts (HCIA). (1991). *Changing Profitability: Investor-owned versus Public and Nonprofits*. Baltimore: HCIA.

Hemesath, M., and Pope, G. (1988). "Linking Medicare Capital Payments to Hospital Occupancy Rates." *Health Affairs* 8:3 (Fall), 104–115.

Herr, W. (1991). "Capital Payments." *Healthcare Financial Management* 45:4 (April), 19–32.

Herzlinger, R., and Krasker, W. (1987). "Who Profits from Nonprofits?" *Harvard Business Review* 65:1 (January - February), 93–106.

Hultman, C. (1991). "Uncompensated Care before and after PPS: the role of hospital ownership and location". *Health Services Research* 26:5 (December), 585–601.

Institute of Medicine. (1986). *For-Profit Enterprise in Health Care*. Washington, D.C.: NAS Press.

Jaffe, J. (1991). "Taxes and Capital Structure of partnerships, REITs." *Journal of Finance* 46:1 (March), 401–408.

Kazemek, E. (1989). "Why Mergers and Acquisitions Fail." *Healthcare Financial Management* 44:1 (January), 94–97.

Klein, A., and Rosenfeld, J. (1991). "PE Ratios, Earnings Expectations, and Abnormal Returns." *Journal of Financial Research* 14:1 (Spring), 51–63.

Laddaga, L., and Haynes, J. (1991). "Anti-dumping Law." *Healthcare Financial Management* 45:3 (March), 84–88.

Lewin, L., Derzon, R., and Margulies, R. (1981). "Investor-Owneds and Nonprofits Differ in Economic Performance." *Hospitals* 55:13 (July 1), 52–58.

Loebs, S. (1989). "The Future of the Tax-exempt Status for Hospitals." *Frontiers of Health Services Management* 5:3 (Spring), 3–22.

Longsdorf, R. (1985). "The Medical-Industrial Complex: A Growing Problem for Health Care." *Private Practice* 11:2 (February), 39–41.

Luke, R. (1991). "Spatial Competition and Cooperation in Local Hospital Markets." *Medical Care Review* 48:2 (Summer), 207–37.

Luke, R., Ozcan, Y., and Begun, J. (1990). "Birth Order in Small Multihospital Systems." *Health Services Research* 25:2 (June), 305–325.

Lynch, J., and McCue, M. (1990). "Effects of For-Profit Multihospital System Ownership on Hospital Financial and Operating Performance." *Health Services Management Research* 3:3 (November), 33–44.

Maturi, R. (1989). "ESOP Financing." *Financial Manager* 22:4 (July/August), 34–39.

McCue, M., and Furst, R. (1986). "Financial Characteristics of Hospitals Purchased by Investor-owned Chains." *Health Services Research* 21:4 (October), 515–528.

McCue, M., McCue, T., and Wheeler, J. (1988). "An Assessment of Hospital Acquisition Prices." *Inquiry* 25:2 (Summer), 290–296.

McCue, M., Pawlukiewicz, J., and Eastaugh, S. (1992). "Effects of Price Regulation on Healthcare Industry Stock Returns." *Health Services Management Research* 6:4, forthcoming.

Millbank, Tweed, Hadley, and McCloy (MTHM). (1991). *The Proctor and Gamble Solution: An Innovative ESOP*. New York: Chase Manhattan Plaza.

Modern Healthcare. (1991). "Annual Survey on Multi-institutional Systems." *Modern Healthcare* 22:21, 4–106.

Nemes, J. (1991a). "Not-for-Profits Gain an Edge by Purchasing For-Profits." *Modern Healthcare* 21:1 (January 7), 46.

———. (1991b). "Two Agencies Downgrade Lutheran General Debt." *Modern Healthcare* 21:1 (January 7), 52.

O'Brien, R., and Haller, M. (1985). "Investor-owned or Nonprofit? Issues and Implications for Academic and Ethical Values in a Catholic Teaching Hospital." *New England Journal of Medicine* 313:3 (July 18), 198–201.

O'Donnell, J., and Taylor, J. (1990). "The Bounds of Charity: Current Status of the Hospital Property Tax Exemption." *New England Journal of Medicine* 322:1 (January 4), 65–68.

Parks, C., Cashman, S., Winickoff, R., and Bicknell, W. (1991). "Quality of Acute Episodic Care in Investor-owned Ambulatory Health Centers." *Medical Care* 29:1 (January), 72–86.

Pattison, R. (1986). "Response to Financial Incentives among Investor-owned and Not-for-Profit Hospitals: An Analysis of the California Data, 1978–1982." In Institute of Medicine, *For-Profit Enterprise in Health Care*, Appendix. Washington, D.C.: National Academy of Sciences.

Pattison, R., and Katz, H. (1983). "Investor-owned and Not-for-Profit Hospitals." *New England Journal of Medicine* 309:6 (August 11), 347–353.

Pauly, M. (1986). "Advent and Implications of For-Profit Delivery." Paper presented at the EBRI Policy Forum, "The Changing Health Care Market" (June 3), Washington, D.C.

Potter, M. (1992). "Taxation of Nonprofit Hospitals: a Cost impact Model." *Hospital and Health Services Administration* 37:1 (Spring), 89–102.

Press, S., and Sherwin, J. (1989). "Financing Growth through REITs." *FAH Review* 22:1 (January–February), 57–63.

Rammell, P., and Parson, R. (1989). "Utah County v. Intermountain Health Care: Utah's Method of Determining Charitable Property Tax Exemptions." *Journal of Health and Hospital Law* 22:1, 73–90.

Reinhardt, J. (1986). "The Nature of Equity Financing." In Institute of Medicine, *For-Profit Enterprise in Health Care*, 67–73. Washington, D.C.: National Academy of Sciences.

Relman, A. (1986). "Ethics and For-Profit Medicine." In Institute of Medicine, *For-Profit Enterprise in Health Care*, Appendix. Washington, D.C.: National Academy of Sciences.

———. (1983). "Investor-owned Hospitals and Health Care Costs." *New England Journal of Medicine* 309:6 (August 11), 370–372.

———. (1980). "The New Medical-Industrial Complex." *New England Journal of Medicine* 303:17 (October 23), 963–970.

Relman, A., and Reinhardt, U. (1986). "Debating For-Profit Health Care and the Ethics of Physicians." *Health Affairs* 5:2 (Summer), 5–29.

Robinson, J., and Luft, H. (1988). "Competition, Regulation, and Hospital Costs." *Journal of the American Medical Association* 260:18 (November 11), 2676–2681.

Salmon, J. (1991). *The Corporate Transformation of Health Care*. Part 2, *Perspectives and Implications*. Amityville, N.Y.: Baywood.

Saywell, R., Zollinger, T., and Chu, D. (1989). "Hospital and Patient Characteristics of Uncompensated Hospital Care." *Journal of Health Policy, Politics and Law* 14:2 (Summer), 287–307.

Sear, A. (1991). "Comparison of Efficiency and Profitability of Multihospital Systems." *Health Care Management Review* 16:2 (Spring), 31–37.

Shortell, S., Morrison, E., and Friedman, B. (1990). *Strategic Choices for America's Hospitals: Managing Change in Turbulent Times*. San Francisco: Jossey-Bass.

Shultz, M. (1991). "Strategic Capital Planning: Systems Look toward the Future." *Trustee* 44:10 (October), 10–12.

Sloan, F., and Vraciu, R. (1983). "Investor-owned and Not-for-Profit Hospitals: Addressing Some Issues." *Health Affairs* 2:1 (Spring), 25–37.

Smith, D., Wheeler, J., and Clement, J. (1991). "Donations and the Behavior of Nonprofit Firms." University of Michigan, unpublished paper, School of Public Health.

Southwick, K. (1988). "AMI Unloads 37 Hospitals in Wake of Takeover Threat." *Health Week* 5:23 (June 8), 1–2.

Starkweather, D. (1981). *Hospital Mergers in the Making*. Ann Arbor, Mich.: Health Administration Press.

Starr, P. (1982). *The Social Transformation of American Medicine*. New York: Basic Books, 146–153.

Starshak, J. (1991). "Tax-exempt Bond Financing." *Healthcare Financial Management* 45:3 (March), 106.

Teitelman, R. (1988) "An ESOPs Fable." *Financial World* 157:17 (August 9), 34–35.

Valdmanis, V. (1990). "Ownership and Technical Efficiency of Hospitals." *Medical Care* 28:6 (June), 552–561.

Vraciu, R., and Virgil, P. (1986). "The Impact of Investor-owned Hospitals on Access to Health Care." In R. Southby and W. Greenberg (eds.), *For-Profit Hospitals: Access, Quality, Teaching, Research*. Columbus, Ohio: Battelle Press.

Watt, J., and Derzon, R. (1986). "Effects of Ownership and Multihospital System Membership on Hospital Functional Strategies and Economic Performance." In Institute of Medicine, *For-Profit Enterprise in Health Care*, Appendix. Washington, D.C.: National Academy of Sciences.

Watt, J., Derzon R., Renn, S., Schram, C., Hahn, J., and Pillari, G. (1986). "The Comparative Economic Performance of Investor-owned Chain and Not-for-Profit Hospitals." *New England Journal of Medicine* 314:2 (January 9), 89–96.

Weisbrod, B. (1988). *The Nonprofit Economy*. Cambridge, Mass.: Harvard University Press.

Wheeler, J., and Clement, J. (1990). "Capital Expenditure Decisions and the Role of the Not-for-Profit Hospital: An Application of a Social Goods Model." *Medical Care Review* 47:4 (Winter), 467–486.

Young, D. (1991). "Planning and Controlling Health Capital: Attaining an Appropriate Balance between Regulation and Competition." *Medical Care Review* 48:3 (Fall), 261–293.

Chapter 13

Evaluation of Financing Alternatives

Under an easily identified set of circumstances, lease financing can be cost effective. Recent developments in finance make it possible to not only evaluate the financial attractiveness of a given lease, but also to accurately predict bounds within which the terms of the lease must fall. Hospital administrators armed with this information should be able to negotiate more favorable lease terms.

—Mark Bayless

Finance is somehow both the implicit culprit and the expected savior of an industry rapidly approaching bankruptcy. The health field, in large part, has been managed by professionals who often had a clear view of part of their external and internal environment without being able to relate these to financial realities.

—J. B. Silvers

Hospitals have an excessive reliance on debt relative to other sectors of the economy. Public utilities borrow on the average about 60 percent of total capitalization, and manufacturing firms about 40 to 50 percent. Hospital debt loads currently are in the 80 to 90 percent range. According to Standard & Poor's (1991), total debt offerings in the hospital industry increased from $2.2 billion in 1974 to $18 billion in 1990. As sources of philanthropy and free Hill-Burton funds dramatically declined from 1972 to 1983, 50 percent of hospitals planning a capital expansion or modernization were forced into the private debt markets. In addition to the simple replacement concept of capital maintenance, society may wish to consider adding on a technological maintenance factor to assure that the hospital has funds for updating capital to keep pace with peer institutions. Given that medical technology is likely to be cost-increasing in the future, preservation of capital position implies both capital replacement and a capital-improvement concept that keeps pace with new technology.

In drawing comparisons between the degree of regulatory involvement in the hospital industry and public utilities, one encounters two important differences. First, the degree of regulatory involvement in hospitals is less rigid, is more variable across state lines and Blue Cross catchment areas, and is handled in an illogical fashion that can best be described as muddling through. Consequently, the hospital sector has the benefit of being less regulated than most public utilities. Second, the ad hoc swings in the reimbursement rules have prevented many hospitals from preserving their capital purchasing power to anywhere near the degree that public utilities are allowed in order to assure future operations. In summary, hospitals have not received the same basic treatment that we accord to other highly regulated utility industries.

While capital costs are a relatively small percentage of total hospital costs (6 to 12 percent in most cases), the importance of equitable capital payment policies exceeds the per annum dollar volumes involved. Adequacy and stability are key in designing a fair payment system for financing both equipment (38 to 40 percent of capital costs annually) and plant. However, defining adequacy is not an easy task. Capital cost varies by geographic region (Pope 1991), and the new Medicare capital payment rules are bad news for the industry (HCFA 1991).

ACCURATE SELF-ASSESSMENT OF RISK AND RETURN

After having taken full advantage of a 36-month slide in interest rates through 1991, hospital executives are beginning to realize that they cannot continue indefinitely increasing the leverage on a service that is leveling off or declining in both volume and earning power. However, borrowing power is needed so that expansion into areas other than inpatient care is not limited. Medicare is starting prospective payment for capital in 1992. The intrinsic advantage of moving hospitals onto a prospective capital payment scheme is in the capital budgeting process. Decisions will be made for rational economic reasons, and borrowing will not be done as a tool to write off some interest expense onto the Medicare program. Decisions will be made on the basis of business risk, and the method of financing will not be largely driven by reimbursement concerns. Unfortunately, a genuine risk assessment of hospital executives on the late end of their hospital's investment cycle may, due to their facility's high accounting age, get dragged down with the poorly managed institutions. This would not happen because of poor judgment, but rather because HCFA refused to incorporate a rolling base of actual cost experience for hospitals with major capital projects (Bromberg 1991).

Given the tighter payment climate, Cleverley (1990) suggested that the organization cannot be too conservative in its assumptions. Often in other business sectors the worst-case forecasts have proven far too optimistic. This was true in the case of the Stanford University debt-capacity analysis (Hopkins, Heath, and Levin 1982). Because capital investment decisions are increasingly complex, a survey of the process is in order.

DESIGNING A CAPITAL PROJECT

Major capital investments should be analyzed in five basic stages:

1. Capital requirements, benefits, and opportunities
2. Project feasibility study
3. Assembly of a financing team and project plan
4. Credit assessment (e.g., bond ratings)
5. Completion of short-term and long-term financing

Stage 1 involves identification of capital requirements to meet shifts in patient demand, clinician referral patterns, or the basic need to keep the facility state-of-the-art (replacement, renovation, modernization, and expansion). The stimulus for assessing capital position may be reactive (e.g., market share is declining because the facility is outdated) or proactive. The opportunity to be first in a new service or in a new, growing marketplace zone (location) is a proactive rationale for major new capital investment. As was pointed out in chapter 5, this process is increasingly driven by consumer preference, supplanting the "empire-building complex" of trustees and medical staff to expand simply for expansion's sake.

Stage 2, the feasibility study, involves a careful conservative assessment of projected cash inflows, cash outflows, the opportunity costs for the resources, and the economic life cycle of the project. The intent of this stage is to develop an accurate estimate of the financial viability and logistical complexity of the various capital-project alternatives. Stage 2 requires approximate answers to the precise problem—not precise answers to the approximate problem. When external consultants are brought in, they must be cognizant of the fact that there is little value in refining an analysis that does not consider the most appropriate alternatives and assumptions for the hospital. The consultants can also point out unreasonable assumptions. If the hospital generates initial cash-flow estimates that are too optimistic to convince its own paid consultants, the facility will have even less success trying to convince the bond-rating agents at Moody's, Standard and Poor's, or Fitch Investor Services (very active in long-term-care-facility financing). Hospital managers and trustees must resist the human temptation among their peers to overstate excessively the growth potential of any new facility or service product line.

Stage 3 involves the formation of a financing team (bankers and lawyers, including hospital counsel, bond counsel, and issuer's counsel) and a team of other key actors in the project plan (e.g., from the architect to the construction manager). Coordination is important. For example, one would not want the architects to waste time and money designing a planned facility that is much too expensive for the debt capacity of the hospital. The individuals involved sometimes number in the hundreds. Consequently, the fixed transaction costs of issuing debt are substantial—that is, it would not be cost-effective to refinance old debt for financial reasons unless the interest rates declined 1.75 to 2.5 percent (depending on volume). Individuals have a number of roles to play and owe allegiances to parties other than the borrower (Elrod and Wilkinson 1985).

The most critical broker of the deal is the commercial banker. Commercial bankers can perform three to four jobs in a single deal, including acting as the lender, investor, debt guarantor, underwriter, and bond or master trustee. Members of the financing team might suggest the purchase of bond insurance to raise the credit rating for the hospital, thus decreasing the rate of interest, if the action is cost-beneficial (without the bond insurance the required volume could not be sold in a reasonable time). Bond insurance clearly makes sense if the decline in interest expense (in discounted dollars) is less than the one time purchase of the insurance, but the decline in interest rates has been low in the early 1990s (Carpenter 1991). Institutional investors do not shy away from buying the higher-yield uninsured hospital bond issues, but individual investors often prefer the lower-risk, lower-yield hospital investment with bond insurance.

Medical technology and consumer demand fueled a capital competition between American hospitals (Institute of Medicine 1991). The expansion in capital per bed, while bed stock declined in the 1980s, was 66 percent debt financed. Hospital indebtedness rose from $4.9 billion in 1980 to $22.5 billion in 1991 (a 360 percent rise), while hospital costs increased only 184.7 percent. Since 1985 hospital bond ratings have fallen in response to increasing debt-to-assets ratios. McCue, Renn, and Pillari (1990) studied 41 hospitals whose ratings had been downgraded from A to BBB and 17 hospitals that had been downgraded to below BBB and concluded that occupancy rate and the ratio of cash to debt service were significantly associated with downgrades.

While the hospital industry is not perceived as being as risky as nuclear power plants (rapid downgrades in creditworthiness and no new debt financing for a decade), the recent trends are disturbing. A downgrade results in more expensive future debt financing. In the period 1987–90 the ratio of hospital downgrades to upgrades was 10.2, compared to a ratio of 4.9 in the initial years of prospective payment (1984–87). Downgrades still exceeded upgrades by 3.3 in the period 1990–91. Given that health care is in competition with other industries for scarce capital, the trends in other sectors are important. For public utilities rated by Standard and Poor's (S & P), the ratio of downgrades to upgrades was 1.1, compared to 1.4 for schools and 2.9 for the transportation industry (1988–91). With hospital ratings dropping, the interest rates at which hospitals borrow will rise, and higher prices will act as a brake on hospital spending for equipment and new services. Interested readers should read the S & P quarterly *Municipal Bond Book*, or the weekly S & P *Credit Watch*.

Stage 4, the credit-assessment stage, involves finalization of the financing documents, inviting in the bond-rating agents for a review, on-site visit, and debt rating. If the issue is for more than $10 million, two independent ratings are required. Standard and Poor's (1991) describes a bond rating as a process to measure relative creditworthiness. Creditworthiness is measured from quantitative factors such as financial ratio analysis (normative time trend, past five years), competitive market position (market share), patient-payer mix, regulatory environment, and feasibility forecasts. To a lesser extent qualitative factors are also considered, such as the management focus of the governing board, characteristics of the medical staff (e.g., age, faithfulness to the hospital), subjective institutional or demographic factors, and legal provisions of the indenture. Moody's summarizes the same concerns under four broad subject headings: debt factors, financial factors, bond security provisions, and hospital-specific factors.

The single most important component in the credit-rating process, in addition to the obvious assessment of the nature of the project to be financed, is the financial ratio analysis of the institution. There are no hard and fast rules, but rating agents clearly prefer facilities with a high debt-service coverage following completion of the project (above 3.0) and a healthy ratio of cash flow to total debt (above 0.4). Other variables considered include the fund balance per adjusted patient day and the operating profit margin. A hospital with a poor rating (e.g., BBB speculative) is likely to have a fund balance ratio of under $300 and a debt-service-coverage ratio below 1.7, whereas an AA-rated facility will most likely have a fund balance per diem above $700 and a debt-service-coverage ratio above 3.7.

Ratings are subject to appeal and may be changed even without a request from the hospital. Ratings may be improved or lowered, but in the current climate, the ratings are most frequently lowered. Rating agencies have a fiduciary responsibility to consider worst-case scenarios in the "visible" future, after the demise of capital-cost pass-through, rather than to focus solely on a hospital's current financial position. One could neatly summarize the increasingly competitive field of capital finance as a transition from the world of Woody Allen ("90 percent of life is just showing up," often true in a rating or feasibility review during the easy era of cost pass-through) to a dog-eat-dog world of Oscar Wilde. Wilde often stated that "it is not enough to succeed, you have to hope your neighbors fail." German hospital administrators refer to this attitude as *Schadenfreude*, or joy in other people's failure. A capital project will no longer be viewed as financeable just because there exists local community support and a "community need"; the organization has to demonstrate that cash flow will be sufficient to make future debt-service payments (Eastaugh 1987).

In a market with many empty hospital beds, investors view financially weak hospitals as "cross-eyed javelin throwers," in that they will not win any awards but will keep the attention of their fearful audience. David Winston (1986) of the Voluntary Hospitals of America (VHA) summarized this issue as follows: "Trustees must resist the temptation of taking off their business hats and putting on their community service hats and making totally foolish decisions on behalf of their hospitals." Grand plans for capital needs often must be scaled back. As we noted in chapter 12, there is strength in numbers when it comes to the capital markets. Multihospital systems utilize master trust indentures that cover all obligated issuers (members or subsets of the system), permitting a better credit rating and borrowing at lower rates of interest.

There is a clear distinction between "making the financial deal" in stages 3 and 4 and "doing the deal" in completion stage 5. In the closing period bonds are printed, certificates written, bonds escrowed with the trustee, and the final boilerplate documents signed. The boilerplate is the basic language of all debt contracts—that is, obligation to pay, events of default, and indemnification. In the case of refinancing and refunding, the closing period also includes completion of legal documents to defease (pay or set aside payment in an airtight escrow account) the prior bond issue before issuing the new debt. Defeasance is the process of removing the liens of old bond documents by escrowing sufficient funds either from proceeds of a new bond issue or from the firm's cash into a special AAA-rated secure escrow trust. This defeasance escrow fund allows debt-service payments to be made on the outstanding old bonds until they mature or can be called (redeemed prior to their stated maturity date).

Refundings are typically done with net cash defeasance (principal and related interest income in escrow is used to pay the principal and interest on the outstanding old bonds), although some hospitals have been forced by existing restrictive covenants to do either (1) full cash defeasance (principal in the escrow must pay principal plus interest on the old bonds) or (2) crossover refunding (principal amount in the escrow is used to pay outstanding bond principal, and interest income is used to reduce interest expense on the refunding bonds). Advance refundings have decreased in popularity since the mid-1980s because the potential gains in lower interest rates have declined, whereas if one borrowed at the peak interest rates in 1980–81, the gains from financing were very substantial, and hospitals were quick to move in 1984–85 (431 refundings). The fewer refundings in the 1990s have been strategic in nature, in order to lift restrictive covenants. Nemes (1990) reported that some small local hospital minisystems have refinanced in violation of restrictive covenants.

In summary, the senior managers, trustees, and hospital counsel must address four major issues:

1. Will payment methods tighten in the future such that sufficient cash flow will not materialize?
2. Will the hospital be in "technical default" with a future modest downturn in patient demand?
3. How can additional debt be issued?
4. How flexible are the terms of the indenture?

Prior to 1986, movable equipment was typically financed with short-term variable-rate debt to minimize interest expense and maximize allowable arbitrage earnings. To expand available debt capacity, hospitals must continue to develop their joint-venture partnerships with their most wealthy client group: the physicians. However, the partnerships are now sold on the basis of business risk versus return and not on the basis of reducing an individual's tax liability, as was done prior to federal tax reform in 1986.

INVESTMENT DECISIONS

Capital is not the same as assets, although the capital of a firm will be invested in many assets at any point in time. This is a distinction with a difference; capital management includes both liability and asset management. The focus is on the residual value to the board or owners, not on a collection of assets on the books. Capital is managed on three basic levels: (1) investment decisions (what to do), (2) financing decisions (the way to acquire it), and (3) capital-structure decisions (what should the mix of debt to equity be, and what type of debt should be incurred?). Investment decisions should be made based on the cash inflows and outflows, yielding a net present value (NPV) (positive, if the project is worth doing; Hampton 1991; Edwards and Bell 1985). Firms should attempt "what if" simulation analysis of the market reaction to a particular investment decision and consider multiplying the NPV by the probability of an event.

The return on investment (ROI) should exceed the cost of capital (Wheeler and Smith 1988). For example, in one recent case the City Hospital of Martinsburg was receiving a return on investment from its state rate commission of 4.9 percent, which was less than its cost of capital (6.9 percent; Eastaugh 1991). This is not a good fiscal result; under good circumstances the hospital would have a ROI (price-level adjusted) that was higher than the cost of capital, and one could label the firm a going concern. In the long run, if this result continues, the hospital's financial viability is threatened (Cleverley 1990; Hsia 1991). If this were one single department with a poor ROI, one could dispose of the business segment (Chow and McNamee 1991). However, if the entire hospital is experiencing an obvious erosion in capital position, it must avoid new capital investment, fight to trim costs, and appeal the geographic equity of such a low ROI (in this context, in a state with a rate-setting commission). The appeal can be made based on vertical equity (other types of hospitals were treated better by the rate setters) and geographic equity. In other states the hospitals received either a fair sufficient rate for a nonteaching hospital (an average 7.0 percent in the state of Maryland) or a generous price-level-adjusted ROI (10 to 11 percent in Oregon and Washington State).

The several state rate-setting commissions define capital costs in a different way from the Medicare program. The major question is whether hospitals should be paid depreciation for buildings and fixed equipment or for the principal payments that they are required to make. Depreciation payments are higher at the start of a facility's life cycle, while principal payments are higher toward the end of the life cycle. Many economic arguments can be provided against the use of depreciation for payment purposes. However, the payment for capital on a basis other than generally accepted accounting principles tends to arouse considerable ire on the part of the hospital industry. The two major options for capital payments are (1) variations on the formulas used by the Maryland and New Jersey hospital rate-setting commissions, which base the payments on the cash requirements of the hospital for capital, or (2) the Medicare definition of capital costs, which bases the payments on the depreciation, interest, and lease costs. This issue causes a great deal of controversy because use of a basis of payment other than depreciation results in paper losses in the financial statements of hospitals. Several states (e.g., Maryland and Connecticut) pay for movable equipment on the basis of replacement-cost depreciation, while others (e.g., New York and Maine) pay according to Medicare cost principles, that is, straight-line depreciation plus interest.

Investment decisions for multihospital systems have been surveyed by Newland and Roma (1989). The selection of an appropriate cost of capital for a single hospital or a multi-institutional system has been analyzed by Wedig, Hassan, and Sloan (1989). If investment analysis answers the question of whether this project, department, or new equipment brings economic returns (adds value to the organization), the decision makers have five ways to distribute the value created: keep it in reserve, let it be absorbed by enhanced perks and redundancy (adding to inefficiency is not a good strategy for ethical managers), enhance the subsidy for education and research done within the firm, distribute the value to consumers (through lower prices), or, in the case of for-profit firms, pay out dividends to owners. The next section surveys how we pay for the investments selected. Capital-structure decisions are covered in chapter 14.

FINANCING DECISIONS

Financing decisions involve contracting with a set of investors or owners for a return required by the parties. For example, the project might be 6.5 percent financed by philanthropy (the gift givers feel an implicit contract that returns a social dividend, "doing good") and 30 percent financed by an explicit contract with owners (an explicit contract with doctors seeking a fiscal dividend and capital appreciation over time). The balance of the project (63.5 percent) might be financed by some mixture of retained earnings, short-term debt, and long-term debt. On the other hand, some projects might better be leased (a topic covered later in this chapter).

Financing decisions are driven by effective cost, which itself is driven by the economywide pool of potential investors and investment options. Health care managers are typically unfamiliar with the investment community (see Weston and Copeland 1991; Standard and Poor's 1991). Health care may be a $1.5-trillion industry in the year 2001, but health care will still only represent 15 to 17 percent of the capital markets. Health care is largely unable to affect the capital markets. On the downside, firms that are denied access to capital may close; for example, some inefficient hospitals may be viewed as being as risky as nuclear power plants. On the upside, some firms may consolidate, merge, integrate, and take advantage of resulting economies of scale and enhanced productivity to become net savers (capital generators). Scale (size) is not the central key to success (witness all the big downgrades in large hospital systems; Nemes 1991). However, efficiency generation and the selection of a good portfolio of appropriately financed investments are the essential ingredients for success.

Financial managers have to adhere to replacement-reserve policies and limit the overexpansion of new-product-development advocates (empire-building risk). The capital budgeting process, guided by NPV and restrained by a limited supply of funds, helps to make the decisions less political. As a general rule of thumb, the hospital should try to generate $40,000 of operating revenue for every $100,000 of total assets (and $30,000 in nursing homes). Such rules of thumb are guideposts, but less relevant than good financial planning. In addition, the financial manager should also support methods to offer incentive pay for those that control costs and enhance productivity.

LIVING WITHIN LIMITS

There are ways for hospitals to cope with the future limits on the availability of capital. Two frequently utilized strategies are sharing and leasing. The multihospital-system approach to health-services management is potentially an effective structure if economies of scale can be captured by pooling financial resources and decreasing the duplication of services and facilities. In addition, multihospital systems make it feasible to hire more sophisticated management and offer an atmosphere conducive to long-range planning. These aspects of multi-institutional systems combine to raise credit ratings, decrease interest costs, and thus make capital financing less expensive and more feasible. The competitive financial advantages of multi-institutional systems in the future may contribute more to the regionalization of health care than health planning (*Modern Healthcare* 1991).

Leasing of equipment can reduce the immediate drain on funds associated with a major purchase. Even overall costs are often reduced as the hospital takes advantage of the economies realized by the leasing firm (Eastaugh 1981). Until 1986 federal tax law encouraged leasing by third parties to nonprofit organizations in the following way. A vendor sold capital equipment to a proprietary intermediary. The intermediary got the benefit of the investment tax credit and accelerated depreciation and was able to lease to the nonprofit organization at a reduced price. The nonprofit organization benefited from this reduced price, whereas it would have reaped no benefit from buying the equipment itself, as the investment tax credit was worthless to an organization that did not pay taxes. In the case of hospitals, leasing provides additional advantages in the form of (1) a hedge against technological obsolescence, (2) an alternative source of funding when debt or equity funding is unavailable, (3) faster reimbursement, and (4) better service. Leasing has continued to grow in popularity since 1988 (Pons 1990).

THE ADVANTAGES OF LEASING

The rapid development of new medical products, in combination with consumer demands for more comprehensive insurance to cover the ever-expanding vista of medical technology, has pressured hospital administrators to replace their equipment more frequently and at a higher cost. Most corporate financial analysts are shocked to learn that hospitals lease less than 20 percent of their capital equipment. Given the nonprofit nature of more than 80 percent of the hospital industry, there are no tax incentives to discourage leasing and favor purchasing. The rule of thumb is that a nonprofit firm should lease two-thirds of its equipment.

The main advantage of lease financing is that it allows the health institution to be more flexible with regard to rapid technological changes in hospital equipment (Gapenski and Langland 1991). The facility can lease equipment for the duration of the equipment's useful life, which is frequently less than the item's physical life. The possibility that the cost of future obsolescence will be built into the contract price is partly offset by the higher residual value the equipment may have for the leasing company, which has greater access to national resale markets.

Leasing is also attractive to the smart health facility administrator because of flexibility in financing. There is no requirement for a large initial payment. Moreover, even if a project is debt financed with low annual payments, a debt contract frequently involves restrictive clauses on future borrowing. Lease financing establishes a new line of credit that is useful as a supplemental financing source in times of high interest rates and limited borrowing opportunities. For example, leasing companies expanded following President Carter's May 1980 Executive Memorandum to all federal agencies asking for a moratorium on hospital-bed construction and capital-project financing in areas with more than 4.0 beds per thousand. They expanded again following the announcement of Medicare prospective payment for capital.

One indirect advantage of leasing is that the administrator may apply leverage on the leasing company through future lease payment options to force the lessee to provide better maintenance service. For example, hospital labs with leased equipment tend to have lower downtime and lower maintenance and repair costs.

Another advantage of leases is the treatment of lease costs by third-party payers. By leasing, the hospital can utilize the services of the asset and be reimbursed for the periodic lease payments. When equipment is bought outright, straight-line depreciation is normally required. Thus the early large cash inflows associated with reimbursement for accelerated depreciation are not realized. This is important in view of the increasingly high time value of money. Moreover, no third-party payers' reimbursement policies include full price adjustments for inflation over the economic life of the equipment. These negative effects of third-party reimbursement can be avoided when a true lease is used for financing. It should be noted that some state rate regulators in Massachusetts and New Jersey have argued that leasing should be discouraged, so as to force hospitals that have purchased equipment that became prematurely obsolete to suffer the full costs of their actions.

There is one other potential reason why leasing may be financially superior to buying. It is currently a moot point to argue whether tax concerns have favored lease or buy decisions. Some analysts argue that the for-profit lessor benefits from the ability to utilize accelerated depreciation and tax credits (not available since 1986) and consequently passes on partial benefits (in the form of slightly lower lease payments) of this asymmetry in the tax treatment to the lessees. On the other hand, some analysts have argued that the lessor simply charges an amount equal in present-value terms to the cost of buying the equipment plus whatever taxes must be paid. This last scenario suggests that it would be financially advantageous for a tax-exempt lessee to buy rather than lease (and pay the lessor's taxes). There is clearly a need for future research to determine which of the two viewpoints is correct (Bayless and Diltz 1985). One might suggest that the former scenario may occur more frequently, especially in urban markets that have many competing medical leasing companies.

CAPITAL LEASES AND OPERATING LEASES

There are two types of leases from the standpoint of the lessee: operating leases and capital leases. A capital lease is viewed as a purchase agreement whereby the risks and benefits of ownership of the asset are transferred to the lessee. This type of lease is not cancellable and is fully amortized, so the asset and related debt must be recorded on the balance sheet.

Under an operating lease, the risks and benefits of ownership are not transferred to the lessee, and the payments under the lease contract are not sufficient to purchase the leased equipment. Thus an operating lease is not fully amortized and does not affect the balance sheet. Operating leases usually contain a cancellation clause and may call for the lessor to maintain and service the equipment.

Two organizations have attempted to classify leases according to whether the contract entered into is viewed as more of a purchase agreement or an actual lease/rental type of agreement. The Financial Accounting Standards Board (FASB) rule 13 distinguishes between a *capital lease*, which is a purchase agreement, and an *operating lease*, which is a rental agreement. On the other hand, the IRS uses the term *financial lease* to signify a purchase and *true lease* to signify a lease agreement. However, because the FASB is more stringent in its criteria, it is possible for a capital lease by FASB standards to be classified as a true lease by the IRS (table 13.1). This inconsistency on the part of the two agencies has led to some confusion in reimbursement by cost-based third-party payers.

The FASB standards must be used for financial statement reporting purposes. However, for third-party reimbursement purposes (Blue Cross and Medicare) the IRS standards are usually applied. If a contract qualifies as a true lease, the rental payments may be expensed on a periodic basis. If the contract is considered

Table 13.1
FASB Criteria for a Capital Lease and IRS Criteria for a Financial Lease

---

FASB Criteria for a Capital Lease (Financial Accounting Standard 13)

1. Ownership is transferred to the lessee by the end of the lease term.
2. The lease contains a bargain purchase option.
3. The lease term is equal to 75% or more of the estimated economic life of the leased property.
4. The present value at the beginning of the lease term of the minimum lease payments equals or exceeds 90% of the excess of the fair value of the leased property over any related investment tax credit retained by the lessor.

IRS Criteria for a Financial Lease (Rule 55-540)

1. The lessee will acquire title upon payment of a stated amount of "rentals" under the contract, i.e., portions of periodic payments are used to establish an equity position to be acquired by the lessee.
2. The "rental" payments materially exceed the current fair rental value, which indicates that the payments include an element other than compensation for the use of property.
3. The total amount which the lessee is required to pay for a relatively short period of use constitutes an inordinately large proportion of the total sum required to be paid to secure transfer of title.
4. Some portion of the periodic payment is specifically designated as interest or is otherwise readily recognizable as the equivalent of interest.
5. The property may be acquired under a purchase option at a price which is nominal in relation to the value of the property at the time when the option may be exercised, as determined at the time of entering into the original agreement, or which is a relatively small amount when compared with the total payments which are required to be made.

---

to be a purchase agreement (or conditional sale), the allowable expenses are interest and depreciation, as period costs.

REIMBURSEMENT

Current reimbursement policy among third-party payers favors true leases over capital leases if revenue maximization is the objective. The capital lease is treated in a fashion similar to debt, with allowable costs being determined for depreciation and interest in a fashion that may not reflect the full costs of the contract (Conbeer 1990).

Medicare and most third-party reimbursement schemes create a disincentive for capital leasing by not allowing the depreciation of an asset below its estimated salvage value and by limiting historical cost to the lower of fair market value or purchase at the current cost of replacement (adjusted only by straight-line depreciation and prorated over the useful life of the asset). On the other hand, a contract defined as a true lease allows full reimbursement of both operating costs and the entire lease payment (Reed 1985). Consequently, true leases give full reimbursement for the current costs of ownership. As a rule, most third-party payers follow the lead of Medicare in creating incentives that favor leasing over purchase. If the machine is purchased with either debt or equity capital, third-party payers reimburse a hospital for depreciation and operating costs. When the machine is financed by debt, hospitals are additionally reimbursed for interest. Depreciation is usually done by the straight-line method. For most movable scientific equipment, the life of the asset as established by the American Hospital Association is assessed as eight to ten years. Medicare has "an unnecessary borrowing" provision that, applied to include capital leases, required that the hospital use all unrestricted liquid assets, including future capital expansion funds, to reduce the amount of the debt lease.

Fortunately for the hospital industry, most third-party payers and Medicaid plans have been slow to adopt the four FASB criteria. Consequently, if the lease is defined as a true lease in the reimbursement contracts, the total rental payment is fully expensed on a period basis, even if the lease is classified as a capital lease for FASB reporting purposes. However, the FASB criteria are being adopted and interpreted in a less flexible fashion by third-party payers concerned with cost containment. What previously passed as a true lease contract allowing for transfer of ownership title at a nominal fee, in violation of FASB criterion 2, is increasingly being appropriately labeled as a variant of the capital lease known as a conditional sales contract or financial lease. An institution that selects a capital lease should require the lessor to document explicitly the interest charges implicit in the lease. The hospital would then have a point of defense against the third-party payer who attempts to impute unfairly low interest costs.

Many smaller hospitals in financial need have opted for a type of operating lease called a "preprocedure rental." A preprocedure rental requires little or no fixed obligation payments, but instead links fees paid by the hospital to the lessor according to the number of procedures performed (Zimmerman and Maier 1989). The costs per procedure are generally higher than for other forms of leasing, but small facilities would not utilize the equipment fully "to scale" (at 90 to 99 percent capacity) in any case. Thus preprocedure rental operating leases might be the least expensive alternative for clinics and small hospitals. One additional benefit of this form of leasing is that it avoids the problem of provider "moral hazard" among doctors who feel pressure to overorder procedures to justify the fixed expense of having the equipment (Eastaugh 1990).

POTENTIAL CHANGES IN REIMBURSEMENT INCENTIVES

Cleverley (1979) suggested two interesting alternatives to the currently popular method of treating depreciation. The first alternative is a form of replacement cost depreciation (RCD) with debt-financing adjustment. In the case of RCD, debt-financing adjustment, it is assumed that third-party payers will reimburse totally for the debt-service costs, both principal and interest. In addition, replacement cost depreciation will be reimbursed, but not totally. A few states recognize RCD in their state Medicaid programs (New Jersey, Minnesota, and Delaware). During the 1980s, in making the transition from historical cost depreciation to RCD, most nursing homes received higher capital payments. RCD is not universally higher in 100 percent of the situations, because when the state pays RCD, it does not pay interest expense, but when the state was paying historical cost depreciation, the interest expense was also a reimbursed cost. The Marshall and Swift index used by Cleverley and other analysts is the standard index to calculate RCD.

In Cleverley's analysis (1991, 1979) the amount of allowed reimbursement will equal replacement cost depreciation times the desired proportion of equity financing—for example, a target proportion of 0.20 in each of the 10 years. This would stimulate containment of total capital-financing costs, since debt would be used to supplement somewhat lower levels of reimbursement. The use of a given proportion of debt is desirable because the nonprofit hospitals can take advantage of the availability of lower tax-exempt interest rates. Moreover, the hospital can adjust the desired equity-financing ratio to suit its financial needs. In the example provided by Cleverley, the target proportion of 0.20 over 10 years resulted in an effective 0.016 decline in the proportion at the end of the period. This decline occurred because the inflation rate was 2 percent higher than the presumed investment-income rate. Thus one disadvantage of this RCD alternative is that if surplus reimbursement funds cannot be invested at a rate of return greater than or equal to the inflation rate, the targeted equity ratio would have to be continually increased to achieve the desired target ratio.

The second practical alternative suggested by Cleverley is an annuity deposit. Under this method, the amount of equity financing necessary to purchase replacement equipment can be accumulated over the life of the present asset. This would allow for replacement of equipment while minimizing financial incentives for overcapitalization. A third alternative is to allow a capital maintenance factor in the reimbursement formulas—that is, a fixed percentage levied against all patients to finance the maintenance of equivalent state-of-the-art equipment and plant assets. This percentage surcharge might range from 3 to 5 percent.

One infrequently mentioned advantage of total replacement cost depreciation, or price-level depreciation, is that it reduces the long-term cost of services to the public. Replacement cost depreciation has been reported in a large number of corporate financial statements since FASB Statement Number 33 in 1979 (Cleverley 1984). In basic economic terms, future capital funds are best held in the hands of the institution that can earn a higher rate of return on the investment over time. The average hospital, because it is a large, nonprofit firm, can earn a rate of return on its investments that is typically more than 4 percentage points higher than that of the average individual, whom we shall call John Q. Public. To make this point clear, let us consider the hypothetical example of a hospital that must replace a piece of equipment in the diagnostic radiology department in five years. The original equipment costs $500,000 in year zero (1992). The equivalent state-of-the-art replacement appreciates in value at the rate of 15 percent per year and will cost $1.006 million in 1997. At the end of the time period the hospital can finance the new equipment in one of two ways: (1) historical cost depreciation of $100,000 per year for five years with a bonus to make up the difference from the rate setters in year 5 (this bonus is called the planned capital service component in some states) or (2) allowing price-level depreciation (with cash inflows of $115,000, $132,000, $152,000, $175,000, and $201,000 for the five years, to net, after adding in the accumulated interest at 12 percent per year from the depreciation fund, a total of $1.006 million).

In the first case the control over the equity of the institution is effectively out of the hands of the trustees and vested under the control of the rate commission (Eastaugh 1991). If the hospital receives $100,000 each year for five years and earns 12 percent annual interest on those funds, it will accrue $635,285 at the end of the period (1997). The differential between replacement costs and accumulated depreciation funds ($370,715) will have to be paid by the consumers in the form of increased rates. If the public had to budget for that difference over the same five-year period, earning 8 percent per annum on the funds, John Q. Public would collectively have to save $63,191 per year for five years to finance the $370,715. However, if hospitals were reimbursed on the basis of price-level depreciation, they could invest the funds at 12 percent interest and would need to save only $58,354 per year for the five years to achieve the $370,715 at the end of 1997. Consequently, it is $31,002 less expensive (future value of savings in 1998, discounted at 12 percent) in the long run for consumers to keep the funds in the hands of the hospital, rather than underreimburse the hospital and pay out the bonus differential ($370,715) in year 5.

Some cynics argue that politicians support rate-setting commissions because they do apparently save money in the short term, irrespective of whether they are perhaps inflationary in the long run. Supporters of rate regulation and planning argue that society could save money in the long run if it could only force some hospitals not to purchase replacement equipment. One might advocate cost containment and still question the wisdom of a regulatory system that treats hospital management like a beggar with a tin cup, where the government rate commission has the right to determine how full the cup should be. Allowing the hospital a return on equity capital is more efficient than letting the government arbitrarily decide how much each hospital deserves and when it should receive the funds (Eastaugh 1991).

Blue Cross plans in eight states and one state rate commission currently recognize some form of price-level depreciation. There is an irony that the one state government (New Jersey) that is progressive concerning the need for inflation-adjusted depreciation has become equally regressive in disallowing reimbursement for future lease contracts. Each New Jersey hospital is allowed a sinking fund for accumulating annually 10 percent of the price-level-depreciable value of the equipment. The New Jersey rate experiment explicitly discourages both leasing and borrowing in future capital decisions. Future lease contracts in New Jersey were not reimbursed by cost payers since 1982. Fortunately, the climate for reimbursement of leases is much better for hospitals outside of New Jersey and Massachusetts.

THE FINANCIAL COST OF LEASING

Leases are not always a cost-beneficial mode of capital financing. One common misconception about leasing is that it conserves capital. For example, the lease payments are frequently larger than the combined principal and interest payments on debt necessary to buy equipment, especially in southern states where leasing companies have a natural monopoly. Henry and Roenfeldt (1978) reported that the majority of hospital financial managers did not know how to correctly determine the charges associated with leasing. Lack of financial expertise did not inhibit the estimated doubling in assets leased by the hospital sector from 1987 to 1991 (Standard and Poor's 1991). After a brief downturn in interest in leasing following federal tax reform in 1986, the leasing industry has taken off in recent years. Approximately $2.7 billion, or 25 percent, of medical equipment was leased in 1988 (Zimmerman and Maier 1989). Leasing should approach $4.0 billion by 1992. Some facilities select leases as a hedge against obsolescence (Conbeer 1990), while other facilities are forced to accept leases because they cannot receive sufficient tax-exempt financing to purchase necessary equipment. If the equipment becomes obsolete, most leasing companies' interest in return business will allow the hospital to trade in the old machine for the newest model for a reasonable upward adjustment in periodic fees (Leonard 1989).

Hospitals and clinics that lease should beware of hidden fees and the "fine print" in the contract (Becker 1990). For example, some lessors require advance rental payments that are not credited against scheduled payments until year five or six, or allow changes in the lease rate on 60 days notice (VA hospitals and other unwary lessees get stuck with this). Grant and O'Donnell (1990) pointed out that health facilities should count each hidden expense, like commitment fees that are not credited against future lease payments or stepped-up implicit lease rates in the inflation adjustment provision.

Another common misconception among hospital managers is that leasing has an intrinsic cash-flow timing advantage. However, some lease contracts require the institution to borrow a sum (for security purposes) in advance, which is comparable to a loan repayable in arrears in annual installments. Consequently, there is no cash-flow advantage to such a leasing agreement if it is correctly compared to a loan of equivalent interest cost and a comparable schedule for repayment. The one advantage that leasing has over purchasing is that the interest costs are typically 1 or 2 percentage points lower. Probably the most widely held misconception concerning leasing is that it represents an undetected mode of debt financing, hidden from regulatory oversight. The hidden-debt argument is at best cosmetic and at worst a zero-sum manipulation in that neither the asset nor the future liability for the lease payments appears on the balance sheet.

Another unanticipated side effect of defining true leases as capital leases is that a number of the financial ratios used to assess the creditworthiness of the facility deteriorate. If the debt ratio or interest-coverage ratio diminishes, then the hospital's bond rating deteriorates, causing the public to pay for incrementally higher interest rates on future capital purchases. We will review the subject of credit ratings and the limits of debt financing in chapter 14.

Claims by lessors that leasing rates are lower than borrowing rates are not always valid. For example, miscellaneous leasing charges can significantly increase the effective interest rate over the quoted rate for the term of the lease. Leases often include hidden charges such as late-payment penalties. The calculated salvage value of the asset also affects the effective interest rate. This means that careful analysis of the net present cost (NPC) of a lease must be carried out to find the effective rate of interest, in order to compare this mode of financing with other alternatives.

NET-PRESENT-COST ANALYSIS OF LEASING, DEBT-FINANCING, AND EQUITY-FINANCING ALTERNATIVES

There are no simple rules to suggest that one form of financing is uniformly superior to another. For example, leases are purported to transfer the risk of medical-equipment obsolescence to the leasing firm. However, the hospital could carry 110 percent (or 90 percent) of the risk in the form of higher (or lower) than "fair" lease-payment terms. One cannot adopt a simple decision rule, such as "purchasing is best because it adds to the hospital's asset base on the balance sheet." Capital leases also add to the asset base, and the asset base is not critical by itself (that is, increases in assets are offset by increases in long-term debt on the same balance sheet).

In the following example, we consider four modes of financing a $100,000 blood analyzer. We assume that the hospital's objective function is to minimize the net present cost to the institution. One way to do this, although not the only way, is by selecting the method of financing that maximizes reimbursement from third-party payers. One could also minimize net present cost (NPC) by selecting the alternative that has a lower present cost because it had a lower initial cost, whether or not it had higher reimbursement. The net-present-cost estimates that we derive are sensitive to discount rates, interest rates, the time span of the lease or loan, the size of the down payment, the percentage of cost-based reimbursement, and the estimated salvage value.

In considering the cash flows for the four financing options in tables 13.2 and 13.3, we have assumed that the hospital uses straight-line depreciation. The blood analyzer is assumed to have a useful life of 5 years and a book life of 10 years. The debt-financing option calls for a $20,000 down payment, payments on principal of $8,000 per year for ten years, and an interest rate of 15 percent.

In the case of both the capital and true (operating) leases, the lease contract is for a period of 5 years. The payment is at the beginning of the year for both leases. An interest rate of 13 percent is implicit in the capital lease, and the bargain purchase option (nominal $1) is exercised. The reimbursement rate for the following example is taken as 50 percent; 50 percent of patients are cost-payers covering three-quarters of allowable costs. This reimbursement rate is assumed to be constant over the 10-year period. (In other markets cost payers have declined to 25 percent.)

Given these assumptions, the true lease is the best alternative, given a discount rate of either 8 percent or 12 percent without salvage value. However, it is important to remember that the choice of alternative is sensitive to the assumptions that were made at the beginning. For example, debt financing could be brought into parity with the true lease option if the interest charge were to decrease relative to the discount rate by more than 2 to 3 percentage points. Likewise, debt would be the preferred option if the salvage value were to increase to more than $28,000 or 28 percent, or if the down payment were 10 percent or less, given a 25 percent salvage value. In addition, the time span of the loan or lease and the reimbursement rate will each affect the choice of financing method. Debt financing in table 13.3 (line 14) is slightly superior to a true lease at a 12 percent discount with $25,000 salvage value.

In this example capital leases were assumed to have a 13 percent interest rate; however, such leases are not competitive with true leases, even if the interest rate is dropped substantially. Capital leases are basically debt financing with a higher down payment (in this example). Thus capital leases are intermediate between equity and debt financing, because as the down payment increases, reimbursement for interest decreases. Why then do so many hospitals currently hold capital leases? Their popularity is largely due to clever marketing efforts on the part of leasing companies who are able to obscure the actual cost of the lease by quoting low interest rates and then adding on miscellaneous charges. It may also be that hospitals that cannot obtain debt financing go instead with a capital lease. Prior to the adoption of FAS 13 in 1977, hospitals had the cosmetic advantage that the debt incurred through a capital lease did not affect their financial ratios; however, this is no longer the case.

A number of factors have been ignored in this simple analysis. The really

Table 13.2
Net-Present-Cost Calculations with an 8 Percent Discount Rate

		A True Lease[a]	B Capital Lease[b]	C Debt Financing[c]	D Equity Financing
1.	Principal payments	-	-	73,680	-
2.	Interest payments	-	-	49,348	-
3.	Maintenance (at $2,000/yr.)	-	7,985	7,985	7,985
4.	True lease payments	112,116	-	-	-
5.	Capital lease payments	-	108,496	-	-
6.	Cash purchase	-	-	-	100,000
	Net Outlay	112,116	116,481	131,013	107,985
7.	Reimbursement for depreciation (years 1-5)[d]	-	14,973	14,973	14,973
8.	Capital asset[e] write-off ($50,000)[f]	-	12,761	12,761	12,761
9.	Reimbursement for maintenance (at 50%)	-	3,993	3,993	3,993
10.	Reimbursement for interest (at 50%)	-	11,045	24,674	-
11.	Reimbursement of true lease (at 50%)	56,058	-	-	-
	Net Reimbursement	56,058	42,772	56,401	31,727
12.	NPC without salvage value	56,058	73,709	74,612	76,258
	Ranking	1	2	3	4
13.	Salvage value ($25,000)	-	17,015	17,015	17,015
14.	NPC with salvage value	56,058	56,694	57,597	59,243
	Ranking	1	2	3	4

a$26,000 per year for five years (includes maintenance, service, and insurance). The FASB term is operating lease.

b13 percent interest, five equal payments of $25,160.58 per year. The IRS term is financial lease.

c15 percent interest and 20 percent down payment.

d($75,000 ÷ 5) x 0.5 = $3,750 per year for 5 years.

eThe asset is not fully depreciated at the time at which the useful life of the asset expires, so the remaining value of the asset must be written off.

f$7,500 x 5 x 0.5 = $18,750.

Table 13.3
Net-Present-Cost Calculations with a 12 Percent Discount Rate

	A True Lease[a]	B Capital Lease[c]	C Debt Financing[b]	D Equity Financing
1. Principal payments	-	-	65,202	-
2. Interest payments	-	-	43,496	-
3. Maintenance (at $2,000/yr.)	-	7,209	7,209	7,209
4. True lease payments	104,972	-	-	-
5. Capital lease payments	-	101,582	-	-
6. Cash purchase	-	-	-	100,000
Net Outlay	104,972	108,791	115,907	107,209
7. Reimbursement for depreciation (years 1-5)[d]	-	13,519	13,519	13,519
8. Capital asset[e] write-off ($50,000)[f]	-	10,640	10,640	10,640
9. Reimbursement for maintenance (at 50%)	-	3,605	3,605	3,605
10. Reimbursement for interest (at 50%)	-	10,284	21,749	-
11. Reimbursement of true lease (at 50%)	52,486	-	-	-
Net Reimbursement	52,486	38,048	49,513	27,764
12. NPC without salvage value	52,486	70,743	66,394	79,445
Ranking	1	3	2	4
13. Salvage value ($25,000)	-	14,186	14,186	14,186
14. NPC with salvage value	52,486	56,557	52,208	65,259
Ranking	2	3	1	4

[a]$26,000 per year for five years (includes maintenance, service, and insurance).
[b]15 percent interest and 20 percent down payment.
[c]13 percent interest, five equal payments of $25,160.58 per year.
[d]($75,000 + 5) x 0.5 = $3,750 per year for five years.
[e]$7,500 x 5 x 0.5 = $18,750.

crucial decision might not be how to finance the $100,000 blood analyzer, but rather, "Shall we purchase the new blood analyzer under any conditions?" The answer to this question is normally yes if the net present value is greater than zero, or if the net present cost is less than zero. In the example any income streams associated with the purchase of the blood analyzer were not considered, other than the cash inflows associated with 50 percent cost-based reimbursement. If such income is considered, a net present cost of less than zero is required if a decision to purchase the machine is to be made on purely financial grounds.

The choice of discount rate is critical in determining the net present cost or net present value of a proposal (Bower and Oldfield 1981). There are two factors to consider when determining the appropriate discount rate: the cost of funds and the yield from alternative uses of the funds. The correct figure to use depends on where the money is coming from. If equity is being spent (anything that is not debt), then the appropriate discount rate is the return from the best alternative use of the funds (including depositing the money in a bank). If the money is obtained via a debt issue, then the appropriate discount rate for evaluating a specific project is the borrowing rate or the rate of return for the best alternative use of funds, whichever is higher. If the rate of return for the best alternative project and the rate of return on the proposed project both exceed the borrowing rate, then both projects should be completed if enough money can be borrowed (otherwise do the one with the higher NPV).

Reed (1985) argued that a complete financial analysis should include a multivariate sensitivity analysis for a range of interest rates, purchase functions, lease-cost functions, salvage values, and discount rates. Burns and Bindon (1988) pointed out the potential for linear programming applications in buy/lease decisions. However, these models are severely limited by our ability to estimate discount rates and the age at which obsolescence will occur.

The trend toward heavier debt financing may be replaced by a trend toward leasing options in the 1990s. The decision to lease rather than buy and borrow should be analyzed in each individual case. We have reviewed the important net-present-cost-analysis assumptions that must be made explicitly. Inappropriate cost analysis is often published in the medical journals (Eastaugh and Eastaugh 1991).

We have briefly reviewed the topic of capital management: the set of decisions involving financing, assets, and other resources that either improve, maintain, or erode the capital value entrusted to the firm by "investors," be they stockholders, government, a religious organization, or a community board. Board members are fiduciaries with legal responsibility for the preservation of a firm's equity in order to accomplish the purposes for which the institution was founded. Cleverley (1991) outlined the problem that insufficient reimbursement frequently prevents the accumulation and retention of sufficient earnings from operations to establish and maintain the equity reserves necessary for future capital needs. Some rate regulators respond by saying that the payment is not too low, but that inefficiency is too high. Regulators also say that there is an excess supply of beds and equipment per bed (a medical arms race), so they do not want all firms to "maintain the equity reserves necessary for future capital needs" (please close the inefficient bed supply). On the other side, hospital managers say, "Please don't underpay all of us by 10 percent, simply don't pay (contract with) some of us." In this latter sense, selective contracting can be seen as an attempt to channel payments to the more efficient providers and simply to avoid certain providers (Eastaugh 1990). If the hospital or other organization is offered a contract for nonemergency service provision, it has the freedom of choice to sign or renegotiate the terms, but it cannot claim that the reimbursement formula confiscated the institution's capital.

CLOSING ACUTE-CARE BEDS: WHERE ARE THE SAVINGS?

The American Hospital Association (AHA) has taken the position that national occupancy rates indicating that hospitals are one-third empty are a "clear" sign that hospitals are efficiently managed. Under the AHA logic, only patients who require inpatient care are admitted to hospitals, and inpatient stays in the expensive hospital bed are as short as medically appropriate. Services previously performed on an inpatient basis are done at alternative sites (e.g., home care or outpatient care), which helps explain why outpatient services rose to 30 percent of hospital revenues in 1991. However, patients, third-party payers, and employers have one difficult question to ask the hospital industry: Where is the piece dividend from using a smaller piece of the inpatient hospital-bed supply? Estimates of how many acute-care beds are empty for 100 percent of the year—never used for any outpatient service or inpatient case—vary from 100,000 to 176,000 beds. How can we as a nation reap the benefits of closing excess beds in order to finance the extra services provided for the elderly, for outpatients of all ages, and for home care and long-term care?

The intent of this section is not to play the health-planning game and set a normative estimate on benefits to society from having an additional reserve supply of empty beds weighed against the cost of adding to that reserve pool. There will always be people who will claim that some influx of patients will fill those beds in a few years, even if each "excess" bed has remained empty for the past decade. Rather, we shall ask the more practical question: What does it cost to maintain a fully empty excess acute-care hospital bed? Estimates vary from a low of $29,000 in 1991 dollars (Pauly and Wilson 1986) to a high estimate of $65,000 by Anderson (1991).

Anderson (1991) offered the better estimate because he included the recent rise in outpatient demand at the hospitals as a variable in the analysis, and he had department estimates over the budget year for safety margins against surges in demand for a sample of 39 Maryland hospitals. This last point is clearly more refined than simply having a hospitalwide estimate of the fluctuation in occupancy rates over the year (Pauly and Wilson 1986; Friedman and Pauly 1981). Pauly's concept (Pauly and Wilson 1986) of a subjective undercapacity crowding cost of having hospitals too full does not offer a rate regulator any guideposts to constrain capital payments to overbuilt, overcapitalized hospitals. The theoretical model of asserting that 100 percent of hospitals are efficient and that in the long run no excess capacity exists offers a poor description of the world.

Anderson (1991) calculated the cost of an excess hospital bed with a three-year standard hospital cost function (chapter 1) for a national sample of 5,068 hospitals. An excess bed cost 29 percent of the average cost of an occupied bed ($224,000), or $65,000 in 1991 dollars. The definition of a bed was the AHA statistical bed, a bed set up and staffed for use (regularly maintained). The average cost of an occupied bed was only $177,500 in 1985.

Pauly and Wilson (1986) used a sample of Michigan hospitals and concluded that the cost of an excess bed was 13 percent (or less) of the average cost of an occupied bed, or $29,000 in 1991 dollars. However, they distinguished unforeseen empty beds from planned excess capacity (foreseen empty beds). In their cost function, short-run marginal cost was 57 percent of average cost; therefore, the residual, or 43 percent of the average cost of an occupied bed, was the cost of an unforeseen empty bed, but the cost of a foreseen empty bed was 13 percent of the average cost of an occupied bed.

Politicians may be surprised to discover that closing beds at hospitals that remain in business or bankrupting entire hospitals will only save 13 to 29 percent of the average cost of an occupied bed (or $29,000 to $65,000 per bed). The high estimate is probably more reliable because the data base was larger, was more recent, included higher capital spending patterns in recent years, and incorporated day-to-day department variations in workload.

Many noneconomists were under the false impression that closing a bed would save 100 percent of the average cost of an occupied bed. The marginal benefit (cost savings) of closing a bed is under 30 percent of the average cost. The optimal statewide occupancy rate may range from 75 percent for a rural state with many small hospitals to above 85 percent for a highly urbanized state. By 1992–93 the average capital cost per bed, occupied or empty, will exceed $25,000. The average annual variable cost of maintaining an empty bed, including light, heat, and labor expenses (maintenance, cleaning, and security) will exceed $50,000.

MEDICARE PROSPECTIVE PAYMENT FOR CAPITAL

In January 1992 the Medicare program began to phase in $6.4 billion of prospective payment for capital (HCFA 1991). "Old" (preexisting) hospital capital will continue to be partially cost reimbursed, but at a 10 percent discount. This phase-in schedule allows hospitals to adjust their capital spending patterns in line with the new limited revenue stream. Over the past three decades capital spending as a fraction of operating expenses increased from 5.1 to 9.13 percent of costs. This inflation was largely fueled by cost reimbursement and expanding medical technology. When Congress began to phase in DRGs in 1983, it delib-

Table 13.4

Simulation of the Impact of the Medicare Capital Payment Scheme for 1992 on a National Sample of 219 Hospitals

Quartiles for Capital Expense per Admission	Medicare Capital Payment per Patient	Financial Change from 1991-92a	
		Winners	Losers
		(number of hospitals)	
Low expense (bottom quartile)	$395	3	0
2nd quartile	530	14	6
Median	677b	-	-
3rd quartile	846	17	11
High expense (top quartile)	1,085	5	23

aWinners gain more than $90 per Medicare patient in inflation-adjusted dollars from 1991-92. Losers lose more than $90 per case.

bMedian 9.7 percent higher than 1991. The plan is revenue neutral, but has redistributive impact.

erately ducked the issue of capital payments and continued to pay for capital on a cost-reimbursement basis. However, each year the federal government tightened the reimbursement formula, paying only 85 percent of Medicare's fair share (market share) in the late 1980s. Starting in 1992, the average hospital will receive $692 per case in capital payments. A low-cost hospital that spends less than its capital allowance will be allowed to keep the difference and spend it in other areas (e.g., enhanced labor productivity or quality assurance). However, a high-cost hospital spending too much on capital (exceeding its allowance) will have to either defer expensive capital expenses or find the extra dollars elsewhere (from non-Medicare patients).

The American tradition of fair rate setting translates into an ever-complex PPS setting of the capital allowance payments. For hospitals with exceptionally high capital costs (150 percent above the new flat payments), Medicare will make an additional payment equal to three-quarters of the costs above the 150 percent level (to assist young "newer" hospitals). To help the poor and rural communities, large urban hospitals with a high share of low-income patients and rural sole community hospitals will get the extra payments when actual costs are 125 percent above the basic flat rates of payment.

No payment scheme will be without winners and losers, given the variation in efficiency, payer mix, and debt-service burden. Table 13.4 offers a projection of the impact of the 1992 capital payment rules on a sample of 219 of the 232 hospitals surveyed in chapter 2. Only 219 of the hospitals could provide sufficient information on their prior and projected capital expenses. The middle group, average-cost hospitals between the 25 and 75th percentiles in the distribution, is expected to have 3 in 10 big gainers (gaining more than $90 per case in additional Medicare payments in inflation-adjusted dollars), but 2 in 10 will be big losers (losing more than $90 per patient under the new capital payment system). In the most expensive 25 percent of the capital spending distribution, the biggest losers will be the newer for-profit hospitals and the tax-exempt large teaching hospitals not serving a disproportionate fraction of low-income patients. These losers in this simple static model are not predestined to be losers throughout the mid-1990s if they cut capital spending and enhance capital productivity (to defer the need to purchase new equipment) by improved maintenance programs.

Congress requested that HCFA develop a 1996 Medicare capital payment plan taking into account new technology and shifts in occupancy rates. A capital payment rate linked to occupancy rate would pay hospitals with more empty beds less for being inefficient. While any introduction of an occupancy adjustment would establish an incentive for efficient capacity selection in the long run (closing more foreseen empty beds), the hospital with an occupancy rate above the minimum level would have less restraint on capital spending (Hemesath and Pope 1989). An occupancy adjustment penalizes excess bed capacity but not excessive purchase of capital per bed. The 1992 prospective payment system per Medicare case is intended to restrain capital expense per patient. Given that more cost shifting onto private patients is not a viable option, more and more hospitals will have to utilize a more cost-minimizing mix of capital and labor (get closer to those theoretical cost curves [chapter 1]). Will all inefficiency ever be eliminated in any industry? No. However, inefficiency is like sin: It would be nice to reduce some of it even if we cannot eliminate it.

REFERENCES

Anderson, G. (1991). "The Number and Cost of Excess Hospital Beds." AHSI consulting report, Johns Hopkins University.

Arnold, J. (1986). "Assessing Capital Risk: You Cannot Be Too Conservative." *Harvard Business Review* 64:5 (September–October), 113–121.

Bayless, M., and Diltz, J. (1985) "Leasing Strategies Reduce the Cost of Financing Healthcare Equipment." *Healthcare Financial Management* 39:10 (October), 38–48.

Becker, E. (1990). "Formal Plan for Major Equipment Purchases Saves Money." *Healthcare Financial Management* 44:8 (August), 26–32.

Bower, R. and Oldfield, G. (1981). "Of Lessees, Lessors, and Discount Rates and Whether Pigs Have Wings." *Journal of Business Research* 9:1 (March), 29–38.

Bromberg, M. (1991). "The Capital Issue." *Health Systems Review* 24:1 (January-February), 4.

Burns, J., and Bindon, K. (1988). "Evaluating Leases with Linear Programming." *Management Accounting* 61:8 (February), 48–53.

Carpenter, C. (1991). "Marginal Effect of Bond Insurance on Hospital Tax-exempt Bond Yields" *Inquiry* 28:1 (Spring), 67–73.

Chow, C., and McNamee, A. (1991). "Pitfalls of Discounted Cash Flow Techniques." *Healthcare Financial Management* 45:4 (April), 34–44.

Claiborn, S. (1985). "Alternative Financing Approaches for Health Care Institutions." *Topics in Health Care Financing* 10:4 (Summer), 33–41.

Cleverley, W. (1991). *Hospital Industry Financial Report*. Oak Brook, Ill.: Healthcare Financial Management Association.

———. (1990). "Return on Investment: Its role in Voluntary Hospital Planning." *Hospital and Health Services Administration* 35:1 (Spring), 71–82.

———. (1986). "Assessing Present and Future Capital Expense Levels under PPS." *Healthcare Financial Management* 40:9 (September), 62–72.

———. (1984). "A Proposal for Capital Cost Payment." *Health Care Management Review* 9:2 (Spring), 39–50.

———. (1979). "Reimbursement for Capital Costs." *Topics in Health Care Financing* 6:1 (Fall), 127–139.

Cohodes, D. (1983). "Which Will Survive? The $150 Billion Capital Question." *Inquiry* 20:1 (Spring), 5–11.

Conbeer, G. (1990). "Leasing Can Add Flexibility to Asset Management." *Healthcare Financial Management* 44:7 (July), 27–34.

Conley, C., and Peppe, R. (1984). "Municipal Bond Insurance May Create Two Tiers of Healthcare Borrowers." *Modern Healthcare* 14:9 (September), 182–192.

Council of Economic Advisers. (1991). *Economic Report of the President, 1991*. Including data from the American Hospital Association Annual Survey. Washington, D.C.: U.S. Government Printing Office.

Dandion, J., and Weil, R. (1975). "Inflation Accounting: What Will General Price Level Adjusted Income Statements Show?" *Financial Analysts Journal* 15:1 (January–February), 30–38.

Eastaugh, S. (1991). "Affidavit on City Hospital of Martinsburg vs West Virginia: What Is a Sufficient ROI Price Level-Adjusted?" Charleston, West Virginia.

———. (1990). "Financing the Correct Rate of Growth of Medical Technology." *Quarterly Review of Economics and Business* 30:4 (Winter), 54–60.

———. (1987). "Capital Financing and Refinancing." *Healthcare Financial Management* 41:1 (January), 107–108.

———. (1984). "Hospital Diversification and Financial Management." *Medical Care* 22:8 (August), 704–723.

———. (1981). *Medical Economics and Health Finance*. Dover, Mass.: Auburn House.

Eastaugh, S., and Eastaugh, J. (1991). "Economic Malpractice: Inappropriate Use of Cost Analysis." *Annals of Emergency Medicine* 20:8 (August), 944–945.

Edwards, E., and Bell, P. (1985). *The Theory and Measurement of Business Income*. Berkeley: University of California Press.

Elrod, J., and Wilkinson, J. (1985). *Hospital Project Financing and Refinancing under Prospective Payment*. Chicago: American Hospital Publishing.

Financial Accounting Standards Board (1979). *Professional Standards: Accounting*. Vol. 3. Chicago: Commerce Clearing House.

Friedman, B., and Pauly, M. (1981). "Cost Functions for a Service Firm with Variable Quality and Stochastic Demand: The Case of Hospitals," *Review of Economics and Statistics* 63:4 (November), 610–624.

Graham, J. (1985). "More States Selling Bond Issues to Funded Pooled Equipment." *Modern Healthcare* 15:15 (July 19), 76.

Grant, L., and O'Donnell, D. (1990). "Watch for Pitfalls When Analyzing Lease Options." *Healthcare Financial Management* 44:7 (July), 36–43.

Grimmelman, F. (1986). "Borrowing for Capital: Will It Empty Your Pockets?" *Hospital Financial Management* 39:12 (December), 19–25.

Grossman, R. (1983). "Leasing versus Buying Equipment." *Applied Radiology* 12:6 (November–December), 69–72.

Guy, A. (1976). "Six Leasing Considerations." *Hospital Financial Management* 6:6 (June), 40–46.

Gapenski L., and Langland, B. (1991). "Leasing Capital Assets and Durable Goods." *Health Care Management Review* 16:3 (Summer), 73–81.

Hampton, J. (1991). *Financial Decision Making*. Reston, Va.: Reston Publishing.

Health Care Financing Administration (HCFA) (1991). "Regulations on Prospective Payment for Hospital Capital-related Costs." *Federal Register* 56:40, February 28, 8476–8536.

Health Care Investment Analysts (HCIA). (1991). *Changing Profitability: Investor-owned versus Public and Nonprofits*. Baltimore: HCIA.

Hemesath, M., Pope, G. (1989) "Medicare Capital Payment Rates and Hospital Occupancy Rates." *Health Affairs* 8:3(Fall), 104–116.

Henry, J., and Roenfeldt, R. (1978). "Cost Analysis of Leasing Hospital Equipment." *Inquiry* 15:1 (March), 33–42.

Hopkins, D., Heath D., and Levin, P. (1982). "A Financial Planning Model for Estimating Hospital Debt Capacity." *Public Health Reports* 97:4 (July–August), 363–372.

Horvitz, R. (1979). "Accounting Management Impact of FAS 13." *Hospital Financial Management* 9:8 (August), 16–21.

Hsia, C. (1991). "Estimating a Firm's Cost of Capital." *Journal of Business Finance & Accounting* 18:2 (January), 281–287.

Institute of Medicine. (1991). *The Changing Economics of Medical Technology*. Washington, D.C.: NAS Press.

Joskow, P. (1980). "The Effect of Competition and Regulation on Hospital Bed Supply and the Reservation Quality of the Hospital." *Bell Journal of Economics* 11:2 (Autumn), 421–447.

Kane, J. (1990). "Negotiate End-of-Lease Options up Front." *Healthcare Financial Management* 44:1 (January), 88–89.

Kidder-Peabody and Company, The Health Finance Group (1989). Public report: *Review of Health Care Finance*. New York.

Kowalski, J. (1991). "Inventory to Go: Can Stockless Deliver Efficiency?" *Healthcare Financial Management* 45:11 (November), 20–34.

Leonard, E. (1989). "Strategies for Nonprofit Hospital Capital Financing in the 1990's." *HealthSpan* 6:4 (April), 16–19.

Marr, J., and Patricola, S. (1984). "FHA Mortgage Insurance for Health Care Providers." *Healthcare Financial Management* 38:10 (October), 52–58.

McCue, M., McCue, T., and Wheeler, J. (1988). "An Assessment of Hospital Acquisition Prices." *Inquiry* 25:2 (Summer), 290–296.

McCue, M., Renn, S., and Pillari, G. (1990). "Factors Affecting Credit Rating Downgrades of Hospital Revenue Bonds." *Inquiry* 27:3 (Fall), 242–254.

Midyette, S., and Pryor, W. (1978). "Equipment Ownership Financing Has Advantages for Hospitals." *Hospital Financial Management* 8:3 (March), 64–69.

Miller, J. (1979). "Hospital Equipment Leasing: The Breakdown Discount Rate." *Management Accounting* 25:3 (July), 21–25.

Modern Healthcare. (1991). "Annual Survey on Multi-institutional Systems." *Modern Healthcare* 22:21, 4–106.

Modigliani, F., and Miller, M. (1958). "The Cost of Capital, Corporation Finance, and the Theory of Investment." *American Economic Review* 48:2 (May), 261–297.

Nemes, J. (1991). "Two Agencies Downgrade Lutheran General Debt." *Modern Healthcare* 21:1 (January 7), 52.

———. (1990). "Healthcare Bonds That Violate Covenants Can Be Refinanced." *Modern Healthcare* 20:11 (March 19), 42.

Neumann, B., Suver, J., and Zelman, W. (1992). *Financial Management: Concepts and Applications for Health Care Providers.* Baltimore: National Health Publishing.

Newland, D., and Roma, S. (1989). "Allocating Capital in a Multihospital System." *Healthcare Financial Management* 43:3 (March), 36–45.

Pallarito, K. (1992). "Hospital Fund Raising." *Modern Healthcare* 22:1 (January 6), 74–75.

Pauly, M., and Wilson, P. (1986). "Hospital Costs." *Health Services Research* 21:2 (Summer), 403–427.

Pons, T. (1990) "Should You Buy or Lease Your New Office Equipment?" *Medical Economics* 67:8 (August), 93–97.

Pope, G. (1991). "Measuring Geographic Variations in Hospitals' Capital Costs." *Health Care Financing Review* 12:4 (Summer), 75–85.

Press, S., and Sherwin, J. (1989). "Financing Growth through REITs." *FAH Review* 22:1 (January–February), 57–63.

Reed, J. (1985). "How Bankers Can Help Their Customers Decide Whether to Lease or Buy." *Journal of Commercial Bank Lending* 22:3 (March), 28–40.

Sandrick, K. (1986). "What If Equipment Loan Pools Dry Up?" *Hospitals* 60:2 (January 20), 60.

Schwartz, G., and Stone, C. (1991). "Strategic Acquisitions by Academic Medical Centers." *Health Care Management Review* 16:2 (Spring), 39–47.

Simpson, J. (1978). "The Health Care Dilemma and Corporate Debt Capacity." *Hospital and Health Services Administration* 23:3 (Summer), 54–67.

Standard and Poor's Corporation. (1991). *Debt Ratings Criteria: Municipal Overview.* New York: Standard and Poor's.

———. (1984–1991). *Municipal Bond Book.* Quarterly issues. New York: Standard and Poor's.

Starshak, J. (1991). "Tax-exempt Bond Financing." *Healthcare Financial Management* 45:3 (March), 106.

Stover, R. (1991). "Bond Ratings and New Municipal Bond Pricing." *Quarterly Journal of Business and Economics* 30:1 (Winter), 3–16.

Suver, J., and Neumann, B. (1978). "Cost of Capital." *Hospital Financial Management* 8:2 (February), 20–26.

Toomey, R., and Toomey, R. (1976). "Political Relations of Capital Formation and Capital Allocations." *Hospital and Health Services Administration* 21:2 (Spring), 11–27.

Wedig, G., Hassan, M., and Sloan, F. (1989). "Hospital Investment Decisions and the Cost of Capital." *Journal of Business* 62:4 (October), 517–537.

Weston, J., and Copeland, T. (1991). *Managerial Finance*. New York: Holt and Rinehart.

Wetzler, D. (1986). "Tax-Exempt Financing for Hospitals." Address at the 29th Congress of Administration, Annual Meeting, American College of Healthcare Executives (February 12), Chicago.

Wheeler, J., and Smith, D. (1988). "Discount Rate for Capital Expenditure Analysis in Health Care." *Health Care Management Review* 13:4 (Spring), 43–51.

Winston, D. (1986). "Access to Capital: The Health Care Market in Flux." Keynote address at the Washington Health Letter Conference on Capital (February 6), New York.

Wood, S. (1986). "Survey Shows Changing Sources of Capital." *Hospital Capital Finance* 3:3 (Fall), 4–6.

Zimmerman, M., and Maier, R. (1989). "Leasing Equipment Minimizes Capital Investment." *Healthcare Financial Management* 43:13 (March), 62–66.

Chapter 14

Access to Capital and
Debt Financing

The typical hospital should be viewed as a more risky venture, and will pay higher interest rates unless they can demonstrate DRG profitability. Hospitals shall no longer have government as a "Sugar Daddy" paying the interest on their debt coupon by coupon. One thousand hospitals may close. We view such hospitals as "cross-eyed javelin throwers" in that they will not win any awards, but they will keep the attention of their fearful audience.

—Investment banker

The penalty for a "wrong" decision a decade ago was usually no more than the effort of persuading some donor to make good a relatively small financial loss. The decisions were private affairs, usually made intuitively. Now they are public affairs involving large sums of borrowed money. Intuition has been replaced by discounted cash flows and debt capacity analysis.

—Walsh McDermott, M.D.

In many situations providers may have reached maximum debt capacity which implies that the next phase may be rapid aging and deterioration of present health facilities in this country.

—William O. Cleverley

Prospective payment by DRG is done in every state for the elderly, 14 states for Medicaid, and 13 other states for Blue Cross. A new era of total revenue controls and decreasing numbers of hospital beds does not preclude the need to allow hospital capital to keep pace with inflation and meet the demand for more tests and procedures per day of care. The first section in this chapter will survey capital-structure decisions facing the health care industry. Autonomy will be lost for those hospitals unable to maintain a reasonable income margin (Grimaldi 1991; Harris and Ravid 1991). To ensure against this, the payers should allow for a small but significant profit margin. Three equations are derived in this chapter to measure the impact that private-sector financing authorities could have on hospital growth as a function of various suggested financial ratio ceiling requirements. After a sensitivity analysis, it is concluded that a 3 percent operating margin would be barely sufficient to reduce the case-study hospital's high dependence on debt. The definition of an adequate operating margin will vary among different-size hospitals and different ownership arrangements. Teaching hospitals may require a 4 to 6 percent margin. Payment formulas fixed in this manner would not only diminish the incentives for excessive reliance on debt financing but also allow new capital to be equally equity financed (47 percent equity and 47 percent debt, instead of 81 percent debt and 13 percent equity). Philanthropy will continue to have a minor role to play (6 percent of new capital stock).

CAPITAL STRUCTURE DECISIONS

Capital structure rules of thumb, even when price and age adjusted, are seldom useful guideposts. It may be a problem if the facility has more than $75,000 of long-term debt per bed or over $100,000 of plant and equipment per bed, but management decisions must be more rational in approach. In this context, Silvers and Kauer (1986) have been long-time advocates of taking a more aggressive financial approach rather than an accounting approach. They have often stated that the risk taking of medical researchers is seldom matched by managerial imagination and aggressiveness. Having covered investment analysis and financing decisions in chapter 13, we are left with the two basic questions in capital structure decisions: (1) What is the appropriate balance between debt and equity financing? (2) Given the level of debt, what is the best mix of long-term and short-term debt?

The standard answer to the first question, trade-off theory, is provided by Modigliani and Miller (1963). They suggested that the optimal capital structure occurs when the marginal costs of debt financing equal the marginal benefits. Marginal benefits, depending on ownership type, include access to lower-cost tax-exempt debt or the tax deductibility of interest payments (Weston and Copeland 1991). Why do the marginal cost and marginal benefit curves intersect? The benefits increase at a constant rate because each additional dollar of debt reaps approximately the same marginal benefit, but the marginal costs start low and increase at an accelerating rate as the debt-to-assets ratio gets higher (0.4 to 0.6) and faster still for ratios above 0.6. Very few hospitals would try to defend an optimal mix of debt in excess of 0.7 (even in financially stressed markets, like New York and Boston).

Prior to 1992 a third marginal benefit stimulating debt financing included the Medicare capital pass-through of interest payments. If local payers like Blue Cross and Medicaid still offer this "benefit," the hospital should include it in the equation to derive an optimal debt level (Berman, Weeks, and Kukla 1991). However, more and more payers are opting for a unilateral or bilateral selective contracting system that includes no specific payment for interest payments (Neumann, Suver, and Zelman 1992). Government tax policy stimulates debt financing, but within the constraint that very high debt levels are too costly. Borrowing becomes more expensive as fewer and fewer firms will lend to you, the hospital's creditworthiness erodes, and interest rates are higher. With higher reliance on debt the probability of default increases, and investors demand higher interest payments to compensate for this risk.

An Alternative for For-Profits

For-profit firms sometimes employ an alternative to trade-off theory in answering the debt-level issue (question 1). This less popular "pecking-order" theory departs from the well-balanced trade-off theory, given that equity funds are either pegged at the bottom of the pecking order (new common-stock sales) or at the top of the pecking order (retained earnings). According to Myers and Majluf (1984), when for-profit managers think that their stock is undervalued, they will be motivated to use debt financing, but if the stock is overvalued, they will issue new common stock. In the finance professors' ideal world investors fully recognize the bias of managers to issue new common stock when it is overvalued, because it helps to maximize the wealth of the current shareholders. Therefore, stock prices typically dip 3 to 4 percent after the announcement of a forthcoming new stock issue, and managers try to make debt their first choice. New common stock is the last choice in the pecking order of alternatives.

Small fast-growth companies that have large capital demands have little choice but to issue new stock (selling a large piece of the company). By contrast, some mature companies have had to go private and stop selling common stock because the price is so undervalued on the market (HCA and AMI are examples; see chapter 12). It is better to go private than continue selling the stock at a low price.

Many mature for-profit firms with too much debt (overleveraged) issue new stock and use the money to refund debt in order to get the debt-to-assets ratio below some target (e.g., 0.52). A few mature companies that are using too little debt (underleveraged) acquire more debt financing and use the funds to repurchase stock. As we demonstrated with the example in table 12.2, tax-exempt firms have less flexibility in their capital-structure options. Tax-exempt organizations have access to tax-exempt long-term, but access to short-term debt is restricted to taxable bank credit. However, the flexibility attributed to for-profit firms is somewhat overstated if nobody will buy their stock at a sufficient price.

Short-Term or Long-Term Debt

We must address the second capital-structure question: Given the level of debt, what is the best mix of long-term and short-term debt? Gapenski (1990) outlined three general approaches to the short-term or long-term debt mix. The first approach, the aggressive approach relying the most on short-term debt, allows some fraction of the firm's permanent assets to be financed with short-term borrowing. This contrasts with the traditional approach to finance all permanent assets with permanent capital (Neumann et al. 1991). Why prefer short-term debt? Short-term debt is normally less costly than long-term taxable debt, and short-term debt is sometimes a little less costly than long-term tax-exempt debt. What is the downside in comparison to variable-rate long-term borrowing? There is a renewal risk that downturns in financial ratios could result in lenders refusing to renew the credit. However, if the borrowing is long run, there is no risk that the renewal can be turned down over the next 9 to 12 months.

The second approach outlined by Gapenski is the conservative approach that centers on the maximum use of long-term debt. Advocates of this approach emphasize the reduced fixed costs (legal fees and so on) of borrowing over the life cycle of the institution. Interest rates may be a bit higher, or much higher under taxable long-term debt, but the facility does not face a renewal risk each year. The third approach is a middle-of-the-road alternative between the two extremes. Under the maturity-matching method, the manager matches the maturities of the liabilities with the maturities of the assets being financed, resulting in a moderate level of reliance on each type of debt (Brick and Ravid 1991).

Shift from Equity to Debt Financing

In the 1970s we saw an explosion in the use of debt financing by hospitals to help support and expand their operations. Later in this chapter we will identify the reasons for an explosion in debt, the constraints on future increases in the debt ratio, and the implications of debt ratios for hospitals in a state of expansion or decline. In addition, the often-neglected reimbursement issue concerning definition of an adequate rate of return on equity to assure sufficient private market financing of hospital capital needs will be discussed.

Two basic policy initiatives by the federal government have fueled the trend since 1972 toward bonded indebtedness. First, Medicare and Medicaid substantially reduced the risk involved with debt financing by reimbursing 100 percent of interest and allowing full amortization of bonded indebtedness. Second, the Nixon administration, acting in the spirit of what it termed ''off-budget financing,'' encouraged investment banking firms and local governments to create tax-exempt financing authorities to issue tax-exempt hospital bonds in 42 states in the period 1970–73. Tax-exempt bonds offered health facilities the advantages of longer payback periods, no down payment or equity requirements, and lower interest rates relative to taxable bonds.

The 1980 Congressional Budget Office report entitled ''Tax Subsidies for Medical Care'' suggested either eliminating the tax-exempt status of hospital bonds or containing the rate of issue of tax-exempt bonds by requiring that they be declared the general-obligation issue of the state or local government unit issuing them. Placing hospital bonds under general-obligation status would force hospitals to compete for capital with schools and public projects on an equal basis. Hospitals barely escaped this fate in the process of 1986 federal tax reform. Currently, state and local government units have no financial responsibilities for hospital bond issues; consequently, they have no direct interest in limiting them. However, the marketplace for general-obligation bond issues would undoubtedly reduce the ability of hospitals to borrow. Some analysts have argued that the relative ease of borrowing in the hospital industry has exacerbated the shortfall of capital available to other public-sector building projects.

Hospitals financially strong enough to be undergoing a major building program, especially in the 1988–91 era of declining inpatient demand, are somewhat less reliant on debt. For example, the $2.4 billion of construction in progress in 1991 was only 50 percent debt financed, 29 percent coming from internal reserves, 10 percent from equity, 6.8 percent from philanthropy, and 4.2 percent from other sources.

Regardless of ownership type, responsibility for protection of assets, quality of care, and facility reputation rests with the governing board. Hospital trustees have a fiduciary responsibility for the preservation or enhancement of a facility's equity. When the equity capital of an institution is eroded due to insufficient reimbursement, inflation, and poor profitability, the ability of that facility to continue meeting community needs will be reduced or eliminated. Some combination of insufficient payment rates and suboptimal financial management can create a shortfall in the retained earnings necessary to maintain sufficient replacement reserves. Cleverley (1991) reported that the average hospital only has enough equity funds to finance 10 percent of its present replacement needs. Therefore, 80 to 85 percent debt financing is required to maintain the average facility adequately.

Philanthropy has declined from 21 percent of tax-exempt hospital capital-project financing in 1968 to 6 percent since 1990. Charitable contributions will not solve our future problems of access to capital. Lenders do respect a successful fund-raising effort, as it may provide a proxy measure of community support and cash flow for the institution; however, the sum total of charitable contributions and grants was less than 6.5 percent of the average tax-exempt hospital's revenues in 1989 (Kidder-Peabody Company 1989). Excessive reliance on debt is viewed by many hospital administrators as a critical problem. In the past few years debt-to-equity ratios have increased dramatically. A facility's ability to issue debt is highly dependent on both the degree to which it is already leveraged and the capital market's estimation of the default risk of the firm. Capital management is becoming increasingly important in the 1990s (Booth 1991; Prezas 1991; Siegel and Hoban 1991).

INTERNAL CAPITAL PLANNING: LONG-RUN PLANS AND SHORT-RUN INVESTMENTS

It is a basic tenet for fiscal managers that the capital process must be managed in order to properly manage the institution. Kaufman and Hall (1991) and Neumann, Suver, and Zelman (1992) offered a comprehensive approach to the long-run issues: strategic capital planning, basics of credit ratings, basic corporate financial tools for investment decisions, and an outline of fixed-rate, insured-rate, and variable-rate financing. Krohm, Merrill, and Talarczyk (1991) offered a more practical guide for management of short-run investments for the smaller-scale organizations (not in multihospital systems). The typical hospital financial manager has to utilize sound principles in selecting and using investment managers. The investment plan should be conservative. Krohm, Merrill, and Talarczyk (1991) surveyed the categories of fixed-income and equity investments and described how health care institutions can measure and maximize investment performance. Their short book offers guidelines for working effectively with investment managers and benchmarks for evaluating their results. The interested reader looking to take more risks and maximize return on invested assets should read Ibbotson and Sinquefield (1991). However, the most interesting information to utilize is often unfamiliar territory for the health care manager, for example, Gibson's (1991) range of volatility or risk of the investment portfolio.

Hospital capital costs as a percentage of total costs increased from 7.1 percent in 1984 to 9.1 percent in 1991. Southern hospitals and for-profit hospitals tend to spend a little bit more on capital (as a percentage of total costs), and state and local public hospitals spend two points less on capital. Why has spending on capital increased? Medical technology and short-run reimbursement concerns are the major culprits. Providers spend more in an area without strict price controls. In the last decade Medicare and other payers cost-reimbursed capital while placing price controls on operating expenses. This is not to suggest that controversy did not exist under cost reimbursement of capital. To reduce payment levels, Medicare liked to select the longest estimated lives for depreciable assets. Therefore Medicare clung to the 1983 American Hospital Association version of the estimated asset lives (years) long after the 1988 edition was published. (A new edition of the estimated asset lives will be published in 1993.) The new Medicare pricing scheme for prospectively paying for capital costs will create a new pressure to decrease or stabilize capital spending (Berman, Weeks, and Kukla 1991). The new prospective payment approach to hospital capital spending will do some harm to hospitals with the unfortunate bad luck of being at the end of their investment life cycle (requiring a replacement program or major modernization in the mid-1990s, not in 15 to 25 years).

Investment Life Cycles

Many published studies have suggested that hospitals make capital investments in identifiable life cycles (Eastaugh 1984; Howell 1984; Rodgers 1988). More basic research is needed concerning the length of these investment cycles, timing, and negative ramifications of deferred investment (Cohodes and Kinkead 1984). A number of professional estimates of the capital needs of the health care industry have been made. The estimates are highly dependent on the assumptions concerning the number of facilities that should survive, capacity utilization (occupancy), facility size, growth in technology, alteration of services, and expansion of different services (Cohodes 1983; Anderson and Ginsburg 1983; Eastaugh 1987; Pillari 1990; Kidder-Peabody 1989). Even with health expenditure growth at 5 to 6 percent per annum and technology growth at 1 to 2 percent per annum, capital needs from 1992 to 1999 could vary widely: $110 to $130 billion for hospital renovation and modernization, $20 to 30 billion for hospital expansion, $90 to 140 billion for skilled nursing facilities, and $70 to 100 billion for intermediate-care/rehabilitation facilities.

Will the health care sector receive the professionally defined estimate of capital needs? Will capital suppliers satisfy capital needs? As with every industry (except perhaps the defense industry from 1982 to 1985), effective capital demands will be some fraction of capital "needs." However, it may be important to the future health of the population that this fraction of demand-to-need be closer to 0.8 than 0.4 to 0.5. Capital-financing availability will significantly shape the structure, access, quality, and cost of our health care system well into the twenty-first century. Hospitals at the end of the investment cycle are most in need of capital for physical plant and modernization. At the level of individual programs, Brown (1988) suggested that certain "orphan investments" would be undercapitalized, such as preventive, social, and rehabilitative services. All through the investment cycle, hospitals require capital for new program development, working capital, and debt service. A number of hospital managers may have to lengthen the investment life cycle.

The degree to which hospitals adjust their investment cycles may vary according to size, ownership, membership in a multihospital system, and the amount of retained earnings on hand. The capital investment cycle is crudely captured by the hospitalwide accounting age (under 9 years representing the "early stage" and over 24 the "late stage"). Accounting age is calculated as a ratio of accumulated depreciation to the original value of plant and equipment. There have been a number of simulation models of hospital investment cycles, including the Schneider, Mager, and Dummit (1986) study of 150 California hospitals, the ICF model of 4,000 American Hospital Association member hospitals, and the Krystynak (1985) study. For policy makers the most critical issue has been assigning an equitable capital add-on payment (CAPPAY), expressed as a percentage of operating revenues. A simple model would include the ratio of the first year's operating revenue to project cost R (e.g., 0.4 to .55), the life of the asset T (e.g., 28 to 35 years), the percentage of the capital investment debt financed B (e.g., 0.85), and the present value of capital reimbursement less principal and interest payments over the life of the asset expressed as a percentage of project cost CF (e.g., cash flow $CF = .22$). If $T = 28$ and $R = 0.47$, solving for CAPPAY:

$$CAPPAY = (B + CF)/(T \times R) = 0.081.$$

The facilities with better financial position are clearly more likely, ceteris paribus, to make major capital investments. Investment behavior also depends on accounting age, profit margin, plant fund, retained earnings, fully funded depreciation accounts, and occupancy rate. The variables are interrelated, and it is difficult to associate empirically the unique contribution of each factor. For example, it is more difficult to achieve higher occupancy rates in smaller hospitals. If one assumes that half of the admissions are nonscheduled, both a 68 percent occupied 65-bed hospital and an 88 percent occupied 500-bed hospital are at 100 percent occupancy three days a year. Physicians and patients prefer newer facilities (lower accounting age). This preference will in turn affect profitability and occupancy. Schneider, Mager, and Dummit (1986) assumed that for every year of decrease in accounting age, a hospital's admission rate will increase by 0.3 percent. In the microsimulation model presented in this text, we shall assume a more generous 0.5 elasticity of the effect of facility age on admissions (chapter 8). The model's critical assumptions for investment probability are presented in table 14.1. Current and projected profit margins are increasingly critical factors in whether a facility initiates a major capital project.

The smaller and less profitable hospitals in the 8 to 16 age category will not be likely to make a major capital investment in the coming decade (table 14.1). Typically, hospitals with recent large capital investments have higher capital expenses and lower operating profit margins. However, hospitals that avoid replacement and modernization decisions also tend to have lower profit margins. This problem of underinvestment or delayed investment can be either involuntary (e.g., the facility is financially distressed) or voluntary (e.g., the trustees and managers are overly timid about the potential for new assets generating sufficient income). Organizations with moderate-range capital expenses are usually the hospitals that have made recent major capital investments, but not in the immediate past.

From the simulation results reported in table 14.2 it appears that the hospitals in a poor financial position are older and less capable of spending the average amount of funds on equipment and plant improvement. Profitability erodes if a facility does not invest. Hospitals not smart enough to invest heavily in the mid-1980s and to receive as much cost reimbursement as possible prior to 1992 are in bad shape for the 1990s. The Bush administration could justify the closure of 100,000 beds from this category on the grounds that they are too expensive to save, and that payments should be channeled to the newer (more recently rebuilt or modernized) hospitals. The financially distressed hospitals would be expected to lobby Congress for a more generous Medicare capital payment system and a second Hill-Burton capital spending program.

Multihospital systems might be better able to adapt to the 1992 capital payment scheme because they are capable of risk spreading. For example, systems could smooth out the "lumpiness" of investments by spacing them over time among chain members. Chains can allocate expensive new investments to member

Table 14.1
Capital Investment Probability as a Function of Hospital Accounting Age,
Occupancy, Size, and Profitability (GT Denotes Greater Than)

Accounting Age	Occupancy	Size (beds)	Operating Margin	Probability of Investment per Annum
25+	GT 50%	20-100	GT .015	0.010
"	GT 60%	GT 100	GT .012	0.012
"	any	any	GT .040	0.020
"	other combinations		--	0.005
17-24	GT 50%	20-100	GT .025	0.011
"	GT 60%	101-300	GT .020	0.014
"	GT 70%	101-300	GT .050	0.090
"	GT 70%	GT 300	GT .040	0.088
"	GT 80%	GT 300	GT .060	0.170
"	other combinations		GT .035	0.050
"	other combinations		.0-.034	0.010
8-16	GT 50%	20-100	GT .025	0.007
"	GT 60%	101-300	GT .020	0.009
"	GT 70%	101-300	GT .050	0.040
"	GT 70%	GT 300	GT .040	0.035
"	GT 80%	GT 300	GT.060	0.070
	other combinations		GT .035	0.010
"	other combinations		.0-.034	0.001
4-7	GT 80%	GT 300	GT .080	0.015
	other combinations			0.0

facilities that are currently operating under the capital cap (the payment add-on) and increasingly share such capital-intensive departments (e.g., MRI).

The upturn in capital spending was predictable in the context of what economists refer to as an "announcement effect." The federal government announced in 1983 that Medicare would end cost reimbursement by 1986 (the eventual date was extended to start for FY 1992). Hospital managers, as rational economic

Table 14.2
Profit Margins as a Function of Accounting Age and Capital Expense per Bed in 1993 and 1995

	Operating Margin 1993	Operating Margin 1995
Accounting age		
0-7	0.008	0.013
8-11	0.024	0.021
12-16	0.013	0.003
17-24	0.011	-0.002
25+	0.001	-0.009
Annual capital expense per bed		
Under $4,500	0.013	-0.010
$4,500-$7,499	0.020	-0.014
$7,500-$10,999	0.015	0.025
$11,000-$13,999	0.011	0.019
$14,000 +	0.000	-0.001

Source: Based on a simulation of 219 hospitals surveyed in chapter 2.

actors, made their capital investment decisions so as to maximize their Medicare payments before the "free lunch" of a cost pass-through ended. Indebtedness skyrocketed, especially in the tax-exempt bond market, where volume increased from $9 billion in 1982 to $9.9 billion in 1983, $10.2 billion in 1984, and $29.9 billion in 1985. According to the 1986 *Bond Buyer Statistical Supplement*, the average interest rate for new A-rated hospital bonds declined from 12.82 percent to 7 percent in 1986 and 6.6 percent in 1992 (Nemes 1992).

Hospitals rushed to the bond markets to take advantage of the Medicare cost-reimbursement formulas, to refinance old debt at lower rates of interest, and to hedge against any possibility that the tax reform in 1986 would eliminate or cap the volume of tax-exempt debt issued to health care facilities. Fortunately, tax-exempt hospitals were spared from most of the restrictions that were placed on tax-exempt bonds in the 1986 tax-reform bill (the one major exception being the Dole provision concerning abusive arbitrage—that is, risk-free gain obtained by borrowing funds at a tax-exempt rate and investing these funds at taxable interest rates for a sure 2 to 3 percent profit). To cap the volume of hospital bonds at a fixed dollar amount per capita per state would have been a textbook example of "nude federalism"—that is, stripping state and local governments of the resources necessary to provide basic services (health care, schools, sewers, and other infrastructure programs).

Capital replenishment is a long-range issue that should not be subject strictly to short-run cost-cutting goals. Policy makers should consider the proverb of the old man who, in the interest of cost cutting, decided not to feed his ox. The ox did fine, so the man did not feed him for nine more days. The ox dropped dead on the tenth day. Do we as a society want the ox of medical technology that promotes quality patient care to drop dead? Like most analogies, this one is imperfect. The ox of quality care is more likely to erode slowly, almost imperceptibly, rather than to drop dead suddenly. More critically, the hospital sector may be overcapitalized on average, but certain poor hospitals in poor neighborhoods are less well positioned to survive the 1990s.

A formula cannot ensure that all hospital closings will be nonharmful (Brown 1988). Future developments in capital spending, the quality of service, and the health status of certain populations are difficult to foresee, and the need for monitoring changes is apparent. Kalison and Averill (1985) suggested allowing hospitals with high capital costs (defined as above 10 percent of total costs) to select a one-time capital-adjustment option patterned on accelerated depreciation.

Reasons for the Increase in Debt Financing

Hospital administrators are not entirely to blame for the critical leverage problems facing their hospitals. Administrators had been blessed with large external sources of funds for many years. The abandonment of government programs such as Hill-Burton, the rise and fall of cost reimbursement, and the dramatic drop in philanthropy have left hospitals groping for new capital sources.

Many factors underlie the shift from equity to debt financing. The most important factor is the shift from cost-plus to simple cost reimbursement. This has created a shortfall in both net income and working capital, forcing hospitals to seek funds externally. The Hill-Burton program, which provided federal funds for the construction of new beds, has been eliminated. Philanthropic contributions as a percentage of total contributions have declined. In 1968 philanthropy accounted for 21.1 percent of capital funds. By 1976 philanthropy accounted for just 7.5 percent of the funding for new projects (Lightle 1981); declining to 6.5 percent in 1990. One should also point out that states with hospital-rate regulatory programs eroded the incentives to seek philanthropy by requiring hospitals to spend a fraction of such unrestricted funds on bad debts and charity care. On the supply side, the 1986 tax reform diminished the tax benefits of giving to tax-exempt organizations. Finally, new technologies and equipment obsolescence have put a strain on larger hospitals in particular to come up with the funds to maintain state-of-the-art technology. This drain on funds is frequently overlooked, yet the rapid turnover in new technologies has proven to be a major cause of increasing hospital costs.

The approach taken in the second half of this chapter will be to suggest why we might stimulate equity financing rather than simply reduce the availability of debt options. Government and third-party insurance carriers have resisted the explicit recognition of an operating margin that would sufficiently cover capital replacement and the technological updating of equipment. Until 1992 interest on debt was an allowable cost passed through under the Medicare program. Hospitals that fund new equipment with debt find the actual cost of purchase to be much lower than the purchase price. To quickly see why, consider the following simplified example of hypothetical hospital A. Hospital A is anticipating the purchase of a new piece of capital equipment. It can fund the purchase through debt or internally generated funds. The financial officer considering these two alternatives faces the following cash flows. Hospital A could debt finance the equipment in 1977 through a 20-year bond issue paying interest of 10 percent per annum with repayment at maturity.

Three-quarters of hospital A's revenues are paid by cost payers who reimburse for all interest expense. Therefore, in the decade 1977–86, 75 percent of interest payments was reimbursed as allowable costs, and management would have assumed that this percentage would remain constant throughout the time period (1977–96). The appropriate discount rate for computing the net present value of the cash flow is 10 percent—that is, the cost of borrowing. The effective cost of the debt-financed purchase to the hospital in 1977 is $36,148 (the $36,148 is composed of the net present value of the 25 percent unreimbursed interest payments, equal to $21,284, plus the debt repayment of $100,000 in the year 2001, which has a net present value of $14,864). The effective cost of the internally funded purchase alternative in 1977 is $100,000. In summary, the time value of money and full reimbursement for interest expense create powerful incentives for hospitals to fund new capital acquisitions with debt. Decision makers had no way of projecting that by 1991 hospital A's revenues paid by cost payers would decline to 20 to 30 percent as Medicare refused to continue its pass-through of interest expense (Medicare would only pay 85 percent of its fair share in 1991).

WANTED: A RETURN ON EQUITY

Analysts should draw a distinction between return *of* capital and the return *on* capital. Return of capital is embodied by the returns generated by the assets for the institution. It is a moot point whether an equitable return of capital would be based on the original cost or the state-of-the-art replacement cost of the capital asset. Price-level depreciation obviously keeps pace with advances in medicine but does not encourage better productivity among providers or manufacturers of hospital assets. Too generous a level of price-level depreciation would obviously be highly inflationary. However, historical cost depreciation erodes capital stock if inflation is greater than zero (Cleverley 1982).

The return on capital is the effective cost of capital. In a for-profit firm, the cost of capital is the average rate per annum a company must pay for its equities.

This figure changes over time with economic circumstances and shifts in perceived risk from investment in the facility (e.g., it may be 8 percent this year and 10 percent next year). As a firm believer in efficient capital markets, Conrad (1986) defined the cost of capital as the discount rate that equates the expected present value of all future cash flows to common stockholders with the market value of common stock at a given time. The problems with calculating a cost of capital for tax-exempt hospitals are more difficult (Wedig, Hassan, and Sloan 1989).

The cost of capital for tax-exempt organizations is best shadow priced by focusing on the motivation of donors (Pauly 1986). Lenders clearly value parting with their capital at the interest rate negotiated in the deal. But donors and certain generous third-party payers may have other motivations. The key issue is whether the donors or quasi-donors want simply a tax deduction or a tax deduction plus social dividends (e.g., the joy of seeing better health care delivered in their community). One could carry the argument to the extreme and suggest that if the donor is forgoing the dollar return from investing in the business world, then the donor does bear an opportunity cost equal to the competitive rate of return of for-profit equity capital.

Unfortunately for hospital managers, as a matter of public policy the government and other payers have not made reimbursement a ''level playing field'' by granting tax-exempt organizations a return on equity to match that of the for-profit chains. Instead, as was reported in chapter 12, Medicare decided to phase out paying any return on equity to the investor-owned sector by 1990. Silvers and Kauer (1986) effectively dismissed the regulators' traditional argument that paying hospitals a return on equity is a ''forced'' contribution to capital stock. Restoration of a return-on-equity (ROE) payment, with a higher rate for for-profit hospitals and a lower rate for tax-exempt firms, represents an ex post payment for a return on ex ante donated capital of contributors. To shadow-price contributions in a weighted average cost of capital as zero assumes that the capital has no worth and will be equally easy to access each year in the future in perpetuity. In this last respect, federal tax reform, by reducing the tax benefits of giving, makes it more difficult for hospitals to attract donations.

MARKETING THE DEBT

Financing authorities organized by state governments have greatly aided hospitals in issuing tax-free debt. The need for a debt-service reserve fund has been eliminated in many cases. These securities typically offer high yields and have proven to be very attractive to fire and casualty companies, banks, and mutual funds. The federal government's National Mortgage Association has similarly enabled hospitals to issue debt at reduced interest costs by reducing the riskiness of the security.

For two decades a large number of private security brokers have been offering hospital securities. They have also helped hospitals to better tailor their debt to the needs of both the hospital and the lender. If the issue is large enough ($10 million or more), it will attract secondary-market interest, which increases its liquidity and lowers its cost enough to make it competitive with other high-volume tax-exempt bonds (such as municipal bonds). The increased demand for debt financing has been matched by an enlarged infrastructure for the issuing of that debt (Zimmerman 1991).

Federal issuing agencies, institutional lenders, and bond-rating agencies must evaluate the creditworthiness of the institution through quantitative measures (financial ratio analysis) and qualitative criteria (such as community support volunteers). Ratio analysis should not be univariate. The superior alternative is to consider simultaneously the patterns in changes of a number of ratios over time. This approach has been labeled a multidiscriminant-analysis methodology by Altman (1978). This method of multidiscriminant profile analysis reduces a number of problems of misclassification encountered in simple comparisons of single ratios. The obvious objective of the credit analysis is to establish whether the borrower can generate sufficient cash flows to service its debt requirements and meet other financial obligations. As President Nixon contracted the Hill-Burton program and encouraged private borrowing, the hospital feasibility study developed as the document to assess creditworthiness. Such studies were first used in the mid-1970s by state and municipal authorities monitoring bond issues. It is somewhat ironic that taxable corporations often borrow from tax-exempt lenders, such as pension funds, whereas the tax-exempt sector has largely relied on taxable buyers of their tax-exempt debt. Pension funds may begin to question the appropriate risk premium and interest rates for lending to hospital chains, given declining earnings rates and falling investor confidence in the stock market.

Government hospitals utilize general-obligation (tax-exempt) bonds as their primary source of capital. Tax-exempt hospitals do most of their borrowing with tax-exempt revenue bonds. Tax-exempt hospitals also have used industrial development bonds (IDBs), a government-backed debt security issued in amounts of $10 million or less, as an additional source of capital. Hospitals frequently formed proprietary subsidiaries and utilized the funds to build nursing homes, surgicenters, or ambulatory-care centers. Starting in 1985, government restrictions and volume caps made IDBs a less attractive source of capital for the hospital industry.

FINANCIAL CONSTRAINTS ON HOSPITALS ISSUING DEBT

As a hospital becomes highly leveraged, it becomes increasingly susceptible to default. To protect themselves, lenders look at many financial indicators to determine the riskiness of a debt issue. Increasingly, hospitals find lenders placing restrictions on hospital finances to insure against the possibility of default. Constraints are often placed on financial ratios such as those mentioned earlier. Even if the constraints are not explicit in the loan agreement, hospitals find that if their leverage position deteriorates, the cost of new debt increases. Eventually, lenders will refuse to purchase any debt as the investment becomes too risky.

Hospitals must maintain their financial stability, as reflected in their leverage and coverage ratios, if they are to continue to finance growth through debt. If other sources of capital remain scarce, maintaining ceilings on financial ratios can severely limit hospitals' ability to grow. Yet such ceilings may be the only way to ensure the solvency of the hospitals.

Once a hospital has reached the limit of one of the constraints, it is possible to determine the maximum growth rate a hospital can maintain and still be within the constraint. This has been done before under some very limiting assumptions, but one can actually derive equations to solve for the maximum growth rate under more relaxed assumptions. We do assume that net income may be used to help meet capital requirements in the year it is earned. Additionally, we assume straight-line relationships between revenue and the capital needed to generate that revenue and between net income and revenue. Under these two assumptions, it will be shown that in order to maintain a reasonable rate of capital expansion, hospitals must rely on external sources of funds. The extent of this reliance on debt is determined largely by the hospital's ability to generate profits internally. The sensitivity of three key financial ratios to net income margin will be demonstrated in the next section.

HOW FINANCIAL RATIOS MAY RESTRICT HOSPITAL GROWTH

To demonstrate how a ceiling on the ratio of debt to total capital can restrict growth, consider the case of County General Hospital (CGH), currently operating with a debt/total-capital ratio ceiling of 50 percent. CGH has a net income margin of 2 percent of revenues and requires $1.15 of capital investment (plant and equipment) and working capital to support each dollar of revenue. Under these conditions the hospital is constrained in the next year to a maximum growth rate in real dollar terms of 3.6 percent.

To see that this is so, let us say that CGH generates $1,000,000 in total revenues this year. Next year the hospital will generate total revenues of $1,036,000 (see figure 14.1). Net income will be $20,720, which can be matched by $20,720 in new debt, maintaining the 50 percent debt/total-capital ratio. The sum, $41,440, is exactly equal to the additional working capital and capital investment required to generate the $36,000 of additional revenue (except for rounding off the growth rate). At higher growth rates the capital requirements exceed the total funds that can be obtained from debt and equity. The hospital would have to become more highly leveraged (issue more debt) to maintain a higher growth rate. At lower growth rates the required new capital can be generated without reaching the debt-financing limit.

A formal equation can be derived to calculate the maximum growth rate for any debt/total-capital ratio. This equation can be used to see the effects each variable has on the growth rate.

Figure 14.1
Capital Growth under the Debt/Total-Capital Restriction

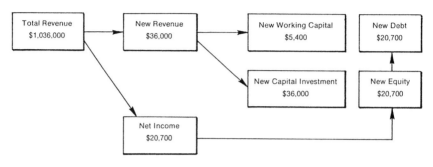

Table 14.3
Maximum Growth Rates under Debt/Total-Capital Restriction

| | | | *Net Income Margin* | | |
Debt/Total Capital	0%	1%	2%	3%	4%
0.50	0	2	4	6	8
0.67	0	3	6	9	12
0.70	0	3	7	10	13
0.75	0	4	8	12	16
0.80	0	5	10	15	21
0.90	0	9	21	35	53

G = maximum growth rate

CI = $ of capital investment required to support $1 of revenues

WC = $ of working capital required to support $1 of revenues

$$X = \frac{\text{debt/total capital}}{1 - \text{debt/total capital}}$$

= maximum debt/equity ratio

M = net income margin

funds generated by growth = funds required to suppport growth

$$(1 + X)(M + G)(M) = (CI + WC)G$$

$$G = \frac{(X + 1)(M)}{(CI + WC) - M - (X)(M)}$$

Table 14.3 presents the maximum allowable growth rates for various values

Figure 14.2
Hospital Growth under the Debt/Plant Restriction

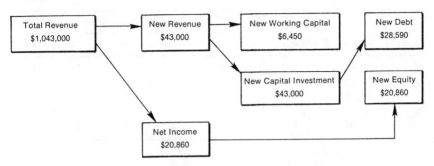

of debt/total capital. For the purposes of these calculations, $M \times CI + WC$ is assumed to equal 1.15. Higher values of CI and WC would result in lower maximum growth rates.

Debt/Plant Ratio

This second constraint limits hospital growth in much the same way as the first constraint. If CGH was at its debt/plant limit of 0.67, it would be restricted to a maximum growth of 4.3 percent next year. This can be seen in figure 14.2. Here, CGH generates $43,000 in new revenues and requires $43,000 in new plant and equipment and $6,450 in new working capital to support this growth—a total cash requirement of $49,450. Net income of $20,860 is generated during the year, leaving the debt requirement at $28,590. This maintains exactly the 0.67 debt/plant ratio.

If the growth rate exceeded 4.3 percent, the additional debt required to support operations would exceed 0.67 times the additional plant and equipment. A lower growth rate would reduce the debt requirement below the maximum allowable level. Again, we can derive an equation to determine the maximum growth rate for a hospital that has reached the limit of its debt/plant constraint.

G = maximum growth rate

CI = $ of capital investment required to support $1 of revenue

WC = $ of working capital required to support $1 of revenue

X = maximum allowable debt/plant ratio

M = net income margin

funds generated by growth = funds required to suppport growth

$$(CI)(X)(G) + M(1 + G)$$
$$= (CI + WC)G$$

Table 14.4
Maximum Growth Rates under Debt/Plant Restriction

Level of Constraint: Debt/Total	Net Income Margin				
	0%	1%	2%	3%	4%
0.67	0	2	4	7	9
0.70	0	2	5	7	10
0.75	0	3	5	8	11
0.80	0	3	5	8	13
0.90	0	4	9	14	19

$$G = \frac{M}{(CI + WC) - (CI)(X) - M}$$

Table 14.4 presents the maximum growth rates for various values of X. Again, $M.CI + WC$ is assumed to equal 1.15.

Debt-Service Coverage

It is reasonable to expect a lender to want some guarantee that a hospital will generate enough income during the year to repay principal and interest. The ability to repay principal and interest is reflected in the debt-service-coverage ratio. This is the ratio of the cash flow available to repay debt to the required debt payments. Specifically, the debt-service-coverage ratio equals

$$\frac{\text{Net Income + Depreciation + Interest}}{\text{Interest + Principal Payments}}$$

Depreciation is added because it is a noncash charge on the income statement.

Typically, this ratio is required to be at least 1.0 to 1.5, with higher coverage ratios being more restrictive to the use of debt. Suppose that CGH has a required margin of 1.50. Depreciable life on new capital investments at CGH averages 20 years, and any new debt would be paid back in equal principal payments over 20 years. If the current interest rate on debt is 10 percent, then it can be shown that the maximum allowable growth rate is just under 3.4 percent.

In this case, CGH would generate $34,000 in new revenues. This growth would require additional plant and equipment of $34,000, to be depreciated over 20 years at $1,700 per year. Additional working capital of $5,000 is needed as well. Net income for next year would be $20,680. Additional debt of $18,420 is required to support operations. The debt will be paid back in annual installments of $921. The first year's interest due is $1,842, and the total interest plus principal due in the first year is $2,763. We can now see that the coverage ratio will be maintained at 1.5.

Additional net income is $680. Depreciation is $1,700. Interest is $1,842.

Table 14.5
How County General Hospital Meets Its Debt-Service-Coverage Ratio

Cash Inflow	=	1.5 × Required Payments
Additional Net Income	$ 680	Principal $ 920
Additional Depreciation	1,700	Interest $1,842
		$2,762
Interest	1,842	
	$4,222 = 1.5 × $2,762	

The sum is $4,222, which, except for rounding errors, is exactly 1.5 times the required interest and principal payments. Table 14.5 summarizes these figures. Again, faster growth would require additional debt, and CGH would be unable to maintain its coverage ratio.

Deriving an equation to determine the maximum growth rate under various situations is a simple task. The final equation is presented below.

G = maximum allowable growth rate

CI = $ of capital investment required to support $1 of revenue

WC = $ of working capital required to support $1 of revenue

C = required coverage ratio

I = rate of interest on debt

RP = repayment period of principal

M = net income margin

DL = depreciable life of new plant and equipment

$$G = [(C \times M)/RP + (C \times I \times M) - (I \times M)]/[((WC + CI) \times C)/RP + ((WC + CI) \times C \times I) - M - (CI/DL) - ((WC + CI) \times I)]$$

Table 14.6 presents the maximum growth rates for coverage ratios of 1.25 and 1.5. As the coverage ratio approaches 1, the maximum allowable growth rate approaches infinity.

For the purposes of calculations for table 14.7, working capital and capital investment needs are assumed to be $1.15 for each dollar of revenue. The repayment period on new debt is 30 years, and the average depreciable life of new capital investment is 25 years. These are typical figures for most hospitals, although depreciable life in proprietary hospitals tends to be a bit shorter (21 years), and depreciable life in voluntary hospitals tends to be longer (27 years) (unpublished data provided by the Capital Finance Division of the American Hospital Association).

As fewer patients are covered under a health plan that recognizes interest expense as an allowable expense for cost-based reimbursement, the coverage ratio as normally calculated in business increasingly reflects a hospital's ability

Table 14.6
Maximum Growth Rates under Debt-Service Constraint

Prevailing Interest Rates	1.25 Coverage Net Income Margin				1.50 Coverage Net Income Margin			
	0%	1%	2%	3%	0%	1%	2%	3%
6%	0%/yr	3%/yr	10%/yr	23%/yr	0%/yr	2%/yr	4%/yr	8%/yr
8%	0	2	7	24	0	1	3	7
10%	0	2	6	15	0	1	3	6
12%	0	2	5	11	0	1	3	5
14%	0	2	4	9	0	1	3	5
16%	0	2	4˙	8	0	1	3	5

Table 14.7
Maximum Growth for Different Capital Investment Requirements

CI	Maximum Growth
0.8	12%/year
0.9	10
1.0	8
1.1	7
1.2	6

to repay its debt. The figures used to calculate the coverage ratio should be the unreimbursable portion of the interest expense. Assume that CGH has cash flows (which include interest expense) of $20,000 and interest and principle payments of $15,000, or a coverage ratio of 1.33. If 50 percent of CGH's $5,000 in interest expense is reimbursed (because 50 percent of CGH's volume is reimbursed on a cost basis), then these figures should be adjusted to $17,500 [$20,000 − 0.5 (5,000)] in cash inflow and $12,500 [$15,000 − 0.5 (5,000)] in required debt service. The coverage ratio increases to 1.40. To calculate a maximum growth rate, one can simply use I' instead of I in the given equation, where $I' = I \times V$ and V is the percentage volume not cost based.

Under typical conditions, a hospital that has reached its debt ceiling and has a small net income margin will often be limited to an annual growth rate of 4 percent or less. For hospitals with a high percentage of revenues coming from uninsured indigent-care patients, the net income margin is often 1 percent or less. In the future these hospitals will find it increasingly difficult to generate new funds from any source.

Hospitals that are not presently near their debt capacity may find their leverage positions weakening quickly as growth continues unabated. For example, if CGH currently has a debt/total-capital ratio of 0.5, an annual revenue growth of 10

Table 14.8
Maximum Growth for Different Working Capital Requirements

WC	Maximum Growth
0.10	10%/year
0.15	8
0.20	7
0.25	6

percent per year, and a net income margin of 2 percent, the debt/total-capital ratio would increase to 0.67 in just nine years. If the debt/plant ratio is currently 0.5, then under these conditions this ratio would increase to 0.67 in just six years.

Sensitivity Analysis

The growth rates presented in tables 14.3, 14.4, and 14.6 are sensitive to changes in each of the variables used to derive the rates. Tables 14.7, 14.8, 14.9, and 14.10 indicate how small changes in these variables can affect the maximum growth rate under the debt-service-coverage constraint, which is the constraint most sensitive to small changes in a hospital's finances. Unless otherwise indicated, the variables will be assumed to have the following values:

CI = capital investment = 1.00

WC = working capital = 0.15

DL = depreciable life = 25 years

RP = repayment period = 30 years

I = interest rate = 0.10

M = net income margin = 0.02

C = required coverage ratio = 1.25

The results in tables 14.7 and 14.8 indicate that small changes in the capital investment and working capital requirements can lead to pronounced changes in the constraint on growth. Increasing efficiency through better working capital management and general productivity increases can greatly reduce a hospital's dependence on debt. Tables 14.9 and 14.10 demonstrate that long repayment periods for debt issues and a short depreciable life for new assets will place the least short-term financial strain on the institution. However, over the life of the debt these conditions may be more restrictive than typical conditions would be.

Philanthropic donations can improve a hospital's leverage position slightly. A hospital that receives enough donations to fund 11 percent of total capital expansion may increase its maximum annual growth rate by as much as a full percentage point or more, depending on the other variables.

Table 14.9
Maximum Growth for Different Depreciable Lives of New Assets

DL	Maximum Growth
20 years	20%/year
23	10
25	8
27	6

Table 14.10
Maximum Growth for Different Repayment Periods of Debt

RP	Maximum Growth
20 years	4%/year
23	5
27	7
30	8

Finally, these conditions assume level principal payments. If loans are paid back through level debt service (principal plus interest) instead, then the loan would prove less constrictive to growth in the first few years but would be more constrictive in the last few years of the debt. This is due to the different timing of the cash flows associated with each method of repayment.

A FEDERAL RESERVE BANK FOR HOSPITAL CAPITAL?

Many analysts claim that the hospital sector has reached the limits of its debt capacity and will reach a point in the early 1990s when it is unable to generate enough capital to meet demand (Herr 1991). However, such analysis ignores the subtle difference between sufficient resources to meet capital maintenance and sufficient resources to meet the physicians' goal of unabated capital improvement. In other words, a national policy for cost containment might involve limiting the ability of hospitals to expand or improve their capital position and perhaps constrain their ability to maintain the high current levels of fixed capital assets. A number of studies in the United States (Fuchs 1986) and England (Cullis, Forster, and Frost 1979) have argued that erosion of hospital capital will have negligible effects on quality, availability of nonelective care, and health-status indexes of the population. If hospitals do not cut back on their capital demands in the future, they may face financial disaster.

Brown (1988) suggested a coordinated intervention into the hospital capital process. To allocate capital irrespective of the wealth of the patient mix, he suggested a local Federal Reserve–style hospital capital bank, presumably to correct or substitute for marketplace imperfections of what some refer to as the current policy of "muddling through." Unfortunately, a hospital capital bank might be as inefficient an investment in the ideal of equity as community-based hospital planning. The "cure-all of regulation" does, however, appeal to small and poorly managed hospitals that are desperate for access to capital. Hospitals turned to debt financing because it was cheap and because other sources of funding (grants and gifts) had declined. As hospitals become more and more highly leveraged, new debt issues will be perceived as being more and more risky. Interest rates will rise, increasing the cost of hospital debt. Some of this increase will be passed along to consumers through reimbursement mechanisms, but hospitals will increasingly have to shoulder much of the burden themselves.

Hospitals that have small net income margins must become highly leveraged in order to maintain growth rates above 4 or 5 percent annually. Hospitals that have been unable to generate funds internally have brought themselves to the brink of default. The three important financial ratios considered herein do not define all conditions necessary to determine the correct operating margin for assuring the hospital sector of adequate private-market financing. For example, the definition of an adequate operating margin will vary among hospitals as a function of size and ownership. It could be argued that the 3 percent operating margin suggested for the 200-bed case-study hospital is niggardly for a 1,000-bed university medical center. Obviously, differences among hospitals do affect their capital needs and, consequently, the "correct" operating margins sufficient to freeze or reduce the amount of capital that is debt financed. The dependence on debt financing will increase if the third-party payers continue to prevent an adequate return on equity, fail to adjust depreciation schedules in line with inflation, and pay for only a miserly share of bad-debt cases. Payers want hospitals to earn a return on equity by improving productivity.

REFERENCES

Altman, E. (1978). "Financial Ratios, Discriminant Analysis, and the Prediction of Corporate Bankruptcy." *Journal of Finance* 23:4 (September), 589–607.

Anderson, G., and Ginsburg, P. (1983). "Prospective Capital Payments to Hospitals." *Health Affairs* 2:3 (Fall), 52–63.

Berman, H., Weeks, L., and Kukla, S. (1991). *The Financial Management of Hospitals.* Ann Arbor, Mich.: Health Administration Press.

Booth, L. (1991). "Influence of Production Technology on Risk and the Cost of Capital." *Journal of Financial and Quantitative Analysis* 26:1 (March), 109–27.

Brick, I., and Ravid, S. (1991). "Interest Rate Uncertainty and the Optimal Debt Maturity Structure." *Journal of Finance and Quantitative Analysis* 26:1 (March), 63–81.

Brief, R., and Lawson, R. (1991). "Approximate Error in Using Accounting Rates of Return to Estimate Economic Returns." *Journal of Business Finance & Accounting* 18:1 (January), 13–20.

Bromberg, M. (1991). "The Capital Issue." *Health Systems Review* 24:1 (January/February), 4.

Brown, J. (1988). *Health Capital Financing: Structuring Politics and Markets to Produce Community Health.* Ann Arbor, Mich.: Health Administration Press.

Brown, J., and Saltman, R. (1985). "Health Capital Policy in the United States: A Strategic Perspective." *Inquiry* 22:2 (Summer), 122–131.

Claiborn, S. (1985). "Alternative Financing Approaches for Health Care Institutions." *Topics in Health Care Financing* 10:4 (Summer), 33–41.

Cleverley, W. (1991). *Hospital Industry Financial Report.* Oak Brook, Ill.: Healthcare Financial Management Association.

———. (1986). "The Ten Commandments of Financial Policy Development." *Healthcare Executive* 1:4 (May/June), 120.

———. (1984). "A Proposal for Capital Cost Payment." *Health Care Management Review* 9:2 (Spring), 39–50.

———. (1982). "Return on Equity in the Hospital Industry: Requirement or Windfall?" *Inquiry* 19:2 (Summer), 150–159.

Cleverley, W., and Harvey, R. (1992). "Competitive Strategy for Hospital Management." *Hospital and Health Services Administration* 37:1 (Spring), 53–69.

Cohodes, D. (1983). "Which Will Survive? The $150 Billion Capital Question." *Inquiry* 20:1 (Spring), 5–11.

Cohodes, D., and Kinkead, B. (1984). *Hospital Capital Formation in the 1980s.* Baltimore: Johns Hopkins University Press.

Conrad, D. (1986). "Returns on Equity for Not-for-Profit Hospitals: A Commentary and Elaboration." *Health Services Research* 21:1 (April) 17–20.

Cullis, J., Forster, D., and Frost, C. (1979). "Demand for Inpatient Treatment: Some Recent Evidence." *Applied Economics* 12:2 (December), 43–60.

Durance, P., Jacobs, L., and Kerr, C. (1991). "Setting Priorities for Equipment Acquisition." *Health Care Management Review* 16:2 (Spring), 73–85.

Durenberger, D. (1986). "Capital Cost Pass-Through Phase-Out: A 6-Year Simplified Approach." Washington, D.C., United States Senate (January) (amended in S.2121, February 27, 1986, as a seven-year phase-in).

Eastaugh, S. (1987). "Capital Financing and Refinancing." *Healthcare Financial Management* 41:1 (January), 107–108.

———. (1984). "Hospital Diversification and Financial Management." *Medical Care* 22:8 (August), 704–723.

———. (1982). "Effectiveness of Community-based Hospital Planning: Some Recent Statistical Evidence." *Applied Economics* 14:5 (October), 475–490.

Elrod, J., and Wilkinson, J. (1985). *Hospital Project Financing and Refinancing under Prospective Payment.* Chicago: American Hospital Publishing.

Fuchs, V. (1986). *The Health Economy.* Cambridge, Mass.: Harvard University Press.

Gapenski, L. (1990). "Risk Factor Helps Determine Debt Maturity Mix." *Healthcare Financial Management* 45:11 (November), 82–84.

Gibson, R. (1991). *Asset Allocation: Balancing Financial Risk.* Homewood, Ill.: Dow Jones–Irwin.

Ginzberg, E. (1986). "The Destabilization of Health Care." *New England Journal of Medicine* 315:12 (September 18), 757–761.

Goldschmidt, Y., and Gafni, A. (1991). "A Managerial Approach to Costing Fixed Assets: The Role of Depreciation and Interest." *Health Care Management Review* 16:4 (Fall), 55–66.

Grimaldi, P. (1991). "Capital PPS: Trekking through the Labyrinth." *Healthcare Financial Management* 45:11 (November), 72–87.

Grimmelman, F. (1986). "Borrowing for Capital: Will It Empty Your Pockets?" *Hospital Financial Management* 6:12 (December), 19–25.

Hampton, J. (1991). *Financial Decision Making*. Reston, Va.: Reston Publishing.

Harris, M., and Ravid, A. (1991). "The Theory of Capital Structure." *Journal of Finance* 46:1 (March), 297–355.

Health Care Investment Analysts (HCIA). (1991). *Changing Profitability: Investor-owned versus Public and Nonprofits*. Baltimore: HCIA.

Herr, W. (1991). "Capital Payments." *Healthcare Financial Management* 45:4 (April), 19–32.

Howell, J. (1984). "Evaluating the Impact of CON Regulation Using Measures of Ultimate Outcome: Some Cautions from Experience in Massachusetts." *Health Services Research* 19:5 (December), 557–613.

Ibbotson, R., and Sinquefield, R. (1991). *Stocks, Bonds, Bills, and Inflation 1991 Yearbook*. Chicago: Ibbotson Associates.

Iglehart, J. (1986). "Early Experiences with Prospective Payment of Hospitals." *New England Journal of Medicine* 314:22 (May 29), 1460–1464.

Institute of Medicine. (1986). *For-Profit Enterprise in Health Care*. Washington, D.C.: National Academy of Sciences.

———. (1976). *Controlling the Supply of Hospital Beds*. Washington, D.C.: National Academy of Sciences.

Johnson, J. (1992). "Dynamic Diversification." *Hospitals* 66:3 (February 5), 20–26.

Kalison, M., and Averill, R. (1985). "Building Capital into Prospective Payment." *Business and Health* 2:7 (June), 34–37.

Kauer, R., and Silvers, J. (1991). "Hospital Free Cash Flow." *Health Care Management Review* 16:4 (Fall), 67–78.

Kaufman, K., and Hall, M. (1991). *The Capital Management of Health Care Organizations*. Ann Arbor, Mich.: Health Administration Press.

Kidder-Peabody and Company. (1986). *Tax-Exempt Hospital Revenue Bonds: A Database*. New York: Kidder-Peabody, Inc.

Kidder-Peabody and Company, The Health Finance Group (1989). Public report: *Review of Health-Care Finance*. New York: Kidder-Peabody, Inc.

Krohm, G., Merrill, M., and Talarczyk, A. (1991). *Investment Program Management for Health Care Institutions*. Chicago: American Hospital Publishing.

Krystynak, L. (1985). "Prospective Payment for Capital: The Financial Nature of Capital Allowances." *Healthcare Financial Management Association Monograph*, Series 83, Oak Brook, Illinois.

Levine, S. (1991). *Dow Jones–Irwin Business and Investment Almanac*. Homewood, Ill.: Dow Jones–Irwin.

Lightle, M. (1981). "Changes in the Sources of Capital." *Hospital Financial Management* 11:2 (February), 42–47.

Long, H. (1982). "Asset Choice and Program Selection in a Competitive Environment." *Healthcare Financial Management* 36:8 (August), 34–50.

Lyles, A., and Schneider, D. (1984). "Development of the Office of Health Facilities Microsimulation Model for Hospital Financing Analysis: An Analysis of Investment Behavior in California." Research report, Center for Hospital Finance, Johns Hopkins University.

Mann, S., and Sicherman, N. (1991). "Agency Cost of Free Cash Flow: Acquisition Activity and Equity Issues." *Journal of Business* 64:2 (April), 213–227.

McCue, M. (1991). "Use of Cash Flow to Analyze Financial Distress in California Hospitals," *Hospital and Health Services Administration* 36:2 (Summer), 223–241.

Mitchell, S. (1991). "Medicare's Capital PPS." *Health Systems Review* 24:2 (March/April), 57–58.

Modigliani, F., and Miller, M. (1963). "Taxes and the Cost of Capital." *American Economic Review* 53:3 (June), 433–443.

Myers, S., and Majluf, N. (1984). "Corporate Financing Decisions When Firms Have Information That Investors Do Not Have." *Journal of Financial Economics* 22:3 (June), 187–221.

Nemes, J. (1992). "Healthcare Bond Volume Jumped 32 percent." *Modern Healthcare* 22:2 (January 13), 34–35.

Neumann, B., Suver, J., and Zelman, W. (1992). *Financial Management: Concepts and Applications for Health Care Providers.* Baltimore: National Health Publishing.

Pauly, M. (1986). "Returns on Equity for Not-for-Profit Hospitals." *Health Services Research* 21:1 (April), 1–16.

Pillari, G. (1990). "U.S. Hospital Trends in the 1990s: Fewer Beds, Less Debt." *HealthSpan* 7:1 (January), 13–15.

Press, S., and Sherwin, J. (1989). "Financing Growth through REITs." *FAH Review* 22:1 (January–February), 57–63.

Prezas, A. (1991). "Inflation, Investment and Debt." *Journal of Financial Research* 14:1 (Spring), 15–26.

Rodgers, J. (1988). *Including Capital Expenses in the Prospective Payment System.* Washington, D.C.: Congressional Budget Office (August).

Schneider, D., Mager, R., and Dummit, L. (1986). "Hospital Investment Behavior: An Analysis Using the Office of Health Facilities (OHF) Model." Final report (October) under Health Resources and Services Administration, HRSA–240–85–0060.

Siegel, F., and Hoban, J. (1991). "Measuring Risk Aversion: Allocation, Leverage and Accumulation." *Journal of Financial Research* 14:1 (Spring), 27–36.

Silvers, J. (1975). "How Do the Limits to Debt Financing Affect Your Hospital's Financial Status?" *Hospital Financial Management* 5:2 (February), 32–41.

Silvers, J., and Kauer, R. (1986). "Returns on Equity for Not-for-Profit Hospitals: Some Comments." *Health Services Research* 21:1 (April), 21–28.

Standard and Poor's Corporation. (1984–1991). *Municipal Bond Book.* Quarterly issues. New York: Standard and Poor's.

Sykes, C. (1986). "The Role of Equity Financing in Today's Health Care Financing Environment." *Topics in Health Care Financing* 11:3 (Spring), 1–3.

Wedig, G., Hassan, M., and Sloan, F. (1989). "Hospital Investment Decisions and the Cost of Capital." *Journal of Business* 62:4 (October), 517–537.

Weston, J., and Copeland, T. (1991). *Managerial Finance.* New York: Holt and Rinehart.

Zimmerman, M. (1991). "Survey: Hospitals Looking for New Ways to Fund Capital Projects." *Healthcare Financial Management* 45:2 (February), 72.

Part Seven

THE BUMPY ROAD AHEAD

Chapter 15

Future Policy Options: What Form
Could Universal Entitlement Take?

Demands are infinite, whereas the resources are finite, regardless of whether the care is funded through health insurance or from public funds. The marketplace system encourages demand and diversity, whereas the controlled system leads to uniformity, rationing, and possibly mediocrity.

—John Lister, M.D.

American doctors should begin to build up a social ethic and behavioral practices that help them decide when medicine is bad medicine: not simply because it has absolutely no payoff or because it hurts the patient, but also because the costs are not justified by the marginal benefits.

—Lester Thurow

The highest quality providers are also the most cost-effective because they make fewer mistakes and know how to treat conditions properly, avoiding traumatic expensive procedures when there are less intensive but equally effective alternatives.

—Charles Jacobs

Policy trends in American health care currently point in all different directions, like a pile of jackstraws. Support can be found in Congress for deregulation, reregulation, planned competition, and free competition. Pauly et al. (1991) advocated a "responsible national health insurance plan" founded upon the belief that resource allocation should be based on individuals' choice of insurance, in light of their different needs and desires. If one wants to spend a little extra and preserve consumer choice, one can adopt the Japanese model of universal entitlement. The premiums are kept affordable in Japan because the law requires that the premium be based on a percentage of income rather than on actuarial risks (Eastaugh 1991). However, if people want their doctors and nurses to serve them like postal workers, a planned government-run national health insurance system will suffice. Americans prefer a quality service and a health care delivery system that is more than adequate, that does more than suffice. A nationalized system offers bureaucrats to whom the consumer can appeal and from whom consumers can experience inaction, insensitivity, and occasionally relief.

If health care is a necessary basic commodity like food, society should underwrite a minimum basic-needs coverage policy for all. We have attempted to mainstream the Medicaid-eligible "covered poor" into the great majority of hospitals, so that equity is better served than in the market for education. However, as with the food stamp program, there has been little social pressure to federalize Medicaid in an egalitarian spirit. Federal policy making has always operated on the "big-wheel principle"—he who is now first will later be last, and he who is last will be first. Consequently, the winds of change may make the egalitarians powerful again in a few years. Then we may have an equitable federal indigent-care policy, even if national health insurance is judged too expensive. Americans have the highest aspirations for the right of access to the best care for everyone, but we never have the necessary amount of resources to do this on a fee-for-service basis. Managed care is one strategy whereby we institutionalize the right to care with an efficient mode of service delivery (Congressional Budget Office 1992).

CAPITATION: THE MEDICINE TO CURE UNBUNDLING

Many employers and government regulators fear that unbundling of services has co-opted attempts at stringent price controls, discount purchasing, and rate regulation. Capitation payment is the ultimate defense against unbundling. Without capitation, when payers squeeze down on one end of the cost-inflation problem, the balloon pops up on the other end in the form of an increased quantity of different transitional-care services. The problem may not be solved through invention of a better regulatory control system. For example, tinkering with the DRGs by adding a severity measure may only open a trapdoor to bottomless grief. The price system may be made more equitable, but does this substantially reduce the incentive to game the system? Capitation can cure the potential for gaming the system through inflated transitional care and can leave the health-system partners the discretion for dividing fair payment rates between institutions and individuals (especially if payers use The Anderson-Steinberg PACS methodology described in chapter 3).

Enthoven (1989) outlined the economics of a system for competing medical plans. Noneconomists incorrectly understand "competition" to be present if there are multiple suppliers in the marketplace (Jones 1990). By that definition the insurance marketplace is competitive in Virginia if there are 363 suppliers. However, the marketplace is not competitive in the economic (price-competition) sense if most employers pay 80 to 90 percent of the premium dollar. Employers should pay a fixed dollar amount for health care, equal to 100 percent of the premium for the lowest-cost local health plan, and employees should pay the excess if they want to sign up with a more expensive insurance plan. As premium expenses rise for the Cadillac health care plans, if employees are paying 100 percent of the added expense (rather than only 10 to 20 percent), they will make a more cost-conscious consumer choice. Ginzberg (1990) pointed out that reform has been slow in this marketplace, but Enthoven (1990) counterargued that the blame rests with employers and the federal government. Employers should get tough and set the company contribution at a fixed amount. Moreover, employers should pressure Congress to advocate limits on tax-free employer contributions to health care premiums. The employers are currently sensitive to the employee wishes that premiums be paid in "cheaper" tax-free dollars (rather than after-tax dollars). If we want more poor people to get insurance coverage, we should stop subsidizing extra expensive health care premiums. A minimum tax subsidy should be offered, and the underlying tax collections could be channeled to expanded Medicaid coverage.

If risk selection forced sicker employees to purchase the more expensive health plans (Jones 1990), one might suggest special risk pools run by employers or the federal government to underwrite certain individuals (e.g., for AIDS or sickle cell). A better alternative, with less administrative expense, might involve the Japanese approach of requiring that the premium be based on a percentage of income rather than on actuarial risks. More healthy individuals should not be allowed to act as free riders and sign up with the least-cost health plans to avoid subsidizing their sicker peers. A third approach, which has been tried in Norway and North Dakota, is to set the per capita annual payments to reflect the likely higher use of services by certain chronic-disease risk groups, thus forcing an implicit subsidy of the sick by the healthy. However, we should not scrap the idea of competition between health plans and thus place no pressure on insurers to be cost-effective just because there is wide variation in health status within the population.

Employers may have an easier time of deriving per capita rates for employed populations with lower coefficients of variation in health status per person compared to the elderly population. A crude morbidity adjustment in the aggregate for nonelderly groups may be sufficient to set capitation rates in an AAPCC formula. The current American climate of enthusiasm for substantial payment reform may follow the path in the 1990s that Norway followed in 1980. After eight years of a prospective payment price system, Norway initiated a population-based, morbidity-adjusted capitation formula in 1980 (Crane 1985). This capitation approach achieved a more equitable distribution of resources among the 89 hospitals and redistributed more resources to chronic-long-term-care services. A 1991 Office of Technology Assessment report on physician payment systems singled out capitation as the best long-term solution to paying for care. However, in the fall of 1991 less than four percent of Medicare enrollees were paid on a per capita basis.

In the American spirit of piecemeal movement toward a major policy shift, we may move state by state and employer by employer to a fully capitated health care system sometime in the 1990s. Gradualist policies will not bring the majority of public patients under capitation in the near future, but future success with private managed-care systems might prompt all payers to push for capitation.

Some regions already have experience with capitation payments. Two rural hospitals in Maryland are paid on a per capita basis by the state rate-setting commission. Blue Cross and the Hartford Foundation have financed a number of additional capitation experiments. A capitation experiment for rural inpatient care was initiated in North Dakota (five hospitals within the state and a sixth hospital over the state line in Minnesota) and in Massachusetts (four hospitals) in 1981. Mangion (1986) reported on the results from one hospital. Significant savings were produced in the first three years, with the hospital retaining 75 percent of the savings and Blue Cross retaining the balance. Employer-based managed-care systems will undoubtedly be less generous than Blue Cross in setting the rates, but the hospital would be fully at risk to retain 100 percent of the savings (or losses). The per capita fixed-payment programs provide hospitals with obvious incentives to economize.

PHYSICIAN REACTION IS NOT MONOLITHIC

Many conservative clinicians dislike guidelines and fear that they will be stripped of admitting privileges if their practice profile exhibits an inability to adjust to the ''new medicine'' of decision analysis, PPS, PPOs, and HMOs. These clinicians argue that ''personal care'' gets lost in the shuffle as DRG trees, software, outliers, economic grand rounds, and ''think-adjustment'' sessions force professionals toward ''cookbook medicine.'' Carrying their case to the extreme, conservative physicians often make four points:

1. If the practice profile is too expensive relative to excessively low government or third-party payment rates, the doctor is labeled ''a dyscodic outlier heterogenicist'' and faces loss of admitting privileges.
2. ''True'' doctors cannot join a PPO or a system because they are ''neither providers nor preferred'' (medicine is a ''calling,'' not a commercial enterprise, and should be preferred for quality caring, not price discounts).
3. Doctors are forced to provide only the admissions that are profitable to the hospital and jettison the nonprofitable services.
4. Doctors are forced to abide by market analysis and selling strategies.

Hospital managers and medical-staff leaders should develop a cogent response to each of these four points of misunderstanding.

First, data-based ''credentialing'' for membership on the medical staff is a negotiated process. If the chief of medical staff can build a reasonable case for retaining an individual whose practice habits are more expensive for uncontrollable reasons (for receiving more severely ill cases than evidenced simply by the DRG or for specializing in treatment of intrinsically unprofitable DRGs the trustees want admitted), then the doctor should be retained on the medical staff and not declared a "shameless statistical deviate." As to the second point, patients do value economic attributes, such as lower out-of-pocket payments for health care, lower premiums, and higher wages because costs are more under control (i.e., so the employer does not have to pay much of the wage increase to health care providers; because they have less funds for wage hikes if they spend more and more on health care costs).

In response to the third point, hospital executives should point out that cost accounting is required to financially plan the institution's future. Moreover, clinicians should rid themselves of the myth that hospital charges are highly correlated with actual resource costs. All parties concerned need accurate standard cost accounting, as was pointed out in chapter 2. The hospital is never required to make a profit on each service product line. However, trustees need to know how much they lose on certain product lines so they can expand or initiate money makers such that the final bottom line is sufficient to maintain a quality hospital. If clinicians do not trust the dollar figures derived from accounting or the CFO, the data can be presented in opportunity-cost terms. A nonphysician manager should never say the "unthinkable" and claim that a given product line is a $500,000 example of "economic malpractice." Instead, the clinicians working in this inefficient service area can be told that the "opportunity costs of this service require that we fire 20 people hospitalwide plus your postgraduate fellow to underwrite the cost of this money-losing product line."

As to the fourth point, physician disdain for marketing is both archaic and antipatient. Health marketing places the consumers as kings and asks how best to meet their medical needs with quality service at an affordable cost. Marketing is simply doing right by the patients, channeling them to the service mode of delivery that is most appropriate. Effective marketing is not "hucksterism" or selling. Good marketing involves open communication, development of trust, and instilling in the public the differential advantages and abilities offered by a given provider. Social marketing programs determine what consumers need, tailor services to meet those needs, and suggest that patients utilize services in a timely preventive manner—that is, before something more serious develops.

SUPPORT FROM THE MEDICAL STAFF

Offering stock in a firm or franchise was an unusual financing arrangement until the passage of tax reform in October 1986. Even well-known firms, such as the Boston Celtics professional basketball team, were selling up to a 40 to 49 percent stake in the franchise under a master limited partnership. Most hospitals do not have the national marketability of the Boston Celtics or the Mayo Clinic, but they have a local captive group of potential investors—their physicians. The master limited partnership could be presented to the medical staff in general terms—that is, if you do not invest in this facility, the workshop where you perform patient care will erode (i.e., plant and equipment will become obsolete). In addition, one could appeal to clinicians' specific (individual) self-interest with various "perks." For example, physicians who invest in the partnership would be provided the best operative time slots, the best work schedules, and relief from bureaucratic burdens. Financially distressed facilities may have to charge those who do not invest in the master limited partnership a monthly "rent" for the right to admit their private-pay patients to the hospital. At the extreme, those doctors not wishing to invest cash in their workshop/hospital would have to pay with their time for the right to be on the medical staff and have admitting privileges. The shift from a field dominated by doctors as non-paying "partners" (keeping the hospital at financial risk) to one where they must invest their funds to keep the facility state-of-the-art destroys the obsolete philosophy of professional dominance. Moreover, the organizations that employ or rent admitting rights to physicians will demand that managers share in decisions regarding professional roles and dominate decisions involving capital acquisitions. In a world where the climate for dialogue between payers and providers has never been worse, the opportunity for joint deals between hospitals and physicians has never been better.

One would hope that most hospitals could still base medical-staff membership decisions on the professional input and not the financial input of the individual doctor. However, in a basic economic sense, if the hospital and the doctor are involved in joint production, and the hospital is under severe financial pressure, the institution may have to demand financial resources from the producer group experiencing higher rates of return—the physician community. Lower physician investment will lead to more hospital closings, to longer travel time to reach the workshop/hospital, or perhaps even to many physicians lacking admitting privileges at any hospital.

OLIGOPOLY OF MINISYSTEMS OR DUOPOLY?

Paul Elwood's "supermed" theory predicted that rapid consolidation should soon produce eight major health corporations providing and insuring 80 to 90 percent of the health services in the nation by 1995 (Elwood 1986). Elwood suggested that only one of these eight firms would be nonprofit. His theory failed, and big systems retrenched (chapter 12). A nonbeliever in both the supermed theory and the conventional wisdom should consider past examples of markets where the experts predicted rapid consolidation. In 1960 the experts predicted that we would have only two auto companies worldwide by 1968; yet we now have six dozen. In 1968 the experts predicted that we would have 90 percent fewer microchip firms by 1975; yet we had 1,200 percent more in 1991. Experts like to predict consolidation in the name of a well-ordered world, but the world continues to be a messy, complex place.

Single free-standing hospitals are much like the mom-and-pop grocery stores of old; many survived by banding together. The strategy typically goes beyond simple horizontal integration of like institutions and usually involves vertical integration through common ownership or control of multiple (nonequivalent) enterprises, one of which can use as its input the output of another. Some analysts have argued that informal networking and formal systems development can provide small and costly rural and urban hospitals with the only opportunity to retain local community control. High-cost medical centers increasingly seize the opportunity to sell their expertise in alternative care services to lower-cost local hospitals and facilitate formal referral patterns for easy cases out of the medical center (so their managed-care contracts can remain cost competitive). This builds a minisystem strong enough to withstand pressures to sell or close. Autonomous hospitals can band together locally, go it alone, or become franchises in a national firm. In either of the last two cases hospitals should avoid going so heavily into debt that their survival is unlikely. Johns Hopkins Hospital, Northwestern, Rush-Presbyterian-St. Luke's Medical Center, and the Mayo Clinic expanded into small hospital groups in their respective cities during the late 1980s. But few hospitals have such access to capital. Avenues for capital include insurance companies interested in regional or local health systems, ex-partners of failed supermed ventures, nursing home chains, local dominant employers in the city, and ultimately the individual hospital's medical staff. As to this last possibility, the marketing points to the physician community could include the following: "You don't want to become an AMI or Humana physician? Then make a financial investment in your local hospitals."

Experts are nearly united in predicting substantial increases in multihospital systems' market share. In this era of rapid change, there is so much written about what "will be" that it is easy to forget current market conditions. In times of stress we often "circle the wagons" and join together in groups, but the circle need not be too large. One should question whether economics suggests that consolidations favor large over small groups of hospitals. Consider the contrast to another market, the toaster industry. Quality in health care is more heterogeneous and costs are more labor-intensive. Unlike the kitchen toaster market, the product/service in health care varies widely in quality across geographic regions of the country—that is, the Humana brand of quality service varies more widely than the GE brand of toaster. Unlike a stockpiled manufactured good, health services are produced and consumed locally. The postulated economies of scale in running a big chain are likely due to the fact that the principal cost input is locally sourced labor. Consequently, if a small hospital reaps purchase discounts through membership in a group buying agreement, the facility need not experience scale economies inferior to those of a 50,000-bed hospital chain (Zuckerman and Kaluzney 1991). The first generation of alliances born in the 1970s involved shared services and multihospital systems (Eastaugh 1981), but the second generation of alliances involves continuity of care, HMOs, and PPOs—a new challenge of cooperation in the 1990s.

In the context of hospital care, local hospitals need not always join a for-profit chain or the nonprofit group with 600 member hospitals if they can find a local market niche. This point is doubly true in a local service-delivery industry like health care, in contrast to microchips and automobiles where there is less concern for distance between the firm and the customer. By 1995 some 20 megasystems may control 50 percent of the market, but 200 to 400 local minisystems may control 60 to 80 percent of their local market shares with a locally developed and controlled insurance product. Consolidation begins to offer few advantages when the service cannot be stockpiled as inventory and the central office becomes too removed from the local community. Minisystems should be capable of out-competing against the megasystems if they remain flexible, adaptive, and non-bureaucratic in response to their market (Shortell 1991; Fein 1991).

The principal disadvantage of small hospital minisystems is the aforementioned reduced access to low-cost capital. However, this is counterbalanced in that local control and small size offer the ability to be quick and flexible in adapting to changing community needs (Peters and Austin 1985). Flexibility often beats size, and size often breeds rigidity and bureaucracy. The investor-owned megasystems are beginning to respond to this last point and are attempting to trim corporate staff and lone (single) hospitals with poor profitability. Local hospitals must sacrifice a little autonomy, initiate master limited partnerships, and band together as minisystems. Enhanced productivity will trim staff-obese institutions with excess overhead. In the 1990s one cannot ignore the productivity/quality challenge.

PROMOTING GOOD ECONOMICS AND GOOD MEDICINE

Preferred practice patterns (PPPs) are necessary for enhanced productivity. They include workload-driven staffing, gainsharing incentive pay to employees, and increased reliance on nurse extender/technicians (chapters 9 and 10). PPPs are also necessary for better investment decisions, financing decisions, and capital-structure decisions (chapters 12–14). With regard to these issues, some recent texts have suggested substantial recent improvement in the state of the practice (Kovner and Neuhauser 1991), while other texts have documented major shortfalls in management performance (Gapenski 1991).

A number of authors have suggested that we adopt a Canadian model to achieve the twin goals of cost containment and universal entitlement (Himmelstein and Woolhandler 1989; Davis et al. 1990). The argument is simply presented as follows: Because Canada spends under 9.2 percent of gross national product (GNP) on health care, it must be superior to the United States in cost containment. This same sort of flawed logic was presented to the author when he was an economist at the National Academy of Sciences. When Canadian spending on health care as a percentage of gross domestic product (GDP) declined from 7.47 percent in 1971 to 6.88 percent in 1974, officials promoting the "efficiency gain" were quick to label Canada as a superior example of cost containment. However, any economist worth his weight in oil knows that it is necessary to look for both currency shifts and real resource shifts. If the Canadian health care system improved its efficiency, it would be using less inputs (e.g., fewer nurses).

Unfortunately for the cheerleaders quick to jump to a conclusion, nurses as a percentage of the work force increased from 1.766 percent to 1.834 percent in the relevant period 1973–74. From the point of view of technical efficiency, the "efficiency gain" was nonexistent. Moreover, it is easy to demonstrate that the efficiency differential between Canada and the United States is equally illusionary.

If we update the Canadian example to the current context, we find that from 1970 to 1990 Canada's real inflation-adjusted per capita GNP increased 72.1 percent, while the real growth in the American GNP per capita was only 35.6 percent. In the 1960s the two nations had equal average annual growth rates. A higher relative GNP gain explains why Canada spends less of its GNP on health care. If one factors out currency exchange rates, utilizes per capita spending in constant dollars in each nation's own currency (factoring out population-growth differences and currency shifts), and adjusts for inflation by the local GNP deflator, one finds that Canada and the United States had the exact same rate of cost inflation from 1970 to 1990, and each nation has dedicated a cumulative increase of 2.55 percent in real health care spending per capita. A health care system relying more on some overall control of spending (like Canada) has better control of health care costs than those relying on a more decentralized mechanism of control (the United States).

How Much Administrative Waste Can We Cut?

Advocates of a one-payer national health care system like Canada frequently claim that the transition can be self-financing. That is, the cut in administrative waste can more than make up for the additional dollars needed to cover uninsured Americans. For example, Woolhandler and Himmelstein (1991) offer the inflated claim that in 1987 dollars the U.S. health care system could save $69.0–83.2 billion by attaining the Canadian level of administrative efficiency. Two-thirds of the assumptions in this article are based upon personal communications that no reader can independently verify. The authors assume that administrative costs are overhead costs, so they count supplies, rent, equipment, and professional liability insurance as if they were an administrative expense that would disappear under their advocated one-payer national health insurance scheme. The appropriate method of cost analysis is marginal cost analysis, or what an accountant calls differential cost analysis. Even if one could accept that American physicians spent 43 percent of office expenses on administrative costs, the expected savings in moving to a universal one-payer system would not be $30 billion. The cost of operating a physician's office, utilities, supplies, and rent cannot be counted as administrative waste in the American health care system. The authors self-select for their comparison Quebec, because this province has the lowest physician fees, and thus the lowest ability to employ enough clerical personnel. The Canadian health care system might be eroding productivity and economic efficiency by having physicians do too many clerical tasks. Woolhandler and Himmelstein also utilize 1972–73 data from Quebec for their analysis.

The American figures on physicians' administrative expense in the Woolhandler and Himmelstein (1991) study are overstated because the data is self-reported to the AMA by individual physicians. Physicians have a reporting bias to overstate administrative time, to in turn pressure government and other third party payers to trim red tape. No provider reports there is too little paperwork and not enough administrative duties. Himmelstein and Woolhandler (1991) also double count time spent on medical records and claims, by adding an additional $4.5 billion of opportunity cost (6 minutes per patient) to their already bloated estimate. Rather than spending $170,000 per physician office in administrative tasks, a more careful range of estimates would peg the potential savings in moving to a one-payer system at between $10,000–27,000. The Canadian figures on doctor offices are more valid and reliable, because they are drawn from tax records (Eastaugh and Eastaugh 1991).

The Woolhandler and Himmelstein (1991) analysis is an even worse comparison between apples and oranges for the hospital sector. It is a surprise that these two New England based authors select California hospitals for their yardstick of hospital administrative expense in the United States (this entire ad hoc article is designed to make Canada look efficient and the U.S. look bad). With more commercial insurance carriers doing business, and competitive bidding programs, California has higher administrative costs per average than the typical American hospital. California has 30 more employees per 100 beds than the average American hospital. The figures for the Canadian health care system are low-ball estimates because: the education department pays for teaching hospital expenses not included in the health budget; Canadian government officials do not record the administrative indirect expenses like processing claims; and the additional costs of collecting more revenue through the tax system are not considered in the Woolhandler and Himmelstein article. The administrative benefit of going to a one-payer national system in the United States is an open question for future analysis. This article is an example of advocacy posing as evidence. Gray (1991) provides a better example: balance evidence and advocacy, present the numbers (the Dragnet "just the facts" approach), and then advocate the policy positions favored by the particular analysts. The process of health policy making can be viewed through a variety of prisms, but we do not need more studies offering biased evidence in the name of advocacy.

Downsizing Capacity: Lessons from Other Lands

Americans want "affordable health care," but there is no clear definition of the goal or the methods to achieve it (Etheredge 1991). We know costs are out of control. The average cost of a hospital stay increased from 8.8 percent of median family income in 1979, to 15.1 percent in 1991. The average nursing home stay increased from 49 percent of median family income in 1979, to 63 percent in 1991. In the United States excess hospital beds are going out of business. American policy makers should begin to realize that (1) hospital closure is a lagged function of local economic activity (many hospitals closed in Texas and Michigan four to eight years after downturns in economic activity), and (2) health care spending follows an adapted expectations model (blips up in health spending track with an exponential-smoothed average of the last six years of economic growth; Eastaugh 1992). The critical point is that health care cost inflation is a worldwide problem. No nation, including Canada, offers a magic formula to resolve the worldwide problems of access and cost control. It is easy to put down the American medical care system with glib lines like ''We have no health care system; rather, we have a disjointed sickness-care nonsystem.'' A disjointed American delivery system experiences as much health care cost inflation as a ''jointed'' government planned delivery system like those in Canada or the Netherlands.

Mandatory employer-based health insurance will not cover all uninsured Americans and will introduce a new set of problems (a classic example of John Thompson's rule: Our current problems are past solutions). Korea mandated health insurance by employer group, phased in over 12 years (1977–89), and has the most rapid rate of medical cost escalation. Germany has 11 decades of experience with social insurance, but its health care system appeared to be in severe trouble even prior to German reunification in 1990 (Iglehart 1991). The German economy is concentrating high-risk patient groups in local sickness funds, many of which are in severe economic trouble (Schneider 1991). However, the German system of Global Based Budgets (GBB) makes their health economy one of the least inflationary for the past two decades (Eastaugh 1992; Rublee and Schneider 1991; Getzen 1990).

DOES A ONE-PAYER NATIONALIZED APPROACH MAKE SENSE?

A number of analysts have suggested a statewide one-payer approach to statewide insurance coverage (Beauchamp and Rouse 1990). Physicians for a National Health Program has advocated abolishing all private and public insurance plans to create a one-payer plan to cover everyone, financed entirely by taxes, with a system of state and regional boards negotiating with providers on compensation (Himmelstein and Woolhandler 1989). The benefits of such a one-payer system are obvious to many: less paperwork, less administrative expense, and fewer financial barriers to access. Himmelstein and Woolhandler may have been over-optimistic in assuming that administrative expense could be trimmed from 15 to 20 percent of health spending to 3 to 4 percent.

Other progressive/left-wing groups have attacked the administrative expense implicit in our current multipayer patchwork system of health insurance coverage. Citizen Action claimed in October 1990 that the 200 commercial insurance firms covering 70 million Americans spent 25 percent of expenses on administration and marketing. Carl Schramm, president of the Health Insurance Association of

America, claimed that the more appropriate fair-cost comparison for small-scale organizations was 13 percent. However, Citizen Action went on to say that the comparable figure was 2.4 percent for Medicare and 3.0 percent for Canada.

The problem with the Canadian approach is that the local government can ration care through inconvenience: long waits for elective surgery, tests, and checkup visits (Grumet 1989). Many managed-care health plans have been cited for having these same problems, but to a lesser degree. Rather than copy the Canadian model, Enthoven (1989) advocated preserving an employer-based approach, offering tax incentives, and mandating "universal coverage for all" through a competition health care plan approach. The many health plans, contracting with both employers and statewide "public sponsors," would compete for enrollees based on price and quality. A third alternative, advocated by the National Leadership Commission on Health Care (Simmons 1990), would keep Medicare and the present health insurance system, but spend an additional $15 billion in public funds to guarantee a basic adequate benefits package. To avoid the unpopular word "taxes," the commission advocated premiums and fees in the form of income-tax surcharges. The Pepper Commission report (Rockefeller 1990) was a little bit more realistic in scaling the price tag to the range of $60 to $90 billion, depending on how much new access is financed in the long-term-care arena (a topic covered in chapter 4).

Levey and Hill (1989) coined a phrase to neatly summarize why no national health plan can be passed (or done cheaply): The inertia surrounding the issue is the product of a long American tradition of equivocation on health policy. "Equivocation triumphs" each decade because the public is willing to pay 5 to 10 percent more in the administrative expense to maximize the diversity of health plans available. The lack of widespread discontent with our expensive medical system seems to ensure slow marginal change in existing programs. On the other hand, optimists can point out that progressive reforms were passed by Congress despite a diffuse 1980s mood of skepticism and barebones reimbursement. It was a Congress plagued by deficits that passed the Hospice Act in 1982 and the Catastrophic Health Benefit Act for the elderly in 1988 (Davis et al. 1990). A cost-effective national system is easy to outline on paper: access reform ("buy in" for the working poor), supply reform ("competition" between providers), and information reform ("buy-right" consumerism based on value shopping for providers based on technical quality, amenities, and cost). Many nations have retrenched from this ideal and have encouraged their citizens to purchase more customized private insurance (New Zealand, Korea, Japan, and the United Kingdom).

WANTED: STABLE FINANCING AND BETTER MANAGEMENT

A stable, sufficient source of financing indigent care is critically needed, but better management among the "suffering" providers is also a necessity. These two issues are linked, but a public policy solution for one problem will not assure the resolution of the other. The hospital sector, disturbed to varying degrees by the absence of revenue for providing service for the uninsured, is the major advocate of improved public insurance programs. The uninsured poor, often described as the medically indigent, are financially unable to pay their hospital bills. The hospital sector, in response to price competition and revenue controls, has been accused of limiting the care that it will provide to the poor (Schiff et al. 1986) or of exhibiting signs of financial distress (National Association of Public Hospitals [NAPH] 1991). However, financial distress can be reduced or eliminated by better management and cost-reduction techniques (Eastaugh 1985). Because the poor are often more severely ill, they may be presumed to cost more per case treated. Hospitals serving a high volume of uninsured individuals, however, have the twin problems of inadequate revenues and inefficient levels of productivity.

The best hospital managers will improve efficiency per department while continuing the public effort to lobby for better reimbursement per patient. One cannot finance indigent care with productivity improvements alone; but without better productivity and increasing reliance on ambulatory care, the money invested in indigent care merely props up inefficient institutions. Policy analysts should be concerned with how resources raised for indigent care can be most effectively allocated. Then we can ask for increasing stewardship of public funds and a stable sufficient level of financing for indigent care.

The problem of indigent care is not simply a hospital finance and cost-shifting issue (Rosko 1990). Indigent service provision is a much broader social problem. The delivery of appropriate and effective medical care for the poor encompasses ethical issues such as the right to care, systemic issues such as access and new modes of service delivery (managed care), and financial issues such as who will pay for uncompensated care. Competition has made indigent care an important endemic "priority problem" for policy makers, rather than simply another "back-burner" issue of concern for the public health community. Hospital executives have a valid point when they note that managing a facility in a system of set prices and prospective contracts for 50 to 70 percent of the patients threatens their ability to provide service to nonpaying patients. Nonpayment for charity care is already seriously limiting the ability of some hospitals to continue to provide their historic share of indigent care (American Hospital Association [AHA] 1989).

Hospital lobbyists call for a "level playing field" and argue that the current situation is like telling Bloomingdale's and Sears to compete for customers and capital with the proviso that Sears must give away its goods to the poor, while Bloomingdale's is allowed to transfer its poor customers to Sears. There is no "free lunch"; if the poor cannot pay for their own care, and government will not, then someone else must bear the burden.

Two states have some limited experience trying to mandate that employers purchase health insurance for their employees. Hawaii since 1974 and Massachusetts in 1988 (but with implementation delayed to 1993) shared the same general approach: (1) to strengthen the existing employer-based insurance system, (2) to mandate that every employed worker be able to obtain health insurance, and (3) to counteract the tendency of small business firms to save money by underinsuring their work force. Differences do exist between the two states. Massachusetts has been slow to start the program supported by Governor Michael Dukakis in 1988. The Hawaii program specifies both a defined benefit package (e.g., at least 120 days of hospitalization) and defined contribution "guidelines" (i.e., employers pay at least half the premium, and employees cannot pay more than 1.5 percent of gross income on health insurance premiums). The Massachusetts program does not define a minimum benefit package, but instead mandates a defined contribution requirement of at least $1,680 per worker by the employer.

All firms in Massachusetts employing six or more workers may someday have to pay a 12 percent tax on the initial $14,000 of wages (up to a maximum of $1,680) for eligible employees not insured. This "pay or play" strategy means that the state of Massachusetts would operate an insurance fund for the uninsured (or provide service directly through managed-care contracts) with the taxes collected. An eligible employee must work at least 30 hours per week for three months, or only 20 hours for heads of households or employees on the payroll for more than six months. A former interest group supporting the Dukakis approach was the state hospital association, which viewed 10 to 15 percent bad-debt rates for teaching hospitals as a major problem. Massachusetts has the highest density of medical students and residents per capita of any state in the nation. The prevalence of bad debt, teaching costs, and low hospital productivity explain the high hospital costs in the state. Hospital spending per capita in Massachusetts, highest in the nation, was 38 percent above the national average in 1991. Hospital executives' support for mandating employer-based coverage has declined as they have come to view this law as being an insufficiently focused hospital-financing mechanism (Goldberger 1990).

Due to the state fiscal crisis and a downgrading of the Massachusetts credit rating, newly elected Republican Governor William Weld had to delay implementation of the 1988 Health Security Act to some future date (1993). The question remains as to whether employers in the state will be able to afford $580 million in 1993 to provide insurance for 345,000 uninsured workers (only 51 percent of the total uninsured population in the state). Will a mandatory contribution cause the loss of 10,000 jobs or 25,000 jobs in a state with high unemployment?

In contrast to the recent experience in this one northeastern state, the Hawaii program has worked reasonably well. Hawaii is a small state with very low levels of unemployment. The insurance industry supported the concept of mandatory benefits (Kim 1991). It enjoyed the small increment of new business in an insurance market dominated by only two players (Blue Shield and Kaiser). The president of the Hawaii Blue Shield plan estimated that the mandated-benefits law assisted only 5,000 to 10,000 workers to gain insurance coverage, and that

30,000 citizens received improved coverage because of the improved benefits package. The law still left 51,000 citizens without health insurance in 1991. It is disappointing that the Hawaii program helps only 15 percent of the previously uninsured, and that Massachusetts demonstration projects with managed care in 1991 may have assisted only 1.5 percent of the uninsured. The most successful and least successful mandatory state-mandated insurance programs do nothing to help the vast majority of the uninsured. More could be done for the working poor at less expense to the state economy if we would sufficiently fund public health clinics to provide the working poor with inexpensive basic care. This approach would upgrade the public health system and not increase the local unemployment rate.

AVOIDING THE PROBLEM OF "YOUR JOB OR YOUR HEALTH"

American industry opposes the ideological concept of mandating any fringe benefits and estimates, according to the *Wall Street Journal* (October 2, 1990), that a Kennedy-Waxman mandatory insurance bill would cost 3.5 million jobs. The microeconomic theorem is easily summarized: Make labor more expensive by mandating that health premiums be paid by the employer, and the firms will utilize less labor. However, the author estimates that the Chamber of Commerce overestimates the job loss at 3.5 million jobs, and liberals underestimate the national job loss at only 50,000 jobs. Some 300,000 to 400,000 jobs might be lost, with a compensating gain of 45,000 jobs in the health industry serving 5 to 6 million newly accessed consumers of health service. The net loss of jobs to the general economy should be weighed against the positive benefits of improved health status, including enhanced productivity on the job and less job turnover and absenteeism (workers can stay working longer rather than attending to an undertreated illness in their family). In the language of economics, health insurance is an investment in human capital, not just an expense. Considering the expense side of the benefit-cost equation, employers will be crafty at passing on the cost of new health coverage to the employees by depressing future wages and reducing the work force. As Needleman (1990) and Friedman (1990) have pointed out, mandating benefits is a very regressive secret payroll tax on the workers. Of the $14 billion of additional expense that small businesses would have to finance under a Kennedy-Waxman plan, 90 percent would eventually be transferred onto the employees through forgone wages, cuts in other fringe benefits, direct payments (e.g., cost-sharing hikes), or loss of jobs.

With a low level of political support, the Kennedy-Waxman mandated-benefits package will not become law in the near future. Too few people would benefit. Many providers might benefit, but efficiency might be reduced. Allocation efficiency might be harmed—for example, if mandating health insurance coverage reduced hospital bad debt from $11.6 billion to $8.0 billion, would the net $3.6 billion go to (1) reducing health care costs, (2) improved hospital financial reserves (and retirement of some long-term debt), or (3) new high-cost hospital technologies? Only a fool would suggest that the majority of the $3.6 billion would be given to the public as a rebate for reduced hospital bad debt (option 1). It might be more efficient to spend a fraction of that $3.6 billion on public health clinic services, with low copayments, for the working poor. The federal government may have to do more to assist local governments in funding basic primary care (Chang and Holahan 1991; Berwick and Hiatt 1989).

The one positive externality of the federal budget crisis debate for FY 1991 was the add-on to state finances by mandating medical services for children of the poor. Even an additional $550 million over the period 1991–95 will help. Children are often the forgotten group in American society; for example, the Hawaii program does not require coverage of dependents. The progressive aspect of the child-coverage bill is that each year the age will move up until children have full health protection to age 18. States are also required to act as the "medigap" insurer for the elderly poor, paying deductibles, copayments, and Medicare Part B premiums that Medicare does not pay. For the elderly above the poverty line, only Part B premiums will be covered by state funds.

FISCAL PROBLEMS FOR STATE AND LOCAL GOVERNMENTS

Uncompensated hospital care, adjusted for inflation, increased from $6.6 billion (in 1991 dollars) to $13 billion between 1981 and 1991. During the same decade, unsponsored care (the costs of uncompensated care that are not offset by payments from state and local governments) increased from $4.7 billion in 1981 to $10.4 billion in 1991. Unsponsored care rose more rapidly than uncompensated care over the decade because only 20 percent of uncompensated care was offset by state and local governments in 1991, compared with 27 percent in 1980 (Congressional Budget Office [CBO] 1991).

State governments have less capacity to expand Medicaid programs (NAPH 1991). The provision of the federal budget bill mentioned in the last section requires states to expand Medicaid funds to pay Medicare premiums of 2.53 million low-income and disabled persons. Starting in 1991, Congress required states to phase in coverage of children through age 18 in poor families, beginning with children under age 6 prior to October 1990 and with the age limit of the law rising to age 18 by the year 2003. While this federal law is progressive, federal dollars do not finance the burden. Federal mandates are crippling the ability of state governors to finance public education, streets, sewers, and other infrastructure support. Medicaid represented 13.1 percent of the average state budget in 1991 ($33.4 billion), but this figure will rise to 16 percent or $52 billion by 1995. Given that a state government cannot run a deficit or print currency, where should the governors cut spending to finance the growing needs of the elderly (including chronic nursing care, covered in chapter 4)? Some Oregon politicians have an answer to this question.

A physician, John Kitzhaber, president of the Oregon Senate, advocated confronting the reality of limits by defining an adequate level of care to which all should have access. Oregon Medicaid program management is trying to allocate funds by linking service costs to expected benefits within the context of available revenue. The plan is expected to be implemented by 1993. The list of conditions under study now exceeds 1,800. The issue of defining services that are sufficiently effective and beneficial compared to other basic health services is a problem for all third-party payers. For example, we spend $4.2 billion on neonatal intensive-care units, but millions of pregnant women do not receive prenatal care. The nation spends $70 billion annually on patients in their last six months of life, but pediatric clinics in poor neighborhoods are being closed for lack of funding. Antidumping laws are little help for facilities in financial trouble (Laddaga and Haynes 1991; Eastaugh 1992) and more leaders call for some form of rationing. A list of 1,800 procedures, rank ordered by cost-benefit, is a new form of explicit economic rationing (Tresnowski 1991).

One study suggested an interesting alternative to the standard analysis of quality-adjusted life years (QALYs). Mehrez and Gafni (1991) suggested healthy-year equivalents (HYEs) as a measure of health status that combines the two attributes of interest, the quantity and quality of life. Unlike normative QALYs, HYEs fully represent patients' preferences, because they are calculated from each individual's utility using the standard gamble approach—that is, the approach uses a combination of lottery questions to assess the individuals' utility preferences. More research is needed to measure the validity and reliability of the HYE concept. Mehrez and Gafni suggested that the reproducibility of the measures is satisfactory, in line with previous studies (Eastaugh 1991, 1983).

The American tradition of implicit rationing is becoming more explicit. State Medicaid directors are in some cases defining classes of individuals that should receive certain types of transplants. Is the expenditure of $200,000 justified by 5 expected extra years of life or by 10 years? Should the decision be different if the person is wealthy and can pay for the treatment as compared with the payment being made from public funds? Medical technology will continue to improve in that area and has the potential to spend vast sums of money.

Until and unless someone in a decision-making position is willing to address these types of questions, health care will continue to absorb an ever-increasing proportion of the gross national product. It is not the job of biomedical researchers, physicians, or hospital administrators to make these sorts of global resource-allocation decisions. It is the job of the elected officials to decide the trade-offs between health care and alternative uses of the available funds. The state of Oregon is attempting to make just this type of decision for its Medicaid program, and it will be interesting to see how these laudable efforts are distorted or thwarted by the legal system.

IDEALS AND POSSIBLE ACTION

What seems new about the 1990s is that corporate America, including all three automotive companies in Detroit, has endorsed the concept of national health insurance. What do health policy analysts make of the current situation? Some of us "old dogs" draw an analogy between what we thought about HMOs in 1970 and what we think about national health insurance lobbying efforts in 1990. Advocates of prepaid HMO care in 1970 resided in one of two groups: idealists in search of equity or managers in search of HMO cost-efficiency (and "soft rationing"). Analogously, advocates of national health insurance fall into categories: idealists in the health professions in search of health care as a right, managers of hospitals interested in getting paid for uncompensated care, or managers of large corporations interested in decreasing their insurance expenses (Griffith 1989; Eastaugh 1990; Employee Benefits Research Corporation [EBRC] 1991).

During this time of health-sector turbulence, many hospital managers encapsulate the policy issue under one label: "uncompensated care." This language signifies the direction, context, and vigor of the hospital lobby in generating improved cash flow for its sector. Alas, in a political world few people will fight for the cause of cash flow. What matters is not uncompensated care in and of itself. What matters is "uncovered people" not getting the required level of care or having to settle for substandard care. Protection of equity and access in the delivery of health services will make a better election-year issue than fighting to get better cash flow for hospitals. One would hope that the current preemption of concern for access by economic priorities will erode, especially as careful studies demonstrate that short-run cost savings in ignoring the poor produce long-run life-cycle cost explosions for society 8 to 20 years in the future (Shapiro, Ware, and Sherbourne 1986). Deterioration in health status among those poor or uninsured may not show up in annual survey data (Brook et al. 1983), but the untreated health care problems can become very significant over decades.

Two caveats are in order. First, numerous studies have been done to measure the marginal costs of hospitals and hospital educational programs (Berry 1986). The literature on the subject can be used to justify estimates of marginal cost as a fraction of average cost ranging from 0.5 to 0.7. The 0.6 figure represents the most frequently cited midrange figure, and it was also the figure adopted by Medicare to make outlier payments. Hospital-industry representatives dislike the cost-containment rationale for paying indigent care at marginal cost rather than at actual costs or full charges. Davis et al. (1990) and Blendon, Aiken, and Freeman (1986) suggested a more generous payment system for an expanded federalized Medicaid program. However, given that the medical care system is being leeched for dollars to compensate in some way for years of free spending under blank-check retrospective cost reimbursement, a stringent formula would be the most politically feasible. In other words, the hospital sector should be happy with 0.6 of a loaf in lieu of no loaf or payment at all for the nonpaying patients. Consequently, by only receiving marginal-costs payments, we as a society are recognizing the burden on nonindigent patients to cover the fixed costs of operating a hospital.

Payment changes have caused significant changes in political viewpoints. In

May 1991 the entire AMA leadership endorsed the idea of national health insurance. A decade ago American health care providers were best described as a fragmented group of fiercely independent organizations. Over 90 percent of the physicians were independent operators in private practice, and hospitals engaged in cost-increasing fierce competition for prestige and the newest capital equipment. Now physicians and hospitals are being subjected to a cost-decreasing mode of competition that is both consumer driven and payer driven. The nature of health-services delivery is changing. We can no longer deny that health care is a blend of art, business, life-style, and science. Providers' traditional objectives have been expanded to include consumer-sensitive service in a more economical style, advocating patient compliance and health promotion while offering the best technical quality of care. Overemphasis on any one aspect may spell disaster for the provider. Providers who pursue only business interests will be no more protected or respected than a used-car dealership. Likewise, those who disrespect business skills, marketing, and consumers' shifting tastes may face an early retirement in the 1990s. Changes in payment systems occur so rapidly that providers and medical suppliers are hard put to keep pace and react, much less plan proactively. There is still room for improved efficiency in a health sector that spends $1 billion every 19 hours. Some of the resources do little good, but the majority of the care averts death, pain, and erosion of functional health status. However, we must be careful not to discount quality or access in the name of economic efficiency. There is a delicate balance to maintain between health care as a social good and health care as a consumer good.

INNOVATION OR STAGNATION AND UNBALANCED GROWTH

The health economy should not be viewed as completely independent from the general economy. The health sector is in some sense a microcosm of Baumol's model of unbalanced growth for the economy (Baumol, Blackman, and Wolfe 1985). An oversimplified health economy might divide into three productivity-growth sectors, one "stagnant" (inpatient) and two "progressive" (ambulatory care and long-term care). The share of the gross national product devoted to inpatient care may rise to above 5 percent. We will spend more on the "miracles of modern medical technology," but the hospital census may remain in a permanent recession relative to 1980–83 levels. The share of health expenditures invested on the stagnant inpatient sector may increase in the long run as our appetite for transplants and high-tech medicine expands. However, the progressive sectors' share of the labor force might increase with the aging of the population and the decline in hospital workers. Productivity improvements may have to underwrite the volume expansion in numbers of services within the two progressive sectors. The progressive ambulatory-care clinics are already innovating themselves out of their cost-dominating market position. If shoddy-quality operators tarnish the service reputation of certain market segments, interest in universal entitlement and regulatory solutions may experience a rebirth.

Some health policy makers have tended to reduce health economics to the level of a forensic science, full of rhetoric and devoid of research results. A main objective of this book has been to engage the interests of policy makers and managers in the research results of academicians. Policy makers, like institutional managers, are too occupied with putting out daily brush fires and reacting to symptomatology to adequately keep abreast of the health-services research literature.

The health industry and the regulators have taken a largely defensive stand. Each party has become preoccupied with the actions and expectations of the other. However, an internal cost-containment ethos and fair reimbursement of total institutional financial requirements are necessary if we are to develop a more rational national health policy; rhetoric concerning "fat" providers and mindless "bureaucrats" is counterproductive. Will the 1990s be a period of uncontrolled growth and expansion of the health economy? Can the recent record of poor performance and sluggish productivity be reversed? The public has come to recognize that the key problems for health policy are cost containment and access to care. The solution to containing costs may be found in better implementation of management strategies and better research in the areas of finance and health economics. In our pluralistic society, better information is a necessary, but not sufficient, condition for achieving a healthier health economy.

The quality of discharge data should improve in 1993 with implementation of the new ICD-10 diagnosis coding system. The new system is responsive to calls for greater specificity and differentiation between services and illnesses. The new "Z codes" offer an expanded category of codes for asymptomatic HIV status, required administrative medical exams, antenatal screening, contraceptive management, drug use, and housing status (homelessness and inadequate insurance). All nations will not utilize every code field; for example, Korea currently codes only three digits (resulting in 340 Korean DRGs, not 490; Eastaugh 1991).

In the spirit that half a loaf of reform is better than having no reform in the American health care system, this author supports the Ginzberg (1991) list of four priorities:

1. All persons below the poverty line should be covered by Medicaid, a proposal that has the support of both the American Medical Association and the Health Insurance Association of America.

2. States should experiment with buying into Medicaid for persons with incomes between 100 and 200 percent of the poverty level.

3. Private insurance companies, after amendment of the Employee Retirement Income Security Act, should offer stripped-down policies for catastrophic care at an affordable price, around $1,000 per year, to younger employed persons with incomes above 200 percent of the poverty level, who represent a sizable proportion of the uninsured.

4. States should develop a funding pool for reimbursing providers, particularly in the public sector, who take care of large numbers of indigent patients; revenues could be generated through sin taxes and other levies.

Long-time advocates of national health insurance will seize on any prediction of major disruptions in the industry as a rationale for passing just such a universal program. In the near future their hopes and dreams may come to fruition if the clamor for quality care and indigent care peaks. The attention cycle in support of universal health insurance coverage has gone up and down. National health insurance has appeared forever imminent on a number of occasions between 1933 and 1979 (Fein 1986). If the current push for competition results in too many scandals of poor quality or poor access, the politicians might pass a national program.

A fifth reform idea, which is already being implemented by the Agency for Health Care Policy and Research (AHCPR), is the development of practice guidelines for providers. Physician education, if given sufficient time and funding, can assist the provider community in developing a cost-effective clinical decision-making mindset. Even if all American physicians practiced in salaried HMO settings, guidelines would still be as helpful as fiscal incentives in achieving the elusive goal of cost containment. The lack of clear clinical guidelines for efficient quality medical care, as defined by Ott (1991) and others, is one major reason why industrial nations are all plagued with the cost-containment problem. Canadian physicians could profit from these guidelines, especially in view of the longer lengths of stay and higher hospitalization rates in Canada relative to the United States (Anderson et al. 1990). Having visited with clinicians and managers from dozens of industrial countries, this author can verify that the physicians of the world will be the consumers of these future AHCPR guidelines (cooks everywhere need a good cookbook as a guide). The "invisible hand" of financial incentives is typically all thumbs, but clinical guidelines offer a light touch: the chance to distinguish necessary tests and procedures from discretionary or inappropriate care. When directed by the willingness-to-pay valuation technique, the guidelines can offer the humanistic quality-adjusted-life-year metric into our resource allocation decisions.

QUALITY-ENHANCING BIDDING

A sixth reform idea is to pay in proportion to service quality. Some analysts have suggested patching up the system of hospital price controls (DRGs) by including a severity-adjustment factor (see chapters 8 and 11) and operating the system on refined DRGs (RDRGs). This new and improved prospective payment system (PPS) would make for a fair "prudent buyer" and help preserve the biomedical capacity of the nation. In theory this approach could save money, and the savings could be redistributed to finance the rising demand for long-term care. One should consider ways to design a PPS scheme that better protects the four basic dimensions of equity:

1. Vertical equity, ensuring that different types of hospitals, such as specialty hospitals or teaching facilities, are treated equally

2. Horizontal equity, ensuring that within a peer category, the facilities with equivalent case mixes are paid equally

3. Financial equity, ensuring that pay is for performance, considering service quality and volume, and not just in proportion to the number of cases

4. Geographic equity, ensuring that national DRG rates do not let "windfall profits" accrue beyond what is judged fair, given operating efficiency and effectiveness

Quality of service is the one major element missing in the analysis.

Ideally, one would want a payment system that fosters improvement in quality of care, pays less than average price for less than average quality, and stimulates closure of unnecessary low-quality hospitals. A reform in the current PPS should offer incentives for low-quality performers to improve and should provide punishment for those who do not improve their quality and efficiency. A quality-enhancing bidding (QEB) system could achieve these stated goals, minimize extra administrative costs, and address the issues of geographic inequity and windfall profits. Under a QEB system, Medicare could receive annual sealed competitive bids along the lines of the California MediCal system (Johns, Anderson, and Derzon 1985; Christianson 1985). QEB would differ from MediCal contracting in three crucial ways:

1. The sealed bids would not involve catchall per diems, but rather average payment per DRG with a cost weight equal to 1 (e.g., if the bid were $4,000 and the DRG weight for that condition equaled 1.25, the payment would be $5,000).

2. Hospitals would be required to bid if they were judged to have below-average quality by their local PRO, and in the pilot-test phase of QEB if they existed in a windfall-profit state.

3. Retrospective incentive compensation for quality improvements would be offered one to two years later (e.g., if a hospital bid $4,100 in a market where the national price would have been $4,900 and it improved its quality rating by 10 percent relative to the PRO moving average, the hospital would receive a retrospective 10 percent kicker bonus for quality improvement). The total payment would not exceed national DRG prices, so this proviso is budget neutral.

Some representatives of the hospital industry are likely to object to QEBs by claiming that "capping the most costly institutions always erodes quality," based on the false premise that the "most costly hospitals are the best and serve the most severely ill." However, equitable compensation for severity can be incorporated into the bidding system either (1) directly, by continuous measurement of severity as a new sixth digit code, or (2) indirectly, on a sampling basis by factoring a reasonable incidence of retrospectively measured case severity into each class of hospital (university medical center, major teaching, moderate teaching, minor teaching, and nonteaching). Quality does not increase cost as a general rule, but rather decreases cost: The skilled and adroit are more cost-efficient than the slow and clumsy users of excess procedures or inappropriate therapeutic adjuvants. It is necessary to invest in quality by designing a bidding system that constrains costs and encourages better service and convenience. The quality-oriented PPOs and HMOs already aggressively seek competitive bids for referral hospital care based on the cost/quality/convenience mix their enrollees desire. The elderly and poor should be equally protected, with PROs defining a floor on quality and HCFA managing the bidding process.

Quality-enhancement payments would give physicians more leverage to go to trustees and management and say, "Do not forgo this quality-improvement investment." If it helps patient care, the facility will get paid for it. To avoid the liar's dice dilemma, QEB would encourage the development of quality and efficiency in tandem. Restricting QEB to low-quality hospitals is important because these hospitals have the greatest potential for improvement, much as the worst-run companies are often the easiest to turn around. At least until QEB is judged cost-beneficial (Eastaugh and Eastaugh 1986), incentive pay to improve quality should be restricted to those hospitals where the investment is most likely to change behavior. Wringing the windfall profits out of suboptimal hospitals—and redistributing the resources to more efficient, quality-enhancing providers—represents financial equity at its best. A QEB program would help inject the Smith-Barney slogan into medicine: "We earn patients the old-fashioned way: We treat them better."

TRY TO MANAGE CHANGE, OR IT WILL MANAGE YOU

Some members of organized medicine express fear that prepaid Medicare is an invitation to create medical ghettos for the elderly. One noted economist argued that we may soon turn to a false form of national health insurance—one offering a voucher for minimum coverage but leaving the individual to fend for a large share of medical costs (Ginzberg 1991). Politicians frequently seek headlines by claiming that the bulk of the medical cost problem is caused by the fraud and abuse of a few providers. This contributes to piecemeal attention being given to such infrequent problems as Medicaid kickbacks and HMO scandals, rather than the more insidious problem of inflationary or quality-eroding incentive structures. A quality-enhancing bidding system would go a long way toward promoting good medicine and good economics.

In visiting Chinese hospitals and medical schools in 1980, I was interested to discover that the ancient proverb, "May you live in interesting times," was often misinterpreted by Caucasian visitors as a curse. The opportunity for substantial reform is best in just such times of stress and strain. In fact, the Chinese term *wei ji* has a simultaneous dual interpretation: opportunity and danger. Over the next five years our health system faces immense opportunity and danger in a reformation on four fronts: access, efficiency, effectiveness, and quality of life. The challenge for providers and managers during this period of unparalleled opportunity is to win a clear victory on all four fronts and not erode either access or quality in the name of efficiency. This is a clear challenge for both managers and policy makers. The job is doubly tough for our physicians. The challenge to physicians will be to carry on one shoulder lifesaving technology and the concomitant financial burden and, on the other shoulder, the will and imagination to apply modern management techniques.

How well the physicians and managers work together will determine whether we experience the bad or good side of the "invisible hand." Bad competition will result in overemphasis on a narrow business focus and an attempt to avoid providers' social obligations. This dark side of competition attacks the special moral importance of health care in society. Warden (1990) argued that health care derives its moral importance from its impact on the normal range of opportunities in society; and opportunity is reduced when illness impairs functioning. However, any balanced view of health care should consider it as both a social good and a consumer good. Good competition will invoke a broader business focus and health-delivery orientation. Good competition can stimulate neighboring providers to offer better services at more reasonable expense through specialization, economies of scale, and quality assurance. This process can improve, and not erode, patient access to quality services throughout all market segments.

The rate of hospital mergers may increase in the 1990s. Mergers are like human relationships; they can range from love and marriage to courtship followed by friendship or fast pillage and one-night stands. Employees often experience turmoil and confusion in merging companies, which often undermine the most careful financial and strategic plans. Financial managers do a good job by avoiding the "Noah's ark" syndrome and cutting administrative fat rather than keeping two of every job position following a merger. Morrisey, Sloan, and Valvona's (1989) study of hospital markets suggested that mergers are not likely to harm competition. Neither urban nor rural markets are that highly concentrated. With the exception of one California chain that had to divest one of a town's three hospitals because of an 81 percent market share, mergers are no antitrust threat to competition.

Under perfect competition a large number of buyers and sellers will drive the producers to outprice, outvalue, and outmaneuver each other to the benefit of all consumers (with the ability to pay). Under an oligopoly the market is composed of a handful of producers whose pricing decisions are interdependent and thus higher than purely competitive market prices (Eastaugh 1981). If a chain has a monopoly on the area market due to a natural monopoly (e.g., a one-hospital town) or because antitrust enforcement is weakened, it has no competitors to dissuade it from charging higher prices and reaping classic monopoly profits. In the case of a duopoly, the two firms can better collude to reap more profits than in an oligopoly situation. Consolidation of the health sector into a few supermeds may have some advantages for large corporations (reaping super discounts), but competition is not among them. Minisystems and the preservation of the freestanding autonomous hospital will best assure a competitive market if and only if such facilities fight hard to trim excess costs and invest in quality-enhancing activities. The aforementioned quality-enhancing bidding schemes (QEBs) may support this more competitive marketplace.

REFERENCES

American Hospital Association. (1989). *The Cost of Compassion.* Chicago: American Hospital Association.

Anderson, M., Pulcins, I., Barer, M., and Evans, R. (1990). "Acute Care Hospital Utilization under Canadian National Health Insurance: British Columbia Experience." *Inquiry* 27:4 (Winter), 352–358.

Baumol, W., Blackman, S., and Wolfe, E. (1985). "Unbalanced Growth Revisited: Asymptotic Stagnancy and New Evidence." *American Economic Review* 75:4 (September), 806–817.

Beauchamp, D., and Rouse, R. (1990). "Universal New York Health Care: A Single-Payer Strategy Linking Cost Control and Universal Access." *New England Journal of Medicine* 323:10 (September 6), 640–644.

Berry, R. (1986). "Cost Functions and Production Functions in a Sample of 45 Hospitals." Final Report of the Arthur Young Graduate Medical Education Study, Vols. 2 and 3, DHHS Contract 100–80–0155 ASPE (October).

Berwick, D. (1991). "Blazing the Trail of Quality." *Frontiers of Health Services Management* 7:4 (Summer), 47–50.

Berwick, D., and Hiatt, H. (1989). "Who Pays?" *New England Journal of Medicine* 321:8 (August 24), 541–542.

Blendon, R., Aiken, L., and Freeman, H. (1986). "Uncompensated Care by Hospitals or Public Insurance for the Poor: Does It Make a Difference?" *New England Journal of Medicine* 314:18 (May 1), 1160–1163.

Blendon, R., and Edwards, J. (1991). "Caring for the Uninsured: Choices for Reform." *Journal of the American Medical Association* 265:19 (May 15), 2563–2566.

Brecher, C., and Nesbitt, S. (1985). "Factors Associated with Variation in Financial Condition among Voluntary Hospitals." *Health Services Research* 20:3 (August), 267–300.

Brook, R., Ware, J., Rogers, W., and Newhouse, J. (1983). "Does Free Care Improve Adults' Health?" *New England Journal of Medicine* 309:22 (December 8), 1426–1434.

Brown, E. and Cousineau, M. (1991). "Loss of Medicaid and access to health services." *Health Care Financing Review* 12:4 (Summer), 17–26.

Butler, S. (1991). "Tax Reform Strategy to Deal with the Uninsured." *Journal of the American Medical Association* 265:19 (May 15), 2541–2545.

Chang, D., and Holahan, J. (1991). *Medicaid Spending in the 1980s: The Access-Cost Containment Trade-off Revisited.* Washington D.C.: Urban Institute Press.

Chassin, M., and McCue, S. (1986). "A Randomized Trial of Medical Quality Assurance." *Journal of the American Medical Association* 256:8 (August 29), 1012–1016.

Christensen, S. (1992). "Volume Responses to Exogeneous Change on Medicare Payment." *Health Services Research* 27:1 (April), 55–68.

Christianson, J. (1985). "Competitive Bidding: The Challenge for Health Care Managers." *Health Care Management Review* 10:2 (Spring), 39–53.

Cleverley, W. (1990). "ROI: Its Role in Voluntary Hospital Planning." *Hospital and Health Services Administration* 35:1 (Spring), 71–82.

Congressional Budget Office (1992). *Selected Options for Expanding Health Insurance Coverage.* Washington, D.C.: U.S. Congress.

Congressional Budget Office. (1991). *Trends in Health Expenditures for Medicare and Medicaid.* Washington, D.C.: CBO, U.S. Congress.

Crane, T. (1985). "Hospital Cost Control in Norway: A Decade's Experience with Prospective Payment." *Public Health Reports* 100:4 (July/August), 406–417.

Davidson, G., and Moscovice, I. (1989). "Health Insurance and Welfare Reentry." *Health Services Research* 24:5 (December), 599–614.

Davis, K., Anderson, G., Rowland, D., and Steinberg, E. (1990). *Health Care Cost Containment.* Baltimore: Johns Hopkins University Press.

Doolittle, R. (1991). "Biotechnology: The Enormous Cost of Success." *New England Journal of Medicine* 324:19 (May 9), 1360–1362.

Eastaugh, S. (1992). *Health Economics: Efficiency, Quality, and Equity.* Westport, Conn.: Auburn House.

———. (1991). "Impact of National Health Insurance in Korea." *Hospital Topics* 70:4 (Fall), 55–60.

———. (1985). "Improving Hospital Productivity under PPS: Managing Cost Reductions without Quality and Service Reductions." *Hospital and Health Services Administration* 30:4 (July/August), 97–111.

———. (1983). "Placing a Value on Life and Limb: The Role of the Informed Consumer." *Health Matrix* 1:1 (Spring), 5–21.

———. (1981). *Medical Economics and Health Finance.* Dover, Mass.: Auburn House, 318–322.

Eastaugh, S., and Eastaugh, J. (1991). "Administrative efficiency: Canada Is Not Vastly Better than America." *New England Journal of Medicine* 325:18 (October 31), 1316–1317.

———. (1986). "Prospective Payment Systems: Further Steps to Enhance Quality, Efficiency, and Regionalization." *Health Care Management Review* 11:4 (Fall), 37–52.

Elwood, P. (1986). "Supermed Concept Gaining Ground." *Federation of American Executives Review* 19:2 (March/April), 69–71.

Elwood, P., and Paul, B. (1984). *Here Come the SuperMeds.* Excelsior, Minn.: Interstudy.

Employee Benefits Research Corporation. (EBRC). (1991). *Assessing the Access Problems.* Washington, D.C.: Employee Benefits Research Institute.

Enthoven, A. (1990). "Multiple Choice Health Insurance: The Lessons and Challenge to Employers." *Inquiry* 27:4 (Winter), 368–373.

———. (1989). *Theory and Practice of Managed Competition in Health Care Finance.* Amsterdam: North-Holland.

Etheredge, L. (1991). "Negotiating National Health Insurance." *Journal of Health Politics, Policy and Law* 16:1 (Spring), 157–167.

———. (1990). "Universal Health Insurance: Lessons of the 1970s, Prospects for the 1990s." *Frontiers of Health Services Management* 6:4 (Summer), 1–35.

Fein, O. (1991). "Restructuring Services in the Academic Medical Center: One Approach to Primary Care Services for the Urban Poor." *Bulletin of the New York Academy of Medicine* 67:1 (January–February), 59–65.

Fein, R. (1986). *Medical Care, Medical Costs: The Search for a Health Insurance Policy.* Cambridge, Mass.: Harvard University Press.

Friedman, E. (1990). "Health Insurance in Hawaii." *Business and Health* 8:4 (June), 52–59.

Fuchs, V., and Hahn, J. (1990). "How Does Canada Do It? A Comparison of Expenditures for Physician Services in the U.S. and Canada." *New England Journal of Medicine* 323:13 (September 27), 884–890.

Gapenski, L. (1992). *Healthcare Financial Management.* Ann Arbor, Mich.: Health Administration Press.

Getzen, T. (1990). "Macro Forecasting of National Health Expenditures" in *Advances in Health Economics and Health Services Research,* ed. by Scheffler, R., Greenwich, Conn.: JAI Press, 27–47.

Ginzberg, E. (1991). *The Contribution of Health Services Research to National Health Policy.* Cambridge, Mass.: Harvard University Press.

———. (1990). "Health Care Reform: Why So Slow?" *New England Journal of Medicine* 322:20 (May 17), 1464–1466.

Goldberger, S. (1990). "The Politics of Universal Access: The Massachusetts Health Security Act of 1988." *Journal of Health Politics, Policy, and Law* 15:4 (Winter), 857–859.

Gray, B. (1991). *The Profit Motive and Patient Care: The Changing Accountability of Doctors and Hospitals.* Cambridge: Harvard University Press.

Griffith, J. (1989). "The Struggle Is the Essence." *Frontiers of Health Services Management* 6:2 (Winter), 31–34.

Grumet, G. (1989). "Health Care Rationing through Inconvenience." *New England Journal of Medicine* 321:9 (August 31), 607–611.

Himmelstein, D., and Woolhandler, S. (1989). "A National Health Program for the United States: A Physicians' Proposal." *New England Journal of Medicine* 320:2 (January 12), 102–108.

Hollingsworth, J., Hage, J., and Hanneman, R. (1991). *State Intervention in Medical Care: Consequences for Britain, France, Sweden, and the United States.* Ithaca, N. Y.: Cornell University Press.

Holoweiko, M. (1992). "Health Care in Hawaii." *Medical Economics* 69:3 (February3), 158–174.

Hughes, J. (1991). "How Well Has Canada Contained the Cost of Doctoring?" *Journal of the American Medical Association* 265:18 (May 8), 2347–2351.

Iglehart, J. (1991). "Germany's Health Care System." *New England Journal of Medicine* 324:7 (February 14), 503–508.

Johns, L., Anderson, M., and Derzon, R. (1985). "Selective Contracting in California: Experience in the Second Years." *Inquiry* 22:4 (Winter), 335–347.

Jones, S. (1990). "Multiple Choice Health Insurance: The Lessons and Challenge to Private Insurers." *Inquiry* 27:2 (Summer), 161–166.

Kim, H. (1991). "Hawaii: Life after Mandatory Insurance." *Modern Healthcare* 21:7 (February 18), 21–25.

Kirkman-Liff, B. (1991). "Health Insurance Values and Implementation in The Netherlands and Germany." *Journal of the American Medical Association* 265:19 (May 15), 2496–2503.

Kirkman-Liff, B., and van de Ven, W. (1989). "Improving Efficiency in the Dutch

Health Care System: Current Innovations and Future Options." *Health Policy* 13:4 (October), 35–53.

Kovner, A., and Neuhauser, D. (1991). *Health Services Management: Readings and Commentary*. 4th ed. Ann Arbor, Mich.: Health Administration Press.

Krasny, J., and Ferrier, I. (1991). *The Canadian Healthcare System in Perspective*. Toronto: Bogart Delafield Ferrier.

Kronick, R. (1991). "Can Massachusetts Pay for Health Care for All?" *Health Affairs* 10:1 (Spring), 26–43.

Laddaga, L., and Haynes, J. (1991). "Anti-dumping Law." *Healthcare Financial Management* 45:3 (March), 84–88.

Levey, S., and Hill, J. (1989). "National Health Insurance: The Triumph of Equivocation." *New England Journal of Medicine* 321:25 (December 21), 1750–1754.

Lister, J. (1986). "The Politics of Medicine in Britain and the United States." *New England Journal of Medicine* 315:3 (July 17), 168–173.

Mangion, R. (1986). "Capitation Reimbursement: A Progress Report." *Hospital and Health Services Administration* 31:1 (January–February), 99–110.

Mehrez, A., and Gafni, A. (1991). "Healthy-Year Equivalents (HYE): How to Measure Them Using the Standard Gamble Approach." *Medical Decision Making* 11:2 (April–June), 140–146.

Moore, F., and Priebe, C. (1991). "Board-certified Physicians in the United States, 1971–1986." *New England Journal of Medicine* 324:8 (February 21), 536–543.

Morrisey, M., Sloan F., and Valvona, J. (1989). *Cost of Capital and Capital Structure in U.S. Hospitals*. Washington, D.C.: National Center for HSR and Technology Assessment, report 209903.

National Association of Public Hospitals. (1991). "Financing and Provision of Health Care to the Medically Indigent." Updated status report.

Needleman, J. (1990). "Mandating Employee Health Benefits? A New Look." *Bulletin of the New York Academy of Medicine* 66:1 (January–February), 80–93.

Nemes, J. (1991). "Hospitals Signaling Distress." *Modern Healthcare* 21:9 (March 4), 37–40.

Neuschler, E. (1990). *Canadian Health Care: The Implications of Public Health Insurance*. Washington, D.C.: Health Insurance Association of America.

Organization for Economic Cooperation and Development. (1991). *National Accounts of OECD Countries, 1950–1990*. Paris: OECD.

Ott, J. (1991). "Competitive Medical Organizations: A View of the Future." in J. Moreno (ed.), *Paying the Doctor*, 83–92. Westport, Conn.: Auburn.

Pauly, M. (1990). "Objectives for Changing Physician Payment." *Frontiers of Health Services Management* 6:1 (Fall), 44–47.

Pauly, M., Danzon, P., Feldstein, P., and Hoff, J. (1991). "A Plan for Responsible National Health Insurance." *Health Affairs* 10:1 (Spring), 5–25.

Peters, T., and Austin, N. (1985). *A Passion for Excellence*. New York: Random House.

Powell, M., and Anesaki, M. (1991). *Health Care in Japan*. New York: Routledge, Chapman, and Hall.

Rachlis, M., and Kushner, C. (1990). *Second Opinion: What's Wrong with Canada's Health-Care System and How to Fix It*. Toronto, Ontario: Collins.

Rakich, J. (1991). "The Canadian and U.S. Health Care Systems: Profiles and Policies." *Hospital and Health Services Administration* 36:1 (Spring), 24–42.

Rockefeller, J. (1990) "The Pepper Commission Report on Comprehensive Health Care."
   New England Journal of Medicine 323:14 (October 4), 1005–1007.

Rosko, M. (1990). "All-Payer Rate-setting and the Provision of Hospital Care to the
   Uninsured in New Jersey." *Journal of Health Politics, Policy, and Law* 15:4
   (Winter), 815–31.

Roybal, E. (1991). "The U.S. Health Care Act." *Journal of the American Medical
   Association* 265:19 (May 15), 2545–2549.

Rublee, D., and Schneider, M. (1991). "International Health Spending Comparisons."
   Health Affairs 10:3 (Fall), 187–197.

Ryan, J., Ward, M., and Kolb, D. (1990). "Capital Management." *Healthcare Financial
   Management* 44:3 (March), 32–40.

Saltman, R. (1990). "Competition and Reform in the Swedish Health System." *Milbank
   Quarterly* 68:4 (December), 597–617.

Schiff, R., Ansell, D., Schlosser, J., Idris, A., Momson, A., and Whitman, S. (1986).
   "Transfers to a Public Hospital: A Prospective Study of 467 Patients." *New
   England Journal of Medicine* 314:9 (February 27), 552–557.

Schneider, M. (1991). "Health Care Cost Containment in the Republic of Germany."
   Health Care Financing Review 12:3 (Spring), 87–101.

Shapiro, M., Ware, J., and Sherbourne, C. (1986). "Effects of Cost Sharing on Seeking
   Care for Serious and Minor Symptoms." *Annals of Internal Medicine* 104:2
   (February), 246–251.

Sherman, B. (1990). "How Investors Evaluate Hospitals' Creditworthiness." *Healthcare
   Financial Management* 44:3 (March), 24–30.

Shortell, S. (1991). *Effective Hospital-Physician Relationships*. Ann Arbor, Mich.: Health
   Administration Press.

Simmons, H. (1990). *Report of the National Leadership Commission on Health Care:
   The Health of the Nation—A Shared Responsibility*. Ann Arbor, Mich.: Health
   Administration Press.

Skarupa, J., and Matherlee, T. (1989). *The Hospital Medical Staff: Closed Medical Staffs
   Are Not Inevitable*. Chicago, Ill.: American Hospital Publishing.

Thorpe, K., Hendricks, A., and Newhouse, J. (1992). "Reducing the Number of Uninsured by Subsidizing Employment-based Insurance." *Journal of the American
   Medical Association* 267:7 (February 19), 945–948.

Tresnowski, B. (1991). "Oregon's Initiative Promises Wealth of Experience to Guide
   Health Care Reform." *Inquiry* 28:3 (Fall), 207–208.

Tuckman, H., and Chang, C. (1991). "Proposal to Redistribute the Cost of Hospital
   Charity Care." *Milbank Quarterly* 69:1 (Spring), 113–142.

Warden, G. (1990). "Future Directions for Urban Health Care." *Henry Ford Hospital
   Medical Journal* 38:3 (Fall), 178–183.

Williams, D., Hadley, J., Pettengill, J. (1992). "Profits, Community Role, and Hospital
   Closure." *Medical Care* 30:2 (February), 174–186.

Woolhandler, S., and Himmelstein, D. (1991). "Deteriorating Administrative Efficiency
   of the U.S. Health Care System." *New England Journal of Medicine* 324:18 (May
   2), 1253–1258.

Zuckerman, H., and Kaluzney, A. (1991). "Strategic Alliances in Health Care: The
   Challenges of Cooperation." *Frontiers of Health Services Management* 7:3 (Winter), 3–22.

Author Index

Note: Page numbers followed by n refer to full bibliographic references.

Subject Index

About the Author

STEVEN R. EASTAUGH is Professor of Health Economics and Finance at George Washington University. The winner of numerous awards, including the American College of Healthcare Executives Edgar Hayhow Award, Eastaugh has published widely in the areas of health care finance and economics. His companion volume, *Health Economics: Efficiency, Quality, and Equity*, will also be issued by Auburn House in 1992.